The Palgrave Handbook of African Entrepreneurship

"From a development policy perspective, this book is unique among recent literature on the subject in some important respects. It discusses not only the challenges such as weak and unstable institutional environment that prevent many African economies from unleashing entrepreneurial drive, but more importantly, it draws on critical empirical and case studies across multiple countries, sub-regions, and economic agents (women-entrepreneurs and the role of diaspora finance for entrepreneurship) within the African continent. Such critical multifaced discussion on the entrepreneurial landscape has been lacking in the African context. Taken together, the connections made between entrepreneurship theory and methodological discussions, and the breadth of critical issues addressed with sound empirical evidence are at the heart of the major contributions of this book. This has resulted in a great study on one of the most important discussions for Africa's sustainable development – entrepreneurship – to date."
—Prof Eugene Bempong, *Chief Research Scientist, African Development Bank*

"Throughout the book's 24 chapters, the authors offer insightful analyses of a large gamut of challenges on the continent, as African countries struggle to overcome the crippling effects of free and unfair global trade and the hegemony of foreign extractive industries at one level, and the multiple ramifications of internal violent conflicts and malgovernance at another level. The authors go beyond the empirical scrutiny of problems and obstacles by methodically challenging the prevailing narrative that often presents Africa under a cloud of doom and gloom…The book harmoniously combines wide-frame analyses of entrepreneurship across the continent and informative case studies that put the analyses in context. The case studies involve countries as diverse as Nigeria, Kenya, Libya, South Africa, Zambia, and Ethiopia, and the issue areas examined include SME (small and medium enterprises) and foreign ventures; emergence and success of nascent entrepreneurship at the national level; the role of financial remittances from Africans of the Diaspora in fostering an entrepreneurial ecosystem on the continent; entrepreneurship education; the rise of young and female entrepreneurs; and so on."
—Professor Mohamed S. Camara, *Chair, Department of African Studies, Howard University*

"The Palgrave Handbook Of African Entrepreneurship is a welcome addition to the expanding literature on how Africa can turn its entrepreneurship focus to sustainable growth. With empirical insights and case studies from countries across the continent, this book illuminates peculiarities and practical insights that can inform policy and practice. A major issue is a one-size-fits-all approach to entrepreneurship issues across the continent, this book differs in this regard. Its thematic sections are comprehensive enough that its relevance across the continent is not in doubt. Entrepreneurs, governments and international agencies should find it beneficial as we all seek to transform Africa economically."

—Wale Fatade, *Commissioning Editor, The Conversation, Africa*

Oluwaseun Kolade · David Rae ·
Demola Obembe · Kassa Woldesenbet Beta
Editors

The Palgrave Handbook of African Entrepreneurship

palgrave
macmillan

Editors
Oluwaseun Kolade
Department of Management &
Entrepreneurship
De Montfort University
Leicester, UK

Demola Obembe
De Montfort University
Leicester, UK

David Rae
Department of Management &
Entrepreneurship
De Montfort University
Leicester, UK

Kassa Woldesenbet Beta
De Montfort University
Leicester, UK

ISBN 978-3-030-75893-6   ISBN 978-3-030-75894-3 (eBook)
https://doi.org/10.1007/978-3-030-75894-3

© The Editor(s) (if applicable) and The Author(s), under exclusive license to Springer Nature Switzerland AG 2022

This work is subject to copyright. All rights are solely and exclusively licensed by the Publisher, whether the whole or part of the material is concerned, specifically the rights of translation, reprinting, reuse of illustrations, recitation, broadcasting, reproduction on microfilms or in any other physical way, and transmission or information storage and retrieval, electronic adaptation, computer software, or by similar or dissimilar methodology now known or hereafter developed.

The use of general descriptive names, registered names, trademarks, service marks, etc. in this publication does not imply, even in the absence of a specific statement, that such names are exempt from the relevant protective laws and regulations and therefore free for general use.

The publisher, the authors and the editors are safe to assume that the advice and information in this book are believed to be true and accurate at the date of publication. Neither the publisher nor the authors or the editors give a warranty, expressed or implied, with respect to the material contained herein or for any errors or omissions that may have been made. The publisher remains neutral with regard to jurisdictional claims in published maps and institutional affiliations.

Cover illustration: Panther Media GmbH/Alamy Stock Photo

This Palgrave Macmillan imprint is published by the registered company Springer Nature Switzerland AG
The registered company address is: Gewerbestrasse 11, 6330 Cham, Switzerland

Foreword

I am delighted to write this Foreword to a timely collection by Seun Kolade, David Rae, Demola Obembe and Kassa Woldesenbet Beta. Africa is dear to me. It is a rich continent with gold, copper and diamonds, and at first, I did not understand how its people were so far from rich.

I first worked on the continent in 1984, when a Canadian firm sent me to Zaire, the "new" name of the formerly Belgian Congo. I recall once we had an expert flown from Brussels to Kinshasa because a machine was not working. He explained that the reason was that nobody had plugged it in. Perhaps what impressed me most there was how everything was delayed and the reason was always explained as being "counter-time."

I later became an academic and contributed my ethnographic findings in Namibia[1], Mozambique[2] and Lesotho[3] to the *Journal of Small-Management*. A comparative study of Ghana and Togo[4] later appeared in the *Journal of African Business*. Africa was not much more developed than was the case in 1984. The flagship of entrepreneurship was micro-business. I wrote, "Both

---

[1] Léo-Paul Dana, "An Analysis of Strategic Intervention Policy in Namibia," *Journal of Small Business Management,* 31, 1993, pp. 90–95.

[2] Léo-Paul Dana, "Small Business in Mozambique After the War," *Journal of Small Business Management* 34 (4), October 1996, pp. 67–71.

[3] Léo-Paul Dana, "Voluntarily Socialist Culture and Small Business in the Kingdom of Lesotho," *Journal of Small Business Management* 35 (4), October 1997, pp. 83–87.

[4] Léo-Paul Dana, "Promoting SMEs in Africa: Some Insights from An Experiment in Ghana and Togo," *Journal of African Business* (The official publication of the International Academy of African Business and Development) 8 (2), October 2007, pp. 151–174.

Ghana and Togo have a multitude of micro-businesses, one-man operations, such as peddlers selling crocodile skulls and dead parrots…such self-employed individuals call themselves entrepreneurs. A. Joseph is proud to distribute his business card…He is engineer of voodoo forces at Stand Nº 7B…Others have no address: a man from Mali selling camel-hides in the street; peddlers from Ghana and Nigeria roaming around Togo; a boy from Togo selling his services to tourists in Ghana. Indigenous people try to sell watches at an intersection; while they haggle over prices they are complaining that the Lebanese control the textile industry and gold trade, preventing new entrants. Housewives sell snacks through the windows of a bus…A self-ordained priest and witch doctor boards the bus to advertise and sell his medicine. The passengers respond, 'Amen.' A woman walks off the street, into a restaurant (with which she is not affiliated) and takes a client's order. From the plate she carries on her head, she makes a sandwich for the client and leaves before the establishment's waiter arrives. At the local market, cans of sardines are being offered for sale, although they are labelled 'DONATED BY THE GOVERNMENT OF JAPAN' and 'NOT FOR SALE'" (Dana, 2007, p. 163). I recall an opportunist on the Ghana side of the border with Togo. He would arrange for a public bus to be delayed and arrive after the border closed, in order to boost the occupancy rate at his hotel.

Entrepreneurship in Africa today is no longer focused on arbitrage often facilitated by corruption. Africa today has a new class of high-flying entrepreneurs. Among them is Bilikiss Adebiyi Abiola the award-winning entrepreneur who established a recycling business in Lagos, creating jobs for Nigerians in a cleaner Nigeria. Given the limited infrastructure in Nigeria, traffic is extremely heavy; recognising the value of circumventing traffic, Chinedu Azodoh and Adetayo Bamiduro cofounded a motorbike ride-hailing and delivery service Metro Africa Xpress. Their phone and web-based platform is similar to Uber, helping consumers are contributing to the infrastructure.

In Kenya, Diana Esther Wangari, MD, cofounded Checkups Medical Centre. This firm introduced medical teleconsultation, allowing patients to seek advice from doctors remotely. Also in Kenya, Jacob Maina Rugano established AfricarTrack International Ltd., allowing employers to monitor the driving and speeding of their employees and also helping the police find stolen vehicles.

In Sierra Leone, Nthabiseng Mosia, Eric Silverman and Alexandre Tourre established Easy Solar (known abroad as Azimuth), providing homes with electricity. These entrepreneurs help poorer consumers with a rent-to-own option, allowing for the possibility to pay off a solar panel at one's own pace.

We are witnessing a new Africa, with a new generation of entrepreneurs introducing not only product and service innovations, but also a new mindset. It is an appropriate time indeed for *The Palgrave Handbook of African Entrepreneurship*, and I salute the editors.

Leo-Paul Dana
Professor
Dalhousie University
Halifax, Canada

Contents

1 **Introduction** 1
Oluwaseun Kolade, David Rae, Demola Obembe, and Kassa Woldesenbet Beta

Part I Institutional Environments and Entrepreneurial Ecosystems

2 **The Importance of Dynamic Capabilities in the Post North African Market Survival of African SMEs International New Ventures (INVs)** 19
Michael Mustafa and Louise Scholes

3 **Uncovering the Role of Institutional Context for Nascent Entrepreneurial Ventures** 45
A. I. Ogunsade, Demola Obembe, and Kassa Woldesenbet Beta

4 **The Interaction Between Family Businesses and Institutional Environment in Africa: An Exploration of Contextual Issues** 67
William K. Murithi and Kassa Woldesenbet Beta

5 **Enterprise Survival and Growth: A Conceptual Exposition of Entrepreneurial Activities in Sub-Saharan Africa** 93
Deji Olagboye, Demola Obembe, and Godwin Okafor

6 The Institutional Context of Community
Entrepreneurship Behaviour in Nigeria: Lessons
from Three Case Communities 115
Rotimi Olaniyan

7 The Impact of Entrepreneurship Framework
and Behaviour on Diaspora Remittance: An African
Perspective 145
*Samuel Salia, Javed G. Hussain, Yahaya Alhassan,
and Masud Ibrahim*

Part II Entrepreneurship Education

8 Left Behind: A Reflection on Lags in the Development
of Entrepreneurship Education in South Africa 173
Natasha Katuta Mwila

9 Risk Society as a Framework for Exploring
Entrepreneurship Education in Nigeria 187
Samson O. Oladejo and Oluwasoye P. Mafimisebi

10 The Nexus Between Nigerian Universities'
Entrepreneurship Training and Digital Technology:
Influence on Graduates' New Venture Creations 215
*Mojolaoluwa O. Alabi, Oluwasoye P. Mafimisebi,
and Samson O. Oladejo*

11 Co-creation of Entrepreneurship Education: Challenges
and Opportunities for University, Industry and Public
Sector Collaboration in Nigeria 239
*Oluwaseun Kolade, Evans Osabuohien, Ayotola Aremu,
Kehinde Adefiola Olanipekun, Romanus Osabohien,
and Patience Tunji-Olayeni*

Part III Technology Entrepreneurship and Innovation Ecosystem

12 Are African Economies Open for Entrepreneurship: How
Do We Know? 269
David Rae, Oluwaseun Kolade, and Adebowale Owoseni

13 African Youth Rising: The Emergence and Growth
of Youth-Led Digital Enterprises in Africa 303
Wheeler R. Winstead and Jean T. Wells

14	Technology Entrepreneurs: Surviving the Valley of Death in the Nigerian Innovation Ecosystem *Oluwaseun David Adepoju*	329
15	ICT Usage Behaviours by SMEs in Varying Operational Environments: A Nigerian Case Study *Ibrahim Rufai*	351

Part IV Entrepreneurship in Conflict Zones

16	Picking up the Pieces: Social Capital and Entrepreneurship for Livelihood Recovery Among Displaced Populations in Northeast Nigeria *Oluwaseun Kolade, Robert Smith, and Saliba James*	385
17	Barriers and Opportunities for Refugee Entrepreneurship in Africa: A Social Capital Perspective *Tracy Luseno and Oluwaseun Kolade*	407
18	Entrepreneurial and SME Activity in Libya: Reviewing Contextual Obstacles and Challenges Leading to Its Fractured Enterprise Culture *Abdulmonem Ahmed Esaudi, Robert Smith, and Veronica Scuotto*	437
19	Application of the People, Context, Deal and Opportunity (PCDO) Model for Entrepreneurship Advancement in Africa *Ovo Imoedemhe*	463

Part V Gender and Diversity Issues in African Entrepreneurship

20	'Longing to Grow My Business': The Work–Life Interface of Women Entrepreneurs in Ethiopia *Konjit Hailu Gudeta, Marloes van Engen, Pascale Peters, Kassa Woldesenbet Beta, Brigitte Kroon, and Atsede Tesfaye Hailemariam*	493
21	Deconstructing the Myth: African Women Entrepreneurs' Access to Resources *Kassa Woldesenbet Beta, Natasha Katuta Mwila, and Olapeju Ogunmokun*	517

22 An Empirical Insight into the Factors Affecting
    the Oscillation of Women Between Self- and Paid
    Employment in South Africa   543
    *Bridget Irene, Promise Opute Abdullah,
    and William K. Murithi*

Part VI Researching African Entrepreneurship:
         Methodological Considerations

23 Conducting Surveys in Africa: Reflections from National
    Surveys in Nigeria   573
    Abiodun Egbetokun

24 A New Look at Case Study Approach in African
    Entrepreneurship Research   595
    Oluwasoye P. Mafimisebi and Frank Nyame-Asiamah

Index   619

Notes on Contributors

Dr. Promise Opute Abdullah is a freelance academic and management consultant with GPROM Academic and Management Solutions, Paderborn, Germany. He also supports organisations with technical advice in several management streams. His research interest includes inter-functional integration, relationship management, cross cultural management, consumer behaviour, entrepreneurship and SMEs, strategic management accounting, etc.

Oluwaseun David Adepoju is a Global Challenges Faculty at the African Leadership University, Kigali Rwanda. Before joining the University, he was the founder and the manager of TECHmIT Africa, a Technology and Innovation Ecosystem Advocacy Organisation in Nigeria. He is currently a Ph.D. researcher in Creative Technologies at the COLAB, Auckland University of Technology, New Zealand.

Mojolaoluwa O. Alabi is a doctoral researcher at the Institute of Youth and Community Research, School of Education and Social Sciences, University of the West of Scotland, Paisley, United Kingdom. His research interests include vocational education and training, higher education, informal sector entrepreneurship, educational ethnography, and self-directed learning.

Dr. Yahaya Alhassan is a Principal Lecturer in Finance and Strategic Management at University of Sunderland in London. He has over 20 years' teaching and management experience in the higher education sector. He holds a Ph.D. in Business Management from Anglia Ruskin University and is a Senior Fellow of HEA.

Ayotola Aremu is a Professor of Educational Technology at the University of Ibadan, Nigeria. She has researched extensively in innovative strategies, tools and technology. She is engaged in facilitating online pedagogy and technology skills amongst lecturers at the University. She is the Director of the office of International Programs.

Abiodun Egbetokun has more than a decade of experience designing, conducting or managing surveys. He holds a Ph.D. in Economics and is currently Assistant Director, Research at the National Centre for Technology Management (NACETEM), Nigeria. His research focuses on the emergence, evolution and economic impact of entrepreneurship and innovation. He tweets @egbetokun and blogs at www.egbetokun.com/blogs.

Abdulmonem Ahmed Esaudi is a Ph.D. Researcher in School of Business and Creative Industries at the University of the West of Scotland. He obtained an MBA from Cardiff Metropolitan University. He got B.B.A from Tripoli University/Libya. He is a member at CAREED (Centre for African Research on Enterprise and Economic Development). His interests in Entrepreneurship & SMEs.

Dr. Konjit Hailu Gudeta is a Researcher at Maastricht University at the Faculty of Arts and Social Studies and an Assistant Professor at Addis Ababa University. Her research interests include work-life interface, boundary management, decent work and wellbeing and women entrepreneurship.

Atsede Tesfaye Hailemariam is an assistant professor at School of Commerce, Addis Ababa University, Ethiopia. She holds a Ph.D. from Tilburg University, The Netherlands. Her research focuses on women entrepreneurship development and policy in Ethiopia, such as women's entrepreneurial motivations, access to finance and their interest and orientation towards business growth.

Javed G. Hussain is a Professor of Entrepreneurial Finance at Birmingham City University. He has extensively published in refereed journal articles and has been nominated for prestigious national and international awards. Currently, he is working with colleagues from UK, Ghana and Pakistan on research linking entrepreneurial finance entrepreneurship and microfinance.

Dr. Masud Ibrahim is currently a senior-lecturer in accounting and associate member of CFCI-research centre at Coventry University. Dr Ibrahim holds a Ph.D. in Oil and Gas Accounting from Robert Gordon University.

His research explores issues such as sustainability, smart cities, governance, accountability, climate-risk disclosures, and corporate reporting.

Dr. Ovo Imoedemhe is currently Associate Professor at Dar Al Hekma University Jeddah Saudi Arabia, where she is a part-time lecturer in Property Law and Intellectual Property Law. Ovo obtained her Ph.D. in Law from the University of Leicester in 2015 and has occupied different academic positions within and outside the UK.

Bridget N. Irene is an Assistant Professor in Enterprise and Entrepreneurship at the International Center for Transformational Entrepreneurship, Coventry University. Her scholarly interests focus on the culturally instantiated facets of the debate on gender entrepreneurship, entrepreneurial competencies, family businesses, entrepreneurship education, and the informal economy.

Prof. Saliba James is a Professor of Asian and International Studies. He was Head of the Department of History, University of Maiduguri, Nigeria, where he coordinated research on Boko Haram Insurgency, in collaboration with the Nigerian Army. His other publications cover international migration and foreign policy.

Dr. Oluwaseun Kolade is an Associate Professor in Strategic Management at De Montfort University, where he leads the African Entrepreneurship Cluster. His research covers the broad areas of transformative entrepreneuring, digital transformation, refugee entrepreneurship, and SMEs strategies in turbulent environments. He has chaired and presented his research at various international conferences.

Dr. Brigitte Kroon is assistant professor Human Resource Studies at Tilburg University. She publishes on HRM and decent work in various contexts. She is program director of the Bachelor HRS—People Management and a member of the European Labour Authority.

Tracy Luseno is currently a Ph.D. researcher and Associate Lecturer in Business and Management at De Montfort University. She is researching refugee entrepreneurship in Africa and the ecosystems in which refugee entrepreneurs operate. Prior to her Ph.D. research, Tracy worked in business analyst roles both in the UK and Kenya.

Dr. Oluwasoye P. Mafimisebi is an Associate Professor/Reader in Management, Entrepreneurship, Risk & Resilience at Leicester Castle Business School, De Montfort University. He holds Ph.D. in Strategy, Enterprise and

Innovation and he is a Certified Business & Management Educator (CMBE). He is on the Editorial Board of Journal of Management & Organisation.

William K. Murithi is a Lecturer in Entrepreneurship at the Leicester Castle Business School, De Montfort University, UK. His Ph.D. investigates strategic behaviours of family and non-family businesses in developing economies. His research interests include entrepreneurship, strategic management, family business, regional development, and socio-cultural and institutional context within developing economies.

Michael Mustafa is an Associate Professor in Entrepreneurial Management at the University of Nottingham, where he obtained a Ph.D. in Applied Psychology. His current research focuses on family firms, transnational entrepreneurship and corporate entrepreneurship. He is the editor of Entrepreneurship Research Journal, Journal of Employment Studies as well as Associate Editor of Journal of Entrepreneurship in Emerging Economies.

Natasha Katuta Mwila has a Ph.D. in business management and is a senior lecturer at Leicester Castle Business School. Natasha is a case method enthusiast with research interests in entrepreneurship and women's work. She is a fellow of the Higher Education Academy and a Chartered Management and Business Educator.

Frank Nyame-Asiamah is Senior Lecturer in Business Management at Leicester Castle Business School, De Montfort University. He obtained a Ph.D. in Management Studies from Brunel University, London. His research interests include organisational learning, information systems, and entrepreneurship. Frank has published in top ranking journals such as Social Science and Medicine, and Technological Forecasting and Social Change.

Demola Obembe is Associate Professor of Strategic Management and Head of Department for Management and Entrepreneurship at De Montfort University, UK. His research interests are in the areas of; strategy process and practice, entrepreneurship and SMEs, knowledge and innovation management, and social capital.

Olapeju Ogunmokun is a Ph.D. researcher and a part-time lecturer in the department of Management and Entrepreneurship at De Montfort University. Her research interests focus on finance, risk and entrepreneurship and her doctoral research investigates the influence of risk perception on access to debt financing of small enterprises.

A. I. Ogunsade is an academic with a wealth of knowledge in business development and a considerable experience of working with corporate stakeholders. He leverages on industry and research experience to advance excellent teaching and innovative classroom practice. His research interests are around institutional entrepreneurship, small business innovation, entrepreneurship education and business start-ups.

Godwin Okafor is a Senior Lecturer in Economics at De Montfort University, UK. He has a Ph.D. from Bournemouth University, UK. Godwin's research interests are in the areas of International Economics and Economic Development. Godwin's research interests have generated outputs in top quality journals.

Samson O. Oladejo is a doctoral researcher at the Institute of Youth and Community Research at the University of the West of Scotland, UK. His Ph.D. research focuses on discourses of risk that obfuscate educational access in the context of Universal Basic Education for young people in urban-poor areas of Lagos, Nigeria.

Deji Olagboye is Associate Lecturer at De Montfort University. He is also undertaking doctoral research in Entrepreneurship in the Department of Management and Entrepreneurship. Deji currently teaches courses on entrepreneurship and enterprise, contemporary business issues, and global contemporary business issues.

Kehinde Adefiola Olanipekun holds a Ph.D degree in Technology Management from African Institute of Science and Policy Innovation (AISPI), Obafemi Awolowo University, Ile- Ife, Nigeria. She works with the Centre for Entrepreneurship and Innovation, University of Ibadan. She is a seasoned entrepreneur both in teaching and practice.

Rotimi Olaniyan has a D.B.A. from Nottingham Business School, where he is Senior Lecturer in Marketing and course leader for the Full time M.B.A. His research interests lie in Entrepreneurial Marketing, and Services Systems. He has had 30 years of industry experience in four countries, prior to joining academia.

Romanus Osabohien is a Lecturer at Department of Economics and Development Studies, and a Research Fellow at Centre for Economic Policy and Development Research (CEPDeR), Covenant University, Nigeria. His research focuses on food security and social protection where he has published numerous peer-reviewed papers in rated journals.

Evans Osabuohien is a Professor of Economics and Head, Department of Economics & Development Studies, Covenant University, Nigeria. He has executed research projects, published three books and over 135 papers. He has been recognised as youngest HOD (2016), Youngest Professor (2017) and One of the 6 Youngest Professors in Nigeria.

Dr. Adebowale Owoseni is a Senior Lecturer in Information Systems at De Montfort University. Prior to joining the academia, he worked as a software developer and solution architect in the financial services sector for 13 years. He researches and teaches on computing for small business, digital transformation and ICT for development.

Pascale Peters is a Full Professor in Strategic Human Resource Management (HRM) at Nyenrode Business Universiteit, Netherlands. Her research interests relate to Sustainable HRM, flexible working, new ways of working, work-life balance and boundary management.

Professor David Rae is a Professor of Enterprise and Director of the Centre for Enterprise & Innovation at Leicester Castle Business School, De Montfort University. He is an innovator and researcher in entrepreneurial learning, leadership, and management who has held senior academic roles at six universities. He won the European Entrepreneurship Education Award in 2020.

Dr. Ibrahim Rufai is a Senior Lecturer in Business and Management and Programme Lead, Senior Leadership Management Degree Apprenticeship at De Montfort University, UK. His research interests are in the areas of SMEs' Performance Outomes from ICTs' Deployment, Anticorruption Initiatives in Business Management and Strategic Management in SMEs.

Dr. Samuel Salia is a Senior Lecturer in Accounting and Finance at De Montfort University. He holds a Ph.D. in Finance from Birmingham City University. Dr Salia's research interest is multidisciplinary with specific focus on diaspora finance, entrepreneurial finance and financial market development.

Louise Scholes is a Reader in Entrepreneurship at Loughborough University London and the Director of the Institute for Innovation and Entrepreneurship. Her main research interests focus on family firms, and management buyouts and their consequences. She is on the editorial board of the International Small Business Journals and has also published on many top-ranking journals.

Veronica Scuotto is a Full Professor at the University of Turin (Italy). She previously worked at the University of the West of Scotland and the Pôle Universitaire Léonard de Vinci in Paris. She has published several articles in international peer-reviewed journals (3* and 4* ABS list). She is an international guest speaker and conference organiser.

Dr. Robert Smith is on special research leave from the UN Office for the Coordination of Humanitarian Affairs, where he has previously worked on humanitarian strategic planning, the humanitarian-development-peacebuilding nexus, and the World Humanitarian Summit. He has published on social capital in humanitarian crises, land reform and other topics.

Robert Smith is an Independent Scholar and Consultant based in Aberdeen, Scotland and was formerly a Professor of Enterprise and Innovation at the University of the West of Scotland and a Reader in Entrepreneurship at Robert Gordon University, Aberdeen. He has 200 publications in international peer-reviewed journals and book chapters.

Patience Tunji-Olayeni is Senior Lecturer at Department of Building Technology and the Chair, Regional Centre of Expertise Ogun (RCE Ogun), Covenant University, a Centre that serves as a learning space for sustainable development with focus on financial and digital literacy of SMEs and youths in the region.

Marloes van Engen is Associate Professor at the Center of Strategy, Organisation and Leadership at Nyenrode Business Universiteit, and also works at the Department of Human Resource Studies, Tilburg University, The Netherlands. Her research interest in understanding and advancing Diversity, Equality and Inclusion in Organisations, and in sustainability in Work and Home.

Jean T. Wells a licensed CPA and attorney, is an Associate Professor at Howard University School of Business where she teaches tax, business law and accounting courses. Ms. Wells earned a Bachelor's in Business Administration (B.B.A.) Accounting from Howard University and a Juris Doctorate from George Washington University.

Wheeler R. Winstead, Ph.D., M.B.A. is the Assistant Director for the Center for African Studies and faculty in the Department of African Studies, Howard University. Winstead is a Fulbright Specialist and Lusofone cultural scholar. He received his Ph.D. in African Studies from Howard. His area of interest is African Entrepreneurship.

Kassa Woldesenbet Beta, Ph.D. is an Associate Professor in Research and Deputy Director of the Centre for Enterprise and Innovation at the Leicester Castle Business School, De Montfort University. His research interests cut across various themes including dynamic capabilities, family business, inclusive entrepreneurship, institutions, SMEs, and transition economies.

List of Figures

Fig. 2.1	Conceptual model and summary of key findings	30
Fig. 3.1	World Bank average of ease of doing business among regional economies (*Source* World Bank doing business report [2019])	52
Fig. 3.2	Entrepreneurial enabling institutional framework	57
Fig. 4.1	Conceptual framework	77
Fig. 4.2	Models and propositions—Interaction between institutions and family businesses	84
Fig. 5.1	The informal economy in SSA, 2010 to 2014 average as a share of gross domestic product (GDP) (*Source* Medina et al. [2016]. *Note* Data excludes Cape Verde, Eritrea, Ethiopia, The Gambia, São Tomé and Príncipe, Seychelles, and South Sudan due to lack of an informality measure)	97
Fig. 6.1	The research purpose	116
Fig. 6.2	Conceptualising the effect of institutional context on community entrepreneurship behaviour	123
Fig. 6.3	The three case communities	125
Fig. 6.4	The table of hypotheses	125
Fig. 6.5	An analysis of the case community contexts of three Nigerian community enterprises (*Source* Adapted from DeBruin and Dupuis [1995]; Hindle [2010] and Welter [2011])	126
Fig. 6.6	Rating the institutional context of three Nigerian community enterprises	128
Fig. 6.7	Chi-square values for institutional rules	130
Fig. 6.8	A comparative assessment of institutional factor communalities across three Nigerian community enterprises	131

List of Figures

Fig. 6.9	Strength and direction of institutional factor communalities on community entrepreneurial behaviour across three Nigerian community enterprises	133
Fig. 6.10	The institutional context and community entrepreneurial behaviour	137
Fig. 9.1	Young Hawkers on Lagos streets (*Source* Authors [2019])	204
Fig. 11.1	A Triple Helix model of EE provision and outcomes (*Source* The Authors)	246
Fig. 11.2	Unemployment rate in Nigeria (Trading Economics, 2021)	249
Fig. 12.1	African states showing all index scores A–Z	285
Fig. 12.2	African states ranked by mean score	286
Fig. 12.3	Afro-continental map of mean scores	287
Fig. 12.4	Regional mean scores	288
Fig. 12.5	Connecting data sources and themes	291
Fig. 12.6	Institutional, human capital and technology factors influencing open entrepreneurship	292
Fig. 13.1	Developing regions with the highest potential for solar, wind, hydro, and geothermal energy (*Source* Adapted from "Development of Wind Energy in Africa" by Alli D. Mukasa, Emelly Mutambatsere, Yannis Arvanitis, and Thouraya Triki, March 2013, in Working Paper Series N° 170 African Development Bank)	317
Fig. 13.2	Five Biggest Wind Markets in Africa (*Source* "The five biggest wind energy markets in Africa" by Tony Tiyou (2016), October 19, in Renewable Energy Focus.com, International Solar Energy Society)	319
Fig. 16.1	The triple nexus framework (*Source* Howe, 2019)	388
Fig. 16.2	Social capital and entrepreneurship in situations of forced displacement (authors)	393
Fig. 17.1	Social determinants of refugee entrepreneurships and levels of analysis (*Source* Author(s))	411
Fig. 17.2	Sub-Sahara Africa refugee population 1990–2018	411
Fig. 17.3	Map of Kenya showing its neighbouring countries (*Source* cia.gov)	414
Fig. 17.4	Map of designated refugee camps and urban refugee areas (*Source* UNHCR.org)	415
Fig. 17.5	Social capital framework for refugee entrepreneurship (*Source* Authors)	426
Fig. 18.1	Phases of Libyan enterprise development (author generated)	443
Fig. 18.2	Factors affecting Libyan SME success (author generated)	450
Fig. 18.3	The Libya Enterprise Centre and entrepreneurial ecosystem (Author generated)	452
Fig. 21.1	Yearly trend of publications (*Source* Authors)	520
Fig. 21.2	Research methods across articles (*Source* Authors)	521

Fig. 22.1	Theoretical framework	552
Fig. 22.2	Drivers of entrepreneurial motivation identified by the respondents (Figures represent the number of counts not participants) (*Notes* Each participant identified multiple factors that motivated them to engage in entrepreneurial activities)	556
Fig. 22.3	Drivers of Oscillation identified by the respondents in this study (Figures represent the number of counts not participants) (*Notes* Each participant identified multiple factors that influenced their oscillation between paid and self employment)	561
Fig. 23.1	Geographical coverage of the World Bank Enterprise Surveys (WBES) (*Source* https://www.enterprisesurveysorg/en/survey-datasets, accessed April 22, 2020)	583

List of Tables

Table 2.1	Key characteristics of case firms	27
Table 2.2	Summary of key dynamic capabilities and their content	29
Table 3.1	Highlight of enabling institutional features for select African economies	56
Table 5.1	MSMEs: definition and typical numbers in SSA	96
Table 5.2	Sub-Saharan Africa (SSA) countries ranking on 'Enterprise conditions' among 54 countries	101
Table 7.1	Variables and sources	152
Table 7.2	Summary statistics—mean and standard deviation of EFC and EBA variables	156
Table 7.3	Summary statistics—mean and standard deviation of control and instrumental variables (including dependent variable)	159
Table 7.4	Correlation of the sample variables for DFS, EBA and EFC	161
Table 7.5	Multivariate regression results for diaspora financing strategy and entrepreneurship framework conditions	162
Table 7.6	Multivariate regression results for diaspora financing strategy and entrepreneurial behaviour and attitudes	163
Table 10.1	Graduate entrepreneur digital tools and social media usage	232
Table 11.1	Barriers to effective implementation of entrepreneurship education in Nigeria	252
Table 12.1	Indices covering economic openness in African countries	278
Table 12.2	Overview of data source and indicators included	283
Table 12.3	Regional average scores	288
Table 12.4	Mapping of indicators into thematic categories	290

List of Tables

Table 14.1	Profile of respondents	337
Table 14.2	Representative quotes supporting the interview themes	339
Table 14.3	Nigeria's Global Innovation Ranking (2007–2020)	342
Table 14.4	Comparative Global Innovation Ranking of Nigeria, Kenya, South Africa, Egypt and Rwanda	343
Table 15.1	Sample table	362
Table 15.2	Most used communication technology medium by the sampled companies	366
Table 15.3	Respondents' views on communication technology media as catalysts for business performance improvement	367
Table 15.4	Current state of performance of communication technology-driven companies compared to their pre-ICT experience	367
Table 15.5	Major influencing factor in local context	368
Table 16.1	Profile of respondents	398
Table 17.1	Social capital amongst refugees in Kenya	419
Table 18.1	Methods of Islamic banking	447
Table 18.2	Types of Libyan SMEs	448
Table 20.1	Summary of results	502
Table 21.1	Geographical coverage of publications	520
Table 21.2	Theoretical perspectives	522
Table 21.3	Main issues covered in thematic areas	523
Table 22.1	Description of Sample	554
Table 22.2	Challenges facing women entrepreneurs in SSA	562
Table 23.1	A comparison of administrative and micro surveys	574
Table 23.2	African countries in the World Bank Enterprise Surveys (WBES), 2006–2020	584
Table 23.3	Country and variable coverage in the African Sector Database (ASD)	585
Table 23.4	Sector coverage in the African Sector Database (ASD)	586
Table 23.5	African countries in the Living Standards Measurement Study (LSMS)	587
Table 23.6	African countries in the Global Entrepreneurship Monitor	589
Table 24.1	Guidance on using case study in African entrepreneurship	609

1

Introduction

Oluwaseun Kolade, David Rae, Demola Obembe, and Kassa Woldesenbet Beta

For a long time, the dominant narrative about the African continent was one associated with wars, poverty and underdevelopment. In the years immediately following independence from colonialism, a wave of nationalist fervour swept through Sub-Saharan Africa. The new African governments embarked on big infrastructural projects and agrarian reforms aimed at linking remote rural areas with big urban centres and driving up agricultural production. Farm settlements were launched and smallholder rural farmers were organised into cooperatives. The agrarian reform, supported by newly established agricultural research institutes and extension agencies, sought to harness comparative advantage in the agricultural sector to shore up export and

---

O. Kolade (✉) · D. Rae
Department of Management & Entrepreneurship, De Montfort University, Leicester, UK
e-mail: seun.kolade@dmu.ac.uk

D. Rae
e-mail: david.rae@dmu.ac.uk

D. Obembe · K. Woldesenbet Beta
De Montfort University, Leicester, UK
e-mail: dobembe@dmu.ac.uk

K. Woldesenbet Beta
e-mail: kwoldesenbet@dmu.ac.uk

generate revenue that could be invested in public services and other sectors of the economy.

The modest gains of the agrarian reform, however, were limited, partly because of the unstable international market and volatility in commodity prices. In addition, the subsequent discovery of crude oil and the increasing dominance of the extractive sector as the principal source of foreign exchange in many countries contributed to reduced investment and attention on the agricultural sector. This precipitated the emergence of rent-seeking, resource conflicts and political upheavals across the continent. The continent also became caught up in the cold war, thereby exacerbating already volatile political conditions and institutional environments.

In the intervening years, bilateral organisations and multilateral agencies such as the IMF and World Bank spearheaded a range of free-market economic reforms on the continent, supporting strategies such as structural adjustment programmes (SAP), privatisation schemes and, latterly, poverty reduction strategy papers. These interventions have had mixed impacts, and many stakeholders and scholars have argued that the top-down approach of international aid regime has exacerbated, rather than mitigated, undedevelopment and inequality on the continent (Geo-JaJa & Mangum, 2001; Riddell, 1992).

Since the turn of the millennium, many stakeholders, including African scholars and policymakers, have called for a paradigm shift in the model of international engagement with African countries. Specifically, there have been growing calls for a departure from a dependency-inducing, paternalistic aid model to a new era of partnership underpinned by the agency of African peoples. This new approach, it is argued, will be defined by ambitious, innovative entrepreneurs driving a new era of shared prosperity and inclusive development on the continent. However, while the vision of a new Africa led by ambitious entrepreneurs is compelling, questions and challenges remain on how these grand ideas can be operationalised in countries characterised by institutional volatility and political instability, cultural contexts with limited opportunities for women, and where entrepreneurs struggle to access funding.

Given the foregoing, this book brings together empirical insights and case studies from various countries across the sub-regions to illuminate contextual peculiarities and common theoretical and practical insights that can inform policy and practice. These are explored within the framework of the following thematic sections: institutional environments and entrepreneurial ecosystems; entrepreneurship education; technology entrepreneurship and innovation ecosystems; entrepreneurship in conflict zones; gender and diversity issues in African entrepreneurship; and methodological considerations for African entrepreneurship research.

The first part recognises that weak and unstable institutional environments pose a major obstacle to entrepreneurship in African countries. The business environment in African countries is typically characterised by institutional voids, volatile market environment, derelict infrastructure and political instability, among others. Turbulent environments are generally characterised by high levels of inter-period change that creates uncertainty and unpredictability, sharp discontinuities in supply and demand, and low barriers to entry and exit (Calantone et al., 2003). Political instability is defined as "the propensity of change in the executive, either by constitutional or unconstitutional means" (Alesina & Perotti, 1996, p. 3). In a sense, entrepreneurs thrive in some forms of instability (Lechler et al., 2012). For example, profit opportunities are often associated with market disequilibrium, and the ability of entrepreneurs to identify and act on these opportunities to "equilibrate" the market (Holcombe, 2003). However, other forms of instability tend to have net negative impacts, precipitating more difficulties than they generate opportunities (Shumetie & Watabaji, 2019).

Furthermore, recent studies have also found that differences in the types and qualities of physical infrastructures, such as transport, energy, broadband, etc., account for differences in regional and national levels of entrepreneurial activity and productivity. While start-up activities were found to be positively associated with good infrastructure in general, some types of infrastructures, such as broadband, were found to have more significant impact (Audretsch et al., 2015). Many African countries face significant challenges with infrastructure, and these have had significant impacts especially on nascent entrepreneurs grappling with the liabilities of newness and smallness. Nevertheless, there are also country-specific peculiarities, unique sectoral challenges and regional differences in infrastructural development, and how these influence business activities on the continent (Agbemabiese et al., 2012; Aworemi, 2013; Igwe et al., 2013). Thus, the chapters in Part I seeks to explore these institutional challenges, while exploring new models that can be used to help budding entrepreneurs overcome the challenges associated with doing business in turbulent environments. The six chapters in this part deal with the links between the institutional environment and entrepreneurship in Africa. Chapter 1 by Mustafa and Scholes, using the dynamic capabilities perspective, examines the key capabilities that are critical to the survival of Zambian SME international ventures post North Africa market entry. Their chapter highlights the importance of sensing and seizing capabilities to the post-entry performance and survival of Zambian SME international ventures. In Chapter 2, Ogunsade, Obembe and Woldesenbet Beta examines the impact of formal and informal institutional contexts on the emergence and success of nascent entrepreneurship in the context of Nigeria. The chapter provides judicious insights into the links between the entrepreneurial governance and public policy and a recursive relationship between the various dimensions of institutions (normative, regulative, and cultural-cognitive) and entrepreneurship-enabling ecosystem for fostering venture creation. This is followed by Chapter 3 where Murithi and Woldesenbet Beta analyse the mutual influence of institutional environment and family business in Africa. Drawing on institutional theory, institutional voids, social capital and family business literatures, the authors develop a conceptual model and advance several theoretically and contextually driven propositions to guide future research on the bi-directional relationship (positive or negative) between the entrepreneurial activities of family business and the institutional environment.

In Chapter 4, Olagboye and colleagues explore enterprise categorisations and the implications for survival and growth. They propose the establishment of a new Nano Enterprise classification to promote legitimisation and institutionalisation of hitherto informal enterprises, and consequently enable their survival and growth within the Sub-Saharan region. This resonates with Olaniyan's contribution in Chapter 5, which adopts a case approach to examine perceived debilitating impacts of institutional environments on community enterprises in a national context and proposes a diagnostic model for fostering favour interactions between the institutions and target entrepreneurial communities. Then, in Chapter 6, Salia and colleagues further examine the role of financial remittance from Africans in diaspora in facilitating entrepreneurial ecosystem development. They argue that diaspora will increase remittances in response to good entrepreneurship framework conditions created by home countries, to boost enterprise development, and equally for the need to engage international finance and governance organisations in facilitating enabling institutional environments and identifying funding sources.

Part II follows on from this with its focus on entrepreneurship education. This is an area that has attracted increasing attention from scholars and practitioners within the last decade. It offers new paths for enquiries and opportunities to develop new research agendas in a continent where increasing population growth presents a unique set of challenges and opportunities for shaping the future of job opportunities and inclusive growth through entrepreneurial training. Entrepreneurship has a crucial role in generating future employment, prosperity and providing tradeable goods and vital services in a rapidly modernising and digitising context (Dana et al., 2018). Youth unemployment and underemployment with undesirable social, economic and political consequences is the alternative which must be addressed and prevented through multiple approaches (British Council, 2018). There is increasing demand, even hunger for entrepreneurship from young people, and growing engagement and innovation from actors in technology, education, business and community activism.

The part explores the roles of entrepreneurship education and learning at a Pan-African level. While there have been studies at national and subnational scope, and at different levels of education, these have tended to be of limited applicability to the scale of the challenges which are faced. New approaches are required and are being developed, such as action-oriented "bootcamps" for venture creation, enabling open access to education and learning for entrepreneurship (Rae, 2019), and innovation in terms of the curriculum, learning processes and effective support within the existing business ecosystems for start-ups. Thus, in Chapter 7, Mwila explores the gaps and opportunities for embedding entrepreneurship education in secondary school curricula in South Africa. This is against the backdrop of disproportionate focus on university undergraduates and the need to provide entrepreneurial training opportunities for those "left behind". Oladejo and Mafimisebi extend this conversation in Chapter 8, where they use a "risk society" framework to propose some new ideas to provide entrepreneurship education at basic education level in Nigeria. This approach, they argued, will promote inclusive entrepreneurship. It will help "bridge the gaps and challenges of risk society and connect them to sustainable enterprise solutions". In Chapter 9, Alabi and colleagues take a new look at university-level entrepreneurship education. Using a community of practice approach, they discuss the importance of entrepreneurship training as a driver of increased competencies in, and uptake of digital technologies, and higher rates of successful new venture creation. Finally, in Chapter 10, Kolade and co-authors propose a new model of co-produced entrepreneurship education, based on the triple helix framework of university, industry and government collaboration. Using the empirical context of the Nigerian higher education sector and the single case study of a leading Nigerian university, the authors argued that the co-creation model can more effectively pool and integrate the best that all stakeholders can offer towards the design and delivery of entrepreneurship education programmes, not only in Nigeria but across the continent.

Part III addresses the theme of technology entrepreneurship. Many scholars and stakeholders have argued that recent developments in digital economies offer an auspicious opportunity for countries and regions at economic margins to "transcend spatial, organisational, social, and political constraints" (Graham, 2019, p. 1) in the drive to launch themselves into the mainstream of global growth and prosperity. Digital technologies are already transforming African economies in terms of retail payment systems, financial inclusion, sustainable business models and revenue administration (Ndung'u, 2018). Other scholars have argued that the fourth industrial revolution offers new and dynamic opportunities for Africa's industrial strategy, with options in automation, additive manufacturing, and the industrial internet (Ayentimi & Burgess, 2019; Naudé, 2017). Chapters 11–14 explore this theme in different conceptual directions and empirical contexts. In Chapter 11, Rae and colleagues pose the question: "are African economies open for entrepreneurship?" To address this question, the authors selected five internationally recognised indices to develop a composite pan-African framework which maps and compares differences and similarities in economic openness and opportunities for digital and entrepreneurial learning across 54 African states. Winstead and Wells bring this conversation to the micro level in Chapter 12. There, they argued against the often-dominant narrative of gloom that the emergence and growth of youth-led digital entrepreneurship is setting a new and positive tone for the rising future of the continent. Adepoju brings us back to the present in Chapter 13, where he discusses the difficult realities of Nigerian digital entrepreneurs struggling to escape the proverbial "valley of death". He provides practical and policy recommendations to support the development and resilience of the Nigerian innovation ecosystem. Finally, in Chapter 14, Rufai highlights location-specific factors that explain differences in levels of ICT uptake among SMEs across affluent and disadvantaged districts of Lagos. He proposes a new concept of "symbiotic interactionism" which, he argues, better explains and integrates the roles of social factors and technological determinism in shaping SMEs' attitudes and responses to technology.

Part IV focuses on entrepreneurship in conflict zones. Within the past decade, two important and related concepts have gained traction within the entrepreneurship literature. The first is the idea of emancipatory entrepreneurship, and the other is the better-developed theory of transformative entrepreneuring. Emancipatory entrepreneuring is linked more closely with Sen's ideas around capabilities and functionings (Hick, 2012; Sen, 2008), and it has been explored in the contexts of poverty and forced displacement (Al-Dajani et al., 2015). It emphasises the scope for the poor and the displaced to exercise their agency to beat the poverty trap and break "free from the authority of another". Similarly, transformative entrepreneuring has been defined as "the process of addressing and ultimately transforming conditions of protracted socio-economic constraint through entrepreneurship" (Tobias et al., 2013, p. 728).

At the heart of most man-made conflicts is the over-arching question of resource struggle (Humphreys, 2005). This can be about the struggle for resources either in their primary or secondary forms, which may be related to greed overabundance or grievance induced by scarcity (Brunnschweiler & Bulte, 2009). Conflicts typically arise when resources are appropriated by dominant groups and distributed unequally. Poverty is often associated with lack of access to resources or the lack of capacity to transform resources and create value from them. The resource-scarcity-poverty-conflict nexus is exacerbated by population growth and density (Magnus Theisen, 2008; Urdal, 2005). The more people live in smaller areas of usable land, for example, the more likely there will be violent struggle for resources. Conflict and poverty induced by resource conflict are especially common in developing countries, where there is heavy reliance on natural resource rent. Entrepreneurship can facilitate a positive change in a population's interaction with resources (Hart, 1995). Instead of engaging in violent conflict over limited natural resources, citizens can be co-opted as co-creators of new resources for the benefit of all. The entrepreneurship process has several direct practical implications on the dynamics of poverty and conflict. Entrepreneurship can create new employment opportunities, and therefore raise household income and welfare. Furthermore, by creating new resources, entrepreneurship invariably makes new resources available for the population, thereby reducing resource poverty.

Thus, the chapters in Part IV draw from different empirical contexts to explore strategies employed by entrepreneurs in conflict zones to overcome resource and institutional constraints, cope with danger, and recover their livelihoods in the aftermath of destruction and disruption precipitated by violent conflicts. Thus, in Chapter 15, Kolade and colleagues explore the case of forcibly displaced households in Northeast Nigeria, where Boko Haram insurgency has precipitated a severe humanitarian crisis. There, rather rely only on humanitarian aid, displaced peoples are drawing on bridging and linking networks to create and harness new entrepreneurial opportunities to recover their livelihoods. In Kenya, the contextual focus of Chapter 16, Luseno and Kolade discuss how refugees are drawing on their bridging and linking networks to overcome the strains and constraints of the host government's encampment policy. They are deploying these network resources to access entrepreneurial opportunities for livelihood recovery and contribution to the host country's economic outcomes. In Chapter 17, Esaudi, and co-authors draw on historical and cultural evidence to discuss the special case of Libya, a country trapped in seemingly intractable internecine war, and where SME activities and entrepreneurial endeavour have suffered significant setbacks. Finally, in Chapter 18, Imoedemhe brings a legal perspective to analysis of the patterns of conflicts fuelled by internal and external forces in some African countries, and how they inhibit entrepreneurial development and SME growth.

Part V addresses live issues around diversity and gender in African entrepreneurship. Women make significant contributions to employment and wealth creation, innovation, uplifting of living standards, and reducing poverty in all economies (Brush et al., 2009; De Vita et al., 2014) not least in African countries (GEM, 2013). While an estimated 163 million women around the world are involved in new business ventures, a significant "gender gap" persists in entrepreneurship (Jennings & Brush, 2013; Kelley et al., 2017) and creates challenges to women's entrepreneurship. However, the ability of women to start and grow their businesses and to achieve empowerment is hindered where legal, institutional and cultural barriers exist and combine with resource constraints and domestic responsibilities that affect women's enterprises to a greater extent than men's (Carter et al., 2015; Jennings & Brush, 2013).

Women's entrepreneurship research evidence indicates that "entrepreneurship is a gendered and highly contextual phenomenon (Henry et al., 2016). While women entrepreneurs might share similar motivations and hurdles, specific contexts, certain socio-economic and political geographies uniquely pattern issues and opportunities they experience. As such, women in developing countries suffer more from underdeveloped institutional, resource and family environments, whereas the women in Africa suffer less from internal family restrictions (Pand, 2008). The gendered assumptions also confer detriment upon women in terms of creating or growing new ventures (Marlow & McAdam, 2015). Gudeta and co-authors, in Chapter 19, offer theoretical and practical insights to the field of (women) entrepreneurship and the work-family literature by exploring the relationship between the work-family roles and business growth in a less researched Sub-Saharan African country, Ethiopia. Chapter 20 probes the challenges and opportunities associated with African women entrepreneurs' access to and use of enterprising resources. By undertaking the systematic review of studies undertaken from 1990–2020, Woldesenbet Beta and colleagues found that studies on African women's access to, and use of, resources have been a very recent phenomenon, were theoretically fragmented, mainly quantitative, and thus unable to develop a nuanced understanding of gender and entrepreneurship in Africa. Irene and coauthors, in Chapter 21, provide judicious empirical insights into why women entrepreneurs in South Africa move back and forth from self-employment to paid employment. Their study illuminates the factors that influence South African women's entrepreneurial venture on the one hand, and consequential impact on their reverting back to regular paid employment.

The final Part VI, discusses methodological issues in African entrepreneurship research. African research in general, and African business research especially, is beset by a range of practical challenges associated with limited access to data (Klingebiel & Stadler, 2015), gaps in quality assurance mechanisms (Gimbel et al., 2017) and difficulties and ambiguities often inherent in adopting operational variables and units of analyses from empirical studies carried out in western contexts (Fadahunsi, 2000; Kolk & Rivera-Santos, 2018). Thus, the chapters in this part include reflective practitioner commentaries and practical suggestions that can be employed to deal with various field work challenges in African entrepreneurship research. Egbetokun, in Chapter 22, considers challenges and opportunities associated with conducting national surveys, drawing from the author's experience with the Nigerian Innovation Surveys. In Chapter 23, Mafimisebi and Nyame-Asiamah reflect on challenges of carrying out case study research in Africa, providing practical suggestions on data management and triangulation of data, among others.

Overall, the chapters across these six parts offer a unique insight into the often simplified but quite multi-layered, complex world of African entrepreneurship. As well as identifying threads of common challenges and practices, the book weaves an intricate tapestry around problems and prospects, cultures and contexts, and the features and future of entrepreneurship and innovation in the African continent.

We now offer some final thoughts on the future challenges and opportunities, as well as recommendations for future research.

First, we observe that the digital transformation of the global economic landscape offers an auspicious opportunity for African countries to chart a new course for inclusive development and shared prosperity on the continent. The advent of the "fourth industrial revolution", driven by new technologies, has captured popular imagination and attracted significant scholarly interest. This new wave of disruptive technologies presents both significant risks as well as enormous opportunities for African countries. On the one hand,

African countries face the risk of falling further behind in a fast-paced knowledge economy dominated by disruptive innovations. On the other hand, Africa is presented with enormous opportunities to catch up, or even leapfrog developed countries to play a leading role in the unfolding fourth industrial revolution.

Technology-based entrepreneurship is set to play a key role if African countries are to harness the opportunities of the fourth industrial revolution. The last five years have witnessed a rapid expansion of tech hubs in Africa. One report indicated that, as of 2015, there were 117 tech hubs in Africa. The vast majority of these were owned or led by the private sector, with only nine led by academic institutions and 10 of them government-owned (Kelly & Firestone, 2016). Between 2016 and 2019, African countries witnessed a significant expansion of tech hubs, from 314 in 2016 to 442 in 2018 and 643 as of October 2019 (Giuliani et al., 2019). In other words, African tech hubs have more than doubled within the last three years leading to 2019.

One of the key areas in which disruptive technologies can have a major impact is entrepreneurial financing. While we have seen a lot of positive stories of development and progress over the last decade, a majority of African entrepreneurs continue to struggle with the big problem of funding. The formal finance institutions continue to operate under old models that shut scores of millions of entrepreneurs out of funding opportunities. New fintech organisations are now disrupting the sector with innovative models which expand access to small and micro enterprises and start-ups, while effectively controlling the risks. Crowdfunding platforms are rapidly expanding across the continent, and e-money has taken hold in East African countries like Kenya. There is also a strong wave of interest in cryptocurrency and the opportunities it holds to drive enterprise growth, financial inclusion and better integration with the global market. These new opportunities are also fraught with risks for which there is a need for focused scholarly engagement. However, given that these disruptive innovations are happening despite static and often negative institutional environments, a new research agenda should interrogate the potential opportunities for technologies to drive institutional transformation on the continent.

Furthermore, for these promises to be realised, stakeholders and scholars need to give more attention to interrogating the facilities and opportunities for training and development of high-tech, high-impact entrepreneurs in Africa. Researchers have begun to investigate the impact of education policy on the supply of "high quality entrepreneurs" in Africa (Olofiyehun et al., 2018). However, there are still significant gaps and opportunities to investigate innovative structures, approaches and programmes that higher education actors can deploy to support the development of home-grown entrepreneurs that are better equipped to take advantage of local contexts and peculiarities as well as compete on the global scale. There are numerous new initiatives bringing the triple helix of university, industry and government stakeholders to develop new models of entrepreneurship education and facilities for start-ups. There are rooms to generate new ideas and knowledge regarding the future of university education on the continent. Beyond this, there is much activity, yet little is known from a scholarly perspective, about opportunities and structures for entrepreneurial learning and development outside the university system. New spaces for entrepreneurial learning and peer mentoring include tech hubs, DIY labs, social media platforms and other virtual spaces. There is a need for a new research agenda investigating the contributions and impacts of these channels in diffusing and nurturing new models of entrepreneurial activities on the continent. We have confidence that the capabilities of African entrepreneurs and researchers will rise to the challenges of achieving combined progress in both entrepreneurial innovation and in researching it.

References

Agbemabiese, L., Nkomo, J., & Sokona, Y. (2012). Enabling innovations in energy access: An African perspective. *Energy Policy, 47*, 38–47. https://doi.org/10.1016/j.enpol.2012.03.051.

Al-Dajani, H., et al. (2015). Entrepreneurship among the displaced and dispossessed: Exploring the limits of emancipatory entrepreneuring. *British Journal of Management, 26*(4), 713–730. https://doi.org/10.1111/1467-8551.12119.

Alesina, A., & Perotti, R. (1996). Income distribution, political instability, and investment. *European Economic Review, 40*(6), 1203–1228.

Audretsch, D. B., Heger, D., & Veith, T. (2015). Infrastructure and entrepreneurship. *Small Business Economics, 44*(2), 219–230. https://doi.org/10.1007/s11187-014-9600-6.

Aworemi, J. R. (2013). Impact of integrated transport system on the productivity of smes in selected South-Western states of Nigeria. *Journal of Economic and Sustainable Development, 4*(8), 1–6.

Ayentimi, D. T., & Burgess, J. (2019). Is the fourth industrial revolution relevant to sub-Sahara Africa? *Technology Analysis & Strategic Management, 31*(6), 641–652. https://doi.org/10.1080/09537325.2018.1542129.

Banerjee, A. V., & Duflo, E. (2011). *Poor economics: A radical rethinking of the way to fight global poverty*. Public Affairs.

Bates, T. (1997). Financing small business creation: The case of Chinese and Korean immigrant entrepreneurs. *Journal of Business Venturing, 12*(2), 109–124.

Belleflamme, P., Lambert, T., & Schwienbacher, A. (2014). Crowdfunding: Tapping the right crowd. *Journal of Business Venturing, 295*(5), 585–609.

Brune, L., Giné, X., Goldberg, J., & Yang, D. (2015). Facilitating savings for agriculture: Field experimental evidence from Malawi. *Economic Development and Cultural Change, 64*(2), 187–220. https://doi.org/10.1086/684014.

Brunnschweiler, C. N., & Bulte, E. H. (2009). Natural resources and violent conflict: Resource abundance, dependence, and the onset of civil wars. *Oxford Economic Papers, 61*(4). https://doi.org/10.1093/oep/gpp024.

Brush, C. G., De Bruin, A., & Welter, F. (2009). A gender-aware framework for women's entrepreneurship. *International Journal of Gender and Entrepreneurship, 1*, 8–24.

Bruton, G., Khavul, S., Siegel, D., & Wright, M. (2015). New financial alternatives in seeding entrepreneurship: Microfinance, crowdfunding and peer-to-peer innovations. *Entrepreneurship Theory and Practice, 39*(1), 9–26.

Buckley, P. J., Clegg, J., & Wang, C. (2002). Impact of inward FDI on the performance of Chinese manufacturing firms. *Journal of International Business Studies, 33*(4), 637–655.

Calantone, R., Garcia, R., & Droge, C. (2003). The effects of environmental turbulence on new product development strategy planning. *Journal of Product Innovation Management, 20*(2), 90–103. https://doi.org/10.1111/1540-5885.2002003.

Carter, S., Mwaura, S., Ram, M., Trehan, K., & Jones, T. (2015). Barriers to ethnic minority and women's enterprise: Existing evidence, policy tensions and unsettled questions. *International Small Business Journal, 33*(1), 49–69.

Coleman, S., & Robb, A. (2015). Financing high-growth women-owned enterprises: Evidence from the United States. In C. Díaz-García, C.G. Brush, E.G. Gatewood & F. Welter (Eds.), *Women's entrepreneurship in global and local contexts* (pp. 183–204). Cheltenham: Edward Elgar.

Cosh, A., Cumming, D., & Hughes, A. (2009). Outside entrepreneurial capital. *The Economic Journal, 119*, 1494–1533.

Cumming, D., Deloof, M., Manigart, S., & Wright, M. (2019). New directions in entrepreneurial finance. *Journal of Banking and Finance, 100*, 252–260.

Dana, L. P., Ratten, V., & Honyenuga, B. (Eds.). (2018). *African entrepreneurship: Challenges and opportunities for doing business*. Palgrave Macmillan.

De Vita, L., Mari, M., & Poggesi, S. (2014). Women entrepreneurs in and from developing countries: Evidences from the literature. *European Management Journal, 32*, 451–470.

Denis, J. D. (2004). Entrepreneurial finance: An overview of the issues and evidence. *Journal of Corporate Finance, 10*(2), 301–326.

Duflo, E., Banerjee, A., Glennerster, R., & Kinnan, C. G. (2013). *The miracle of microfinance? Evidence from a randomized evaluation* (Working Paper No. 18950). National Bureau of Economic Research. https://doi.org/10.1257/app.20130533.

Dupas, P., & Robinson, J. (2013). Savings constraints and microenterprise development: Evidence from a field experiment in Kenya. *American Economic Journal-Applied Economics, 5*(1), 163–192. https://doi.org/10.1257/app.5.1.163.

Fadahunsi, A. (2000). Researching informal entrepreneurship in Sub-Saharan Africa: A note on field methodology. *Journal of Developmental Entrepreneurship, 5*, 249. Article.

Flory, J. A. (2016). *Banking the poor: Evidence from a savings field experiment in Malawi* (Working Paper). Robert Day School of Economics and Finance, Claremont McKenna College.

Fu, H., Yang, J., & An, Y. (2019). Made for each other: Perfect matching in venture capital markets. *Journal of Banking & Finance, 100*, 346–358.

GEM. (2013). *Global entrepreneurships monitor 2013 global report: Fifteen years of assessing entrepreneurship across the globe.* Global Entrepreneurship Research Association, London Business School, London.

Geo-JaJa, M. A., & Mangum, G. (2001). Structural adjustment as an inadvertent enemy of human development in Africa. *Journal of Black Studies, 32*(1), 30–49. https://doi.org/10.1177/002193470103200102.

Gimbel, S., et al. (2017). Improving data quality across 3 Sub-Saharan African countries using the Consolidated Framework for Implementation Research (CFIR): Results from the African health initiative. *BMC Health Services Research, 17*(S3), 53–63. https://doi.org/10.1186/s12913-017-2660-y.

Graham, M. (Ed.). (2019) *Digital economies at global margins.* The MIT Press. https://doi.org/10.7551/mitpress/10890.001.0001.

Giuliani, D. et al. (2019). *Building a conducive setting for innovators to thrive a qualitative and quantitative study of a hundred hubs across Africa.* Available at: https://www.afrilabs.com/wpcontent/uploads/2019/11/AfriLabs-Innovation-Ecosystem-Report.pdf.

Hart, S. L. (1995). A natural-resource-based view of the firm. *Academy of Management Review.* https://doi.org/10.5465/amr.1995.9512280033.

Henry, C., Foss, L., & Ahl, H. (2016). Gender and entrepreneurship research: A review of methodological approaches. *International Small Business Journal, 34*(3), 217–241.

Hick, R. (2012). The capability approach: Insights for a new poverty focus. *Journal of Social Policy, 41*(2), 291–308. https://doi.org/10.1017/S0047279411000845.

Holcombe, R. G. (2003). The origins of entrepreneurial opportunities. *Review of Austrian Economics, 16*(1), 25–43. https://doi.org/10.1023/A:1022953123111.

Huang, Y., Khanna, T. (2003). Can India overtake China? *Foreign Policy, 137* (July–August).

Hulme, D., Moore, K., & Barrientos, A. (2015). Assessing the insurance role of microsavings. In R. Vos, N. Islam & M. Koparanova (Eds.), *Financing for overcoming economic insecurity.* Bloomsbury Publishing.

Humphreys, M. (2005). Natural Resources, conflict and conflict resolution. *Journal of Conflict Resolution, 49*, 508–537. https://doi.org/10.1177/0022002705277545.

Igwe, C. N., et al. (2013). A review of Nigeria' transportation system and the place of the entrepreneurs. *Journal of Sustainable Development Studies, 3*(2), 168–180. https://doi.org/10.1111/j.1467-8519.2005.00302_27.x.

Jennings, J. E., & Brush, C. G. (2013). Research on women entrepreneurs: Challenges to (and from) the broader entrepreneurship literature? *The Academy of Management Annals, 7*(1), 663–715.

Karlan, D., & Linden, L. L. (2014). *Loose knots: Strong versus weak commitments to save for education in Uganda* (Working Paper No. 19863). National Bureau of Economic Research.

Karlan, D., Ratan, A. L., & Zinman, J. (2014). Savings by and for the poor: A research review and agenda. *Review of Income and Wealth, 60*(1), 36–78. https://doi.org/10.1111/roiw.1210.

Kelley, D., Benjamin, B., Candida, B., & Patrica, G., et al. (2017). *Global entrepreneurship monitor 2016/2017*. Report on Women's Entrepreneurship. Babson College.

Klingebiel, R., & Stadler, C. (2015). Opportunities and challenges for empirical strategy research in Africa. *Africa Journal of Management Taylor & Francis, 1*(2), 194–200. https://doi.org/10.1080/23322373.2015.1026758.

Kolk, A., & Rivera-Santos, M. (2018). The state of research on Africa in business and management: Insights from a systematic review of key international journals. *Business and Society, 57*(3), 415–436. https://doi.org/10.1177/0007650316629129.

Ladge, J., Eddleston, K. A., & Sugiyama, K. (2019). Am I an entrepreneur? How imposter fears hinder women entrepreneurs' business growth. *Business Horizons, 62*(1), 615–624.

Lechler, T. G., Edington, B. H., & Gao, T. (2012). Challenging classic project management: Turning project uncertainties into business opportunities. *Project Management Journal, 43*(6), 59–69. https://doi.org/10.1002/pmj.21304.

Magnus Theisen, O. (2008). Blood and soil? Resource scarcity and internal armed conflict revisited. *Journal of Peace Research, 45*(6), 801–818. https://doi.org/10.1177/0022343308096157.

Marlow, S., & McAdam, M. (2015). The influence of gender upon entrepreneurial legitimacy. *Entrepreneurship Theory and Practice, 39*(4), 719–995.

Naudé, W. (2017). *Entrepreneurship, education and the fourth industrial revolution in Africa* (IZA Discussion Paper No. 10855).

Ndung'u, N. (2018). Harnessing Africa's digital potential: New tools for a new age. In *Foresight Africa* (pp. 84–99).

Nielsen, T. M., & Riddle, L. (2009). Investing in peace: The motivational dynamics of diaspora investment in post-conflict economies. *Journal of Business Ethics, 89*, 435–448.

Olofinyehun, A. O., Adelowo, C. M., & Egbetokun, A. A. (2018). The supply of high-quality entrepreneurs in developing countries: Evidence from Nigeria. *Science and Public Policy, 45*(2), 269–282. https://doi.org/10.1093/scipol/scx065.

Rae, D (2019). Entrepreneurship in the open space: A new dynamic for creating value? In D. Higgins, & P. Jones, (Eds.), *Creating entrepreneurial space: Talking through multi voices, reflections on emerging debates* (pp. 153–172). McGowan, P. Emerald.

Ramamurti, R. (2004). Developing countries and MNEs: Extending and enriching the research agenda. *Journal of International Business Studies, 35*(4), 277–283.

Riddell, J. B. (1992). Things fall apart again: Structural adjustment programmes in Sub-Saharan Africa. *The Journal of Modern African Studies, 30*(1), 53–68. https://doi.org/10.1017/S0022278X00007722.

Sen, A. (2008). Well-being, agency and freedom: The Dewey lectures 1984. *The Journal of Philosophy, 82*(4), 169–221.

Shumetie, A., & Watabaji, M. D. (2019). Effect of corruption and political instability on enterprises' innovativeness in Ethiopia: Pooled data based. *Journal of Innovation and Entrepreneurship, 8*(1), 11. https://doi.org/10.1186/s13731-019-0107-x.

Tobias, J., Mair, J., & Barbosa-Leiker, C. (2013). Toward a theory of transformative entrepreneuring: Poverty reduction and conflict resolution in Rwanda's entrepreneurial coffee sector. *Journal of Business Venturing, 28*(6), 728–742. https://doi.org/10.1016/j.jbusvent.2013.03.003.

Urdal, H. (2005). People vs. Malthus: Population pressure, environmental degradation, and armed conflict revisited. *Journal of Peace Research.* https://doi.org/10.1177/0022343305054089.

Walz, U., & Hirsch, J. (2019). The financing dynamics of newly founded firms. *Journal of Banking & Finance, 100*, 261–272.

Weston, M. (2018). *Next generation: Africa overview.* British Council.

Part I

Institutional Environments and Entrepreneurial Ecosystems

2

The Importance of Dynamic Capabilities in the Post North African Market Survival of African SMEs International New Ventures (INVs)

Michael Mustafa and Louise Scholes

Introduction

Continued globalization and technological advancements have led to increased firm internationalization behavior (Lu & Beamish, 2001; Scholes et al., 2015). Internationalization involves the expansion of business operations across country borders into geographic or global regions new to the organization (Hitt et al., 1994; McDougall & Oviatt, 2000). Evidence suggests that internationalization is a major driver of sustained economic growth, especially for the emerging economies of Africa (Ibeh, 2003; Ibeh et al., 2012; Kuada, 2006; Tvedten et al., 2014).

African SMEs are becoming increasingly active in the global arena (Marco & Patterson, 2010) as well as in intra-regional internationalization, the latter due to increased integration among some African economies (Boso et al., 2018; Mellahi & Mol, 2015). While African SMEs' ability to internationalize is a crucial ingredient for economic growth and development (Ruzzier et al., 2006), limited research exists on the processes, and especially how African

---

M. Mustafa (✉)
The University of Nottingham Malaysia, Semenyih, Malaysia
e-mail: Michael.mustafa@nottingham.edu.my

L. Scholes
Institute for Innovation and Entrepreneurship, Loughborough University, London, UK

SMEs survive and thrive in foreign markets post initial foreign market entry (Anderson, 2011; Calof & Viviers, 1995; Matanda, 2012; Mtigwe, 2004; Okpara, 2009).

The past 30 years have seen a growth in scholarly interest in the activities of international new ventures (INVs) from emerging economies (Autio et al., 2011; Coviello & Munro, 1997; Knight & Cavusgil, 2004). Current research into the internationalization of INV's has largely focused on the early internationalization phases of such enterprises (Autio et al., 2000; Coviello, 2006; Weerawardena et al., 2007). Consequently, the issue of how the early internationalization of developing economy INVs impacts their 'continued' growth and 'survival' in foreign markets remains highly understudied in the literature (Cavusgil & Knight, 2015; Gerschewski et al., 2018; Mudambi & Zahra, 2007; Sapienza et al., 2006; Zahra, 2005). This is particularly the case with SME INVs from Africa (Matanda, 2012; Mellahi & Mol, 2015; Mtigwe, 2004; Okpara, 2009). Research suggests that INVs from Africa can significantly increase their risk of failure by entering into international markets (Timmons, et al., 2004). Therefore, understanding the post-entry survival of African SME INVs may be of critical importance as such firms are likely to be subject to liabilities of foreignness, newness, smallness and social connectedness (Brüderl & Schüssler, 1990; Zaheer & Mosakowski, 1997; Zahra, 2005). The developing economy context may be particularly revealing here because of the accentuated need for capability development due to adverse external conditions such as political instability and lack of domestic finance (Khan & Lew, 2018; Riviere & Suder, 2016; Rutashobya & Jaensson, 2004).

With regard to the African context, considerable differences in institutional arrangements may be observed between the economies of Northern Africa (relatively more developed) versus Southern Africa (relatively less developed), wherein colonial, socio-economic legacies and geographic proximity to Europe and the Middle-east have resulted in significant differences with respect to capital, technology, knowledge and financing endowments (Arora & Vamvakidis, 2005). Such differences may provide SME INVs from the south opportunities to not only broaden their global market share (Anderson, 2011) but also to develop their existing resources and capabilities (Köksal & Özgül, 2010). The ability of INVs from developing economies to survive the organizational shock of foreign market expansion will depend on whether they are capable of developing new streams of capabilities and improving their existing ones (Hashai, 2011; Knight & Cavusgil, 2004; Sapienza et al., 2006). Specifically, the survival of developing economy SME INVs may require higher order capabilities (e.g., dynamic ones), which somewhat differ from those needed for daily business operations in domestic markets (e.g., ordinary or functional ones) (Agarwal & Helfat, 2009; Audretsch, 1995; Teece, 2014). In this respect, Teece (2007,p. 1341) conceptualized dynamic capabilities as being related to sensing, seizing and reconfiguring dimensions.

This chapter therefore draws on Teece's (2007) sensing, seizing and reconfiguring perspectives to explore which key capabilities are critical to the survival of African SME INVs post international market entry. Specifically, we focus on the early internationalization experiences of Zambian SMEs to North African markets in terms of the speed, scope and scale of the internationalization. Zambia is a resource-rich country in southern Africa with impressive economic growth (Dana & Ratten, 2017). Since the late 1990s, Zambia has developed numerous initiatives aimed at encouraging entrepreneurial activities and supporting the nation's many SMEs, significant contributors to the nation's socioeconomic development (Azmat & Samaratunga, 2009). However, many of Zambia's SMEs continue to suffer significant barriers to their development such as limited financing, human capital and knowledge (Anand, 2015). In this respect, we consider the rapid internationalization activities of Zambian SMEs to more developed North African markets as an opportunity for them to overcome some of these institutional constraints in their own countries.

Based on the above discussion this particular chapter seeks to answer the following questions:

a. *What is the speed, scale and scope of African SME INVs internationalization to North African markets?*
b. *Which key capabilities are critical for the post-entry survival of Southern African SME INVs in North African markets?*

Our study is based on five internationally active Zambian INVs from the service sector. The main contributions of this study are twofold. First, we address calls to explore the South-North African internationalization of African SMEs (Misati et al., 2017; Øyna & Alon, 2018). Specifically, we show that Zambian SMEs may internationalize rapidly with characteristics similar to other INVs discussed in the literature. Secondly, by drawing on Teece's (2007) dynamic capabilities approach, we address recent calls in the internationalization literature to consider the specific capabilities necessary for INVs from developing economies to survive and thrive after foreign market entry (Kiss et al., 2012). In particular, we highlight the importance of sensing and seizing capabilities to the post-entry performance and survival of Zambian SME INV. Specifically, we suggest that despite their limited home country resources, Zambian SME INVs were able to survive and thrive in North African markets by creating entrepreneurial initiatives, developing their networks, having a niche market and product focus, along with transforming and renewing existing capabilities.

Literature Review

International New Ventures (INVs) and African SMEs

Early research by Autio et al. (2000) and McDougall et al. (1994) showed how INVs were able to rapidly internationalize into foreign markets by utilizing their key resources and learning capabilities. Specifically, such research has typically suggested that the internationalization process of INV may differ significantly from more traditional and incremental approaches to internationalization, as INV often invest aggressively in building capabilities in their internationalization processes based on their home-based learning and country-specific advantages (Luo & Tung, 2007; Ramamurti & Singh, 2009). Additionally, recent developments in internationalization theory have further pointed to the liability of outsidership by highlighting the importance of developing business networks to learn about foreign markets (Johanson & Vahlne, 2009; Lew et al., 2016). Hence, INVs need to develop capabilities for their growth and survival in foreign markets as they have to regularly deal with the liabilities of smallness, newness and foreignness (Sui & Baum, 2014; Zaheer & Mosakowski, 1997; Zahra, 2005). In this respect, various studies have highlighted the significance of SMEs' dynamic capabilities in their internationalization success (Al-Aali & Teece, 2013; Dietmar et al. 2013; Swoboda & Olejnik, 2016; Villar et al. 2014).

Recently there has been a growth in scholarly interest concerning the internationalization activities of African SMEs (Boso et al., 2018; Ibeh et al., 2012; Teagarden Von Glinow & Mellahi, 2018). A combination of fierce competition from foreign enterprises in local markets (Moini et al., 2016) and un-favorable domestic operating environments (Puffer et al., 2016) are thought to deter many SMEs from internationalizing (Tvedten et al., 2015; Kiss et al., 2012). Yet, despite limited human, financial and tangible resources, many African SMEs are choosing to engage in international entrepreneurial activity (Acs & Amorós, 2008; Marco & Patterson, 2010).

The internationalization of African SMEs has attributed to the continents' rapid economic growth which in turn has galvanized more SMEs to take the risk of internationalizing to both regional and non-African markets

(Boso et al., 2016, 2018; Ibeh et al., 2012; Jones et al., 2018). Goncalves and Smith (2019) showed how African firms can leverage new technologies to internationalize rapidly, while Misati et al. (2017) demonstrated how Ugandan SMEs internationalized close to inception and rapidly into various African and non-African markets (Kundu & Katz, 2003). Such internationalization behaviors were largely akin to that of born-globals or INVs (Knight & Cavusgil, 1996; Øyna & Alon, 2018). However, the existing research on the internationalization of INVs from Africa has largely remained silent on the issue of which capabilities are necessary for their survival and growth once foreign market entry has been achieved.

Dynamic Capabilities and the Post-Entry Survival of African SMEs

Specific resources and capabilities are of crucial importance for INVs from developing economies to develop and sustain their competitive advantage in foreign markets (Barney, 2001; Hitt et al., 2001; Mudambi & Zahra, 2007; Sapienza et al., 2006; Wernerfelt, 1984). Thus, identifying the value-creating processes adopted by INVs to overcome their liabilities of foreignness and smallness necessary for post-entry survival and performance is worthy of further investigation, especially among INVs from emerging economies that are considered as being resource poor.

Given that many African INVs suffer from resource constraints (Chacar et al., 2010; Granér & Isaksson, 2002), a key concern for such enterprises remains securing the necessary amount of resources, and developing and diversifying their capabilities in order to ensure their growth and survival in international markets (Autio et al., 2011; Mudambi & Zahra, 2007; Sui & Baum, 2014). Resources themselves may not be sufficient for growth; however, as research has shown, the capability of deploying any resources is what is necessary for enterprise growth and survival (Verona, 1999). Dynamic capability refers to the organizational and strategic routines through which managers or enterprise owners alter their enterprises' resource base via the acquisition, shedding, integration and recombination of resources to generate new value creation (Autio et al., 2011; Eisenhardt & Martin, 2000). Specifically, dynamic capabilities highlight an enterprise's ability to reconfigure itself to adapt to its environment (Sapienza et al., 2006; Zott, 2003). Therefore, specific dynamic capabilities may be essential for post-entry survival and growth of African SME INVs in foreign markets (Teece, 2000).

Teece (2007) conceptually structured competence processes as 'sensing-seizing-reconfiguring' capabilities (i.e., dynamic capabilities). A sensing capability may enable African SME INVs to identify opportunities and threats present in foreign markets, thus explaining such enterprises' entrepreneurial risk-taking or risk-avoiding behaviors as well as its learning behaviors (Johanson & Vahlne, 2009). A seizing capability may help to explain African SME INVs innovation-creating process through the 'seizure' of opportunities and the accompanying development of capability and resource allocations. Finally, a 'reconfiguring' capability is related to African SME INVs' organizational value-capturing abilities, expressed by the re-alignment of resources, the re-designing of the organizational architecture followed by seizing opportunities. Teece's (2007) notion of dynamic capabilities provides a general framework to explore how African SME INVs develop the necessary capabilities to survive post-entry in dynamic foreign market environments.

Research Context and Post-Entry INV Capabilities

Internationalization to unfamiliar markets and new institutional environments poses significant challenges to INVs due to their limited ability to overcome the liabilities of foreignness and differences in institutional arrangements (Eden & Miller, 2004; Zaheer, 1995; Zaheer & Mosakowski, 1997). This may be particularly the case with African SME INVs internationalization from the less developed African economies of the South to more advanced African markets in the North (Chandra et al., 2012; Misati et al., 2017; Yoo & Reimannb, 2017; Kujala & Törnroos, 2018). Differences in institutional environments between the economies of Northern and Southern Africa exist because their colonial and socioeconomic experiences have resulted in considerable differences with respect to capital, technology, knowledge and financing (Arora & Vamvakidis, 2005). The research context for this particular study is Zambian SMEs in the service industry.

Zambia is a landlocked and resource-rich country and has recorded impressive economic growth since 2000 (Dana & Ratten, 2017). It has been considered one of the fastest growing economies in the world (Choongo, 2017; Phillips & Bhatia-Panthaki, 2007; Jones et al., 2018). In Zambia SMEs comprise of about 97% of private businesses, thus contributing to a significant proportion of employment and economic development (Azmat & Samaratunge, 2009). Since the 1990s, the Zambian government has pursued policies designed to encourage the competitive and sustainable growth and development of SMEs. The resulting entrepreneurial focus along with economic liberalization has resulted in the opening up of the service sector to significant foreign and local competition thus catalyzing internationalization activity, particularly among local SMEs.

Evidence suggests that SMEs from Southern African economies may choose to rapidly internationalize in order to remain competitive and to escape constraints in their domestic markets (Anand, 2015; Chacar et al., 2010; Granér & Isaksson, 2002; Mengistae & Pattillo, 2004). However, the rapid internationalization of Zambian SMEs to the more lucrative markets of Northern Africa may not be sufficient for their survival if they fail to develop the necessary capabilities to succeed in such markets (Misati et al., 2017; Sapienza et al., 2006). Hence, the Zambian context provides scope for the understanding of the post-entry survival of Southern African SME INVs to Northern Africa where the conditions may hinder its capability development and survival.

Method

An exploratory multiple case study approach was chosen (Yin, 2003). According to Eisenhardt (1989) and Yin (2003), multiple case studies allows for in-depth investigations of specific phenomena while also permitting researchers to explain cause-and-effect relationships. Our chosen approach allows for a deeper understanding of the internationalization process of SME INVs in Africa as perceived by those individuals who are most involved in the process and is consistent with prior studies investigating such phenomena.

Case Selection

We focus on INV SMEs from Zambia internationalizing to the more developed North African economies of Tunisia, Morocco, Algeria, Libya and Egypt. Our sample consisted of five INV SMEs from the Zambia's services sector. The Zambia Chamber of Small and Medium Business Associations (ZCSMBA) was contacted to identify potential member firms which met the following key criteria. Firstly, case firms had to meet the formal definition of an SME as outlined by the Zambian Small Enterprises Development Act of 1996, in that they employ up to 30 people and that their annual turnover does not exceed US$40,000; second, case firms had to be part of the Zambian services sector; third, case firms should have been engaged in international activities since or near inception; finally 25% of firm revenues should have come from foreign markets in North Africa within three years of inception. Based on the above criteria, five case firms were identified and selected for further investigation. Table 2.1 provides a summary of the key characteristics of the case study firms.

Data Collection and Analysis

The owner and key employees were chosen to be interviewed as they had the most in-depth knowledge regarding their firms' internationalization. All interviews were conducted in English, lasted approximately 45–60 min in duration and followed a semi-structured interview protocol. Eisenhardt (1989) suggested this approach can be used to facilitate some level of standardization and cross-case analysis. All interviews were digitally recorded and transcribed verbatim. Specific interview questions include: *What factors enabled your company to succeed once in the North African market? Could you explain how your company developed the skills and ability to successfully compete in North Africa? How did you manage to survive and prosper in the North African market?*

Yin (2003) argued that case studies allow the researcher the opportunity to use different sources of evidence, which assists in triangulation with the information given by the informants. Accordingly, webpages, company reports, financial records, meeting minutes and brochures were also utilized as secondary sources of data. Such secondary data enabled a deeper understanding of each case firm's history and their products as well as understanding the circumstances behind certain events during internationalization.

Data analysis began by transcribing individual cases. Both within and cross-case data analysis techniques as suggested by Eisenhardt (1989) and Miles and Huberman (1994) were utilized for analysis. The within-case and cross-case analyses were used to concentrate on the emergent themes related to the factors affecting the continued post-entry performance of the selected INVs in the North African markets. As patterns emerged from the data individual codes were combined into groups that were then categorized (see Table 2.2). Once a category was identified through the pattern analysis (e.g. capability), it was further differentiated by breaking it down into subcategories. Emergent categories were compared and contrasted with the literature (Yin, 2003). These key capabilities are discussed in the following section.

Table 2.1 Key characteristics of case firms

Case firm	Founding/industry	Interviewees	No. of employees/annual turnover (USD$)	Year of first internationalization/% of foreign sales over total sales	First international market served	Subsequent international markets served (Yr)	Initial market entry mode	Subsequent entry modes
A	2004/Tourism/Travel	Founder, managing director, operations and planning director, sales and marketing manager	30/11.43mil	2005/40%	Tunisia (2004)	Algeria (2007), Morocco (2009), Mali (2005), Uganda (2013)	Direct exporting	Various modes—Small Joint Venture and distributors
B	1998/Retail sales	Founder, sales director, online projects director, marketing and operations director, employee	21/3.4mil	1998/35%	Egypt (1998)	Algeria (2002), Morocco (2004), Mali (2009), Tanzania (2011)	Direct exporting	Various modes—JV, alliance, agents/distributor

(continued)

Table 2.1 (continued)

Case firm	Founding/industry	Interviewees	No. of employees/ annual turnover (USD$)	Year of first internationalization/% of foreign sales over total sales	First international market served	Subsequent international markets served (Yr)	Initial market entry mode	Subsequent entry modes
C	1995/Health & safety products	CEO, engineering director, R&D director, sales director	18/0.83mil	1997/29%	Tunisia (1995)	Morocco (1999), Uganda (2005)	Direct exporting	Move to higher commitment—sales subsidiary
D	2005/IT technologies	Managing director, Chief Information Officer, new operations director, software engineer	13/2.1 mil	2005/45%	Libya (2005)	Algeria (2009), Zimbabwe (2018)	Indirect exporting	Move to higher commitment—Strategic alliance
E	2008/Bio technologies	Founder, sales director, lead scientist, marketing and sales director	27/1.1mil	2009/32%	Egypt (2008),	Morocco (2011), Uganda (2017)	Indirect exporting	Move to higher commitment—JV

Table 2.2 Summary of key dynamic capabilities and their content

Capabilities	Firms
Sensing capability: entrepreneurial initiatives and network relationship development	
Identifying new business opportunities	All firms
Openness to new ideas	A, B and D
Knowledge of product and market	B, C and E
Accessing co-ethnic networks	All firms
Leveraging partners for new market knowledge	All firms
Encouraging partner equity investments	A, B and C
Seizing capability: product and Niche market development	
Investing in R&D for product development	A, C, D and E
Knowledge about market and changing customer needs	All firms
Investing in brand development and extension	B, C and E
Utilizing retained profits toward	
Reconfiguration capability: transformation and renewal capabilities	
Organizational restructuring	A, B, C and D
Teamwork	A, B, C
Professionalization of HR function	All firms
Enhanced recruitment and selection for staff	C, D and E

Findings

Speed Scale and Scope of African SME INVs Internationalization to North African Markets

In terms of research question one, our analysis of the firms showed that they had varying experiences with respect to their speed, scope and scale of internationalization. Regarding, the speed of internationalization, all case firms internationalized rapidly within the first two years from inception. For two of the case firms (B and D), internationalization occurred as of inception in that their first sales were to foreign markets in North Africa. The average time between the case firms' initial foreign market entry into North Africa and subsequent internationalization efforts into the region was 2.8 years.

With regard to scope, all case study firms internationalized to multiple markets in Northern Africa, albeit with a distinct pattern. For example, some case firms first internationalized into geographically and culturally distant markets such as Tunisia (A and C), Egypt (B, and E) or Libya (D). Subsequent internationalization efforts continued to remain in the North African region and included countries such as Algeria (A, B and D), Morocco (A, B, C and E) or Mali (A and B). Surprisingly only after approximately 8 years of international activity did the case firms internationalize to more geographically and culturally close markets such as Uganda (A, C and E), Tanzania (B) or Zimbabwe (D).

Finally, regarding the scale of internationalization, data shows that initial market entry into North Africa consisted solely of either direct (A, B, C) or indirect exporting (D and E). Regarding their subsequent internationalization activity, besides continuing exporting activities, four case firms (A, B, C and D) moved toward higher commitment internationalization modes. For instance, at firm D, issues dealing with distributors in Libya encouraged the top management team to seek further control over their operations in the region by establishing a sales subsidiary when entering the Algerian market. Similarly, firm C sought to take advantage of the large Algerian market not only by exporting directly, but also by establishing a small sales office. Cases A and B adopted higher commitment modes such as joint ventures and strategic alliances when entering new markets such as Algeria (B) and Morocco (A).

In terms of research question two, respondents were asked to reflect on and indicate how the internationalization activities of their firms affected the development of their existing resources and capabilities. Through cross-case analysis, the development of three specific resources and capabilities were identified, namely: managerial human capital development, networking capabilities and marketing capabilities and these were mapped onto the Teece framework as shown in Fig. 2.1. The findings are discussed in detail below.

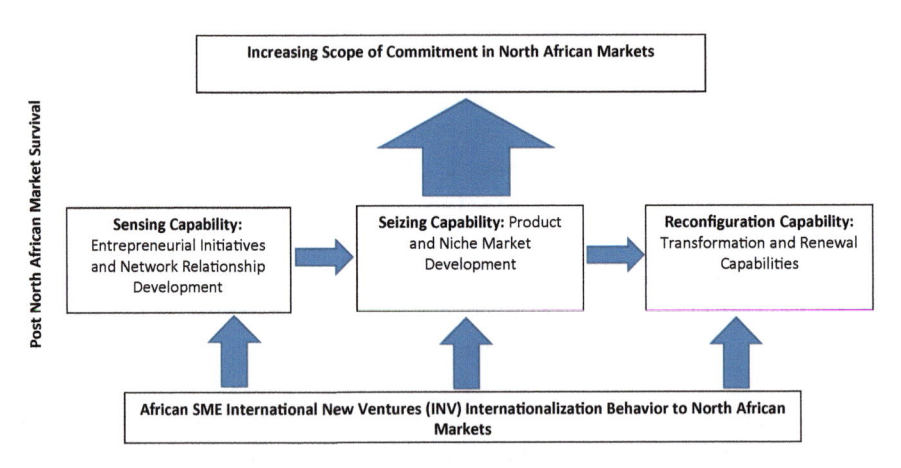

Fig. 2.1 Conceptual model and summary of key findings

Sensing Capability: Entrepreneurial Initiatives and Network Relationship Development

All case firms were found to have engaged in various entrepreneurial initiatives post market entry which was critical for their growth and survival in those markets. Most case firm owner/managers indicated that despite encountering several new market opportunities in North Africa, they nevertheless continued to focus on a particular product or service even though it was considered risky to do so. According to the Sales Director of firm E:

> *being too focused on a particular product is always a gamble, but it is one we took by investing capital and energy in it… so far it has been one of our more successful decisions in Egypt.*

Additionally, nearly all case firm owner/managers believed that in order to survive in the North African markets, they needed to outperform their competitors. This they suggested required the exploration of high-risk and high-reward products or services rather than simply offering their current product or service mixes. For example, in the case of firm B, once they entered the Egyptian market and began distributing their products, they quickly focused on exploring key areas in the market where existing clients were underserved and where they could offer their expertise. As the Sales Director from Firm B stated:

> *As a company, we keep our product lines simple, but that has not stopped us from constantly trying to anticipate the current and future needs of our key customers.*

Similarly, case firm C found that although their core product was well received by the Zambian consumers, those in Tunisia and beyond wanted additional features. Accordingly, the firm modified its original product significantly to meet the future needs of those North African clients. As the CEO of firm C commented:

> *Initially, we thought our initial products were fine for market… We discovered quickly that that Tunisian clients had additional needs which we felt we could easily meet. So we stripped our product down and rebuilt it from the ground up to satisfy their future wants.*

The above evidence suggests that the capability of sensing and seizing market opportunities helped the case firms thrive and survive in the North African market by not only focusing on core products, but also successfully anticipating changes in consumer demands and engaging in riskier new product development.

Networking was also important. The majority of participants interviewed indicated that relationships (personal or professional) played a crucial role in their initial market entry into North African, and that they were even more important for their continued growth and post-entry survival. For instance, for firms A, C and D, informal relationships with former alumnus (A and D) or with kin abroad (C) were used to learn about new markets in North Africa (D), to seek out new opportunities (A and D) or to overcome the liability of newness in highly developed markets such as Tunisia (A and C). Similarly, for firms B and E, informal relationships based around close friends (B), or with fellow business partners (E) who had some prior experience in North African markets, were considered crucial to their initial market entry efforts into North Africa. Evidence suggests that investing in and maintaining relationships post initial market entry was a key aspect of their ongoing growth and survival, as they had developed key products and gained knowledge through their networks. For instance, the founder of firm A commented on the importance of investing in and maintaining relationships with clients and network partners in the North African markets:

> *In our line of work, deep and trusting relationships matter a lot. So, once we enter a new market our focus quickly switches to not only offering a good product and service, but also to building stronger and deeper relationships with our clients and with potential clients.*

Additionally, investing in and maintaining the relationships post market entry enabled some of the case firms to gain complementary capabilities, such as superior market knowledge and technologies (A and D), access to financial capital (B, C and D) and to overcome market liabilities and regulations (C and E). Similarly, investments and efforts at maintaining relationships lead to increased levels of trust between partners as well as investments in higher commitment market entry modes such as joint ventures and strategic alliances (A and B) or sales subsidiaries (C). For instance, at firm C, the CEO talked about the following benefits of cultivating relationships with regard to trust. According to him, trust:

> *...allowed us to gain respect. We are also able to benefit from the significant knowledge spill over, it's important for a small company like us, when we have a relationship in place with a registered government-linked corporation [in Morocco].*

Such evidence highlights the significance of developing and maintaining relationship to the post-entry survival of African SME INVs from the South in North African markets.

Seizing Capability: Product and Niche Market Development

Evidence suggests that nearly all of the case firms actively began specializing in order to survive post-initial market entry in the North African markets. Specifically, findings showed that developing specific product knowledge, along with the development of niche products based on market differentiation, allowed the case firms to achieve post-entry survival. For instance, in nearly all case firms, owner/managers and senior management placed considerable emphasis on developing proprietary and domain-specific knowledge, as such knowledge was highly valued by customers in the North African markets. For instance, the Chief Information Officer for firm D commented that:

> *"In all honesty, this firm would not have survived in this region if the owners had decided to only focus on a particular specialist domain area of IT. Survival in a tough and new market such as Algeria really requires you to really think about either experimenting with or developing various domains of specialist IT knowledge..."*

Similarly, the R&D Director of firm C also talked about the importance of distinguishing yourself from your competitors by developing proprietary knowledge regarding the Morocco market.

> *Since entering the market [Morocco], we have been fortunate enough to develop our unique knowledge about the market. I would go on to say that our knowledge of the Moroccan market is at times much better than the local competition. This knowledge about the market has really served us well because it's something highly sought after and valued by our customers and allows us to compete in a tough market.*

Besides developing specialist knowledge, a focus on niche market and product development was also considered an important capability by all case firms regarding their initial post-entry market survival. Specifically, data suggests that once the case firms entered the North African markets, they quickly moved toward developing a product or service-based specialization. Evidence suggests that by developing specialist products and services for niche segments in North African, the case firms were able to develop an edge over their competitors. For instance, at firms B, C and D, new product innovation was reported as an instrumental outcome of internationalization into North Africa. In the case of firm C, this meant the development and launching of a new line of products specifically tailored toward the Mining industry in Morocco. Likewise, firm A used their profits from internationalization and an opportunity in the Algerian market to set up R&D activities with a local partner there. This initiative led to the development of several online platforms offering customizable travel solutions for customers. As the Sales and Marketing director from firm A explained:

> our operations now span the breadth of North Africa. All these customers need and want specific products. Our research team has allowed us to develop novel solutions to each particular customer segment...

The above evidence suggests that once African SME INVs from the South internationalized to the markets in the North and established their presence in those markets, their capacity to further grow and to survive was dependent on their ability to develop proprietary and product-specific knowledge along with shifting their focus more toward the refinement of their products and services.

Reconfiguration Capability: Transformation and Renewal Capabilities

Evidene suggests that the case firms were able to develop new products and services tailored to the North African markets by focusing on their clients' specific needs. In particular, the case firms were able to meet their customers' niche needs through either exploitation of their renewal capabilities (e.g. developing new products (A, B, C and D) and through identifying and exploiting opportunities through actively engaging with their customers (A, C, D and E), or via their regenerative capabilities (e.g. reconfiguring existing product offerings (A, B and E) and resource bases (A, B, C and E). Accordingly, several of the case firms (A, B, C and D) began to restructure their enterprises' internal processes to provide one-stop solutions to their customers. Such changes were deemed critical to helping the case firms identify customer needs early on and to act upon those needs to offer their customers better solutions. The Operations and Planning Director of firm A commented that:

Since I have started, there has been a lot of change internally in this company, mostly internal and structural. For example, we have now created a customer development and retention team that continuously engage with our customers to better anticipate the changing market realities in Morocco and Algeria. Of course, the benefit of this is that we are able to improve our product offerings to customers.

Evidence further showed that the case firms at times made significant investments in diversifying and developing their workforce. Investing in the development of their workforce was seen by many case firms as building and establishing their domain niches throughout North African markets. Interview evidence suggests that majority of case firms began investing in basic Human Resource Management (HRM) practices (C, D and E) as means of adding much-needed expertise to their workforce and motivating them. For example, the owner of firm saw it as important to implement improved recruitment and selection policies, aimed at attracting and selecting individuals who possessed the relevant international management skills and knowledge of North Africa. Consequently, this led to the recruitment of two new area managers with experience in North African markets. Similarly, firm C changed its compensation policy in order to retain and motivate staff who had to regularly travel to Algeria for business. According to the Sales Director from firm C:

In my first role, I simply conveyed others' decisions to my staff, I had little responsibility. I was then asked to head up our first overseas branch [in Alegeria], it was a challenge at first, but I had to learn quickly to navigate the Algeria market place and culture and make, at times, riskier than normal decisions. This made a big difference to me.

The above findings highlight the importance of reconfiguring and renewing capabilities in order to survive in the North African markets post initial entry.

Conclusions and Implications

The aim of this study was to provide insights into the internationalization behavior of Zambian SME INVs to North African markets, and which key capabilities were critical to their post-entry survival. Applying the dynamic capability perspective from Teece (2007) to developing economy INV post-entry survival issues, our study helps to better understand why and how SME INVs from Africa's South can survive in the often culturally and institutionally different markets of North Africa; a topic that remains under-explored in the current literature. By doing so, our study contributes to the scant literature on African SMEs' internationalization in several ways (Boso et al., 2018). Broadly, we note that Zambian SMEs INV internationalization pattern with respect to their speed, scope and scale was similar to that of INVs from both developed and developing economies (Knight & Cavusgil, 1996; Øyna & Alon, 2018). More specifically, and contrary to expectations, we found that Zambian SMEs INV were willing and able to commit to higher commitment and riskier internationalization entry modes such as strategic alliance/JVs and sales subsidiaries. Our cases also showed that the highly entrepreneurial mindsets of the Zambian SMEs INV as well as commitment to learn from their internationalization efforts were instrumental in overcoming their resource deficiencies as they leveraged their unique capabilities and strengths. Our finding here is unique in that it has rarely been considered or observed in the previous literature. However, this comes as no surprise as the resource and capabilities deficit that many of the case firms began with, may have actually encouraged entrepreneurial ways of thinking by their owner/managers in order to overcome many of the issues they faced post market entry.

Secondly, in applying a dynamic capabilities perspective, our study represents one of the few attempts in the existing literature to understand the post-entry survival of African SMEs. In particular, our study highlights the significance of investing in the development of capabilities (Andersson, 2011; Fleming & Waguespack, 2007; Gabrielsson & Gabrielsson, 2013; Hashai, 2011; Sarasvathy, 2001; Teece, 2014) with respect to African SMEs INVs survival in foreign markets. African SME INVs from the South that internationalize rapidly into North African markets are likely to suffer from the liabilities of foreignness, newness and smallness, and also from the limited domestic resources available in their home markets. In this regard it is critical for such African SME to rely on network relationships, in order to enhance their competitiveness and survival in international markets (Mort & Weerawardena, 2006; Sepulveda & Gabrielsson, 2013). Not surprisingly our findings showed that developing and maintaining network relationships is a key capability that helps to explain the post entry survival of the African SME INVs in North African markets.

The domestic resource base in Zambia is considered as weak, thus leaving local enterprises with limited opportunities to benefit from local networks (Choongo, 2017; Phillips & Bhatia-Panthaki, 2007; Jones et al., 2018). Accordingly, the reliance on international networks goes someway in explaining the survival of the case firms in North Africa markets, as the development of networking capabilities positively influences the post-entry survival (Makadok, 2001; Zott, 2003) as they served as a means of *sensing* foreign market opportunities (Forsgren, 2016; Lew et al., 2016). More interestingly though, all case firms demonstrated a willingness to aggressively seek out new relationships in foreign markets post market entry and more importantly, were willing to invest significant financial and non-financial resources in order to further develop and maintain such relationships.

Additionally, case evidence showed that *seizing*, an increase in product and market specialization, is also an important capability explaining the post-entry survival of African SME INVs in North African markets. A common finding among the case firms was their rapid move toward offering highly niche products and services to very specific segments of the North African market. Specifically, findings showed that the case firms actively brought about improvements to their products and service offerings by developing priority and specific knowledge about the North African markets they operated in. Hence, the development of specialization capabilities positively influences African SMEs' INV post-entry survival and performance in North African markets.

Evidence further demonstrated that the case firms went through a *reconfiguration*, a renewal and transformation of their existing capabilities, in order to survive and grow in the North African markets. Specifically, transformative dynamic capabilities were found to be embedded in the process of each of the case firms. For instance, some of the case firms were able to renew their previous knowledge and pursue specialization in product and service offerings by changing their organizational cultures or their human resource practices. Such additions and changes to their process allowed the case firms to proactively engaging with their customers and to better anticipate changes in the dynamic North African markets [refer to Fig. 2.1 for our key findings].

Implications for Practice

Our study also has a number of practical implications for owner/managers of African SMEs and African government policy makers in general. For African SME owner/managers, our study highlights that internationalization should be viewed not simply as leveraging of existing resources but as an opportunity to learn. The value of internationalization to more advanced African Northern markets may therefore not only be economical in nature, but may also result in changes to managerial attitudes and firm capabilities that lead to future success. Additionally, African SMEs and their owners/managers should think beyond simply exporting as their primary mode of international engagement. We suggest that higher commitment modes such as strategic Alliances/JVs, if possible, may bring about significant and valuable learning opportunities for African SME. From a policy perspective, African governments especially from less developed economies, could do well to lower transaction costs (Lu & Beamish, 2001), reduce political and economic instabilities (Fosu, 2003) and focus on developing innovation, human resources and marketing capabilities in the local economies (Ibeh et al., 2012). Such capabilities have been identified by the existing literature as significant barriers to the internationalization of Africa SMEs. They also represent an important step in encouraging African SMEs to take the risk of internationalizing.

References

Acs, Z. J., & Amorós, J. E. (2008). Entrepreneurship and competitiveness dynamics in Latin America. *Small Business Economics, 31*(3), 305–322.

Agarwal, R., & Helfat, C. E. (2009). Strategic renewal of organisations. *Organisation science, 20*(2), 281–293.

Al-Aali, A. Y., & Teece, D. J. (2013). Towards the (strategic) management of intellectual property: Retrospective and prospective. *California Management Review, 55*(4), 15–30.

Anand, B. (2015). Reverse globalization by internationalization of SME's: Opportunities and challenges ahead. *Procedia-Social and Behavioral Sciences, 195*, 1003–1011.

Anderson, W. (2011). Internationalization opportunities and challenges for small and medium-sized enterprises from developing countries. *Journal of African Business, 12*(2), 198–217.

Arora, V., & Vamvakidis, A. (2005). The implications of South African economic growth for the rest of Africa. *South African Journal of Economics, 73*(2), 229–242.

Audretsch, D. B. (1995). Innovation, growth and survival. *International Journal of Industrial Organisation, 13*(4), 441–457.

Autio, E., George, G., & Alexy, O. (2011). International entrepreneurship and capability development—Qualitative evidence and future research directions. *Entrepreneurship Theory and Practice, 35*(1), 11–37.

Autio, E., Sapienza, H. J., & Almeida, J. G. (2000). Effects of age at entry, knowledge intensity, and imitability on international growth. *Academy of Management Journal, 43*(5), 909–924.

Azmat, F., & Samaratunga, R. (2009). Responsible entrepreneurship in developing countries: Understanding the realities and complexities. *Journal of Business Ethics, 90*(3), 437–452.

Barney, J. B. (2001). Resource-based theories of competitive advantage: A ten-year retrospective on the resource-based view. *Journal of Management, 27*(6), 643–650.

Boso, N., Adeleye, I., White, L. (Eds.). (2016). Africa-to-Africa internationalization: Emerging trends and key issues. In *Africa-to-Africa Internationalization*. AIB Sub-Saharan Africa (SSA) Series. Palgrave Macmillan.

Boso, N., Annan, J., Adeleye, I., Iheanachor, N., & Narteh, B. (2018). Examining the paths from export strategic orientations to export performance: The mediating role of export resource transformation capability. *Thunderbird International Business Review, 60*(2), 207–230.

Brüderl, J., & Schüssler, R. (1990). Organizational mortality: The liabilities of newness and adolescence. *Administrative Science Quarterly*, 530–547.

Calof, J. L., & Viviers, W. (1995). Internationalization behavior of small-and medium-sized South African enterprises. *Journal of Small Business Management, 33*(4), 71.

Cavusgil, S. T., & Knight, G. (2015). The born global firm: An entrepreneurial and capabilities perspective on early and rapid internationalization. *Journal of International Business Studies, 46*(1), 3–16.

Chacar, A. S., Newburry, W., & Vissa, B. (2010). Bringing institutions into performance persistence research: Exploring the impact of product, financial, and labor market institutions. *Journal of International Business Studies, 41*(7), 1119–1140.

Chandra, Y., Styles, C., & Wilkinson, I. F. (2012). An opportunity-based view of rapid internationalization. *Journal of International Marketing, 20*(1), 74–102.

Chetty, S., & Campbell-Hunt, C. (2004). A strategic approach to internationalization: A traditional versus a "born-global" approach. *Journal of International Marketing, 12*(1), 57–81.

Choongo, P. (2017). A longitudinal study of the impact of corporate social responsibility on firm performance in SMEs in Zambia. *Sustainability, 9*(8), 1300.

Coviello, N., & Munro, H. (1997). Network relationships and the internationalisation process of small software firms. *International Business Review, 6*(4), 361–386.

Coviello, N. E. (2006). The network dynamics of international new ventures. *Journal of International Business Studies, 37*(5), 713–731.

Dana, L. P., & Ratten, V. (2017). International entrepreneurship in resource-rich landlocked African countries. *Journal of International Entrepreneurship, 15*(4), 416–435.

Eden, L., & Miller, S. R. (2004). Distance matters: Liability of foreignness, institutional distance and ownership strategy. *Advances in International Management, 16*(4), 187–221.

Eisenhardt, K. M., & Martin, J. A. (2000). Dynamic capabilities: What are they? *Strategic Management Journal, 21*(10–11), 1105–1121.

Eisenhardt, K. M. (1989). Agency theory: An assessment and review. *Academy of Management Review, 14*(1), 57–74.

Fleming, L., & Waguespack, D. M. (2007). Brokerage, boundary spanning, and leadership in open innovation communities. *Organisation Science, 18*(2), 165–180.

Floyd, S. W., & Lane, P. J. (2000). Strategizing throughout the organisation: Managing role conflict in strategic renewal. *Academy of Management Review, 25*(1), 154–177.

Forsgren, M. (2016). A note on the revisited Uppsala internationalization process model—The implications of business networks and entrepreneurship. *Journal of International Business Studies, 47*(9), 1135–1144.

Fosu, A. K. (2003). Political instability and export performance in sub-Saharan Africa. *Journal of Development Studies, 39*(4), 68–83.

Gabrielsson, P., & Gabrielsson, M. (2013). A dynamic model of growth phases and survival in international business-to-business new ventures: The moderating effect of decision-making logic. *Industrial Marketing Management, 42*(8), 1357–1373.

Gerschewski, S., Lew, Y. K., Khan, Z., & Park, B. I. (2018). Post-entry performance of international new ventures: The mediating role of learning orientation. *International Small Business Journal, 36*(7), 807–828.

Goncalves, M., & Smith, E. C. (2019). Lusophone-African SME internationalization: A case for born global and international joint ventures. *Journal of Transnational Management, 24*(3), 231–258.

Granér, M., & Isaksson, A. (2002). Export performance in the Kenyan manufacturing sector. *Structure and Performance of Manufacturing in Kenya*. Palgrave Macmillan.

Hashai, N. (2011). Sequencing the expansion of geographic scope and foreign operations by "born global" firms. *Journal of International Business Studies, 42*(8), 995–1015.

Hitt, M. A., Hoskisson, R. E., & Ireland, R. D. (1994). A mid-range theory of the interactive effects of international and product diversification on innovation and performance. *Journal of Management, 20*(2), 297–326.

Hitt, M. A., Ireland, R. D., Camp, S. M., & Sexton, D. L. (2001). Strategic entrepreneurship: Entrepreneurial strategies for wealth creation. *Strategic Management Journal, 22*(6–7), 479–491.

Ibeh, K., Wilson, J., & Chizema, A. (2012). The internationalization of African firms 1995–2011: Review and implications. *Thunderbird International Business Review, 54*(4), 411–427.

Ibeh, K. I. (2003). Toward a contingency framework of export entrepreneurship: Conceptualisations and empirical evidence. *Small Business Economics, 20*(1), 49–68.

Johanson, J., & Vahlne, J. E. (2009). The Uppsala internationalization process model revisited: From liability of foreignness to liability of outsidership. *Journal of International Business Studies, 40*(9), 1411–1431.

Jones, P., Maas, G., Dobson, S., Newbery, R., Agyapong, D., & Matlay, H. (2018). Entrepreneurship in Africa, part 1: Entrepreneurial dynamics in Africa. *Journal of Small Business and Enterprise Development, 25*(3), 346–348.

Khan, Z., & Lew, Y. K. (2018). Post-entry survival of developing economy international new ventures: A dynamic capability perspective. *International Business Review, 27*(1), 149–160.

Kiss, A. N., Danis, W. M., & Cavusgil, S. T. (2012). International entrepreneurship research in emerging economies: A critical review and research agenda. *Journal of Business Venturing, 27*(2), 266–290.

Knight, G. A., & Cavusgil, S. T. (1996). The born global firm: A challenge to traditional internationalization theory. *Advances in International Marketing, 8*(1), 11–26.

Knight, G. A., & Cavusgil, S. T. (2004). Innovation, organisational capabilities, and the born-global firm. *Journal of International Business Studies, 35*(2), 124–141.

Kuada, J. (2006). Internationalisation of firms in developing countries: Towards an integrated conceptual framework. *International Business Economics, 43*, 1–22.

Kujala, I., & Törnroos, J. Å. (2018). Internationalizing through networks from emerging to developed markets with a case study from Ghana to the USA. *Industrial Marketing Management, 69*, 98–109.

Kundu, S. K., & Katz, J. A. (2003). Born-international SMEs: Bi-level impacts of resources and intentions. *Small Business Economics, 20*(1), 25–47.

Lu, J. W., & Beamish, P. W. (2001). The internationalization and performance of SMEs. *Strategic Management Journal, 22*(6–7), 565–586.

Luo, Y., & Tung, R. L. (2007). International expansion of emerging market enterprises: A springboard perspective. *Journal of International Business Studies, 38*(4), 481–498.

Lew, Y. K., Khan, Z., Rao-Nicholson, R., & He, S. (2016). Internationalisation process of Chinese SMEs: The role of business and ethnic-group-based social networks. *International Journal of Multinational Corporation Strategy, 1*(3–4), 247–268.

Makadok, R. (2001). Toward a synthesis of the resource-based and dynamic-capability views of rent creation. *Strategic Management Journal, 22*(5), 387–401.

Marco, F., & Patterson, S. (2010). Africa's outlook. *OECD Observer, 279*, 64–65.

Matanda, M. J. (2012). Internationalization of established small manufacturers in a developing economy: A case study of Kenyan SMEs. *Thunderbird International Business Review, 54*(4), 509–519.

McDougall, P. P., & Oviatt, B. M. (2000). International entrepreneurship: The intersection of two research paths. *Academy of Management Journal, 43*(5), 902–906.

McDougall, P. P., Shane, S., & Oviatt, B. M. (1994). Explaining the formation of international new ventures: The limits of theories from international business research. *Journal of Business Venturing, 9*(6), 469–487.

Mellahi, K., & Mol, M. J. (2015). Africa is just like every other place, in that it is unlike any other place. *Africa Journal of Management, 1*(2), 201–209.

Mengistae, T., & Pattillo, C. (2004). Export orientation and productivity in sub-Saharan Africa. *IMF Staff Papers, 51*(2), 327–353.

Miles, M. B., & Huberman, A. M. (1994). *Qualitative data analysis: An expanded sourcebook.* Sage.

Misati, E., Walumbwa, F. O., Lahiri, S., & Kundu, S. K. (2017). The internationalization of African small and medium enterprises (SMEs): A South-North pattern. *Africa Journal of Management, 3*(1), 53–81.

Mtigwe, B. (2004, April). Expositions of African entrepreneurial firm internationalization behavior. In *Proceedings of the 5th international conference of the international academy of African business and development* (pp. 7–10), Georgia State University.

Moini, H., Kuada, J., & Decker, A. (2016). Internationalisation of family—Owned businesses in a geographically remote area. *International Journal of Entrepreneurial Venturing, 8*(2), 143–169.

Mort, G. S., & Weerawardena, J. (2006). Networking capability and international entrepreneurship: How networks function in Australian born global firms. *International Marketing Review, 23*(5), 549–572.

Mudambi, R., & Zahra, S. A. (2007). The survival of international new ventures. *Journal of International Business Studies, 38*(2), 333–352.

Okpara, J. O. (2009). Strategic choices, export orientation and export performance of SMEs in Nigeria. *Management Decision., 47*(8), 1281–1299.

Øyna, S., & Alon, I. (2018). A review of born globals. *International Studies of Management & Organisation, 48*(2), 157–180.

Phillips, C., & Bhatia-Panthaki, S. (2007). Enterprise development in Zambia: Reflections on the missing middle. *Journal of International Development: The Journal of the Development Studies Association, 19*(6), 793–804.

Puffer, S. M., McCarthy, D. J., & Jaeger, A. M. (2016). Institution building and institutional voids can Poland's experience inform Russia and Brazil? *International Journal of Emerging Markets, 11*(1), 18–41.

Ramamurti, R., & Singh, J. V. (Eds.). (2009). *Emerging multinationals in emerging markets.* Cambridge University Press.

Riviere, M., & Suder, G. (2016). Perspectives on strategic internationalization: Developing capabilities for renewal. *International Business Review, 25*(4), 847–858.

Rutashobya, L., & Jaensson, J. E. (2004). Small firms' internationalization for development in Tanzania: Exploring the network phenomenon. *International Journal of Social Economics, 31*(1/2), 159–172.

Ruzzier, M. H., Hisrich, R. D., & Antoncic, B. (2006). SME internationalization research: Past, present, and future. *Journal of Small Business and Enterprise Development., 13*(4), 476–497.

Sapienza, H. J., Autio, E., George, G., & Zahra, S. A. (2006). A capabilities perspective on the effects of early internationalization on firm survival and growth. *Academy of Management Review, 31*(4), 914–933.

Sarasvathy, S. D. (2001). Causation and effectuation: Toward a theoretical shift from economic inevitability to entrepreneurial contingency. *Academy of Management Review, 26*(2), 243–263.

Scholes, L., Mustafa, M., & Chen, S. (2015). Internationalization of small family firms: The influence of family from a socioemotional wealth perspective. *Thunderbird International Business Review, 58*(2), 131–146.

Sepulveda, F., & Gabrielsson, M. (2013). Network development and firm growth: A resource-based study of B2B born globals. *Industrial Marketing Management, 42*(5), 792–804.

Sui, S., & Baum, M. (2014). Internationalization strategy, firm resources and the survival of SMEs in the export market. *Journal of International Business Studies, 45*(7), 821–841.

Swoboda, B., & Olejnik, E. (2016). Linking processes and dynamic capabilities of international SMEs: The mediating effect of international entrepreneurial orientation. *Journal of Small Business Management, 54*(1), 139–161.

Teagarden, M. B., Von Glinow, M. A., & Mellahi, K. (2018). Contextualizing international business research: Enhancing rigor and relevance. *Journal of World Business, 53*(3), 303–306.

Teece, D. J. (2014). A dynamic capabilities-based entrepreneurial theory of the multinational enterprise. *Journal of International Business Studies, 45*(1), 8–37.

Teece, D. J. (2007). Explicating dynamic capabilities: The nature and microfoundations of (sustainable) enterprise performance. *Strategic Management Journal, 28*(13), 1319–1350.

Teece, D. J. (2000). Strategies for managing knowledge assets: The role of firm structure and industrial context. *Long Range Planning, 33*(1), 35–54.

Timmons, J. A., Spinelli, S., & Tan, Y. (2004). *New venture creation: Entrepreneurship for the 21st century* (Vol. 6). New York: McGraw-Hill/Irwin.

Tvedten, K., Hansen, M. W., & Jeppesen, S. (2014). Understanding the rise of African business. *African Journal of Economic and Management Studies, 5*(3), 249–268.

Verona, G. (1999). A resource-based view of product development. *Academy of Management Review, 24*(1), 132–142.

Villar, C., Alegre, J., & Pla-Barber, J. (2014). Exploring the role of knowledge management practices on exports: A dynamic capabilities view. *International Business Review, 23*(1), 38–44.

Weerawardena, J., Mort, G. S., Liesch, P. W., & Knight, G. (2007). Conceptualizing accelerated internationalization in the born global firm: A dynamic capabilities perspective. *Journal of World Business, 42*(3), 294–306.

Wernerfelt, B. (1984). A resource-based view of the firm. *Strategic Management Journal, 5*(2), 171–180.

Yin, R. K. (2003). Designing case studies. *Qualitative Research Methods*, 359–386.

Yoo, D., & Reimann, F. (2017). Internationalization of developing country firms into developed countries: The role of host country knowledge-based assets and

IPR protection in FDI location choice. *Journal of International Management, 23*(3), 242–254.

Zaheer, S. (1995). Overcoming the liability of foreignness. *Academy of Management Journal, 38*(2), 341–363.

Zaheer, S., & Mosakowski, E. (1997). The dynamics of the liability of foreignness: A global study of survival in financial services. *Strategic Management Journal, 18*(6), 439–463.

Zahra, S. A. (2005). A theory of international new ventures: A decade of research. *Journal of International Business Studies, 36*(1), 20–28.

Zott, C. (2003). Dynamic capabilities and the emergence of intrandustry differential firm performance: Insights from a simulation study. *Strategic Management Journal, 24*(2), 97–125.

3

Uncovering the Role of Institutional Context for Nascent Entrepreneurial Ventures

A. I. Ogunsade, Demola Obembe, and Kassa Woldesenbet Beta

Introduction

The role of contexts for nascent entrepreneurship and new venture creation has continued to attract attention among scholars and practitioners alike (Roundy et al., 2018). This is rightly so, as entrepreneurial activities constitute a key driver of economic growth (Wigren-Kristofersen et al., 2019; Wu et al., 2020). An economy thrives when institutions and supportive business environment provide nascent entrepreneurs and small businesses the opportunity to grow, innovate and survive (World Bank, 2019). This means that when institutions are robust and healthy for entrepreneurial activities, small and local businesses flourish, generate employment and contribute to economic growth. As such, the absence of a robust and efficient institutional environment would be at variance with promoting entrepreneurial activities and economic development (Autio & Fu, 2015; Escandon-Barbosa et al., 2019; Lajqi & Krasniqi, 2017).

A. I. Ogunsade (✉) · D. Obembe · K. Woldesenbet Beta
De Montfort University, Leicester, UK
e-mail: adekunle.ogunsade@dmu.ac.uk

D. Obembe
e-mail: dobembe@dmu.ac.uk

K. Woldesenbet Beta
e-mail: kwoldesenbet@dmu.ac.uk

Notwithstanding the increased attention and initiatives by entrepreneurship scholars, government and global policymakers, the institutional environments and cost of doing business continue to pose a significant challenge for nascent and small businesses in Sub-Saharan Africa (SSA). The World Bank (2019) study of ease of doing business across 190 economies indicates that the regulatory environment in most Sub-Saharan African countries still ranks below the desirable general average. For example, the quality of governance, access to financing, infrastructure, electricity, registering property and enforcing contracts, among other factors, still pose institutional burdens to entrepreneurial activities, and therefore need significant improvement. The entrepreneurial ecosystem and many business indicators that drive nascent and small business development for inclusive and sustainable economic growth across developing economies and particularly for Sub-Sharan Africa remain low at best (Acs et al., 2008; Bosma et al., 2001; Liñán & Fernandez-Serrano, 2014; Reynolds et al., 2005; World Bank, 2019). Nascent entrepreneurs in developing economies are often confronted with institutional burdens and/or challenges in bringing their desires for new business creation into fruition (Chigunta, 2017; Wennekers et al., 2005). While the likes of Mauritius (a global top 20 economy for ease of doing business in 2020), Rwanda and Kenya exemplify countries on a positive trajectory, most SSA countries seem to be lagging behind other developing regions in terms of institutional framework performance for nascent and high growth venture start-ups. According to the World Bank (2020), the majority of countries in the bottom 20 of their ease of doing business survey are from Sub-Saharan Africa region with a count of 12. The substantial differences in performance even among Sub-Saharan African economies thus call for a new policy framework that could deliver skills, innovation and entrepreneurial inclusive economic growth.

Entrepreneurs and entrepreneurial activities in SSA are impacted by institutional contextual challenges derived from underdevelopment (Goel & Ranjan, 2020; McMillan & Woodruff, 2002; Peng & Shekshnia, 2001). Studies have argued that institutional contexts play an important role in the emergence of robust human economic activities in both developed and emerging economies (Ogunsade & Obembe, 2016; Wigren-Kristofersen et al., 2019). However, many dimensions of institutions remain underexplored, particularly how different levels of formal and informal institutions impact nascent entrepreneurial activities in emerging economies. Bearing in mind the contextual challenges in SSA, we argue for much-needed research on the institutional framework for nascent entrepreneurial and SME policies. We suggest that it is time for policy direction and entrepreneurial governance for institutional restructuring framework that will deliver needed support for nascent entrepreneurial activities aimed at inclusive growth.

We further examine the impact of formal and informal institutional contexts on the emergence and success of nascent entrepreneurship. We explore a range of entrepreneurship-enabling institutions and policies that can eliminate institutional voids, as well as revitalise entrepreneurial ecosystems for the emergence of nascent/high growth venture start-ups, and inclusive economy growth. To put the study in perspective, we leverage on the concept of institutionalism (North, 1990) and institutional theory (Scott 2013) to argue that the dimensions of institutional context can act as constraining and enabling factors affecting entrepreneurial activities in different contexts.

First, we theorise that entrepreneurial governance and public policy can provide direction and support for nascent entrepreneurs, through seed funding and local embeddedness to eliminate institutional voids. Secondly, we provide a framework that explains a recursive relationship among the institutional context dimensions and entrepreneurial enabling institutional policies that will eliminate institutional voids. In addition, our framework provides policy implications, through which African governments can focus interventions and investments to improve entrepreneurial capacity and engagement. This can help alleviate poverty and produce more inclusive growth needed for wealth creation and development in Africa. Overall, our study offers a multi-dynamic view of embeddedness through institutional framework to uncover the barriers to nascent entrepreneurial activity in Africa.

This chapter is divided into four main sections. In the following sections, we try to uncover the institutional and contextual challenges for nascent entrepreneurship and new venture creation. Furthermore, we explore formal and informal institutional embeddedness for entrepreneurship behaviour. Finally, drawing on empirical work on institutional change and entrepreneurial governance, we provide a possible policy framework to uncover the needed foundation that will trigger nascent entrepreneurial activity, sustained value creation both in the short and long term within SSA.

Nascent Entrepreneurship and New Venture Creation

Although, various models have been proposed to understand the importance of the process involved in business transition from gestation to the advancement and development of business ideas (Kim et al., 2006; Reynolds et al.,

2005), studies on nascent and emerging enterprises are still limited. This limitation is partly due to the difficulty in identifying nascent stages of start-ups and the associated costs. However, what is consistent from these models is that entrepreneurial process for new venture creation involves different stages. These stages include the cognitive recognition of opportunity, the propensity and desire to exploit a given opportunity as well as the decision to follow through in starting a new enterprise (Dimov, 2007; Wiklund & Shepherd, 2005). Nascent entrepreneurs are enterprising individuals in the pursuit of entrepreneurial opportunities with aims of introducing new products and services to the market for economic growth and development (AFDB, 2016; Wennekers et al., 2005). The importance of small business for the overall productivity and wellbeing of the economy cannot be overemphasised. A number of empirical studies on Africa identified entrepreneurship and small business start-ups, and SMEs as having potential for job creation and development within the region, contributing 50–70% of national employment and productivity (Legas, 2015; Ogunsade et al., 2020; Okafor, 2011).

The evolution and continuous development of new innovative ventures is very important for the economic development and growth across the African continent. In this regard, a key focus for entrepreneurial development strategies for many African economies should involve the facilitation of sustainable and inclusive growth policies that will facilitate jobs and poverty reduction (Goel & Ranjan, 2020; Wu et al., 2020). Despite the economic value of micro, small and medium enterprises (MSMEs), SMEs and new business start-ups are constrained in SSA and little seems to be done to provide thriving environmental conditions. While small businesses generally vary in size and capacity for growth, they face common challenges arising at similar phases of their development. Nascent entrepreneurs are often faced with myriads of problems including, obtaining customers, delivering products and services and generating sufficient income to break even or cover costs of capital and asset replacement. In addition, economic recessions, unstable economic policies, coupled with infrastructural challenges such as unstable power supply, affect entrepreneurial activities. The acquisition of venture capital is another challenge that is generally facing business start-ups. It is however a challenge that is more pronounced within developing African economies, where corrupt practices hamper the ability to secure government grants and bank loans.

We elaborate on these factors as determinants of nascent entrepreneurs' subjective decisions and judgements towards new ventures. We argue that the evolution and continuous development of new ventures is dependent on the perception of opportunities, capacity and judgement of nascent entrepreneurs

(Kor et al., 2007). In this sense, the dynamic interactions of positive institutional environment are imperative for a sustained entrepreneurial effort. Entrepreneurial activities particularly emerging new businesses require conviction and sufficient confidence for risk-taking decisions by individual entrepreneurs. Therefore, it is imperative to uncover institutional factors and policies that will encourage and trigger entrepreneurial capacity to the level at which entrepreneurial activities will impact regional economic growth.

In this regard, nascent entrepreneurs in the pursuit of entrepreneurial opportunities, and aiming to introduce new products and services to the market, need the right environment to succeed. According to Dimov (2007), opportunity seeking within the market economy is perceptual in nature. However, successful business opportunity is contingent on certain favourable economic, social and institutional framework in which entrepreneurship occurs (Mair et al., 2012; Weiss & Montgomery, 2005). In this sense, uncovering the needed or expected institutions and ecosystems within an economy to affect the propensity and emergence of new ventures is very important. A sustained entrepreneurial effort for the creation of new business start-ups not only requires a supportive ecosystem, it equally requires effective and adequate policy frameworks. This is required to stimulate innovation, growth and enterprise culture that could lead to the generation of high-growth ventures. We thus argue that nascent entrepreneurs in Africa as well as other developing economies are confronted with institutional voids/burdens in bringing their desires for new business creation into fruition. Our position therefore is that instituting effective entrepreneurial ecosystems and governance is key to the realisation and creation of value, as well as innovation and the emergence of entrepreneurial market opportunities and new ventures.

In the following section, we uncover these institutional and contextual challenges and present a policy framework that may provide the needed foundation to trigger sustained value creation both in the short and long terms.

Formal and Informal Institutional Burdens to Entrepreneurship Development

There are growing studies on how formal and informal institutions significantly influence entrepreneurship (Autio & Fu, 2015; Escandon-Barbosa et al., 2019; Lajqi & Krasniqi, 2017; Lim et al., 2010; Wigren-Kristofersen et al., 2019). The formal and informal institutional contexts influence entrepreneurship and new business development through the level of regulatory support, and through prevailing support from the social and cultural environments (Acs et al., 2012; Audretsch et al., 2015). Furthermore, both institutional contexts are recognised as key influences for new venture creation and development, and thereby as triggers for economic growth and development (Acs et al., 2012; Audretsch et al., 2015; Goel & Ranjan, 2020; Memili et al., 2015).

Institutions may not only determine economic action and decision towards the emergence of new business start-ups, they can also impact on the availability of critical resources for which nascent and new ventures depend upon for survival (Blackburn & Ram, 2006; McMullen et al., 2008). New ventures usually require considerable amounts of financial capital, which may be raised through individual private financing or external credit given by micro-angel investors (Bowen & De Clercq, 2008). For example, the institutional context of a country, such as the political structure, policies, rules and regulations, social networks, trust and cooperative norms, may influence the formation and performance of organisations and development within the country. This is particularly so in many African contexts where political governance structures are the main institutional pillars.

Formal Institutional Environment and Challenges to Entrepreneurial Activities

Extensive research shows that formal institutional environments significantly influence entrepreneurship (Autio & Fu, 2015; Escandon-Barbosa et al., 2019; Lajqi & Krasniqi, 2017; Lim et al., 2010; Wigren-Kristofersen et al., 2019). Research further establishes that formal environmental structures, such as the regulatory framework for the introduction and existence of new business start-ups, can often impact the development of economic activities and entrepreneurship (Van Stel et al., 2007). The formal aspects of institutional contexts consist of laws, regulations, incentives, punishments, sanctions and procedures that possess the capacity to establish and monitor behaviours and actions as well as influence certain conducts.

The formal environment also provides the regulatory structures of laws, government enactments, rules and policy directions that encourage and promote certain set of behaviours while controlling or limiting others. The importance of the regulatory environment to facilitating nascent entrepreneurial development cannot be underestimated. According to the World Bank (2019), of all regions surveyed, Sub-Saharan Africa faces more regulatory challenges than any other, both in terms of regulatory structures and quality of regulation. For meaningful regional economic development, it is therefore expedient to gain insight into factors within the formal environment, which may enable or pose specific challenges to entrepreneurial venture development in the region.

First, we note that formal institutional frames that greatly affect entrepreneurial activities include contract and bankruptcy laws, social policies and welfare structures for families and women, as well as property law. All of these represent important aspects of institutions that are under the structure of the State, and can directly or indirectly influence values, behaviour or decisions of individual members of the society towards committing resources to entrepreneurial activities. For example, property right is a key element of institutions that offers incentives and motivation for entrepreneurs to exploit opportunities within the market.

Furthermore, formal institutional contexts are deemed as critical determinants of entrepreneurial activities and behaviours As the regulatory dimension of institutional environment influences, among other things, the quality of governance, ease of doing business, access to financing, infrastructure and importantly the individual entrepreneur's perceptions and mindset (Acs, et al., 2008; Baumol, 1990). The entrepreneurial ecosystem and the prevalence of, or type of, entrepreneurial activities found in any society can be impacted by the regulatory environment directly or indirectly (Roundy et al., 2018).

The regulatory dimension can thus be positioned as the institutional environment that includes key policy measures which acknowledge the differences in policy direction for SMEs and entrepreneurship, and which provides policy measures, remove administrative and regulatory burdens, as well as removing constraints for creation of new venture. These institutional structures should also facilitate access to capital, pre-seed and other financing. They can also improve knowledge/information flow, enable training infrastructures and provide technical assistance and incubator centres that stand as anchors for entrepreneurial mindset development and creation of business start-ups among youths.

The World Bank's (2020) study of ease of doing business and starting a new venture, compared 190 economies, over 40 of which were economies in Sub-Saharan Africa. The survey ranking indicates that the regulatory environment in most Sub-Saharan African countries still ranks well below the general desirable average. The factors such as dealing with construction permits, getting electricity, registering property, getting credit, protecting investors, paying taxes, trading across borders, enforcing contracts, resolving insolvency

Average ease of doing business score (0-100)

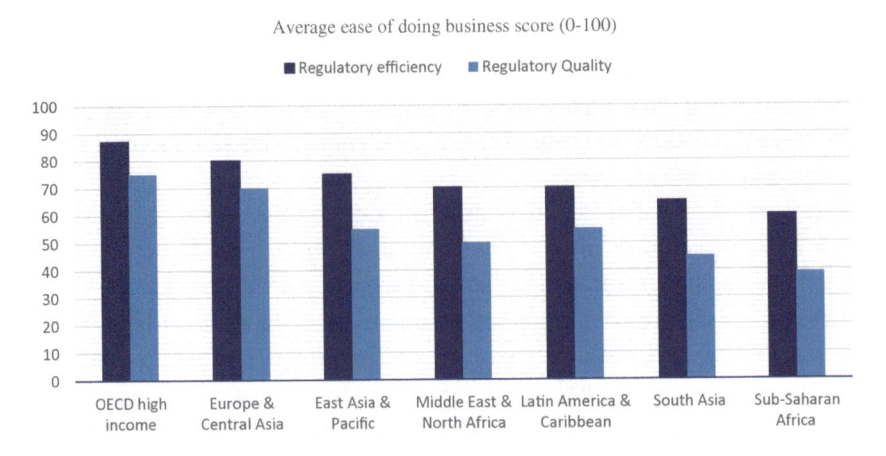

Fig. 3.1 World Bank average of ease of doing business among regional economies (*Source* World Bank doing business report [2019])

and employing workers that contribute to the ease of starting a business still require significant improvement in most Sub-Saharan African countries. These factors impose restrictive conditions which inhibit entrepreneurial mindsets and new venture creation among young people. In this context, entrepreneurial efforts to acquire pre-seed financing and venture capital as well as infrastructural amenities are not favourable to stimulate predispositions towards entrepreneurial engagement among youths. Therefore, the regulatory institutions affect the motivation, the energy and incentives for entrepreneurial engagement. Government policy to stimulate or encourage productivity and innovation should be put in place for the development of the right entrepreneurial ecosystem (Fig. 3.1).

Informal Institutional Contexts and Challenges to Entrepreneurial Development

Institutionally, countries vary substantially in respect to how the informal environment encourages new business starts-ups (Lim et al., 2010; McMullen et al., 2008). The informal aspect of institutional contexts such as trust, social expectations, social network, social capital, cooperative cultural norms and even corruption can impact on nascent entrepreneurial activity and success of new ventures. These occur at national and local levels, and the informal institutional environment impacts both nascent entrepreneurial activities and the prevalent cultures. For entrepreneurial culture, we focus on a mix of local cultural norms, expectations and attitudes for business practices that motivate individual young entrepreneurs to start and grow new ventures. The informal institutional context for entrepreneurship includes the normative structures within a society. These normative institutions consist of the system of beliefs, cultural norms, societal values and certain assumptions or world views that are shared and taken for granted by members or individuals with a social institution (Autio & Fu, 2015; Bowen & De Clercq, 2008). The informal environment, such as the cultural environment, impacts greatly on behaviour, and influences/determines the kind of orientation that is dominant within a culture. It also determines the winning mentality, achievement orientation, risk orientation of entrepreneurs as well as the legitimate means of achieving them. Studies show that perceptions and attitudes towards risk and fear of business failure can also negatively impact business start-ups.

This is particularly so, in African cultures where business failure is perceived as shortcoming rather than as a learning curve (Dheer, 2017; Shane, 1993). As such we emphasise that within the African context, cultures, norms and the immediate social environment can significantly affect individual entrepreneurial orientation and entrepreneurial choice. The instance of social networks and social capital presents a relevant perspective of the unique and important process through which informal networks, within an institution, impact entrepreneurship and business start-ups (Dheer, 2017; Escandon-Barbosa et al., 2019). Social capital is not only built through the structures of personal resources accrued over time but also through networks of cooperative norms, families and friends to achieve economic and social objectives (Escandon-Barbosa et al., 2019; Lin, 2001). As many African societies are collectivist in nature, research shows that the normative and cultural-cognitive environments present significant opportunities and funding support for nascent entrepreneurial ventures (Ogunsade & Obembe, 2016).

Scott (2013) noted that societal norms are not only constructed, they influence behaviour and cognitive structures. Similarly, studies indicate that social stability and order are functions of rules, regulations and societal norms (Lee & Peterson, 2000; Williams et al., 2010). For example, scholars have identified how corrupt illegal behaviour and social insecurity affect the capacity for economic growth and development (Dheer, 2017). Corrupt practices and illegal behaviours within social institutions tend to impact on entrepreneurial activities and new business formation. Furthermore, corruption and insecurity not only increase transactional costs, they also decrease the motivation for investment (Escandon-Barbosa et al., 2019; Anokhin & Shulze, 2009). Where corrupt behaviour becomes the social norm, individual motivation and perceptions for new business creation are invariably impacted.

Informal institutions also affect the cognitive structures, social knowledge and beliefs that influence human behaviour and actions. The elements of informal institutions can therefore shape investment, competition, and entrepreneurial activities. The cultural-cognitive dimension thus reflects the mindset, schemas and inferences in which reality, meaning and certain decisions are based (Scott, 2013). The cognitive institutional environment is also reflected in the set of beliefs, perceptions and assumptions that are deeply shared within the society (Scott, 2013). On a macro level, there is a wide range of data associating the national culture within a country to entrepreneurship behaviours of its people, organisations and governments. Literature also highlights the importance of cultural norms, values and beliefs in facilitating entrepreneurial venture and business start-ups. For instance, on a wider scale, cultural values have also been found to impact on the growth of national income, gross domestic product and competitiveness (Bruton & Ahlstrom, 2003).

We note that Sub-Saharan Africa is diverse and has a very large number of dispersed communities with different cultural beliefs, norms and values. However, most countries across the region are oriented towards similar cultural values and social relations. Vershinina et al. (2017) observed that country-specific national cultures, such as Ubuntu in Southern Africa, Humanism in Central African countries, Harambee in Eastern African countries, have the potential to enable or constrain entrepreneurial mindsets and venture creation. Similarly, Murithi et al. (2019) argue that socio-cultural institutions present unique opportunities and complex challenges for venture creation and economic activities, particularly in contexts that are characterised by institutional voids within the formal institutions such as Sub-Saharan Africa.

Institutional Change for Entrepreneurial Emergence and Implications for Policy Framework in Africa

Entrepreneurial governance frameworks must facilitate policy formulation contingent upon the stability and innovativeness of the socio-cultural, political and economic context. This is represented through entrepreneurial governance, public policy and ecosystem frameworks (EGPFs) for institutional change and innovation. Our position is that the quality of entrepreneurial governance, public policy and ecosystems at both national and local levels must include specific, deliberate and evidence-based policies for entrepreneurial finance, taxes and bureaucracy, business incubators.

A fundamental problem is that some of these institutions lack policy direction and focus for nascent business ventures in SSA. For instance, In Nigeria and South Africa, although there are many potential support institutions, business angels and foundations, for various reasons, the funds do not get to individuals who need them, so transparency is still an issue. Whereas in countries like Angola, Madagascar and Mozambique, these important regulations and business support institutions are gradually undergoing reforms and improvement, but more improvements are still required (Herrington & Coduras, 2019; Herrington et al., 2017). The substantial variations that exist when compared across 190 economies in terms of quality of governance, access to finance, infrastructure and ease of doing business call for policy framework direction for entrepreneurial activities. Table 3.1 demonstrates similarities and differences of efforts being made to strengthening regulations within some Sub-Saharan African economies.

Entrepreneurial Governance and Public Policy for SAA

In our framework, we recognise the critically important role of various stakeholders which include policymakers, private sectors, non-governmental organisations and educational institutions in facilitating and creating the enabling institutions and ecosystem for nascent entrepreneurial emergence. Our framework prescribes that governments need to invest in regulation, build physical infrastructure and socio-cultural norms to enable internal market dynamics, development and economic growth. Firstly, specific policy on venture capital, knowledge and innovation is vital in order to stimulate the economy and encourage productivity. This will come with government and private sector coming together to identify entrepreneurial opportunities and specific policy oriented for five to ten-year plans to provide guidelines and incentives for entrepreneurs. Secondly, the symbiotic relationship between government, private and non-governmental actors, including local associations and universities, is important for decision-making. Also, essential are specific policies for normative and social network opportunities, policies for both rural and urban infrastructural development that will impact on economic structures as well as create incentives and market opportunities.

We further emphasise that the objective of governance is the creation of value through effective policies that enable opportunity, knowledge and innovation within business environments. We elaborate on this policy framework in the following sections (Fig. 3.2).

Table 3.1 Highlight of enabling institutional features for select African economies

Features	Economies	Highlights
Simplified preregistration and registration formalities (publication, notarization, inspection, and other requirements)	Burundi; Côte d'Ivoire; Ethiopia; Mauritania; Morocco; Nigeria; South Africa; Sudan; Togo;	While Nigeria, Ethiopia, South Africa etc., made some improvement in the area of easy of starting a business by eliminating process in multiple application forms and tax registration, more is still needed in the area of areas like transparency of procedures, capital requirements and reliable electricity
Abolished or reduced minimum capital requirement	Central African Republic; Togo	Togo, CAR eliminated paid-in minimum capital requirement and made business start-ups much easier
Introduced or improved online procedures	Nigeria; Tanzania; Togo	Nigeria improved online platform for registration and paying stamp duties, Togo and Tanzania introduced online business registrations platform for easy of doing business
Increased transparency of information	Gabon; Rwanda; Togo; Tunisia	Gabon and Israel upgraded their official websites to include relevant information to the public at large regarding land registry services
Facilitated more reliable power supply and transparency of tariff information	Angola; Gabon; Mozambique; Rwanda; South Africa; Togo	Angola, Gabon, South Africa, and Rwanda, recorded good improvement in regulatory frameworks for electricity generation and capacity

Source World Bank doing business report (2019)

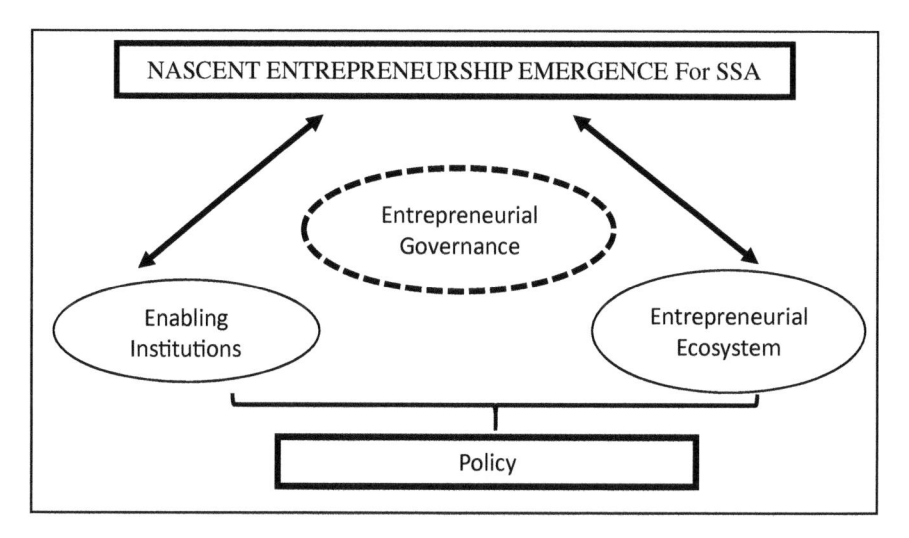

Fig. 3.2 Entrepreneurial enabling institutional framework

Enterprise Enabling Institutions (EEIs)

Entrepreneurship support organisations are products of policy initiatives for the creation of private and public institutions that are meant to build viable and successful new business start-ups for young people who do not have the finances, skills, experience or expertise to start a profitable new venture by themselves. In this regard, enterprise-enabling institutions such as business incubators, venture capitalist, microfinance banks, informal networks and non-governmental organisations have been found to be remarkable in providing the needed support in fostering entrepreneurial activities and new ventures in low-income economies, such as are characteristic of Sub-Saharan Africa (Smith et al., 2016). However, the promise of these supportive institutions to alleviate poverty and create inclusive and sustainable economic growth in the region has not been realised (Goel & Ranjan, 2020; Smith et al., 2016).

Therefore, we suggest that enabling entrepreneurial start-ups, through embryonic activities, business angels, education and business incubators, will provide individuals with needed resources and skills to not only take on business opportunities but foster the ability and self-confidence to act on them. For instance, local enterprises enabling support foundations, such as the Mowgli Foundation in North Africa, and Middle East, have been found to be effective in alleviating poverty by providing vital resources for new businesses (Smith et al., 2016).

Many studies have further demonstrated the impact of entrepreneurship education to include opportunity recognition, ability to evaluate business risk when starting a business and skills to successfully run the business (De Clercq & Arenius, 2006; Dickson et al., 2008). Invariably, it also impacts attitudes, values and personal developments of young entrepreneurs in business opportunity recognition. In this regard, it is important for policymakers to create policy frameworks and structures that will enable early stage business venture to successfully launch their business.

Supporting Entrepreneurial Ecosystem

Entrepreneurial ecosystems that promote the emergence of entrepreneurial economy and high growth entrepreneurship prospects are characterised by factors such as supporting local and regional policies, new ideas, innovation, infrastructure, stable power supply and individual motivation for economic activities (Brenner, 2004; Jessop, 2002). Similarly, Isenberg (2011) identifies key components of business ecosystem environments to include economy, support structures, human resources, markets, capital, culture and policies. This perspective indicates that the key success factor for entrepreneurial emergence and survival is based on foundations with a mix of these components within the business environment or ecosystem. We argue that whereas biological ecosystems do occur naturally, entrepreneurial ecosystems have to evolve through deliberate policy initiatives that will trigger the development of new venture creation and entrepreneurial advancement. More recently, South Africa for instance, has been attempting to promote efficient business ecosystems in which the State is directly helping to formulate business supports, offer additional seed finance, start-up loans, entrepreneurial training program and business incubators to facilitate entrepreneurship (Holt & Littlewood, 2017; Kasseeah & Tandrayen-Ragoobur, 2016; Kiggundu & Ogola, 2017; Lux et al., 2016). In this sense, specific policies for a supportive ecosystem with a robust and dynamic institutionally embedded interaction of knowledge and information among individuals are key critical. Institutions and other informal linkages are also critical to the advancement and allocation of resources for entrepreneurial activities within a society (Acs et al., 2012; Roundy et al., 2018). As an important part of the entrepreneurial ecosystem, universities and other institutions of higher education have a central place in the development of entrepreneurship. Therefore, promoting effective entrepreneurial training, education and policy framework, is critical to fostering students' entrepreneurial mindsets and capability. Effective entrepreneurship knowledge, policy support as well as the general supportive normative and cognitive environment for, and within, institutions of higher education is crucial to providing the necessary capacity for entrepreneurial mindsets and orientation among young people (Dickson et al., 2008; Jabeen et al., 2017; Matlay, 2008).

Policy Implications

Many studies on institutional context for entrepreneurship indicate that the support of institutional structures such as business incubators, seed financing, microfinance, micro-angels, local cultural associations, networks and other foundations are very key in entrepreneurs' efforts to start new venture in social contexts and environments with institutional voids (De Clercq et al., 2010). While we acknowledge the importance of this perspective in solving issues created through institutional voids, our model place emphasizes on the importance of entrepreneurial governance and public policy for the right ecosystem and entrepreneurship-enabling institutions in bridging this issue. Our model helps to provide the understanding of the key roles of formal and informal institutions in the process of new business development and inclusive growth through entrepreneurial economic and national development.

Entrepreneurship-enabling institutions and governance can direct economic actions towards new business start-ups through the provision of vital resources upon which new ventures may be dependent to survive (McMullen et al., 2008). While, Van Stel et al. (2007) found that the regulatory environment and support affect the rate of new business, Mitchell et al. (2002) noted that prevailing socio-cultural values within a particular context impact the rate of new business start-ups. Bowen and De Clercq (2008) further emphasised the importance of the formal institutions in channelling vital resources such as finance which new business ventures require to thrive. New businesses often require significant external capital resources for start-up, and financing may be derived from personal savings or network resources, as well as from external financial sources which may come from banks and angel investors.

Additionally, our model emphasis that entrepreneurial governance goes beyond access to finance; instead, it gives nascent and early stages entrepreneurs exposure to skills, information, network and knowledge that are required for success. Our model of entrepreneurial governance framework policy focuses more on government, private local and international actors partnering together to invest in creating infrastructure and business ecosystems that will enable the development of entrepreneurial opportunity, reliable and affordable electricity, digital infrastructure.

Theoretical Implications

The present study provides opportunities to enrich the entrepreneurship literature on nascent entrepreneurship and institutions governance in SSA. The study contributes to the understanding of how institutional environments and entrepreneurial governance can influence nascent entrepreneurial activities and the success of SMEs in SSA. In our opinion, entrepreneurial success, transforming beyond the gestation stage to start-up, is dependent on different dynamics and characteristics of societies. Sub-Saharan Africa has different variations and incidences of institutional change which makes institutional environments more pertinent in understanding entrepreneurial emergence.

We extend studies on institutional embeddedness for entrepreneurship by identifying institutional voids and contextual challenges limiting high growth and nascent entrepreneurship in Africa; and we provide a policy framework and direction to bridge these voids. Policy framework conditions based on entrepreneurial governance, public policy and entrepreneurial ecosystem for institutional change and innovation can help to focus resources that will positively impact institutional environments. We derive our policy framework from a basic assumption that entrepreneurial emergence is a result of institutional contexts that impact individual entrepreneurial decisions to pursue a given opportunity while considering associated risks, skills and other normative sentiments occurring within this business environment. As such, institutional voids within the socio-economic environment are likely to impact entrepreneurial propensity and nascent entrepreneurs. We surmise that socio-economic structures represent a central focus in the development of well-functioning social and institutional settings for sustained economic growth and entrepreneurial emergence. Furthermore, unlike many single-layered perspectives of contextual determinant, our study offers a multi-layered account to further understand entrepreneurial engagement (Wigren-Kristofersen et al., 2019). We demonstrate the importance of embeddedness, entrepreneurial governance and supportive ecosystem for nascent entrepreneurial activities (Jabeen et al., 2017; Welter et al., 2019). Accounting for the contextual challenges, we theorise that entrepreneurial governance and public policy must focus on policy-direction support for nascent entrepreneurs, seed funding and local embeddedness in order to eliminate institutional voids. We thus submit that this will help to create new ventures, inclusive growth and effective diffusion of formal and informal institutional structure in Sub-Saharan Africa.

Conclusion

We contended that institutionally, the business environment presents many challenges to nascent entrepreneurs and new business survival in SSA. Some of the constraints identified are issues of market opportunity, corruption, low education, access to credit or finance and skills and knowledge to successfully transform business ideas from gestation to start-ups. In addition to challenges of the regulatory environment, the normative and cultural-cognitive environments all come together to impact nascent and opportunity-driven entrepreneurial activities among young people. It has been shown that individuals with the required skills, technical know-how and wealth of informal network of social capital, are able to be successful business owners. Therefore, our study presents a policy framework that identifies the importance of enterprise-enabling institutions and entrepreneurial governance to direct economic actions towards new business start-ups through provision of vital resources upon which new ventures may depend for survival. As a result, entrepreneurial governance and public policies must focus on policy-direction support for nascent entrepreneurs, seed funding and local embeddedness to eliminate institutional voids. We submit that this will help to create new ventures, inclusive growth and effective diffusion of formal and informal institutional structures. Furthermore, we propose an institutional framework based on a recursive relationship between institutional contexts and entrepreneurship-enabling institutions. Finally, we conclude that there is need for government policy initiatives that promote investments in order to improve entrepreneurial capacity and engagement. This will contribute towards poverty alleviation and produce more inclusive growth needed for wealth creation and development in Africa.

References

Acs, Z. J., Audretsch, D. B., Braunerhjelm, P., & Carlsson, B. (2012). Growth and entrepreneurship. *Small Business Economics, 39*(2), 289–300. https://doi.org/10.1007/s11187-010-9307-2.

Acs, Z. J., Desai, S., & Hessels, J. (2008). Entrepreneurship, economic development and institutions. *Small Business Economics, 31*(3), 219–234. https://doi.org/10.1007/s11187-008-9135-9.

AFDB, A. (2016). *North Africa-working paper—The role of nascent entrepreneurship in driving inclusive economic growth in North Africa*. African Development Bank.

Anokhin, S., & Schulze, W. S. (2009). Entrepreneurship, innovation, and corruption. *Journal of Business Venturing, 24*(5), 465–476.

Audretsch, D. B., Belitski, M., & Desai, S. (2015). Entrepreneurship and economic development in cities. *The Annals of Regional Science, 55*(1), 33–60. https://doi.org/10.1007/s00168-015-0685-x.

Autio, E., & Fu, K. (2015). Economic and political institutions and entry into formal and informal entrepreneurship. *Asia Pacific Journal of Management, 32*, 67–94.

Baumol, W. J. (1990). Entrepreneurship: Productive, unproductive and destructive. *Journal of Political Economy, 98*(5), 893–921.

Blackburn, R., & Ram, M. (2006). Fix or fixation? The contributions and limitations of entrepreneurship and small firms to combating social exclusion. *Entrepreneurship and Regional Development, 18*(1), 73–89.

Bosma, N., Stigter, H., & Wennekers, S. (2001). *The long road to the entrepreneurial society*. Global Entrepreneurship Monitor.

Bowen, H. P., & De Clercq, D. (2008). Institutional context and the allocation of entrepreneurial effort. *Journal of International Business Studies, 39*(4), 747–767.

Brenner, N. (2004). Urban governance and the production of new state spaces in Western Europe, 1960–2000. *Review of International Political Economy, 11*(3), 447–488.

Bruton, G. D., & Ahlstrom, D. (2003). An institutional view of China's venture capital industry: Explaining the differences between China and the West. *Journal of Business Venturing, 18*(2), 233–259.

Chigunta, F. (2017). Enterprise as a possible solution to youth unemployment. *Labour and Learning, 10*. 433–451.

De Clercq, D., & Arenius, P. (2006). The role of knowledge in business start-up activity. *International Small Business Journal, 24*(4), 339–358.

De Clercq, D., Danis, W. M., & Dakhli, M. (2010). The moderating effect of institutional context on the relationship between associational activity and new business activity in emerging economies. *International Business Review, 19*(1), 85–101.

Dheer, R. (2017). Cross-national differences in entrepreneurial activity: Role of culture and institutional factors. *Small Business Economics, 48*, 813–842.

Dickson, P., Solomon, G., & Weaver, K. (2008). Entrepreneurial selection and success: Does education matter? *Journal of Small Business and Enterprise Development, 15*(2), 239–258.

Dimov, D. (2007). Beyond the single-person, single-insight attribution in understanding entrepreneurial opportunities. *Entrepreneurship Theory and Practice, 31*(5), 713–731.

Escandon-Barbosa, D., Urbano-Pulido, D., & Hurtado-Ayala, A. (2019). Exploring the relationship between formal and informal institutions, social capital, and entrepreneurial activity in developing and developed countries. *Sustainability, 11*(2), 550.

Goel, S., & Ranjan, K. (2020). Entrepreneurial aspirations and poverty reduction: The role of institutional context. *Entrepreneurship & Regional Development, 32*(1–2), 91–111.

Holt, D., & Littlewood, D. (2017). Waste livelihoods amongst the poor—Through the lens of bricolage. *Business Strategy and the Environment, 26*(2), 253–264.

Herrington, M., & Coduras, A. (2019). The national entrepreneurship framework conditions in Sub-Saharan Africa: A comparative study of GEM data/national expert surveys for South Africa, Angola, Mozambique and Madagascar. *Journal of Global Entrepreneurship Research, 9*(1), 60.

Herrington, M., Kew, P., Singer, S., Carmona, J., Wright, F., & Coduras, A. (2017). GEM 2016–2017 global report. *Global Entrepreneurship Monitor*, 1–177.

Isenberg, D. (2011). *The entrepreneurship ecosystem strategy as a new paradigm for economy policy: Principles for cultivating entrepreneurship*. The Babson Entrepreneurship Ecosystem Project, Babson college, MA.

Jabeen, F., Faisal, M. N., & Katsioloudes, M. I. (2017). Entrepreneurial mindset and the role of universities as strategic drivers of entrepreneurship: Evidence from the United Arab Emirate. *Journal of Small Business and Enterprise Development, 24*(1), 136–157.

Jessop, B. (2002). *The future of the capitalist state*. Polity Press.

Kasseeah, H., & Tandrayen-Ragoobur, V. (2016). Ex-garment female workers: A new entrepreneurial community in Mauritius. *Journal of Enterprising Communities: People and Places in the Global Economy, 10*(1), 33–52.

Kiggundu, M. N., & Ogola, F. O. (2017). Kenya's Safaricom, CEO Bob Collymore and m-pesa: Extended notes from keynote address. *Africa Journal of Management, 3*(1), 30–52.

Kim, P. H., Aldrich, H. E., & Keister, L. A. (2006). Access (not) denied: The impact of financial, human, and cultural capital on entrepreneurial entry in the United States. *Small Business Economics, 27*(1), 5–22.

Kor, Y. Y., Mahoney, J. T., & Michael, S. C. (2007). Resources, capabilities and entrepreneurial perceptions. *Journal of Management Studies, 44*(7), 1187–1212.

Lajqi, S., & Krasniqi, B. (2017). Entrepreneurial growth aspirations in challenging environment: The role of institutional quality, human and social capital. *Brief Entrepreneurial Finance, 26*, 385–401.

Lee, S., & Peterson, S. (2000). Culture, entrepreneurial orientation, and global competitiveness. *Journal of World Business, 35*(4), 401–416.

Legas, H. (2015). Challenges to entrepreneurial success in Sub-Saharan Africa: A comparative perspective. *European Journal of Business and Management, 7*(11), 23–35.

Lim, D., Morse, E., Mitchell, R., & Seawright, K. (2010). Institutional environments and entrepreneurial cognitions: Comparative business systems perspective. *Entrepreneurship Theory & Practice, 34*(3), 491–516.

Liñán, F., & Fernandez-Serrano, J. (2014). National culture, entrepreneurship and economic development: Different patterns across the European Union. *Small Business Economics, 42*(4), 685–701.

Lux, S., Lamont, B. T., Ellis, K. M., Ferris, G. R., & Muchira, J. (2016). Developing and utilizing efficient ties in entrepreneurial networks in Africa. *Africa Journal of Management, 2*(1), 73–92.

Mair, J., Marti, I., & Ventresca, M. J. (2012). Building inclusive markets in rural Bangladesh: How intermediaries work institutional voids. *Academy of Management Journal, 55*(4), 819.

Matlay, H. (2008). The impact of entrepreneurship education on entrepreneurial outcomes. *Journal of Small Business and Enterprise Development, 15*(2), 382–396.

Mitchell, R. K., Busenitz, L., Lant, T., McDougall, P. P., Morse, E. A., & Smith, J. B. (2002). Toward a theory of entrepreneurial cognition: Rethinking the people side of entrepreneurship research. *Entrepreneurship Theory and Practice, 27*(2), 93–104.

McMillan, J., & Woodruff, C. (2002). The central role of entrepreneurs in transition economies. *Journal of Economic Perspectives, 16*(3), 153–170.

McMullen, J. S., Bagby, D. R., & Palich, L. E. (2008). Economic freedom and the motivation to engage in entrepreneurial action. *Entrepreneurship Theory and Practice, 32*(5), 875–895.

Memili, E., Fang, H., Chrisman, J. J., & De Massis, A. (2015). The impact of small-and-medium-sized family firms on economic growth. *Small Business Economics, 45*(4), 771–785.

Murithi, W., Vershinina, N., & Rodgers, P. (2019). Where less is more: Institutional voids and business families in Sub-Saharan Africa. *International Journal of Entrepreneurial Behavior & Research, 26*(1), 158–174.

North, D. C. (1990). *Institutions, institutional change and economic performance*. Cambridge University Press.

Ogunsade, I. A., & Obembe, D. (2016). The influence of informal institutions on informal sector entrepreneurship: A study of Nigeria's XE "Nigeria" hand-woven textile industry. *Journal of Small Business & Entrepreneurship, 28*(6), 413–429.

Ogunsade, I. A., Murithi W., & Mafimisebi, O. (2020). Entrepreneurship education for youth in Africa: Institutional determinants of entrepreneurial mind-set and action among university educated youths. In S. Dobson, P. Jones, D. Agyapong & G. Maas (Eds.), *Enterprising Africa: Transformation through entrepreneurship*. Routledge.

Okafor, E. E. (2011). Youth unemployment and implications for stability of democracy in Nigeria. *Journal of Sustainable Development in Africa, 13*(1), 358–373.

Peng, M. W., & Shekshnia, S. V. (2001). How entrepreneurs create wealth in transition economies. *The Academy of Management Executive, 15*(1), 95–111.

Reynolds, P., Bosma, N., Autio, E., Hunt, S., De Bono, N., Servais, I., Lopez-Garcia, P., & Chin, N. (2005). Global entrepreneurship monitor: Data collection design and implementation 1998–2003. *Small Business Economics, 24*(3), 205–231.

Roundy, P. T., Bradshaw, M., & Brockman, B. K. (2018). The emergence of entrepreneurial ecosystems: A complex adaptive systems approach. *Journal of Business Research, 86*, 1–10.

Scott, R. W. (2013). *Institutions and organisations* (4th ed.). Sage.

Shane, S. (1993). Cultural influences on national rates of innovation. *Journal of Business Venturing, 8*(1), 59–73.

Smith, A., Judge, W., Pezeshkan, A., & Nair, A. (2016). Institutionalizing entrepreneurial expertise in subsistence economies. *Journal of World Business, 51*(6), 910–922.

Van Stel, A., Storey, D., & Thurik, R. (2007). The effect of business regulations on nascent and young business entrepreneurship. *Small Business Economics, 28*(2–3), 171–186.

Vershinina, N., Barrett, R., & McHardy, P. (2017). Logics and rationalisations underpinning entrepreneurial decision-making. *Journal of Small Business and Enterprise Development*.

Weiss, J., & Montgomery, H. (2005). Great expectations: Microfinance and poverty reduction in Asia and Latin America. *Oxford Development Studies, 33*(3–4), 391–416.

Welter, F., Baker, T., & Wirsching, K. (2019). Three waves and counting: The rising tide of contextualization in entrepreneurship research. *Small Business Economics, 52*(2), 319–330.

Wennekers, S., Van Wennekers, A., Thurik, R., & Reynolds, P. (2005). Nascent entrepreneurship and the level of economic development. *Small Business Economics, 24*(3), 293–309.

Wigren-Kristofersen, C., Korsgaard, S., Brundin, E., Hellerstedt, K., Agnete Alsos, G., & Grande, J. (2019). Entrepreneurship and embeddedness: Dynamic, processual and multi-layered perspectives. *Entrepreneurship & Regional Development, 31*(9–10), 1011–1015.

Wiklund, J., & Shepherd, D. (2005). Entrepreneurial orientation and small business performance: A configurational approach. *Journal of Business Venturing, 20*(1), 71–91.

Williams, C. C., Round, J., & Rodgers, P. (2010). Explaining the off-the-book enterprise culture of Ukraine: Reluctant or willing entrepreneurship? *International Journal of Entrepreneurship Small Business, 10*(2), 165–180.

World Bank Group. (2019). *Doing business 2019: Reforming to create jobs: Comparing business regulation for domestic firms in 190 economies.* International Bank for Reconstruction and Development/World Bank.

World Bank Group. (2020). *Doing business 2020: Comparing business regulation in 190 economies.* International Bank for Reconstruction and Development/World Bank.

Wu, A., Song, D., & Yang, Y. (2020). Untangling the effects of entrepreneurial opportunity on the performance of peasant entrepreneurship: The moderating roles of entrepreneurial effort and regional poverty level. *Entrepreneurship & Regional Development, 32*(1–2), 112–133.

4

The Interaction Between Family Businesses and Institutional Environment in Africa: An Exploration of Contextual Issues

William K. Murithi and Kassa Woldesenbet Beta

Introduction

Scholars are interested in the intersection between family businesses and institutional environment literature due to the several characteristics that emerge as family businesses interact with the institutional environments in unique ways (Soleimanof et al., 2018). Some unique features emerge due to embeddedness of family businesses at the intersection of multiple institutional logics (Fairclough & Micelotta, 2013) such as the family, market (business), the state, community, etc. (Miller & Le Breton-Miller, 2014; Thornton et al., 2012). Such embeddedness in multiple logics significantly influence beliefs, values, preferences, behaviours, and actions of family businesses. For instance, family logics focus on preserving core family values and beliefs, whereas business logics naturally aim at norms and standards related to business efficiency and effectiveness (Soleimanof et al., 2018). Simultaneously, the family as an institution has its own idiosyncratic norms, values, and beliefs that help to pursue its interests via the family businesses in broader institutional contexts (Miller et al., 2011).

W. K. Murithi (✉)
Centre for Enterprise and Innovation, De Montfort University, Leicester, UK

K. Woldesenbet Beta
De Montfort University, Leicester, UK

Despite some family business scholars attempts to using an institutional perspective in their research (e.g. Leaprott, 2005; Melin & Nordqvist, 2007; Parada et al., 2010), this strand of research has not yet developed due to lack of consistency and unhelpful biases (Soleimanof et al., 2018). Addressing such 'uneven development and unproductive biases' (Soleimanof et al., 2018, p. 33) entails researchers to move beyond examining the bidirectional influence of family business and the institutional environment to investigate 'whether or when those reciprocal influences are positive or negative' (Wright et al., 2014, p. 1248). Additionally, attempts to draw on institutional logics of the family are yet to be fully explored within the realm of institutional theory and research (Fairclough & Micelotta, 2013). Therefore, this chapter seeks to address these gaps by examining the influence of institutional environment on family businesses and vice versa within the African context.

Institutional voids which refer to the prevalence of underdeveloped and dysfunctional formal institutions in Africa impact businesses significantly. In this chapter, 'institutional void' is defined as the absence or the weakly presence of the formal 'rules of the game' (North, 1990) that support market activities and that shape the behaviour of family businesses and entrepreneurs (Khanna & Palepu, 1997; Mair et al., 2012). We focus on how the institutional environment in Africa shapes the behaviours of family businesses and how the family businesses also shape the changes in institutional environments. This focus is motivated by the following factors: First, to extend to the ongoing debate on whether family businesses have an advantage or disadvantage in developing economies (Gedajlovic et al., 2012). While scholars such as Gedajlovic and Carney (2010), Luo and Chung (2013) and Miller et al., (2009) contend that family businesses have an advantage because of their social capital and stability which help to fill institutional voids (Banalieva, et al., 2015), others argue that family businesses lack the required competence in developing economies due to their resistance to change and emphasis on family control (see Claessens et al., 2000). These conditions force African family businesses to navigate through the demands of multiple institutional logics (Fairclough & Micelotta, 2013) such as family, business, market, and state. Second, to address the research gap in family business in the African context as the they received scant attention hitherto despite their prevalence and contributions to regional economic and social development (Acquaah, 2016; Khavul et al., 2009). In doing so we seek to address the research question: How do family businesses affect and are affected by the institutional environment in Africa?

The chapter is organised as follows: The next section briefly presents institutional environment followed by an overview of family businesses and their significance in Africa in section three. In section four a series of theoretically—and contextually driven propositions are advanced on the interaction between family businesses and institutional environments. Section five presents the conclusion.

Institutional Environment

Institutions are the 'rules of the game' in a society (North, 1990). Institutions such as regulative, normative, and social-cognitive show high degree of persistence (Scott, 2001); change over time, are not uniformly assumed, and have results that are exclusive (Dacin et al., 2002). However, the institutional approaches differ significantly on the conceptualisation of these institutions, their level of analysis and their explanations of how these institutions matter to the interplay of business and society (Hotho & Pedersen, 2012). Generally, institutional theorists have focussed on investigating the institutional limitations that exist within market-driven economies, however, stabilities, constraints, and dynamics resulting from the various dimensions of institutions and may vary by contexts (Hotho & Pedersen, 2012).

The extant literature identifies formal and informal institutions (Scott, 2001). Both forms of institutions co-exist and influence business management and performance in Africa differently as opposed to the Western and Anglo-American context (Khavul et al., 2009; Murithi et al., 2020). The formal institutions refer to the laws, regulations, policies, and government structures, while informal institutions capture traditions, customs, religious believes and norms, ideologies, and culture (Kaufmann et al., 2018; Salimath & Cuhen, 2010).

Our interest in this chapter is to explore how the understudied informal institutions affect and are affected by the family business entrepreneurial activities. The institutional support perspective states that entrepreneurial activity thrives in countries with formal institutions that support entrepreneurial behaviours (Zahra & Wright, 2011). In contrast, the institutional voids perspective argues that entrepreneurial activities flourish in resource-constrained environments where individuals are forced to act entrepreneurially to provide services and products that governments do not provide (Estrin et al., 2013). Institutional voids also exacerbate prevailing social inequalities due to local institutional arrangement that determine access to market and opportunities (Crow, 2001). Khanna and Palepu (2010) identified institutional voids that hinder market functioning such as underdeveloped capital, labour, and product markets. Institutional voids also affect not only the operation of markets but their developments to begin with (Estrin et al., 2013; Mair & Marti, 2009) because of the lack of enforcement of formal rules and regulations, which create exchange uncertainties and stalls market development. Chakrabarty (2009) in the study of the influence of national culture and institutional voids on family ownership at the country-level found that both the national culture and institutional voids influence the ownership patterns of family businesses and that the effects of national culture are strong where institutional voids are prevalent and weak where intuitional voids are less prevalent.

Family business is simply a business that is owned and/or managed by more than one member of the family (i.e. either close-nuclear family members or diverse-extended family members). Though less studied, the value of the family business as a form of ownership is important in Africa as it acts as a substitute for a lack of strong regulatory framework or efficient market supporting institutions (Betrand & Schoar, 2006; Visser & Chiloane-Tsoka, 2014). Family businesses have their roots embedded in the family unit which is governed by certain behaviours, values, and norms. Additionally, family businesses not only create value and wealth, but also enable intergenerational and/or geographical transmission of wealth in developing economies (Carney, 2005). Family businesses in Africa, we argue, use informal institutions to overcome the challenges paused by institutional voids. Informal institutions such as strong traditions, customs societal norm, culture and unwritten codes of conduct are dominant in African societies and co-exist with formal institutions left by the colonial systems of governments (Khavul et al., 2009; Leaprott, 2005; Zoogah et al., 2015). With a varied degree of influences, we contend that family businesses are, 'simultaneously embedded' in both formal and informal institutions and these shape entrepreneurial intention, creation, management, and performance of family businesses in Africa (Khavul et al., 2009). Moreover, important stakeholders such as families, communities, politicians, and government agents' behaviours are also shaped by both formal and informal institutions and vice versa.

Family Businesses and Their Significance in Africa

This section of the chapter explores the family businesses, their economic significance and family business entrepreneurship within the African context.

Understanding Family Businesses Within the African Context

To date, there is no universally accepted definition of family business. Scholars define family businesses based on both demographic components and essence approach. Such definitions may involve criteria such as: self-identification (Westhead & Cowling, 1998); ownership, management, governance (Chua et al., 1999); level of family involvement in the business (Chrisman et al., 2012); interdependent subsystems (Litz, 2008); generational transfer with focus on intra-family succession and intentions for transgenerational transition (De Massis et al., 2008); and family identity (Zellweger et al., 2012). The most widely cited definition is provided by Chua et al. (1999). They defined family business as:

> a business governed and/or managed with the intention to shape and pursue the vision of the business held by a dominant coalition controlled by members of the same family or a small number of families in a manner that is potentially sustainable across generations of the family or families (p. 25).

This is the most widely used definition within the family business research as it combines both the demographic components and family essence approach, which are necessary and sufficient conditions for family to influence firm behaviours, strategic direction, and performance (De Massis et al., 2014). According to De Massis et al. (2014), these conditions not only evaluate the ability of the family but also their willingness to influence the strategic behaviours of the business.

In Africa, although a large proportion of firms are family businesses, their ownership is not typically captured as a 'family-owned business'; their contribution is less recognised and support mechanisms are less available (*Tharawat Magazine*, 2016). This is echoed by a prominent family business magazine 'Tharawat' where they argue that the institutional environment does not recognise and support family businesses. They state that:

> The institutional environment family businesses operate within [Africa] may not always recognise their importance and do not provide much support. Therefore, while family businesses undoubtedly have an impact on the economy at large, the question is often raised of whether economic institutions are engaging enough to safeguard the survival of family-owned companies. (*Tharawat Magazine*, 2016, online)

Most of the enterprises in Africa are simply categorised as micro, small, and medium enterprises (MSMEs); with no clear distinctions established whether the business belongs to a family or not. MSMEs are organised around the family system with direct or indirect control of the business because of tradition, customs, and collectivist culture (Acquaah, 2016; Khavul et al., 2009).

While the 'family business' as an organisation seems to have received considerable attention in respect of its operationalisation, 'the family' as an institution on the other side has received less attention (Leaprott, 2005; Murithi et al., 2020; Randerson et al., 2016). This stems from the recognised heterogeneity of families and the contemporary changes witnessed regarding the composition of families (extended, nuclear, single parent, gay couples, surrogacy, etc.) (Randerson et al., 2016). For instance, one of the criticisms of the above definition is that the 'family' referred to in most of the articles reviewed is based on studies that adopt the 'nucleus family'[1] as perceived in Western and North American context (Khavul et al., 2009; Randerson et al., 2016). In this context, family refers to a group of individuals with tight circles of immediate relatives connected through blood or marriage (Khavul et al., 2009; Naldi et al., 2007). On the contrary, in Africa, the foundation of family is kinship ties,[2] which can include extended family members[3] consisting of a broader lineage (Stewart, 2003). According to Reis and Sprecher (2009), kinship ties include lineal generational bonds (children, parents, grandparents, and great grandparents), collateral bonds (siblings, cousins, nieces and nephews, and aunts and uncles), and ties with in-laws. Although this chapter's focus is not about presenting debates on how to define family businesses in the African context, it might be necessary to consider the different branches of the 'family', comprising both younger and older generations, and including members of the extended family such as cousins, uncles, and aunts as well as distant relatives or community members given power or authority to oversee matters of the family by the patriarch[4] or matriarch.[5] This is likely to be especially important in cultures where family denotes a relationship beyond that of parents and children living together in regions such as Latin America, Asia, and Africa. We acknowledge that not all kinship ties may extend to

---

[1] A family consisting of two parents and their children, but not including aunts, uncles, grandparents etc (Cambridge Dictionary).
[2] Ties based on blood and marriage. In H. T. Reis & S. Sprecher (Eds.), *Encyclopaedia of human relationships* (pp. 951–954). Sage.
[3] A family unit that includes grandmothers, grandfathers, aunts, and uncles etc. in addition to parents and children (Cambridge Dictionary).
[4] A male head of the family.
[5] A female head of the family.

the business context, but there is evidence that suggest that entrepreneurs in Africa, draw on their kinship ties to raise financial resources which in itself is uniquely attributed to the social ties and collectivist cultures prominent in the African informal institutions (Khayesi et al., 2014; Murithi et al., 2020). The more extensive the family and their networks are, the more opportunities for accessing resources; however, this comes at cost to family businesses as they are expected to share their resources with their extended family network. We, therefore, have reasons to, in our notion of a family, include a broader, extended family group and more than two generations. This means that our view of family includes relatives, of both affine[6] and kin (Stewart, 2003) and other members of the society or community with a mandate to foresee or influence the family and business decisions. An affine is a person related by marriage, i.e. an in-law; and kin refers to a group of persons of common ancestry, i.e. relatives of various distances.

The majority of MSMEs that operate in an informal economy consist of a huge proportion of family businesses (Khavul et al., 2009). The informal economy consists of various economic activities that are conducted outside of the formal institutional boundaries but are considered legitimate by large segments of the society (Webb et al., 2014). Schneider (2005,p. 600) defines economic informality as 'all market based legal production of good and services that are deliberately concealed from public authorities', for purposes of taxation, employment, and administrative regulation. Addressing the family business definition in an African context thus needs capturing businesses operating in the informal markets as they form the backbone of entrepreneurial activities in African economies (Khavul et al., 2009). Thus, it is time to review the appropriateness of western originated family business definition.

Socio-economic Importance of Family Businesses in Africa

Although comprehensive reliable data is rare, family businesses are assumed to make significant contributions to socio-economic development in Africa. Available evidence shows that family businesses constitute over 90% of all private businesses in most African countries (Acquaah, 2016). We highlight below the contribution of family businesses in Nigeria (West Africa), South Africa (Southern Africa), Zimbabwe (Central Africa), and Kenya (Eastern Africa).

---

[6] A relative by marriage.

In Nigeria, which is the largest economy and most populous country in Africa, 78.5% of MSMEs are family-owned (Nigeria National Bureau of Statistics, 2007). Family businesses contribute significantly to the economic growth, employment, and wealth creation in Nigeria (Onuoha, 2013). Nigeria is home to some of the largest African family businesses such as Dangote, Ibru Organisation, Chisco Transport, Innoson Motors, and Cutix Industries to mention but a few with founding family controlling a large proportion of the shareholding and capital invested in the businesses. Most of the family business conglomerates operate internationally including across Africa and other regions of the world.

In South Africa, which is the second largest economy in Africa, family businesses are a predominant way of doing businesses; they comprise an estimated 80% of all South African businesses and 60% of corporates listed in the Johannesburg Stoke Exchange (JSE) (Maas & Diederichs, 2007). Further, family businesses account for 50% of economic growth in South Africa (Fishman, 2009). Over the past two decades, FBs in South Africa have experienced rapid growth due to the rationalisation process within many large organisations (Van der Merwe et al., 2009; Visser & Chiloane-Tsoka, 2014).

In Zimbabwe, it is reported that most enterprises start as family businesses and thrive under the leadership of the founding member (Nyamwanza et al., 2018). Their presence in the economy is vitally important as they account for 80% of the small and medium firms. However, their growth intentions were stifled by either the lack of well-thought-out succession planning (Sikomwe et al., 2012) or succession being affected by the presence of polygamous families (Nyamwanza et al., 2018) or lack of communication and preparedness regarding succession (Dumbu, 2018).

Family businesses are the backbone of the Kenyan economic and social development with prominent medium and large family-run businesses contributing substantially to GDP, employment opportunities, and wealth creation. The absolute financial contribution of family businesses to GDP in Kenya was more than 59% (World Bank, 2014). It is estimated that family businesses account for 60–80% of all employment in Kenya (Waweru, 2014). According to a report by PwC on private firms, 95% of Kenyan FBs that predicted growth were confident of achieving it, with 32% aiming for aggressive growth over a five-year period, while another 56% expected steady growth (2014, p. 6).

In recent times, evidence has emerged that shows the extent and effects of family businesses in Africa. In Eastern Africa region, considering only the large-sized family businesses in East Africa, there exist 645 family-owned businesses with turnover between $10 million and $100 million (Asoko

Insight, 2020). Of these family businesses, about three-quarters are Kenyan, 17% Ethiopian, 5% Zambians and Uganda, Rwanda and Tanzania are each home to 2% of the region's family businesses. For instance, in Rwanda, there are 14 large family-owned businesses with revenues over $10 million, three of which operate in the construction industry. Some of the renowned family businesses in Kenya include Bidco Oil refineries, Ramco group, Chandaria Industries, Nakumatt and Tuskys Supermarkets and Kenyatta Family. The recent report by Asoko Insight (2020) shows the existence of 490 large Kenyan family businesses earning revenues more than $10 million across a wide range of industries. Of the 490, 14.3% or 70 companies earn more than $50 million and 22 earn over $100 million per annum. The 22 Kenyan family companies with turnover over $100 million operate across various sectors, from banks to air freight and logistics. This diversification is unlike other countries in sub-Saharan Africa where the leading family businesses are largely concentrated in the industrial manufacturing sector. Family-owned businesses in Kenya, however, face challenges of corruption and lack of robust succession structure which limit their growth and longevity. The study by PWC showed that family businesses that reported as having a clear and communicated succession plan have fallen from 24% in 2016 to 17% in 2018; 30% of them made it through the second generation and only 13% passed three generations (Asoko Insight, 2020). One such example is Nakumatt Supermarket, one of the most successful retail businesses in Africa that folded amidst controversies of poor management, lack of transparency, unwarranted expansion and in ability to service its debts. The Nakumat case shows the challenges family businesses face in achieving sustained good performance and intergenerational succession.

Family Business Entrepreneurship

Entrepreneurship occurs at the nexus of individuals and opportunities. Most of the entrepreneurial behaviours of individuals is rooted in the family context, giving rise to the concepts of business families and family business. Business families are families that own various businesses while family business is a business owned by a family (or families) (Steir et al., 2015). Prior studies have failed to take into consideration the heterogeneity of business families and family business entrepreneurship. Entrepreneurial behaviours within the business families and family businesses are driven by the intersection of 'individual members, controlling family unit and business unit' subsystems (Habbershon et al., 2003). The survival of both the family and business entities depends on the individual and collective entrepreneurial behaviours (Randerson et al., 2015). Scholars in the field of family business argue that the interplay between the individuals, family group, and business unit contribute to entrepreneurial behaviours that lead to emergence of two significant fields of study: family entrepreneurship and family business entrepreneurship (Bettinelli et al., 2014).

Family entrepreneurship field is defined as research that 'studies entrepreneurial behaviours of family, family members and family business' (Bettinelli et al., 2014, p. 4) while family business entrepreneurship 'studies the entrepreneurial behaviours of the management team and firm itself and how risk-taking, innovativeness and proactiveness are present in strategic decisions, the management of resources available and how the firm is developed over time' (Wright et al., 2016, p. 8). According to prior studies, entrepreneurial behaviours of the family and family business can take different outcomes: start up with no previous business experience within the family (Randerson et al., 2015), serial business families with transgenerational experience and success which turn their acquired business experience in creating new family business ventures (Habbershon, 2006), corporate entrepreneurship (Zahra et al., 2013) referring to the 'gamut of informal and formal activities the firm actually undertakes in identifying, evaluating and exploiting opportunities through internal (e.g., the creation of new venture units) and external (e.g., alliances) means' (2013, p. 364)—and more specifically corporate family entrepreneurship (Bettinelli et al., 2017).

As a result of the collectivism culture within developing economies such as Africa, both business families and family businesses can leverage on the culturally embedded or social relational networks within the informal sociocultural institutions to propagate their business activities. Given that entrepreneurial activities within the business emerge as a result of the family needs and challenges (Michael-Tsabari et al., 2014), entrepreneurial family businesses would be willing to influence their formal and informal social relationships and networks in order to protect their socioemotional wealth (Gomez-Mejia et al., 2007). In the next section, we advance theoretically driven propositions to guide future studies on the influence of institutional environment on family businesses and vice versa in the context of Africa (Fig. 4.1).

```
                    ┌─────────────────────┐
                    │ Institutional Voids │
                    └─────────────────────┘
                     ↙                   ↘
┌──────────────────────────┐       ┌──────────────────────────┐
│ Institutional Environment│       │   Family and Family      │
│  (Formal and Informal    │ ←───→ │ Business Entrepreneurship│
│      Institutions)       │       │                          │
└──────────────────────────┘       └──────────────────────────┘
```

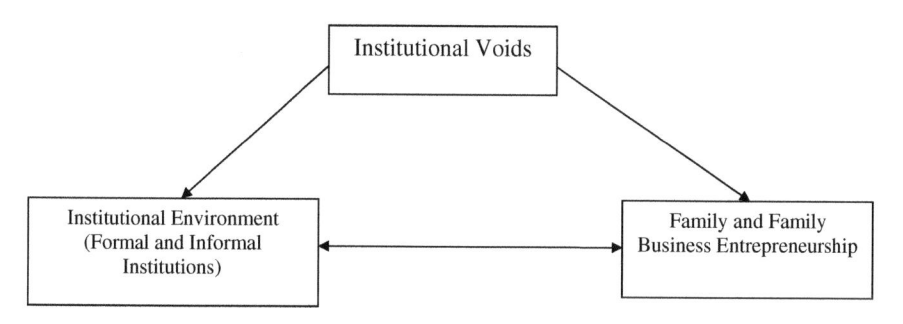

Fig. 4.1 Conceptual framework

Interaction Between the Institutional Environments and Family Businesses—Advancing Propositions

Family businesses have been the subject of research within the Western and North American context over the last three decades. However, there is a limited understanding on how the family businesses' entrepreneurial behaviours influence the institutional environment and vice versa in emerging and developing economies. Several researchers have called for research that explore the effects of the institutional context on entrepreneurial activities (Zahra et al., 2014), business families (Murithi et al., 2020) and family businesses' behaviours (Randerson et al., 2020; Reay et al., 2009). Kolk and Rivera-Santos (2018) also call for studies which accounts for the diversity across contexts and which avoid a generalised approach, or what is referred to as 'broad brush strokes' (Wainaina, 2005). This chapter seeks to address these gaps by providing propositions that guide future studies.

From an institutional perspective, the family is an important social unit in the society. The family refers to the institution while the family businesses refer to an organisation. According to Randerson et al. (2020, p. 4), 'the family is an institution in its own right', and thus deserves to be considered as such using the regulative, normative and cognitive domains (Scott, 2001) because of the institutional pressure it exerts on the business and environment. In developing economies, family, kinship, and sociocultural systems exert pressures on management of family businesses. For instance, in the case of Igbo tribe in Nigeria, Iqwe et al. (2020) study shows that Igbo businesses are organised in a family, kindred and kinship system and, early entrepreneurial learning and an informal tribe-based apprentice system support entrepreneurial behaviours and access to resources (Randerson et al., 2020). The prevailing African societal ties, both affine and kinship ties relating to families and communities, propagate the collectivist culture that promotes reciprocity and dependency culture (Zoogah et al., 2015). For instance, the family patriarch or matriarch in African families is responsible for the maintenance of family members because of the high dependency culture of family members who do not work and community welfare (Khayesi & George, 2011). Such dependence on family businesses becomes a cost to family business resources, and this in turn limits their performance and potential contribution to local and regional development. Thus, the bonding social and network ties seen from this perspective present the 'dark side' of social networks prevalent in African socio-cultural context (Khayesi et al., 2014). However, said this, such contributions to family members and community may help smoothing consumption and improving social well-being of the community as well as promote family cohesion and harmony among the family business and local communities.

According to Murithi et al. (2020), focussing on the family unit, as opposed to the family business only, in sub-Saharan Africa, showed that the family and the business are not competing subsystems. Instead, they complement each other and enable the businesses to navigate the complex institutional environment in contexts mired by institutional voids. For instance, the involvement of the extended family becomes a major source of capital, expertise, and information even for the informal entrepreneurial activities at the family level (Khavul et al., 2009; Murithi et al., 2020). Evidence from small firms in Kampala, Uganda, showed that the larger the entrepreneur's network (i.e. kinship networks) the more resources they could raise; however, this came at a higher cost (Khayesi et al., 2014). Thus, the interdependence between family business and, extended family and community ties has both positive and negative outcomes to family businesses. Based on the foregoing discussion we propose:

> *Proposition 1a*: In the context of institutional, relying on the extended family and community ties limits family businesses' expansion/growth.
>
> *Proposition 1b*: In the context of institutional void, extended familial and communal ties serve as conduit for acquiring resources such as financial and human capital for family business growth.

Informal institutions which originate from the strong traditions, customs, societal norm, culture, and unwritten codes of conduct are dominant in African societies and co-exist with formal institutions left by the colonial governments (Khavul et al., 2009; Murithi et al., 2020; Zoogah et al., 2015).

According to Murithi et al (2020), there are three types of informal institutions within sub-Saharan Africa: political, economic, and socio-cultural institutions. They argue that in the complex sub-Saharan African institutional environment, the family drives the business family engagement in institutional entrepreneurship via their 'embeddedness within the social relationships and relational familial logics' (Murithi et al., 2020, p. 158).

Family businesses operate at the interface of family, business, and institutional environments. For family businesses, familial ties and societal relationships bring important resources to the business. However, possessing such critical network resources may not necessarily contribute to the competitive advantage of the family business as this might not necessarily translate into relational assets (McGrath, 2010). McGrath and O'Toole (2018, p. 197) argue that entrepreneurial family firms must actively pursue related connections, 'beyond early social network ties, to gain access to and use a broader pool of resources and capabilities external to the firm'. To access external resources, family businesses need to be open and willing to partner (Dyer & Singh, 1998), to have the ability to coordinate competencies and combine knowledge across corporate boundaries (Lorenzo & Lipparini, 1999) as well as sustain their innovativeness by creating and managing overall architecture of their network over time (Capaldo, 2007). Therefore, we posit that:

> *Proposition 2*: Sustained performance of family businesses is related to their ability and willingness to leverage external network resources beyond their familial and close community ties.

Institutional voids exist in the 'situations where institutional arrangements that support markets are absent, weak, or fail to accomplish the role expected of them' (Mair & Marti, 2009, p. 419). In most African countries, weak regulatory systems and inefficient economic markets give rise to a culture of corruption, nepotism, fraud in the procurement processes and favouritism within the public agencies and institutions. These factors deprive these countries of the needed finances for economic and infrastructure development leading to regularity inefficiencies and ineffectiveness. An increase in bureaucracy increases unnecessary institutional pressures on private businesses including family businesses.

The prevalence of informal payments, corruption, and related irregularities forces family business to part with a significant amount of their wealth to overcome their uncompetitive behaviours in the economy to guarantee their sustainability and for accessing markets (Bassetti et al., 2015). Families that engage in such corruptive practice may be able to insulate the family business from risky ventures, compensate for the managerial inefficiencies as well as protect their socioemotional wealth. Similarly, the strong association of family businesses with political leaders within the African countries can be used to protect the businesses from uncertain markets, compensate for the lack of professional management and enable preservation of family wealth. It is common for some family firms to exploit their political connections for resource appropriation, engage in multiple business lines, and navigate dysfunctional formal institutions. New entrepreneurial firms however would find it more difficult to venture into business than incumbents in corruptive environments.

Businesses which navigate through a corrupt environment could adjust their behaviour to the corresponding informal norms in order to mitigate the negative impacts of corrupt practices (Tonoyan et al., 2010) by developing contacts and social networks (Estrin et al., 2013). Estrin et al. (2013) liken the notion of corruption with the concept of rent seeking and argue that such informal norms allow incumbents to share private benefits with government administrators at the cost of newcomers (Aidis et al., 2008). Therefore, we propose that in the context of institutional voids:

Proposition 3a: Large families and family businesses are more likely to exploit their political connections for resource appropriation and to protect their businesses from uncertainty in developing market environments than smaller businesses.

Proposition 3b: Large family businesses are more likely to engage in corruptive practices (bribe and lobby government officials and politician) to grow their businesses and gain competitive advantages. But such engagement acts as an implicit tax on resources as well limit the entry of new firms.

The exploration of family businesses' behaviours and outcomes in less developed institutional contexts such as those found in Africa provides an important insight into the interaction of the family/family business and the institutional environment. Previous research in this area indicates that operating as a family business serves as a calculated response to underdeveloped formal institutional contexts (see, Jøsrgensen et al., 1986; Murithi & Woldesenbet, 2021). Family businesses are ubiquitous in such contexts due to the agency costs, resources, and governance advantages that family governance provides for firms (Carney, 2005; Soleimanof et al., 2018). Employing family members reduces uncertainty associated with agency costs that results from 'lack of general interpersonal trust, underdeveloped monitoring mechanisms, and inefficient labour markets' (Soleimanof et al., 2018, p. 35).

Webb et al. (2015) underscored that family ties are used to acquire essential resources and to enact underdeveloped capital markets, weak property right systems, and inefficient contract enforcement mechanisms that typify developing economies. Family relations and resources, being strategic and intangible, allow firm growth and survival especially in the base-of-the-pyramid markets with underdeveloped formal institutions (Webb et al., 2015). In short, families provide 'a level of trust, solidarity and resources that is otherwise inefficient and risky to secure' (Webb et al., 2015, p. 120) for entrepreneurs in less developed institutional contexts. Therefore, we posit that.

Proposition 4: Family as an institution enables access to relevant resources and help overcome the challenges posed by the underdeveloped capital markets, weak property right systems, and inefficient contract enforcement mechanisms.

Family businesses fill institutional voids within turbulent sectors in emerging markets by drawing on the communal relational connections that positively influence firm performance (Miller et al., 2009; Murithi et al., 2020). They are known to use familial and extended social networks including external business networks and links with community and political leaders (Acquaah, 2012) to create portfolio of businesses. Some family business scholars argue that the existence of links between family businesses and political systems within African countries with some of the renowned family businesses being controlled by political families that control resources and power (Murithi et al., 2020). For example, in Kenya, these include business families such as President Kenyatta's family—Brookside Dairy, Heritage Hotels, Commercial Bank of Africa and Media Max; former President Moi's family—Kenya Time Network, Maritime, Signon Freight, Kabarak University; and former Prime Minister Odinga's family—Spectra International, and East Africa Spectre. Several other renowned business families within sub-Saharan Africa are associated with political families, politicians, and regimes to benefit their businesses economically, through access to strategic resources and lobbying for favourable policies.

Using political informal institutions and political capital, renowned political families establish strong social and relational networks, hence build business families that contribute to economic growth of developing countries. Such business families can influence both formal and informal institutional environments in economies characterised by institutional voids (Murithi et al., 2020). For instance, business families can positively overcome institutional voids in financial credit by being institutional investors. Arguably large business families can leverage on institutional resources to finance entrepreneurial activities in environments where financial institutions fail to offer credit facilities (Chakrabarty, 2009; Murithi et al., 2020). Families can act as institutional entrepreneurs as they have interest in institutional arrangements and by leveraging resources to create new institutions by transforming existing ones (Lawrence & Philips, 2004). We state that thus:

> *Proposition 5a*: Large family businesses are more likely to be embedded in strong political networks than small family businesses and can be controlled by political families which allow them unrestricted access to strategic resources that enables them to engage in multiple business lines.

> *Preposition 5b*: The ways in which business families enact entrepreneurial ideas within institutional voids is likely to shape the changes in formal and informal institutions.

In Africa, informal economic activities prevail (Khavul et al., 2009). A large proportion of these businesses operate informally without formal structures of ownership or right to property recognised by law, which can facilitate the trade, sale, or transfer of property or ownership rights to the immediate family members. In the absence of such legal framework, the ownership or properties of these businesses are subject to African traditional inheritance practices which allows distant family members (linked by kinship ties) to have a right of inheritance to the business or property in case of death or incapacitation of the founder (Kelly et al., 2008). Such context also appreciates the value of family businesses as they act as a substitute for lack of strong regulatory framework or efficient financial markets which provide protection to minority shareholders in developing economies (Betrand and Schoar, 2006; Visser & Chiloane-Tsoka, 2014). Additional behaviours observable in family businesses is how unified ownership and control provide them with organisational proclivities that are beneficial in less developed contexts (Carney, 2005). Family businesses are cost-efficient in underdeveloped labour-intensive contexts because of their prudence in using family resources, availability of cheap labour, patient capital, and reduced administrative overhead costs because of their direct management (Soleimanof et al., 2018). Therefore, we propose:

> *Proposition 6a*: The stewardship and governance mechanism of family firms operating informally are likely to be governed by informal institutions within the context and such conditions are likely to affect the transition to formality.

In view of influencing local development, it is not yet clear which institutional logics primarily influence the decisions and behaviours of family businesses in Africa. This is because the beliefs, values, actions, and behaviours of the firms could be influenced by the combination of the family, the business, the community, and the state logics. Further, family businesses combine different sociological and cultural qualities to overcome institutional voids (Murithi et al., 2020). Empirical evidence from family firms in emerging economies has shown that top level managers (TLMs) are more likely to develop strong social capital with managers from other firms, communities, and political leaders, which increases their community involvement (Acquaah, 2012; Murithi, 2020). Family businesses in Kenya, for instance, are capable of developing strong bonding and network capital, and in using different coping strategies in response to institutional pressures. They are able to do so because of the existence of strong collectivist cultures and social-cultural institutions (Murithi et al., 2020; Murithi & Woldesenbet, 2021) which leverage both communal and institutional resources, both formal and informal, to improve business performance and contribute to regional economic and social development (Murithi, 2020). Based on the foregoing analysis, we propose:

Proposition 6b: The strong collectivist culture and social-cultural institutions provide family businesses with rich social resources that promote business growth and socio-economic development.

Figure 4.2 visually summarises the propositions advanced above.

Conclusion

This chapter sought to examine the interaction between institutional environments and family businesses within the under researched African context. The chapter reviewed the existing literatures extensively to derive theoretically and contextually driven propositions to guide future research on the links between family, family businesses, and institutional environments in Africa. The core argument of the chapter is that Africa's diverse institutional environments provide a golden opportunity to examine the interaction between institutions and family/family businesses, that is, how the formal and informal institutions shape business family and family businesses' entrepreneurial behaviours in subtle but pervasive ways (Estrin et al., 2013; Scott, 1995).

Propositions advanced in this chapter would help to further our understanding of not only how family/family businesses value, beliefs, actions, and

Institutions	Institutional Voids	Business families and Family Business

[Diagram content:]

Family & Community Ties → Limits/Constrains Growth → P1(a) → Family Business Growth
Family & Community Ties ↔ P2 ↔ Family Business Growth
Family & Community Ties → Financial and human Capital resources → P1(b) → Family Business Growth

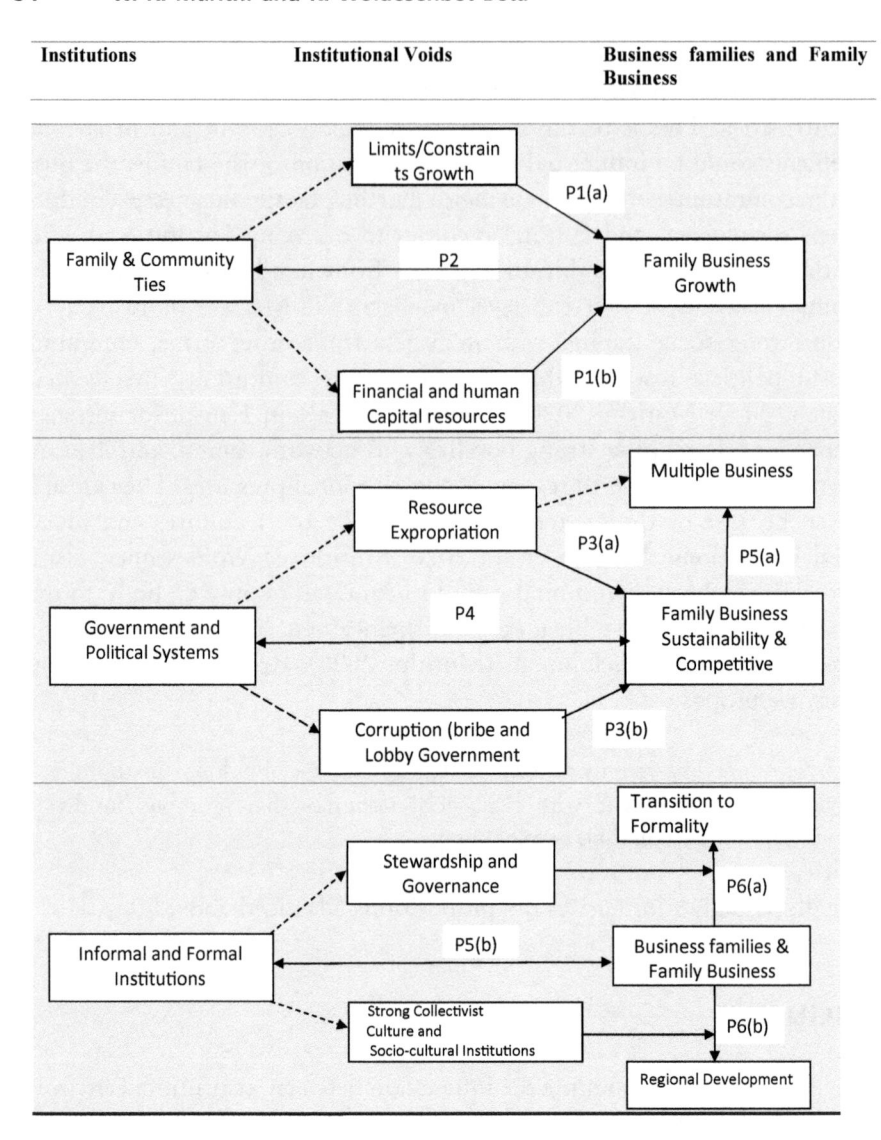

Government and Political Systems → Resource Expropriation → P3(a) → Family Business Sustainability & Competitive
Resource Expropriation ⇢ Multiple Business
Family Business Sustainability & Competitive → P5(a) → Multiple Business
Government and Political Systems ↔ P4 ↔ Family Business Sustainability & Competitive
Government and Political Systems → Corruption (bribe and Lobby Government) → P3(b) → Family Business Sustainability & Competitive

Informal and Formal Institutions → Stewardship and Governance → Transition to Formality
Stewardship and Governance → P6(a) → Business families & Family Business
Informal and Formal Institutions ↔ P5(b) ↔ Business families & Family Business
Informal and Formal Institutions → Strong Collectivist Culture and Socio-cultural Institutions → P6(b) → Regional Development

Fig. 4.2 Models and propositions—Interaction between institutions and family businesses

behaviours are influenced by formal and informal institutions but also vice versa. The propositions also would help to guide studies with focus on various institutional logics such as family, business, state, and community as well as on institutional voids and institutional support perspectives. For example, the institutional support perspective states that entrepreneurial activity thrives in countries with formal institutions that support entrepreneurial behaviours. In contrast, the institutional voids perspective argues that entrepreneurial activities flourish in resource-constrained environments where individuals are forced to act entrepreneurially to provide services and products that governments do not provide.

This chapter makes four important contributions to relationship between family businesses and institutional environments. First, while prior institutional theorists have explored the dichotomous effects of institutional effects on organisations, this chapter advanced propositions that help examination of the bidirectional effects of the interaction between institutional environments and family business within the African context. In doing so, the chapter shows how, in what aspects and contexts family businesses shape the institutional environments and vice versa. For instance, the pervasiveness of corruptive practices, co-opting of powerful policy and state officials, and the family businesses run by politicians in power all influence the behaviour of both the businesses and the formal and informal institutions.

Second, we extend the institutional theory and a related notion of institutional voids in an Africa context which had been hitherto under-explored. The propositions advanced in this chapter thus would help further scholarly understanding of the interplay between formal and informal institutions and institutional voids, and family/family businesses (Kolk & Rivera-Santos, 2018; Murithi & Woldesenbet, 2021; Murithi et al., 2020). This is because, several studies continue to acknowledge that the African institutional and contextual environments uniquely influence organisational and business behaviours, which in turn affect performance and contribution to development (Acquaah, 2016; Murithi & Woldesenbet, 2021; Murithi et al., 2020; Zoogah et al., 2015).

Third, the chapter provides a basis for extending a limited understanding of how the family businesses' entrepreneurial behaviours are influenced by or influence the institutional environment within developing economies in Africa. In so doing, the chapter responds to calls for further research on the effects of the institutional context on entrepreneurial activities (Welter, 2011; Wright et al., 2014), business families (Murithi et al., 2020), and family businesses behaviours (Randerson et al., 2020; Reay et al., 2009). It is also in a response to Kolk and Rivera-Santos' (2018) plea for careful studies on African context which consider diversities across the continent and to avoid a generalised approach, or what is referred to as 'broad brush strokes' (Wainaina, 2005).

Fourth, the review and propositions make clear how the family businesses' beliefs, values, behaviours, actions, and decisions are subject to influences by multiple institutional logics such as family, business/market, community, and state, to name a few. It would be of great interest to know in-depth how the interplay of these competing, at times, conflicting institutional logics influence family businesses' norms, behaviours, and actions in Africa context.

References

Acquaah, M. (2012). Social networking relationships, firm-specific managerial experience, and firm performance in a transition economy: A comparative analysis of family owned and nonfamily firms. *Strategic Management Journal, 33*(10), 1215–1228.

Acquaah, M. (Ed.). (2016). *Family businesses in sub-Saharan Africa: Behavioral and Ssrategic perspectives*. Springer, Palgrave Macmillan.

Aidis, R., Estrin, S., & Mickiewicz, T. (2008). Institutions and entrepreneurship development in Russia: A comparative perspective. *Journal of Business Venturing, 23*(6), 656–672.

Asoko Insight. (2020). *Asoko East Africa's family businesses report*. Available at: https://asokoinsight.com/content/developments/east-africa-family-owned-businesses-report. Accessed on 24 April 2020.

Banalieva, E. R., Eddleston, K. A., & Zellweger, T. M. (2015). When do family firms have an advantage in transitioning economies? Toward a dynamic institution-based view. *Strategic Management Journal, 36*(9), 1358–1377.

Bassetti, T., Dal Maso, L., & Lattanzi, N. (2015). Family businesses in Eastern European countries: How informal payments affect exports. *Journal of Family Business Strategy, 6*(4), 219–233.

Bertrand, M., & Schoar, A. (2006). The role of family in family firms. *Journal of Economic Perspectives, 20*(2), 73–96.

Bettinelli, C., Fayolle, A., & Randerson, K. (2014). Family entrepreneurship: A developing field. *Foundations and Trends® in Entrepreneurship, 10*(3), 161–236.

Bettinelli, C., Sciascia, S., Randerson, K., & Fayolle, A. (2017). Researching entrepreneurship in family firms. *Journal of Small Business Management, 55*(4), 506–529.

Capaldo, A. (2007). Network structure and innovation: The leveraging of a dual network as a distinctive relational capability. *Strategic Management Journal, 28*(6), 585–608.

Carney, M. (2005). Corporate governance and competitive advantage in family-controlled firms. *Entrepreneurship Theory and Practice, 29*(3), 249–265.

Chakrabarty, S. (2009). The influence of national culture and institutional voids on family ownership of large firms: A country level empirical study. *Journal of International Management, 15*(1), 32–45.

Chrisman, J. J., Chua, J. H., Pearson, A. W., & Barnett, T. (2012). Family involvement, family influence, and family—centred non—economic goals in small firms. *Entrepreneurship Theory and Practice, 36*(2), 267–293.

Chua, J. H., Chrisman, J. J., & Sharma, P. (1999). Defining the family business by behavior. *Entrepreneurship Theory and Practice, 23*(4), 19–39.

Claessens, S., Djankov, S., & Lang, L. (2000). The separation of ownership and control in East Asian corporations. *Journal of Financial Economics, 58*, 81–112.

Crow, B. (2001). *Markets, class and social change: Trading networks and poverty in rural South Asia*. Palgrave Macmillan.

Dacin, M. T., Goodstein, J., & Scott, W. R. (2002). Institutional theory and institutional change: Introduction to the special research forum. *Academy of Management Journal, 45*(1), 45–57.

De Massis, A., Chua, J. H., & Chrisman, J. J. (2008). Factors preventing intra-family succession. *Family Business Review, 21*(2), 183–199.

De Massis, A., Kotlar, J., Chua, J. H., & Chrisman, J. J. (2014). Ability and willingness as sufficiency conditions for family-oriented particularistic behavior: Implications for theory and empirical studies. *Journal of Small Business Management, 52*(2), 344–364.

Dumbu, E. (2018). Challenges surrounding succession planning in family owned businesses in Zimbabwe: Views of the founding entrepreneurs of the businesses at Chikarudzo Business Centre in Masvingo district. *The International Journal of Business Management and Technology, 2*(2), 38–45.

Dyer, J. H., & Singh, H. (1998). The relational view: Cooperative strategy and sources of interorganisational competitive advantage. *Academy of Management Review, 23*(4), 660–679.

Estrin, S., Korosteleva, J., & Mickiewicz, T. (2013). Which institutions encourage entrepreneurial growth aspirations? *Journal of Business Venturing, 28*(4), 564–580.

Fairclough, S., & Micelotta, E. R. (2013). Beyond the family firm: Reasserting the influence of the family institutional logic across organisations. In M. Lounsbury & E. Boxenbaum (Eds.), *Research in the Sociology of Organisations, 39*(B), 63–98.

Fishman, A. (2009). When business is kept in the family. *Sunday Times Newspaper, Business Times/Careers, 13*(2).

Gedajlovic, E., & Carney, M. (2010). Markets, hierarchies, and families: Toward a transaction cost theory of the family firm. *Entrepreneurship Theory and Practice, 34*(6), 1145–1172.

Gedajlovic, E., Carney, M., Chrisman, J. J., & Kellermanns, F. W. (2012). The adolescence of family firm research: Taking stock and planning for the future. *Journal of Management, 38*, 1010–1037.

Gómez-Mejía, L. R., Haynes, K. T., Núñez-Nickel, M., Jacobson, K. J., & Moyano-Fuentes, J. (2007). Socioemotional wealth and business risks in family-controlled firms: Evidence from Spanish olive oil mills. *Administrative Science Quarterly, 52*(1), 106–137.

Habbershon, T. G., Williams, M., & MacMillan, I. C. (2003). A unified systems perspective of family firm performance. *Journal of Business Venturing, 18*(4), 451–465.

Habbershon, T. G. (2006). Commentary: A framework for managing the familiness and agency advantages in family firms. *Entrepreneurship Theory & Practice, 30*(6), 879–886.

Hotho, J. J., & Pedersen, T. (2012). 'Beyond the "rules of the game": Three institutional approaches and how they matter for international business.' In Demirbag, M. & Wood, G. (Eds.), *Handbook of Institutional Approaches to International Business, 236*.

Igwe, P. A., Madichie, N. O., & Amoncar, N. (2020). Transgenerational business legacies and intergenerational succession among the Igbos (Nigeria). *Small Enterprise Research, 27*(2), 165–179.

Jøsrgensen, J. J., Hafsi, T., & Kiggundu, M. N. (1986). Towards a market imperfections theory of organisational structure in developing countries. *Journal of Management Studies, 23*(4), 417–442.

Kaufmann, W., Hooghiemstra, R., & Feeney, M. K. (2018). Formal institutions, informal institutions, and red tape: A comparative study. *Public Administration, 96*(2), 386–403.

Kelly, L., Lewa, P. M., & Kamaria, K. (2008). Founder centrality, management team congruence and performance in family firms: A Kenyan context. *Journal of Developmental Entrepreneurship, 13*(4), 383–407.

Khanna, T., & Palepu, K. (1997). Why focused strategies may he wrong for emerging markets. *Harvard Business Review, 75*(4), 41–51.

Khanna, T., & Palepu, K. G. (2010). *Winning in emerging markets: A road map for strategy and execution*. Harvard Business Review Press.

Khavul, S., Bruton, G. D., & Wood, E. (2009). Informal family business in Africa. *Entrepreneurship Theory and Practice, 33*(6), 1219–1238.

Khayesi, J. N., & George, G. (2011). When does the socio-cultural context matter? Communal orientation and entrepreneurs' resource accumulation efforts in Africa. *Journal of Occupational and Organisational Psychology, 84*(3), 471–492.

Khayesi, J. N., George, G., & Antonakis, J. (2014). Kinship in entrepreneur networks: Performance effects of resource assembly in Africa. *Entrepreneurship Theory and Practice, 38*(6), 1323–1342.

Kolk, A., & Rivera-Santos, M. (2018). The state of research on Africa in business and management: Insights from a systematic review of key international journals. *Business & Society, 57*(3), 415–436.

Lawrence, T. B., & Phillips, N. (2004). From moby dick to free willy: Macro-cultural discourse and institutional entrepreneurship in emerging institutional fields. *Organisation, 11*(5), 689–711.

Leaprott, J. (2005). An institutional theory view of the family business. *Family Business Review, 18*(3), 215–228.

Litz, R. A. (2008). Two sides of a one-sided phenomenon: Conceptualizing the family business and business family as a Möbius strip. *Family Business Review, 21*(3), 217–236.

Lorenzoni, G., & Lipparini, A. (1999). The leveraging of interfirm relationships as a distinctive organisational capability: A longitudinal study. *Strategic Management Journal, 20*(4), 317–338.

Luo, X. R., & Chung, C. N. (2013). Filling or abusing the institutional void? Ownership and management control of public family businesses in an emerging market. *Organisation Science, 24*(2), 591–613.

Maas, G. & Diederichs, A. (2007). *Manage family in your business.* Northcliff: Frontrunner Publishing (Pty) Ltd.

Mair, J., & Marti, I. (2009). Entrepreneurship in and around institutional voids: A case study from Bangladesh. *Journal of Business Venturing, 24*(5), 419–435.

Mair, J., Martí, I., & Ventresca, M. J. (2012). Building inclusive markets in rural Bangladesh: How intermediaries work institutional voids. *Academy of Management Journal, 55*(4), 819–850.

McGrath, H., & O'Toole, T. (2018). Extending the concept of familiness to relational capability: A Belgian micro-brewery study. *International Small Business Journal, 36*(2), 194–219.

McGrath, R. G. (2010). Business models: A discovery driven approach. *Long Range Planning, 43*(2–3), 247–261.

Melin, L., & Nordqvist, M. (2007). The reflexive dynamics of institutionalization: The case of the family business. *Strategic Organisation, 5*(3), 321–333.

Michael-Tsabari, N., Labaki, R., & Zachary, R. K. (2014). Toward the cluster model: The family firm's entrepreneurial behavior over generations. *Family Business Review, 27*(2), 161–185.

Miller, D., & Le Breton-Miller, I. (2014). Deconstructing socio-emotional wealth. *Entrepreneurship Theory and Practice, 38*(4), 713–719.

Miller, D., Le Breton-Miller, I., & Lester, R. (2011). Family and lone founder ownership and strategic behavior: Social context, identity, and institutional logics. *Journal of Management Studies, 48*(1), 1–25.

Miller, D., Lee, J., Chang, S., & Breton-Miller, I. (2009). Filling the institutional void: The social behavior and performance of family vs. non-family technology firms in emerging markets. *Journal of International Business Studies, 40*, 802–817.

Murithi W. K. (2019). *Exploring the effects of the strategic behaviours of family and non-family businesses on regional development: Evidence from Kenya.* Doctoral dissertation, De Montfort University.

Murithi, W., Vershinina, N., & Rodgers, P. (2020). Where less is more: Institutional voids and business families in Sub-Saharan Africa. *International Journal of Entrepreneurial Behavior & Research.* Available at: https://doi.org/10.1108/IJEBR-07-2017-0239.

Murithi, W. K., & Woldesenbet Beta, K. (2021). Comparing family and non-family firms' strategic effects on regional development evidence from Kenya. In R. Basco, R. Stough & L. Suwala (Eds.), *Family Business and Regional Development* (pp. 177–192). Routledge.

Naldi, L., Nordqvist, M., Sjöberg, K., & Wiklund, J. (2007). Entrepreneurial orientation, risk taking, and performance in family firms. *Family Business Review, 20*(1), 33–47.

National Bureau of Statistics. (2007). *National Account of Nigeria 1981–2006* (p. 2019). Federal Republic of Nigeria.

North, D. G. (1990). *Institutions, institutional change and economic performance.* Cambridge University Press.

Nyamwanza, S. T., Mavhiki, S., & Ganyani, R. (2018). Succession planning in polygamous family businesses: A case of a family business in Zimbabwe. *IOSR Journal of Business and Management (IOSR-JBM), 20*8, 32–39.

Onuoha, B. C. (2013). Challenges and problems of professionalizing family businesses in South-East Nigeria. *American International Journal of Contemporary Research, 3*(4), 130–139.

Parada, M. J., Nordqvist, M., & Gimeno, A. (2010). Institutionalizing the family business: The role of professional associations in fostering a change of values. *Family Business Review, 23*(4), 355–372.

PricewaterHouse Coopers. (2014). *Navigating the owner's agenda: Kenya private company survey.* Available at: https://www.pwc.fr/fr/assets/files/pdf/2015/01/pwc_africa_business_agenda2014.pdf. Accessed on 4 June, 2020.

Randerson, K., Bettinelli, C., Fayolle, A., & Anderson, A. (2015). Family entrepreneurship as a field of research: Exploring its contours and contents. *Journal of Family Business Strategy, 6*(3), 143–154.

Randerson, K., Dossena, G., & Fayolle, A. (2016). The futures of family business: Family entrepreneurship. *Futures, 75*, 36–43.

Randerson, K., Seaman, C., Daspit, J. J., & Barredy, C. (2020). Institutional influences on entrepreneurial behaviours in the family entrepreneurship context: Towards an integrative framework. *International Journal of Entrepreneurial Behavior & Research, 26*(1), 1–13. https://doi.org/10.1108/ijebr-01-2020-824.

Reay, T., & Hinings, C. R. (2009). Managing the rivalry of competing institutional logics. *Organisation Studies, 30*(6), 629–652.

Reis, H. T., & Sprecher, S. (2009). Goal pursuit, relationship influences. *Encyclopedia of Human Relationships.* Thousand Oaks, CA: SAGE Publications.

Salimath, M. S., & Cullen, J. B. (2010). Formal and informal institutional effects on entrepreneurship: A synthesis of nation-level research. *International Journal of Organisational Analysis, 18*(3), 358–385.

Schneider, F. (2005). *Shadow economies of 145 countries all over the world: What do we really know?* (CREMA Working Paper 2006–01). Basel, Center for research in Economics, Management and the Arts.

Scott, W. R. (1995). *Institutions and organisations.* Sage.

Scott, W. R. (2001). *Institutions and Organisations* (2nd ed.). Thousand Oak, CA: Sage.

Sikomwe, S., Mhonde, C., Mbetu, K. C., Mavhiki, S., & Mapetere, D. (2012). Critical perspectives on succession planning in the commuter transport sector in Zimbabwe. *International Journal of Business and Social Science, 3*(5), 230–241.

Soleimanof, S., Rutherford, M. W., & Webb, J. W. (2018). The intersection of family firms and institutional contexts: A review and agenda for future research. *Family Business Review, 31*(1), 32–53.

Steier, L. P., Chrisman, J. J., & Chua, J. H. (2015). Governance challenges in family businesses and business families. *Entrepreneurship Theory and Practice, 39*(6), 1265–1280.

Stewart, K. J. (2003). Trust transfer on the world wide web. *Organisation Science, 14*(1), 5–17.

Tharawat Magazine. (2016). *Family business: The art of communication.* [Online] Available at: http://www.tharawat-magazine.com/family-business-articles/governance/1524-family-businessthe-art-of-communication. Accessed on 4 May 2020.

Thornton, P. H., Ocasio, W., & Lounsbury, M. (2012). *The institutional logics perspective: A new approach to culture, structure, and process.* Oxford University Press.

Tonoyan, V., Strohmeyer, R., Habib, M., & Perlitz, M. (2010). Corruption and entrepreneurship: How formal and informal institutions shape small firm behavior in transition and mature market economies. *Entrepreneurship Theory and Practice, 34*(5), 803–832.

Van der Merwe, S., Venter, E., & Ellis, S. M. (2009). An exploratory study of some of the determinants of management succession planning in family businesses. *Management Dynamics, 18*(4), 1–17.

Visser, T., & Chiloane-Tsoka, E. (2014). An exploration into family business and SMEs in South Africa. *Problems and Perspectives in Management, 12*(4), 427–432.

Wainaina, B. (2005). *How to write about Africa.* Available at: https://granta.com/how-to-write-about-africa/. Accessed on 12 April 2020.

Waweru, N. (2014). Factors influencing quality corporate governance in Sub Saharan Africa: An empirical study. *Corporate Governance, 14*(4), 555–574.

Webb, J. W., Ireland, R. D., & Ketchen Jr, D. J. (2014). Toward a greater understanding of entrepreneurship and strategy in the informal economy. *Strategic Entrepreneurship Journal, 8*(1), 1–15.

Webb, J. W., Pryor, C. G., & Kellermanns, F. W. (2015). Household enterprise in base-of-the-pyramid markets: The influence of institutions and family embeddedness. *Africa Journal of Management, 1*(2), 115–136.

Welter, F. (2011). Contextualizing entrepreneurship—Conceptual challenges and ways forward. *Entrepreneurship Theory and Practice, 35*(1), 165–184.

Westhead, P., & Cowling, M. (1998). Family firm research: The need for a methodological rethink. *Entrepreneurship Theory and Practice, 23*(1), 31–56.

World Bank. (2014). *Global financial development report 2014: Financial inclusion.* Washington, DC: World Bank.

Wright, M., Chrisman, J. J., Chua, J. H., & Steier, L. P. (2014). Family enterprise and context. *Entrepreneurship Theory and Practice, 38,* 1247–1260.

Wright, M., De Massis, A., Scholes, L., Hughes, M., & Kotlar, J. (2016). *Family business entrepreneurship.* Available at: https://www.ifb.org.uk/media/1874/ifbrf-entrepreneurship-report.pdf. Acessed on 12 March 2020.

Zahra, S. A., Randerson, K., & Fayolle, A. (2013). Part I: The evolution and contributions of corporate entrepreneurship research. *Management, 16*(4), 362–380.

Zahra, S. A., Wright, M., & Abdelgawad, S. G. (2014). Contextualization and the advancement of entrepreneurship research. *International Small Business Journal, 32*(5), 479–500.

Zahra, S., & Wright, M. (2011). Entrepreneurship's next act. *Academy of Management Perspectives, 25*, 67–83.

Zellweger, T. M., Kellermanns, F. W., Eddleston, K. A., & Memili, E. (2012). Building a family firm image: How family firms capitalize on their family ties. *Journal of Family Business Strategy, 3*(4), 239–250.

Zoogah, D. B., Peng, M. W., & Woldu, H. (2015). Institutions, resources, and organisational effectiveness in Africa. *Academy of Management Perspectives, 29*(1), 7–31.

5

Enterprise Survival and Growth: A Conceptual Exposition of Entrepreneurial Activities in Sub-Saharan Africa

Deji Olagboye, Demola Obembe, and Godwin Okafor

Introduction

This chapter establishes a theoretical foundation for the establishment of a Nano Enterprise (NE) classification as an enabler for the institutionalisation of informal economy enterprises in Sub-Saharan Africa by defining NE in the context of SSA. Entrepreneurial activities are globally recognised and acknowledged as catalysts for economic growth (Acs et al., 2008; Wright & Marlow, 2012; Wright & Stigliani, 2013) and considered critical for countries transitioning to market economies as well as the developing countries of SSA (Puffer et al., 2010). While the entrepreneurial capacity of a nation is often defined in terms of the formal institutional environment comprising political, economic, and legal structures (Acs et al., 2008), these formal structures alone do not adequately depict the different dynamics within the environment in which entrepreneurial activities occur in SSA. Institutional theorists (Pache & Santos, 2013; Powell & DiMaggio, 1991) suggest that many dynamics in the entrepreneurial environment stem not from technological or material imperatives, but rather they stem from cultural norms, symbols, beliefs, and rituals (Suchman, 1995).

D. Olagboye (✉) · D. Obembe · G. Okafor
De Montfort University, Leicester, UK
e-mail: deji.olagboye@dmu.ac.uk

Sub-Saharan Africa is faced with numerous economic and social challenges, including high unemployment rates, corruption, institutional weakness, poor infrastructure, poverty, etc. These have intensified the push for policies directed towards the development of entrepreneurship as well as micro, small, and medium-scale enterprises (MSMEs) (Kongolo, 2010; Mamman et al., 2019; Obeng & Blundel, 2015; Rogerson, 2001). Sub-Saharan African countries such as Nigeria, South Africa, Democratic Republic of Congo, Kenya, Senegal, Angola etc., and the development institutions that support them, have been initiating policies designed to stimulate the emergence of vibrant MSME sectors, which many expect to catalyse growth, produce employment, and reduce poverty (Poole, 2018). Belief in the transformational power of MSMEs in SSA has been spurred on by both the significant role that small and medium-scale enterprises (SME) are credited to have played in more advanced economies and by the overt promotion of SMEs by major development agencies, including specialist units of the World Bank and the United Nations Industrial Development Organisation (Poole, 2018).

Consequently, enterprise policies that have been developed and implemented in SSA comprise policies directed at both start-ups (entrepreneurship) and existing firms classified as SMEs. Typically, virtually all organs of governments have policy initiatives which qualify as either entrepreneurship policies (EP) or small and medium-scale enterprise policies (SMEP). These are most often not coordinated and as such not measured for impact in SSA (Mamman et al., 2019; Wapshott & Mallett, 2018). In addition to the state-led interventions, there are other non-governmental forms of influence and support for entrepreneurship and MSMEs in Sub-Saharan Africa. An example of such non-governmental form of influence is the Tony Elumelu Foundation (TEF), a private sector-led philanthropic organisation empowering African entrepreneurs to create jobs in the African continent.

However, central to the MSME phenomenon is the informal economy. The view posited in the 1970s when the informal economy was apparently 'discovered' by the international development sector (Charmes, 2012) suggests that as economies grew and regions developed, workers in the informal economy would be absorbed in the formal economy (Jackson, 2012). Today, the informal economy appears to be an expanding and permanent fixture in SSA. As the discourse on the seemingly perpetual existence of the informal economy continues, the need for a careful and even-handed synthesis is becoming increasingly apparent, more so in SSA where the economic contribution of the informal economy is hugely significant.

This chapter provides such a synthesis as the study establishes a theoretical foundation by defining Nano enterprises (NE); highlighting ambiguities in the conventional definition and usage of Micro enterprise in Sub-Saharan Africa, and exploring the distinction between micro enterprises and NEs. The study further provides a treatise on the institutional environment and the informal economy in SSA to explain the growth and permanence of the informal economy in SSA. In addition, we use Oliver's (1991) five institutional antecedents to provide propositions as to how institutional antecedents can be a determinant of conformity or resistance of the informal economy enterprises in Sub-Saharan Africa to the establishment of an NE classification as an enabler for institutionalisation. The study concludes with future research directions.

Theoretical Foundations

Defining Nano Enterprises

Over the years, countries and regional bodies have used the following criteria in defining micro enterprises (i) the number of employees and (ii) the turnover or balance sheet value. These criteria however provide definitions of micro enterprises, with varying degree of specificity and lack of uniformity. For the European Union, SME categorisation of micro enterprises is; 1–9 employees and a turnover less or equal to €2million, whereas the United State classifies micro enterprises as having 1–4 employees (Poole, 2018). Similarly, in Nigeria micro enterprises are classified as having 1–9 employees and assets equivalent to < €10,450 (excluding land and building) (Kale, 2019). SSA countries use more or less the same criteria in terms of number of employees as shown in Table 5.1.

These varying definitions are confusing and the adopting of the 1–9 employee definition for micro enterprises in SSA highlights conformity to the European Union definition rather than overt self-justification of the nature of enterprises especially in developing countries of SSA, where over 70% of micro enterprises are typically non-employing enterprises with assets/turnover predominantly less than €2,090 as against the commonly used less than €10,450 asset/turnover definition of micro enterprises as highlighted in Table 5.1. For example, in Nigeria, 99% of MSMEs are micro enterprises and 97% of them are unregistered non-employing enterprises (Kale, 2019).

Based on existing scholarly work around the informal economy (Fox & Sohnesen, 2012; Ogunsade & Obembe, 2016; Porta & Shleifer, 2008),

Table 5.1 MSMEs: definition and typical numbers in SSA

	Employees	Total asset/turnover	
Micro	1–9	< €10,450	
Small	10–49	≥ €10,450 < €104,480	
Medium	50–199	≥ €104,480 < €1,044,799	
Distribution patterns in a representative economy in SSA			
Categories	Share of all firms (%)	Share of emp (%)	Remark
Micro	90	30	Typically over 70% non-employing sole traders
Small	8	20	
Medium	1.5	10	
Large	0.5	40	

Source Adapted from Fjose et al. (2010)

we propose an inclusive definition of NE that explicitly acknowledges and incorporates enterprises in both the formal and informal economy, run and managed by single individuals. That is:

> **Nano enterprises (NE)** are non-employing registered and unregistered enterprises operated by a single individual or with the help of family members and undertaking legitimate economic activities and services—in the formal and informal economy.

Why Nano Enterprise?

While there is little, if any, reference to NE in the entrepreneurship and MSMEs literature, the Australian Bureau of Statistics (ABS) refers to Nano businesses as largely sole traders, trusts and self-managed superannuation funds. According to the Australian Tax Office (ATO) data set, there are Nano-sized businesses that report business revenue but have no Goods and Services Tax (GST) activity (the mandatory GST registration threshold is the equivalence of €46,500 turnover). These Nano businesses are however excluded from the ABS small business counts.

While the individual economic contribution of these Nano businesses is said to be correspondingly small, their number is significant overall. For every ten small businesses with GTS activity in the ATO data there are six other Nano businesses without GST activity (about 1.2 million in total). Extrapolating these figures would give a potential gross domestic product (GDP) contribution of Nano businesses of roughly 2% of GDP. However, in Sub-Saharan African countries, the relevance and contribution of the informal economy is significant with an average as a share of GDP that ranges from a low of 20 to 30% in Mauritius, South Africa, Namibia, and Botswana to a high of over 50% in Benin, Tanzania and Nigeria as shown in Fig. 5.1 (Medina et al., 2016).

The IEE are often non-employing individuals doing business and classified as micro enterprises is SSA countries, which we define as NEs in this context. We argue for the need to legitimise the IEE in SSA through institutionalisation with the establishment of an NE classification, as against current reference to these enterprises as unregistered, unmonitored, unregulated etc. Businesses seek legitimacy for many reasons, and conclusions may depend on the objectives against which these efforts are measured (Suchman, 1995).

In the context of SSA where the informal economy is deemed vital, we theorise that legitimacy through the establishment of an NE classification will affect not only how people act towards the IEE, but also how they understand them (Díez-Martín et al., 2013; Suchman, 1995). This is because society perceives legitimate organisations not only as worthier, but as also more trustworthy, more meaningful, and more predictable. PwC Nigeria (2020), further noted that the playing field can be made even for all by relaxing the

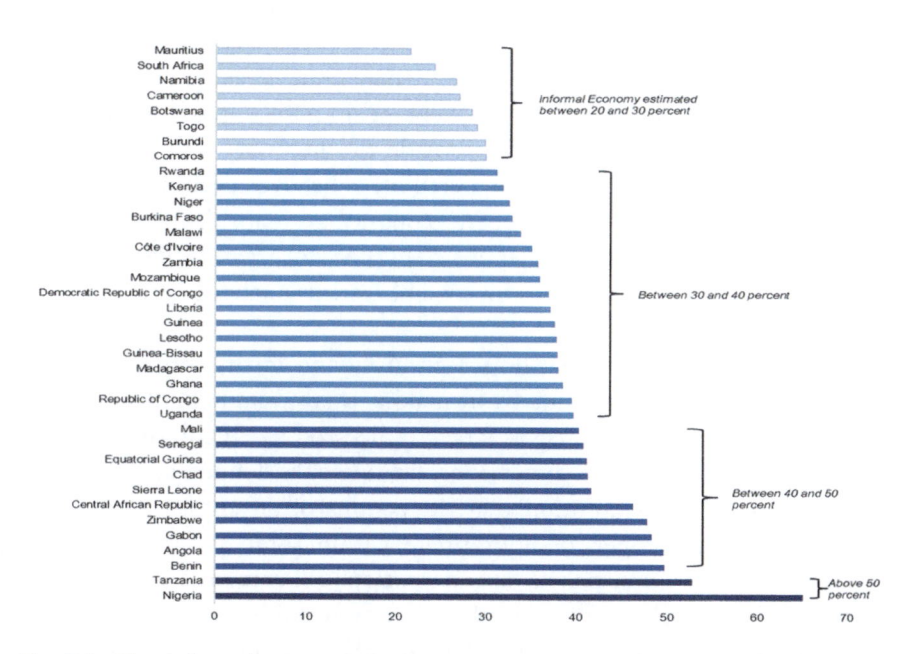

Fig. 5.1 The informal economy in SSA, 2010 to 2014 average as a share of gross domestic product (GDP) (*Source* Medina et al. [2016]. *Note* Data excludes Cape Verde, Eritrea, Ethiopia, The Gambia, São Tomé and Príncipe, Seychelles, and South Sudan due to lack of an informality measure)

entry rules and easing barriers for informal businesses to get into the formal economy.

Institutional researchers argue that organisations do not simply extract legitimacy from the environment in a feat of cultural strip mining; rather, external institutions construct and interpenetrate the organisation in every respect (DiMaggio & Powell, 1983; Jawahar & Mclaughlin, 2001; Stenholm et al., 2013; Zucker, 1987). Traditional definitions determine how these enterprises in the informal economy are built, how they are run, and, simultaneously, how they are understood and evaluated (Díez-Martín et al., 2013; Suchman, 1995; Zimmerman & Zeitz, 2002).

In reality NEs in both the informal and formal economies face operational challenges and institutional constitutive pressures (such as multiplicity of taxation, stringent loan conditions, lack of targeted support, corruption, etc.). We incorporate this duality into the larger picture of the establishment of an NE categorisation to highlight ways in which legitimacy can act like a manipulatable resource for institutionalisation and access to resources for IEE, and the recognition of taken-for-granted NEs currently classified as micro enterprises in the formal economy of SSA countries.

There have been previous attempts at institutionalising the IEE, but these attempts provide an explicitly evaluative cast or a merely passive acquiescence to dealing with the issue of informality (Benjamin et al., 2014; Lund & Skinner, 2004; Tokman, 2001, 2007; Webb et al., 2009). Institutionalisation must be grounded in legitimacy to provide the necessary cultural congruence that will create the existence of a credible collective account or rationale explaining what NE in the informal economy are capable of doing and why (Jepperson, 1991; Suddaby et al., 2017). As Suchman (1995) suggests, within culture and tradition, legitimacy and institutionalisation are virtually synonymous.

The proposition here is that both legitimacy and institutionalisation can empower these enterprises primarily by making them seem natural and meaningful, while access to resources is largely a by-product. Incorporating both the evaluative and cognitive dimensions, legitimacy is defined as the "generalised perception or assumption that the actions of an entity (in this case NE) are desirable, proper, or appropriate within some social constructed system of norms, values, beliefs, and definition" (Suchman, 1995, p. 574). Consequently, we take a theoretical approach to addressing the need for the institutionalisation of IEE in SSA and the recognition of the taken-for-granted NEs currently classified as micro enterprises in SSA with the proposition of the establishment of an NE classification as an enabler for institutionalisation.

Institutional Environment and the Informal Economy in SSA

Researchers have in the past developed various typologies as representation of institutions. North's (1990) typology that distinguishes between formal institutions (rules and regulations) and informal institutions (norms and culture) is adopted for this study. Despite the foregoing distinction in the two institutional dimensions, some scholars maintain that, in practice, many enterprises in the developing, emerging, and transitional economies are neither wholly formal nor wholly informal. They argue that enterprises operate somewhere in the middle of these two extremes, exhibiting various levels of informalisation (de Castro et al., 2014; Welter et al., 2015; Williams & Shahid, 2016). Others argue that the lack of symmetry between these institutional dimensions, which is said to be at a greater extent in SSA, continues to endear entrepreneurs to the informal economy where entrepreneurs can avoid the stifling formal institutional barriers and demands to doing business (Aidis, 2005; Aidis & Adachi, 2007; Isenberg, 2010; Mamman et al., 2019; Urbano & Alvarez, 2014).

Formal institutions also known as the regulatory component of a country's institutional environment is made up of rules, laws and the general regulatory environment governing the formal economy (Aidis, 2005; Bohatá & Mládek, 1999). Beyond these government regulations and laws, the regulatory environment in SSA also includes land allocation, taxation policies, trade policies, infrastructure development, business registration, licensing requirements, social security, as well as other macroeconomic policies that presumably should provide support for new businesses, reduce the risk for individuals starting a new venture, and enable entrepreneurial efforts to acquire venture capital, but in reality, this has not been the case (Ogunsade & Obembe, 2016).

While societies globally have both formal and informal economies, IEEs are prevalent in SSA where there is a constant struggle with institutional weakness and inefficiencies with policy formulation and implementation challenges that has continued to undermine developmental efforts (Dolowitz & Marsh, 2000; Herrington & Kelley, 2012; Ogunsade & Obembe, 2016; Mamman et al., 2019; PwC Nigeria, 2020; Williams & Shahid, 2016). This is exacerbated by the existence of institutional barriers and enterprise conditions that hinder venture creation, survival, and growth. The entrepreneurship literature suggests that the combination of these factors has allowed the informal economy to flourish in SSA as entrepreneurs seek ways of doing business within the boundaries of what the informal institutions consider acceptable (Mamman et al., 2019; Webb et al., 2009, 2013, 2014).

The term micro covers widely different types of IEEs in SSA. Everything is included, but largely fragile zero growth and non-employing micro-firms managed by individuals (often with family members' support) generating subsistence-level revenues. These are often informal NEs that are pivotal for survival in the developing countries of SSA where unemployment and poverty levels are high. The role that these NEs play in the economies of SSA countries and the challenges they face are often completely different. They struggle with fluctuating revenues, red tape complexity, multiple taxation, lack of knowledge and relevant competences, lack of finance, and access to stable electricity (Fjose et al., 2010). A measure of the enterprise conditions created by the regulatory environment in SSA countries is seen in the ranking of SSA countries in Table 5.2.

Where reforms to formal institutions have occurred in SSA, they tend to favour large-scale businesses as governments seek to attract foreign direct investment (Hegerty, 2009; Williams & Vorley, 2015). These reforms are generally premised around providing foreign investors low-cost labour. However, it most often means that as well as being disadvantaged in cash credit markets, the IEE in SSA are also displaced from potential markets by foreign competition. While a stable legal framework with well-protected property rights promotes coordination and planning and also prevents ad hoc dispossession of rewards from entrepreneurship, the experience of entrepreneurs in SSA has been that of legal systems incapable of adequately protecting property rights and resolving business disputes (Manolova & Yan, 2002; Williams & Vorley, 2015).

Enterprise Conditions in SSA Countries and Regional Highlights

The 2019/2020 Africa Prosperity Report by the Legatum Institute focused on understanding how prosperity is created and perpetuated in Africa. The report ranks the prosperity of African countries based on predefined domains/pillars. The eight defined pillars included 'Enterprise Conditions'—which measures the degree to which regulations enable businesses to start, compete, and expand. Table 5.2 shows the ranking of all the SSA countries among the 54 African countries ranked based on the enterprise conditions pillar. The ranking essentially measures the impact of institutional regulations on start-ups, survival, and growth of businesses in African countries (Legatum Institute, 2019).

Table 5.2 Sub-Saharan Africa (SSA) countries ranking on 'Enterprise conditions' among 54 countries

A–C	Ranking	D–K	Ranking	L–R	Ranking	S–Z	Ranking
Angola	50	Dem. Rep. of the Congo[a]	47	Lesotho	29	Sao Time & Prin	14
Benin	18	Djibouti	15	Liberia	25	Senegal	13
Botswana	7	Equatorial Guinea	27	Madagascar	38	Seychelles	4
Burkina Faso	26	Eritrea	49	Malawi	24	Sierra Leone	42
Burundi	23	Ethiopia	41	Mali	34	Somalia	53
Cameroon	37	Gabon	19	Mauritius	1	South Africa[a]	3
Cape Verde	17	Gambia	28	Mozambique	43	South Sudan	44
Central African Rep	52	Ghana	6	Namibia	12	Swaziland	30
Chad	54	Guinea	16	Niger	35	Togo	36
Comoros	31	Guinea-Bissau	33	Nigeria[a]	32	Uganda	8
Congo	48	Kenya[a]	5	Rwanda	2	Tanzania	22
Côte d'Ivoire	21					Zambia	9
						Zimbabwe	46

Source Adapted from the 2019/2020 Legatum Institute Africa Prosperity Index
[a] Denotes largest economies by GDP in the four regions of Sub-Saharan Africa

Enterprise conditions in the largest economies by GDP in the four regions of SSA as denoted in Table 5.2 reveal a ranking that suggests that the size of the GDP of a country in SSA is not an indication of how availing the enterprise conditions are in that country. Below are the highlights of the largest economies by GDP in the central, eastern, southern, and western regions of SSA.

Central region—Democratic Republic of the Congo (DRC): The central region of SSA has a total of nine countries, namely; Angola, Cameroun, Central African Republic, Chad, Congo, Gabon, Equatorial Guinea, DRC, and Sao Tome and Principe. The DRC has the biggest economy in the region with a GDP size of $48.994 billion in 2019 which was up from the $47.099 billion recorded in 2018. However, the DRC has 30–40% informal economy as shown in Fig. 5.1 and is ranked 47th out of the 54 countries ranked in Africa on enterprise conditions. Sao Tome and Principe has the highest ranking of 14th in the region followed by Gabon ranked 19th. The investment environment is said to be down largely as a result of the deteriorating property rights and investor protection conditions due to political instability in the DRC.

Eastern region—Kenya: The eastern region of SSA has a total of 12 countries, namely: Burundi, Comoros, Djibouti, Ethiopia, Eritrea, Kenya, Uganda, Rwanda, Seychelles, Somalia, Tanzania, and South Sudan. Kenya with a GDP of $98.607 billion in 2019 up from the $87.928 billion in 2018 has the biggest economy in the region. Ranked 5th, Kenya has the third highest ranking on the enterprise conditions ranking in the region behind Rwanda and Seychelles who are ranked 2nd and 4th respectively. As seen in Fig. 5.1, Kenya also has 30–40% informal economy. The introduction of M-PESA, a tech-innovative mobile banking system used by many Kenyans has greatly helped improve the investment environment in Kenya.

Southern region—South Africa: The region has a total of 11 countries, namely: Botswanamary>, Lesotho, Madagascar, Malawi, Mauritius, Mozambique, Namibia, South Africa, Swaziland, Zambia, and Zimbabwe. South Africa has the biggest economy in the region and second biggest in Africa with a GDP of $358.839 billion in 2019 down from $368.135 billion in 2018. South Africa is ranked 3rd on the overall enterprise conditions ranking and is the second highest ranked country in the region behind Mauritius, ranked 1st overall. Botswana is the third highest ranked in the region with a ranking of 7th overall. The informal economy in South Africa is among the lowest in SSA at 20–30% informality as seen in Fig. 5.1. However, safety and security remain a challenge in South Africa, with particularly high rates of violence and property crimes.

Western region—Nigeria: The region is home to the highest number of countries in SSA with 15 countries, namely: Benin, Burkina Faso, Carpe Vade, Côte d'Ivoire, Gambia, Ghana, Guinea, Guinea-Bissau, Liberia, Mali, Niger, Nigeria, Senegal, Sierra Leone, and Togo. With a GDP of $446.543 billion in 2019 up from the $398.186 billion recorded in 2018, Nigeria is the biggest economy in the western region of SSA and indeed the biggest economy and most populous country on the continent. However, Nigeria is ranked 32nd on overall enterprise conditions ranking and 10th within the region. This is perhaps not surprising considering the fact that alongside Tanzania, Nigeria has over 50% informal economy. Nigeria suffers from oil dependency and poor labour force engagement while safety and security remains a big challenge with the continuous attacks from Boko-Haram insurgence.

Characteristic Features of the Informal Economy Entrepreneurs in SSA

The characteristic features of informal economy entrepreneurs in Sub-Saharan Africa may also be an explanation for their choice of the informal economy. As Mamman et al. (2019) suggests, researchers of MSMEs and entrepreneurship in Africa have attempted to profile the characteristic features of an African entrepreneur and MSME operator (Kropp et al., 2008; Spring, 2007). They conclude that in terms of personality characteristics, 'real' African entrepreneurs share similar psychological characteristics with their counterparts from other parts of the world. On the other hand, their motivation is said to differ from that of other entrepreneurs, especially from those that come from Western individualistic societies, where communal interests do not form part of their motivation (Benzing & Chu, 2009; Sriram & Mersha, 2010).

The second dimension of the profile suggests that not all the business operators are entrepreneurs in the strictest sense of the term. At times, some people are attracted by the ease of access to start-up capital provided by the state, while others are driven to seek alternative means of livelihood or a secondary source of income (Mamman et al., 2019). Therefore, acknowledging and understanding these varying characteristics is important for policy-makers in SSA to ensure that enterprise development policy formulation and implementation are directed at providing the enabling institutional environment specifically for entrepreneurs and enterprises with growth motives for better economic impact and forestall the current practice of muddling poverty alleviation schemes with enterprises development programmes (Benzing & Chu, 2009).

It is estimated that the average size of the informal economy as a percentage of gross national income in SSA is 42.3% and the informal economy in SSA is dominated by trade-related activities, while services and manufacturing only appear to account for a small percentage of informal activity (Medina et al., 2016). Studies reveal that in Angola, Nigeria, South Africa, DRC, Kenya, and Uganda, the majority of informal economy workers are in retail trades, mostly self-employed (Jackson, 2012; Medina et al., 2016). The studies estimate that these self-employed retail traders account for seventy per cent of informal workers in SSA, with the remainder in wage employment. Petty trading and street vending is especially prevalent in the continent.

Wages in SSA are also low and irregular, and the informal economy entrepreneurs in SSA provide goods and services mainly for low-income consumers and not wholly in small scale, and frequently involves women as entrepreneurs—as many as half the total number (Barratt Brown, 1995). However, the existence of such a large informal economy has ensured that low-income families in SSA can defy the implications of such low-recorded gross domestic product (GDP) per capita figures and actually survive the economic hardship. We thus argue that there is a need for institutionalisation in order to ensure that the informal economy actors engaged in corrupt activities do not continue to undermine the aforementioned positive impact of the informal economy entrepreneurs in SSA (Williams & Vorley, 2015).

The entrepreneurship literature reveals the extensive use of institutional theory in trying to explain and understand the characteristic features of entrepreneurial activities and venture creation decision in the informal economy. However, as highlighted by Oliver (1991), early versions of institutional theory placed particular emphasis on the taken-for-granted character of institutional rules, myths, and beliefs as shared social reality. It also emphasises processes by which businesses tend to become instilled with value and social meaning. Subsequent proponents of institutionalisation have elaborated the nature and variety of these institutional processes (DiMaggio & Powell, 1983; Jawahar & Mclaughlin, 2001; Stenholm et al., 2013; Zucker, 1987) and the varying influences that these processes exert on the structural characteristics of businesses (Meyer et al., 1987; Singh et al., 1986) and business change (Tolbert & Zucker, 1983).

Institutional Antecedents as Facilitators of the Institutionalisation of the IEE in SSA

The theoretical reasoning that underpins conformity or resistance to institutional expectations and laws is both the ability and willingness of the IEE to conform to the institutional environment (Oliver, 1991; Zimmerman & Zeitz, 2002). The ability and willingness of these enterprises to conform with institutional requirements for the establishment of an NE classification as an enabler for the institutionalisation of informal economy enterprises in Sub-Saharan Africa may be limited by; enterprises' queries about the validity or legitimacy of the existing institutional rules, enterprises' attempts to retain control over their operations, and the self-serving behaviours among informal economy actors that are in conflict with institutional goals (Pache & Santos, 2010; Scott Richard, 1987).

The confines on the willingness and ability of enterprises to conform drives the propositions in this section, which explores the likelihood that the informal economy enterprises in SSA will accept and conform to the institutional requirements for the establishment of an NE classification as an enabler for institutionalising the informal economy enterprises in SSA countries. As highlighted by Oliver (1991), the five institutional antecedents;—cause, constituents, content, control, and context, correspond, respectively, to five basic questions that the IEE in SSA may want answered about institutionalisation pressures; why the establishment of an NE classification and the pressure to conform—cause?; who is exerting the pressure—constituent?; what these pressures are and seek to achieve—content?; how or by what means the pressure to institutionalise is being exerted—control?, and where the pressures are occurring—context?

Cause of NE Classification

The *cause* of NE classification refers to the reasons, intended goals, or set of expectations that underlie the pressures to institutionalise. Factors engendering the exertion of pressures by institutional constituents, including the state, are underspecified in institutional theory, which in itself may create conflict among actors (Díez-Martín et al., 2013; Zucker, 1987). If the establishment of an NE classification is to be effective as an enabler for the institutionalisation of informal economy enterprises in SSA countries, it has to be; (i) capable of increasing the legitimacy of the informal economy enterprise in SSA for social acceptability and fitness as to being perceived as economic citizens with access to otherwise inaccessible institutional support; and (ii) create logical economic reasons and accountability expressed in terms of the accruable economic benefits for institutionalisation.

Constituent Exerting Pressures

In reality, the collective normative structures of the institutional environment is not necessarily coherent or in unitary and enterprises are often faced with multiple, conflicting demands that hinder their ability to conform (Jawahar & Mclaughlin, 2001; Oliver, 1991). The level of multiplicity of institutional constituents (local, state, and federal agencies) and the level of dependence of IEEs on these constituents will determine conformity or resistance to the establishment of an NE classification as an enabler for the institutionalisation of informal economy enterprises in SSA countries. Conformity to institutionalisation is most likely in contexts where there is low multiplicity of institutional constituents and conflicting requirements and where there is higher dependence of IEEs on institutional constituents. (Jawahar & Mclaughlin, 2001; Oliver, 1991; Peng, 2003; Stenholm et al., 2013).

Content of the Pressures to Institutionalise

The consistency of the institutionalisation pressures with the goals of the IEE in SSA, and the potential loss of decision-making discretion that the pressures foist on the IEE will determine their conformity or resistance to the establishment of an NE classification as an enabler for institutionalisation. If the institutionalisation demands are deemed compatible with the internal goals of the IEE and will not lead to the potential loss of decision-making discretion or loss of freedom, conformity to institutionalisation is the most likely in such a context. Discretion and decision-making independence is important in organisation—environment relationship (Provan, 1982, 1983; Schneider et al., 2017; Whetten & Leung, 1979). The level of resistance by IEEs in SSA will vary with the perceived loss of autonomy related with conforming to institutionalisation pressures from the establishment of an NE classification.

Control Over Enforcement of the Institutionalisation Pressures

Control here refers to the channel through which institutional pressures and expectations are exerted on the IEE in SSA. Institutional pressures are primarily exerted via two distinct processes; legal coercion and voluntary diffusion. Both DiMaggio and Powell (1983) and Scott (1987) suggest that laws or mandates by governments are usually enforced by means of coercion as against pressures in the hope for voluntary adoption. Scholars have argued that the differences in country-specific institutional arrangements determine the levels of entrepreneurial activities (Jennings et al., 2013; Stenholm et al., 2013; Williams & Vorley, 2015). Conformity to the establishment of an NE classification as an enabler for the institutionalisation of informal economy enterprises in SSA is most likely in a context where the degree of legal or state coercion is high with grave consequences and strictly enforced punitive measures (Oliver, 1991; Pache & Santos, 2010, 2013).

Context of the Institutional Environment

The high levels of uncertainty in the institutional environment and the interconnectedness of institutional actors in SSA countries may impact positively on the ability and willingness of the IEE in SSA to conform to the institutionalisation expectations and demands of the establishment of an NE classification as an enabler for institutionalisation (Pfeffer & Salancik, 1978; Sutter et al., 2017; Webb et al., 2014). Institutional environment uncertainty in this context refers to the degree to which the IEE in SSA are able to accurately predict or forecast the future states of the economic environment. While interconnectedness in this context is the compactness of relations among enterprises or operators in the informal economy business environment which can enhances the voluntary or non-mandatory spread of shared information, norms, and values (Meyer & Rowan, 1977; DiMaggio & Powell, 1983). Conformity to institutional expectations and demands can protect enterprises from business environment upheaval or disruption (Mair et al., 2015; Oliver, 1991).

Discussion and Future Direction

This chapter contributes to the theoretical reframing of institutionalisation in the context of the IEE in SSA, which is often given an evaluative cast or a merely passive acquiescence in contemporary discourses on entrepreneurship in two main respects: first, the study theorises the establishment of a unifying classification—Nano Enterprise as an enabler for legitimising, institutionalising, and better understanding the informal economy enterprises in SSA and the taken-for-granted NE in the formal economy, otherwise classified as micro enterprises, to engender effective policy formulation and implementation in SSA (Díez-Martín et al., 2013; Suchman, 1995; Suddaby et al., 2017). This study transcends simplistic passivity by drawing on Suchman's (1995) institutional legitimacy approach to theorise how legitimacy can facilitate the IEE in Sub-Saharan Africa to elicit the external institutional construct and interpenetration that will define the existence and acceptance of the informal economy enterprise as of equal importance in the process of State development in SSA and avail them access to the needed resources for survival and growth (Suchman, 1995; Suddaby et al., 2017).

Secondly, we discuss how the effects of institutional environment and multiple, competing institutional expectations and pressures from different institutional constituents may impact the ability and willingness of informal economy enterprises in SSA to conform to the establishment of an NE classification as an enabler for institutionalisation. The study used Oliver's (1991) five institutional antecedents to provide propositions on how the cause, constituent, content, control, and context of the institutional environment can be the determinant of conformity or resistance of informal economy enterprises in SSA to the establishment of an NE classification. In addition to the theoretical contributions, we hope that the propositions in this study will motivate future empirical research in this area.

As with every study, the present study has limitations which however provide future research directions. While we conceptualise and theorise the case for the establishment of an NE classification as an enabler for the institutionalisation of the IEE in SSA, it is possible that institutionalisation may occur in other ways. However, our approach is in keeping with Kale's (2019) report which highlights the need for the establishment of a classification for the non-employing entrepreneurs. Similarly, other related studies suggest a separate classification or segmentation for self-employed persons (Dvouletý, 2020; Skrzek-Lubasińska & Szaban, 2019). This study thus provides new avenues for entrepreneurship researchers on the topic of institutionalisation of the IEE especially in the context of SSA.

Conclusion

In conclusion, we began by noting that entrepreneurial activities are globally recognised and acknowledged as a catalyst for economic growth and considered critical for countries transitioning to market economies, as well as the developing countries of SSA. This study concludes that, while the proposal presented suggests that the establishment of an NE classification will enhance the legitimacy and institutionalisation of the IEE in SSA for survival and growth and improve their contribution to the economy of SSA, the nature and degree of institutional pressures and requirements (cause, constituents, content, control, and context) will be pivotal determinants of conformity or resistance by the IEE in SSA to the establishment of an NE classification as an enabler for institutionalisation.

Extant entrepreneurship literature provides a passive acquiescence to the institutionalisation of the informal economy without room for context diversity on how entrepreneurship manifests in developing regions such as SSA where the informal economy is socio-economically significant. This chapter presents a complementary view of how the institutional environment and multiple, competing institutional constituent demands impact on the IEE and other institutional actors in Sub-Saharan Africa. With the growing importance of the informal economy in SSA, future research should continue to aid the visibility of the informal economy in Sub-Saharan Africa; challenging traditional conceptualisation of entrepreneurship and the sustenance of the viability and independence of the informal economy.

References

Acs, Z. J., Desai, S., & Hessels, J. (2008). Entrepreneurship, economic development and institutions. *Small Business Economics, 31*(3), 219–234. https://doi.org/10.1007/s11187-008-9135-9.

Aidis, R. (2005). Institutional barriers to small- and medium-sized enterprise operations in transition countries. *Small Business Economics, 25*(4), 305–317. https://doi.org/10.1007/s11187-003-6463-7.

Aidis, R., & Adachi, Y. (2007). Russia: Firm entry and survival barriers. *Economic Systems, 31*(4), 391–411. https://doi.org/10.1016/j.ecosys.2007.08.003.

Benjamin, N. et al. (2014). Informal economy and the World Bank, *World Bank policy research working papers*. https://doi.org/10.1596/1813-9450-6888.

Benzing, C., & Chu, H. M. (2009). A comparison of the motivations of small business owners in Africa. *Journal of Small Business and Enterprise Development, 16*(1), 60–77. https://doi.org/10.1108/14626000910932881.

Bohatá, M., & Mládek, J. (1999). The development of the Czech SME sector. *Journal of Business Venturing, 14*(5–6), 461–473. https://doi.org/10.1016/S0883-9026(98)00025-1.

Brown, B., & Michael. (1995). *Africa's choices: After thirty years of the World Bank*. Penguin.

Charmes, J. (2012). The informal economy worldwide: Trends and characteristics. *Margin: The Journal of Applied Economic Research, 6*(2), 103–132. https://doi.org/10.1177/097380101200600202.

de Castro, J. O., Khavul, S., & Bruton, G. D. (2014). Shades of grey: How do informal firms navigate between macro and meso institutional environments? *Strategic Entrepreneurship Journal, 8*(1), 75–94. https://doi.org/10.1002/sej.1172.

Díez-Martín, F., Prado-Roman, C., & Blanco-González, A. (2013). Beyond legitimacy: Legitimacy types and organisational success. *Management Decision, 51*(10), 1954–1969. https://doi.org/10.1108/MD-08-2012-0561.

DiMaggio, P. J. & Powell, W. W. (1983). The iron cage revisited: Institutional isomorphism and collective rationality in organisational fields. *American Sociological Review, 48*(2), 147–160. Available at: https://www.researchgate.net/publication/246481910_The_Iron_Cage_Revisited_Institutional_Isomorphism_and_Collective_Rationality_in_Organisational_Fields.

Dolowitz, D. P., & Marsh, D. (2000). Learning from abroad: The role of policy transfer in contemporary policy-making. *Governance, 13*(1), 5–23. https://doi.org/10.1111/0952-1895.00121.

Dvoulety, O. (2020). Classifying self-employed persons using segmentation criteria available in the Labour Force Survey (LFS) data. *Journal of Business Venturing Insights, 14*, e00199. https://doi.org/10.1016/j.jbvi.2020.e00199.

Fjose, S., Grünfeld, L. A., & Green, C. (2010). *SMEs and growth in Sub-Saharan Africa: Identifying SME roles and obstacles to SME growth*. Available at: http://www.menon.no. Accessed: October 12, 2019.

Fligstein, N. (1985). The spread of the multidivisional form among large firms, 1919–1979. *American Sociological Review, 50*(3), 377. https://doi.org/10.2307/2095547.

Fox, L. & Sohnesen, T. P. (2012). *Household enterprises in Sub-Saharan Africa: Why they matter for growth, jobs, and livelihoods*. Available at: http://econ.worldbank.org.

Hegerty, S. W. (2009). Capital inflows, exchange market pressure, and credit growth in four transition economies with fixed exchange rates. *Economic Systems, 33*(2), 155–167. https://doi.org/10.1016/j.ecosys.2009.02.001.

Herrington, M. & Kelley, D. (2012). *African entrepreneurship Sub-Saharan African regional report*. Available at: http://www.babson.edu/Academics/centers/blank-center/global-research/gem/Documents/GEM%202012%20Africa%20Report.pdf.

Isenberg, D. J. (2010). How to start an entrepreneurial revolution. *Harvard Business Review, 88*(6), 40–50. Available at: www.hbr.org. Accessed: November 22, 2019.

Jackson, T. (2012). Cross-cultural management and the informal economy in Sub-Saharan Africa: Implications for organisation, employment and skills development. *The International Journal of Human Resource Management, 23*(14), 2901–2916. https://doi.org/10.1080/09585192.2012.671510.

Jawahar, I. M., & Mclaughlin, G. L. (2001). Toward a descriptive stakeholder theory: An organisational life cycle approach. *Academy of Management Review, 26*(3), 397–414. https://doi.org/10.5465/amr.2001.4845803.

Jennings, P. D., et al. (2013). Institutions, entrepreneurs, and communities: A special issue on entrepreneurship. *Journal of Business Venturing, 28*(1), 1–9. https://doi.org/10.1016/j.jbusvent.2012.07.001.

Jepperson, R. L. (1991). Institutions, institutional effects, and institutionalization. In W. W. Powell & P. J. DiMaggio (Eds.), *The new institutionalism in organisational analysis* (pp. 143–163). University of Chicago Press. Open Access Available at: http://www.oalib.com/references/9344472. Accessed: March 10, 2020.

Kale, Y. (2019). Micro, Small, and Medium Enterprises (MSME) national survey 2017 report. *National Bureau of Statistics (NBS) and Small & Medium Enterprises Development Agency of Nigeria (SMEDAN)*. Available at: http://www.nigerianstat.gov.ng/download/967.

Knoke, D. (1982). The spread of municipal reform: Temporal, spatial, and social dynamics. *American Journal of Sociology, 87*(6), 1314–1339. https://doi.org/10.1086/227595.

Kongolo, M. (2010). Job creation versus job shedding and the role of SMEs in economic development. *African Journal of Business Management, 4*(11), 2288–2295. Available at: http://www.academicjournals.org/AJBM. Accessed: October 10, 2019.

Kropp, F., Lindsay, N. J., & Shoham, A. (2008). Entrepreneurial orientation and international entrepreneurial business venture startup. *International Journal of Entrepreneurial Behavior & Research, 14*(2), 102–117. https://doi.org/10.1108/13552550810863080.

Lagatum Institute. (2019). *The Africa prosperity report 2019/20*. Available at: www.li.com.

Lund, F., & Skinner, C. (2004). Integrating the informal economy in urban planning and governance: A case study of the process of policy development in Durban, South Africa. *International Development Planning Review, 26*(4), 431–456. https://doi.org/10.3828/idpr.26.4.5.

Mair, J., Mayer, J., & Lutz, E. (2015). Navigating institutional plurality: Organisational governance in hybrid organisations. *Organisation Studies, 36*(6), 713–739. https://doi.org/10.1177/0170840615580007.

Mamman, A., et al. (2019). SME policy formulation and implementation in Africa: Unpacking assumptions as opportunity for research direction. *Journal of Business Research, 97*, 304–315. https://doi.org/10.1016/j.jbusres.2018.01.044.

Manolova, T. S., & Yan, A. (2002). Institutional constraints and entrepreneurial responses in a transforming economy. *International Small Business Journal: Researching Entrepreneurship, 20*(2), 163–184. https://doi.org/10.1177/0266242602202003.

Medina, L. et al. (2017). *The informal economy in Sub-Saharan Africa: Size and determinants* (Working Paper: WP/17/156). International Monetary Fund (IMF). Available at: https://www.imf.org/en/Publications/WP/Issues/2017/07/10/The-Informal-Economy-in-Sub-Saharan-Africa-Size-and-Determinants-45017.

Meyer, J., Scott, W. R., & Strang, D. (1987). Centralization, fragmentation, and school district complexity. *Administrative Science Quarterly, 32*(2), 186. https://doi.org/10.2307/2393125.

Meyer, J, W., & Rowan, B. (1977). Institutionalized organizations: Formal structure as myth and ceremony. *American Journal of Sociology, 83*(2), 340–363. https://doi.org/10.1086/226550.

North, D. C. (1990). *Institutions, institutional change, and economic performance*. Cambridge University Press.

Obeng, B. A., & Blundel, R. K. (2015). Evaluating enterprise policy interventions in Africa: A critical review of Ghanaian small business support services. *Journal of Small Business Management, 53*(2), 416–435. https://doi.org/10.1111/jsbm.12072.

Ogunsade, I. A., & Obembe, D. (2016). The influence of informal institutions on informal sector entrepreneurship: A study of Nigeria's hand-woven textile industry. *Journal of Small Business & Entrepreneurship, 28*(6), 413–429. https://doi.org/10.1080/08276331.2016.1202093.

Oliver, C. (1991). Strategic responses to institutional processes. *Academy of Management Review*, 16(1), 145–179. https://doi.org/10.5465/amr.1991.4279002.

Pache, A. C., & Santos, F. (2010). When worlds collide: The internal dynamics of organisational response to conflicting institutional demand. *Academy of Management Review*, 35(3), 455–476. https://doi.org/10.5465/AMR.2010.51142368.

Pache, A. C., & Santos, F. (2013). Inside the hybrid organisation: Selective coupling as a response to competing institutional logics. *Academy of Management Journal*, 56(4), 972–1001. https://doi.org/10.5465/amj.2011.0405.

Peng, M. W. (2003). Institutional transitions and strategic choices. *Academy of Management Review*, 28(2), 275–296. https://doi.org/10.5465/amr.2003.9416341.

Pfeffer, J., & Salancik, G. R. (1978). *The external control of organisations: A resource dependence perspective*. Harper & Row.

Poole, D. L. (2018, October [2017]). Entrepreneurs, entrepreneurship and SMEs in developing economies: How subverting terminology sustains flawed policy. *World Development Perspectives*, 9, 35–42. https://doi.org/10.1016/j.wdp.2018.04.003.

Porta, R., & Shleifer, A. (2008). *The unofficial economy and economic development* (Working Paper Series No. 14520). National Bureau of Economic Research (NBER). Available at: http://www.nber.org/papers/w14520. Accessed: February 7, 2020.

Powell, W. W. & DiMaggio, P. (Eds.). (1991). *The new institutionalism in organisational analysis*. University of Chicago Press. Available at: https://www.press.uchicago.edu/ucp/books/book/chicago/N/bo3684488.html. Accessed: March 8, 2020.

Provan, K. G. (1982). Interorganisational linkages and influence over decision making. *Academy of Management Journal*, 25(2), 443–451. https://doi.org/10.5465/256003.

Provan, K. G. (1983). The federation as an interorganisational linkage network. *Academy of Management Review*, 8(1), 79–89. https://doi.org/10.5465/amr.1983.4287668.

Puffer, S. M., McCarthy, D. J., & Boisot, M. (2010). Entrepreneurship in Russia and China: The impact of formal institutional voids. *Entrepreneurship Theory and Practice*, 34(3), 441–467. https://doi.org/10.1111/j.1540-6520.2009.00353.x.

PwC Nigeria. (2020). PwC's MSME survey. *Building to last: Nigeria report*. Available at: www.pwc.com/ng.

Rogerson, C. M. (2001). In search of the African miracle: Debates on successful small enterprise development in Africa. *Habitat International*, 25(1), 115–142. https://doi.org/10.1016/S0197-3975(00)00033-3.

Schneider, A., Wickert, C., & Marti, E. (2017). Reducing complexity by creating complexity: A systems theory perspective on how organisations respond to their environments. *Journal of Management Studies*, 54(2), 182–208. https://doi.org/10.1111/joms.12206.

Scott Richard, W. (1987). *Organisations: Rational, natural, and open systems* (2nd ed.). Prentice Hall. Available at: https://www.scribd.com/doc/312871394/W-Richard-Scott-Organisations-Rational-Natural-And-Open-Systems-5th-Edition-Prentice-Hall-2003-6. Accessed: March 8, 2020.

Singh, J. V. Tucker, D. J. & House, R. J. (1986). Organisational legitimacy and the liability of newness. *Administrative Science Quarterly, 31*(2), 171. https://doi.org/10.2307/2392787.

Skrzek-Lubasińska, M., & Szaban, J. M. (2019). Nomenclature and harmonised criteria for the self-employment categorisation: An approach pursuant to a systematic review of the literature. *European Management Journal, 37*(3), 376–386. https://doi.org/10.1016/j.emj.2018.11.001.

Spring, A. (2007). African women in the entrepreneurial landscape: Reconsidering the formal and informal sectors. *Cadernos de Estudos Africanos, 11*(12), 19–38. https://doi.org/10.4000/cea.924.

Sriram, V., & Mersha, T. (2010). Stimulating entrepreneurship in Africa. *World Journal of Entrepreneurship, Management and Sustainable Development, 6*(4), 257–272. https://doi.org/10.1108/20425961201000020.

Stenholm, P., Acs, Z. J., & Wuebker, R. (2013). Exploring country-level institutional arrangements on the rate and type of entrepreneurial activity. *Journal of Business Venturing, 28*(1), 176–193. https://doi.org/10.1016/j.jbusvent.2011.11.002.

Suchman, M. C. (1995). Managing legitimacy: Strategic and institutional approaches. *Academy of Management Review, 20*(3), 571–610. https://doi.org/10.5465/amr.1995.9508080331.

Suddaby, R., Bitektine, A., & Haack, P. (2017). Legitimacy. *Academy of Management Annals, 11*(1), 451–478. https://doi.org/10.5465/annals.2015.0101.

Sutter, C., et al. (2017). Transitioning entrepreneurs from informal to formal markets. *Journal of Business Venturing, 32*(4), 420–442. https://doi.org/10.1016/j.jbusvent.2017.03.002.

Tokman, V. E. (2001). Integrating the informal sector in the modernization process. *SAIS Review, 21*(1), 45–60. https://doi.org/10.1353/sais.2001.0027.

Tokman, V. E. (2007). *Modernizing the informal sector*. Available at: http://www.un.org/esa/desa/http://www.un.org/esa/desa/papers. Accessed: November 15, 2019.

Tolbert, P. S., & Zucker, L. G. (1983). Institutional sources of change in the formal structure of organisations: The diffusion of civil service reform, 1880–1935. *Administrative Science Quarterly, 28*(1), 22. https://doi.org/10.2307/2392383.

Urbano, D., & Alvarez, C. (2014). Institutional dimensions and entrepreneurial activity: An international study. *Small Business Economics, 42*(4), 703–716. https://doi.org/10.1007/s11187-013-9523-7.

Wapshott, R., & Mallett, O. (2018). Small and medium-sized enterprise policy: Designed to fail? *Environment and Planning C: Politics and Space, 36*(4), 750–772. https://doi.org/10.1177/2399654417719288.

Webb, J. W., et al. (2009). You say illegal, I say legitimate: Entrepreneurship in the informal economy. *Academy of Management Review, 34*(3), 492–510.

Webb, J. W., et al. (2013). Research on entrepreneurship in the informal economy: Framing a research agenda. *Journal of Business Venturing, 28*(5), 598–614. https://doi.org/10.1016/j.jbusvent.2012.05.003.

Webb, J. W., Ireland, R. D., & Ketchen, D. J. (2014). Toward a greater understanding of entrepreneurship and strategy in the informal economy. *Strategic Entrepreneurship Journal, 8*(1), 1–15. https://doi.org/10.1002/sej.1176.

Welter, F., Smallbone, D., & Pobol, A. (2015). Entrepreneurial activity in the informal economy: A missing piece of the entrepreneurship Jigsaw Puzzle. *Entrepreneurship & Regional Development, 27*(5–6), 292–306. https://doi.org/10.1080/08985626.2015.1041259.

Whetten, D. A., & Leung, T. K. (1979). The instrumental value of interorganisational relations: Antecedents and consequences of linkage formation. *Academy of Management Journal, 22*(2), 325–344. https://doi.org/10.5465/255593.

Williams, C. C., & Shahid, M. S. (2016). Informal entrepreneurship and institutional theory: Explaining the varying degrees of (in)formalization of entrepreneurs in Pakistan. *Entrepreneurship & Regional Development, 28*(1–2), 1–25. https://doi.org/10.1080/08985626.2014.963889.

Williams, N., & Vorley, T. (2015). Institutional asymmetry: How formal and informal institutions affect entrepreneurship in Bulgaria. *International Small Business Journal: Researching Entrepreneurship, 33*(8), 840–861. https://doi.org/10.1177/0266242614534280.

Wright, M., & Marlow, S. (2012). Entrepreneurial activity in the venture creation and development process. *International Small Business Journal: Researching Entrepreneurship, 30*(2), 107–114. https://doi.org/10.1177/0266242611432793.

Wright, M., & Stigliani, I. (2013). Entrepreneurship and growth. *International Small Business Journal: Researching Entrepreneurship, 31*(1), 3–22. https://doi.org/10.1177/0266242612467359.

Zimmerman, M. A., & Zeitz, G. J. (2002). Beyond survival: Achieving new venture growth by building legitimacy. *Academy of Management Review, 27*(3), 414–431. https://doi.org/10.5465/amr.2002.7389921.

Zucker, L. G. (1987). Institutional theories of organisation. *Annual Review of Sociology, 13*(1), 443–464. https://doi.org/10.1146/annurev.so.13.080187.002303.

6

The Institutional Context of Community Entrepreneurship Behaviour in Nigeria: Lessons from Three Case Communities

Rotimi Olaniyan

Introduction

It has long been suggested that entrepreneurship research has not paid sufficient attention to the community in which entrepreneurship is acted out (Martinez et al., 2011). Other authors have posited that a better understanding of the underlying relationship between entrepreneurship and community may indeed be the next true frontier for entrepreneurship researchers (Coase & Wang, 2011). This chapter contributes to the global discourse within this underrepresented area by exploring the nature, relationships and effects of the institutional context on African entrepreneurship behaviour at the community level within Nigeria.

A community-based enterprise is conceptualised along the lines of Peredo and Chrisman (2006), as a 'socio-economic arrangement in which the community acts entrepreneurially to create and operate a new enterprise embedded in its existing social structure'. By association, the notion of 'community entrepreneurship' in this study is one which points more to the entrepreneurship development challenges of groups of geographical and spatially proximate and/or culturally homogeneous people who on account of their shared socio-cultural structures, hold a strong collectivist view which

R. Olaniyan (✉)
Nottingham Trent University, Nottingham, UK
e-mail: rotimi.olaniyan02@ntu.ac.uk

they manifest in a set of 'communal' entrepreneurial behaviours, rather than an individualistic entrepreneurial orientation in the more classical sense of the construct.

Of particular theoretical interest, is how Nigerian community-based entrepreneurs are impacted by institutional rules and entrepreneurship development policy measures. The author theorises that the unique combinations of these factors which encompass the economic, political and socio-cultural factor conditions within which all entrepreneurial actors must operate, (the institutional context), impact on the entrepreneurial behaviours of various communities such as: venture opportunity recognition, resource allocation and deployment of an entrepreneurial strategy, in ways uniquely different from each other. The specific research questions are as articulated in the following Fig. 6.1.

By drawing upon earlier frameworks offered by Shane (2003), Stevenson and Lundstrom (2007), Peredo and Chrisman (2006), Ben Letaifa et al. (2016) and others, the study focuses attention on the nature, relevance, impact and interrelatedness of institutional factors on the entrepreneurial behaviour of community entrepreneurs in such a dynamic and emerging economy as Nigeria between 1990 and 2018 which most of the data gathered covers.

The chapter considers how entrepreneurship is described in the literature and in particular how it plays out in the African context. Secondly, it explains the nature of community entrepreneurship as a guiding construct to this study before explaining the contextual elements in light of relevant literature. Next, it expatiates on the research design before presenting the findings of the study. A discussion on the relevance of these findings and a conclusions section detailing the contributions to the emerging fields of both community entrepreneurship and developmental entrepreneurship, which Koveos (2006) and Adusei (2016) see as being concerned with the special developmental challenges and conditions of adversity faced by entrepreneurs, not least in the developing world follows. Finally, suggestions for future research bring the chapter to a close.

Research Aim	To better understand the effect of the institutional context on community entrepreneurship behaviour			
	RQ 1	RQ 2	RQ 3	RQ 4
Research Questions	How Do Members of the Community Ventures Rate the Institutional Context Within Which They Venture?	Is the Perception of the Institutional Context of Community Entrepreneurial Behaviour Independent of Location?	Do Institutional Factors Impact the Communities' Entrepreneurial Behaviour in Similar Ways Across Each of the Three Case Communities?	Are the direction and degree of influence of all Institutional factors on the entrepreneurial behaviour of the community enterprises similar across all three case communities?

Fig. 6.1 The research purpose

Entrepreneurship is a multi-dimensional concept (Audretsch et al., 2007) which as a social construct is neither new, nor alien to Africans. The study of this focal area has been recognised by researchers such as (Adusei, 2016; Wennkers et al., 2002), as having achieved activity of varying levels systematically across time and countries. The determinants and dynamics of African entrepreneurship might be said to be significantly similar to those found in other economies in such ways as; the theoretical impact of cultures and national environments (Hayton et al., 2002; Tan, 2002; Hofstede, 2001,) or single cultural factors such as post-materialism on entrepreneurship (Uhlaner et al., 2002) or contextual quality (Ben Letaifa et al., 2016).

The basis for understanding the institutional context of entrepreneurship has traditionally been through the assessment of, and relational aspects to economic and cultural values (Schumpeter, 1947; Hofstede, 2001); the influence of the formal and regulatory framework (Davidsson et al., 2006; Klapper et al., 2009; North, 1990); the influence of informal institutions on entrepreneurship (Manolova et al., 2008), and the interplay of more temporal societal factors (Baumol, 1990; Davidsson, 2005).

Empirical African studies have provided mixed findings on these links, based fundamentally on the cultural dimensions proposed by Hofstede (1994, 2001) and commonly used in cross-cultural research. Some suggest that entrepreneurs share a common set of values regardless of culture (McGrath et al., 1992), while others such as Vershinina et al. (2017) have recently argued that culture will affect entrepreneurship in unique ways. For example, some African studies have generally concluded that psychological variables (Frese, 2000), and race and ethnicity (Ramachandran & Shah, 1999) are important predictors of entrepreneurial activity, while research on resource landlocked African countries (Dana & Ratten, 2017) or Africans in diaspora (Ojo et al., 2013) suggest that entrepreneurial tensions exist in every country while entrepreneurial development can be fostered with appropriate cultural orientation and institutional frameworks.

This study is inspired by a proposition that sees institutional factor conditions as being different within communities and argues that these differences present contextual typologies that could have significant consequences on how an otherwise monolithic national entrepreneurship development policy should be articulated and eventually deployed within African nations.

Understanding Community Entrepreneurship

Community enterprises may be characterised as those enterprises, which are controlled by their members and which 'have social as well as economic aims (Somerville & McElwee, 2011), that are 'controlled by people living within their area of benefit (the 'community'), and their surpluses (if any), are principally invested or used to benefit people within that area. (Though not necessarily the same people as has been suggested by Hayton (1996). Community-based entrepreneurship manifests as a type of enterprise in which the community operates and grows from within the enterprise and the entrepreneurial process. The result is 'local communities, which create collective business ventures and through them or their results, aim to contribute to both local economic and social development' (with 'Community' meaning a 'shared geographical location, generally accompanied by collective culture and/or ethnicity and potentially other shared relational characteristics' (Peredo & Chrisman, 2006). They explain that the community, 'is simultaneously both the enterprise and the entrepreneur'. It 'acts as an entrepreneur when its members, acting as owners, managers, and employees, collaboratively create or identify a market opportunity and organise themselves to respond to it', while, 'the community acts as an enterprise when its members work together to jointly produce and exchange goods and/or services using the existing social structure of the community as a means of organising those activities' (Julien, 2007; Hindle, 2010; Peredo & Chrisman, 2006, Somerville & McElwee, 2011).

This identification of entrepreneurial effort at the level of the community, and the extension of the traditional view of human capital to incorporate the social context, is a radical shift, away from the traditionally held view of the sole individual being the principal actor in the entrepreneurial process and provides a more collectivist view of entrepreneurship. De Bruin and Dupuis (1995) further suggest that not only do the theoretical underpinnings of community entrepreneurship lie in neo-Schumpeterian ideas of innovation, creative and adaptive responses to the challenges thrown by economic cycles but in practice, such a notion also comprises other elements, such as socio-cultural capital which may be particular kinds of knowledge and social styles (Codd et al., 1985) and involves the familiarity and ease of language and socio-cultural milieu which is ingrained and embodied within a homogenous group. Bourdieu (1984) had suggested that this might be symbolised by the way cultural artefacts such as food, craft, music, clothing and dance are consumed. Other elements include market-leading orientation, which, much in the Schumpeterian fashion of creative response, is where the community deliberately stages its affairs in ways that create demand for their offering of social, cultural and other resources empowerment and the leadership seeks to transform the community through the mobilisation of these temporal factors towards a collective vision shared by members of the community. In addition to this is the treatise on the contextual nature of the community highlighted by the likes of Welter (2011) which the study integrates with that of De Bruin and Dupuis (1995) and Hindle (2010) as a more comprehensive theoretical way to understand the operating logic behind such ventures.

The Institutional Context of Community Entrepreneurship

Baumol (1990) had long identified the lingering influence of institutional factors on entrepreneurial behaviours and had even gone as far as to assert that the entrepreneur's level of innovative or unproductive practices depends on the existing institutional arrangement, or 'rules of the game'. A term which North (1990) mentions as 'defining and limiting the opportunity and choices available to individuals within a particular social context which itself in located within the environment which the entrepreneur has to play'.

This institutional environment refers to the economic, political and social factor conditions within which entrepreneurship occurs. Shane and Venkataraman (2000) building on the work of North (1990) describe these formal institutions as laws, regulations, and the supporting apparatuses such as agencies and regulatory bodies. Through a wide range of mechanisms such as enforcement, incentives and precepts, the formal institution establishes the boundaries of entrepreneurial behaviour. The informal institution on the other had refers to the social norms, values and cultural beliefs that define socially acceptable behaviour. While North (1990) offers a compelling and celebrated theoretical framework for exploring institutional context, the author has chosen to build on seven specific institutional factors offered by Shane (2003) which are seen as being better suited to a detailed analysis of the impact of factor conditions. Studying these more granular factors (which are expatiated upon below) is important for two reasons: firstly, because they have been proven by Shane and others to influence the entrepreneurial behaviour of individuals and, secondly, they are manifestly easier to observe.

Indeed, the effect of the manipulation of policy which regulatory authorities might be able to use to influence the degree and quality of 'institutional munificence' (defined by the author as the quality of the context of these factor conditions) within which community entrepreneurial behaviour is expected to manifest, has been a major source of concern for many researchers focused on the African entrepreneurial context. Fadahunsi and Rosa (2002) and, Ogunsade and Obembe (2016) for instance had highlighted the absence of well-developed formal institutions in most African economies as being major barriers for entrepreneurial development within the continent. Yet, as observed by North (2005), entrepreneurs will adapt their activities and strategies to fit the opportunities and limitations provided through formal and informal institutional frameworks. Formal rules are usually designed to reduce transaction costs and facilitate exchange and are likely to impact on different groups and individuals differently. He asserts that since rules and institutions are creations of individuals and groups, sometimes as a result of their private interest, they do not always operate in the interest of the common social wellbeing. This poses the question, whether this holds true within the community entrepreneurship context.

The four key economic institutional factors enumerated by Shane (2003) to influence entrepreneurial behaviour are: societal wealth, economic stability, capital availability and taxation. The political environment equally influences the exploitation of entrepreneurial opportunity, by influencing perceived risks and returns (Harper, 1996). The most notable dimensions within the political environment as suggested by Shane (2003) are freedom, property rights and centralisation of power. The socio-cultural environment influences the exploitation of entrepreneurial opportunity, in three ways: through societal attitudes towards entrepreneurial activity, social norms and cultural beliefs. All of these are integrated as underpinning theoretical constructs, into the conceptual framework that guides the study.

Entrepreneurship Policy Context of Nigerian Community Entrepreneurship

A critical institutional factor condition for entrepreneurship is entrepreneurship development policy and measures, and it is important that this is comprehensively analysed as part of the larger aim of this research study.

Nigeria had developed two entrepreneurship policy documents between 2005 and 2015. Before this was a series of ad-hoc and uncoordinated economic instruments, measures and institutions that the government initiated to deal with issues around credit and finance, rural and small farmer incentives, business support services, tax concessions and other predominantly microfinance initiatives targeted at individual small and informal sector businesses. However, it might be argued that the policy context within which the Nigerian community entrepreneurs operate is weak and has been for well over twenty-five years.

For all the statements of best intentions and rhetoric, the policy documents made (particularly the 2005 document which has been the most vigorously implemented), faltered along several important structural lines. The first, is that the 2005 document was predominantly a small business policy document rather than an entrepreneurial development policy document. This might be understandable given that it was initiated as part of the NEEDS (National Economic Empowerment Development strategy) programme of the then Obasanjo administration which in 2003 established SMEDAN (Small and Medium Scale Enterprises Development Agency of Nigeria. This policy document was replaced by the National Enterprise Development Programme (NEDEP) in 2014/2015 with a more far-reaching mandate of nurturing a well-structured MSME sub-sector with a particular focus on micro-enterprises. No categorical mention was made of community entrepreneurship within the content of both policy documents, while the closest mention to a clearly defined institutional support for community enterprises contained within the 2014–2015 document focused on local government areas and cooperative societies as vehicles and units for policy interventions (SMEDAN, 2019). With the change in ruling party and government in 2015, the NEDEP programme, however, seemed to have been discontinued in its original form and largely replaced with the Nigerian Economic Recovery and Growth Plan (2017–2020).

Audretsch et al. (2001) and Stevenson and Lundstrom (2007) explain that while a small business policy focuses more on the post start up stage and seeks to create the required institutional framework to promote the growth of firms, an entrepreneurship development policy model is more encompassing and ideally includes instruments and measures taken to stimulate more entrepreneurial behaviour in communities, regions or nations. It places the required attention on the entrepreneurial behaviour arc as derived from Shane (2003) as a basis for crafting a supporting environment rather than just the supply of SMEs.

The 2005 policy document was incomplete in addressing such entrepreneurial benchmarks and cross-comparisons between states and communities as a policy metric and faltered in its structural frame-working, particularly as suggested by UNCTAD (2012). The absence of several keywords and its thematic paucity when compared to the literature, evidence its failure to address some of the critical contemporary issues that a national entrepreneurship development agenda must contend with, such as social networks. The UNCTAD (2012) framework overlaps with Stevenson and Lundstrom (2007) in certain areas and offers a slightly different focus in others. The UN institution suggests that six key components should make up the policy areas to be addressed in crafting the optimal mix of policy measures. These are (1) formulating national entrepreneurship strategy; (2) optimising the regulatory environment; (3) enhancing entrepreneurship education and skills; (4) facilitating technology exchange and innovation; (5) improving access to finance; and (6) promoting awareness and networking.

Conceptualising the Effect of Institutional Context on Community Entrepreneurship Behaviour

The multi-dimensional nature of this study demonstrates that several concepts and constructs can be integrated into one broad organising conceptual framework. At the heart of this organising, framework is the linear model of the entrepreneurial behavioural process proposed by Shane (2003) which is applied here to the processes that community-based entrepreneurs go through. It is these behaviours that the external institutional factors will influence, and the study's reading of such influences will largely be measured by how the respondents perceive of such behaviours. Positive outcomes of such behaviours will invariably be the intended objectives of policy measures (which also forms part of the regulatory environment). Theoretical models for understanding institutional factors (Shane, 2003) are also incorporated into this framework, as are conceptual frameworks for better understanding community-oriented enterprises (De Bruin & Dupuis, 1995; Hindle, 2010); contextualisation (Ben Letaifa et al., 2016) and policy measures (Stevenson & Lundstrom, 2007), to comprise an integrated conceptual framework that guides the study as shown in Fig. 6.2.

Research Context and Methods

The research design used was a multiple case-study of three communities, utilising predominantly quantitative methods with three distinctive features by way of design: (1) Measuring perception with ordinal scales, (2) explanatory in its intent through the use of an abductive approach and (3) a non-experimental comparative study which builds on a cross-sectional data gathering process. This was supplemented by field notes, observations and the content analysis of existing official Nigerian government entrepreneurship development policy documents on micro, small and medium enterprises,

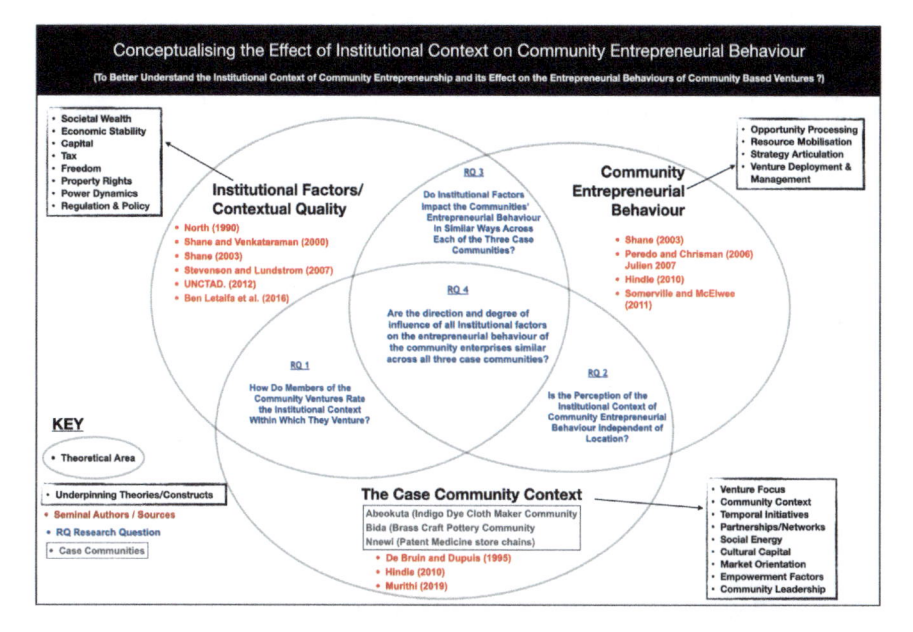

Fig. 6.2 Conceptualising the effect of institutional context on community entrepreneurship behaviour

between 1990 and 2015, chief of which was the 2005 MSME policy document.

One hundred and fifty-four respondents were recruited from across the three communities (Bida—fifty-three, Nnewi—fifty-one, Abeokuta—fifty) using convenience sampling parameters from the population of members of the community-based venture. A survey questionnaire was administered in the local language, while responses were translated back into English and filled out appropriately.

Nineteen closed questions were asked using a 5-point ordinal scale. Respondents were first asked to rate their perception of the current entrepreneurial situation, practices and influences within the community, secondly to provide an assessment of the community's outward entrepreneurial behaviour along the lines of Shane's (2003) model, thirdly, to answer specific questions assessing their behavioural responses to specific institutional factor conditions and, finally, to give an assessment of the institutional context within which they currently operate.

The analysis of the quantitative data followed three sequential steps using SPSS. The first allowed for descriptive statistics that used mean scores to plot respondents' relative perception of environmental context. The next stage utilised inferential statistics (chi-square) to engage in hypothesis testing by establishing whether there were non-spurious relationships between selected variables and location. Factor analysis, which is a test for the strength of (albeit non-directional in nature) such relationships, revealed commonalities across various institutional factors, and their influence on the outward manifest entrepreneurial behaviour of the community entrepreneurs along the lines of Shane's (2003) model. Fourthly, ordinal regression analysis was utilised to establish the direction and relative strength of those variables, in such a way as to predict likely odds of direction and strength of influence across variables.

Introducing the Nigerian Case Communities

Often referred to as an oil-rich nation, Nigeria emerged as Africa's largest economy in 2013 after a statistical rebasing of its economic data. It peaked with an annual GDP of $568 Billion, a GDP per capita of $2,533 in 2014. However, a slowdown in its economic affairs influenced by the crash of crude oil prices has seen GDP figures fall to $397.27 Billion as at 2018 with a population of over two hundred million across two hundred and fifty ethnic language groups living in seven hundred and seventy-four local government areas (World Bank, 2020). In a 2018 analysis of ease of starting a new business, it was ranked 105th out of one hundred and eighty-three countries. (World Bank, 2020). It is also a country beset with several developmental challenges, chiefly being mass poverty, corruption, income inequalities, mass youth unemployment and weak infrastructures such as power.

Although the selection of the three community-based entrepreneurial case studies provides a limited representation of Nigeria, they do have paradigmatic value (Yin, 2003) given their status as prime examples of indigenous semi-urban community ventures in Nigeria. See Fig. 6.3 for case details.

Findings and Discussion

The Research Hypotheses

Each of the four research questions were reformulated into Null hypotheses which the study worked to reject. These hypotheses are listed in Fig. 6.4.

Location	Abeokuta (South West Nigeria)	Nnewi (South East Nigeria)	Bida (North Central Nigeria)
Community Venture	The Abeokuta Indigo Fabric Dye Community	The Nnewi Patent Medicine Store Chains	The Bida Brass Pottery Community
Brief Description	• Abeokuta is an ancient provincial town with 4 million inhabitants situated 100 kilometres north of the commercial capital city of Nigeria, Lagos. • The indigenes are predominantly members of the Yoruba tribe, the second largest Nigerian ethnic group. The Yoruba are famous for their cultural heritage as well as commercial spirit. The Egbas of Abeokuta have long been famous for the indigo dye fabric they produce, which is as much a cultural artefact as it is a business. • The fabric dye community venture operates out of two clusters within the heart of the city and is predominantly a female-dominated enterprise engaging several thousands of people, particularly women and their children.	• Nnewi, a small provincial town in Abia state, south eastern region of Nigeria, is home to 1 million inhabitants of the Igbo ethnic group. Its enterprising people are predominantly Christians and traders as well as small scale manufacturers who have an established reputation as a centre of commerce in Nigeria. • While not a community venture in the sense that we might expect, patent medicine dealerships are one of the business areas where the Nnewi have built a national dominance, through a network of stores and branches they have established through a very successful apprenticeship and sub franchising programme open to their kith and kin.	• Bida is a small provincial town located in Niger state in north central Nigeria with 1 million inhabitants from the Nupe ethnic group who are predominantly Muslims and farmers. • The Bida potteries have long had an established reputation as a centre of indigenous art and craft. Family groups, who have inherited the business, and skills from their forebears, drive the community venture.

Fig. 6.3 The three case communities

Research Aim	To better understand the effect of the institutional context on community entrepreneurship behaviour			
	RQ 1	RQ 2	RQ 3	RQ 4
Research Questions	How Do Members of the Community Ventures Rate the Institutional Context Within Which They Venture?	Is the Perception of the Institutional Context of Community Entrepreneurial Behaviour Independent of Location?	Do Institutional Factors Impact the Communities' Entrepreneurial Behaviour in Similar Ways Across Each of the Three Case Communities?	Are the direction and degree of influence of all Institutional factors on the entrepreneurial behaviour of the community enterprises similar across all three case communities?
	H0 1	H0 2	H0 3	H0 4
Hypotheses	Members of the Community Ventures will NOT Rate the Institutional Context Within Which They Venture similarly	The Perception of the Institutional Context of Community Entrepreneurial Behaviour is NOT Independent of Location	Institutional Factors do NOT Impact the Communities' Entrepreneurial Behaviour in Similar Ways Across Each of the Three Case Communities	The direction and degree of influence of all Institutional factors on the entrepreneurial behaviour of the community enterprises are NOT similar across all three case communities

Fig. 6.4 The table of hypotheses

The Case Community Contexts (Community Entrepreneurship in Nigeria)

The research question going into the study was built on the seminal works of a few writers such as Shane and Venkataraman (2000) and others who posit that institutional factors influence entrepreneurial behaviour. The study confirms this within the context of the indigent, collective and socio-culturally networked entrepreneurial endeavour. However, it also goes further to suggest that the institutional framework and context are different across the case communities, creating different behavioural typologies that must ultimately be recognised when developing national entrepreneurship development policy and programmes.

In order to better understand how these institutional factor conditions have impacted on the entrepreneurial behaviour of these communities, it is useful to first understand how the community enterprises structure and operate themselves, utilising a conceptual framework adapted from the works of DeBruin and Dupuis (1995), Hindle (2010) and Welter (2011). Figure 6.5 highlights how the communities have tapped into these 9 key dimensions in varying ways. Driven by a shared focus and led by varying loose leadership structures, the three community enterprises have relied heavily upon important unique qualities such as their context, social energy, cultural capital and closely bound social networks, to develop and drive their set of community initiatives.

There are in the author's view, within the three cases, a position that the informal institutional arrangement seems to have an impact in regulating the boundaries of behaviour at the community enterprise level. It supports the earlier view by Gywali and Fogel (1994) that socio-cultural norms and values are evident regulators of entrepreneurial behaviour. The strong sense of community and exploitation of the power of socially energised networks that is seen within the three cases, serve as protection and cohesive counter-balancing forces in the absence of legally binding contracts and other forms of more formal regulations. The findings, however, seem to challenge a long-held view by Harper's (1997), that the prevalence of such non-legal binding contracts limits the supply of entrepreneurship, as we see that the ventures have thrived over the years despite such challenges.

	The Abeokuta Indigo Fabric Dye Community	The Nnewi Patent Medicine Store Chains	The Bida Brass Pottery Community
Community Venture Focus	The design, manufacture and wholesale of traditionally inspired indigo dyed fabrics	Patent medicine stores	The design, manufacture, polishing and sale of traditionally inspired brass and glass pottery
Community Context	Spatial, Ethnic, Network	Ethnic, Network	Spatial, Ethnic, Religious
Community (Temporal) Initiatives	• Apprenticeship and skills development • Community Thrift and micro credit schemes	• Apprenticeship and skills development, • Community Thrift and micro credit schemes, • Lobby and interest group protection schemes	• Apprenticeship and skills development, • Community thrift and micro credit schemes
Partnerships/Networks	• No established formal partnerships, loose informal networks of suppliers, customers and peers. • A quasi-democratic business management system	• No established formal corporate partnerships, loose informal networks of suppliers, sub franchisors	• No established formal corporate partnerships, loose informal networks of suppliers, customers and peers. • There is however a strong informal partnership with the traditional Islamic emirate
Social Energy	Jointly fighting poverty (Gbamiboshe)	Achievement orientation and a persecution complex	Sustenance of a divinely inspired heritage
Cultural Capital	• The ancient fabric dying process and design patterns passed down from generation to generation.	• Kinship • Inherited trades	• The ancient pottery process and design patterns passed down from generation to generation. • Islamic influences
Market Orientation	An informal commercial trading structure, largely wholesale oriented	An informal commercial trading structure, largely retail oriented	An informal commercial trading structure, largely wholesale oriented • Significantly supported by royal patronage of the emir
Empowerment Factors	• Peer inspired and consensus driven communal tactical action. Also, heritage	• Apparently more individualistic. Achievement orientation, supported with a strong union.	• Royal Patronage
Community Enterprise Leadership	The Iya Oloja. The matriarch leader of the community venture	More republican; a fairly sophisticated democracy, with an elected president of the trade group as head.	The Emir. The royal and patron leader of the community venture. Sarkin Aiki (The Master Craftsman)

Fig. 6.5 An analysis of the case community contexts of three Nigerian community enterprises (*Source* Adapted from DeBruin and Dupuis [1995]; Hindle [2010] and Welter [2011])

However, we also see a hint of North's (2005) theory about the unproductive impact of formal institutional rules and frameworks on entrepreneurial behaviour in places like Nnewi where a prevalence of fake and adulterated drugs by a few of the practitioners has occasioned what is seen by the community leaders as an overbearing regime of regulation by government agencies. What is curious in this instance is to note whether the entrepreneurs who have engaged in such *unproductive* entrepreneurial acts have done so in response to their reading of the institutional context, which paradoxically was assessed by the Nnewi respondents as strong. However, the issue of adulterated drugs and the resultant legal regulation and enforcements witnessed within this community, represents one of this study's striking examples of the coercive impact and effect of formal institutional rules towards what is akin to isomorphic behaviour of community-based entrepreneurs (DiMaggio & Powell, 1983).

The Key Findings

RQ 1

> H_{01}: Members of the community ventures will **NOT** rate the institutional context within which they venture similarly
>
> Decision: Accept null hypothesis.

The analytical procedure used in this section was based on a 5-point ordinal scale (where 1.0–2.9 is scored as a poor context; 3.0–3.9 is scored as a weak context and 4.0–5.0 is scored as a strong context) to evaluate the contextual ratings that members of the three respective community ventures gave the various institutional factors (Shane & Venkataraman, 2000), within their communities.

The respondents interviewed perceived the institutional context within their communities to be relatively weak (see Fig. 6.6) with the average score across all three cases being 3.6 as shown in the figure below. The exception, however, is in Nnewi where it was perceived to be strong, with a score of 4.1. Bida respondents perceived that the taxation system is not fair but were satisfied with their sense of freedom and property rights. We accept the Null Hypothesis in this case.

The respondents interviewed in both Abeokuta and Bida perceive the formal institutional context within their communities to be relatively weak, suggesting the lack of an enabling institutional environment. They single

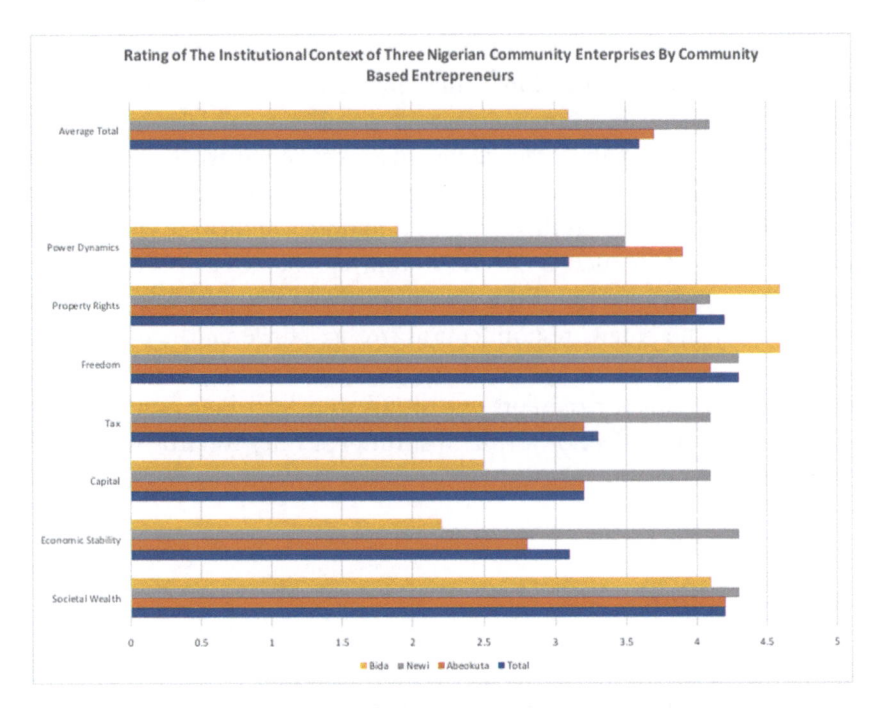

	Total	Abeokuta	Newi	Bida
Societal Wealth	4.2	4.2	4.3	4.1
Economic Stability	3.1	2.8	4.3	2.2
Capital	3.2	3.2	4.1	2.5
Tax	3.3	3.2	4.1	2.5
Freedom	4.3	4.1	4.3	4.6
Property Rights	4.2	4	4.1	4.6
Power Dynamics	3.1	3.9	3.5	1.9
Average Total	3.6	3.7	4.1	3.1

Fig. 6.6 Rating the institutional context of three Nigerian community enterprises

out economic stability and power dynamics/distance as the weakest of the institutional rules' determinants, which perhaps may be seen as an indictment on their part on macroeconomic managers as well as the political leadership. But the reading from Bida where we see the emergence of power dynamics as a third communality factor challenges views held by Harper (1997) and Shane (2003) that where the internal locus of control is low or power distance is high, there is a reduction in entrepreneurial propensities. The Bida case proves that even in the face of feudal rulership, the community venturing spirit exists and flourishes. It further suggests that such traditional institutions must be recognised for the powerful influences they have on community behaviour and indeed how they may be utilised in engendering entrepreneurship development going forward.

Also, interesting, however, is the near corroboration of the postulation given by Audretsch and Acs (1990) that societal wealth enhances entrepreneurial behaviour, particularly in the exploitation of opportunity. All three communities view their societies as being wealthy, which may be viewed as being contrary to official economic data. The literature is thick with suggestions that the supply of indigent African entrepreneurship is constrained by such lack of societal wealth. The author argues that these community ventures are viewed by their members as legacies of entrepreneurial opportunity passed down from generation to generation to help in the collective communal fight against poverty not as a result of societal wealth, but rather *despite* it.

H_{02}: The perception of the institutional context of community entrepreneurial behaviour is **NOT** independent of location.

Decision: Reject null hypothesis.

Chi-Square analysis is used as a test of independence, based on a bivariate contingency table ($r \times c$) under the null hypothesis rule of independence, where X^2 has an asymptotic chi-squared distribution, with $(r - 1)(c - 1)$ degrees of freedom (Bryman & Bell, 2007).

The acceptable level of statistical significance in this case is established by the P value 0.0005 with the degrees of freedom based on the net number of column and row combinations being 8. The result of the SPSS computation is given in Fig. 6.7.

In this case, the null hypothesis is rejected as not independent ($p < 0.05$) of the three case communities/locations in Nigeria (see Fig. 6.7). This implies that institutional context is dependent on the community and the way institutional rules as articulated are perceived by the various community actors

	CHI SQUARE VALUE	DEGREE OF FREEDOM	P-VALUE	DECISION
Institutional Context by Location	298.658	8	0.0005	Reject Null Hypothesis

Fig. 6.7 Chi-square values for institutional rules

to affect them differently. This provides a stronger empirical basis for understanding the current reality of the entrepreneurship policy environment at the community level while also strengthening the argument against monolithic policy approaches.

Perhaps it throws up an important question about who should be crafting community enterprise policy within a federal operating government such as Nigeria. National policy, in this case, comes from a federal government that in most instances is four to five layers separated from indigenous communities. It underscores the challenge that such instruments and their authors have to be relevant, resonant and intimate, with the peculiarities to be found in individual sub-national communities.

It also underscores a scholarly disconnect, between policymakers eager to utilise entrepreneurship as a development instrument and harbinger of economic prosperity to the populace, and the intellectual underpinning required to understand, how to design and deploy effective enterprise development policy. The sometimes-wholesale importation of Western models without regard to the peculiarity of the policy context has been another major constraint to the achievement of policy success in several countries in Africa.

H_{03}: Institutional factors do **NOT** impact the communities' entrepreneurial behaviour in similar ways across each of the three case communities.

Decision: Accept null hypothesis.

Using principal component (factor) analysis, the study was able to assess if each of the seven institutional factors were perceived to impact on the communities' entrepreneurial behaviour in similar ways across all three communities and more specifically identify which combination of factors seem to work together. The evidence points to the null hypothesis being accepted. The study found that there are three broad buckets of institutional factor commonality across the three case communities as shown in Fig. 6.8.

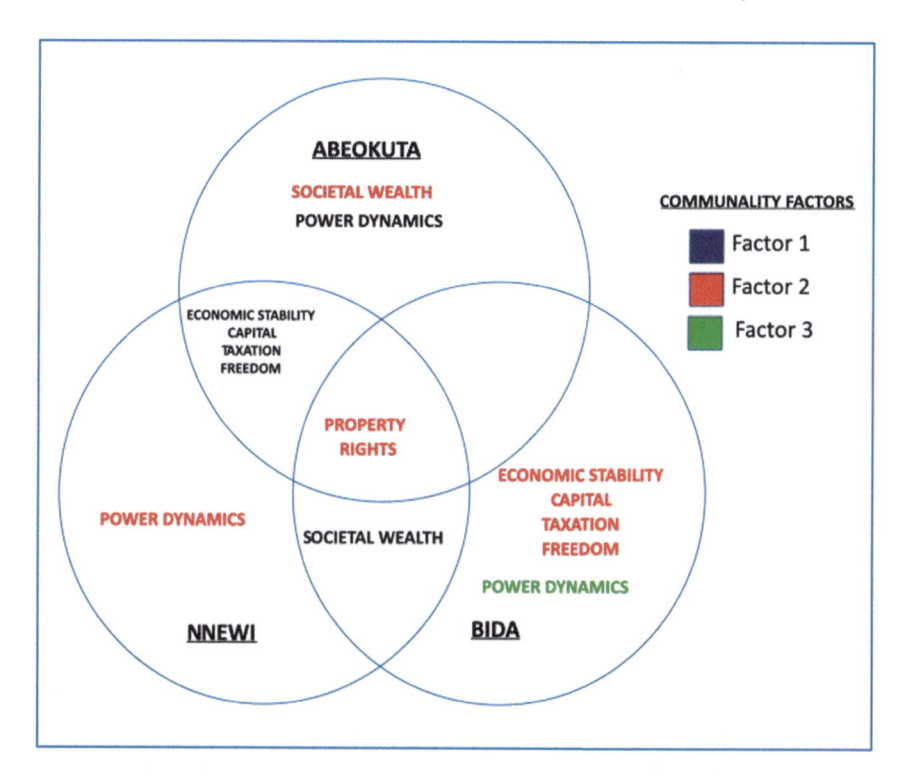

Fig. 6.8 A comparative assessment of institutional factor communalities across three Nigerian community enterprises

The single common factor across all three communities as regards institutional rules was property rights, which had strong perception scores. It suggests that most respondents believe that they have adequate title protection and rights over their properties. This is in contrast to Power dynamics (which measures the balance of power and role of the leadership in determining the action of the followership) being established a third communality factor in Bida. This unique analysis perhaps underscores the extremely influential role of the Emir in Islamic communities where he is viewed as both a spiritual, political and economic leader of his people. There might be a need to better understand religion and entrepreneurship in Northern Nigeria, and how Islam impacts entrepreneurship arrangements. Islamic economics, which differs from Western capitalism by several measures, claims that Islam provides an 'all-encompassing model for social, economic, and political life'. Heftier (2006) Commercial shariah, for instance, differs drastically from Western business laws in several notable respects Khan (2006) and requires further assessment in follow up research.

The results of the factor analyses suggest that the null hypothesis must be accepted in this case. Institutional factors are perceived by the respondents as influencing community entrepreneurial behaviour in significantly different ways across the case community ventures studied. The implications of this are re-enforcement of the emerging argument for a more customised approach to 0 development policy at the community level which will be discussed in greater details in the latter part of the chapter.

Existing literature has sufficiently documented the influence of institutional factor conditions on venture performance (Ben Letaifa et al., 2016; Klapper et al., 2009). Policy measures and other political factors such as Freedoms, Tax and Property rights constitute the arrowhead by which governments attempt to not only intervene but also more importantly direct the course of socio-economic activity, (UNCTAD, 2012; World Bank, 2020). Incorporating these dimensions into the study might have initially seemed ambitious given the sheer complexity of the regulatory environment and the presence of institutional voids in emerging economies. Yet being arguably the least intimate of all the institutional factors, the perception of respondents of these factor conditions constitutes an important assessment of the direction of policy munificence. Africans, have on account of the pervasiveness of globalisation, begun to expect and indeed demand more of their governments, with policy frameworks increasingly being seen as socio-economic contracts between the government and the citizenry.

H_{04}: The direction and degree of influence of all institutional factors on the entrepreneurial behaviour of the community enterprises are **NOT** similar across all three case communities.

Decision: Accept null hypothesis.

The final analysis of the institutional factors influencing entrepreneurial behaviour at the community level studied the odds of explicit outcomes across the four established manifest variables based on Shane's (2003) articulation of the four stages of entrepreneurial behaviour; Opportunity Processing, Resource mobilisation, Strategy articulation, and venture deployment. Here the study sought to ascertain the strength and direction of a causal effect of one variable upon another (see Fig. 6.9).

This study shows a uniquely different set of strong relationships between combinations of institutional factor conditions or contexts and the manifested characteristics of community-based entrepreneurs to pursue community-based ventures along lines of entrepreneurial behaviours across all three locations. As shown in Fig. 6.9. The null hypothesis is accepted.

COMMUNITY VENTURE	FACTOR CLUSTERS	INSTITUTIONAL FACTOR COMMUNALITIES	OPPORTUNITY PROCESSING	RESOURCE MOBILIZATION	STRATEGY ARTICULATION	VENTURE DEPLOYMENT & MANAGEMENT
The Abeokuta Indigo Fabric Dye Community	FACTOR ONE	• Economic Stability • Capital • Taxation • Freedom • Power Dynamic	2X	3X	2X	2X
	FACTOR TWO	• Societal Wealth • Property Rights	1X	1X	1X	1X
The Nnewi Patent Medicine Store Chains	FACTOR ONE	• Societal Wealth • Economic Stability • Capital • Taxation • Freedom	1X	1X	1X	1X
	FACTOR TWO	• Property Rights • Power Dynamic	1X	1X	1X	1X
The Bida Brass Pottery Community	FACTOR ONE	• Societal Wealth • Freedom • Property Rights	2X	1X	1X	2X
	FACTOR TWO	• Economic Stability • Capital • Taxation • Freedom • Property Rights	3X	1X	1X	2X
	FACTOR THREE	• Power Dynamic	1X	1X	1X	1X

Fig. 6.9 Strength and direction of institutional factor communalities on community entrepreneurial behaviour across three Nigerian community enterprises

The study found that factor 1 variables for Institutional Rules (Economic Stability, Capital, Taxation, Freedom, and the Power Dynamic) are twice (2×) more likely to influence how opportunity is processed and enterprise strategy is developed by the Abeokuta indigo cloth dyers, than those communalities classified as factor 2 (Societal Wealth and Property rights), and three times (3×) more likely to influence how they mobilise resource and go on to develop the community enterprise.

In the case of the Nnewi patent medicine sellers, the findings show that the direction and strength of influence of institutional covariates classified as factor 1 (Societal Wealth, Economic Stability, Capital, Taxation and Freedom) is about the same (1×) as those classified as factor 2 (Property Rights and Power Dynamics) on resource mobilisation, strategy articulation and venture development while it is only marginally higher on opportunity process (1×).

The study finds an interesting occurrence regarding the institutional context in Bida, with the emergence of a third distinct factor. Here, the respondents, perceive the odds of the strength and direction of influence for factor 1 (Societal Wealth, Freedom and Property Rights) as being twice (2×) those of factor 3 (Power Dynamics) on how entrepreneurial opportunity is processed, while that of factor 2 (Economic Stability, Capital, Taxation,

Freedom and Property Rights) is about three times (3×) higher than those of factors 1 and 3, respectively.

The odds of the strength and direction of all three factor communalities (F1, F2 and F3) are about the same on resource mobilisation. The odds of factors 1 and 2 are about the same but each of them is only marginally higher than that of factor 3 on strategy articulation. Those of factors 1 and 2 are about two times (2×) higher than factor 3 on venture development.

The search for relevance and intimacy with the peculiarities of the contextual challenges communities face, requires policy authors and development consultants to be data and process driven. Hindle (2010) argues for the development of diagnostic tools as practice-oriented contributions to the field of entrepreneurship. The author argues that the findings from the fourth research question offers an important foundational premise from which to theorise along these lines. Indeed, the development of such a model or framework helps answer the study's strategic question by helping relevant stakeholders in the entrepreneurship development space within Africa to pay particular attention to the efficacy of communities being the effective units of performance measurement of policy and factor condition impact, and not just nations.

Factor One institutional commonalities in the Abeokuta case as well as the Factor One and Factor Two commonalities in the Bida case, are suggestive of peculiar institutional arrangements that must be paid attention to in their ability to have such uniquely significant and directional impact on the identified range of community entrepreneurship behaviours across these communities, respectively.

So, while societal wealth and capital availability might have long been argued to enhance the processing of entrepreneurial opportunity generally, it can be seen from the evidence, that members of a community (as individuals, groups or the community as a whole) can be better aided to learn and practice entrepreneurship (across the spectrum of entrepreneurial activities) in other ways (such as the promotion of *Factor One* commonalities on resource mobilisation in the South Western community of Abeokuta or Factor Two commonalities on opportunity recognition in the northern community of Bida) in a strong recognition of community diversity that yet seeks to preserve and enhance community integrity.

Conclusion

This chapter presented the findings on how institutional factor conditions, made up of both formal political and economic systems of regulations, incentives and institutional arrangements that enforce them, as well as informal set of values and conventions, influence community entrepreneurial behaviour. The research question and proposition going into the study was built on the seminal works of several authors who have long argued that institutional factors create contextual conditions of varying qualities which influence entrepreneurial behaviour. The study has sought to test this within community entrepreneurship settings and indeed confirms this. However, it also goes further to suggest that the institutional framework and context are different across the case communities, creating different typologies, which ultimately must be recognised when developing national entrepreneurship development policy.

The strategic question that the study has sought to answer is how the relationships between institutions factor conditions and community entrepreneurship behaviour might be better understood, with an argument that such an insight might help increase the supply and success of community-based entrepreneurs in African countries such as Nigeria through policy readjustments. The research challenge has been to unearth the truth about whether the range of environmental contexts these factors create, based on the various combinations of possible outcomes observed can be calibrated into distinct prognostic typologies to which interventionist policy measures and programmes may be bespoke.

The single common impacting institutional factor across all three communities studied was property rights, which had strong perception scores, suggesting that most respondents believe that they have adequate title protection and rights over their properties. The factor is however not as critical as other factors such as the perception of economic stability and tax, (which are seen by the majority of respondents in Abeokuta, and Bida as being contextually weak), in influencing entrepreneurial behaviour. Busenitz et al. (2000) propose that cross-national differences in entrepreneurship are best explained by a broader set of institutions, while Dia (1996) had provided an intriguing interpretation of the effects of social status, social relations and social transfers for African entrepreneurship. His approach to the subject explains institutional failures in Africa in terms of institutional disconnects, and consequently builds his argument for a solution in terms of institutional reconnection: reconciliation, twinning, linkages and capacity building of formal institutions.

Formal Institutional rules have traditionally been thought to be weak in Africa, with the broadly held view being that it is the informal institutional rules which tend to govern, by primarily granting legitimacy to widely held social conventions. The findings from Bida, where the emergence of power dynamics isolates the critical role of the traditional monarch as being more influential than the government establishment in directing the affairs of the citizens within that community, as a separate factor in its own right, suggests that is right and calls attention to the need to work with this emergent reality in the articulation of entrepreneurship development programs.

Ultimately, this research throws up the need for major institutional reforms. In developing a stronger institutional context, local as well as state (regional) governments will need to focus on strengthening macroeconomic stability, promoting accessible capital markets and progressive tax policies, as these factors have been shown within the research to have a significant impact on community entrepreneurial alertness; how community-based entrepreneurs process opportunity, as well as manage the community-based ventures.

Research Implications (Towards a New Diagnostic Model for Institutional Munificence for Community Entrepreneurship)

Hindle (2010) argues for the development of diagnostic tools as practice-oriented contributions to the field of entrepreneurship. He emphasises that the word 'diagnostic' should be preferred to the word 'analytical' because of the greater precision it offers. The essence of diagnosis as a formal activity is that it employs standard procedures to define a unique situation. This study invariable supports the development of such diagnostic frameworks as entrepreneurship development instruments that may be used to better categorise communities (as individuals, groups or the community as a whole) into clusters with contextual similarities. There is a contribution here in being able to help members of a community to learn and practice entrepreneurship (across the spectrum of entrepreneurial activities) in ways that both recognise community diversity, but which also seek to preserve and enhance community integrity. In developing such a diagnostic tool, the researcher believes that the findings from this study will be particularly helpful, in mapping the interrelatedness of various institutional factors (as suggested in Fig. 6.10) across community entrepreneurial behaviour.

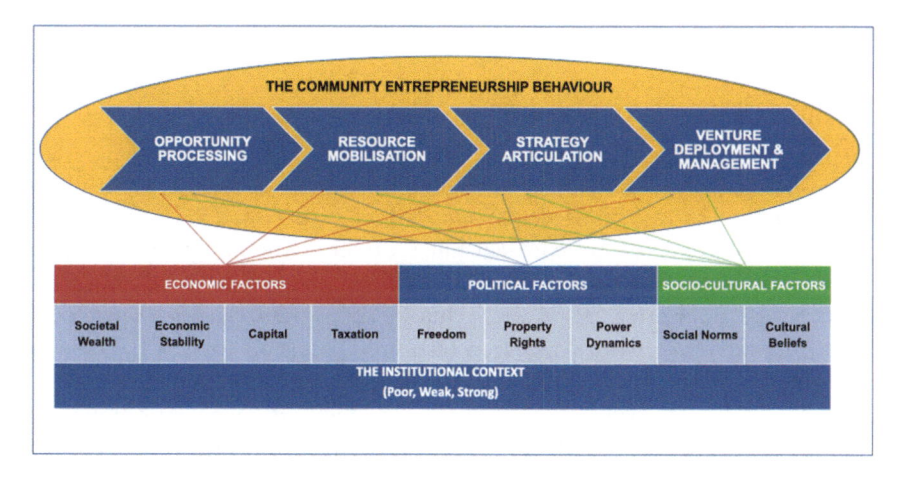

Fig. 6.10 The institutional context and community entrepreneurial behaviour

Limitations and Themes for Further Research

The results of this study offer several avenues for future research. The area of environmental factors and how they influence the human condition in business is always a fertile area for inquiry This study has been limited in part as to the generalisability of the findings on account of the scale of this study, thus it would be particularly useful to extend this study to many more communities with Nigeria and perhaps West Africa if not other regions to get a sense of how applicable these broad findings in how environmental conditions influence the entrepreneurship process.

It would also be expedient to return to the 'why' side of the research equation (behaviour and motivation), at some time, to better understand why these factors established as being significant influence the respondents in such a manner; why for instance is the Emir's role that dominant in commercial life and how do the respondents, and the cultural agent himself (The Emir), believe that such factors might be utilised to add further impetus to the vision of exploiting entrepreneurship as a veritable tool of fighting poverty in similar African countries. (Baum & Locke, 2004; Smith et al., 2001; Gartner, 1985).

Nigeria like several of its African peers still lacks imagination concerning the meaning of an entrepreneurial economy and a clear and properly coordinated framework for implementing entrepreneurship at all policy levels. What is needed most, is an intellectual and munificent environment, which encourages creative work and risk-taking behaviour at the community level. It is hoped that this research helps to move the discourse in that direction.

References

Acs, Z. J., & Audretsch, D. B. (1990). *Innovation and small firms*. Cambridge, MA: MIT Press.

Acs, Z., & Karlsson, C. (2002). Introduction to institutions, entrepreneurship and firm growth: The case of Sweden. *Small Business Economics, 19*, 63–67.

Adusei, M. (2016). Does entrepreneurship promote economic growth in Africa? *African Development Review, 28*(2), 201–214.

Audretsch, D. B., Carree, M. A., & Thurik, A. R. (2001). *Does entrepreneurship reduce unemployment?* Tinbergen Institute Discussion Paper T1. Tinbergen Institute.

Audretsch, D. B., & Keilbach, M. (2007). The localization of entrepreneurship capital: Evidence from Germany. *Papers in Regional Science, Wiley Blackwell, 86*(3), 351–365.

Baum, J. R., & Locke, E. A. (2004). The relationship between entrepreneurial traits, skills, and motivation to subsequent venture growth. *Journal of Applied Psychology, 89*(4), 587–598.

Baumol, W. J. (1990). Entrepreneurship: Productive, unproductive, and destructive. *Journal of Political Economy, 98* (5, Part 1).

Blanchflower, D. G. (2000). Self-employment in OECD countries. *Labour Economics, 7*(5), 471–505.

Blanchflower, D. G., & Meyer, B. (1994). A longitudinal analysis of the young self-employed in Australia and the United States. *Small Business Economics, 6*, 1–20.

Ben Letaifa, S., & Goglio-Primard, K. (2016). How does institutional context shape entrepreneurship conceptualizations? *Journal of Business Research, 69*(11), 5128–5134.

Bourdieu, P. (1984). *Distinction: A social critique of the judgment of taste*. Harvard University Press.

Bryman, A., & Bell, E. (2007). *Business research methods*. USA: Oxford University Press.

Busenitz, L. W., Gomez, C., & Spencer, J. W. (2000). Country institutional profiles: Unlocking entrepreneurial phenomena. *Academy of Management Journal, 43*, 994–1003.

Codd, J., Harker, R., and Nash, R. (Eds). (1985). *Political issues in New Zealand education*. Palmerston North.

Covin, J. A., & Slevin, D. P. (1991). A conceptual model of entrepreneurship as firm behavior. *Entrepreneurship: Theory and Practice*, 7–25.

Coase, R. H., & Wang, N. (2011). The industrial structure of production: A research agenda for innovation in an entrepreneurial economy. *Entrepreneurship Research Journal, 1*(2), 1–11.

Creswell, J. W. (1998). *Qualitative inquiry and research design*. Sage Publications.

Dana, L. P., & Ratten, V. (2017). International entrepreneurship in resource landlocked African countries. *Journal of International Entrepreneurship, 15*(4), 416–435.

Dana, L. P. Ratten, V., & Honyenuga, B. Q. (2018). Introduction to African entrepreneurship. In L. P. Dana., V. Ratten & B. Honyenuga (Eds.), *African entrepreneurship*. Palgrave Studies of Entrepreneurship in Africa. Palgrave Macmillan.

Davidsson, P. A. (2005). *Researching entrepreneurship*. Springer.

Davidsson, P. A., & Wiklund, J. (1997). Values, beliefs and regional variations in new firm formation rates. *Journal of Economic Psychology, 18*(2), 179–199.

Davidsson, P., Hunter, E., & Klofsten, M. (2006). Institutional forces: The invisible hand that shapes venture ideas? *International Small Business Journal, 24*(2).

De Bruin, A., & Dupuis, A. (1995). A closer look at New Zealand's superior economic performance: Ethnic employment issues. *British Review of New Zealand Studies, 8*, 85–87.

De Bruin, A. A., & Power, T. (2001). The role of community employment creation: Lessons and challenges for a new era. In P. Morrison (Ed), *Labour employment and work in New Zealand*. Proceedings of the Ninth Conference. Victoria University Wellington.

Dia, M. (1996). *Africa's management in the 1990s and beyond: Reconciling indigenous and transplanted institutions* (2nd ed.). World Bank.

DiMaggio, P. J., & Powell, W. (1983). The iron cage revisited institutional isomorphism and collective rationality in organisational fields. *American Sociological Review, 48*(1983), 147–160.

Fadahunsi, A., & Rosa, P. (2002). Entrepreneurship and illegality: Insights from the Nigerian cross—Border trade. *Journal of Business Venturing, 17*(5), 397–429.

Frese, M. (2000). *Success and failure of micro business owners in Africa: A psychological approach*. Quorum Books.

Gartner, W. (1985). A conceptual framework for describing the phenomenon of new venture creation. *The Academy of Management Review, 10*.

Gnyawali, D., & Fogel, D. (1994). Environments for entrepreneurship development: Key dimensions and research implications. *Entrepreneurship: Theory and Practice, 18*(4), 43–62.

Harper, D. A. (1996). *Entrepreneurship and the market process: An enquiry into the growth of knowledge*. Routledge.

Harper, D. A. (1997). Institutional conditions for entrepreneurship. *Advances in Austrian Economics, 5*, 241–275.

Hayton, K. (1995). Community involvement in economic regeneration lessons from North East England. *Community Developement Journal, 30*(2), 169–179.

Hayton, K. (1996). A critical examination of the role of community business in urban regeneration. *Town Planning Review, 67*(1), 1–20.

Hayton, J., Gerard, G., & Shaker, Z. (2002). National culture and entrepreneurship: A review of behavioral research. *Entrepreneurship Theory and Practice., 26*, 33–52.

Heftier, R. W. (2006). Slamic economics and global capitalism. *Society, 44*(1), 16–22.

Hindle, K. (2010). How community context affects entrepreneurial process: A diagnostic framework. *Entrepreneurship and Regional Development, 22*(7), 599–647.

Hofstede, G. N. (1984). The cultural relativity of the quality of life concept. *Academy of Management Review, 9*(3), 389–398. Also, In G. Redding (Eds), *International cultural differences*, 1995.

Hofstede, G. N. (1994). Management scientists are human. *Management Science, 40*(1), 4–13.

Hofstede, G. N. (2001). Cultures consequences. *Effect of cultural values and ESE on intentions* (2nd ed). Sage.

Hofstede, G. N. (2004). Culture's role in entrepreneurship: Self-employment out of dissatisfaction. In T. E. Brown & J. Ulijn (Eds.), *Innovation, entrepreneurship and culture: The interaction between technology, progress and economic growth*. Edward Elgar Publishing.

Hofstede, G. N., & McCrae, R. R. (2004). Personality and culture revisited: Linking traits and dimensions of culture. *Cross-Cultural Research, 38*(1), 52–88.

Jennings, P. D., Greenwood, R., Lounsbury, M. D., & Suddaby, R. (2013). Institutions, entrepreneurs, and communities: A special issue on entrepreneurship. *Journal of Business Venturing, 28*(1), 1–9.

Julien, P. A. (2007). *A theory of local entrepreneurship in the knowledge economy*.

Kallon. (1990). *The economics of Sierra Leonean entrepreneurship*. University of America press.

Khan, A. (2006). The interaction between sharia and international law in arbitration. *Chicago Journal of International Law, 6*(2), 791–802.

Kiggundu, M. N. (2002). Entrepreneurs and entrepreneurship in Africa: What is known and what needs to be done. *Journal of Developmental Entrepreneurship, 7*, 239–258.

Klapper, L., Lewin, A., & Delgado, J. M. Q. (2009). The impact of business environment on the business creation process, *The World Bank Policy*. Research Working Paper Series 4937.

Kinunda-Rutashobya, L. (1999). African entrepreneurship and small business development: Emerging research issues. In L. Rutashobya. & D. Olomi (Eds.), *African entrepreneurship and small business development* (pp. 19–52). Dar es sallam University Press.

Kleymeyer, C. (1994) Introduction. In C. Kleymeyer (Ed.), *Cultural expression and grassroots development*. Lynne Rienner Publishers.

Koveos, P. A. (2006). Shaping the field of developmental entrepreneurship. *Journal of Developmental Entrepreneurship (JDE), 11*(4), 275–276.

Luthans, F., Stajkovic, A., & Ibrayeva, E. (2000). Environmental and psychological challenges facing entrepreneurial development on transitional economies. *The Journal of World Business, 35*(1), 95–110.

Manolova, T., Eunni, R., & Gyoshev, B. (2008). Institutional environments for entrepreneurship: Evidence from emerging economies in eastern Europe. *Entrepreneurship Theory and Practice, 32*, 203–218.

Martinez, M. A., Yang, T., & Aldrich, H. E. (2011). Entrepreneurship as an evolutionary process: Research progress and challenges. *Entrepreneurship Research Journal, 1*(1) Article 4.

McGrath, R. G., MacMillan, I. C., Yang, E. A., Tsai, W. (1992). Does culture endure, or is it malleable? Issues for entrepreneurial economic development. *Journal of business venturing, 7*, 115–135.

Morris, M. H., Davis, D. L., & Allen, J. W. (1994). Fostering corporate entrepreneurship: Cross-cultural comparisons of the importance of individualism versus collectivism. *Journal of International Business Studies, 25*(1), 65–89.

Murithi, W. (2019, 9–13th August). *Dynamics of family businesses and their implications on creation of social value: Evidence from Kenya a Sub-Saharan Africa country.* 79th Annual Meeting of the Academy of Management: Understanding Inclusive Organisation.

North, D. C. (1990). *Institutions.* Institutional Change and Economic Performance. New York: Cambridge University Press.

North, D. C. (2005). *Understanding the process of economic change.* University Press.

Ogunsade, I. A., & Obembe, D. (2016). The influence of informal institutions on informal sector entrepreneurship: A study of Nigeria's hand-woven textile industry. *Journal of Small Business & Entrepreneurship, 28*, 1-17.

Ojo, S., Nwankwo, S., & Gbadamosi, A. (2013). African diaspora entrepreneurs navigating entrepreneurial spaces in 'home' and 'host' countries. *Entrepreneurship and Innovation, 14*(4), 289–299.

Peredo, A. M., & Chrisman, J. J. (2006). Toward a theory of community-based enterprise. *Academy of Management Review, 31*(2), 309–328.

Portes, A., & Jensen, L. (1989). The enclave and the entrants: Patterns of ethnic enterprise in Miami before and after Mariel. *American Sociological Review., 54*, 929–949.

Portes, A., Fernandez-Kelly, P., & Haller, W. (2005). Segmented assimilation on the ground: The new second generation in early adulthood. *Ethnic and Racial Studies, 28*, 1000–1040.

Ramachandran, V., & Shah, M. K. (1999). Minority entrepreneurs and firm performance in Sub- Saharan Africa. *Journal of Development Studies, Taylor & Francis Journals, 36*(2), 71–87.

Rees, H., & Shah, A. (1986). An empirical analysis of self-employment in the UK. *Journal of Applied Econometrics, 1*, 95–108.

Sackmann, S. A., & Phillips, M. E. (2004). Contextual influences on culture research: Shifting assumptions for new workplace realities. *International Journal of Cross-Cultural Management, 4*, 370–390.

Schumpeter, J. A. (1947). *Capitalism, socialism and democracy.* New York: Harper & Brothers Publishers.

Shane, S. (1994). Are champions different from non-champions? *Journal of Business Venturing, Elsevier, 9*(5), 397–421.

Shane, S. (2003). *A general theory of entrepreneurship*. Edward Elgar.

Shane, S., & Venkataraman, S. (2000). The promise of entrepreneurship as a field of research. *Academy of Management Review, 25*(1), 217–469.

Singh, K., & Mitchell, W. (1995). The effect of partner performance on business survival in the U.S. hospital software systems industry, 1961–1991.

SMEDAN. (2007). *Public presentation of draft national policy on MSME in Kano and Lagos* (Online). Available at: https://smedan.gov.ng/downloads/. Accessed 17 June 2019

SMEDAN. (2019). *National policy on MSMEs* (Online). Available at: https://smedan.gov.ng/downloads/. Accessed 17 June 2019.

Smith, K., Baum, J., & Locke, E. (2001). A multi-dimensional model of venture growth. *The Academy of Management Journal, 44*(10).

Somerville, P., & McElwee, G. (2011, June). Situating community enterprise: A theoretical exploration.*Entrepreneurship & Regional Development, 23*(5–6), 317–330

Steensma, H. K. (2000). Attitudes toward cooperative strategies: A cross cultural analysis of entrepreneurs. *Journal of International Business Studies, 31*, 591–609.

Stevenson, L., & Lundstrom, A. A. (2007). Dressing the emperor: The fabric of entrepreneurship policy. In D. B. Audretsch, I. Grilo, & A. Thurik (Eds.), *Handbook of research on entrepreneurship policy*. Edward Elgar Publishing.

Tan, W. L. (2002). Entrepreneurship challenges ahead for Singapore. Extrepreneurship in Asia expert workshop, Hong Kong, 28 June 2002. Research Collection Lee Kong Chian School Of Business.

Themba, G., Chamme, M., Phambuka, C. A., & Makgosa, R. (1999). A framework for understanding the role of culture in Sub-Sahara Africa. *Journal of Business Venturing, 8*, 91–98.

Thurik, R., Lorraine, U., & Jan, H. (2002). *Post-Materialism as a cultural factor influencing entrepreneurial activity across nations*. EIM Business and Policy Research, Scales Research Reports.

Tiessen, J. H. (1997). Individualism, collectivism and entrepreneurship: A framework for international comparative research. *Journal of Business Venturing, 12*, 367–384.

Triandis, H. C. (1994). Cross-cultural industrial and organisational psychology. In H. C. Triandis, M. D. Dunette & L. M. Hough. (Eds.), *Handbook of industrial and organisational psychology*. (Vol. 4, pp. 103–172).

Trompenaar, A., & Hampen-Turner, C. (1997). *Riding the waves of culture: Understanding diversity in global business*. Irwin Professional (burr Ridge, III).

UNCTAD. (2012). *Development-centred globalization: Towards inclusive and sustainable growth and development*.

Venkataraman, S. (1997). The distinctive domain of entrepreneurship research: An editor's perspective. In J. A. Katz & R. H. Brockhaus (Eds.), *Advances in entrepreneurship, firm*.

Vershinina, N., Woldesenbet, B. K., & Murithi, W. (2017). How does national culture enable or constrain entrepreneurship? Exploring the role of Harambee in Kenya. *Journal of Small Business and Enterprise Development, 25*(4), 687–704.

Welter, F. (2011). Contextualizing entrepreneurship—Conceptual challenges and ways forward. *Entrepreneurship Theory and Practice, 35*(1), 165–184.

Wennkers, A. R. M., Uhlaner, L. M., & Thurik, A. R. (2002). Entrepreneurship and its conditions: A macro perspective. *International Journal of Entrepreneurship Education, 1*(1), 25–64.

World Bank. (2020). *Nigeria's macroeconomic data* (Online). Available at: https://data.worldbank.org/. Accessed 25 August 2020.

Yin, R. K. (2003). *Case study research: Design and methods* (3rd ed.). Sage.

Zahra, S. (1993). A conceptual model of entrepreneurship as firm behaviour: A critique and extension. *Entrepreneurship: Theory and Practice, 17*(4), 5–21.

7

The Impact of Entrepreneurship Framework and Behaviour on Diaspora Remittance: An African Perspective

Samuel Salia, Javed G. Hussain, Yahaya Alhassan, and Masud Ibrahim

Introduction

Diaspora remittance[1] into Africa is widely considered a poverty reduction tool through smoothing household consumption and fulfilling government balance of payment. As a result, the empirical evidence is focused on balance of payment and household consumption as drivers of remittance into Africa (Ajefu et al., 2020; Amidu et al., 2019; Huay & Bani, 2018; Siani, 2020). However, a significant population of the diaspora are interested in remitting finance into the home country to set up enterprises (Jia & Sun, 2020; Saadi,

---

[1] Arthur et al. (2020) defines migrant remittance as the amount of funds remitted by the diaspora to the home country during a given period.

S. Salia (✉)
De Montfort University, Leicester, UK
e-mail: samuel.salia@dmu.ac.uk

J. G. Hussain
Birmingham City University, Birmingham, UK

Y. Alhassan
University of Sunderland, London, UK

M. Ibrahim
Coventry University, Coventry, UK

2020; Williams, 2020). Therefore, whether the format of entrepreneurial ecosystem in African countries drives remittance inflow is an important question that this study wishes to address.

It is widely documented that Africa is one of the poorest continents in the world despite its abundant resources (Lone & Ahmad, 2020). In terms of poverty and debt, according to the World Bank indicators, the continent has persistently underperformed, thus the need to develop policy to address the malaise of the continent. Most African nations have gained their independence largely from European colonies in the 1950s and 1960s; that in theory may have enabled the countries to develop through retained resources, however, the evidence is contrary. As agrarian societies, Africa consistently struggle with stagnating economic growth, skills shortage and declining commodity prices (e.g. oil). In response to these challenges in the 1980s, most countries in the continent embraced International Monetary Fund (IMF) structural adjustment programmes (SAP) aimed at creating an enabling environment for the private sector to contribute and stimulate economic growth. As a result, initiatives such as creating business-friendly environments and promoting economic integration were widely adopted (Cummings et al., 2020; Nwankwo, 2011) in an attempt to alleviate poverty and foster skills development. Whilst the programmes were widely embraced by African nations, most of the drawbacks have been widely associated with resource mismanagement and lack of source of finance (Lall, 1995). Also, government efforts without wider stakeholder engagement are insufficient to develop an entrepreneurial ecosystem based around creating supportive environments to foster innovative start-ups (Acs et al., 2017; Cavallo et al., 2019; Premand et al., 2016).

Following the three debt reliefs launched in 1996 (the Heavily Indebted Poor Countries Initiative, HIPC), 1999 (The enhanced HIPC initiative) and 2005 (Multilateral Debt Relief Initiative, MDRI) various attempts to understand the effect of these programmes on African countries have yielded some interesting patterns (see Cassimon et al., 2015; Djimeu, 2018) for the positive fiscal response effects of the debt relief initiatives. The focus of donor institution policies has been to encourage African economies to reduce public sector cost and encourage private sector to align domestic market conditions with WTO rules (see Cheru, 2002).

However, the prognosis to address entrepreneurship under development is a complex one. There is a tendency for African countries to import rather than develop self-sufficiency; this practice stagnates development of home-grown firms over time (Romero-Barrutieta et al., 2015). The other common theme amongst African economies is ill-conceived privatisation approaches that instead of promoting enterprise tends to reduce competition and gives rise to monopolies. Such models limit the ability of the poor to access finance and engage with enterprise. The situation is further worsened as the WTO trade rules, as extension of liberalisation policies, tend to hamper the capacity of African governments to support indigenous enterprise development. Hence, African nations need strategies that promote innovation, development of skills and attract finance (Adeoye et al., 2020; Efobi et al., 2019).

The propositions put forward by academics (Letiche, 2010; Mijiyawa, 2017; Nissanke, 2019) are that certain conditions and transformational actions, with a focus on entrepreneurship, are necessary for African nations to attract finance and to exit poverty (Brixiova, 2010). Whilst, there has been an increased emphasis to promote the private sector (William Lyakurwa, 2009), there seems to be lack of partnership amongst decision-makers and the African diaspora,[2] in order to attract remittance for meaningful enterprise development. A key element of that partnership is the creation of an entrepreneurship ecosystem that attracts diaspora resources (Minto-Coy et al., 2018).

Irrespective of this, most of the previous literature tends to focus on household consumptions and government balance of payment as drivers of diaspora remittance. This study aims to bridge the gap to aid policy formulation regarding response to the drivers of Diaspora remittance and to enhance understanding of how to help entrepreneurs and entrepreneurial ecosystems thrive (Abubakar et al., 2018; Efobi et al., 2019).

Our study makes significant contribution to academic literature and policy implication. First, it explores the potential ways through which an ecosystem can be developed to link entrepreneurship with access to finance. Diaspora remittance can be an important funding source for entrepreneurship activities in Africa—a continent associated with a long history of financing challenges (Plaza & Ratha, 2011). Second, our evidence shed light on the crucial role entrepreneurial behaviour and attitudes combined with entrepreneurship framework play in driving diaspora remittance inflows into Africa. Whilst prior studies (Amidu et al., 2019; Lartey et al., 2012) provide extensive empirical evidence on household consumption and balance of payment as drivers of remittance, a paucity of study demonstrates how entrepreneurial behaviour and attitudes are likely to impact diaspora remittance. We further shed light on how some country-specific attributes such as a country's capacity to attract talent and retain human capital; enables the population

---

[2] From the African Union (2005) perspective, the diaspora is 'peoples of African heritage living outside the continent, irrespective of their host country's citizenship, and who remain committed to contribute to the development of the continent and the building of the African Union'.

to innovate and use technology. We argue that a holistic policy framework is required from international organisations such as World Bank, Africa Development Bank and African Union towards raising awareness of this key source of finance to promote entrepreneurial related projects.

The paper proceeds as follows: the next section provides a review of previous studies, followed by presentation of the data and the empirical model for the study with the identification strategy and estimation method discussed. The empirical results with discussions are then reported and the final section presents the conclusion of the study.

Literature Review

Entrepreneurship ecosystem is credited as a regional economic development approach based around creating supportive environments to foster innovative start-ups (Acs et al., 2017; Cavallo et al., 2019). Most recently, institutional structures and collaborating networks of entrepreneurial activities are documented as supportive environments that open up channels for small businesses to access finance (Anton & Bostan, 2017). Access to affordable finance, which can make businesses competitive, remains a major barrier to entrepreneurship growth and the entrepreneurship ecosystem in Africa is underdeveloped (Atiase et al., 2018).

Attributes of an entrepreneurial ecosystem as described by (Acs et al., 2017; Cavallo et al., 2019) are incorporated in the entrepreneurial framework and entrepreneurial attitudes developed by Global Entrepreneurships Monitor (GEM) to aid understanding of how to help entrepreneurs and entrepreneurial ecosystems thrive (Abubakar et al., 2018; Efobi et al., 2019). However, the literature search suggest there is limited evidence that examines the entrepreneurial framework and entrepreneurial behaviour (see Brixiová et al., 2015) required in the home country to attract remittance from the diaspora. Over the recent past, studies have started to examine the 'gap'; however (Ahuja & Purankar, 2018; Brixiova, 2010; Dalmarco et al., 2018) suggest, the government and policy-makers at large lack the realisation of the importance of Africans in the diaspora.

Diaspora population presence and participation within the economies of Western countries have been praised in terms of their engagement with enterprise and their contribution to the economy (Flisi & Murat, 2011; Kloosterman & Rath, 2010; Kourtit et al., 2013; Priebe & Rudolf, 2015). For example, a study of Chinese and Indian entrepreneurs in Silicon Valley shows that companies founded by immigrants employed 45,000 workers and generated $52 billion in revenue (Hill & Ram, 2010). Furthermore, evidence suggests overwhelming rise of entrepreneurial skills amongst diaspora residing in diversified economies such as Germany, France, United Kingdom and United States of America (Kloosterman & Rath, 2010; Kotabe et al., 2013). Therefore, the existing evidence proves a growing acknowledgement of the potential resources in the emigrant populations towards problem-solving which translates into the current academic interests.

What is more significant, despite turbulence amongst African countries, the outlook in remittance is somewhat larger or equivalent to, the official foreign exchange reserves, in the case of many Africa countries (Ratha, 2016). Diaspora remittance, wield a positive effect on the receiving country's balance of payment position, increase household consumption and lead to greater savings amongst the population (Caballé & Santos, 1993; Cattaneo, 2005; Rapoport & Docquier, 2006). The suggestion is that effective utilisation of diaspora remittance in priority areas such as, investment in entrepreneurial activities will lead to increase in job creation and rise in income levels (Amuedo-Dorantes & Bansak, 2014). Notwithstanding the stylised facts about shifting diaspora remittance into the form of diaspora finance[3], their impact will depend on African countries financial innovativeness and capacity to build trust to mobilise the resources of diaspora through special investment vehicles (Plaza & Ratha, 2011).

Technology intensive economies experiences suggest the growth in the use of technology is accompanied by demand for well-equipped and skilled employees. This structural change has led to outflow of human capital from developing to developed economies, further creating shortage of trained employees in Africa and other emerging economies. The outward migration flow from Africa has increased the pool of diaspora, hence the increased level of remittance. The positive impact of Silicon Valley entrepreneurs connecting their homeland to California through technological transfers and the impact of return to rural China is well documented (Mayer et al., 2015). Thus, aside from sharing of finance, the diaspora can also benefit the home country through skills transfer and expectations of how business should be conducted. Given their mixed life experiences, a diaspora is able to obtain the benefits of the institutional environments of their host country and their home country (Brzozowski et al., 2014). Besides, the dual entrepreneurial cultures acquired through the process of living in both home and host countries are sensitive to institutional contexts (Estrin et al., 2016) and impacts entrepreneurial activity

---

[3] Finance provided by the diaspora for investment in their country of origin. This finance is often devoted to investment in financial assets or enterprise (Salia et al., 2020).

in the home country. The role model 'demonstration effect', whereby residents in the diaspora's country of origin are encouraged to emulate and accept skills of the diaspora returnee that generates significant benefits in countries with low levels of innovative or disruptive skills (Mayer et al., 2015).

It is imperative for African countries to develop appropriate entrepreneurial frameworks and inculcate entrepreneurial attitudes to harness the much-needed capital: financial, human, physical and social for enterprise development. Historically, African countries have not developed a supportive business environment to leverage on the resources of their diaspora (Chand, 2016) as a more predictable source of financial inflow. Contrary, the documented evidence suggest Africa has focused on drivers of household consumption and setting balance of payment measures to boost remittance (Lartey et al., 2012; Ratha, 2011). This viewpoint is a contrast to several developing countries in Asia (such as, China, India and Philippines etc.) that have recognised the importance of their diaspora and developed entrepreneurial ecosystems to attract remittance. This has enabled them to develop specific capabilities to attract opportunities for entrepreneurial activities (Strielkowski et al., 2017). Such approaches have led to improvement within local economies, job creation and poverty alleviation (Chand, 2016). The impact and importance of diaspora remittance suggests African countries needs to have a broader view of the diaspora beyond a mere source of remittances; they need to build a substantial and meaningful entrepreneurship framework and behaviour to attract diaspora remittance to contribute to enterprise development.

Data and Methodology

Data and Sources

We discussed in this section, the data sources and sampling description used to operationalise the key independent variable of interest (Entrepreneurship ecosystem), the dependent variable (Diaspora remittance) and the control variables for the study. Following Atiase et al. (2018), information on entrepreneurship ecosystem is obtained from global entrepreneurship and development institute platform via global entrepreneurship monitor (GEM) database. Data from this platform includes information on the measure of inter-country entrepreneurial performance relating to quality and depth of entrepreneurship ecosystem reported for 137 countries. Because we are interested in Africa, we obtain a list of all the 54 African countries, which have been reported on during our period of study. We started by generating descriptive observations related to all variables for the 54 African countries. From the descriptive observations, we were able to retrieve data for 20 African countries, which did not have missing data.

We focused exclusively on the list of the 20 African countries. Using this list we were able to obtain annual remittance inflow data for these countries from the World Bank migrant remittance database reported for 214 countries and territories. Because we are interested in African countries, we excluded all remittances from one African country to the other. Information from this database has been extensively used by several studies (Aggarwal et al., 2006; Amuedo-Dorantes & Pozo, 2006; Lartey et al., 2012). Finally, we merged the two datasets with Global Competitive index on aggregate country-specific attributes relating to talent and innovation from 2007–2018 to obtain our final panel sample involving 20 African countries for 2007–2018. Please see Table 7.1 for detailed definition and construction of this index.

Variables Definition

Dependent and Independent Variable

The primary dependent variable for the study is Diaspora remittance. The study seeks to understand the sensitivity of remittance inflow to level of entrepreneurship ecosystem in the sample countries. Thus, the aim is to collect data on remittance inflows in the countries in our sample. In line with this, we employ Arthur et al. (2020) definition of migrant remittance as the amount of funds remitted by the diaspora to the home country during a given period.

The primary independent variable is entrepreneurship ecosystem, which is measured via the GEM adult population survey (i.e. entrepreneurial behaviour and attitudes) and the national expert survey (i.e. entrepreneurial framework conditions). This is consistent with Atiase et al. (2018). Measures of the entrepreneurial behaviour and attitudes are focus on entrepreneurial activity, attitudes and aspirations of respondents. Whilst measures of the entrepreneurial framework conditions are focused on entrepreneurial finance, government programmes and policies, market regulations, cultural and social norms, R&D transfer and education. Detailed definitions of each of these variables can be found in Table 7.1.

Table 7.1 Variables and sources

Concept	Variable	Sources	Remark
Diaspora financing strategies (DFS)	Migrant remittance inflows (MRI)	World Bank	This concept has been used in the past to understand diaspora strategies (see Aggarwal et al., 2006; Amuedo-Dorantes & Pozo, 2006 Lartey et al., 2012)
Entrepreneurship framework conditions (EFC)	• Financing for entrepreneurs (FfE) • Governmental support and policies (GSP) • Taxes and bureaucracy (TxB) • Governmental programmes (GPr) • Basic school entrepreneurial education and training (BSE) • Post-school entrepreneurial education and training (PSE) • R&D transfer (RDT) • Cultural and social norms (CSN)	Global entrepreneurship monitor (GEM)	This term has been conceptualised in the previous literature (see Audretsch & Belitski, 2017; Valliere, 2010)
Entrepreneurial behaviour and attitudes (EBA)	• Perceived opportunities (POp) • Perceived capabilities (PCp) • Entrepreneurial intentions (EnI) • Total early-stage Entrepreneurial Activity (TEA) • Motivational Index (MoI) • Female/Male TEA (FMT) • High Job Creation Expectation (HJE) • Innovation (Inn) • High Status to Successful Entrepreneurs (HSE)	Global entrepreneurship monitor (GEM)	O'Gorman, C. (2019) This term has been conceptualised in the previous literature (see O'Gorman, 2019)

(continued)

Table 7.1 (continued)

Concept	Variable	Sources	Remark
Control variables	• Country capacity to retain talent (CRT) • Country capacity to attract talent (CAT) • Capacity for innovation (CfI) • Availability of latest technology (ALT) • FDI & technology transfer (FTT) • Attitude towards entrepreneurial risk (AER) • Companies embracing disruptive ideas (CDI) • Multi stakeholder collaboration (MSC)—*Instrumental variable* • Collaboration between companies (CBC)—*Instrumental variable* • Entrepreneurship (Ent)—*Instrumental variable*	IMF	

Source Authors analysis based on research design

Control Variables

In line with previous studies (Micozzi & Lucarelli, 2016), several country-specific characteristics are controlled for, namely: Country capacity to retain talent, Country capacity to attract talent, Capacity for innovation, Availability of latest technology, FDI & technology transfer, Attitude towards entrepreneurial risk and Companies embracing disruptive ideas. Detailed definitions of these variables can be found in Table 7.1.

Multivariate Regression Models

We employ the following baseline multivariate regression equations for our empirical model specification for this study. In order to test our hypotheses, we employ the following model specifications for diaspora remittances in relation to (1) behaviour and attitudes measurements or attributes, (2) entrepreneurial framework conditions and (3), we employ transformational entrepreneurship related variables to remittance in addition to the set of control variables.

$$DFS_{i,t} = \text{Intercept} + \beta_1 EFC_{i,t} + \beta_2 EBA_{i,t}$$
$$+\beta_3 \text{Control\_variables}_{i,t} + \varepsilon_{i,t} \quad (7.1)$$

$$EBA_{i,t} = \text{Intercept} + \beta_1 EFC_{i,t} + \beta_2 DFS_{i,t}$$
$$+\beta_3 \text{Control\_variables}_{i,t} + \varepsilon_{i,t} \quad (7.2)$$

where $DFS_{i,t}$ is the dependent variable in model 1, which is measured by country's level of migrant's remittance inflows at period t. $EFC_{i,t}$ indicates entrepreneurship framework conditions in each country at time t, measured by a set of variables as presented in Table 7.1. EBA stands for entrepreneurial behaviour and attitudes in country i, at time t, measured by a set of variables presented in Table 7.1.

In order to examine the impact of the EFC on the DFS, we use Eq. 7.1 where set of variables representing EFC and EBA are regressed against the MRI. We are equally interested in the coefficient results from interaction between DFS and EFC (DFCxEFC) in order to affect the EBA within a given country. Hence, we argue that if more diaspora remittances interact with favourable entrepreneurship conditions, the entrepreneurial behaviour and attitudes in a country will flourish. In order to identify the important variable to be used in establishing entrepreneurial behaviour and attitudes, we carry out exploratory factor analysis.

Instrumental Variables Approach

To examine the association between diaspora remittance and transformational entrepreneurship in Africa, we adopt an instrumental variable approach (two-stage least squares) to deal with any potential endogeneity issue. The instrument must satisfy two conditions to be valid. First, the endogenous variable and the instrumental variable must be correlated (the relevance condition). Second, our instrument must satisfy the exclusion condition, meaning that it should not be correlated with the error term of the second-stage equation. We estimate Eq. 7.1 using an instrumental variable regression (IV) with region dummies and country dummies with country-level clustered standard errors. We include several country-level variables to control for cross-sectional differences in country characteristics that have potential to affect the relationship between diaspora remittance and transformational entrepreneurship in Africa.

Robustness Check

We carried out several diagnostic checks to obtain reasonable evidence of the fitness of our model to the data and in satisfaction of the fundamental OLS assumptions.

Results and Discussions

We start by examining the basic characteristics of our variables with summary statistics focusing on mean and standard deviation of each variable across the three tiers namely: DFS, EBA and EFC. Tables 7.2 and 7.3 provide descriptive statistics of the variables we use in the study for our selected sample of 20 African countries. From Table 7.2, we find that standard deviation for most of the variables are low meaning there is not much deviation from mean values. The results show the slow nature of African countries in developing entrepreneurship activities vis-à-vis entrepreneurship framework conditions and entrepreneurial behaviour and attitudes. A few exceptions are countries that introduced some reforms and funding targeting entrepreneurship like Algeria, Angola, Cameroon, Egypt, Nigeria, Tunisia and Uganda (that have witnessed rapid improvement in its entrepreneurial intentions).

In Table 7.3, we find that diaspora remittance inflow has massively increased for some countries such as Algeria, Burkina Faso, Ghana and Nigeria. This may not be unrelated with the current transformational measures being taken to boost some entrepreneurship activities and make their economics diversified and attractive to the outsider community including diaspora. Other countries that recently experienced Arab spring— e.g. Egypt and Libya are yet to witness high diaspora remittances possibly because of economic destruction led by the spring. However, Tunisia indicates some progress with some economic restructuring that is attracting diaspora investments. We show correlation analysis in Table 7.4.

Table 7.5 presents the regression results based on OLS estimation. We find that diaspora remittance is influenced by many factors that build up country-specific entrepreneurship framework conditions and many other country-specific attributes included as control variables. More specifically, financing for entrepreneurs, basic entrepreneurial education and training are

Table 7.2 Summary statistics—mean and standard deviation of EFC and EBA variables

Economy	Variable	FfE	GSP	TxB	GPr	BSE	PSE	RDT	CSN	PcO	PCp	EnI	TEA	MoI	FMT	HJE	Inn	HSE
Algeria	Mean	3.19	3.21	2.66	2.98	2.29	3.05	2.81	3.12	52.55	55.32	30.33	9.90	1.92	1.08	17.00	17.42	76.31
	Std. Dev	0.26	0.07	0.12	0.2	0.14	0.34	0.08	0.11	7.16	3.19	10.17	4.93	0.88	0.00	7.42	5.15	12.17
Angola	Mean	2.35	2.55	2.21	2.13	1.86	2.26	1.75	2.86	68.06	65.14	51.51	28.60	1.34	0.87	16.74	17.61	76.73
	Std. Dev	0.45	0.3	0.06	0.21	0.14	0.11	0.06	0.05	6.53	9.84	20.20	7.76	0.42	0.15	6.46	3.89	7.46
Botswana	Mean	2.65	2.61	2.50	2.54	2.39	2.95	2.27	2.81	61.89	69.82	64.09	28.63	1.66	0.82	32.11	23.30	79.28
	Std. Dev	0.15	0.12	0.17	0.14	0.32	0.20	0.15	0.07	5.11	3.26	5.51	5.77	0.28	0.04	1.23	4.54	4.62
Burkina Faso	Mean	2.03	2.76	3.04	2.78	1.34	2.81	1.76	2.96	61.20	73.55	50.63	28.33	1.71	0.82	15.04	16.05	86.99
	Std. Dev	0.21	0.37	0.19	0.30	0.11	0.10	0.09	0.14	2.82	6.67	11.43	6.04	0.57	0.06	1.78	5.71	5.11
Cameroon	Mean	2.26	2.9	2.53	2.77	2.03	3.07	2.20	3.02	64.63	74.21	41.01	30.10	1.16	0.87	15.77	14.89	67.01
	Std. Dev	0.15	0.25	0.24	0.10	0.14	0.26	0.14	0.18	4.35	1.39	12.62	6.39	0.14	0.06	2.74	0.97	3.10
Egypt	Mean	2.37	2.40	2.07	2.09	1.27	1.95	1.80	2.35	44.25	51.25	45.26	10.39	0.69	0.85	26.98	22.05	84.61
	Std. Dev	0.15	0.30	0.19	0.18	0.10	0.17	0.16	0.22	7.32	8.88	14.68	3.11	0.19	0.17	9.12	5.84	3.49
Ghana	Mean	2.34	2.55	2.22	2.24	2.11	2.77	2.05	3.03	74.76	82.23	58.26	32.10	1.37	0.80	12.42	12.47	92.04
	Std. Dev	0.23	0.26	0.04	0.06	0.08	0.13	0.03	0.05	5.08	6.57	11.76	5.59	0.46	0.00	3.42	3.20	1.79
Libya	Mean	2.14	2.01	2.63	1.75	1.41	2.30	1.83	2.51	52.26	58.63	62.07	11.15	7.41	1.05	28.28	26.14	84.35
	Std. Dev	0.00	0.00	0.00	0.00	0.00	0.00	0.00	0.00	0.00	0.00	0.00	0.00	0.00	0.00	0.00	0.00	0.00
Madagascar	Mean	1.87	2.14	2.20	1.89	1.47	3.20	2.03	2.32	27.48	53.43	36.24	21.25	1.76	1.04	1.74	17.14	77.40

7 The Impact of Entrepreneurship Framework ...

Economy	Variable	FfE	GSP	TxB	GPr	BSE	PSE	RDT	CSN	PcO	PCp	EnI	TEA	MoI	FMT	HJE	Inn	HSE
	Std. Dev	0.16	0.11	0.31	0.11	0.06	0.08	0.06	0.02	4.36	2.80	5.10	0.72	0.57	0.17	0.83	5.31	0.54
Malawi	Mean	1.95	2.30	2.18	2.12	2.16	3.02	1.90	2.42	76.60	87.01	68.48	31.84	0.85	0.75	1.22	32.41	0.00
	Std. Dev	0.02	0.01	0.4	0.1	0.03	0.18	0.00	0.01	3.26	3.50	2.52	5.27	0.25	0.00	0.54	5.94	0.00
Morocco	Mean	2.24	2.27	2.39	2.18	1.3	2.31	1.74	2.29	39.84	51.46	32.36	8.23	1.56	1.02	14.42	15.16	65.82
	Std. Dev	0.23	0.19	0.13	0.12	0.07	0.21	0.12	0.13	6.70	16.21	5.46	4.49	0.20	0.07	4.36	2.55	11.51
Namibia	Mean	2.57	2.96	2.28	2.44	2.73	3.09	2.11	3.22	71.77	73.98	48.73	25.75	0.99	0.79	20.53	36.70	70.84
	Std. Dev	0.05	0.01	0.23	0.07	0.06	0.01	0.14	0.03	4.89	0.04	5.18	10.74	0.01	0.00	0.00	4.79	6.99
Nigeria	Mean	2.06	1.93	1.83	2.09	2.11	2.73	1.8	3.24	84.13	86.22	60.69	36.63	1.70	1.00	23.35	18.84	70.42
	Std. Dev	0.14	0.06	0.16	0.13	0.02	0.27	0.07	0.07	1.74	2.24	26.24	2.80	0.32	0.00	2.56	0.88	7.51
Senegal	Mean	2.10	2.65	3.16	2.75	1.23	2.27	1.52	2.14	69.91	89.05	66.64	38.55	1.92	0.78	22.70	8.21	0.00
	Std. Dev	0.18	0.17	0.27	0.29	0.13	0.24	0.04	0.33	0.00	0.00	0.00	0.00	0.00	0.00	0.00	0.00	0.00
South Africa	Mean	2.65	2.75	2.06	2.08	1.91	2.53	2.06	2.56	37.41	39.89	11.78	8.07	1.24	0.91	25.05	34.66	71.46
	Std. Dev	0.29	0.19	0.15	0.14	0.16	0.15	0.14	0.22	4.18	3.43	2.56	1.85	0.28	0.07	5.06	9.05	6.50
Sudan	Mean	2.33	1.66	1.81	1.73	1.63	2.35	1.89	2.64	70.98	74.52	66.65	22.17	1.68	0.75	23.13	13.37	85.30
	Std. Dev	0.00	0.00	0.00	0.00	0.00	0.00	0.00	0.00	0.00	0.00	0.00	0.00	0.00	0.00	0.00	0.00	0.00
Tunisia	Mean	2.83	3.69	2.88	2.96	1.56	2.75	2.33	2.75	33.45	53.87	32.01	7.62	2.26	0.93	21.09	28.87	88.18

(continued)

Table 7.2 (continued)

Economy	Variable	FfE	GSP	TxB	GPr	BSE	PSE	RDT	CSN	PcO	PCp	EnI	TEA	MoI	FMT	HJE	Inn	HSE
	Std. Dev	0.22	0.98	0.81	0.61	0.33	0.52	0.44	0.36	14.12	9.86	14.67	2.57	1.20	0.00	13.26	4.67	10.73
Uganda	Mean	2.35	2.47	2.02	2.32	2.13	3.02	2.00	3.22	75.18	84.54	60.38	31.70	1.59	0.90	8.48	8.98	88.06
	Std. Dev	0.10	0.22	0.18	0.20	0.21	0.19	0.19	0.23	7.03	3.00	14.27	3.77	1.00	0.03	3.29	1.24	4.16
Zambia	Mean	2.07	2.42	2.54	2.35	2.09	2.64	1.82	2.58	78.68	80.30	55.60	38.00	1.23	0.93	6.18	11.38	73.91
	Std. Dev	0.14	0.27	0.17	0.29	0.18	0.31	0.13	0.06	2.38	3.17	11.31	4.71	0.24	0.00	2.44	4.98	4.13

Table 7.3 Summary statistics—mean and standard deviation of control and instrumental variables (including dependent variable)

Economy	Variable	CRT	CAT	ALT	FTT	AER	CDI	MSC	CBC	Ent	MRI
Algeria	Mean	2.19	2.57	3.59	3.63	2.93	2.92	2.98	3.01	134.00	2,039.33
	Std. Dev	0.18	0.65	0.33	0.28	0.08	0.02	0.07	0.23	1.41	165.42
Angola	Mean	3.79	2.12	3.38	4.36	3.38	2.19	2.05	1.91	138.00	20.59
	Std. Dev	0.05	0.55	0.13	0.38	0.00	0.00	0.00	0.00	0.00	25.44
Botswana	Mean	3.75	3.05	4.52	4.33	3.62	3.29	3.33	3.05	87.50	0.00
	Std. Dev	0.25	0.50	0.22	0.30	0.03	0.20	0.21	0.26	9.19	0.00
Burkina Faso	Mean	2.34	2.76	3.60	4.24	3.56	3.22	3.21	2.79	116.00	264.18
	Std. Dev	0.14	0.45	0.35	0.24	0.00	0.00	0.00	0.00	0.00	140.72
Cameroon	Mean	2.72	3.22	3.96	4.30	3.64	3.16	3.44	2.95	96.00	229.82
	Std. Dev	0.14	0.80	0.31	0.41	0.06	0.03	0.04	0.04	2.83	67.32
Egypt	Mean	2.54	2.94	4.27	4.65	3.26	3.02	3.36	3.64	107.50	0.00
	Std. Dev	0.24	0.24	0.36	0.35	0.11	0.10	0.11	0.06	9.19	0.00
Ghana	Mean	3.69	3.27	4.25	4.34	4.02	3.83	3.78	3.63	46.00	1996.45
	Std. Dev	0.29	0.83	0.34	0.17	0.06	0.09	0.21	0.12	2.83	1640.76
Libya	Mean	2.25	2.28	3.93	3.61	0.00	0.00	0.00	0.00	0.00	0.00
	Std. Dev	0.03	0.21	0.56	0.64	0.00	0.00	0.00	0.00	0.00	0.00
Madagascar	Mean	3.13	3.19	4.04	4.12	0.00	0.00	0.00	0.00	0.00	334.57
	Std. Dev	0.13	0.56	0.27	0.30	0.00	0.00	0.00	0.00	0.00	49.93
Malawi	Mean	3.29	2.97	3.81	3.88	3.51	2.94	2.90	2.65	106.50	30.30
	Std. Dev	0.29	0.38	0.33	0.44	0.01	0.16	0.02	0.12	6.36	10.00
Morocco	Mean	3.60	3.04	4.98	4.82	3.61	3.17	3.25	2.88	98.50	6911.67
	Std. Dev	0.28	0.50	0.26	0.17	0.05	0.10	0.04	0.05	4.95	425.38
Namibia	Mean	3.61	3.14	5.07	4.63	4.00	3.37	3.47	3.23	66.00	57.82
	Std. Dev	0.17	0.68	0.39	0.25	0.03	0.01	0.01	0.06	5.66	23.50
Nigeria	Mean	3.72	3.46	4.27	4.50	4.77	3.44	3.12	2.78	15.00	20436.87
	Std. Dev	0.10	0.37	0.36	0.27	0.10	0.00	0.08	0.07	2.83	1678.92

(continued)

Table 7.3 (continued)

Economy	Variable	CRT	CAT	ALT	FTT	AER	CDI	MSC	CBC	Ent	MRI
Senegal	Mean	3.56	3.45	5.13	4.46	3.44	3.14	3.62	3.22	109.50	1699.37
	Std. Dev	0.09	0.65	0.30	0.30	0.04	0.00	0.06	0.08	0.71	298.69
South Africa	Mean	3.67	4.02	5.43	4.89	4.32	3.88	4.12	3.78	34.50	919.52
	Std. Dev	0.21	0.60	0.22	0.28	0.01	0.02	0.07	0.01	4.95	130.05
Sudan	Mean	0.00	0.00	0.00	0.00	0.00	0.00	0.00	0.00	0.00	731.25
	Std. Dev	0.00	0.00	0.00	0.00	0.00	0.00	0.00	0.00	0.00	523.60
Tunisia	Mean	2.53	3.56	5.00	4.79	3.47	2.89	3.17	2.65	120.50	2028.17
	Std. Dev	0.27	0.28	0.42	0.51	0.22	0.18	0.21	0.18	10.61	190.16
Uganda	Mean	3.02	3.11	4.08	4.74	4.30	3.60	3.63	3.18	49.00	895.31
	Std. Dev	0.05	0.60	0.44	0.30	0.05	0.02	0.01	0.02	1.41	217.84
Zambia	Mean	3.79	3.20	4.28	4.62	3.95	3.21	3.43	3.26	66.00	56.64
	Std. Dev	0.29	0.69	0.46	0.28	0.00	0.00	0.00	0.00	0.00	16.49

significant conditions that affect the level of migrant remittance inflows in the African continent and this is observed in (Adeoye et al., 2020; Efobi et al., 2019). This implies on average that migrant remittance inflows decrease by average of 9,611 where a country has set up financing for entrepreneurs and decrease by up to 4,796 where government has just attempted to provide basic school entrepreneurial education and training in its constituency. This finding supports previous evidence (Andonova et al., 2020) that suggest diaspora will invest in an environment where the population understands entrepreneurship beyond basic entrepreneurial education and training in its entrepreneurship transformation policies. However, it can be observed that cultural and social norms in Africa are very significant in promoting migrant remittance inflows. This is not a surprise in Africa as culture is so invaluable and a great asset to attract economic activities in a given territory thereby promoting some entrepreneurship activities.

Similarly, consistent with Strielkowski et al. (2017), we find so many country-specific attributes to be significant attractive factors to migrant remittance inflows into the African continent. For example, our results show that existing framework that include country's capacity to attract talent; country's capacity to retain talent; capacity for innovation; availability of latest technology; FDI & technology transfer; and attitude towards entrepreneurial

Table 7.4 Correlation of the sample variables for DFS, EBA and EFC

	GSP	FeF	GPr	TxB	BSE	PSE	RDT	CSN	Pop	PCp	EnI	TEA	MoI	FMT	HJE	Inn	HSE	MRI
GSP	1.00																	
FeF	0.46	1.00																
GPr	0.58	0.73	1.00															
TxB	0.42	−0.05	0.24	1.00														
BSE	0.41	0.26	0.42	0.02	1.00													
PSE	0.31	−0.05	0.15	0.22	0.54	1.00												
RDT	0.56	0.58	0.60	0.25	0.48	0.60	1.00											
CSN	0.58	0.32	0.35	0.02	0.77	0.39	0.35	1.00										
POp	0.34	−0.07	−0.08	−0.09	0.66	0.15	0.02	0.76	1.00									
PCp	0.29	−0.29	−0.21	−0.06	0.51	0.32	0.03	0.64	0.87	1.00								
EnI	−0.02	−0.44	−0.44	0.10	0.28	0.15	−0.16	0.40	0.68	0.72	1.00							
TEA	0.04	−0.50	−0.27	−0.05	0.51	0.29	−0.17	0.55	0.74	0.83	0.69	1.00						
MoI	0.11	0.23	−0.02	−0.25	−0.23	−0.08	0.12	−0.02	−0.04	−0.03	−0.04	−0.32	1.00					
FMT	0.17	0.07	0.10	0.39	−0.35	0.09	0.13	−0.31	−0.46	−0.42	−0.36	−0.43	0.40	1.00				
HJE	−0.18	0.31	0.15	−0.54	−0.08	−0.48	−0.17	−0.04	−0.09	−0.24	−0.33	−0.26	0.18	−0.37	1.00			
Inn	−0.10	0.45	0.38	−0.33	0.10	−0.12	0.00	0.03	−0.30	−0.35	−0.46	−0.21	−0.08	−0.16	0.64	1.00		
HSE	−0.12	0.20	0.07	−0.22	0.36	0.29	0.32	0.30	0.30	0.25	0.28	0.15	0.12	−0.31	−0.17	−0.11	1.00	
MRI	0.02	−0.19	−0.35	−0.06	−0.15	−0.08	−0.31	0.07	0.10	0.08	0.04	0.02	0.20	0.35	0.04	−0.14	−0.49	1.00

Note Presents the Pearson correlation coefficients amongst the sample variables used in our study. As it can be observed from the results, there are no serious issues related to multicollinearity. We also find that most variables are significantly correlated with all dependent variable. This lends support to our earlier projection about our assumed direction of relationship. Our correlation results indicate significant correlation of the coefficients mostly between 1 and 5% probability values. Based on this, we present our regression results in the following tables

Table 7.5 Multivariate regression results for diaspora financing strategy and entrepreneurship framework conditions

Variables	Obs	Parms	RMSE	R-Sq	F	P
MRI	26	15	1832.70	0.9207	9.119056	0.0004
	Coef	Std. Err	t	P > t	[95% Conf. Interval]	
FFE	−9611.606	2547.277	−3.77	0.003	−15,218.12	−4005.087
GSP	−1291.68	3087.646	−0.42	0.684	−8087.543	5504.183
TXB	−1036.33	2642.498	−0.39	0.702	−6852.428	4779.769
GPR	1212.723	3170.858	0.38	0.709	−5766.29	8191.735
BSE	−4796.094	2499.816	−1.92	0.081	−10,298.15	705.9643
PSE	−2547.391	3123.097	−0.82	0.432	−9421.281	4326.498
RDT	5661.634	3833.558	1.48	0.168	−2775.97	14,099.24
CSN	10,464.07	2599.053	4.03	0.002	4743.591	16,184.54
CRT	−11,120.64	3240.44	−3.43	0.006	−18,252.8	−3988.481
CRT	10,275.63	2419.43	4.25	0.001	4950.501	15,600.76
CAT	−4494.102	1088.475	−4.13	0.002	−6889.819	−2098.385
ALT	6063.616	1758.672	3.45	0.005	2192.804	9934.428
FTT	−5620.715	2069.618	−2.72	0.002	−10,175.91	−1065.515
AER	−567.4095	154.7695	−3.67	0.004	−908.0548	−226.7642
_CONS	24,579.19	9581.398	2.57	0.026	3490.678	45,667.71

risk are significant in shaping the diaspora financing strategy. All these variables that are significant are 1% probability level. We interpret that diaspora financing strategy is a great source of financing entrepreneurship activities in Africa where finance is one of the major problems hindering entrepreneurship development. However, the entrepreneurship framework conditions defined in our study is also relevant when some minimum country-specific attributes are achieved.

In this regard, our interpretation of entrepreneurship environment in terms of framework conditions is relevant in defining diaspora remittance strategy but the conditions are dependent upon the existing framework that can demonstrate successful entrepreneurship activities and commitments. We do not find governmental support and policies and governmental programmes to be significant in attracting migrant remittance inflows. This is consistent with the previous studies that found governments' efforts in support and programmes for entrepreneurial skills development are not enough in developing entrepreneurship activities (Premand et al., 2016). We do not also find any significant influence of post school entrepreneurial education and training and R&D transfer simply because of similar problem noted for the earlier variables due to non-commitments of many governments. Our model r-squared is strong with up to 92% of the variation in the diaspora financing strategy explained by the set of explanatory variables that represent the framework African as a continent requires for migrant remittance inflows to grow. Also, the F test is found to be significant indicating the fitness of the model for our dataset. Furthermore, we explore the effect of the entrepreneurial behaviour and attitudes on the diaspora financing strategy. Table 7.5 presents the results based on multivariate analysis.

Table 7.6 presents the regression results based on OLS estimation in order to examine the effect of entrepreneurial behaviour on the diaspora remittances in African countries. Consistent with our results from the previous section, total early-stage entrepreneurial activity and high status to successful entrepreneurs in a country are highly significant in attracting investments by diaspora in the home country perceived from entrepreneurial perspective. This is expected and in line with the previous interpretation because diaspora will be confident in channelling remittances only when the environment is conducive for entrepreneurship activities. A country that has a sound framework will ensure that total early-stage entrepreneurial activity is in place for the citizens (Escandon-Barbosa et al., 2019). Additionally, diaspora will be interested in the level of or high status to successful entrepreneurs as indication of how their investments will behave. The evidence that can support how conducive the environment is can be associated with the two highly significant variables noted above.

Table 7.6 Multivariate regression results for diaspora financing strategy and entrepreneurial behaviour and attitudes

Variables	Obs	Parms	RMSE	R-Sq	F	P
MRI	20	15	973.2211	0.9894	33.28374	0.0006
	Coef	Std. Err	t	P > t	[95% Con f. Interval]	
POp	−62.7966	49.92133	−1.26	0.264	−191.124	65.53026
PCp	−23.9779	64.05436	−0.37	0.724	−188.635	140.679
EnI	5.180275	72.00089	0.07	0.945	−179.904	190.2645
TEA	454.1684	121.3736	3.74	0.013	142.1677	766.1691
MoI	2223.224	1269.196	1.75	0.14	−1039.35	5485.796
FMT	−3879	6411.657	−0.6	0.572	−20,360.7	12,602.69
HJE	−101.241	108.3929	−0.93	0.393	−379.873	177.392
Inn	−52.1245	85.13608	−0.61	0.567	−270.974	166.7247
HSE	−184.532	42.29928	−4.36	0.007	−293.266	−75.7985
CRT	−12,946.6	2804.512	−4.62	0.006	−20,155.8	−5737.33
CAT	10,308.59	2773.021	3.72	0.014	3180.309	17,436.87
CfI	−2774.34	1341.637	−2.07	0.093	−6223.13	674.4443
ALT	2618.87	1476.387	1.77	0.136	−1176.3	6414.045
FTT	−816.459	119.4307	−6.84	0.001	−1123.47	−509.453
_cons	27,681.61	9070.004	3.05	0.028	4366.423	50,996.8

Other variables that indicate entrepreneurial behaviour and attitudes such as perceived opportunities, perceived capabilities and entrepreneurial intentions do not significantly influence the inflow of diaspora remittances. This outcome is supported by previous studies (Meseguer et al., 2017). Reflecting on the previous results of this study and the set of control variables, non-significance of the variables can be attributed to the fact that diaspora are interested in establishing strong evidence to remit funds into Africa only when it is beyond reasonable doubt that a safe environment is available in addition to the capacities to retain/attract talents and innovation.

Similarly, we document evidence that all the country-specific variables such as country's capacity to attract talent; country's capacity to retain talent; capacity for innovation; FDI & technology transfer; and attitude towards entrepreneurial risk are significant in shaping the diaspora financing strategy with the exception of availability of latest technology. All these variables are significant are 1% probability level. We interpret that diaspora financing strategy as a great source of financing entrepreneurship activities in Africa where finance is one of the major problems hindering entrepreneurship development (Plaza & Ratha, 2011). However, the entrepreneurship ecosystem remains essential in attracting funds from diaspora.

In this regard, our interpretation of entrepreneurship environment in terms of framework conditions is relevant in defining diaspora financing strategy but the conditions are dependent upon the existing framework that can demonstrate successful entrepreneurship activities and commitments. Our modelled r-squared is strong with up to 98% of the variation in the diaspora financing strategy explained by the set of explanatory variables that represent the framework African as a continent requires for migrant remittance inflows to grow. Also, the F test is found to be significant indicating the fitness of the model for our dataset.

Summary and Conclusion

This study explored the entrepreneurial and behavioural attributes required in African countries to attract remittances from their diaspora. Thus, the paper outlines a range of topical issues that provide promising hunting grounds for policy-makers and academic. For example, it was shown that presence of entrepreneurship framework conditions such as; entrepreneurial education, government programmes, culture and social norms impacts positively on remittance inflows. The diaspora will increase remittances in response to good entrepreneurship framework conditions created by the home country to boost enterprise development. In particularly, country-specific attributes such as ability to attract and retain talent significantly impacts positively on remittance inflows. Entrepreneurial behaviour and attitudes such as; perceived opportunities, motivation and entrepreneurial intentions are found to be sensitive to remittance inflows. Thus, the results are instrumental in understanding entrepreneur attributes that motivate the diaspora to remit resources for problem-solving in the home country. Although studies on this topic are limited because of data availability, recent development and access to global data from the World Bank/IMF/OECD and Global Entrepreneurship Monitor have created an opportunity to extensively research on this topic.

The study makes significant contribution to academic literature and policy implication. In line with our findings, we provide the following action points. Africa should implement the policy of embedding entrepreneurship into education and training at both formal and informal institutions. This will indicate a need for entrepreneurship education at primary (entailing provision of infrastructure at school like books, games, online tools), secondary (entailing extracurricular activities in addition to raising entrepreneurship awareness); vocational and higher education (where the main practical courses and training programmes should be exposed with link to incubation centres). Second, governments of Africa nations should ensure STEM (science, technology, engineering and math) skills are taught at the right levels with appropriate development of curriculum. Enactment of mentorship and role model programmes will also go a long way to boost development of home-grown entrepreneurship.

We argue that a holistic policy framework is required from international organisations such as World Bank, Africa Development Bank, African Union towards raising awareness of this key source of finance to promote entrepreneurial related projects.

References

Abubakar, I., Aldridge, R. W., Devakumar, D., Orcutt, M., Burns, R., Barreto, M.L., ... Hargreaves, S. (2018). The UCL–Lancet Commission on Migration and Health: The health of a world on the move. *The Lancet, 392*(10164), 2606–2654.

Acs, Z. J., Stam, E., Audretsch, D. B., & O'Connor, A. (2017). The lineages of the entrepreneurial ecosystem approach. *Small Business Economics, 49*(1), 1–10. https://doi.org/10.1007/s11187-017-9864-8

Adeoye, B. W., Nwokolo, C. I., & Igboanugo, N. I. (2020). Migrant remittance inflow and industrialization in Africa: What role does financial development play? In *Financing Africa's Development* (pp. 191–220). Springer, Cham.

Aggarwal, R., Demirguc-Kunt, A., & Martinez Peria, M. S. (2006). *Do Workers' Remittances Promote Financial Development ?* https://doi.org/10.1596/1813-9450-3957

Ahuja, V., & Purankar, S. (2018). Quality Business School education and the expectations of the corporate-A research agenda. *Procedia Computer Science, 139*, 561–569. https://doi.org/10.1016/J.PROCS.2018.10.209

Ajefu, J. B., Demir, A., & Haghpanahan, H. (2020). The impact of financial inclusion on mental health. *SSM Population Health, 11*, 100630.

Amidu, M., Abor, J. Y., & Issahaku, H. (2019). Left behind, but included: The case of migrant remittances and financial inclusion in Ghana. *African Finance Journal, 21*(2), 36–63.

Amuedo-Dorantes, C., & Bansak, C. (2014). Employment verification mandates and the labor market outcomes of likely unauthorized and native workers. *Contemporary Economic Policy, 32*(3), 671–680. https://doi.org/10.1111/coep.12043

Amuedo-Dorantes, C., & Pozo, S. (2006). Migration, remittances, and male and female employment patterns. *American Economic Review, 96*(2), 222–226. https://doi.org/10.1257/000282806777211946

Anton, S. G., & Bostan, I. (2017). The role of access to finance in explaining cross-national variation in entrepreneurial activity: A panel data approach. *Sustainability, 9*(11), 1947.

Arthur, E. K., Musau, S. M., & Wanjohi, F. M. (2020). Diaspora remittances and financial inclusion in Kenya. *European Journal of Business and Management Research, 5*(2).

Atiase, V. Y., Mahmood, S., Wang, Y., & Botchie, D. (2018). Developing entrepreneurship in Africa: Investigating critical resource challenges. *Journal of Small Business and Enterprise Development*.

Audretsch, D. B., & Belitski, M. (2017). Entrepreneurial ecosystems in cities: Establishing the framework conditions. *The Journal of Technology Transfer, 42*(5), 1030–1051.

Brixiova, Z. (2010). Unlocking productive entrepreneurship in Africa's least developed countries*. *African Development Review, 22*(3), 440–451. https://doi.org/10.1111/j.1467-8268.2010.00255.x

Brixiová, Z., Ncube, M., & Bicaba, Z. (2015). Skills and youth entrepreneurship in Africa: Analysis with evidence from Swaziland. *World Development, 67*, 11–26. https://doi.org/10.1016/j.worlddev.2014.09.027

Brzozowski, J., Cucculelli, M., & Surdej, A. (2014). Transnational ties and performance of immigrant entrepreneurs: The role of home-country conditions. *Entrepreneurship & Regional Development, 26*(7–8), 546–573. https://doi.org/10.1080/08985626.2014.959068

Caballé, J., & Santos, M. S. (1993). On endogenous growth with physical and human capital. *Journal of Political Economy, 101*(6), 1042–1067. https://doi.org/10.1086/261914

Cassimon, D., Van Campenhout, B., Ferry, M., & Raffinot, M. (2015). Africa: Out of debt, into fiscal space? Dynamic fiscal impact of the debt relief initiatives on African Heavily Indebted Poor Countries (HIPCs). *International Economics, 144*, 29–52. https://doi.org/10.1016/J.INTECO.2015.04.007

Cattaneo, C. (2005). *International migration and poverty: A cross country analysis.* Retrieved from https://www.researchgate.net/publication/267261100.

Cavallo, A., Ghezzi, A., & Balocco, R. (2019). Entrepreneurial ecosystem research: Present debates and future directions. *International Entrepreneurship and Management Journal, 15*(4), 1291–1321. https://doi.org/10.1007/s11365-018-0526-3

Chand, M. (2016). Leveraging the Diaspora for Africa's economic development. *Journal of African Business, 17*(3), 273–290. https://doi.org/10.1080/15228916.2016.1160856

Cheru, F. (2002). Debt, adjustment and the politics of effective response to HIV/AIDS in Africa. *Third World Quarterly, 23*(2), 299–312. https://doi.org/10.1080/01436590220126658

Cummings, E. M., Davies, P. T., & Campbell, S. B. (2020). *Developmental psychopathology and family process: Theory, research, and clinical implications.* Guilford Publications.

Dalmarco, G., Hulsink, W., & Blois, G. V. (2018). Creating entrepreneurial universities in an emerging economy: Evidence from Brazil. *Technological Forecasting and Social Change, 135*, 99–111. https://doi.org/10.1016/J.TECHFORE.2018.04.015

Djimeu, E. W. (2018). The impact of the Heavily Indebted Poor Countries initiative on growth and investment in Africa. *World Development, 104*, 108–127. https://doi.org/10.1016/J.WORLDDEV.2017.11.002

Efobi, U., Asongu, S., Okafor, C., Tchamyou, V., & Tanankem, B. (2019). Remittances, finance and industrialisation in Africa. *Journal of Multinational Financial Management, 49*, 54–66.

Escandon-Barbosa, D., Urbano-Pulido, D., & Hurtado-Ayala, A. (2019). Exploring the relationship between formal and informal institutions, social capital, and entrepreneurial activity in developing and developed countries. *Sustainability, 11*(2), 550.

Estrin, S., Mickiewicz, T., & Stephan, U. (2016). Human capital in social and commercial entrepreneurship. *Journal of Business Venturing, 31*(4), 449–467. https://doi.org/10.1016/J.JBUSVENT.2016.05.003

Flisi, S., & Murat, M. (2011). The hub continent. Immigrant networks, emigrant diasporas and FDI. *The Journal of Socio-Economics, 40*(6), 796–805. https://doi.org/10.1016/j.socec.2011.08.025

Hill, T., & Ram, M. (2010). Far from Silicon Valley: How emerging economies are re-shaping our understanding of global entrepreneurship. *Journal of International Management, 16*(4), 321–327. https://doi.org/10.1016/J.INTMAN.2010.09.003

Huay, C. S., & Bani, Y. (2018). Remittances, poverty and human capital: Evidence from developing countries. *International Journal of Social Economics*.

Iraj Hashi, B. A. K. (2011). Entrepreneurship and SME growth: Evidence from advanced and laggard transition economies no title. *International Journal of Entrepreneurial Behavior & Research, 5*(17), 456–487.

Kloosterman, R., & Rath, J. (2010). Immigrant entrepreneurs in advanced economies: Mixed embeddedness further explored. *Https://Doi.Org/*https://doi.org/10.1080/13691830020041561. https://doi.org/10.1080/13691830020041561

Kotabe, M., Riddle, L., Sonderegger, P., & Täube, F. A. (2013). Diaspora investment and entrepreneurship: The role of people, their movements, and capital in the international economy. *Journal of International Management, 19*(1), 3–5. https://doi.org/10.1016/j.intman.2012.12.001.

Kourtit, K., Nijkamp, P., & van Leeuwen, E. (2013). New entrepreneurship in urban diasporas in our modern world. *Journal of Urban Management, 2*(1), 25–47. https://doi.org/10.1016/S2226-5856(18)30063-3

Lall, S. (1995). Structural adjustment and African industry. *World Development, 23*(12), 2019–2031. https://doi.org/10.1016/0305-750X(95)00103-J

Lartey, E. K. K., Mandelman, F. S., & Acosta, P. A. (2012). Remittances, exchange rate regimes and the Dutch disease: A panel data analysis. *Review of International Economics, 20*(2), 377–395. https://doi.org/10.1111/j.1467-9396.2012.01028.x

Letiche, J. M. (2010). Transforming sub-Saharan Africa. *Journal of Policy Modeling, 32*(2), 163–175. https://doi.org/10.1016/J.JPOLMOD.2010.01.003

Lone, S. A., & Ahmad, A. (2020). COVID-19 pandemic—An African perspective. *Emerging Microbes & Infections, 9*(1), 1300–1308. https://doi.org/10.1080/22221751.2020.1775132

Lyakurwa, W. (2009). Prospects for economic governance: Resilient pro-poor growth. *Foresight, 4*(11), 66–81.

Mayer, S. D., Aki, H., & Freiling, J. (2015). Entrepreneurial business and economics review. In *Entrepreneurial Business and Economics Review* (Vol. 3). Retrieved from https://www.ceeol.com/search/article-detail?id=305125

Micozzi, A., & Lucarelli, C. (2016). Heterogeneity in entrepreneurial intent: The role of gender across countries. *International Journal of Gender and Entrepreneurship*.

Mijiyawa, A. G. (2017). Drivers of structural transformation: The case of the manufacturing sector in Africa. *World Development, 99*, 141–159. https://doi.org/10.1016/J.WORLDDEV.2017.07.007

Minto-Coy, I. D., Lashley, J. G., & Storey, D. J. (2018). Enterprise and entrepreneurship in the Caribbean region: Introduction to the special issue.

Entrepreneurship and Regional Development, 30(9–10), 921–941. https://doi.org/10.1080/08985626.2018.1515823

Nissanke, M. (2019). Exploring macroeconomic frameworks conducive to structural transformation of sub-Saharan African economies. *Structural Change and Economic Dynamics, 48*, 103–116. https://doi.org/10.1016/J.STRUECO.2018.07.005

Nwankwo, S. (2011). Imagining Africa in the global economy. *Thunderbird International Business Review, 53*(1), 3–8. https://doi.org/10.1002/tie.20385

Plaza, S., & Ratha, D. (2011). *Diaspora for development in Africa*. World Bank.

Premand, P., Brodmann, S., Almeida, R., Grun, R., & Barouni, M. (2016). Entrepreneurship education and entry into self-employment among university graduates. *World Development, 77*, 311–327.

Priebe, J., & Rudolf, R. (2015). Does the Chinese Diaspora speed up growth in host countries? *World Development, 76*, 249–262. https://doi.org/10.1016/j.worlddev.2015.07.007

Rapoport, H., & Docquier, F. (2006). Chapter 17 the economics of migrants' remittances. *Handbook of the Economics of Giving, Altruism and Reciprocity, 2*, 1135–1198. https://doi.org/10.1016/S1574-0714(06)02017-3

Ratha, D. (2011). *Leveraging migration for Africa: Remittances, skills, and investments*. World Bank.

Ratha, D. (2016). *Migration and remittances factbook 2016*. World Bank.

Romero-Barrutieta, A. L., Bulíř, A., & Rodríguez-Delgado, J. D. (2015). The dynamic implications of debt relief for low-income countries. *Review of Development Finance, 5*(1), 1–12. https://doi.org/10.1016/J.RDF.2014.07.003

Siani, J. (2020). International remittances, poverty and growth into WAEMU countries: Evidence from panel cointegration approach. *Economics Bulletin, 40*(2), 1446–1456.

Strielkowski, W., Tcukanova, O., & Zarubina, Z. (2017). Globalization and economic integration: The role of modern management. *Polish Journal of Management Studies, 15*.

Valliere, D. (2010). Reconceptualizing entrepreneurial framework conditions. *International Entrepreneurship and Management Journal, 6*(1), 97–112.

Part II

Entrepreneurship Education

8

Left Behind: A Reflection on Lags in the Development of Entrepreneurship Education in South Africa

Natasha Katuta Mwila

Background

South Africa is worthy of attention in studies of entrepreneurial education on the African continent because it has arguably the most developed educational system in this context (McKeever, 2017) and is one of Africa's largest economies (Macha, 2017).

The South African education system has a controversial past stemming from the apartheid regime of 1948 to 1994. Apartheid was the institutionalisation of segregation and discrimination in South Africa based on four race groups (White, Black, Indian and Coloured) (Union of South Africa, 1950). This meant segregation and discrimination were entrenched in all systems including housing, health, employment opportunities and education. With resulting inequality, entrepreneurship emerged strongly as a livelihood necessity for much of the non-white population. However, much of the population was subjected to 'Bantu Education'; a system that excluded black students from exposure to certain subjects and positioned them to fill only labour related positions (Macha, 2017). 'Whites Only' government schools (also known as Model C schools) followed a more comprehensive curriculum. These two historical elements of the education

N. K. Mwila (✉)
Centre for Enterprise and Innovation, De Montfort University, Leicester, UK
e-mail: natasha.mwila@dmu.ac.uk

© The Author(s), under exclusive license to Springer Nature Switzerland AG 2022
O. Kolade et al. (eds.), *The Palgrave Handbook of African Entrepreneurship*,
https://doi.org/10.1007/978-3-030-75894-3_8

system had a negative effect on stimulating entrepreneurial thought during schooling and nurturing post-education entrepreneurial activity. In 2001, a Global Entrepreneurship Monitor (GEM) report to this effect was released establishing that '…apartheid education damaged people's confidence and self-esteem, which impacted on their initiative and creative thinking. The restrictions created during apartheid limited the access to informal learning and work experience opportunities for many South Africans. These areas are critical in developing the skills and confidence necessary to start a business' (Herrington et al., 2010).

Marking 26 years post-apartheid, it is timely to take stock of where the education system is in the important area of entrepreneurship in the economy. This is especially so if the country is to make any meaningful progress in attaining the Sustainable Development Goal Target 4.4 which is 'By 2030, substantially increase the number of youth and adults who have relevant skills, including technical and vocational skills, for employment, decent jobs and entrepreneurship' (United Nations, 2015). This target is part of Goal 4 which reads 'Ensure inclusive and equitable quality education and promote lifelong learning opportunities for all' (United Nations, 2015). Although the racial divide has been over, the inequality still exists in certain subjects including entrepreneurship. A study[1] that informed this chapter established that entrepreneurial education in South Africa was found in the subject offerings of only private schools and not public schools. Targeting the national curriculum may therefore provide a resolution to this problem.

GEM is South Africa's longest-running entrepreneurship research programme (since 2001) and it conclusively finds that there is indeed a link between a low level of overall education and low levels of entrepreneurial activity; as well as social and entrepreneurial factors that do not encourage entrepreneurship as a career path of choice and low levels of entrepreneurial education (Herrington et al., 2010). The annual GEM reports consistently show 'the importance of education as a predictor of individuals who believe they have the skills to start a business, the possibility that the business will survive beyond start-up phase and the likelihood that the business will be an opportunity-driven business' (Herrington et al., 2010). Notably for this study, Herrington et al. (2010) also draw attention to the 'questionable quality and appropriateness of education in South Africa'.

The first GEM report's most important finding was that there was a lack of suitable entrepreneurial and business education and training among

---

[1] The study was an honours research project conducted by Luke Nicholas Brand, under the supervision of the author, in 2017 titled 'Entrepreneurial Ecosystem: How Entrepreneurs Perceive the Role of Education'. The project received cum laude honours from Monash University.

the youth of South Africa. 19 years following that report, nothing significant has been done to address the situation. The Youth Commission and Umsobomvu Youth Fund which were created in 2005 in response to the report were disbanded by 2008 after being deemed totally unsuccessful. A more embedded approach is therefore warranted, and the curriculum may be the key.

Literary Clarifications

This chapter has been positioned to address entrepreneurial education as conceptualised by Erkkilä (2000). This is defined as a blend of enterprise education, focused on personal development, mindset, skills and ability (Lackéus, 2015); and entrepreneurship education, focused on the erection of a venture and self-employment (Mahieu, 2006).

The author acknowledges that there is an ongoing debate regarding whether educators should be educating 'about entrepreneurship', 'for entrepreneurship' or 'through entrepreneurship' as aptly summarised by Lackéus (2015). This chapter does not engage in this debate but asserts that the role for education is in all three and that for secondary educators it is a blend of the latter two.

Methodology

The study employed archival research as advised in the work of Cuffaro (2011). This called for the extraction of evidence from archival records primarily from the National Department of Basic Education in South Africa (hereafter referred to as 'The Department'). The documents used in this study were as follows: media releases; opinion pieces; newsletters; parliamentary questions; speeches; reports; legislation; policies; publications; national curriculum statements; and curriculum assessment policy statements.

Many consulted sources are archived in online catalogues which are publicly accessible. This made a 'key word' search suitable at the onset of the study protocol to find relevant sources. The key words informing this study were as follows: Curriculum/ Curricula; Subject/ Subjects; Secondary School; Matric; and Entrepreneurship/ Entrepreneur/ Enterprise. Construct validity was considered to not be an issue as the operational words used for the study are exactly the operational words used in practice with no further extensions or assumptions of word usage beyond the context of an education curriculum.

381 word and combination word searches were feasible based on the statistical computation of possible combinations $nCr = n! / r! * (n - r)!$, where n represents the number of items (key words), and r represents the number of items being chosen at a time. Actual searches conducted were 146 after omitting irrelevant searches (those whose combinations included alternative terms).

The author additionally made use of the 'Information for Researchers' facility available from The Department. This put the researcher in contact with clerks able to assist with interpretation of some of the documents as well as accessing material not available in the online public domain (particularly dated material with reference to pre-1994 curriculum matters).

The second part of the study involved comparative narrative analysis of individuals that have experienced the South African secondary curriculum at different points in time. The approach was informed by the work of Riessman (1993). These narrative accounts were offered in a focus group setting and examined and compared to the documentary evidence from the archival investigation.

The profile of participants was as follows:

- Participant A—entrepreneur that attended school under the Bantu Education System
- Participant B—entrepreneur that attended a Model C School
- Participant C—entrepreneur that attended a Private School after 1994 but before the 2005 reforms
- Participant D—entrepreneur that attended a Public School after 1994 but before the 2005 reforms
- Participant E—entrepreneur that attended a Private School after the 2005 reforms
- Participant F—entrepreneur that attended a Public School after the 2005 reforms.

The selection of participants was based on the crucible moments of the curriculum's evolution (the Bantu Education System, the end of apartheid and the introduction of outcomes-based education). All participants had completed the mandatory 12 years of schooling, initiated and run their own businesses and so their insights were deemed crucial regarding any influences the education curriculum had on their entrepreneurial success.

Four focus group meetings were held over a one-month period. All participants attended the meetings. The first meeting discussed the overall research project and focussed on the Bantu Education System. Participants shared their experiences, opinions and knowledge. Participants were also invited to examine some documents related to the time and provide commentary. The first meeting lasted for three hours broken up into one-hour blocks. At the end of the meeting, participants were issued voice recorders to capture any thoughts they had after the meeting before the next one.

The second meeting reviewed any further thoughts from the first meeting. It focussed on the end of apartheid. The activities of the first meeting were replicated. The third meeting followed the structure of the second meeting and focussed on outcomes-based education. At the fourth meeting, the author provided summaries of previous discussions and sought clarity where required. Participants also shared specifics about their entrepreneurial journeys and where they had gaps that could have been filled by some form of education. The fourth meeting was 4 h long and concluded the data collection exercise from participants.

Content analysis was employed during the sense-making process of the data. The approach was informed by the work of Duriau et al. (2007). Patterns that were examined were related to content on curriculum development through subject offering.

Findings

This section integrates the findings from archival research and the narrative accounts of the study participants around the earlier mentioned crucible moments of curriculum development in the South African secondary schooling system.

1954–1994

> I recall the teachers looking very puzzled about what they had to teach when it came to subjects like mathematics. They had to teach us these subjects in English and at that time, 1968, I could barely understand it. To be honest, I learned nothing in school. I learned more from the white children that my mother looked after. They taught me English and Afrikaans. They were younger than me but when I looked at their books, they seemed to be exposed to so much more than we were at my school. These kids were nice to me but

every other white man looked at me like filth. Experiencing daily torrents of racial abuse, all I wanted to be when I grow up is a *baas* (Afrikaans for boss). That is where my entrepreneurial spirit was ignited. (Participant A)

Documents show that there was next to no involvement of teachers in the development of the curriculum during this era (Adu & Ngibe, 2014). This in part explains the experience of Participant A in the classroom with teachers who had either little familiarity with the content they delivered or insufficient capacity, language or otherwise, to do so. In alignment with the apartheid policies and practices of the time there were 15 Departments of Education before 1994 (Mda & Mothatha, 2000). This resulted in vast differences in the curriculum offering across different schools.

I was taught in school, day in and day out, that I was the best. Everything I learned was presented to me in a manner that forced me to engage with the material, critique and think outside the box. Receiving this consistent conditioning, I believe, is the reason why many white folks from my generation ended up getting into business, whether we attended varsity or not. (Participant B)

In contrast to Participant A, Participant B's experience of the classroom was one that built up his mindset for entrepreneurship. Archival documents on the lesson plans in Model C schools confirm this approach to the education of white learners. The education system was a tool for the implementation of the white supremacist agenda that reigned at the time.

1994–2004

The 24 subjects offered over this period included Business Studies (offered in an optional suite of studies including accounting and economics). According to the National Curriculum Statement, Business Studies have the following focus areas, and would therefore be closely related to entrepreneurship education:

1. Challenging business environments: Learners are to investigate the different environments within which a business operates and the effect of these environments on the operations of the enterprise.
2. Achievable business ventures: Learners are to be equipped with the skills to establish successful business ventures. This is to take place through generating ideas and drawing up business plans (which includes investigation of the product and demographics, a SWOT analysis, financial planning

and management planning). Combined with creative thinking, this will enable learners to pursue viable and entrepreneurial business ventures.
3. Business roles: Learners are to be introduced to the essential roles that they need to perform (as a citizen, team member, professional, self-manager and entrepreneur) in a variety of business contexts.
4. Business operations: Learners are to acquire the knowledge and skills necessary to manage essential business functions, such as human resources, public relations, marketing and production, within the context of relevant legislation and other contemporary issues.

> At my school, anything related to entrepreneurship I learned in our business club. We were given guidance on how to come up with business ideas and execute them. This was very hands on and practical. We participated in running the tuck shop and selling all sorts at school fetes and other functions. They also regularly invited some of the parents who run businesses to come and talk to us about how they got started and the challenges they faced. Business Studies was too theoretical for me. The business club was where I got my true taste of entrepreneurship (Participant C).

> Wow! I am amazed that the focus of business studies is what you have pointed out to us from the government document! I did not learn any of that in school and I was really a strong and keen student. If I relied only on what I learned in that subject I would have zero capacity to run a business, let alone even run a *spaza* in the *kasi* (small informal shop situated in the township). Subjects like accounting which were practical were more useful to my entrepreneurial practice. To be frank with you, I learned how to run business from those who were running business in the neighbourhood, and the funny thing is most of them did not even have the privilege of going to school. I am talking about the roadside mechanics, the shebeen queens and the barbers. Our parents told us, "go to school so one day you can be somebody- a doctor, a lawyer, an accountant". Nobody associated going to school with running your own business. Our school system does not support entrepreneurship. That is why I am so shocked at the strong emphasis in the focus areas of business studies that you have shown us. Our schools are missing the mark...I heard Participant C mention a business club at school, the public schools only have JETS clubs (Junior Engineers, Technicians and Scientists) and this reflects where society places value- in the sciences. If we had business clubs as well, we would have considered entrepreneurship much earlier on. (Participant D)

2005

The 2005 curriculum was introduced to implement Outcomes Based Education with a view to enable articulation between education and training. The four Learning Outcomes (LOs) for Business Studies are as follows:

> LO 1: Business Environments—The learner can demonstrate knowledge and analyse the impact of changing and challenging environments on business practice in all sectors.
> LO 2: Business Ventures—The learner can identify and research viable business opportunities and to explore these and related issues through the creation of achievable business ventures.
> LO 3: Business Roles—The learner can demonstrate and apply contemporary knowledge and skills to fulfil a variety of business roles.
> LO 4: Business Operations—The learner can demonstrate and apply a range of management skills and specialised knowledge to perform business operations successfully.

> Business Studies have always had a poor reputation as not really teaching anything that other subjects in the commerce set cover. At my school, business studies were considered a companion subject. This means although they were optional, you were strongly encouraged to take them alongside your core choices. Our parents were also encouraged to motivate us into this option because of the practical business exposure that was possible. I was a strong science student. I knew that all I wanted to study in uni[versity] was robotics. But honestly, business studies sowed a seed in me to think about building my own robotics empire. I just wish it could have been deeper practical knowledge so that I wouldn't have to do an MBA after my robotics degree to have confidence in starting up my own business. The only thing I think I learned was SWOT analysis. (Participant E)

Participant E's experience of missing out on entrepreneurial education in their technology-related subject is confirmed in the study of du Toit and Gaotlhobogwe (2018). They (du Toit & Gaotlhobogwe, 2018) found that the curricula of South Africa and Botswana do not include explicit entrepreneurship content necessary to support technology, nor pedagogical guidance to support teachers in this regard. Du Toit and Gaotlhobogwe sound a warning that without this, reducing youth unemployment is not possible in either country.

> I studied business studies to complete my set of options. Everyone said it was easy and good for someone who didn't really know what they wanted to do

after matric. What did I learn from it? I also only remember SWOT and maybe it's because I found it in all my modules at varsity. I remember most of what I learned in all other subjects except this one. (Participant F)

There is an evident gap in the achievement of the intended learning outcomes whether in the public or private school setting. This brings into question whether they outcomes are achievable in the first instance based on the current subject content offering.

Celebratory Findings

The South African curriculum is largely shaped by current global trends and local needs as is reflected in the national curriculum statement:

> ...the scale of change in the world, the growth and development of knowledge and technology and the demands of the twenty-first century required learners to be exposed to different and higher-level skills and knowledge than those required by the existing South African curricula. Second, South Africa had changed. The curricula for schools therefore required revision to reflect new values and principles, especially those of the Constitution of South Africa. (Department of Education, 2007)

The latest updates to the curriculum have considered the state of industrial revolution and incorporated Coding; Robotics; Technical Mathematics; Technical Sciences; Maritime Sciences; Aviation Studies; Mining Sciences and Aquaponics. To position the schools to deliver the new curriculum, several public schools will be transformed to technical high schools. Furthermore, by April 2019, 43,774 teachers were recruited for training in delivering the new curriculum. Training was delivered over June to September 2019. In addition, there have been laudable partnerships with universities and the corporate sector including multinational organisations like Google to deliver a relevant curriculum and provide delivery platforms in the subject of coding for example.

Such efforts could be replicated in other subjects of relevance including, as argued in this chapter, entrepreneurship. Efforts made in the Business Studies offering are well noted and this area of study has potential to play a part in addressing wider national issues around human rights, inclusivity and social justice if it delivers on its intended outcomes. The argument made however is that Business Studies is insufficient by itself and Entrepreneurship needs to be brought on board.

Problem Findings

Entrepreneurship is still not a part of the curriculum. There has been an ongoing assumption that entrepreneurship is covered in other aspects of the curriculum. Although business studies, by proxy, have some relationship to entrepreneurship, their focus is only on how to function in an enterprise and not how to create one.

There has been a pervasive view of entrepreneurship as an add-on and not a stand-alone part of education. A study by the International Labour Organisation (2017) found that 'students in grade 10 to grade 12 who were undertaking business studies and exposed to an additional component of experiential entrepreneurship education were subjectively more competent and capable of starting a new business, reporting better soft and hard skills than business studies students who did not receive the experiential component. The added entrepreneurship component, however, had no additional impact in terms of entrepreneurial intentions compared to students taking regular business studies'. This finding strongly suggests that simply revamping business studies by including entrepreneurial components is not enough. There is a case for introducing entrepreneurship as a stand-alone subject.

Recent studies (such as that of Uleanya & Gamede, 2017) have looked at entrepreneurship as a vocational route suitable for implementation in further education (the gap between matric and university study). This is more aligned to higher education and does not address the offering of entrepreneurial education at basic level, although these studies recognise that this would be the basis for any meaningful advancement of entrepreneurial activity.

One of the key drivers of any reform in the education curriculum of South Africa has been politics. Although this is expected, given the historical context of the country, this has been crippling in making the necessary content adjustments that may not fit into the political agenda of the government of the day. Emphasis has been on developing how curriculum content is taught but the actual development of curriculum content has lagged.

Limitations

The author acknowledges that the vast majority of archival sources have not been digitised and even where they are, online catalogues are frequently incomplete. In as much as efforts were made to access all key resources, the completeness of data cannot be assured. The study also relied on participant ability to recall and the author acknowledges that the passage of time and other events may cloud memory and our representation of past events. Considering these methodological hurdles, a study that incorporates a higher number of participants and representation from the educator and policy maker perspective as well may be necessary.

Recommendations

1. Benchmarking
   South Africa has an opportunity to benchmark a curriculum proposition for entrepreneurship as a separate subject as has been done in Kenya and Nigeria (Valerio et al., 2014). Perhaps this could be done through school transformation which would include establishment of entrepreneurial high schools just as there is a move to have technical high schools.

   The successful partnership model on coding could be replicated to create the appropriate infrastructure for entrepreneurship education in the curriculum. Incubation hubs have proved largely successful in the South African context (Atiase et al., 2020) and perhaps these could be integrated into secondary schools.
2. Curriculum Transformation
   The study acknowledges that there are other current curriculum transformation needs that could be leveraged. For instance:

   'The robotics curriculum will not require any infrastructure or devices, but will need maker spaces to provide hands on, creative ways to encourage students to design, experiment, build and invent; e.g. through cardboard construction activities', Angie Motshekga (Minister of Basic Education). These outlined requirements have entrepreneurial elements which could be well delivered through a complimentary entrepreneurship subject. The persistent mismatch of the curriculum and labour market needs (African Development Bank, 2017) should be addressed.

   In as much as curriculum transformation is desired, the fundamentals must not be neglected. According to Herrington and Kew (2016) low levels of entrepreneurial activity and management capabilities in South Africa are linked to the country's ineffective entrepreneurial education and inadequate mathematics and science teaching at primary and secondary school levels. This suggests that curriculum transformation must include continued attention to mathematics and science at school.

3. Investment in Education

    In concurrence with the GEM conditions for entrepreneurial success, this paper recommends education and training at each level of the education and training system. This training and education ideally would incorporate the creation and management of new, small or growing business entities. The levels of the system are primary and secondary school entrepreneurship education and training; as well as post-school entrepreneurship education and training. Entrepreneurial education is perceived as a long-term complementary solution, when embedded in school and university curricula, to creating national and regional centres of enterprise excellence (African Development Bank, 2017).

    It cannot be overemphasised that greater investment in human capital is required (African Development Bank, 2017). There is an opportunity to extend education to those outside the traditional boundaries of education policy, i.e. adults that have already started up enterprises. Fostering the business skills of existing entrepreneurs may yield great benefit in contributing to sustainable enterprises.

    There is concern that with the effects of the COVID pandemic, investment in other sectors including education will fall. This is something that must be closely watched as learners have already fallen behind as a consequence of this pandemic. Entrepreneurship education needs to be especially strengthened at this time to minimise youth unemployment and increase economic activity.

4. Public Policy on Education

    There needs to be institutional support for the prioritisation of the various education forms (formal, apprenticeships and vocational) to meet the needs of the labour market (African Development Bank, 2017). Although there is an abundance in the quantity of education sources there is a role for public policy in ensuring that quality is assured through the various education modes. Continuous evaluation must be incorporated into any policy to ensure its effectiveness.

5. Policy and Skills Level Matching

    The evidence shows that even well-intended policies are unsuccessful if blanket approaches are followed. What is therefore recommended is that different policy sets are formulated, with differing priority actions according to the skills level in the country and according to the proportion of survival/necessity entrepreneurs. Entrepreneurship education that is post-schooling in nature is best targeted at opportunity-driven entrepreneurs (Isaacs et al., 2007).

References

Adu, E. O., & Ngibe, N. C. P. (2014). Continuous change in curriculum: South African teachers' perceptions. *Mediterranean Journal of Social Sciences, 5*(23), 983–989.

African Development Bank. (2017). *African economic outlook 2017: Entrepreneurship and industrialisation*. African Economic Outlook. https://www.afdb.org/en/documents/document/african-economic-outlook-aeo-2017-95818. Accessed 22 October 2020.

Atiase, V. Y., Kolade, O., & Liedong, T. A. (2020). The emergence and strategy of Tech Hubs in Africa: Implications for knowledge production and value creation. *Technological Forecasting and Social Change*. https://doi.org/doi.org/10.1016/j.techfore.2020.120307

Cuffaro, M. A. (2011). *Archival research*. Encyclopedia of Child Behavior and Development (pp.140–141).

Department of Education. (2007). *National curriculum statement grades 10–12 (general)*. Learning Program Guidelines: Business Studies. Republic of South Africa.

Du Toit, A., & Gaotlhobogwe, M. (2018). A neglected opportunity: Entrepreneurship education in the lower high school curricula for technology in South Africa and Botswana. *African Journal of Research in Mathematics, Science and Technology Education, 22*(1), 37–47.

Duriau, V. J., Reger, R. K., & Pfarrer, M. D. (2007). A content analysis of the content analysis literature in organisation studies: Research themes, data sources, and methodological refinements. *Organisational Research Methods, 10*(1), 5–34.

Erkkilä, K. (2000). *Entrepreneurial education: Mapping the debates in the United States, the United Kingdom and Finland*. Taylor & Francis.

Herrington, M., & Kew, P. (2016). *South African Report 2015/16: Is South Africa Heading for an Economic Meltdown?* Global Entrepreneurship Monitor, University of Capetown, Development Unit for New Enterprise. Global Entrepreneurship Monitor. http://ideate.co.za/wp-content/uploads/2016/05/gem-south-africa-2015-2016-report.pdf. Accessed 23 October 2020.

Herrington, M., Kew, J., Kew, P., & Monitor, G. E. (2010). *Tracking entrepreneurship in South Africa: A GEM perspective* (pp. 1–174). Graduate School of Business, University of Cape Town.

International Labour Organisation. (2017, October). *Educating entrepreneurs: Can In-school youth be taught to start a business? Evidence from South Africa* (Issue Brief No. 5).

Isaacs, E., Visser, K., Friedrich, C., & Brijlal, P. (2007). Entrepreneurship education and training at the further education and Training (FET) level in South Africa. *South African Journal of Education, 27*(4), 613–630.

Lackéus, M. (2015). *Entrepreneurship in education: What, why, when, how*. OECD.

Macha, W. (2017). *Education in South Africa*. World Education News + Reviews. https://wenr.wes.org/2017/05/education-south-africa accessed 9 May 2019.

Mahieu, R. (2006). *Agents of change and policies of scale: A policy study of entrepreneurship and enterprise in education* (Doctoral thesis). Umeå Universitet.

McKeever, M. (2017). Educational inequality in apartheid South Africa. *American Behavioral Scientist, 61*(1), 114–131.

Mda, T., & Mothatha, S. (2000). *Critical Issues in South African Education after 1994*. Juta.

Riessman, C. K. (1993). *Narrative analysis* (Vol. 30). Sage.

Uleanya, C., & Gamede, B. T. (2017). The role of entrepreneurship education in secondary schools at further education and training phase. *Academy of Entrepreneurship Journal 23*(2), 1–12.

Union of South Africa. (1950). *Population Registration Act: No. 30 of 1950*. SA Government Gazette.

United Nations. (2015). *Transforming our world: The 2030 agenda for sustainable development*. Resolution adopted by the General Assembly.

Valerio, A., Parton, B., & Robb, A. (2014). *Entrepreneurship education and training programs around the world: Dimensions for success*. The World Bank.

9

Risk Society as a Framework for Exploring Entrepreneurship Education in Nigeria

Samson O. Oladejo and Oluwasoye P. Mafimisebi

Introduction

In this study, we demonstrated how the notion of risk society is driving entrepreneurship education among young people in Nigeria using risk society theory as our conceptual lens. The risk society theory is particularly relevant because young people in today's society are vulnerable and exposed to series of unimaginable life experiences. Modern risk theorists has consistently sought to capture the dynamisms of the modern era and consistently argued that risks are embedded in every fabric of human endeavours and that the world is increasingly turning to a risk society surrounded with uncertain and unfortunate unpredictable events such as terrorism, climate change, outbreak of pandemic, nuclear disasters to mention just a few that tends to negatively impact on the way of life for the current generation (Beck, 1992, 2000, 2014; Bialostok, 2015; Giddens, 1999). Beck referred to this as manufactured risks which evolve as a result of routine consequences of technological, scientific and economic advancement with broader international implications

---

S. O. Oladejo (✉)
University of the West of Scotland, Paisley, United Kingdom
e-mail: Samson.Oladejo@uws.ac.uk

O. P. Mafimisebi
Centre for Enterprise and Innovation, De Montfort University, Leicester, UK
e-mail: oluwasoye.mafimisebi@dmu.ac.uk

and boomerang effects (Beck, 1992: 48). Risk theorists posited that risk in the modern society are novel, systematic, inevitable and are usually caused by series of individual or institutional actions or inactions which could sometimes cause significant and damaging impacts that could stretched within and outside the countries. The coronavirus risk and the ensuing crises is a classic example how novel and unconventional risk can transcend across national borders with consequential impact.

In particular, Beck (1992) through the lens of his ground-breaking risk society theory has provided a theoretical framework through which the incidences, transitions, processes and dynamics of the current political, cultural, religious, industrialised and globalised world could be understood, analysed and interpreted (cf. Connolly & Haughton, 2017). Also, Giddens (1990) sees risk as a double-edged sword of the contemporary world embedded with both prospects and calamities which are metamorphosed into opportunity and disaster. Connolly and Haughton (2017) clearly pointed out that risk is not just an art or a term, but as well a daily experience with unimaginable potential future disaster which could pose a threat to many if appropriate theoretical approach is not put in place. In this regard, one of the distinctions of Beck legacy was the applicability of risk society theory to national and international risk communication and management (ibid.). Central to his study are risk, technological advancement, globalisation, industrialisation and reflexive modernisation.

Risks in late modernism is indiscernible because previously danger was tangible and one could see flames from a fire, see the foes approaching, or hear a furious waterfall and evade such peril. However, the five senses are incapable of protecting humans any longer (Beck, 1992) and threats are all around us. Accordingly, the societies which is the natural environment where entrepreneurship activities take are characterised by 'organised irresponsibility', where risk producers are protected at the expense of risk victims and no one can be sure of one's roles as to who will be the aggressor and who will be the victim (ibid). The outcome of human activities across a range of spectrum (entrepreneurship inclusive) have presented novel sources of risk and uncertainty which serve to accentuate the risk(s) involved in constructing daily decisions, and a central irony to the risk society is that these risks are created by the developments of modernisation trying to regulate them (Beck, 1992, 2014; Giddens, 1999,

Beck and other scholars postulated that, risk in the modern society are systematic, inevitable, universal, undetectable where the production of wealth led to the production of risks and poses the threat that could undermine the economic, social, environmental, and entrepreneurial activities and how entities are pursuing their errands individually and collectively (Beck, 1995; Blok, 2018; O'Connor, 2019). This undoubtedly, is contributing to the crisis of unemployment that is crippling the labour market in Nigeria (ILO, 2019) and made worse by the ever-increasing population, precariousness, endemic corruption and bad leadership in the country (NBS, 2018, 2020; UNESCO, 2019). Considering these complexities, systemic failures and associated risk construction despite the country's huge potentials and high level of wealth among its political elites. Research suggests that millions of young people who are supposed to be in employment are at risk of joblessness with unfavourable live opportunity (ILO, 2019). To reverse this trend, we suggest that an all-inclusive entrepreneurship education is crucial and should be integrated across all levels of educational systems in Nigeria.

We note that vulnerable young people in Nigeria have little or no control over the modernised, ever changing demand in the risk society (Beck, 1992). Therefore, our main claim is that entrepreneurship education is critical to develop and promote entrepreneurial and employability skills of young people in Nigeria. There are over 10.5 million children out of school in Nigeria and more than 80% of young people in Nigeria are from poor families (UNESCO, 2019; UNICEF, 2019). This impacted negatively on their access to basic education and partly explains why many young people engaged in entrepreneurship activities like streets hawking and other risky ventures as means of survival and to funding their education in Nigeria (Adekunle, 2019; Babalola, 2013; Onyimadu, 2020; UBEC, 2009). A large number of young people in Nigeria engage in trading and other entrepreneurship activities in hazard-prone environment which exposes them to series of unimaginable risks and dangers. Moreover, while Nigeria is acclaimed to have produced the highest number of educated young people in the whole of Africa, youth unemployment and poverty remains high (Adekunle, 2019). In context, existing studies found that more than 80% of a graduate who finished higher education are without job and are mostly engaged in the informal sector (UNESCO, 2015; ILO, 2019). To illustrate, current unemployment rate stands at 33.5% among the general population but youth unemployment and underemployed rate remains at 55.4% (NBS, 2020). Although unemployment is projected to increase especially among young people, we argue that entrepreneurship education can help reverse this trend.

Research suggests that unemployment situation in Nigeria is made worse by the adverse effect of risk society, weak institutions, endemic corruption and bad governance. Collectively, these factors contribute to the weak entrepreneurial ecosystems and institutional architectures vital to support entrepreneurship in Nigeria. Our review of existing studies found that low skills limit opportunities for employment in the formal economy and that government social programmes (for example, N-Power and other youth empowerment schemes) intended to address problems of poverty and unemployment are ineffective. Therefore, we examine how entrepreneurship education can be used to provide sustainable solution to raising unemployment and poverty situations in Nigeria. We draw on the risk society framework uncover issues that are integral to creating inclusive and entrepreneurial opportunities in Nigeria. In this direction, education play crucial roles in transforming societal problems and promoting economic well-being (Gottfried, 2014; UNESCO, 2016). The role of education in facilitating social development (UNESCO, 2016), reducing poverty and inequalities across societies (Shimeles & Verdier-Chouchane, 2016), raises national and organisational productivity, promotes people's creativity, entrepreneurship and technological advances, and enhancing sustainable development (World Bank, 2008) has been well-documented in the literature.

Moreover, the rate of participation in education has been shown to have a direct impact on entrepreneurship activity of an individual. Albeit research suggests that this partly depends on the commitment of the economic, social and political institutions of a nation (Nieuwenhuizen & Kroon, 2002). As a result, Nigerian government has resulted into formulating basic education and entrepreneurship policies to accelerate access to education and to promote entrepreneurs' culture among its young generation (Abdulraheem et al., 2013; UNESCO, 2011). In this context, entrepreneurship education was introduced in tertiary institutions with the hope of equipping students with appropriate entrepreneurial skills and knowledge required to be able to live a meaningful life and as well contribute to the growth and development of their societies in line with National Policy on Education. This is because entrepreneurship helps in reducing unemployment by creating jobs and entrepreneurship education can be employed as a viable instrument in raising and instilling entrepreneurial mindsets.

Furthermore, the pressure on higher institutions in Nigeria to produce employable graduates and stimulate business start-ups has resulted into compulsory introduction of entrepreneurship education to all students in higher education. The essence was to train them to be able to use critical and creative thinking to identify, analyse, organise, manage activities and solve problems in a proactive and efficient ways. Also, the policy stipulated that students should be equipped with the ability to negotiate and communicate effectively and be curious to experiment innovative ideas. Similarly, entrepreneurial education was introduced at basic education levels in the revised UBE policy in 2008 (UBEC, 2009). This was aimed at preparing students to develop a theoretical base for life-long entrepreneurship and business skills. In this chapter, we reflect on the implications of the Nigerian government approach to entrepreneurship education. In the next section we explore entrepreneurship education and revisit the notion of entrepreneurship education in Nigeria. This is followed by another section on entrepreneurship education and risk society. We discuss the methods and present some emerging ideas and thinking about entrepreneurship education at basic level. In the last two sections, we discuss our findings, reflect on the implications and concluding remarks.

Background, Context and Literature

Entrepreneurship Education: A Conceptual Review

Entrepreneurship education is broadly conceptualised as strategic efforts to support students and graduates with entrepreneurial mindsets including perseverance, trust, determination, risk management, a positive attitude towards change, tolerance of uncertainties, initiatives, the need to achieve, understanding of timeframes, creativity and clear understanding of big picture (Humphreys & Crawfurd, 2015; Taatila, 2010; Uyanga, 2012). The Quality Assurance Agency for Higher Education (QAA) (2018) defined entrepreneurship education as the application of enterprise behaviours, attributes and competencies into the creation of cultural, social or economic value. Albeit the QAA (2018) recognised that entrepreneurship education can, but does not exclusively, lead to venture creation. Recent studies have investigated role of entrepreneurship education in facilitating employable graduates and stimulate business start-ups (Jones & Matlay, 2011; Pittaway & Hannon, 2008). The discourse of entrepreneurship education is driven by factors associated with risk society in which political and institutional actors (e.g. government officials and universities) are under moral obligation to ensure graduates are fit for the twenty-first-century global economy (Gibb, 2008). This view implies that political and institutional actors should develop policy and practice regarding entrepreneurship education which enhance entrepreneurial qualities of students and graduates.

Albeit entrepreneurship education is a complex phenomenon which varies in definition, approach and implementation (Crayford et al., 2012; Jones & Iredale, 2010), we emphasise the value of context when discussing entrepreneurship education. The variations in conceptualization of entrepreneurship education suggest that context moderate its usage and application. In this view, entrepreneurship education is much broader than entrepreneurial learning or teaching students how to develop new business plans, create and manage micro and small start-ups. The new emerging approach to entrepreneurship education takes into consideration pedagogical advances in entrepreneurial learning, development of the teacher-learner experience, life skills and good citizenship (Crayford et al., 2012; Draycott et al., 2011; Jones & Iredale, 2010). This is a more flexible approach to entrepreneurship education. The European Commission's EntreComp Framework is also another useful model of entrepreneurship education. The EntreComp framework is divided into three areas, those ideas and opportunities, resources and into action. Within this framework, entrepreneurship competence includes spotting opportunities, vision, creativity, valuing ideas, taking the initiative, mobilising others, motivation and perseverance, mobilising resources, financial and economic literacy, working with others, learning through experience, coping with ambiguity, uncertainty and risk (EU EntreComp, 2018). However, it is also essential to acknowledge the need to incorporate other variables such as inclusion of marginalise ethnics groups, vulnerable people, resilience, entrepreneurial ecosystems, and inclusive culture towards entrepreneurship as vital components of entrepreneurship education. In practical context, we consider entrepreneurship education as an effective tool to bridge the gaps and challenges of risk society and connE6ect them to sustainable enterprise solutions. In what follows, we consider entrepreneurship education in Nigeria context and specifically discuss how this matter for vulnerable young people in risk society.

Entrepreneurship Education in the Nigerian Context

Over the past few decades, the economies of most African countries have passed through turbulent times which ravaged and plagued entrepreneurial activities. In the Nigeria context, our review of existing literature found that pandemic poverty, unemployment, institutional voids, climate change, terrorism, banditry and communal conflicts complicate entrepreneurial activities. For example, the national poverty and inequality in Nigeria is estimated at 40% and youth unemployment is over 50% (Adeniran et al., 2019; World Bank, 2019). While entrepreneurship education is viewed as vital to develop entrepreneurial capability and can help address issues of poverty, unemployment and job creation, there are several under-explored factors including role of entrepreneurial ecosystems and risk society in Nigeria. Therefore, we argue that entrepreneurship education in Nigeria context is more complex and flexible to accommodate varied practices that facilitate entrepreneurial activities.

Indeed, entrepreneurship has long been recognised for its contribution to societal growth over the past several decades. Also, the relationship between entrepreneurship education and entrepreneurial intentions and development has been analysed in a meta-analytic review (Bae et al., 2014). Bae et al. (2014) found that that entrepreneurship skills can be shaped by entrepreneurship education. We broaden this line of discussion that introducing entrepreneurship education to young people at basic education levels could be used to address the problem of access to free basic education and the risks associated with vulnerable young people in Nigeria. In the Nigeria context, we view entrepreneurship education in a wide sense as any pedagogical programme or process of education for entrepreneurial attitudes and skills which involves developing certain personal entrepreneurial qualities that help overcome challenges, vulnerabilities and risks associated with starting businesses and/or developing employability profile. This conceptualization is therefore not exclusively focused on the immediate creation of new businesses but covers a wide variety of situations, aims, methods and teaching approaches (Alain et al., 2006).

Here, entrepreneurship education is a process of acquiring entrepreneurial skills, behaviours and personal talents which scope spanned beyond the sole aim of establishing an enterprise. However, most of the young people we investigated dabble into enterprise for economic survivals while many others indicated that becoming an entrepreneur is a desirable career choice due to unemployment and poverty in Nigeria. Studies have shown that the economic situation of an individuals is positively related to their entrepreneurship engagement leading to the economic development of their communities (Page & Soderbom., 2015). In context of Nigeria, we found that those who engaged in entrepreneurial activities without adequate entrepreneurial training are disadvantage in the marketplace and at risk of business discontinuity (Edoho, 2015).

Empirical studies have found out that lack of adequate and appropriate entrepreneurship skills could lead to business closure because access to the right information is very crucial for business success (Mutalemwa, 2015). Our review of entrepreneurship studies showed that having access to the right information between actors in the entrepreneurial ecosystems and networks is beneficial especially where entrepreneurial actors share insights and ideas. In addition, actors from diverse backgrounds and groups provide a myriad of informational resources that can be used to stimulate entrepreneurial activities in Nigeria. Therefore, we argue that access to entrepreneurial ecosystems, informational network and entrepreneurship education is critical in enabling entrepreneurial skills and creativity in Nigeria. Hence, we propose that the more diverse the entrepreneurial networks are, the more innovative the entrepreneurs in entrepreneurial ecosystems become. In sum, we argue that entrepreneurship education in Nigeria must penetrate to the basic education level to ensure inclusive entrepreneurship and development. We elaborate upon this view in the next section.

Entrepreneurship Education at Basic Education Level in Nigeria

The Nigeria Universal Basic Education (UBE) policy and National Policy on Education (NPE) (UBEC, 2009) make education at basic level free and compulsory for young people in Nigeria. The UBE policy was designed to address the problem of out-of-school children in Nigeria. In global context, the number of 'out-of-school' children is estimated at 58.4 million (UNESCO, 2019) and more than 250 million children cannot read (The Good Planet Foundation, 2013; UNESCO, 2015). However, the data shows that Nigeria has the highest number of 'out-of-school' children estimated at over 10.5 million and research evidence further revealed that 90% of these 'out-of-school' children never attend school (Humphreys & Crawfurd, 2015; Uyanga, 2012). Consequently, successive Nigerian governments have introduced series of educational policies over the past five decades to solve the grave problem of 'education equity problem'.

However, the introduction of UBE policy with the aim of providing free and compulsory education and make young people self-reliant and a productive member of the society has not help solve these problems (Adekunle, 2019; Adeniran et al., 2019; Babalola, 2013; Humphreys & Crawfurd, 2015). As a result, we argue that ineffectiveness of Nigerian educational policy can be address by focusing on entrepreneurship education at the basic educational level (Uyanga, 2012). In clear context, we note that by extending entrepreneurship education to basic educational level, entrepreneurial learning opportunities become inclusive and available to marginalise or vulnerable groups in Nigeria. This is the most proactive approach to address education equity problem and unemployment in Nigeria. While much of the Nigerian educational policy continues around entrepreneurship education at higher education level, we argue it is actually the introduction of entrepreneurship education at basic education level which is most important.

In view of the discussion above, there is also a clear need to focus on entrepreneurial education that embraces inclusive provision and delivery, experiential learning processes, outcomes and assessment, local participation, community engagement and resilience, and student-employer participation. In this regard, entrepreneurship education is position to instil entrepreneurial knowledge and skills required to students right from the beginning of their education. This will enable them to be able to engage in entrepreneurial activities successfully in a variety of ways. The exercise will involve training, tutoring and providing guidance for them to participants and as well provide the enabling and conducive environment for them to operate (Adekunle, 2019; Mutalemwa, 2015; Onyimadu, 2020). Moreover, this approach will afford young people the entrepreneurial opportunities to discover business opportunity, sharpens their employability skills and creativity as well as apply them for economic, social and cultural gains and for community and national development.

Furthermore, it is imperative to include entrepreneurship education within the context of risk society with emphasis on practicable working models to enhance UBE objectives of making pupils self-reliant through entrepreneurship at the end of their nine years basic education in Nigeria (Edoho, 2015; Mutalemwa, 2015; UBEC, 2009). This is crucial because of the unprecedented challenging times we live in and coupled with the attendant impact resulting in mass unemployment, abject poverty, dwindling economies, millions of children out of school, tribal conflicts, increasing crimes, and various kinds of diseases just to mention a few (Salabson, 2020).

In addition to the above-mentioned points, the uncertainties that characterises the Nigeria business environment and society expose young people to a situation that makes them more disadvantaged and vulnerable in many aspects. The introduction of entrepreneurship education at the basic level is vital to overcome some of these challenges and make young people resilient in Nigeria. Therefore, we call for the affirmation of entrepreneurship education to provide inclusive entrepreneurial opportunities; and also, we emphasise the need for urgent action and innovation in Nigeria educational systems. Our rationale is derived from the empirical research findings which suggest that collaboration, innovation and robust entrepreneurial ecosystems are needed to allo0w effective entrepreneurship education (Edoho, 2015; Humphreys & Crawfard, 2015).

Entrepreneurship Education and Risk Society

Risk society is view as the manner in which society organises in response to risk. We conceptualise contemporary Nigeria as a 'risk society' (Beck, 1992) to indicate the fundamental change in the nature of societal vulnerability and resilience. Albeit the notion of risk society was originally used to describe a fundamental change in the relationship between society and nature. In the Nigeria context, we extend the discussion of risk society as the main factor responsible for the social amplification of risk and creation of new hazards (Mafimisebi, 2017, 2018; Mafimisebi & Thorne, 2017a). In this view, social behaviour and societal reaction to lack of entrepreneurial opportunities create new hazards and risks. The risk society thesis emphasised that modern risks such as climate change, poverty and unemployment are reflexive in the sense that they are self-inflicted (Mafimisebi, 2017). For example, risks in the entrepreneurial ecosystems of Nigeria are broadly external to most citizens and/or entrepreneurs.

Diseases would spread, lack of access to basic education limits entrepreneurial learning, climate change would damage farm harvests, and institutional voids complicate ease of doing business in Nigeria. This perspective conceptualises risks as consequences of human activities (Beck, 1992). According to Douglas (1966), risks are responses to problem within the social arena of a distinct environment and as social cohesion deteriorates, disaster and threats of risks assists as resources for constructing societal demand and protecting social restrictions. Here, we argue that while undertaking entrepreneurial activities is inherently risky; entrepreneurship education is crucial to enable citizens have access to inclusive entrepreneurial opportunities and overcome factors that make them vulnerable in society (Beck, 1992; Giddens, 1999; Mafimisebi et al., 2018; Mafimisebi & Thorne, 2017b). We hypothesise that entrepreneurial learning is crucial in such situations because entrepreneurship actions are socially embedded.

In this sense, describing entrepreneurship education [formal & pedagogic, received] and entrepreneurial learning [naturalistic & learner-centred andragogic, active] will be immensely beneficial to the study at this stage. Although, '*there is no one size fit it all*' definition for entrepreneurship education, However, in the context of this chapter, entrepreneurship education is described as an architectural model for shaping motives and attitudes that helps to equip young people with functional knowledge and skill that assists them in taken informed entrepreneurship decisions through teachings that encourages creative thinking either in a formal and pedagogical manner or through an instruction received in an informal way; Nzokurum & Orji,

2017; Olokundun, 2018; Rae & Wang, 2015). Entrepreneurship education is much wider than entrepreneurship learning as it encompasses a variety range of events.

On the other hand, entrepreneurial learning is crucial to nurturing a wider set of qualities that can form a crucial and key basis for entrepreneurial venturing (European, 2006). This is why the introduction of entrepreneurship education is particularly important at the basic education levels in developing countries such as Nigeria. To this end, over the years, several scholars such as Draycott et al. (2011), Rae and Matlay (2010) have argued that entrepreneurial intents is a compelling and strong determinant of entrepreneurial conduct. In this regard, entrepreneurship scholars have tried to comprehend and evaluate the characteristics and the efficacy (nitty–gritty) of enterprise creation under condition of risk and uncertainty. Therefore, entrepreneurship education and risk society act as a bridge between weak educational governance, institutional voids and educational policy implementation that tends characterise the Nigerian business environment. In this regard, exploring entrepreneurship education through the prisms of risk society brings the future into the present and make it more calculable. This view allows us to theorise about entrepreneurship patterns and activities as embedded in risks, vulnerabilities and resilience (Mafimisebi & Ogbonna, 2016; Mafimisebi & Thorne, 2015). This implies that entrepreneurship education can then be geared towards positioning citizens especially at basic education level to prepared themselves along a focused set of rules directed towards certain set objectives of managing such unexpected events surrounding their entrepreneurial endeavours and/or business activities (Beck & Douglas, 1985).

In a similar vein, the study suggests that introducing entrepreneurship education to young people at the basic education levels could make them acquire the right and needed skills and to help them behave in a way that will make them emerge as successful entrepreneurs in the risk society. This implies that social embeddedness of entrepreneurship education displays itself not only in shaping young people's dispositions but also entrepreneurial mindsets and behaviours to enterprise. In context, it is acknowledged that entrepreneurial mindset and flexibility of response are crucial to deal with uncertainty in risk society. Additionally, drawing upon risk society lens, we further propose that entrepreneurship education will shape the way in which enterprise materials are produced, leveraged and used within the context of the society. Thus, risk society and entrepreneurship education are used to draw the attention of young people in Nigeria to specific types of danger or as a device for improving and increasing their access to inclusive entrepreneurial opportunities, thereby solving the problem of poverty and unemployment in society (Beck, 1999; Mafimisebi, 2017; Mafimisebi & Thorne, 2015).

Methods

We used systematic search approach found in review studies and explore online databases such as Scopus, Web of Science, Google Scholar, EBSCO and their reference lists to identify all relevant published articles in the field of entrepreneurship education and risk society during the past five decades. This search strategy of using several sources helped us to ensure that we have included all notable risk society and entrepreneurship education studies in our research. Moreover, we also focused specifically on studies relating to entrepreneurship education and risk society in Africa context. To locate the most relevant studies in this area, we used keywords such as entrepreneurship education, risk society, inclusive entrepreneurship in Africa, universal basic education, entrepreneurial opportunities in Africa, Africa entrepreneurship, Nigeria national policy on education, vulnerable young people in Nigeria, education and out-of-school children in Nigeria. We exclude studies that did not contain these terms from our final selection of articles. In context, we operationalise the search strategy by ensuring that the final articles contain keywords of specifically mentioned our search terms.

The initial articles collected were reviewed and refined to ensure that we take into consideration entrepreneurship education and risk society in Nigeria context. Furthermore, we are particular about the need to understand and give meaningful interpretations to young people subjective lived experiences in relation to entrepreneurial opportunities in risk society. Therefore, we augment and enrich the review articles by collecting qualitative data through photovoice and community walk. The use of photovoice and community walk allow us to interact with 53 participants (young people of school age, teachers, parents, school principals and ministry of education officials) across different works of lives in Nigeria. In perspective, the first author carried out the data collection in Nigeria as part of a broader project examining risk society and universal basic education. Throughout the process of photovoice and community walk, research field notes on the lived experience of young people and observations were recorded.

Photovoice is an innovative visual qualitative research method that allow participants the opportunity to capture their experiences, perspectives and views about an issue that matters to them and allow them to dialog with the researcher in order to compare pedagogies from themes that evolved from the conversations (Pilcher et al., 2016; Wang & Burris, 1994). It is underpinned by Freire's method to education for critical consciousness, allowing participants to make sense of photos to document and reflect their day to day happenings and involvements that are vital to them (Liebenberg, 2018). Photovoice is an enhanced method of expression and approachability which we observed to be very effective to gather facts from young people (see also Lögdberg et al., 2018).

Similarly, Community Walk (CW) a participatory qualitative approach was employed in this research to solicit information from young people in the study site which took a form of control walk within the participants community as prescribed by Evans and Jones (2011). The researcher engaged young people in an informal walk through a predetermine route already agreed by the two parties (Woodgate et al., 2017). This was utilised to engage young people in a conversational walk which allows them to share their experiences, concerns and relate with the researchers, asking and answering questions that relate to the subject matter. CW enables young people to share their first-hand real-time experiences on their involvement on entrepreneurship activities and education.

Though the photovoice and community walk are adjudged to be innovative and maximise representativeness among other things (Woodgate et al., 2017). However, the methods are said to be subjective, time consuming, and with sets of multiple ethical quandaries- typical features and distinctive characteristics of a qualitative research (Punch & Oancea, 2014). Other shortcomings of photovoice was that it requires huge resources to carry out (Sutton-Brown, 2015). After considering the fact that the advantages of using these methods far outweighed the disadvantages which are clearly enumerated above, it was consequently adopted. The researchers skilfully mitigated the limitations using their expertise, wealth of experiences and training given to the participants as recommended by Wang (1999).

We use photovoice and community walk as data collection tools in this study to collected useful information from young people about their involvement in entrepreneurship activities and access to education. The research field notes and observation records allow us to make sense of entrepreneurship education and risk society in the Nigeria context. In the following section, we present our findings and linked the discussion to the entrepreneurship education and risk society literature.

Empirical Findings—Risk Society and Entrepreneurship Education in Nigeria

In this section, we present our main findings from the literature and reflect upon qualitative data derived from photovoice and community walk to guide our analysis. Recent research on risk society suggested that vulnerability in society is complicated and amplified by the nature of political and institutioal actors' response to institutional problems (Mafimisebi, 2017). In order to shape and give correct meanings to young peole voices and pictures and to critically analyse and interpreted the information they provided about their experiences; an interpretative phenomenological analysis (IPA) was adopted through the lens of risk society. IPA offer an insight into how young people make sense of their individual subjective experiences relating to their entrepreneurial actions and access to education (Creswell, 2014; Robson & McCartan, 2016; Williams, 2018). The data were subjected to processes of IPA of reading and re-reading to familiarise with the contents, then coding and categorising until the key themes evolved (Punch & Oancea, 2014; Smith et al., 2009). We found that three main themes emerge from both our review of existing literature and qualitative data collected via photovoice and community walk in Nigeria. These themes are inclusive entrepreneurship education, institutional problems of risk society, and resilient entrepreneurial activities. We elaborate upon these themes in the following subsections.

Inclusive Entrepreneurship Education

We found that entrepreneurship education is currently introduced at higher education level in Nigeria. Our review shows that this exclusive approach to entrepreneurship education is not sustainable because a large number of individuals are marginalised and vulnerable from the institutional problems created by political and institutional actors. Albeit while there is some evidence that entrepreneurship education is essential at basic and vocational education level, this is largely ignored in current Nigeria educational policy and actions. Our community walk data suggest that some of the young people were unable to attend school because of a lack of money to buy basic materials needed in school, pay transport fare to school and/or buy food to eat during school hours. Although these materials are supposed to be provided for them free as contained in the universal basic education policy (Adekunle, 2019; Onyimadu, 2020; UBE, 2009). The lack of sufficient free education materials for young people from vulnerable and marginalised family's impact on their abilities to access entrepreneurial opportunities.

While entrepreneurship education has largely been at the remit of higher education, there is now increasing need for inclusive entrepreneurship education in Nigeria. We found that current practices of entrepreneurship education fail to account for large number of people who do not attend formal education in Nigeria. This implies that a significant number of them do not have access to entrepreneurial learning. The institutional problems created through educational policy make it difficult for individuals to access entrepreneurship education in Nigeria. In this regard, we argue that there is close interaction between risk society and entrepreneurship education in Nigeria because individuals' experiences are socially embedded in them via constant interactions (Bryman, 2015; Jha, 2008; Punch & Oancea, 2014). Therefore, we suggest that inclusive entrepreneurship education that takes into consideration broader societal and institutional risks as well as household vulnerability is essential to overcome some of the current challenges in Nigeria. For example, we contend that inclusive entrepreneurship education would provide equitable access to entrepreneurial learning and by extension entrepreneurial opportunities discovery and realisation. This calls for the need to revisit deficiencies in the current entrepreneurship education policies and practices in Nigeria. In doing this, the emphasis should be placed on providing entrepreneurship education (both formal and non-formal) and training with a particular focus on young people at the basic education levels where their potentials and skills are resulted into enterprise ventures, incorporating an informal learning to engage those not in formal education develop entrepreneurial behaviours and intentions with or without a profitable objective. In practical context, there is a need to move away from the current practice of entrepreneurial learning to entrepreneurship education which also incorporates entrepreneurial learning. This holistic approach to entrepreneurship education is required to make meaningful impact in a risk society such as Nigeria.

Institutional Problems of Risk Society

In this conversation, our findings suggest that current practices of entrepreneurship education produce risks which are also accompanied by the social amplification of risks in Nigeria. Drawing from the risk society lens, we argue that there is the need to understand the new dimension of entrepreneurship education which not only acknowledges that exclusive entrepreneurial opportunities produces risks, but also systematically and openly seeks to answer how unequal entrepreneurial opportunities could be prevented, minimised and problematized. It is acknowledged that 'unequal entrepreneurial opportunities' cannot be eliminated, but may be minimised with good governance and accountability, equal access to entrepreneurial finance, and standardised ease of doing business in Nigeria. Our argument is underpinned by empirical evidence that one of the factors that could deterred the success of entrepreneurship activities among young people even when properly implemented within the context of risk society is the institutional problems of Nigeria. The persistent institutional problems and failure of entrepreneurial ecosystems and architecture of the Nigeria to provide equitable entrepreneurial opportunities discourages young entrepreneurs and shrink the domestic economy, and eventually inhibit prospects for economic growth (Achumba et al., 2013; Mafimisebi, 2017; Mafimisebi & Thorne, 2015). In this regard, we argue that institutional problems can be a recipe for social unrest which could substantially impact on entrepreneurial activities and thereby compound high unemployment and poverty risks in Nigeria.

Our findings indicate that one of the crucial challenges facing entrepreneurship in Nigeria is the propensity of the crisis of vulnerability in entrepreneurial activities. While entrepreneurial activities in other climates are not immune from risks, Nigeria is faced with uncertainty, social and cultural constrains, identity problem, stress, lack of access to finance, lack of access to modern technologies, incessant power supply and inadequate specialised education. Thus, research findings suggest that these several factors combined partly explain the dynamics of wealth and poverty in Nigeria. Hence, there is need to consider the unique characteristics of business environment and entrepreneurial ecosystems in Nigeria when introducing policies mix to address inequitable entrepreneurial opportunities. In this context, risk and vulnerability analysis work as a natural complement to traditional poverty analysis that can add value to the policy dialogue. The analysis of risk and vulnerability encapsulates two separate specific areas of attention. It focuses on the role of risk in the dynamics of poverty and the strategies households use to address the exposure to various sources of risks. Here, the focus is on the impact of risk on poverty, considering the informal and formal mechanisms of risk reduction, mitigation and coping capacities of individuals. Even though risk and its consequences are not given central importance when studying vulnerable groups, there is a considerable connection since their resilience and opportunities will make individuals liable to further impoverishment in risk society. These undoubtedly are inevitable outcome of risk society factors of poverty, corruption, kleptocracy, lack of access and transparency that impact entrepreneurial opportunities in Nigeria.

Entrepreneurial Activities in Nigeria

The risk society perspective on entrepreneurship education elaborates institutional problems, weak entrepreneurial ecosystems, and vulnerability that inhibit entrepreneurial learning and opportunities. We find that engagement in entrepreneurial activities is limited and most people lack access to entrepreneurship education in Nigeria. Although we find the individuals engage actively in micro and small business entrepreneurship in Nigeria. A number of these individuals are *sole-entrepreneurs* who require access to entrepreneurship education to learn the fundamentals of scaling and growing their micro businesses. In addition, there is considerable connection in the entrepreneurship and education policy arena whereby traditional instruments for social protection and entrepreneurial learning to be used as a springboard to enhance entrepreneurial activities in Nigeria. We find this approach allows young people to take advantage of entrepreneurial activities and opportunities for wealth and job creation while being protected against risk-induced hardship.

Furthermore, entrepreneurial activities in Nigeria require strategic entrepreneurship policy to ensure inclusive entrepreneurship. The photovoice and community walk data suggest that micro and petty trading are mostly done by the you people especially in packed traffics in places like Lagos, Nigeria (Fig. 9.1). In neighbourhoods' busy roads, young people trade a variety of goods including locally grown fruits and vegetables, hoping that passing vehicles will buy their goods, while others rent out gumboots to pedestrians who seek to pass flooded streets (Fig. 9.1). Others act as 'road traffic wardens' when bad roads become jammed-packed with vehicles. However, we find that most of the young people are not adequately trained to start and manage businesses. In this case, a number of these micro and small businesses ended shortly within two years and further contribute to joblessness in the community. This demonstrates the need for inclusive entrepreneurship education to ensure that all citizens have access to entrepreneurial learning. It is important to state that entrepreneurial learning would have to take place within the broader entrepreneurship education context in Nigeria.

Failure to acquire a rudimentary business expertise which could be made available to young people in primary and secondary schools may be attributed to one of the reasons most micro and small businesses fail in Nigeria. Our findings also showed that most individuals do see how entrepreneurship education provided in schools could give them the values and attitudes related to the skills they need to develop a thriving business. Therefore, we empathise

Fig. 9.1 Young Hawkers on Lagos streets (*Source* Authors [2019])

the need for political and institutional actors to help lay an important foundation for entrepreneurial behaviours in Nigeria. Developing an entrepreneurial skills base requires a shift in culture. One of the biggest limitations to developing an entrepreneurial skills base is the lack of support from society and formal institutions. The emphasis must shift from teaching content about entrepreneurship to broader issues of experiential modes of learning, start-ups funding, coaching and mentoring of entrepreneurs, and collaboration from all stakeholders.

Discussion

In this chapter, we have demonstrated how the notion of risk society is driving entrepreneurship education in Nigeria. Research suggests that unemployment and poverty situations in Nigeria is made worse by the adverse effect of weak institutions, endemic corruption and bad governance (Adekunle, 2019; Edoho, 2015; Mafimisebi & Ogbonna, 2016; Onyimadu, 2020). In addition, the economic effects of environmental crises, terrorism and diseases outbreak such as the Ebola health crisis and coronavirus (COVID-19) pandemic crisis are likely to further exacerbate these problems. Collectively, these factors contribute to the weak entrepreneurial ecosystems, institutional voids and entrepreneurial architectures vital to support entrepreneurship in Nigeria. Our review of existing studies found that low skills limit opportunities for employment in the formal economy and that government social programmes (for example, N-Power and other youth empowerment schemes) intended to address problems of poverty and unemployment are ineffective.

Notably, we found that the discourse of entrepreneurship education is driven by factors associated with risk society in which political and institutional actors (e.g. government officials and universities) are under moral obligation to ensure graduates are fit for the twenty-first-century global economy (Gibb, 2008). We emphasised the value of context when discussing entrepreneurship education. The variations in conceptualization of entrepreneurship education suggest that context moderate its usage and application. In this view, entrepreneurship education is much broader than entrepreneurial learning or teaching students how to develop new business plans, create and manage micro and small start-ups. In context, we acknowledged that the new emerging approach to entrepreneurship education takes into consideration pedagogical advances in entrepreneurial learning, development of the teacher-learner experience, life skills and good citizenship (Crayford et al., 2012; Draycott et al., 2011; Jones & Iredale, 2010). We argued that this is a more flexible approach to entrepreneurship education.

In the Nigeria context, we viewed entrepreneurship education in a wide sense as any pedagogical programme or process of education for entrepreneurial attitudes and skills which involves developing certain personal entrepreneurial qualities that help overcome challenges, vulnerabilities and risks associated with starting businesses and/or developing employability profile. This conceptualization is therefore not exclusively focused on the immediate creation of new businesses but covers a wide variety of situations, aims, methods and teaching approaches (Alain et al., 2006). In practical context, we considered entrepreneurship education as an effective tool to bridge the gaps and challenges of risk society and connect them to sustainable enterprise solutions.

Our work makes three main contributions to Africa entrepreneurship literature. First, we extend the discussion of risk society as the main factor responsible for the social amplification of risk and creation of new hazards in Nigeria (Mafimisebi, 2017, 2018; Mafimisebi & Thorne, 2017a). In this view, social behaviour and societal reaction to lack of entrepreneurial opportunities create new hazards and risks. The risk society thesis emphasised that modern risks such as climate change, poverty and unemployment are reflexive in the sense that they are self-inflicted (Mafimisebi, 2017). Second, we make our contribution by arguing that while undertaking entrepreneurial activities is inherently risky; inclusive entrepreneurship education is crucial to enable citizens have access to inclusive entrepreneurial opportunities and overcome challenges that make them vulnerable in society (Beck, 1992; Giddens, 1999; Mafimisebi et al., 2018; Mafimisebi & Thorne, 2017b). Third, and lastly, we used the notion of risk society and entrepreneurship education to draw attentions to specific types of dangers facing individuals in Nigeria and as a device for improving and increasing their access to inclusive entrepreneurial opportunities thereby solving the problem of poverty and unemployment in the society (Beck, 1999; Mafimisebi, 2017; Mafimisebi & Thorne, 2015).

Collectively, our findings have considerable implications for entrepreneurship education policy and practice in Nigeria. First, albeit we found that individuals demonstrate strong resilience in the face of risk society in Nigeria, our work calls for inclusive entrepreneurship education practice. We suggest the need for ensuring entrepreneurship education penetrates every level of education and also includes those who are outside the formal education structures in Nigeria. Second, we recommend that Nigeria drop the current practice of entrepreneurship education that is exclusively for those in the formal educational systems. In this regard, we call for a more equitable distribution of entrepreneurial learning in Nigeria. Third, there is need to consider the unique characteristics of business environment and entrepreneurial ecosystems in Nigeria when introducing policies mix to address inequitable entrepreneurial opportunities.

Conclusion

Drawing on the notion of risk society to explore entrepreneurship education, we suggest that entrepreneurship education should become integral across all educational levels in Nigeria. Albeit the notion of risk society was originally used to described a fundamental change in the relationship between society and nature. In the Nigeria context, we extend the discussion of risk society as the main factor responsible for the social amplification of risk and creation of new hazards (Mafimisebi, 2017, 2018; Mafimisebi & Thorne, 2017a). This is because individuals are exposed to series of unconventional risks and unimaginable life experiences that limit access to entrepreneurial opportunities. We suggest that inclusive entrepreneurship education should become an increasingly essential part of the overall Nigeria educational systems. The high number of people living in poverty and those without jobs increase the demand for entrepreneurial skills that will help them over the challenges of risk society and turbulent environment.

Entrepreneurship education in Nigeria should extend beyond the conventional school structure and incorporate indigenous and local participation from stakeholders to ensure that out-of-school children captured. Successful introduction and effective implementation of entrepreneurship education into the four walls of classrooms at the basic education level will provide young people with knowledge and tools they required to manage and sustain their entrepreneurial activities. Additionally, this will afford individuals to acquire necessary entrepreneurial skills and behaviours that will make them start their own business, be self-reliant, formalised their businesses, and to acquire the needed expertise to maintain professional networks. This in turn will reduce high rate of unemployment in the country by alleviate poverty, eradicate unemployment and increase access to education. Nigerian entrepreneurship education initiatives should focus on the development of robust entrepreneurial ecosystems, enterprising individuals and their ability to remain resilient in risk society, and maintain inclusive approach to entrepreneurial opportunities. In conclusion, we have succinctly proposed how the concept of risk society is powering entrepreneurship education in Nigeria and established that joblessness and poverty situations in the country is made worse by the negative impact of weak institutions, widespread corruption, bad governance and the damaging impact of COVID-19 pandemic. Together, these issues contribute to the weak entrepreneurial ecosystems, institutional voids and poor entrepreneurial designs crucial to support entrepreneurship in Nigeria.

References

Abdulraheem, I., Mordi, C., Yinka, O., & Ajonbadi, H. (2013). Outcomes of planned organisational change in the Nigerian public sector: Insights from the Nigerian higher education institutions. *Economic Insights - Trends and Challenges, 65*(1), 26–37.

Achumba. I.C, Ighomereho. O. S, Akpor-Robaro. M. O. M. (2013). Security challenges in Nigeria and the implications for business activities and sustainable development, *Journal of Economics and Sustainable Development, 4*(2). www.iiste.org. ISSN 2222–1700 (Paper) ISSN 2222–2855 (Online).

Adekunle, A. (2018, December 27). UNICEF laments 10.5m out-of-school children in Nigeria. Vanguard. Retrieve from: www.vanguardngr.com/2018/12/unicef-laments-10-5m-out-of-school-childrenin-nigeria/.

Adekunle, A. (2019). Emerging issues in the achievement of the mandates of the universal basic education programme In Nigeria. *InterdisciplinaryJournal of Education (IJE), 2*(1), 15–26. Retrieved.iuiu.ac.ug/index/ije/article/view/7.

Adeniran, A., Onyekwen, C., Onubedo, G., Ishaku, J., & Amara Ekeruche. M. A. (2019). *Is Nigeria on track to achieving quality education for all? Drivers and implication.* State of the SDGs, Centre for the Study of the Economies of Africa, Abuja, Nigeria

Asongu, S., & Odhiambo, N. (2019). Doing business and inclusive human development in Sub-Saharan Africa. *African Journal of Economic and Management Studies, 10*(1), 2–16. https://doi.org/doi.org/10.1108/AJEMS-05-2018-0132

Babalola. Y. A. (2013). The effect of firm size on firms profitability in Nigeria. *Journal of Economics and Sustainable Development* www.iiste.org ISSN 2222–1700 (Online) Vol.4.

Bae, T. J., Qian, S., Miao, C., & Fiet, J. O. (2014). The relationship between entrepreneurship education and entrepreneurial intentions: A meta-analytic review. *Enterp. Theory Pract., 38*, 217–254.

Beck, U. (1992). *Risk society: Towards a new modernity*. Sage.

Beck, U. (1995a). *Ecological enlightenment: Essays on the politics of the risk society*. Humanities Press.

Beck, U. (1995b). *Ecological politics in an age of risk*. Polity Press; Blackwell

Beck, U. (1999). *World risk society*. Polity Press; Blackwell.

Beck, U. (2000). *The brave new world of work*. Polity Press.

Beck, U. (Ed.). (2014). *Ulrich Beck: Pioneer in cosmopolitan sociology and risk society*. Springer.

Bialostok, S. (2015). Risk theory and education: Policy and practice. *Policy Futures in Education., 13*(5), 561–576.

Bourdieu, P. (1990). *In other words: Essays towards a reflexive sociology*. Stanford University Press.

Bourdieu, P., & Passeron, J. C. (1964). *Les Héritiers. Les étudiants et leurs études*. Ed. de Minuit

Bryman, A. (2015). *Social research methods*. Oxford University Press.

Blok, A. (2018). The politics of urban climate risks: Theoretical and empirical lessons from Ulrich Beck's methodological cosmopolitanism. *Journal of Risk Research, 21*(1), 41–55. https://doi.org/10.1080/13669877.2017.1359203

Budget Office of the Federation. (2018). *Federal Government of Nigeria Appropriation Bill*. Retrieved from: http://placng.org/wp/wp-content/uploads/2018/06/2018-Appropriation-Act.pdf.

Bullough. A., & Renko, M. (2013). Entrepreneurial resilience during challenging times. *Journal of Business Horizons, 56*, 343–350. https://doi.org/10.1016/j.bushor.2013.01.001.

Connolly, M., & Haughton, C. (2017). The perception, management and performance of risk amongst forest school educators. *British Journal of Sociology of Education, 38*(2), 105–124.

Crayford, J., Fearon, C., McLaughlin, H., & Vuuren, W. V. (2012). Affirming entrepreneurial education: Learning, employability and personal development. *Industrial and Commercial Training, 44*(4), 187–193.

Creswell, J. W. (2014). *Research design: Qualitative, quantitative, and mixed methods approach* (3rd ed.). Sage.

Draycott, M., Rae, D., & Vause, K. (2011). The assessment of enterprise education in the secondary education sector. A new approach?. *Education + Training, 53*(8/9), 673–91.

Drucker, P. F. (1985). *Innovation and entrepreneurship: Practice and Principles*. Butterworth.
Federal Ministry of Education. (1999). *Implementation guidelines for the UBE programmes*. F.G. press.
Federal Republic of Nigeria. (1981). *National policy on education* (p. 8). NERDC Press.
Federal Republic of Nigeria. (1998). *National policy on education Lagos*. E Press.
Federal Republic of Nigeria. (2004). *National policy on education*. (4thed.). NERDC
Edoho, F. (2015). Entrepreneurship and socioeconomic development: Catalyzing African transformation in the 21st century. *African Journal of Economic and Management Studies, 6*(2), 127–147. https://doi.org/10.1108/AJEMS-03-2013-0030.
Ejere, E. I. (2011). An examination of critical problems associated with the implementation of the Universal Basic Education (UBE) Programme in Nigeria. *International Education Studies, 4*(1), 221–229.
Liguori, E., Bendickson, J., Solomon, S., & McDowell, W. C. (2019). Development of a multi-dimensional measure for assessing entrepreneurial ecosystems. *Entrepreneurship & Regional Development, Taylor & Francis Journals, 31*(1–2), 7–21. https://doi.org/10.1080/08985626.2018.1537144.
EntreComp: The Entrepreneurship Competence Framework. (2018). https://ec.europa.eu/jrc/en/publication/eur-scientific-and-technical-research-reports/entrecomp-entrepreneurship-competence-framework.
Evans, J., & Jones, P. (2011). The walking interview: *Methodology, mobility and place, 31*(2), 849–858.
Gibb, A. A. (2008). Entrepreneurship and enterprise education in schools and colleges: Insights from UK practice. *International Journal of Entrepreneurship Education, 6* (2).
Giddens, A. (1990). *The consequences of modernity*. Stanford: Stanford University Press.
Giddens, A. (1999). Risk and responsibility. *The Modern Law Review, 62*(1), 1–10. https://doi.org/10.1111/1468-2230.00188.
Good Planet Foundation. (2013). *Accelerating progress to 2015 Nigeria. A report series to the UN Special Envoy for Global Education*. The Good Planet Foundation (pp. 1–30).
Gottfried, M. A. (2014). The achievement effects of tardy classmates: Evidence in urban elementary schools. *An International Journal of Research, Policy and Practice, 25*(1). https://doi.org/10.1080/09243453.2012.728135.
Humphreys, S., & Crawfurd, L. (2015). *Issues of educational access, quality, equity and impact in Nigeria: The EDOREN review of the literature on basic education*. EDOREN, Abuja.
ILO (2019). International Labour Organisation. https://www.ilo.org/dyn/normlex/en/f?p=NORMLEXPUB:12100:0::NO::P12100_ILO_CODE:C107.

Jones, C., & Matlay, H. (2011). Understanding the heterogeneity of entrepreneurship education: Going beyond Gartner. *Education + Training, 53* (8/9), 692–703.

Jones, B., & Iredale, N. (2010). 'Enterprise education as pedagogy. *Education + Training, 52*(1), 7–19.

Jha, N. K. (2008). *Research methodology*. Abhishek Publications.

Liebenberg, L. (2018). Thinking critically about photovoice: Achieving empowerment and social change. *International Journal of Qualitative Methods, 17*, 1–9.

Lögdberg, U., Nilsson, B., & Kostenius, C. (2018). Young migrants' experiences and conditions: A photovoice study. *Sage Journals*, 1–12.https://doi.org/10.1177/2158244020920665.

Mafimisebi, O.P. (2017). *Self-inflicted disasters: moral disengagement in unconventional risk, crisis and disaster management strategy* (Unpublished PhD thesis). University of Portsmouth.

Mafimisebi, O. P. (2018). Risky business: Data on trading results for UK general insurance firms during and after the global financial crisis. *Data in Brief, 21*, 2384–2389.

Mafimisebi, O. P., Nworie, I., & Hadleigh, S. (2018). Resilience and learning from insurance firms: Dataset on British long-term insurance market performance. *Data in Brief, 21*, 2360–2366.

Mafimisebi, O. P., & Nkwunonwo, U. C. (2015). Environmental risk: Exploring organisational resilience and robustness. *International Journal of Scientific & Engineering Research, 6*(1), 1103–1115.

Mafimisebi, O. P., & Ogbonna, O. C. (2016). Environmental risk of gas flaring in Nigeria: Lessons from Chevron Nigeria and Ilaje crisis. *Journal of Economics and Sustainable Development, 7*(1), 180–204.

Mafimisebi, O. P., & Thorne, S. (2015). Oil terrorism-militancy link: Mediating role of moral disengagement in emergency and crisis management. *Journal of Emergency Management, 13*(5), 447–458.

Mafimisebi, O. P., & Thorne, S. (2017a). Strategies for disaster risk reduction and management: Are lessons from past disasters actionable? In C. Kuel & C. N. Madu (Eds.), *Handbook of disaster risk reduction & management* (pp. 843–866). World Scientific Press.

Mafimisebi, O. P., & Thorne, S. (2017b). Vandalism-militancy relationship: The influence of risk perception and moral disengagement. *International Journal of Mass Emergencies and Disasters, 35*(3), 191–223.

Mbakogu I., & Hanley J. (2020). The quest for education as a factor of vulnerability to child trafficking: Reflections on "child rescue" from the perspective of West African children. In j. Winterdyk & J. Jones (Eds.), *The Palgrave international handbook of human trafficking*. Palgrave Macmillan.

Mutalemwa, D. (2015). Does globalisation impact SME development in Africa? *African Journal of Economic and Management Studies, 6*(2), 164–182. https://doi.org/10.1108/AJEMS-01-2015-0012.

National Beuareu of Statistics. (2020). *Poverty and inequality in Nigeria 2019: 40% of total population classified as poor.*

Nieuwenhuizen, C., & Kroon, J. (2002). Identification of entrepreneurial success factors to determine the content of entrepreneurship subjects. *South Africa Journal of Higher Education, 16*(3). https://doi.org/10.10520/EJC36933.

NBS. (2018). *National survey of micro, small, and medium enterprises 2017*. Abuja. NBS.

Nwangwu, I. G. O. (2007). Entrepreneurship in education. Concepts and constraint. *African Journal of Education and Development Studies, 4*(1),196–207

Nzokurum, J. C., & Orji, U. W. (2017). Administration of enterpreneurship lifelong education for early childhood education in rivers state. *International Journal of Academia, 4*(1), 1–12.

O'Connor, C. D. (2019). Social change, risk, and individualization: Young people's perceptions of a large-scale oil extraction project. *Journal of Youth Studies, 22*(2), 273–289. https://doi.org/10.1080/13676261.2018.1497781.

Olawolu, O. E., & Kaegon, L. E. S. (2012, September 17–21). *Entrepreneurship education as tool for youth empowerment through higher education for global workplace in rivers*. A paper presented at the Seventh Regional Conference on Higher Education for a Globalized world organized by the Higher Education Research and Policy Network (HERPNET): holding at the University of Ibadan, Ibadan Nigeria.

Okereke, L. C., & Okorafor, S. N. (2011). Entrepreneurship skills development for millennium development goals (MGDs) in business education. *Business Education Journal, 1*(11), 83–88.

Olokundun, A. (2018). Experiential pedagogy and entrepreneurial intention: A focus on university entrepreneurship programmes. *Academy of Entrepreneurship Journal, 24*(2), 21–57.

Onyimadu, C. O. (2020). Assessing the Nigerian Federal government's financial commitments to its education rights obligations. *Modern Economy, 11*, 475–494. https://doi.org/10.4236/me.2020.112035.

Page, J., & Soderbom, M. (2015). Is small beautiful? Small enterprise, aid and employment in Africa. *African Development Review, 27*(S1), 44–55.

Pilcher, K., Martin, W., & Williams, V. (2016). Issues of collaboration, representation, meaning and emotions: Utilising participant-led visual diaries to capture the everyday lives of people in mid to later life. *International Journal of Social Research Methodology, 19*(6), 677–692.

Pittaway, L., & Hannon, P. (2008). Institutional strategies for developing entrepreneurship education: A review of some concepts and models. *Journal of Small Business and Enterprise Development, 15*(1), 202–226.

Punch, K. F., & Oancea, A. E. (2014). *Introduction to research methods in education.* Sage.

Rae, D., & Matlay, H. (2010). Enterprise education and university entrepreneurship. *Industry and Higher Education, 24*(6), 409–411. https://doi.org/10.5367/ihe.2010.0019.

Rae, D., & Wang, C. L. (2015). *Entrepreneurial learning: New perspectives in research, education and practice* (1st ed.). Routledge.

QAA. (2018). *Enterprise and entrepreneurship education: Guidance for UK higher education providers*. Retrieved from https://www.qaa.ac.uk/docs/qaas/enhancement-and-development/enterprise-and-entrpreneurship-education-2018.pdf?sfvrsn=15f1f981_8.

Robson, C., & McCartan, K. (2016). *Real world research* (4th ed.) Willey.

Shimeles A., & Verdier-Chouchane, A. (2016). The key role of education in reducing poverty in South Sudan. *African Development Review, 28*(2), 162–17. https://doi.org/10.1111/1467-8268.12199/pdf.

Smith, J., Flowers, P., & Larkin, M. (2009). *Interpretative phonomenological analysis: Theory method and research*. Sage.

Sutton-Brown, C. (2015). Photovoice: A methodological guide. *Photography and Culture, 7*(2), 169–185.

Taatila, V. P. (2010). Learning entrepreneurship in higher education. *Education + Training, 52*(1), 48–61.

UBE Information Handbook. (2009). *Role of responsibilities of UBE stakeholders and policy framework for collaboration*. ISBN: 13 978–978–49501–2–1

UNESCO. (2011). *Education for all global monitoring report 2011*. Paris: UNESCO.

UNESCO Institute for Statistics. (2016). *Estimating the number of out-of-school: A methodological problems and alternative approaches*. Retrieved from: unesco.org. http://www.uis.unesco.org.

UNICEF. (2019). *UNICEF Education*. Retrieved from: https://www.unicef.org/nigeria/education

United Nations Development Programme. (2016). *Human Development Report 2016: Human Development for Everyone*.

United Nations Educational, Scientific and Cultural Organisation. (2019a). International Yearbook of Industrial Statistics 2019. Cheltenham: Edward Elgar Publishing (cited on pages 61, 63).

United Nations Educational, Scientific and Cultural Organisation. (2019b). UNESCO Institute for Statistics (UIS) database (cited on pages 39–42).

Uyanga, R. (2012). The provision of universal basic education in Nigeria: Challenges in the 21st century. *International Journal of Diversity in Organisations, Communities & Nations, 11*(6), 31–48.

Wang, C., Morrel-Samuels, S., Hutchison, P. M., & Bell, L. (2004). Flint photovoice: Community building among youths, adults, and policymakers. *American Journal of Public Health, 94*(6), 911–913.

Wang, C. (1999). Photovoice: A participatory action research strategy applied to women's health. *Journal of Women's Health, 8*(2), 185–192.

Wang, C., & Burris, M. (1994). Empowerment through photo novella: Portraits of participation. *Health Education Quarterly, 21*(2), 171–186.

Wang, C., & Burris, M. (1997). Photovoice: Concept, methodology, and use for participatory needs assessment. *Health Education and Behaviour, 24*(3), 369–387.

Williams, N. (2018). *Research methods: The basics* (2nd ed.). Routledge.

Woldemichael & Shimeles. (2020). *African economic outlook 2020*. African Development Bank 2020.

Woodgate, R. L., Zurba, M., & Tennent, P. (2017). Worth a thousand words? Advantages, challenges and opportunities in working with photovoice as a qualitative research method with youth and their families [30 paragraphs]. *Forum Qualitative Sozialforschung/Forum: Qualitative Social Research, 18*(1), Art. 2.

World Bank. (2008). *Nigeria: A review of the costs and financing of public education.* Volume II: Main Report. Report 42418-NG. AFTH3, Human Development.

World Bank. (2013). *Youth employment in Sub-Saharan Africa: Overview*. World Bank.

World Bank. (2015). *Data and statistics.* Retrieved from http://data.worldbank.org.

World Bank. (2019a). *Poverty and Equity database*. Washington (cited on pages 25–27).

World Bank. (2019b). *World Development Indicators database*. Washington (cited on pages 47–55).

10

The Nexus Between Nigerian Universities' Entrepreneurship Training and Digital Technology: Influence on Graduates' New Venture Creations

Mojolaoluwa O. Alabi, Oluwasoye P. Mafimisebi, and Samson O. Oladejo

> Be prepared to sacrifice, and work harder than you've ever thought possible. Be prepared to work around the clock, to be laughed at, called a dreamer, and to be told several times that your ideas will not work. —Nkemdilim Begho

Introduction

The mainstream entrepreneurship literature emphasises the value of entrepreneurship training in boosting the capabilities for new venture creations. Previous studies found that entrepreneurial activities are crucial antecedent of economic competitiveness and innovation capabilities (Galindo & Mendez, 2014). This has necessitated government in most developed economies to invest greatly in entrepreneurship education at universities (Brush et al., 2009). In Nigeria, government investment in entrepreneurship training is driven in part by the raising number of unemployed graduates and youths. For example, the National Bureau of Statistics (NBS) reveals that in the fourth quarter of 2020, the unemployment rate in Nigeria is

---

M. O. Alabi · S. O. Oladejo
University of the West of Scotland, Glasgow, UK

O. P. Mafimisebi (✉)
Centre for Enterprise and Innovation, De Montfort University, Leicester, UK
e-mail: oluwasoye.mafimisebi@dmu.ac.uk

27.1%. This is a significant increase in the unemployment rate which stood at 23.1% in 2018 (NBS, 2020). In recent decades, the Nigerian government has proposed a nation-wide strategic initiative to stimulate innovation and entrepreneurship via the compulsory introduction of entrepreneurship training in Nigeria universities. However, gaps remain in our understanding of the role Nigerian universities play in boosting graduate employability and new venture creations in Nigeria. In context, the purpose of this chapter is to examine the nexus between Nigerian universities entrepreneurship training and digital technology by considering their influence on graduates' new venture creations.

Entrepreneurial activities in the Nigeria informal sector economy have significantly contributed to reducing the population of unemployed graduates. Research suggests that new graduates are relying more and more on the informal sector for survival and sustenance (Adeyemi & Enisan, 2013). While informal employment was understood to exist for people with low-education, opportunities exist for entrepreneurship training to help reduce poverty, unemployment and boost job creations in Nigeria. Entrepreneurship training normally aims to promote entrepreneurial competency, positive attitude and intention towards new venture creations. Recent research found that entrepreneurial training leads to an increase in the acquisition of entrepreneurial skills among graduates of higher education (Kolm & Larsen, 2016). Unemployment and underemployment have made university graduates pursue entrepreneurship since formal sector jobs are oversaturated. Careers in the informal sector are multifaceted, with people having more than one job during their lifetime; in addition, they have multiple sources of income generation.

It has been estimated that more than one million graduates experience unemployment due to limited jobs in the formal sector in Nigeria (Aminu, 2019). Informal activities in Nigeria include; farming, fishing, street vendor, recreational halls, construction, transportation, entertainment and shoeshine workers among others. The entrepreneurial activities in the informal sector of Nigeria are largely facilitated by nascent indigenous entrepreneurs. In this chapter, we posit that universities graduates can leverage on entrepreneurship training and digital technology to start, grow and scale new ventures in Nigeria. The informal sector as recognised the United Nation Development Programme and the World Bank provides unique opportunities for creation of jobs through entrepreneurship. Although the informal sector of Nigeria has several challenges which revolve around structuring, disorganised information, non-compliance with legal regulations, low productivity and poor wages.

However, we believe that these challenges can be overcome through entrepreneurship training and digital technology. Drawing on the concept of Community of Practice by Lave and Wenger (1991), this chapter focuses on how Nigerian universities can use entrepreneurship training to support graduates (students) to create new ventures and make substantial contributions to reduction of poverty and unemployment in Nigeria. It argues that mutual engagement, connection and collaboration among university graduates could help to recognise real-life employment problems and address them. The remainder of this chapter is divided into eight sections. In sections two to five, we review relevant literature relating to new ventures creation in Nigeria, community of practice, graduate preparation for entrepreneurship, and digital technology. In section six, we discuss the research method used in this work. In the final three sections present the findings, discussion and conclusion.

Graduates and New Ventures Creation in Nigeria

Through entrepreneurship training, students are exposed to entrepreneurial mind sets, behaviours and capabilities on how to address anomalies in an uncertain world. Moreover, we argue that entrepreneurship training can inspire students to be self-confident, identifying gaps in their immediate environment, preparing them with various entrepreneurship skills applied to create value (creativity, networking relationship management and risk taking). All these are necessary for founding, leading and transforming new organisations and new ventures start-ups (Akuegwu & Nwi-Ue, 2016; Herrmann et al., 2008). The concept 'new venture creation' is the formation of new organisations through planning, organising, and establishing which does not always follow a coherent pattern, but an interaction between the individual and environment (Metallo et al., 2020; Venesaar et al., 2014). In the context of Nigeria, existing studies that over-dependence on oil has been a major challenge confronting creation and prosperity of new ventures in Nigeria, as well as the risks and crises emanating from the exploration and exploitation of natural resources that complicate entrepreneurial activities (Brien, 2020; Mafimisebi, 2017, 2018; Mafimisebi & Nkwunonwo, 2015; Mafimisebi & Thorne, 2015, 2017). Research also suggest that the available skills and technologies do not match the exploration of those resources, which has caused a total neglect in taking opportunities to creating new ventures.

The discovery and recognition of an opportunity by an innovative and creative person who explores the environment must decide to take advantage to bring the opportunities to fruition. However, not every opportunity results in new firms, before and after the discovery, and not all individuals have the intention to understand the formation of new business venture (Hunjra et al., 2011). Why people do not search and recognise opportunities around them, is a function of their interaction with their ecosystem (Shane & Venkataraman, 2000). Hence, the recognition of an existing opportunity and its value brings entrepreneurial profit on the 'discoverer'. Pursing an identified opportunity is part of developing entrepreneurial mindset from undergraduates and supporting career plans for graduates to create and grow a successful new venture.

Furthermore, the entrepreneurship process involves the identification and exploitation of needs ahead of possible competitors via exceptional and innovative approaches. Prior to the commencement of the new venture, there is a need for strategic preparation and proper implementation of what is analysed and evaluated. The most important key forces to deal with are in the macro-environmental landscape. This requires attention by the entrepreneur in order to achieve successful presence, growth and development (Kirkley, 2016). Research found that entrepreneurial intention and desire towards new venture creation positively impact on their performance (Hunjra et al., 2011). With the growing attention on young graduates knocking at the door of entrepreneurship to create new ventures in Nigeria, there is a growing need for entrepreneurial skills and competencies to allow graduates to start, develop and scale their businesses.

In practical context, entrepreneurship training is vital in order to improve the prospect of Nigerian universities graduates in creating new ventures and developing entrepreneurial capabilities. In addition, research notes that with the Key Performance Indicator (KPI), the evaluation of performance, innovation and behaviours play a crucial role in order to change or continue the strategy in the Nigeria's economy (Nabi et al., 2011). In our review of existing literature, we found four tools and approaches that are instrumental to facilitating new venture creations (Garvin, 1984). We discuss each of these approaches as follow:

<u>Transcendent-based approach:</u> The idea of this approach is traceable to Plato's concept of 'ideal form' beauty. The approach is based on how to introduce new products and services to the market with the aim of meeting and satisfying the market needs. The quality of the product is absolute and universally recognisable, which confirms the uncompromising standards and high

achievement. Quality is ambiguous; but however simple, it can be recognised over a period of time through experience. In developing and designing a product, **quality** of the product is a major concern of entrepreneur. It must meet customers' want and desire, for that reason the entrepreneurs must place emphasis on improving the quality of the products through creative ideas in order to achieve success and progress. An example is the iPhone series where each successive version comes with different unique functionalities.

Product-based approach: Unlike the first approach, here quality is precise and quantifiable with a new and innovative product in order to meet to need of the customer. This approach appears to be based on individual personal choices, which creates a significant impression of 'must have' on customers. This strategy is utilised in a venture inside an existing market that is established, seeking growth and expansion. From an economist's point of view, quality here implies durability of goods which provide a pool of services.

User-based approach: This approach suggests that quality '*lies in the eye of the beholder*' (Garvin, 1984; Kirkley, 2016). The approach further suggests that individual consumers have specific needs and wants, those needs and demands are what best satisfy customer(s) as it is regarded as 'highest quality'. This strategy relies on how end-users have confidence in a product or service that meets their needs. Customers' ability to share their frustrations, demands and worries about a particular product or service with an entrepreneur helps to solve the problem and find a suitable solution (Saatci et al., 2014), which is the actual way of establishing new ventures. The user-based approach is for building products and services to meet by satisfying early market demand, then upgrading to meet and be accepted by the mass market (Kirkley, 2016). Graduate entrepreneurs can leverage on the user-based approach to initiate new businesses that create values for customers and thereby allow them to make profits.

Manufacturing-based approach: This approach is predominantly concerned with the engineering and manufacturing practice to meet industry and regulatory standards (Argyris, 1976; Garvin, 1984). Fundamentally, the quality of manufacturing-based is identified as 'conformance to requirements', conformance is achieving results which depends on having the requirements. After a design or specification has been recognised, any nonconformity suggests a reduction in quality. This method recognises a consumer's preference in quality; when a product specification is deviated from, the product is likely to be poor, giving less satisfaction. The new venture may adopt the approach for growth and expansion likewise an existing firm.

Value-based approach: This approach describes costs and prices as quality (Garvin, 1984). The satisfactory price of a quality product provides performance or conformance. In this approach, material and ingredients are quality indicator examples are shoe, food, clothing, and beauty products. The quality of a product has so much to do with a suitable price. The quality measure should be commensurate to the price, the approach measure quality as 'worth' while the result is 'affordable excellence'.

Which of the above approaches is best suited for a new venture in Nigeria? Considering the socio-economic situations of Nigeria, a user-based approach is the most suitable approach to the challenges facing graduates' entrepreneur in their new venture creation. The entrepreneurs assume they 'know' what is specific to the customer, unfortunately, they may replicate the existing enterprise model, while the resource and the skills required are different from the existing model. It is however important for graduates to carefully understand the target market before launching a business.

Theoretical Framework: Individual Knowledge Among the Community of Practice

In this chapter, we draw on the Community of Practice (CoP) literature (Lave & Wenger, 1998) a concept which describes a group of people who have come together voluntarily with the purpose of sharing a concern, creating knowledge and solving problems. It is important to understand that individual knowledge is the greatest treasure as a form of knowledge which exist among individuals, also it is an essential component of all knowledge among the community (Pyrko et al., 2017). Individual knowledge of members is developed through shared experience of everyday life; hence, trust is required to dwell in a knowledge area with another person. Individual members of the CoP define and sustain the social structures which emerge and grow over time as well as generate output, they meet regularly to share and learn on a set of common interests. CoP can take various forms and come in various sizes with no specific numbers stipulated.

Wenger-Trayner and Wenger-Trayner (2015) suggest that a CoP can be homogenous or heterogeneous, unstructured or deliberate, unrecognised to institutionalised, long or short lived, virtual or face-to-face with the purpose of communicating, connecting, and conducting community activities (Wilson, 2014). The community of practice can be a supporting mechanism for graduates with multiple forms of entrepreneurial competences to flourish as an energetic members of the society and economy (Nabi et al., 2011). Informal communities of practice are reasonably common in the informal sector where members possess different expertise, undertake different hierarchical roles (Collier & Esteban, 1999; Conrad, 2008). It provides a means to shared social capital for practitioners, novice are provided with skills and competence and therefore advance in the completion of meaningful shared goals as part of the community. On the other hand, CoP is relevant to higher education (Barczyk & Duncan, 2013) it impacts the creation and development of knowledge a characteristic common to all disciplines.

From a practical perspective, CoP is valuable and consequential in a developing economy like Nigeria to help new venture creation, skills deployment and develop institutions. However, from an intellectual standpoint, CoP fosters collaborative and supportive learning, distinguishes between a community of learners and a group of individuals who are facing a range of similar professional challenges, strengthen mutual support for university educators and practitioners (Barab et al., 2006). In our view, CoP describes the way individuals work, learn, communicate, network and development their competencies. Digital technology has transformed and widen the CoP, geographic and temporal space are defected (Zhang & Storck, 2001). In this context, membership is open to members willing to join and participate, digital devices such as Facebook, WhatsApp, Instagram, Mobile phone Email and Wide Area Networks; are the dominant communication method among COP.

Individuals among the COP utilise the platforms to market, enquire and share experiences. This makes the CoP the appropriate theoretical framework to underpin our research. There are three structural elements of the CoP. These are: domain of knowledge, community and practice. A domain of knowledge is an area of knowledge that brings the community (graduates) together which gives them identity. In this context, the members' address the socio-economic challenge 'unemployment' which has brought them together. What distinguished the members is the integration of unemployed vs employed graduates. Community is described as the group of people (graduates) who have come together with the aim of interacting, learning and establishing a quality relationship among members (Wenger et al., 2011). We agreed with others (Wilson, 2014) that (new) members do not take centre stage (practice), their interest is to become a practitioner with the emphasis placed on observation, special assistance, close supervision. A new member starts on a periphery which he/she acts (behaves, beliefs and language) like a community (Gherardi & Nicolini, 2000).

Practice entails 'the body of knowledge, methods, tools, stories, cases, documents' (Smith et al., 2017) which graduates are going to develop knowledge and share together. In the CoP literature, practice is described as the act of living in the world and an area of specialisation. The combination of these definitions implied that unemployment (domain) brought graduates' (community) for knowledge generation and creation (practice). Knowledge creation enables an active member of a society to be productive through learning among CoP, skill enhancement and resources acquisition and utilisation (Nabi et al., 2011).

Graduates' Preparation for Entrepreneurship

The small-scale businesses are usually found within the informal sector, which has transformed the production, distribution and consumption of goods and services (Otekhile & Matthew, 2017). The IMF-World Bank Structural Adjustment Program (SAP) gave rise to the informal sector in the late 1980s as a hub of employment generation in Nigeria (Yusuf, 2014). Some literature refers to the informal sector as illegal activity, due to its unregulated activities by the government such as lack of payment of income tax and cruel situation on workers subjecting them to work without pay example is farming, waste disposal carpenters (WorldBank, 2015; Yusuf, 2014).

In our view, the informal sector is seen as a substitute or relief to those who cannot find regular jobs, nevertheless, its nature is dualistic as people have more than one jobs to set-up and run them simultaneously. It can also be seen as a counter to market failure where needs exist not met efficiently by 'formal' sector. Informal sector are income generating and entrepreneurial activities outside formal institutional boundaries (Sassen, 1993; Webb et al., 2009). The informal sector manifests itself in a variety of forms across and within economies (ILO, 2015). ILO further claimed that the informal sector is the greater source of employment as it is an avenue for people to earn their livelihood.

Hence, players in the informal sector have multiple sources of income generation (Yusuf, 2014) reveals that the people in the informal sector lack job security and adequate work condition. Informal entrepreneurship training could be a key economic driver that facilitates life-long learning, intensifies creative freedom, recognises and benefits from development opportunities. The Nigerian universities have placed much emphasis on general education which has only created 'general human capital' (Tilak, 2002). In the Nigerian universities, entrepreneurship education was introduced in the year 2006, with the aim of equipping learners with practical business skills, recognition of new opportunities, which deemed necessary to respond to the crisis of youth unemployment challenges (Adawo & Atan, 2013; Yusuf, 2014).

Several universities developed strategies to promote entrepreneurial education such as the Centre for Entrepreneurial and Development Research (CEDR) of the University of Nigeria, Nsukka and the Directorate of Technical and Entrepreneurship of the University of Ilorin. Since the inception of entrepreneurship training in the Nigerian universities, enormous research carried out on its importance (Akhuemonkhan et al., 2013; Longe, 2017; Oviawe, 2010). However, economic development remains staggered, reliant on external stakeholders with problems of unemployment, underemployment and skill shortages (Ekpoh & Edet, 2011). To respond to this endemic crisis, Babalola (2011) argues that teaching entrepreneurship is an essential course for undergraduate students not minding their course of study.

Despite the rhetoric of reforms in the Nigerian universities, lack of structured curriculum, inadequate finance, and ill-equipped laboratories and technical workshop are partly responsible for the negative attitudes to entrepreneurship among students in universities of science and technology which should have lifted entrepreneurship from survivalist activities. We agreed with others (Afolabi et al., 2017; Anho, 2014) who have observed that entrepreneurship training in the Nigerian universities curriculum is conspicuously absent, which poses a serious concern to the National Universities Commission (NUC) since the policy does not resolve unemployment and poverty problems facing Nigeria. Nigerian universities are expected to have holistic entrepreneurship training and development to build graduates with entrepreneurship culture and mindsets (Afolabi et al., 2017).

The lack of partnership with local economies, resources, and expertise is a stark contrast to the educational systems in leading OECD countries. There is a need for cultural policy the recognition of indigenous knowledge, to be firmly embedded in the entrepreneurship training in the Nigerian universities curriculum. The approach of indigenous knowledge in the Universities is to help develop undergraduates' minds towards the essence of being Africans (Nigerians). Moreover, our stance is that to reverse the colonial domination and post-independence threats placed in the national policy on education which lay emphasis on 'education for paid employment', indigenous knowledge in the university curriculum needs serious consideration to address the vital issue of cultural identity and autonomy in education (Lilemba & Matemba, 2015). As a subset of entrepreneurship, indigenous entrepreneurship as an integral part of the society is fundamental to ensuring that entrepreneurial skills at the university in order to contribute to economic development.

Through entrepreneurial activities, entrepreneurs transform and strengthen the indigenous entrepreneurship and cultural practices (Gallagher & Lawrence, 2012). In fostering connectedness, Lim (2002) acknowledges three instruments, including: (1) enriching relationships within the university through supporting research, connecting with faculty, and the recruitment of graduate students; (2) research consortia participation and (3) collaborating with external companies involved in a scientific relationship. The mechanisms categorise the expectations for significant productivity among the three independent sets (university, companies, and graduates). The universities, companies and graduates capture different knowledge types which contains: scientific knowledge, solutions to specific technical problems, and knowledge embedded in tools and processes. From any of the knowledge source, exploiting existing knowledge and exploring new areas could be balanced as well as increase productivity.

We are of the opinion that entrepreneurship training has a difficult (lack of infrastructure and long-life learning exempted) stance in Nigerian universities, there is some evidence indicating that if students are properly and seriously prepared before becoming graduates it forms a route to societal and global relevance. Similarly, there is literature that pays attention to culture and entrepreneurship culture (Akuegwu & Nwi-Ue, 2016; Gibb, 1999; Schein, 2009). The former aims at instilling in students' soft skills (autonomy, creativity, and a sense of responsibility) and hard skills (entrepreneurial knowledge and skills and management competencies). While the latter is a set of values, beliefs, and attitudes commonly shared by people of any entrepreneurial way of life as being desirable, and in turn supporting the pursuit of effective entrepreneurial behaviour by individuals or groups.

Opportunities and Challenges with Digital Technology

The opportunities that accompanied the admittance of digital technologies have offshoots of creativity, efficiency, and productivity, which have resulted in economic growth and strengthen inclusion (WorldBank, 2015). Technology enables the practical application of knowledge which increases economic productivity. With the introduction of Global System for Mobile (GSM) over the past 20 years, Nigeria has fostered opportunities for empowerment and self-employment. Digital technology has made Nigerians most specifically, graduates to engage in entrepreneurial activities during their studies and after the completion of their degree programmes. Digitalisation has transformed every sector of the economy and quality of life through access to basic services and education in the country (GSMA, 2019). The digital innovation trends has positively created rapid growth in the way people communicate, work, learn and earn over the years on the lives of the people (WorldBank, 2019).

The digital technology has transformed entrepreneurial processes and outcomes in the twenty-first century necessary for employment and participation in the society. The digital technology enables information sharing, collaboration, communication, creation of knowledge, problem solving (Van Laar et al., 2017). In both professional and personal lives, digital technology is efficient for transforming traditional learning and mobilise skills that are required in an emerging digital environment. Knowledge embedded in a digital technology environment provides users with a mindset to perform tasks, and solve problems intuitively. Hence, digital technologies with its unique features have shaped entrepreneurial pursuits (Nambisan, 2017).

At the moment, digital technologies are sources of innovation and entrepreneurship, which have positively impacted hundreds of millions of Nigerians. Digital platforms provide people with avenue to access digital channels such as mobile computing devices, 3D printing, social media, data analytics, computer and internet. For instance, users market goods and services through the use of social media (WhatsApp, Twitter, Facebook and Instagram). New ventures are transformed to create and enhance inward remittance as well as productivity of the economy (WorldBank, 2019). The modern-day significance of digitising of products and services permits countless flexibility that distinguishes content, function, medium and forms (Yoo et al., 2010). All these have made entrepreneurial results to be incomplete, this is as a result of continued progress when they have been introduced to the market.

Furthermore, the absence of power infrastructure is a challenge for most entrepreneurs in Nigeria. Low-level technologies have impacted on innovation negatively, effectives and reliable access to the internet responsible for backwards of digital technology frontiers. Another obstacle of backwardness is poor electricity support. The source of energy is a headache which has led ventures to fail early. Low-level technologies have impacted on innovation negatively, effectives and reliable access to the internet is required to remedy backward area of digital technology frontiers.

Methodology

This study employed an ethnographic qualitative research approach to elicit information from graduate entrepreneurs who are running various enterprises of their own. Similar research studies related to youth unemployment and graduate entrepreneurship activities have been carried out in this context using different research approaches such as case study, and grounded theory, etc. (Creswell & Poth, 2016). However, from our review of literature it was discovered that studies in this line of conversation that employed educational ethnography are very scarce, if available at all. Due to limited qualitative research focusing on graduate entrepreneurial inventions in higher education in Nigeria. This study adopted educational ethnography in investigating the nexus between entrepreneurship training and digital technology among University graduates in the country.

Educational ethnography was employed for the field investigation to contextualise the lived experience of graduate entrepreneurs practice in this context. Similarly, using educational ethnography reveals how the participants make meaning from life and entrepreneurship experiences. It helps us to gain deeper understanding into the world of each participants by asking them questions, using words such as How? Why? and What if? (Kirkley, 2016; Nader, 2011) to build knowledge about the whole phenomenon of graduate entrepreneurship training and digital technology under investigation in this study. The study provided an opportunity to gather relevant information from graduate entrepreneurs using three data collection methods we deemed appropriate for educational ethnography study, namely; observations, interviews and conversation as recommended by (Punch and Oancea, 2014). As this research examined individual personal experience(s) of graduate entrepreneurs', educational ethnography is most suitable for the study because it reveals the lived experiences of the University graduate entrepreneurs within the context of their informal settings.

Educational ethnography is more appropriate due its strengths in understanding the process the learning of each participants, their CoP while focusing on their daily routine. In the field of education, ethnography is often used in educational or organisation settings within and outside the classroom as it helps to understand the new practice in higher education (Antoniadou & Dooly, 2017; Fixsen, 2017; Walford, 2008). This method helps us gather useful information to explore their individual experiences of entrepreneurial inventions. Furthermore, the approach reveals human complexity that may not be available in other methodologies such as quantitative studies or mixed methods. Accordingly, the authors meticulously engaged twelve graduate entrepreneurs in their informal arena as a researcher that was fully embedded in the whole research process 2018 and 2019 having secured all the necessary ethics approval.

Twelve of these universities' graduates were engaged in diverse vocations different from what they have studied in the university. All the participants' consents were sought and they all agreed and took part in the reflective interviews, observations, and informal conversations. The selection of the respondents was done after consultation with the respondents who were willing and interested. With the participants' consent, the first researcher was present at the participants' informal environment to observe actual reality, ways of life, interactions, and actions in order to learn about what takes place (Shagrir, 2017). The multiple sources of data collection employed enabled the researcher to gather a robust and thick data for the study (Mafimisebi, 2017). This also helps to ensure data trustworthiness and to overcome some of the inherent weaknesses associated with educational ethnography studies such as unavoidable subjectivity and difficulties arising in merging several viewpoints due to data triangulation (Silverman, 2013). Here, the 'thick' suggest a sufficient and well detailed account of the field experiences of graduate entrepreneurship activities. The selection of the respondents was done after consultation with the respondents who were willing and interested. With the participants' consent, we were present at the participants' informal environment to observe actual reality, ways of life, interactions, and actions in order to learn about what takes place (Shagrir, 2017).

In each participants' informal arena, we undertook the important task of reflecting, interpreting and ascribing meaning to all actions, words and happenings that were examined (Shagrir, 2017; Van Maanen, 2011). While conversation took place at time the participant was less busy, it enabled us to establish close and ongoing relationships to eradicate unmediated communication (Shagrir, 2017). The reflective interview was conducted at end of the observation after 'long' stay with the participant at the place of their choice. This was recorded and lasted no longer for one (1) hour. Interviews were recorded and subsequently converted into typed transcripts. In Nigeria, the research location was Osun State (South West Nigeria) although the participants' attended Universities across the six geopolitical zones, namely; South West—five, North-East- one, North-West- one, North Central- two, South-East- one, and South-South- two. Regarding the research ethics, the presentation of verbatim excerpts included the university name and the age of the participants. The participants' names were anonymised using a non-identified codes and pseudonyms.

Furthermore, to better understand the digital technology influence on the entrepreneurial activities, we examined how they incorporated social media to shape their entrepreneurial pursuits. The transcript was read repeatedly to understand and ascertain the quality, we also listened to the recording several times so we could transcribe the interviews. We read the field notes and interviews compiled from the data several times, in order to understand the material content. From the process, we were able to come up with common issues that emerged from the data. We cross-checked the identified issues against the aim of the research, from there we were able to recognise the relationships, patterns, themes, and issues were identified and coded (Ary et al., 2010; Ryan & Bernard, 2003). The data analysis was based on observations, interviews and informal conversation, from them two key issues we categorised as themes were captured. The first theme concerns graduates' preparation towards entrepreneurship while the second theme in question coalesced two issues about digital technology.

Graduates' Preparation for Entrepreneurship

In this section, we present the findings of this research. We find that many of the respondents (graduate entrepreneurs) claimed that the entrepreneurship teaching at higher education in Nigeria was theoretical and general, with no practical elements or case study. It was revealed that the entrepreneurship content was developed through a Western system of education (formal), which has no correlation with their enterprise, thus, neglecting the informal sector context. In addition, they are of the view that the formal jobs are no longer available for the graduates as the formal sector is oversaturated with little provision for the newest graduates. Regarding the relationship between what they were taught and their enterprise correlation, two participants note:

> Participant A: I studied physiology and now I am a pig farmer, there is no relationship. laugh...It is totally uncorrelated, if I want to say when it comes to livestock farming, I did human physiology which means I should understand the anatomy of some in this animal if not all since pig can be classified as a mamma also which human beings falls under, so I should be able to understand that this animal has one stomach. (27 years old, LAUTECH, Osun State)

> Participant B: I like Geography, I like the environment and I was very good at Geography, I needed to go to the university that is the way in Nigeria, everybody wants to go to university, if Nigeria is not structured the way it is I wouldn't have attended University. I would have gone to fashion School or

Business School from the scratch. I would have taken my stand and at that time I was young, most of all my teaching at the university was theory. (32 years old, UNIILORIN, Osun State)

On the entrepreneurship content:

Participant A: In my opinion the content of the entrepreneurship are good for advanced countries not we in Nigeria. Here as you can see I do diverse businesses to make ends meet (profit), the entrepreneurship course did not prepare me for that, no practical examples on how Nigerians entrepreneurs build or sustain their enterprise.

Participant B: The entrepreneurship course is not for me, I do not believe in it as my needs are not met. All I was thought was general entrepreneurship with no practical experience, can you believe after graduation I went for a training in fashion which provided me with practical and theoretical knowledge of how to become successful in any environment you find yourself in Nigeria.

As seen from the above quotations, this type of entrepreneurship curriculum has failed to prepare graduates for productive activities, or to address practical activities. These should involve brain storming, problem solving and knowledge creation/generation integrated into the learning activity in the lecture rooms, using real-world situations. However, the application of knowledge of human physiology by Participant 'A' into his enterprise shows critical thinking in understanding and addressing entrepreneurial ventures. For Participant 'B' apart from the lack of correlation between Geography and the enterprise (fashion making), going for training that provided the Participant with specific skills regarding the profession and relevant to indigenous Nigeria would enhance opportunities for new venture creation. The participants noted that due to instability, lack of jobs, and unemployment situations in Nigeria, starting a new business has become a necessity. As such, a holistic paradigm of entrepreneurship education emerged during the study, evidenced by their successful ways of diversifying income-generating portfolio (Participant A), lack of power (electricity), individual self-directed learning to be entrepreneurial and creativity in order to be unique. Knowledge was gained by self-directed learning, experience-based entrepreneurship, observation (apprentice), reflection, practitioners (CoP) and individualised instruction (from parents and community elders).

From the responses captured in this study, we find that while Nigerian universities have incorporated entrepreneurship education as General Education Studies (GES) to be taught in higher education, however, 'nativising' or contextualising entrepreneurship to effectively and adequately meet the aspirations and desires of a developing nation was lacking. This implies that entrepreneurship usefulness and appropriateness at the University answers and adapts to the needs of daily life, hopes, expectation and preparation for an unknown future focusing on theories, content and pedagogical approaches that suit social and economic development (building and creating own economy).

The respondents noted that informal entrepreneurship training should prepare undergraduates' to be 'polypreneur' (more than one vocation). This participant described himself as '*ona kan o wo ja*' in this context it means 'there are many paths to access the Market' and implies that there are various potential means through which one can achieve a single goal. The participant stressed further that informal entrepreneurship training should be taught with the aim of solving more than one problem(s) and the purpose of creating and producing value; but the learner must understand how to search, recognise, and turn new opportunities within the environment into realities, from there profit is certain could be generated. For the respondents, participant 'A' reinforces that there are some who search for opportunities (searcher), there are set of people who can identify opportunities (identifier), and there are some who help to achieve the opportunities (stakeholder), it is either you possess one or two, possessing the three are uncommon. The participant 'A' narrated that;

> Agriculture is a money-making enterprise where people need food but not all people can produce it for themselves, while I make food (pigs) available for them to buy at my price. Before I embark on the enterprise, I told my parents that I want to add to my hustle in the area of agriculture, I gave different examples of agricultural billionaires in Nigeria and that the politicians have farms, which livestock is included, Obasanjo the ex-president has a farm in Ota, Buhari the present president has cattle ranch in his home town, Dogara ex-speaker house of representative has a livestock farm in Bauchi and Afe-Babalola has livestock farm in Ekiti State. With all these examples, my parents welcome the idea of livestock farming starting with pig but with progress. My mom contacted the person that helped on how we got the farm site, likewise, they supported me financially with the payment, the money was divided into two, they paid fifty percent and I paid fifty.

Clearly, the participant was in search for the opportunities, he was also the one who identified the opportunities while the parents are the sponsor (stakeholder). The business enterprise could have been difficult without their support, in contemporary small business enterprise, stakeholders are primary to accomplishing the goals, and nevertheless, their withdrawal can lead to the death of the business, just like the parents warned with no growth they would exit. For instance, both participants explained that they have met and are working with different kinds of people in their enterprises, we observed at the farm that participant 'A' has few persons who are his practitioners in pig farming (Community of Practice CoP) they are the veterinary doctor and his friend who studied health and animal production. While participant 'B' also has professional friends and senior tailors who forms part of his CoP, he described one as 'Egbon X'. From the respondents', it is evident that there was a conceptualised worldview of graduate entrepreneurs on knowledge and wealth creation in the enterprise. In sum, we learnt that in the informal sector which the respondents belong, they do have a CoP which is a way of solving problems, developing knowledge, skills and collaborate for the young and old.

Digital Technology: Self-learning, Marketing and Community of Practice

In response to the use of digital technology, the participants lamented that their universities lack a digital infrastructure which is quick and flexible to connect and promote their products. They explained that the university offers 'information technology' as a General Education Studies (GES) course which is only relevant for academic purposes, not sufficient for professional and personal lives, instead they need digital skills to adapt to their career and job. They added that the situation has contributed to lack of relevant technical skills among few graduates in a knowledge-driven society. We argue that gaining digital skills is important yet, it goes beyond educational setting, and it is a lifetime opportunity that prepares one for present jobs and future jobs.

The respondents noted that since the introduction of Global System for Mobile Communications (GSM) for over twenty 20 years in Nigeria, they have enjoyed diverse opportunities that foster empowerment in their difficult environment. They explained that although private service providers have made access to the internet possible, it is expensive, sometime very fast, other time slow and with no access in many areas (GSMA, 2019). They explained that the knowledge of digital tools has provided graduates with thousands of jobs, as they have worked in the personal, social and technological environment, relocating to industrialised countries, as e-learning consultants, marketing products and services, solving problems and sharing information. We have observed how self-employed graduates use digital technology, to create new business ventures from their home, create value (creativity, network relationship management and risk taking), and transform traditional learning to self-learning.

Perhaps, importantly, we further learnt that the informal entrepreneurship training would be 'very useful' to a significant number of unemployed graduates by the rapid growth and success of good examples of graduate entrepreneurs from new venture who rely on digital tools as they use to collaborate, market and search for information (learn). The table below illustrates the participants' use of digital technology.

Table 10.1 clearly gave us the impression that respondents in the study are utilising digital tools and what they use them for in their enterprises. The most common is 'Communication/Collaboration'. Respondents said they made phone calls (WhatsApp calls, video calls, Facebook call and chat) with their CoPs to help manage and empower their learning, correspondingly, they network with other practitioners in different locations within and outside Nigeria, engage themselves in questions, get familiar with a technique, when there is need to purchase a tool. For instance, the fashion maker said it was on the fashion WhatsApp that a member told him of 'where to get a used embroidery machines'. In addition, the respondents stated that they used three main social media platforms 'WhatsApp, Facebook and Instagram' to 'Communicate/Collaborate, market and solve Problem/creativity, Self-learn and Cultural awareness'. Respondents explained that they share updates in

Table 10.1 Graduate entrepreneur digital tools and social media usage

	Skills mentioned	Digital technology
Participant A	Communication/collaboration Self-learning/design thinking Critical thinking	Facebook YouTube Instagram
Participant B	Communication/collaboration Marketing Cultural awareness	Facebook YouTube Instagram
Participant C	Communication/collaboration Lifelong learning	Email/E-marketing MOOC
Participant D	Communication/collaboration Critical thinking	WhatsApp YouTube
Participant E	Communication/collaboration Problem solving/creativity	Facebook/CoP YouTube Instagram Email
Participant F	Communication/collaboration Marketing	Instagram/CoP Facebook WhatsApp

texts, images, videos and contents on social media networks with the intention of advertising, and promoting marketing. The participants stated that they have gained new customers through social media marketing while deeper relationships are sustained with the existing one.

Some revealed that social media has created avenue to meet customers within and outside Nigeria, that with social media they have reached out to where they have never been before, they communicate with customers, view complaints, signs and symbols speak a volume, 'negotiate price' and follow up on the delivery of products. Respondents said that in self-learning they are supported on the YouTube videos, Massive Open Online Course (MOOC), free website, social media and books; in-depth understanding of what they watch encourage and help them to develop deep sense in their enterprise, shape creativity on doing new things they haven't done before, learn about their products and services which increase growth in the business. Digital technology in Nigeria has helped in promoting social media marketing, shaping thinking and communicating increased online collaborating strategies. Likewise, digital technologies support autonomy, provide personal and professional skills, develop acquisition and competence of indigenous entrepreneurs and enhance decision making in a fast-changing economy. Digital technology in Nigeria has experienced a paradigm shift which impacts on a person and the changes that occur in the environment enhance decision making in a fast-changing economy.

Conclusion

In this chapter, we examined the nexus between Nigerian universities entrepreneurship training and digital technology by considering their influence on graduates' new venture creations. The findings from this research suggest that Nigerian universities entrepreneurship training has little or no influence on graduate entrepreneurs' new venture creations in Nigeria. Prior studies appear to subject mixed effect of entrepreneurship training and some entrepreneurship scholars challenged the notion that entrepreneurship curriculum alone is insufficient to change people's intention to start a new venture. The Nigerian universities entrepreneurship curriculum has not been given adequate attention. Our findings revealed that Nigerian universities graduates are motivated to create new ventures because of necessity in part arising from lack of jobs, saturation in the job market, poverty and unemployment. This allow universities graduates to prepare themselves in a deprived economy like Nigeria in spite of the neglect of entrepreneurship training and digital technology (Arogundade, 2011).

Furthermore, our findings revealed that graduates pursue different careers completely different from their studies in the university. We also found that people are no longer constrained to only one source of making money but are more willing to have two or more sources of income as a 'polypreneur' (more than one vocation) as a participant described himself as '*ona kan o wo ja*'. We discovered that polypreneurs find more opportunities in the Nigerian entrepreneurial space. With different kinds of businesses or portfolios, entrepreneurial initiatives develop with no limitation to any activities that impact on the people and society at large. The transition from higher education to work must be 'value added' to enable graduates to understand the economy and enter the labour market with productive and useful capabilities.

As argued in this chapter, graduate entrepreneurs' identified opportunities, align the opportunity to the available resources, and invest substantial time in the pre-start up planning. Depending on graduates' degree subject, critical knowledge was applied, it is acknowledged that graduates instigate whatever they have studied to meet their enterprise demand. With these, the graduates appear to be capable of embracing entrepreneurial activities or going into any business of their choice and sustain their new venture. Moreover, we found that the academic research community in higher education in Nigeria has a positive CoP. In this regard, there is a need to emphasise CoP (possibly embedded in the curriculum) among graduates to innovatively observe the needs of the society and develop entrepreneurial skills (McDonald & Star, 2006) that solve their individual challenges and the economy. Nigerian universities need to do more in creating specific indigenous entrepreneurial training that meets the industrial needs in Nigeria to create more employment opportunities, thereby promoting national development and process industrialization. In conclusion, graduate entrepreneurs should leverage from their CoP learning experiences to benefit from entrepreneurship training and take advantage of digital technology in order to transform their entrepreneurial activities.

References

Adawo, M. A., & Atan, J. A. (2013). Graduate Unemployment in Nigeria: Entrepreneurship and venture capital nexus. *Journal of Economics and Sustainable Development, 4*, 75–81.

Adeyemi, A., & Enisan, G. (2013). Urban land use and informal sector economy in Nigeria. *International Journal of Science Commerce and Humanities, 1*.

Afolabi, M. O., Kareem, F. A., Okubanjo, I. O., Ogunbanjo, O. A., & Aninkan, O. O. (2017). Effect of entrepreneurship education on self-employment initiatives among Nigerian Science & Technology students. *Journal of Education and Practice, 8*, 44–51.

Akhuemonkhan, I., Raimi, L., & Sofoluwe, A. (2013). Entrepreneurship education and employment stimulation in Nigeria. *Journal of Studies in Social Sciences, 3*.

Akuegwu, B., & Nwi-Ue, F. (2016). Developing entrepreneurship culture among university students in South-South, Nigeria. *Mediterranean Journal of Social Sciences, 7*, 315.

Aminu, A. (2019). Characterising graduate unemployment in Nigeria as education-job mismatch problem. *African Journal of Economic Review, 7*, 113–130.

Anho, J. (2014). Entrepreneurship education: A panacea for unemployment, poverty reduction and national insecurity in developing and underdeveloped countries. *American International Journal of Contemporary Research, 4*, 124–136.

Antoniadou, V., & Dooly, M. (2017). Educational ethnography in blended learning environments. In *Qualitative approaches to research on plurilingual education* (pp. 237–263).

Argyris, C. (1976). Single-loop and double-loop models in research on decision making. *Administrative Science Quarterly*, 363–375.

Arogundade, B. B. (2011). Entrepreneurship education: An imperative for sustainable development in Nigeria. *Journal of Emerging Trends in Educational Research and Policy Studies, 2*, 26–29.

Ary, D., Jacobs, L. C., Sorensen, C., & Razavieh, A. (2010). *Introduction to research in education* (8th ed.). Wadsworth.

Babalola, J. B. (2011). World Bank support for Nigerian higher education: Pleasure, pains and pathway towards a knowledge economy. *An inaugural lecture delivered at the University of Ibadan*.

Barab, S., Warren, S. J., Del Valle, R., & Fang, F. (2006). Coming to terms with communities of practice. In *Handbook of human performance technology* (pp. 640–664).

Barczyk, C. C., & Duncan, D. G. (2013). Facebook in higher education courses: An analysis of students' attitudes, community of practice, and classroom community. *International Business and Management, 6*, 1–11.

Brien, S. (2020). Africa Prosperity Report 2019/20.: Legatum prosperity index. London, UK.

Brush, C. G., de Bruin, A. & Welter, F. (2009). A gender-aware framework for women's entrepreneurship. *International Journal of Gender and Entrepreneurship, 1*(1), 8–24.

Collier, J., & Esteban, R. (1999). Governance in the participative organisation: Freedom, creativity and ethics. *Journal of Business Ethics, 21*, 173–188.

Conrad, D. L. (2008). From community to community of practice: Exploring the connection of online learners to informal learning in the workplace. *The American Journal of Distance Education, 22*, 3–23.

Creswell, J. W., & Poth, C. N. (2016). *Qualitative inquiry and research design: Choosing among five approaches.* Sage.

Ekpoh, U. I., & Edet, A. O. (2011). Entrepreneurship education and career intentions of tertiary education students in Akwa Ibom and Cross River States, Nigeria. *International Education Studies, 4,* 172–178.

Fixsen, A. (2017). *Feeling Our Way: An ethnographic exploration of university staff experiences of 'soft skills' learning and development programmes.* University of Westminster.

Galindo, M., & Mendez, M T. (2014). Entrepreneurship, economic growth, and innovation: Are feedback effects at work? *Journal of Business Research, 67,* 825–829.

Gallagher, B., & Lawrence, T. B. (2012). Entrepreneurship and indigenous identity: A study of identity work by indigenous entrepreneurs in British Columbia. *International Journal of Entrepreneurship and Small Business, 17,* 395–414.

Garvin, D. A. (1984). What does product quality really mean? *Sloan Management Review, 25.*

Gherardi, S., & Nicolini, D. (2000). To transfer is to transform: The circulation of safety knowledge. *Organisation, 7,* 329–348.

Gibb, A. (1999). Creating an entrepreneurial culture in support of SMEs. *Small Enterprise Development, 10,* 27–38.

GSMA. (2019). Connected society the state of mobile internet connectivity. *GSMA Association UKaid.*

Herrmann, K., Hannon, P., Cox, J., Ternouth, P., & Crowley, T. (2008). *Developing entrepreneurial graduates: Putting entrepreneurship at the centre of higher education,* NESTA London.

Hunjra, A. I., Ahmad, H. M., Rehman, K. U., & Safwan, N. (2011). Factors influencing intention to create new venture among young graduates. *Africa Journal of Business Management, 5,* 121–127.

ILO. (2015). Formalization of the informal economy: Area of critical importance.

Kirkley, W. W. (2016). Creating ventures: Decision factors in new venture creation. *Asia Pacific Journal of Innovation and Entrepreneurship.*

Kolm, A.-S., & Larsen, B. (2016). Informal unemployment and education. *IZA Journal of Labor Economics, 5,* 8.

Lave, J., & Wenger, E. (1991). *Situated learning: Legitimate peripheral participation.* New York: Cambridge University Press.

Lave, J., & Wenger, E. (1998). Communities of practice. Retrieved June 9, 2008.

Lilemba, J. M., & Matemba, Y. H. (2015). *Reclaiming indigenous knowledge in Namibia's post-colonial curriculum: The case of the Mafwe people.* UNAM Press.

Lim, D. H. (2002). Perceived differences between classroom and distance education: Seeking instructional strategies for learning application. *International Journal of Educational Technology, 3*(1), 1–10.

Longe, O. (2017). Graduate unemployment in Nigeria: Causes, consequences and remiediable approaches. *Journal of Contemporary Research, 7,* 56–68.

Mafimisebi, O. P. (2018). Risky business: Data on trading results for UK general insurance firms during and after the global financial crisis. *Data in Brief, 21,* 2384–2389.

Mafimisebi, O. P. (2017). *Self-inflicted disasters: Moral disengagement in unconventional risk, crisis and disaster management strategy.* (Unpublished PhD thesis). Portsmouth: University of Portsmouth.

Mafimisebi, O. P., & Thorne, S. (2017). Vandalism-militancy relationship: The influence of risk perception and moral disengagement. *International Journal of Mass Emergencies and Disasters, 35*(3), 191–223.

Mafimisebi, O. P., & Nkwunonwo, U. C. (2015). Environmental risk: Exploring organisational resilience and robustness. *International Journal of Scientific & Engineering Research, 6*(1), 1103–1115.

Mafimisebi, O. P., & Thorne, S. (2015). Oil terrorism-militancy link: Mediating role of moral disengagement in emergency and crisis management. *Journal of Emergency Management, 13*(5), 447–458.

McDonald, J., & Star, C. (2006). Designing the future of learning through a community of practice of teachers of first year courses at an Australian university. Proceedings of the 1st International LAMS Conference: Designing the Future of Learning. LAMS Foundation (pp. 65–76).

Metallo, C., Agrifoglio, R., Briganti, P., Mercurio, L., & Ferrara, M. (2020). Entrepreneurial behaviour and new venture creation: The psychoanalytic perspective. *Journal of Innovation & Knowledge.*

Nabi, G., Liñán, F., Mitra, J., Abubakar, Y., & Sagagi, M. (2011). Knowledge creation and human capital for development: The role of graduate entrepreneurship. *Education+ Training.*

Nader, L. (2011). Ethnography as theory. *HAU: Journal of Ethnographic Theory, 1,* 211–219.

Nambisan, S. (2017). Digital entrepreneurship: Toward a digital technology perspective of entrepreneurship. *Entrepreneurship Theory and Practice, 41,* 1029–1055.

NBS. (2020). Trading economics: Nigeria unemployment rate 2006–2020. National Bureau of Statistics, Nigeria. https://tradingeconomics.com/nigeria/unemployment-rate.

Otekhile, O., & Matthew, O. (2017). An explorative study of the contribution of the informal sector to economic activities in Lagos, Nigeria.

Oviawe, J. I. (2010). Repositioning Nigerian youths for economic empowerment through entrepreneurship education. *European Journal of Educational Studies, 2,* 113–118.

Punch, K. F., & Oancea, A. (2014). *Introduction to research methods in education.* Sage.

Pyrko, I., Dörfler, V., & Eden, C. (2017). Thinking together: What makes communities of practice work? *Human Relations.*

Ryan, G. W., & Bernard, H. R. 2003. Techniques to identify themes. *Field Methods, 15,* 85–109.

Saatci, E. Y., Arikan, S., & Cal, B. (2014). Values? How social entrepreneurs' portrait values differ from commercial entrepreneurs? *International Journal of Education and Research, 2*, 143–160.

Sassen, S. (1993). The informal economy: Between new developments and old regulations. *Yale LJ, 103*, 2289.

Schein, E. H. (2009). *The corporate culture survival guide*. Wiley.

Shagrir, L. (2017). *Journey to ethnographic research*. Springer.

Shane, S., & Venkataraman, S. (2000). The promise of entrepreneurship as a field of research. *Academy of Management Review, 25*, 217–226.

Silverman, D. (2013). *Doing qualitative research: A practical handbook*. Sage.

Smith, S. U., Hayes, S., & Shea, P. (2017). A critical review of the use of Wenger's Community of Practice (CoP) theoretical framework in online and blended learning research, 2000–2014. *Online Learning, 21*, 209–237.

Tilak, J. B. (2002). Education and poverty. *Journal of Human Development, 3*, 191–207.

Van Laar, E., Van Deursen, A. J., Van Dijk, J. A., & De Haan, J. (2017). The relation between 21st-century skills and digital skills: A systematic literature review. *Computers in Human Behavior, 72*, 577–588.

Van Maanen, J. (2011). *Tales of the field: On writing ethnography*. University of Chicago Press.

Venesaar, U., Kallaste, M., & Küttim, M. (2014). Factors influencing students' venture creation process. *Procedia-Social and Behavioral Sciences, 110*, 678–688.

Walford, G. (2008). *How to do educational ethnography*. Tufnell Press.

Webb, J. W., Tihanyi, L., Ireland, R. D., & Sirmon, D. G. (2009). You say illegal, I say legitimate: Entrepreneurship in the informal economy. *Academy of Management Review, 34*, 492–510.

Wenger-Trayner, E., & Wenger-Trayner, B. (2015). *Introduction to communities of practice: A brief overview of the concept and its uses*. Wenger-Trayner.

Wenger, E., Trayner, B., & De Laat, M. (2011). Promoting and assessing value creation in communities and networks: A conceptual framework. *The Netherlands: Ruud De Moor Centrum, 20*, 2010–2011.

Wilson, K. (2014). Communities of practice as a framework for understanding the professional impact of collaborative cultural work.

WorldBank. (2015). *African home-grown innovations take off*. International Finance Corporation EMCOMPASS.

WorldBank. (2019). *Nigeria digital economy diagnostic report*. The World Bank Group Washington, DC.

Yoo, Y., Henfridsson, O., & Lyytinen, K. (2010). Research commentary—The new organizing logic of digital innovation: An agenda for information systems research. *Information Systems Research, 21*, 724–735.

Yusuf, S. A. (2014). Informal sector and employment generation in Nigeria.

Zhang, W., & Storck, J. (2001). Peripheral members in online communities. *AMCIS 2001 Proceedings*, 117.

11

Co-creation of Entrepreneurship Education: Challenges and Opportunities for University, Industry and Public Sector Collaboration in Nigeria

Oluwaseun Kolade, Evans Osabuohien, Ayotola Aremu, Kehinde Adefiola Olanipekun, Romanus Osabohien, and Patience Tunji-Olayeni

Introduction

Since the turn of the millennium, there has been a surge in the rate of higher education enrolment in sub-Saharan Africa. According to one report, the number of higher education enrolment more than doubled from 2,344,000 in year 2000 to 5,228,000 in 2010 (British Council, 2014). As of 2019, the number of enrolments has increased to 8 million (*The Economist*, 2019). However, despite the significant expansion of access to higher education, sub-Saharan African countries continue to grapple with high rates of youth unemployment, and graduate unemployment, in particular. Universities are,

---

O. Kolade (✉)
Department of Management and Entrepreneurship, De Montfort University, Leicester, UK
e-mail: seun.kolade@dmu.ac.uk

E. Osabuohien · R. Osabohien · P. Tunji-Olayeni
Covenant University, Ota, Nigeria

A. Aremu
University of Ibadan, Ibadan, Nigeria

K. A. Olanipekun
Obafemi Awolowo University, Ile-Ife, Nigeria

therefore, under increasing scrutiny from the general public and industry stakeholders who are concerned about the declining quality of university education, the limited absorptive capacity in the labour market, and the employability of university graduates.

Over the past few decades, scholars and practitioners have been grappling with questions around the future of higher education in the global knowledge economy. Universities are no longer seen as the only sites of knowledge production. This is especially the case in the sphere that has been described as mode 2 knowledge, that is, knowledge produced within the context of the application (Gibbons et al., 1994). The new production of knowledge is based on a transdisciplinary, heterarchical, boundary-spanning approach. This approach aggregates and integrates inputs from academic, industry and government stakeholders (Godin & Gingras, 2000; Hessels & van Lente, 2008).

In recognition of the foregoing, universities in the developed world and many emerging economies have been undergoing a process of transformation in response to disruptive and consequential changes occurring in the knowledge-producing sector. The ongoing transformation in the sector is in keeping with epochal transformations of universities, from their profile as storehouses of knowledge in the medieval period to knowledge factory in modern times to current transformations to knowledge and innovation hub. The new and current changes recognise the changing role of universities as facilitators of a multi-sectoral and multi-stakeholder process of knowledge production (Youtie & Shapira, 2008). In line with this, some scholars have proposed a concept of the "entrepreneurial university", which, in addition to the traditional mission of research and teaching, now embraces "economic development" as a third mission (Etzkowitz et al., 2000).

While the imperative of change in universities is underpinned by the same overarching logic of tri-partite mission in the global context, it also presents unique sets of challenges and opportunities in developed to developing country contexts. Compared to developing countries, universities in developed countries are more autonomous and independent in their operational structures, and they operate within more reliable and stable institutional environments. They can, therefore, more effectively harness this autonomy and tap into the existing structures and frameworks in the institutional environment to organise their response to changing needs and requirements in the industry and the labour market (Mosey et al., 2012). For emerging economies and developing countries, the challenges are exacerbated by limited autonomy and national innovation systems that are more oriented towards the diffusion of knowledge and innovation from advanced countries rather than active stimulation of indigenous knowledge to serve local needs (Wong et al., 2007). In the same vein, these unique challenges are also potential opportunities to effect fundamental changes in the higher education sector, making them more sustainable and more responsive to industry needs and societal challenges in the twenty-first century.

While many developing countries are making significant progress in reforming and repositioning the higher education sectors for the twenty-first- century knowledge economy, most African countries are lagging behind. Across African countries, there are tensions and contradictions in expectations of different stakeholders about the role of universities. These expectations range from an ancillary role of transmitting established knowledge rather than generate new knowledge; to a self-governing role prioritising external collaboration driven, not necessarily by local needs but by agenda of international funding agencies; to an instrumentalist role that emphasises expertise exchange and capacity building over production of new knowledge; and finally as the engine of development whereby the university plays a central role in development (Cloete et al., 2011). The engine of development roles includes contributions to improvement in health care and agricultural production, but also include contributions to innovations in the private sector.

The "engine of development" role aligns with the imperative of entrepreneurship education in African universities (Ejemeyovwi et al., 2018). In response to the challenge of widespread unemployment and limited opportunities in the private sector, many African countries have launched new policy interventions to promote entrepreneurship education, in many instances making it compulsory for all students enrolled in higher education sector. In some African countries like Botswana, Kenya and Uganda, entrepreneurship education has been introduced in both public secondary schools and tertiary institutions, with the key objectives of raising skills levels and stimulating innovation and productivity in the private sector (Farstad, 2002). In Nigeria, the federal government launched a policy initiative in 2002, directing all higher education institutions to introduce entrepreneurship as a compulsory course in their curriculum. The overarching intention was to incentivise universities to produce highly skilled entrepreneurs who can inject dynamism and innovation into the private sector (Olofinyehun et al., 2018).

While this policy intervention is well-intentioned, the impact has been modest at best since it was first introduced about two decades ago. In this paper, we propose that the relative lack of success is related to inadequate collaboration and limited synergy between universities on the one hand, and industry and government stakeholders on the other. In Nigeria, the dominant notion of the university has been the ancillary function—essentially a relic of the colonial era—where the universities are expected to produce educated graduates to fill spaces in the now oversaturated public sector. Under this model, in which the university–industry engagement is minimal, universities have struggled to implement successful entrepreneurship education programmes.

Thus, in this chapter, we draw on the Triple Helix model (Etzkowitz, 2008; Etzkowitz & Leydesdorff, 2000) to explore the challenges and opportunities for more effective collaboration and synergistic partnership between university, industry and government for more effective design and delivery of entrepreneurship education in Nigerian universities. The chapter includes a single case study of Covenant University (CU), a leading private university that has attained significant international recognition and national prominence within a relatively short period. It analyses the strategies CU has employed to co-opt industry stakeholders towards the delivery of entrepreneurship education programmes. This paper also discusses the challenges of the CU strategies, for example in terms of limited involvement of industry practitioners in curriculum design, and the under-developed partnership with government agencies. The rest of the chapter is organised as follows. First, we provide the theoretical basis for the work through the review of the extant literature on new knowledge production, university–industry–government partnership, and entrepreneurship education. Next, we set out the empirical context for the present study. This is followed by the case study and the paper then concludes with the discussion of the findings and implications for policy and practice.

Theoretical Framework

The Triple Helix: A Model of University–Industry–Government Innovation

As the world emerges from the industrial society to a knowledge economy, the changing landscape has necessitated debates and discussions around the transformation of knowledge infrastructure in response to the dynamic changes, challenges and opportunities of a knowledge-based economy. Among competing ideas and theories, the Triple Helix has emerged as one of the dominant models of institutional arrangement that is best suited to the new production of knowledge and economic growth. The central thesis of the

Triple Helix is that the expanding role of the knowledge sector has precipitated new interactions among previously distinct and often disconnected institutional domains of university, industry and government (Leydesdorff & Etzkowitz, 1996). These dynamic interactions have led to the emergence of an integrative, boundary-spanning institutional arrangement in which "industry operates in the Triple Helix as the locus of production; government as the source of contractual relations that guarantee stable interactions and exchange; (and) the university as a source of new knowledge and technology, the generative principle of knowledge-based economies" (Etzkowitz, 2003a, p. 295). The Triple Helix is thus characterised by the emergence of hybrid organisations at overlapping institutional spheres (Etzkowitz & Leydesdorff, 2000).

The origins of the Triple Helix can be traced to the analysis of the differences and interactions between the nation-state and the economy, and the two processes that account for this differentiation: the functional differentiation between sciences and the markets; and the institutional separation between private and public control (Leydesdorff & Etzkowitz, 1996). The formation of the Triple Helix begins with collaboration among the trio of university, industry and government, each of them bringing knowledge, expertise and resources from their traditional institutional spheres. This proceeds to the next phase in which the continuing interactions produce a transformative impact on each of the Triple Helix partners. That is, while each partner maintains its distinct identity and primary roles, it begins to develop capabilities and take on roles traditionally associated with the other partners (Etzkowitz, 2003a).

The Triple Helix model is different from the innovation systems approach in several respects. First, within the innovation systems approach, the firm is cast as the primary actor, with the university and government playing supporting roles. In the Triple Helix, the university is the leading actor, in keeping with the requirements of a knowledge-based economy. Nevertheless, the system is heterarchical, owing more to dynamic interactions within fluid institutional boundaries, rather than the dominance of any one actor (Etzkowitz & Zhou, 2017). Furthermore, within the innovation systems approach, the organisation of innovation follows a laissez-faire process of self-regulation and self-correction. In contrast, the Triple Helix highlights the role of a regional innovation organiser, "an individual or organisation with convening capabilities" (Etzkowitz & Zhou, 2017, p. 7).

The innovation processes occur in three growth spaces: the knowledge space, the consensus space, and the innovation space. The knowledge space is the epistemological source of new ideas for industry use, as well as where university research and teaching capabilities are deployed towards the formation of new firms. In the consensus space, various actors from university, industry and government spheres come together to fashion out new ideas and strategies for optimal and effective utilisation of knowledge. The innovation space builds on these by providing new platforms and spaces, such as science parks and incubation hubs, where entrepreneurial ideas can be actualised (Etzkowitz, 2003b).

One major implication of the Triple Helix model is the ongoing transformation of the university system. It is argued that, within the context of the changing landscape of knowledge production, universities need to embrace the third mission of economic and social development, along with the traditional roles of teaching and research. In effect, the university of the future is seen as the entrepreneurial university able to function, not merely as knowledge factory but as a boundary-spanning innovation hub bringing industry actors and government stakeholders together (Bjerregaard, 2010; Etzkowitz et al., 2000; Hussler et al., 2010). For developing countries, there are specific challenges for universities to grapple with in order to make this transition. First, universities in developing countries are relatively younger institutions with a much lower level of autonomy and independence compared to their counterparts in the developed world (Wong et al., 2007). In African countries, especially, a centralised, command-and-control model is unsustainable, in terms of funding and quality assurance (Teferra, 2013; Imogen Mathers, 2016).

Furthermore, it is recognised that universities in Africa and other developing countries typically adopt an imitation model based on diffusing technological knowledge and organisational practices emanating from the West. The organisational model of universities in developing countries does not give enough attention to the significant differences in the institutional environment, or, more crucially, the enormous opportunities to tap into local knowledge and develop indigenous innovations (Wong et al., 2007). These factors make the imperative of the entrepreneurial university in African countries more urgent, as universities need to reinvent themselves, not only about embracing a more sustainable model, but more broadly in keeping with the demands of the twenty-first- century knowledge economy.

Entrepreneurship Education and Economic Development

Entrepreneurship education research has typically focused on how the provision of specific training for students can influence their intentions to create and develop new ventures. These intention-based models of entrepreneurship education draw from the theory of planned behaviour (Ajzen, 1991), which states that the intention to perform one or the other behaviour can be predicted by attitudes towards the behaviour, subjective norms and perceived behavioural control. Thus, within the context of entrepreneurial intentions, scholars have argued that university entrepreneurship programmes can inspire and raise attitudes of students towards entrepreneurial ventures (Souitaris et al., 2007), as well as enhance students' abilities (Walker et al., 2013).

Entrepreneurship education programmes are not homogenous because different entrepreneurs at different stages of their entrepreneurial endeavour require different types of knowledge and competencies. Therefore, an entrepreneurship education programme may be targeted towards creating awareness about opportunities for small businesses or be aimed towards providing practical skills for those seeking to make the transition from traditional employment to self-employment. Finally, it can be aimed towards continuous skill development for existing business owners who want to enhance and update their skills (Henry et al., 2005).

There is a general agreement among scholars that, in order for entrepreneurship education to achieve the main aim of transmitting skills required by the entrepreneur, it has to be modelled and structured differently from conventional, class-room based mode of learning. It has to be action-oriented and practical, focusing on specific tasks, and cognisant of the uncertain and unpredictable environment in which entrepreneurs have to operate and make decisions (Galloway et al., 2005; Gibb, 1987; Rae, 2004; Rasmussen & Sørheim, 2006). However, other scholars have argued that theory should be at the heart of entrepreneurship education, to help entrepreneurs understand the consequences of their actions (Fiet, 2001a, 2001b). It is not enough for students or trainees to learn about the conduct of successful entrepreneurs, because students are unlikely to encounter exact or similar issues in their future experiences, and a focus on ideal entrepreneurial behaviour can be, in fact, demoralising and demotivating for students (Fiet, 2001b). On the other hand, it is more effective if problem-solving tasks and key questions about entrepreneurship are built around well-defined theories, so students can gain a good grasp of general principles they can apply in practice.

From the human capital perspective, entrepreneurship education is seen as an effective channel to develop entrepreneurial, technical and management skills necessary to enhance labour productivity and promote innovation and creativity (Cooney, 2012). Nevertheless, entrepreneurship education does not always produce the desired outcomes. At least one study reported that participation in entrepreneurship education brought participants to have a greater awareness of the risks and challenges, thus making them realise it was not for them. In other words, participation and increased awareness led to contrary intention (Oosterbeek et al., 2010). The success or otherwise of EE programme are also linked to the quality of specific curricula and the effectiveness of delivery approach. For example, didactic and class-based lectures are less effective, and participants also tend to benefit from instructors who have some real-life experience as entrepreneurs or are supported by real-life entrepreneurs (Ahmad et al., 2014).

The central argument of this chapter is that a co-creation model, bringing together the Triple Helix of university, industry and government stakeholders, is best suited for effective design and delivery of entrepreneurship education programme in Nigeria, and by and large in sub-Saharan African countries. In the existing model, there is limited room for involvement of industry stakeholders. Where industry practitioners have been involved at all, it always seems to be piecemeal on the sides, limited in scope and depth. Furthermore, governments appear to have assumed the role of detached clients, waiting at the end for the outcome with little or no involvement in the process. To address this problem, this chapter proposes a conceptual framework (see Fig. 11.1) that frames the process of entrepreneurship education design and delivery within the canvas of the Triple Helix model of university–industry–government partnership. This model allows the universities to retains their primary roles in leading the process of knowledge production

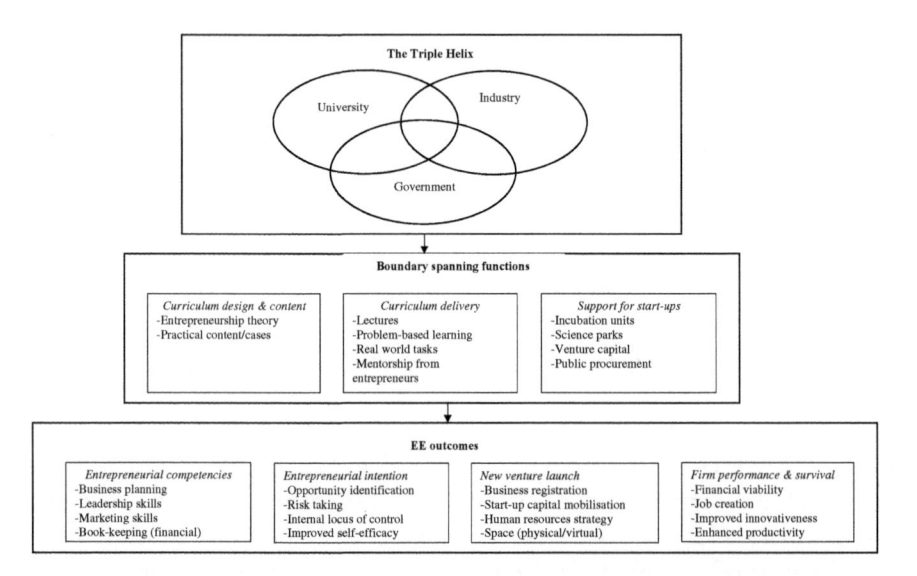

Fig. 11.1 A Triple Helix model of EE provision and outcomes (*Source* The Authors)

through training for skill development and competence building. They are, however, actively joined in this by industry practitioners in designing and delivering EE programmes that are based on problem-based learning and real business/life experience. The government contributes through its active involvement in quality assurance processes, through innovative policy interventions, and by using its convening powers to support and incentivise the Triple Helix partnership.

The model stipulated that the industry takes the lead in market activities including new venture launching in collaboration with the university who would set up incubation units and partner in the creation of science parks and other platforms for innovation and new venture creation. Finally, in this boundary-spanning approach where each of the key actors takes on the role of the other, the government also participates in the market activities, by acting both as buyers as well as venture capitalists. The first market role of the buyer can be achieved through strategic procurement activities aimed at new ventures. This can help stimulate the market and the entrepreneurial ecosystem, making it easier for nascent entrepreneurs to survive the proverbial "valley of death" in the life of new ventures. The same goes to its role as venture capitalists, providing startups with the necessary funding to actualise their entrepreneurial ideas and contribute to national productivity and welfare.

Thus, in the framework, four outcomes of entrepreneurship education can be identified: entrepreneurial competencies and skills, entrepreneurial intention, new venture launch, firm performance/survival. These outcomes are each broken down into a set of key operational metrics. For example, in order to launch a new venture, the entrepreneurs need to mobilise capital, develop a clear strategy for human resources. They will also need a space, either virtual and/or physical, to run their new business. The activities leading to these outcomes, contributed by the whole spectrum of actors in the Triple Helix, are in three broad categories: curriculum design; curriculum delivery; and support for startups.

Empirical Context

According to a recent estimate, Nigeria has 150 private and public universities, with an average intake of 600,000 students, according to Nigeria's National University Commission (NUC, 2014). Nigerian tertiary education institutions are estimated to produce up to 500,000 graduates every year, and some Nigerian graduates study abroad who come home to compete for jobs (Kazeem, 2016). This is in addition to graduates from other institutions of higher Education (Colleges of Education, Polytechnics) and those who dropped out after Basic or Senior secondary Education. The number is daunting.

The Nigerian government, in response to the challenge of rising graduate unemployment in the country graduates mandated in 2008, that all higher education institutions should compulsorily offer at least two courses in Entrepreneurship. Before this intervention by the federal government, some universities had launched awareness workshops and vocational entrepreneurship programmes. Following the government's directive, many universities saw the need to start Postgraduate programmes in Entrepreneurship Education and studies. One of the aims was to provide the needed core of academics who would facilitate the programmes as well as researchers who can offer research-based directions to enterprise development and growth in the country.

The directive on compulsory entrepreneurship education was one in line with policy interventions initiated to stem the tide of the rising unemployment rate and worsening poverty levels in the country. During the military regime in the 80s, the National Directorate of Employment (NDE) was established in 1986 with the vision of "jobs for all". The core mandate of the directorate was to design and implement programmes to combat mass unemployment. In 2003, following the return to civilian rule, the Small and Medium Enterprises Development Agency of Nigeria (SMEDAN) was set up to promote the development of MSME sector of the Nigerian economy.

Similarly, the National Poverty Eradication Programme (NAPEP) was launched in 2001 to train youths in vocational trades and to support microcredit, among others. The overarching aim was to address poverty in Nigeria. Despite all these, the unemployment rate in Nigeria has increased from 22.7% in the second quarter of 2018 to 23.1% in the third quarter of 2018. Unemployment Rate in Nigeria rose from 12.31% in 2006 to 23.10% in 2018, as shown in Fig. 11.2.

Industrial development is essential to the creation of job opportunities However, industrial performance in Nigeria has stagnated in the past few decades. The manufacturing sector, which is the most dynamic component of Nigeria's industrial sector, has declined. According to Ekpo (2014), the reasons for this poor performance include:

- Poor conception of implementation of industrialisation strategies
- Low technological development
- Inadequate infrastructure

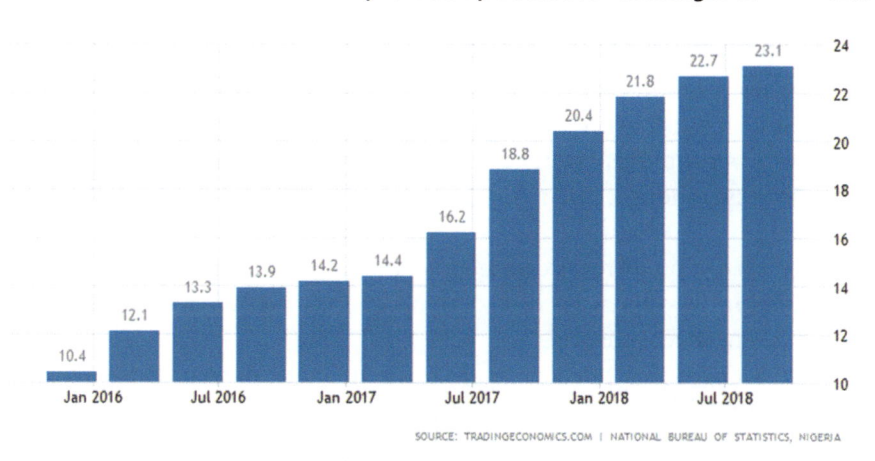

Fig. 11.2 Unemployment rate in Nigeria (Trading Economics, 2021)

- Non-completion and functioning of industrial core projects.

All these hinge on the lack of needed capable human resource. The latter is a sombre failure of Nigeria's HEIs. The non-existent relationship between the HEIs and the industry is greatly faulted for this. University–industry linkages, which could be in different forms and include a different level of commitment (such as research and development [R&D], training and curriculum development, and consultancy Martin, 2000), is a must if the outcomes of EE must be realised. Presently, industry stakeholders are not involved in the design of curricula for teaching in higher education institutions.

In order to effectively address the problem of inadequate synergy between university and industry sectors, stakeholders must first acknowledge the value of industry collaboration. Industry based analysis, including the soft and technical skills needed in the industry, should be the basis of curriculum development. The poor and inadequate learning environment which breeds mediocrity is another reason for the isolation. This is because the captains of the industries find the poor educational infrastructure (inadequate classrooms and teaching resources) as substandard in providing qualified graduates for the industry. This situation is what Othman (2011) referred to as "Splendid Isolation". The lack of awareness among the universities of the possibility of the University–Industry partnership makes it more difficult for collaboration among the two sectors. A strong university linkage, according to Okwelle and Ayonmike (2014), would improve the nation's economy, provide job opportunities, thereby leading to wealth generation, reduce crime rates and encourage creativity and competitiveness in nation-building.

At the time when the Nigerian government, through the National Universities Commission (NUC) gave a directive to Higher Institutions of learning to start entrepreneurship Education, it also came up with the minimum benchmarks for its implementation. The document highlighted the following, among others:

- Nigeria has a quest for accelerated economic growth; therefore, the youth population is to be assisted to develop and convert their innovative ideas into business ventures.
- There is a need to actively promote and train students to be entrepreneurial within Nigeria's educational system.
- The aims of the compulsory entrepreneurial modules should be the re-orientating of students towards a job creation mindset rather than the fixed attitude of job seeking.
- The modules should equip them with the skills required in establishing businesses or making them add value to existing systems if employed in organisations.
- The main objective of the modules is to introduce students to concepts and opportunities available in entrepreneurship and innovation.
- No previous knowledge is assumed.

Further according to the NUC brief, the specific objectives of the courses are to:

- Understand the relationship of enterprise, entrepreneur, business, entrepreneurship, innovation and creativity
- Analyse the historical perspective of entrepreneurship in Nigeria and relate it to the recent trend of unemployment, under-employment and job dissatisfaction, personal, national and global economic recession
- Identify the roles of entrepreneurial development agencies and regulatory bodies
- Cultivate the spirit of entrepreneurship
- Correct wrong attitudes and mindsets and develop high entrepreneurial potential in student
- Select possible business ideas
- Build the capacity to create a business plan to start a business.

The effective implementation of the entrepreneurship modules (as stipulated in the government policy document), is expected to produce graduates who are job creators and employable. These outcomes could not therefore be achieved through the traditional "lecture" mode of delivery in higher institutions. Although the benchmark states that case studies as well as interaction with entrepreneurs be used, it seemed that most institutions were not prepared for these. A number of higher education institutions have tried to incorporate entrepreneurs, captains of organisations to co-teach. These include their alumni, friends of the University and CEO of big corporations who have grants or votes to support the educational sector. However, the involvement of these industry partners are typically on an ad hoc basis, and do not usually involve any input on curriculum design. The entrepreneurship educational policy, in itself, is implicitly embedded in the National Policy for Education. There is no evidence of any significant input or contribution from industry stakeholders in the development of the policy.

Apart from the issue of the methodology of delivery, there are other constraints as highlighted by various authors to the effective implementation of Entrepreneurship Education in Nigeria. These constraints are summarised in Table 11.1.

Case Study: Covenant University Nigeria

Covenant University is a Christian Private University established in 2002 with a vision to raise a new generation of leaders for the African Continent on the platform of holistic, human development and integrated learning curriculum, in order to raise well-equipped and inspired citizens who will go out to develop their world (Covenant University, 2021). Covenant University's commitment to pioneering excellence at the cutting edge of research has been validated by the Times Higher Education rankings of 2018 where Covenant University ranked number 1 in both Nigeria and West Africa and 6 in Africa. At inception, Covenant University introduced the Entrepreneurial Development Studies (EDS) programme housed by the Centre for Entrepreneurial and Development Studies (CEDS). The programme is an all semester programme and compulsory for all students irrespective of the student's chosen course of study. It involves both theory and practice. With the vision of empowering Covenant University graduates entrepreneurially in a bid to make them productive and contribute significantly toward national socio-economic and human development. This innovative effort has yielded results in no small measure. For example, EDS—the entrepreneurship modules designed by Covenant University, has been adopted by the National Universities Commission (NUC) as required course components across Universities in Nigeria. Furthermore, in 2017 and 2018,

Table 11.1 Barriers to effective implementation of entrepreneurship education in Nigeria

Factors	Authors	Highlights/remarks
1. Poor infrastructures	Ojeifo (2012), Brown (2012), and Nwambam et al. (2018)	These include erratic power supply and poor communication and transportation facilities. These hinder the development and growth of SMEs and startups
2. Policy challenges	Unachukwu (2009) and Ojeifo (2012)	Inconsistency in policy processes and designs; discontinuity in policy implementation
3. Human capacity	Unachukwu (2009), Unachukwu (2009) and Blenker et al. (2008)	Lack of adequate trainers to facilitate entrepreneurship education; Limited practical business knowledge of many university tutors in the EE programmes
4. Cultural and societal barriers	Unachukwu (2009)	Poor societal attitude to entrepreneurship and self employment; pressure from parents to get paid government/civil service jobs

Covenant University graduates were ranked as the most employed graduates in Nigeria (Stutern, 2018).

CEDS is the premiere entrepreneurial centre in Nigeria. It was established with the aim to consciously train job creators and a mission to drive the culture of enterprise and innovation, creating and promoting entrepreneurial awareness and opportunities. It aims to impart entrepreneurial skills in the students, staff and members of the external context in contact with the Centre. In line with the policy of the Nigerian federal government under the auspices of the Nigerian Universities Commission, CEDS seeks to enhance the capacity of potential and practicing entrepreneurs who desire to learn practical skills that will make them self-employed and self-dependent. In line with its core objectives the centre aims to inspire Covenant University graduates to become employers of labour, thereby reducing unemployment in Nigeria. In addition, the centre seeks to actively stimulate the development and growth of entrepreneurship in Nigeria; support market linkages; and mentoring of SMEs. In December 2019, Covenant University was recognised as the "Best Entrepreneurship Development University of the Year" (Covenant University, 2019).

In pursuing its goals, the CEDS engages in collaborations with universities, government agencies and multilateral actors. Some of them are highlighted below:

i. Collaboration with the West African regional block—Economic Community of West African States ECOWAS—in fostering trans-border exchanges in entrepreneurship education.
ii. Partnership with the South African Tshwane University of Technology on fostering African content in Entrepreneurship Education.
iii. The Nigerian federal government agency—National Universities Commission under the Education Partnership for Africa (EPA) with Essex University, UK, and Bayero University, Kano, is collaborating with Covenant University to host the Knowledge Exchange for Entrepreneurship Education (KEEP) component of the partnership.
iv. Collaboration with Wadhwani Foundation which is a non-profitable organisation with the primary mission to create jobs, enhance job creation and job fulfilment.

Universities can indeed influence the development of entrepreneurial skills because academic instructions serve as an important environment that enhances the creation of entrepreneurial tendencies in students (Barral, Ribeiro and Canever, 2018). Additionally, students have the opportunity to choose alternative career as a result of exposure to entrepreneurial skills. Since Covenant University started turning out graduates in 2006, several spin-off companies have been created by Covenant University graduates and they are still up and running till date. Notable among these are: Piggy Vest, Softcom; Kora Pay; Thrive Agric, and a host of others. Piggy Vest is an online investment and savings platform launched in 2016. It currently hosts more than 350,000 users and more than 1 billion naira ($2.72 million) saved every month. Softcom focuses on provision of ICT solutions for businesses and individuals, while Kora Pay focuses on provision of financial services. Thrive Agric provides a digital platform where investors can be linked up with farmers.

To ensure that entrepreneurial ideas of more students are nurtured properly and successfully launched into the market (i.e. industry), the Hebron Startup Lab was created by Covenant University in 2017. The Hebron Startup Lab provides Startup trainings for prospective entrepreneurs. It also provides mentorship to interested students by linking them up with suitable mentors in the industry. Some of the Startups that were incubated at Hebron Startup Lab include Invest Naira, Cycles and University Compass. The strong collaborations between Covenant University and some industry partners have facilitated entrepreneurship development in Covenant University. A few of these are highlighted herein.

Partnership Between RCE Ogun, Covenant University and Zenith Bank, PLC

The Zenith Bank PLC in Partnership with the Regional Centre of Expertise, Ogun (RCE Ogun) at Covenant University has contributed immensely to the entrepreneurship development in Ogun State, in particular, and Nigeria, in general. For instance, RCE Ogun as part of her activities for 2019 and in line with her objective of creating Education for Sustainable Development (ESD) in Ogun State through formal, informal and non-formal training, enlightenment programmes and exemplar projects for the sustainable existence of Ogun State, partnered with the Zenith Bank PLC and the Hebron Startup Lab of Covenant University for a four-day training tagged "Digital Skills for Sustainable Wealth Creation" which held from 30th September to 3rd October 2019 (Details are available online at RCE Ogun's website: http://rceogun.covenantuniversity.edu.ng/rce-oguntrains-youths-for-on-digital-skills-for-sustainable-wealth-creation).

Having gone through the four-day training and shown proficiency in digital marketing, the participants were awarded a certificate of completion at the closing ceremony. As the Chair of RCE Ogun reiterated the commitment of the centre in continuous community and entrepreneurial engagement with industrial partner of Zenith Bank PLC and encouraged the participant to put to good use the knowledge learnt during the workshop. The opening session took place on Monday the 30th of September 2019 at Covenant University Centre for Research Innovation and Discoveries (CUCRID) and had in attendance, the Vice-Chancellor of Covenant University, the Monarch of Ota Kingdom (the Olota of Ota), Oba Adeyemi Abdulkabir Obalanlege represented by the Onikotun of Ota, Oba Abdulhakeem Kolawole, and 40 youth participants from Ogun State in view to acquiring entrepreneurial education. The courses taught at the training include: Self Discovery, Venture Creation,

Google Digital Tools for Business (Google Heptics team), Product Development, Marketing, Pitching & Selling (MAPS), Entrepreneurial Mindset, Web Design using WordPress, Graphics Design training and Leadership and Team Building.

Partnership Between Hebron Startup Lab, Covenant University and Softcom

The Softcom partnership with Hebron Startup Lab at Covenant University has helped in enhancing the entrepreneurial development and educational curriculum. Some of the ways in which Softcom has contributed to entrepreneurship development at Covenant University is by providing internship opportunities for the students (both at the undergraduate and at the graduate levels) to exercise, build and learn digital and entrepreneurial skills. One of the notable outcomes from the partnership is that a good number of Covenant University graduates involved at Hebron Startup Lab have been recruited by Softcom (Co-creation Hub, 2017).

The partnership has helped entrepreneurship development at Covenant University through funding. To exemplify this, Softcom funded Covenant University's 6-cohort micro-Venture Acceleration Programme (mVAP) to nurture and support 200 entrepreneurs in 2019. This support is not only in terms of funding in the area of networking, Softcom connects Hebron Startup Lab/Covenant University with their numerous networks by inviting Covenant University to their programmes as well as hosting the startup teams during boot camps.

Partnership Between Hebron Startup Lab, Covenant University and Google

Hebron Startup Lab at Covenant University is also in partnership with Google. In this partnership, Google helps in entrepreneurial development in the following areas: (a) Funding: Google supports the Centres *Edustart* programmes financially; (b) Facilitation: Google also provides free Digital skills training to update student teams with the future skills; and network-building: Google helps to expand the lab's networks through invitation for their programmes and hosting them in the Google office.

Apart from CEDS and Hebron Startup Lab that are actively involved in developing entrepreneurial skills and transmitting such skills for the benefit of the society, other centres have also been established in Covenant University to further provide collaborative measures with the industry in solving societal needs. Some of these include Centre for Economic Policy and Development Research (CEPDeR) and Regional Centre for Expertise, Ogun (RCE Ogun). While CEPDeR provides the platform for linking research to policy and practice, RCE Ogun, creates the avenue for harnessing various forms of knowledge from formal, informal and non-formal education in ensuring education for sustainable development. RCE is one of the globally recognised centres United Nations University Institute for the Advanced Study of Sustainability (UNU-IAS).

Discussion

This chapter examines the landscape of entrepreneurship education in Nigeria, Africa's most populous country and largest economy. The study is set against the backdrop of a 2002 policy directive to Nigerian universities to implement the delivery of compulsory entrepreneurship education in their curricula across all disciplines. This directive was in response to the growing problem of graduate unemployment in the West African country, and recognition of the limited absorptive capacity of the Nigerian labour market. While the policy idea sounds good, the development and implementation of entrepreneurship education have been hampered by a wide range of institutional, pedagogical and practical challenges. In this chapter, we argue that these challenges are in part associated with the top-down approach that underpinned the federal government directive to the nation's higher education providers. While the stakeholders cannot go back in time, they can, in retrospect, implement a new model of partnership that brings university, industry and government actors together towards reform and implementation of more enriching and impactful entrepreneurship education. Thus, we adopt a theoretical model of the Triple Helix to analyse the challenges and opportunities associated with EE design, implementation and outcomes. We also show how the three institutional actors can come together in a co-creation model to tackle the challenges and harness the opportunities to produce, support and incentivise a new generation of innovative entrepreneurs in the country.

The Covenant University (CU) case study highlights several key features that mark out the university as a burgeoning exemplar of an entrepreneurial university actively taking on a leading role in the Triple Helix. CU has become an active regional innovation organiser, especially within Southwest

Nigeria. It has, for example, convened workshops and networking events bringing regional officials and industry actors together with members of the academia. By facilitating these co-creation platforms, the university has spearheaded the development of new ideas and solutions to the pressing problems of unemployment. However, it is not clear how the university's explicit faith background can limit its potential to expand these networks. Nevertheless, the university has established itself as a leading example of university-led innovation and entrepreneurial development. Its specific impact can be highlighted in three key areas.

First, CU has made significant progress in embracing the third mission of economic and social development, along with the traditional roles of teaching and research. In pursuance of this, the university has launched a number of business ventures which it still operates. This is a good example of an institution taking on the role of another in a Triple Helix with fluid institutional boundaries (Etzkowitz, 2003a). In this case, the university, with its core role of teaching and research, has stepped out to take on the core role of industry, which is to launch and operate companies. In doing this, the university is able to bring its advantage to bear in terms of research and knowledge production for innovation development and firm performance. Equally important, this enables the university to provide students with real-world entrepreneurial experiential learning. Thus, students are provided hands-on support from ideation to startup and practical experience of various activities and challenges associated with launching and growing new ventures. This on-campus learning opportunity, complemented with off-campus industry placement, enables the students to engage more fruitfully and make the connection between academic knowledge and practical, real-world entrepreneurship.

Second, CU also appears to have had considerable success in co-opting industry stakeholders as co-creators of entrepreneurship curricula. Industry practitioners have been integrated into the teaching faculty, not only in the Entrepreneurship Education programme but in various modules across the faculties. The productive knowledge exchange among university academic staff and industry practitioners has helped enriched the entrepreneurial learning experience of students. Among others, it provides opportunities for students to interact closely with real-world entrepreneurs and ask practical questions that industry practitioners are better placed to answer. Furthermore, the university has been able to co-opt its alumni who have become successful entrepreneurs into its mentorship programme and as industry placement opportunities for current students. Much has been done to integrate industry actors and entrepreneurs into the curriculum delivery; however, there is little available evidence on if, or to what extent to which the university has co-opted industry practitioners in the curriculum design. This is an important area for the institutional stakeholders to consider for the future development of the entrepreneurship education (EE) programme. Industry partners are not only effective in the delivery of EE curriculum, but they can also have valuable inputs to make to curriculum content and design of summative and formative assessments, among others.

Third, the university has demonstrated the ability to engage with relevant arms and agencies of governments, both at the regional and national levels, towards more effective design and delivery of entrepreneurship education programmes. This engagement enables both the university and industry stakeholders to provide feedback to the government, which can, in turn, influence entrepreneurship education policy. As outlined in the section on the empirical contexts, one of the major criticisms of the Nigerian entrepreneurship education is that it was mostly top-down. In other words, when a directive was issued to Nigerian universities and other higher education providers on the need to implement compulsory entrepreneurship training, there was little consultation and input from the higher education providers during the process of policy implementation. As such, the policy was essentially forced on, rather than co-created by, the universities. By convening network events and workshops bringing government, industry and university stakeholders together, Covenant University has not only provided a feedback mechanism for continuous improvement of entrepreneurship education programmes, it has also provided a template for future partnership and collaboration for development and implementation of future policies for entrepreneurship development.

The objectives and goals of entrepreneurship education in Nigeria are such that neither universities nor industry nor the government can achieve them in isolation. While, as in the Triple Helix, each of the institutional actors has core expertise and competencies to lead specific activities, the flexibility of the Triple Helix model allows them to move across boundaries to take on the role of the other. As such, while the university takes the lead in designing curriculum contents and assessment, industry practitioners have vital input to make to the structure and content of curricula, as does the government in terms of matching curriculum content with national development agenda and growth projections. In addition, industry actors can use the experience of this Triple Helix collaboration to initiate entrepreneurship training programmes of their own- say for current employees or through a reformed apprenticeship system. In doing this, they can co-opt university academic partners to support industry-initiated entrepreneurship training. This is in line with the advent of degree apprenticeships in developed countries, where employers and universities work together in the design and delivery of work-based degree programmes (Bravenboer, 2016; Gessler, 2017; Mulkeen et al., 2019). Nigeria, like many African countries, already has an extensive apprenticeship system operating mainly in the informal sector. The formal sector can draw lessons from this system in the development of an alternative model of new work-based degree programmes, with entrepreneurship training at its core.

Further, government agencies such as the National Universities Commission, play a lead role in quality monitoring processes, again with inputs from university and industry actors to ensure academic excellence and industry relevance, respectively. Finally, to the extent that the ultimate goal of entrepreneurship education is to inspire and support university graduates who have entrepreneurial ambitions, entrepreneurship education programmes need to be backed up with strategic and focused institutional support (Anosike et al., 2018; Kolade, 2018). This includes simplification of the business registration process, provision of startup funds for promising entrepreneurs, strategic use of public procurement to stimulate and incentivise nascent entrepreneurship, provision of co-creation space, market reform and infrastructural development. Again, while the government take the lead in these institutional interventions, it is also expected that universities and industry stakeholders will make essential contributions. For example, industry practitioners can step in as angel investors for university startups, and universities can provide support for new business registrations, in addition to providing co-working spaces for startups. Finally, the university entrepreneurial ecosystem can serve as a mirror of the wider national entrepreneurial ecosystems, thus providing a practical learning environment for entrepreneurs-in-training to engage with various actors, tackle numerous challenges and appropriate new opportunities.

Conclusion and Recommendation

While the immediate empirical context of this chapter is the Nigerian higher education sector, the Triple Helix model of entrepreneurship education has wider relevance and application across, and indeed beyond, the African continent. Here we emphasise the particular relevance to the African context where the university sector is in crisis. Furthermore, national governments are grappling with rising problem of youth unemployment and the mismatch between graduate skills portfolios and industry needs. A Triple Helix model of entrepreneurship education will effectively pool and integrate the best that university, industry and government stakeholders have to offer towards the development of entrepreneurs and human resources suited to the countries' needs and the demands of the twenty-first-century knowledge economy. This model will also address the peculiar circumstances of the African labour markets which require more job creators than job seekers. Finally, it will aid the necessary transformation of African universities into more dynamic, entrepreneurial entities with less reliance on government subventions, and better positioned to drive a new era of inclusive growth in the twenty-first-century knowledge economy.

In the light of the above discussion and conclusions, it is recommended that both public and private universities take more pro-active approach in leading university–industry–government partnerships for entrepreneurship education design and delivery. These can be through intentional and more structured networking activities; universities actively embracing entrepreneurial opportunities, support for industries to break through fluid institutional boundaries by taking on some academic roles such as work-based training and degrees, and working with governments to encourage the emergence of new entrepreneurial universities that are better equipped for both knowledge production and knowledge capitalisation.

References

Ahmad, S. Z., Ismail, M. Z., & Buchanan, F. R. (2014). Examining the entrepreneurship curriculum in Malaysian polytechnics. *International Journal of Management Education, 12*(3), 397–406 (Elsevier Ltd.). https://doi.org/10.1016/j.ijme.2014.06.004.

Anosike, P., Kolade, O., & Ahmed, P. K. (2018). Entrepreneurship education service and socioeconomic development in Sub-Saharan Africa. In *The service sector and economic development in Africa* (pp. 131–144). Routledge.

Ajzen, I. (1991). The theory of planned behavior. *Organisational Behavior and Human Decision Processes, 50*(2), 179–211. https://doi.org/10.1016/0749-5978(91)90020-T

Barral, M. R. M., Ribeiro, F. G., & Canever, M. D. (2018). Influence of the university environment in the entrepreneurial intention in public and private universities. *RAUSP Management Journal, 53*(1), 122–133. https://doi.org/10.1016/j.rauspm.2017.12.009.

Bjerregaard, T. (2010). Industry and academia in convergence: Micro-institutional dimensions of R&D collaboration. *Technovation, 30*(2), 100–108 (Elsevier). https://doi.org/10.1016/j.technovation.2009.11.002.

Blenker, P., Dreisler, P., Færgemann, H. M., & Kjeldsen, J. (2008). A framework for developing entrepreneurship education in a university context. *International Journal of Entrepreneurship and Small Business, 5*(1), 45–63.

Bravenboer, D. (2016). Why co-design and delivery is "a no brainer" for higher and degree apprenticeship policy. *Higher Education, Skills and Work-Based Learning, 6*(4), 384–400. https://doi.org/10.1108/HESWBL-06-2016-0038

Brown, P. B. (2012). *Why everyone will have to become an entrepreneur* (Crowd Sourced Version). http://www.forbes.com/sites/actiontrumpseverything/2012/11/03/why-everyone-will-have-to-become-an-entrepreneur-crowd-sourced-version/.

British Council. (2014). *Can higher education solve Africa's job crisis? Understanding graduate employability in Sub-Saharan Africa.*

Cloete, N., Bailey, T., & Pillay, P. (2011). *Universities and economic development in Africa.* Centre for Higher Education Transformation (CHET). Available at: www.africanbookscollective.comiii. Accessed 3 January 2020.

Co-creation Hub. (2017). Press Release : Co-creation Hub Hosts 3rd Annual Social Change Summit. Press Release. Available at: https://cchubnigeria.com/press-release-co-creation-hub-cchub-hosts-3rd-annual-social-change-summit/.

Cooney, T. M. (2012). *Entrepreneurship skills for growth-orientated businesses, Denish business authority.* Available at: http://www.oecd.org/cfe/leed/Cooney_entrepreneurship_skills_HGF.pdf.

Ejemeyovwi, J. O., Osabuohien, E. S., & Osabohien, R. (2018). ICT investments, human capital development and institutions in ECOWAS. *International Journal of Economics and Business Research, 15*(4), 463–474. https://doi.org/10.1504/IJEBR.2018.092151.

Covenant University. (2019). *Covenant: Nigeria's most outstanding higher institution of the year 2019.* Covenant University News. Available at: https://www.covenantuniversity.edu.ng/News/Covenant-Nigeria-s-Most-Outstanding-Higher-Institution-of-the-Year-2019#.YFO0rp37SUm.

Covenant University. (2021). *About Covenant University, About CU.* Available at: https://www.covenantuniversity.edu.ng/About-Us/About-CU#.YFO27J37SUn.

Ekpo, U. (2014). Nigeria industrial policies and industrial sector performance: Analytical expoloration. *IOSR Journal of Economics and Finance., 3*(4), 1–11.

Etzkowitz, H., Webster, A., Gebhardt, C., & Terra, B. R. C. (2000). The future of the university and university of the future: Evolution of ivory tower to entrepreneurial paradigm. *Research Policy, 29*(2), 313–330. https://doi.org/10.1016/S0048-7333(99)00069-4

Etzkowitz, H. (2003a). Innovation in innovation: The Triple Helix of university-industry-government relations. *Social Science Information, 42*(3), 293–337. Available at: https://journals.sagepub.com/doi/pdf/https://doi.org/10.1177/05390184030423002. Accessed 1 January 2020.

Etzkowitz, H. (2003b). Learning from transition: The triple helix as an innovation system. In *Symposium on "Knowledge based society: A challenge for new EU and accession countries."* Zagreb, Croatia.

Etzkowitz, H. (2008). *The Triple Helix: University-industry-government innovation in action.* https://doi.org/10.4324/9780203929605.

Etzkowitz, H., & Leydesdorff, L. (2000) The dynamics of innovation: From National Systems and "'Mode 2'" to a Triple Helix of university-industry-government relations. *Research Policy, 29*(2), 109–123. Available at: www.elsevier.nlrlocatereconbase. Accessed 1 January 2020.

Etzkowitz, H., & Zhou, C. (2017). *The Triple Helix: University-industry-government innovation and entrepreneurship.* https://doi.org/10.4324/9781315620183.

Farstad, H. (2002). *Integrated entrepreneurship education in Botswana, Uganda and Kenya.* Oslo. Available at: https://www.voced.edu.au/content/ngv%3A25852.

Fiet, J. O. (2001a). The pedagogical side of entrepreneurship theory. *Journal of Business Venturing, 16*(2), 101–117. https://doi.org/10.1016/S0883-9026(99)00042-7.

Fiet, J. O (2001b). The theoretical side of teaching entrepreneurship. *Journal of Business Venturing, 16*(1), 1–24. https://doi.org/10.1016/S0883-9026(99)00041-5.

Galloway, L., Anderson, M., Brown, W., & Wilson, L. (2005). Enterprise skills for the economy. *Education + Training, 47*(1), 7–17. https://doi.org/10.1108/00400910510580593.

Gessler, M. (2017). Educational transfer as transformation: A case study about the emergence and implementation of dual apprenticeship structures in a German automotive transplant in the United States. *Vocations and Learning, 10*(1), 71–99 (Springer). https://doi.org/10.1007/s12186-016-9161-8.

Gibb, A. (1987). Enterprise culture—Its meaning and implications for education and training. *Journal of European Industrial Training.* https://doi.org/10.1108/eb043365

Gibbons, M., Limoges, C., Nowotny, H., Schwartzman, S., Scott, P., & Trow, M. (1994) *The new production of knowledge: The dynamics of science and research in contemporary societies.* Available at: https://uk.sagepub.com/en-gb/eur/the-new-production-of-knowledge/book204307. Accessed 20 December 2019.

Godin, B., & Gingras, Y. (2000). The place of universities in the system of knowledge production. *Research Policy, 29*(2), 273–278. https://doi.org/10.1016/S0048-7333(99)00065-7

Henry, C., Hill, F., & Leitch, C. (2005). Entrepreneurship education and training—Can entrepreneurship be taught? Part I. *Education + Training, 47*(2), 98–111. https://doi.org/10.1108/00400910510586524.

Hessels, L. K., & van Lente, H. (2008). Re-thinking new knowledge production: A literature review and a research agenda. *Research Policy, 37*(4), 740–760. https://doi.org/10.1016/j.respol.2008.01.008

Hussler, C., Picard, F., & Tang, M. F. (2010). Taking the ivory from the tower to coat the economic world: Regional strategies to make science useful. *Technovation, 30*(9–10), 508–518 (Elsevier). https://doi.org/10.1016/j.technovation.2010.06.003.

Imogen Mathers. (2016). *Who is going to pay for higher education in Africa?—SciDev.Net*, Sci Dev Net. Available at: https://www.scidev.net/global/education/feature/higher-education-africa-who-pays.html?__cf_chl_jschl_tk__=ba1e50bbe8cd20723f30f64d964adcc726414b0c-1579775482-0-AVxS4ka0Aym5TWEFuBvlLxO4bcuwPIcAWAninhUfc6vl0DQtUg6ZTZ0UuCYM0ectCVS_Ngkn5_YvyKXpaETUbf2oCZmyYAh. Accessed 23 January 2020.

Kazeem, Y. (2016). *About half of the university graduates in Nigeria cannot find jobs*. https://qz.com/africa/603967/about-half-of-the-university-graduates-in-nigeria-cannot-find-jobs/.

Kolade, O. (2018). Venturing under fire: Entrepreneurship education, venture creation, and poverty reduction in conflict-ridden Maiduguri, Nigeria. *Education + Training, 60*(7–8), 749–766.

Leydesdorff, L., & Etzkowitz, H. (1996). Emergence of a Triple Helix of university-industry-government relations. *Science and Public Policy, 23*(5), 279–286.

Martin, M. (2000). Managing university-industry relations: A study of institutional practices from 12 different countries. A working document in the series "Improving the Managerial Effectiveness of Higher Education Institutions." IIEP/UNESCO. https://www.aau.org/wp-content/uploads/sites/9/2018/04/Managing-University-Industry-Relations.pdf.

Mosey, S., Wright, M., & Clarysse, B. (2012). Transforming traditional university structures for the knowledge economy through multidisciplinary institutes. *Cambridge Journal of Economics, 36*(3), 587–607. https://doi.org/10.1093/cje/bes008

Mulkeen, J., Abdou, H. A., Leigh, J., & Ward, P. (2019). Degree and higher level apprenticeships: An empirical investigation of stakeholder perceptions of challenges and opportunities. *Studies in Higher Education, 44*(2), 333–346. https://doi.org/10.1080/03075079.2017.1365357.

National Universities Commission. (2014). National Universities Commission Benchmark Minimum Academic Standards for Undergraduate Programmes in Nigerian Universities. BMAS Engineering and Technology. www.mciu.edu.ng.

Nwambam, A. S., Nnennaya O. O., & Nwankpu I. S. (2018). Evaluating the entrepreneurship education programme in Nigerian universities for sustainable development. *Journal of Entrepreneurship Education, 21*(1). Print ISSN: 1098-8394; Online ISSN: 1528-2651. https://www.abacademies.org/articles/evaluating-the-entrepreneurship-education-programme-in-nigerian-universities-for-sustainable-development-6996.html.

Ojeifo, S. A. (2012). Entrepreneurship education in Nigeria. *Journal of Education and Practice, 3*(14), 78–82.

Okwelle, P. C., & Ayonmike, C. S. (2014). Towards value re-orientation of youths on the role of technical vocational education and training (TVET) for sustainable development in Nigeria. *Journal of Education and Practice, 5*(8), 186–191.

Olofinyehun, A. O., Adelowo, C. M., & Egbetokun, A. A. (2018). The supply of high-quality entrepreneurs in developing countries: Evidence from Nigeria. *Science and Public Policy, 45*(2), 269–282. https://doi.org/10.1093/scipol/scx065

Oosterbeek, H., van Praag, M., & Ijsselstein, A. (2010). The impact of entrepreneurship education on entrepreneurship skills and motivation. *European Economic Review, 54*(3), 442–454. https://doi.org/10.1016/j.euroecorev.2009.08.002

Othman, N. B. (2011). An assessment of a university-industry partnership in a Malaysian University. *International Journal of Business and Social Science, 2*(8), 94–103.

Rae, D. (2004). Practical theories from entrepreneurs' stories: Discursive approaches to entrepreneurial learning. *Journal of Small Business and Enterprise Development, 11*(2), 195–202. https://doi.org/10.1108/14626000410537137

Rasmussen, E. A., & Sørheim, R. (2006). Action-based entrepreneurship education. *Technovation, 26*(2), 185–194. https://doi.org/10.1016/j.technovation.2005.06.012

Souitaris, V., Zerbinati, S., & Al-Laham, A. (2007). Do entrepreneurship programmes raise entrepreneurial intention of science and engineering students? The effect of learning, inspiration and resources. *Journal of Business Venturing, 22*(4), 566–591. https://doi.org/10.1016/j.jbusvent.2006.05.002

Stutern. (2018). *The Nigerian Graduate Report 2018*. Available at: http://eprints.covenantuniversity.edu.ng/11968/1/2018%2BNigerian%2BGraduate%2BReport.pdf.

Teferra, D. (2013). Funding higher education in Africa: State, trends and perspectives. *Journal of Higher Education in Africa/Revue de l'enseignement supérieur en Afrique*, 19–51. CODESRIA. https://doi.org/10.2307/jhigheducafri.11.1-2.19.

The Economist. (2019). *A booming population is putting strain on Africa's universities—Tertiary Education in Africa*. Tertiary Education in Africa. Available at: https://www.economist.com/middle-east-and-africa/2019/08/10/a-booming-population-is-putting-strain-on-africas-universities. Accessed 5 October 2019.

Trading Economics. (2021). Nigeria Unemployment Rate | 2006–2020 Data | 2021–2023 Forecast | Calendar, Nigerian Unemployment Rates. Available at: https://tradingeconomics.com/nigeria/unemployment-rate. Accessed 11 August 2021.

Unachukwu, G. O. (2009). Issues and challenges in the development of entrepreneurship education in Nigeria. *African Research Review—An International Multi-disciplinary Journal, Ethiopia, 3*(5), 213–226.

Walker, J. K., Jeger, M., & Kopecki, D. (2013). The role of perceived abilities, subjective norm and intentions in entrepreneurial activity. *Journal of Entrepreneurship, 22*(2), 181–202. https://doi.org/10.1177/0971355713490621

Wong, P. K., Ho, Y. P., & Singh, A. (2007). Towards an "entrepreneurial university" model to support knowledge-based economic development: The case of the National University of Singapore. *World Development, 35*(6), 941–958. https://doi.org/10.1016/j.worlddev.2006.05.007

Youtie, J., & Shapira, P. (2008). Building an innovation hub: A case study of the transformation of university roles in regional technological and economic development. *Research Policy, 37*(8), 1188–1204. https://doi.org/10.1016/j.respol.2008.04.012

Part III

Technology Entrepreneurship and Innovation Ecosystem

12

Are African Economies Open for Entrepreneurship: How Do We Know?

David Rae, Oluwaseun Kolade, and Adebowale Owoseni

Introduction

The purpose of this chapter is to explore the economic openness of African national economies to their populations, in the interests of widening access to enterprise and innovation across Africa. Inspired by the concept of entrepreneurship as a fundamental human right (Aerni, 2015), how freely do people have universal access to enterprise and innovation across Africa? How can progress towards this goal be measured? Given the scale of economic, demographic, political and environmental challenges facing African countries, should the question instead be 'why can there not be universal access across Africa'?

In the context of global economic volatility arising from many causes; the impact of the Coronavirus pandemic, with severe social and economic effects on African countries; and population growth especially in Sub-Saharan

---

D. Rae (✉) · O. Kolade
Department of Management and Entrepreneurship, De Montfort University, Leicester, UK
e-mail: david.rae@dmu.ac.uk

O. Kolade
e-mail: seun.kolade@dmu.ac.uk

A. Owoseni
De Montfort University, Leicester, UK

African countries, progress towards open economies may be judged essential. There is an increasing requirement to create employment and economic opportunities for an African population growing at more than 30 million annually (IIAG, 2020). However, structural reforms, availability of technology and data resources alone are not intrinsically capable of providing the social and economic innovation and changes required. Human agency and capability are required, within a context which supports, and does not prevent, human-scale innovation. It is also essential to consider the context of policy and political, economic, educational and infrastructural factors which may create or constrain an open economy, and enable or constrain people from adopting technologies and resources with potential for their economic self-determination through entrepreneurship (Atiase et al., 2018).

The prime question addressed in this chapter is:

How can the readiness of African states for entrepreneurial activity open to all be assessed from existing information sources?

The chapter explores two related strategic issues which concern the mass adoption of innovation and entrepreneurship which are required for economic development and job creation within African countries. These are both accentuated by the impact of the Coronavirus pandemic on African countries and people.

Firstly, the levels of economic openness at national levels and individual freedom to act entrepreneurially;

Secondly, the general availability of open access to entrepreneurial means, resources and opportunities.

A third factor, the ability to track and evaluate progress towards entrepreneurial activity and outcomes, is beyond the immediate scope of this work but flows from it and the proposed framework may contribute towards it.

These three issues directly address the United Nations Sustainable Development Goals (UN SDGs) 8: 'Promote sustained, inclusive and sustainable economic growth, full employment and decent work for all'; and 9: 'Build resilient infrastructure, promote inclusive and sustainable industrialization and foster innovation' (UN, 2015).

The contribution of this chapter is to use existing internationally recognised indices of economic development, governance, corruption and digital access to develop a composite pan-African framework which can indicate national levels of economic openness, and related factors which affect innovation and entrepreneurial development.

What Does an 'Open' Economy Mean, and Why It Matters

The term 'Open' is used in two differing, but complementary senses in this work. The first relates to Open economies and societies; the second to the use of freely available data and related resources within this context (Open definition, 2005). The two are fundamentally connected, since, as demonstrated in this chapter, it is necessary to use freely available data to judge the openness of an economy, though many extant datasets which would be useful to do so are not available in this way. An open economy is one in which individuals enjoy the right to start businesses and to trade without undue restrictions; where government supports businesses on an equal basis and where economic opportunities are equally available, rather than being protected or reserved. These can also be described as conditions of free enterprise. It does not mean there is no role for government, but rather that the state should not try to control all functions of the economy, nor to levy excessive taxes or undue restrictions on businesses. There is fair and open access to opportunities, and protectionism, corruption and cronyism which restrict fair access are prevented.

An open economy also refers to an economy in which a significant percentage of its goods and services are traded internationally. The degree of openness depends on the level of trade restrictions such as tariffs imposed by a country. The merits and demerits of an open, free-market economy have attracted considerable debates among policymakers and scholars of African economy (Dollar & Svensson, 2000; Heidhues & Obare, 2011; Riddell, 1992). For many, including large sections of the African public, free market is often associated with the implementation of the Structural Adjustment Programme (SAP) in African countries, at the behest of IMF and World Bank in 1980s and 90s. That was against the backdrop of significant decline in growth, after the early promise in the late 1950s and the 1960s. In the 1970s, African countries had struggled to implement state-led investment and import substitution strategies (Heidhues & Obare, 2011). SAP comprised of four key components: 'currency devaluation, the removal/reduction of the state from the workings of the economy, the elimination of subsidies in an attempt to reduce expenditures, and trade liberalisation' (Riddell, 1992, p. 53). The ensuing austerity and removal/drastic reduction of state welfare and social programmes contributed significantly to negative perceptions of SAP on the part of the African public. However, the subsequent two decades did not produce significant outcomes in terms of growth and development, as African countries became dependent on foreign exports, and the development of indigenous enterprises fell back further and foreign multinationals dominated the African market (Ratten & Jones, 2018).

So whilst there are both degrees of and disadvantages to a free-market economy, it contrasts with the dangers of a totally state-controlled economy in which production and consumption are highly regulated, usually to the frustration and impoverishment of its citizens. This has been attempted in various ways by some African states at different times, such as the latter years of the Mugabe regime in Zimbabwe (Jones, 2010). In this chapter, we approach the concept of an open economy primarily from the standpoint of openness to citizens' unfettered economic participation, and then, by extension, openness to international trade. We argue that, in order for a country to participate effectively and beneficially in the global economy, it needs to embrace an 'open' paradigm that unleashes the entrepreneurial capabilities of its citizens, and therefore enables them to compete both nationally and internationally. The open enterprise model requires the active involvement of the state in creating this environment.

Finally, an open economy operates within the context of transparency of government and society more generally, where citizens can monitor government spending and activities, where their rights are protected, and where corrupt practices in government, and between businesses and government, are minimised, as argued in Pollock's 'Open Revolution' (Pollock, 2018). The existence of these conditions varies widely across the continent, with some states making significant progress towards them, whilst others contend with complex legacies of poor governance, conflict, and endemic deprivation.

Open is also used to describe the availability of freely shared digital resources, such as data, source code, learning materials and other categories. The definition used for these is: 'Open data and content can be freely used, modified, and shared by anyone for any purpose' (Open definition 2.1, 2005). These are also referred to as Open resources (Rae, 2019).

Open resources are critically important in the African context. Access to them enables African citizens and businesses to find information; use a wide range of resources; develop digital tools with open-source code; and many other effects. These applications would be unavailable if they were reliant on proprietary paid-for solutions, and can stimulate grassroots innovation. An example is the use of OpenStreetMap by country groups to develop detailed mapping and geo-datasets https://wiki.openstreetmap.org/wiki/OSM_Africa. MapUganda quickly developed a COVID-19 response map in 2020 to support public health capacity.

Both forms of 'openness' are essential for entrepreneurial development in an African context, and it has been proposed by the European Union that, in combination, open economies and the use of open resources have very significant potential for economic development, participation and growth (Ramjoué, 2015). In recent years whilst this has been strongly argued (World Bank, 2014), in conducting this research it was evident that the application of data for economic development was quite limited and very uneven across different countries in the African context, though with growing applications in related fields such as health, education and governance (Lansana et al., 2020). There have been a series of initiatives, and the Africa Open Data Network co-ordinated by the Local Development Research Institute has the potential to progress Open data at an African level https://www.developlocal.org/data4development/aodn/.

Open resources are an essential ingredient of Open Entrepreneurship (OE), a new form of entrepreneurship which uses freely available public resources to create wider value. As defined by Rae (2019) this is an activity which creates multiple forms of value (such as economic, social, cultural and environmental) for entrepreneurs and others: investors, co-workers, customers, the community at large. To achieve this, the entrepreneurial person or organisation is able to access, freely and fairly, the resources, means and opportunities for entrepreneurial activities of value creation. OE is open to all members of society; inclusivity regardless of culture, gender, age, ability, or section. OE is a means of personal, economic and social development locally and globally (Rae, 2019: 164).

The African Context for Entrepreneurship

Across a vast continent of 54 nations, whilst there is great diversity within Africa, the conditions for their economic development have many shared factors. Whilst these are not completely unique, they differ in important ways from those in 'developed' continents (Jones et al., 2018a). Geographical factors of size, sparsity of population in vast rural and desert areas, and relatively poor land transport routes have impeded the development of connected markets. There are diverse populations in every sense: geographically, ethnically, linguistically and culturally.

Entrepreneurship within African societies has a long history which predates European and Northern involvement. Ochonu (2018) explored the entrepreneurial communities, trading networks and traditions, especially in West Africa, including Benin, Wangara, and across the Sahara. It is clear from a range of historical explorations that diverse entrepreneurial activities, including agrarian, resource-based and mercantile, with complex commercial organisations had existed and thrived within organised societies before colonisation (Ochonu, 2018; Sambajee & Weston, 2015).

European trading links in the eighteenth and nineteenth centuries, and subsequent colonisation in the late nineteenth and twentieth centuries, can be viewed as primarily focused on value extraction and resource exploitation of African societies. The most extreme form was slavery, but this exploitation was also manifested in many other ways, involving practices from the most brutal, in the case of Belgium and the Congo, to arguably more benign but still oppressive regimes in British and French colonies, for example (Ochonu, 2018).

The postcolonial legacy from 1950 onwards left many states with governance and legal systems mirroring former imperial models, and which were designed for administrative control and value extraction, not entrepreneurship. The French, English and Belgian colonial models certainly did not aim to encourage indigenous entrepreneurship. The postcolonial process of liberating Africans from inappropriate, discriminatory and outdated requirements, for example for creating new ventures, has been slow and uneven (Nkomo, 2011).

Whilst there are many such factors constraining entrepreneurship, the past two decades have seen accelerating growth in both the incidence of entrepreneurship by African people, and the rise in research studies of this phenomenon (Edoho, 2015; Jones et al., 2018a; 2018b; 2018c). Recent generations of African young people have recognised both the possibility of entrepreneurship and its potential in enabling them to create their own jobs, incomes and futures, rather than competing in overcrowded employment markets with many more job seekers than opportunities (Chigunta, 2017). There is a growing recognition that whilst entrepreneurial models, technologies and practices from Western and Northern nations may provide inspiration and starting points, African approaches to entrepreneurship can be more effective by adapting these to local conditions, as well as combining them with existing cultural, trading practices and resources (Dvouletý & Orel, 2019). Simply trying to replicate Western models of entrepreneurship in the African social and economic contexts may not provide an enduring model, and more research is required (Jones & Ratten, 2018).

One major driver for this increase in entrepreneurship is education. There is undoubtedly insufficient educational access and capacity in many parts of Africa (AEO, 2020). However, many of those able to take advantage of it have recognised that entrepreneurship can be an option, though often less culturally prized than a conventional professional, government or corporate career; again, this is a colonial cultural legacy (DeJaeghere & Baxter, 2014). More African learners, though still too few, encounter entrepreneurship education at some point in their studies. But given the large projected increases in population in many African countries (Worldometer, 2020), there is no doubt that a commensurate of greater increase in education at all levels is essential (Jones et al., 2018b). Even now, there are deteriorating educational outcomes, and insufficient places at university level to meet rising demand in countries such as Nigeria. Educational participation rates, progression to secondary education, especially among girls, and university access, are all too low in many countries to provide the skills required for economic development and inclusive growth (AEO, 2020; IIAG, 2017). Unemployment for young people exceeds 50% in most African states. The Coronavirus pandemic is increasing this further.

As African populations grow from 1.3bn to a projected 2bn people by 2040, there will be huge challenges in coming years in meeting the requirements of a growing, young population in many African, especially Sub-Saharan countries (Sheriff & Muffatto, 2014). Housing, health and educational capacity will be high priorities among these, but the primary one must be economic inclusion through employment or other useful activities. According to International Labour Organisation data, African employment grew on average by 18.5 million annually between 2015–2020 (AfDB, 2020). This reflects employment in the formal sectors, and informal employment can only be estimated. But with a continuing annual population increase of over 30 million, significantly more employment will need to be created each year (Chigunta, 2017). However, the Mo Ibrahim Foundation suggests only 3 million jobs are created annually in Sub-Saharan Africa, and that Africa is in danger of losing its youth to migration or extremism (IIAG, 2020). Otherwise, the future is likely to be one of an increasing population, with growing young, poor, under-educated and excluded groups finding outlets in informal and criminal activities; or seeing migration or extremism as their alternatives. It is beyond the ability of any state to create all the jobs required, nor would that be either likely or effective.

Only a continual increase in all forms of entrepreneurship has the prospect of both creating the economic activity and employment, combined with providing the services required by a growing population. No single solution will be adequate. The African Economic Outlook (2017) advocated an integrated approach between industrial strategies and entrepreneurship (AEO,

2017). In addition, continued increases in self-employment, technology-based entrepreneurship, co-operative, collective and social enterprises, inward investment creating new corporate enterprises, and new approaches yet to be developed will all be required (Lashitew & van Tulder, 2017).

The scale of this challenge is immense and may sound implausible. However, the progress made in recent years must be considered, alongside the drivers for economic and employment growth. As educators, we see the tremendous hunger for learning and for entrepreneurship across Africa, as young people recognise that these factors together can provide possible futures, if only they can access them. Africa has limitless resources of human talent, of land, potentially of solar energy and a richness of physical and agrarian resources. There is both the scope and the urgency to convert these into African-directed innovation and entrepreneurship, aided by Open resources, which can address economic, social, educational and material needs and opportunities. One of the factors which has constrained development is governance, which is variable in its effectiveness at national levels, and for this reason is specifically addressed by the Mo Ibrahim Foundation.

As the chapter was written, the impact of COVID-19 pandemic spread across the African continent. Whilst having severe health and longer-term economic consequences, the pandemic has also triggered widespread and innovative uses of Open Data approaches and methods to enable responses to the disease. This has demonstrated the capacity and potential for wider applications of Open working for economic, social and educational development in Africa (Lansana et al., 2020).

African countries were able to skip past several generations of copper-cabled telephone and computer technologies to become ready adopters of digital telephony and App-based devices. The five 'KINGS' countries which are leading digital business innovation, include Kenya, Ivory Coast, Nigeria, Ghana and South Africa, fuelling rapid innovation, technology adoption, and economic growth (Osiakwan, 2017). Recent research shows the growth of 'DiY Labs' and Tech hubs in developing technological innovation at an accessible grassroots level in four African countries, signalling wider potential for innovation and growth through community participation in knowledge production (Atiase et al., 2020).

Yet the phenomenon of the 'KINGS' digital economies also exposes the comparative performance of other African countries, some lagging well behind in digital entrepreneurship and adoption. In almost two-thirds of countries, internet access is available to less than 25% of the population

(AEO, 2020). This and other issues of comparability underscores a fundamental problem. How do we assess the readiness and progress of African countries for enabling open access to entrepreneurial development?

Filling the Gap in Data

At an international level, the Global Entrepreneurship Monitor (GEM) has become recognised as the 'standard' for measuring entrepreneurial orientation and activity, but despite its 'global' aspiration, its progress in including African countries has been very limited. This is largely due to the commitment and costs required by academic national teams who have to raise the finance and undertake the annual research surveys on a continuing basis. According to GEM (2017) GEM adult population survey data for Africa is only available for 8 countries over a 3-year period between 2011 and 2017. GEM is neither global in this respect, nor a useable indicator for more than a small and currently unrepresentative number of African countries. Dvouletý and Orel (2019) explored the application of GEM and other indices to African entrepreneurship development, using World Bank, Transparency International and Heritage Foundation data to study determinants of early-stage entrepreneurial activity, and recommending further data-led research.

Informed by this work and by Kuada (2015), other extant indices were considered for this study which could provide indicators on openness for enterprise at an African level with a high degree of national inclusion. Whilst many studies focus on Sub-Saharan Africa (SSA) only, and classify North Africa within the 'Middle East and North Africa' (MENA) pan-region, this study includes all African continental and the island states of Cabo Verde, Comoros, Madagascar, Seychelles, and São Tomé & Príncipe, as far as possible. This corresponds to the 54 African Union members, with the sole exception of the emergent Sahrawi Arab Democratic Republic. The nine indices considered include those listed in Table 12.1.

These nine indices were reviewed and considered with reference to Mårtensson et al. (2016) 4 C's research quality model for credibility; contributory; communicable and conforming. This included their currency (recency of updating); completeness (coverage of African states); and reliability.

The Open Data Barometer is 'a global measure of how governments are publishing and using open data for accountability, innovation and social impact'. This was considered dated (2016), including only 50% of African states, and no longer representative of the Open Data field in Africa.

Table 12.1 Indices covering economic openness in African countries

Index name & abbreviation	Scope of assessment	No. African states	Latest update	Link to data source
Heritage Foundation: Index of Economic Freedom [IEF]	Free-market system policy implementation	51	2020	https://www.heritage.org/index/
World Bank Doing Business [DB]	11 areas of business regulation	54	2020	https://www.doingbusiness.org/
Corruption perceptions index [CPI]	Perceptions of government and business corruption	54	2019	https://www.transparency.org/en/cpi
GSMA mobile phone connectivity [GSMA]	Measures 4 factors of mobile internet adoption	45	2019	https://www.mobileconnectivityindex.com/
Ibrahim Index of African Governance [IIAG]	National governance using 4 sets of criteria	54	2017	https://mo.ibrahim.foundation/
Global Entrepreneurship Index [GEDI]	composite indicator of e-ship ecosystem	34	2018	https://thegedi.org/
African Development Bank Country Policy and Institutional Assessment [CPIA]	Quality of policies and institutional frameworks performance	36	2018	https://cpia.afdb.org/ http://dataportal.opendataforafrica.org/
Legatum Prosperity Index [LPI]	Preconditions for growth in prosperity	54	2020	https://www.prosperity.com
Open Data Barometer [ODB]	Govt publication & use of Open Data	25	2016	https://opendatabarometer.org

The Open Data Impact map was also consulted and whilst this identified individual organisations it did not provide a usable national index.

The GEDI is potentially valuable as an international index which draws on GEM and other data, but currently includes only 34 African countries. It does not use primary data on some countries but averages data from contiguous states to provide a score. Rather than being included in the framework, it may be useful as a comparator, but this may change in future as its African coverage improves.

The African Development Bank Country Policy and Institutional Assessment (CPIA) assessment currently includes the 36 countries which are included in the African Development Fund (ADF). Whilst it states that all 54 African states are included, the data for the non-ADF countries could not be located as a dataset or on the website. This omits economically significant states including South Africa and Nigeria, as well as North African states. The CPIA uses a 1–6 rating which is not readily compatible with the approach used in collating the framework. Again, it may be used as a comparator with the framework. The Open Data for Africa portal hosted by AfDB includes just 13 African countries.

The Legatum Prosperity Framework (LPF: Legatum, 2020) assesses national capability and progress in 'strengthening the pathways from poverty to prosperity'. The Institute is funded by the Legatum Foundation, which is committed to liberating human potential through poverty reduction, and is in turn funded by Legatum Limited, a Dubai-based private investment firm with a 30-year history of global investment. The framework identifies three domains of 'inclusive societies', 'open economies' and 'empowered people', each comprising four of the twelve 'pillars of prosperity' and within these are 66 elements which are measured from 294 indicators, based on identified public data sources. Twelve of the indicators for social capital use Gallup data, for example. It is a well-developed framework and can be used as a comparator with the approach developed below. It includes several indicators and data sources which are drawn from other indices, such as IEF, DB and GSMA, and there would be a double-weighting effect if the LPF were to be included.

Hence the five indices included in the framework are these.

Ibrahim Index of African Governance (IIAG).

The IIAG dataset is compiled by the Mo Ibrahim Foundation (MIF) which focuses on the importance of governance and leadership in improving the quality of life in Africa. It has been released every two years since 2007, accompanied by an Index Report outlining the main findings of the Index, continental, regional and country data, and other resources and analytical tools. It is significant in being an African-generated study which focuses on the entire continent. It measures governance performance across the four categories of Safety & Rule of Law; Participation & Human Rights; Sustainable Economic Opportunity; and Human Development. These categories contain 14 subcategories and a range of 102 indicators from 35 sources which provide quantifiable measures of the overarching dimensions of governance. The 2018 report commented on the widening gaps between the quality of governance, educational outcomes, population and youth expectations, whilst economic failed to translate into sustainable economic opportunity (IIAG, 2018).

The Heritage Foundation: Index of Economic Freedom (IEF)

The Heritage Foundation is a US-based organisation with a right-wing free-market orientation. Whilst its work can be seen through this ideological lens, the analysis the index provides has legitimate value in the context of world economic competitiveness. It assesses the connections between economic opportunity, individual empowerment and prosperity by focusing on free-market system policy implementation. Twelve aspects of economic freedom measured in the *Index* are grouped into four broad categories:

1. **Rule of law** (property rights, judicial effectiveness, and government integrity);
2. **Government size** (tax burden, government spending, and fiscal health);
3. **Regulatory efficiency** (business freedom, labour freedom, and monetary freedom); and
4. **Market openness** (trade freedom, investment freedom, and financial freedom).

These are grouped into five categories between 'free' and 'oppressed'. Most African countries are classified in the 'mostly unfree' or 'repressed' categories of the global grading. The individualistic free-market orientation of the report is clear in its commentary on African economic freedom:

'The region's continuing underperformance reflects repeated failures to implement policy changes to improve the business and investment climate and strengthen the rule of law. The missed economic opportunities due to corruption and conflict, in particular, represent a tragedy for the region's huge population of young people, who lose developmental ground that is increasingly difficult to make up as such conditions persist. Successful efforts at structural reform have been rare, and the modernization of infrastructure and institutions lags severely throughout most of Sub-Saharan Africa' (IEF, 2020, 100).

World Bank Doing Business (DB)

The World Bank Doing Business (formerly Ease of Doing Business) index covers eleven areas which benchmark functional business regulation. It reflects the World Bank economic outlook with ten of these areas included in the ease of doing business score and ranking: starting a business, dealing with construction permits, getting electricity, registering property, getting credit, protecting minority investors, paying taxes, trading across borders, enforcing contracts and resolving insolvency. It also measures features of labour market regulation, which is not included in the measures. Doing Business relies on information from national laws and regulations, Business survey respondents, governments of the economies covered and World Bank Group regional staff.

Most African countries are ranked between 100 and 190 in the global ranking to 190, with 27 in the 'below average' category. Mauritius, Rwanda and Kenya rank in the top 60 globally. The regional average for ease of starting a business is 80.

Corruption Perceptions Index (CPI) 2018

The 2018 Corruption Perceptions Index is published by Transparency International. Based on national reports, it measures the perceived levels of public sector corruption through business surveys and expert opinions in 180 countries. Given that there is continuing concern about the levels of both government and business corruption in a number of African states, and which represents a constraint for legitimate entrepreneurship, it is a valid index to include. Sub-Saharan Africa is the lowest-scoring region with 32/100. It includes the African Development Bank Country Policy and Institutional Assessment results in the scoring for 2018.

There have been valid critiques of the CPI, such as Søreide (2006), de Maria (2008) and recently Budsaratragoona and Jitmaneeroj (2020) for methodological, cultural bias and other reasons. However, it remains of value and legitimate to use as a comparison of perceptions, as distinct from purely objective data. The aforementioned three indices all include perceptions-based assessments of a range of data sources which include qualitative opinions as well as empirical data; they therefore need to be judged on the basis of possible bias and distortion, especially from non-African perspectives.

GSMA Mobile Phone Connectivity (GSMA)

The lack of a usable indicator for open data access and the high reliance of African businesses on mobile phone and digital connectivity means that inclusion of the GSMA Mobile Connectivity Index is valid as a proxy measure. This is an analytical tool that measures the performance of 163 countries, representing 99% of the World's population, against the four key enablers of mobile internet adoption: infrastructure, affordability, consumer readiness and content and services.

Scores for each of these four key enablers are combined to produce a single composite measure for each country of the strength of the foundations for universal access to and adoption of the mobile internet. There is a limitation in that a single country score does not reflect the variability of connectedness within countries, especially those with large land areas and juxtaposition of urban hotspots and rural digital deserts.

GSMA also provides a proxy for access to e-business and e-banking in the African context where mobile phone connectivity is the normal business platform. Digital inclusion is a vital factor for entrepreneurial participation and the ability to find market information, routes to market and make financial transactions. The speed of analogue to digital network conversion is a factor, especially in the largest countries by land areas. AEO (2020) showed that 2/3 of African states had internet access for below 25% of the population.

Table 12.2 illustrates the data sources and main indicators included in these five indices.

Comparative Method

Each of the five chosen indices provides a composite percentage score for each country derived from the categories and indicators it includes. Consideration was given to extracting certain categories and indicators from some indices, and excluding others, such as the rule of law, personal safety, national security and the issue of construction permits. It was decided against doing this to

Table 12.2 Overview of data source and indicators included

Data source	Key indicators
IIAG (Ibrahim Index of Good Governance)	Safety & Rule of Law; Participation & Human Rights; Sustainable Economic Opportunity; and Human Development
IEF (Heritage Foundation)	Rule of Law; Government Size; Regulatory Efficiency; Market Openness
World Bank Doing Business	starting a business, dealing with construction permits, getting electricity, registering property, getting credit, protecting minority investors, paying taxes, trading across borders, enforcing contracts and resolving insolvency
Corruption Perception Index	Measures the perceived levels of public sector corruption
GSMA mobile phone connectivity (GSMA)	Mobile internet adoption: infrastructure, affordability, consumer readiness and content and services

retain the integrity of each index, and because these issues affect the wider freedoms and ability of citizens to participate in entrepreneurial activities.

It was noted that some of the global indices may be accompanied by an ideological bias, for example that the IEF, and to an extent the DB indices, represent Western and US-oriented free-market perspectives. The CPI may also be more sympathetic to Western liberal concerns about corruption. It is clear from the narratives in these reports that African countries are subject to harsh criticisms of national policy, leadership and conduct. These may be valid at an international level, but do they help African citizens in these countries to address and secure change? The inclusion of the IIAG as an African-only index, which may overlap with the IEF, DB and CPI in some areas, can act as a balance against these concerns. Whilst all these indices are based on significant volumes of data, they are selective and representative in the analysis they provide through their methodologies. They provide a perspective for a period, rather than an objective reality.

The five indices were standardised into a common set of 54 African states, as each index used a slightly different order. The most recently available datasets were used, varying between those published in 2018 up to 2020. An arithmetic mean was calculated from the percentage ratings from each index. Nine countries were not included in at least one index, but only two (Somalia and South Sudan) were omitted from two indices. This is shown as a graph in Fig. 12.1. The countries were then ranked by the mean scores as shown in Fig. 12.2. These figures and the data tables in the Annex enable comparison between all African states and are available for further analysis, for example on a geographical, linguistic, or other basis. A regional comparison is provided to assess whether regional geography is significant.

These tables are interesting and useful because, in the global usage of the four indices IEF, DB, CPI and GSMA, African countries are ranked at global level, or in either the MENA or SSA levels, rather than at a continental all-Africa level. These generally relegate the majority of African states to the lower and lowest performing levels. This is a function of their globally comparative methodologies and the factors they employ, but the effects of this may well be counter-productive in two respects. Firstly, for non-African readers, for example in businesses and government organisations, they perpetuate an impression of African countries as, in the main, rather backward and corrupt laggards. This may disadvantage African states in gaining aid and investment for improvement (Alberto & Weder, 2002). It can also act to reinforce popular, nationalist and even racist perceptions about Africa in wealthy 'developed' countries (Dvouletý & Blažková, 2018). Secondly, for African readers, they can be interpreted in different ways. As above, they show the relegation of African states in global league tables, reducing hope of improvement. They do not show historic causes, such as colonial legacies and periods of poor governance, conflict or recovery from natural disasters. Nor do they include factors which may be unique or distinctive in an African context (Takyi-Asiedu, 1993). The question, again, is how useful they can be in securing improvement.

Whilst it is informative to compare African countries at a global level, this can distract attention from the value of pan-African comparisons which are more likely to share similarities. The framework provides a general indication for the institutional, legal, policy, technological and business factors which can provide the infrastructure and setting for entrepreneurial activities. It may also have value in informing discussions on peer-based African development.

Data Presentation Section

The table which includes national scores for each index and an arithmetic mean is included at Annex 1. It is shown in Fig. 12.1 as a rod graph with a line for the mean, with the countries displayed alphabetically.

The mean score is used to simplify and smooth the five indices. This also facilitates a ranking of the countries by mean. This is shown in Fig. 12.2.

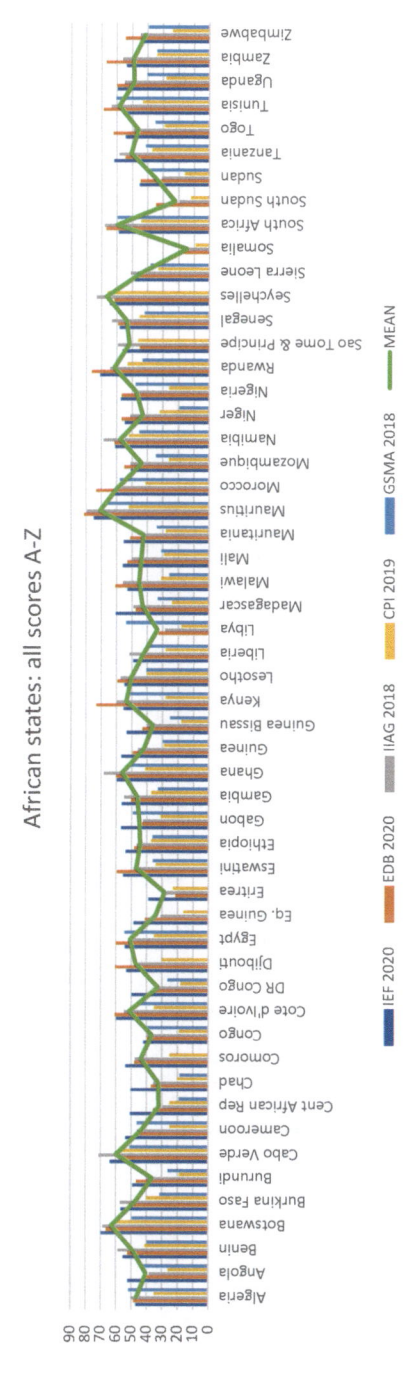

12 Are African Economies Open for Entrepreneurship ...   285

Fig. 12.1 African states showing all index scores A–Z

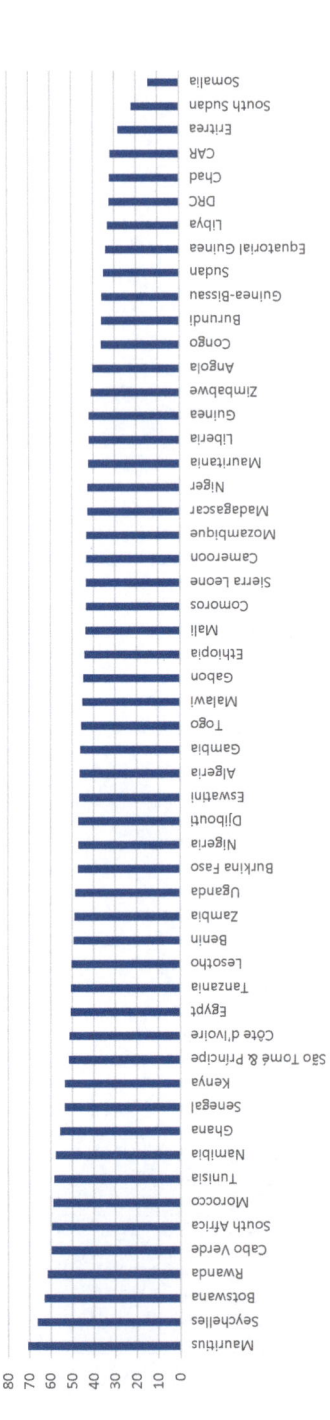

Fig. 12.2 African states ranked by mean score

This graph is informative in starting to shape the analysis. Three of the five most highly scoring countries are island states, atypical of continental African nations by being small in both territory and population, with their economies highly dependent on tourism and services. Possibly they should be regarded as outliers. Botswana, Rwanda, and South Africa are the highest ranked continental countries. Just four countries score 60% or over; 13 between 50 and 59.9; 25 between 40 and 49.9; nine between 30 and 39.9; and just three between 14 and 29.9. These three, Eritrea, South Sudan and Somalia, are subject to long-standing factors of conflict, environmental challenges, famine and other severe disadvantages. The midpoint is 42.45, which corresponds to the proximal ranking of five countries. Hence the range from 30 to 69 includes 47 countries, or 87% of the total.

Country size does not appear to be in itself an advantage; since even excluding island states, relatively small countries including Botswana, Rwanda, Ghana, Senegal and Côte d'Ivoire score highly on the ranked mean. But smallness is not in itself a strength, as can be seen from countries further down the index.

The next question is what influence geographical location may have over the ranking. Figure 12.3 shows a continental map of the mean scores.

This shows the highest (densest) scores in the south, north-west coastal and east, with lowest in central Africa. It does not illustrate the north-east

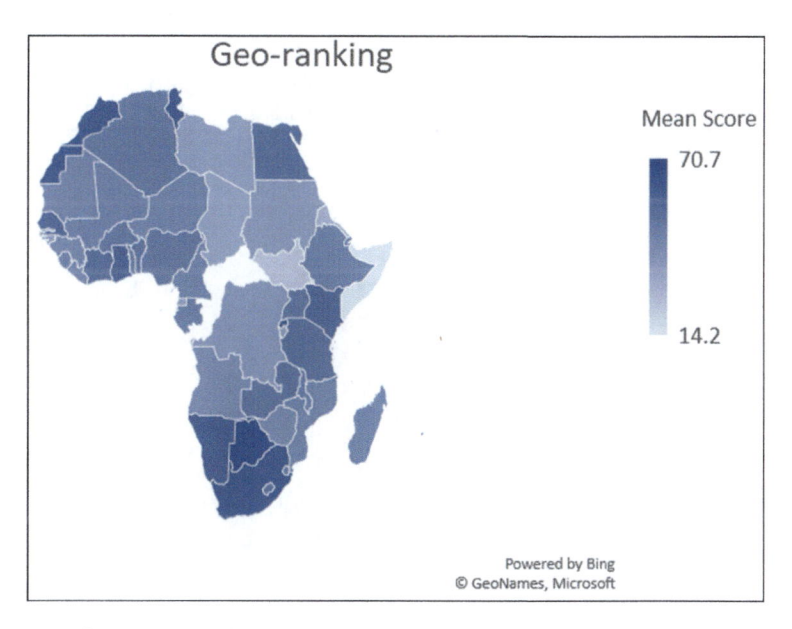

Fig. 12.3 Afro-continental map of mean scores

or small islands. Therefore, to explore the geography, a regional analysis was conducted, using the African Union (AU) five regions structure as a basis. However, it is considered that the six island nations have more in common with each other than they share with the continental regions in which the AU groups them, and from which they are quite distant. These factors include their mainly small landmass and population by African standards, their economic structure and dependence on tourism and trading activities such as financial services. Three of the islands do not have a GSMA score for mobile phone connectivity, which reduces the reliability of their ratings. Hence the Islands form an additional regional group for this analysis. The regional scores are shown in Table 12.3. This is followed by a graph in Fig. 12.4 illustrating this data.

It is interesting that across five of the six regions, including the islands, the average scores for the indices, as well as the overall mean scores, do not vary much. It is only in the case of the Central region that all scores are dramatically lower. Within the Central region, composed of eight countries,

Table 12.3 Regional average scores

	IEF 2020	EDB 2020	IIAG 2018	CPI 2019	GSMA 2018	Mean
North	60.9	54.4	65.2	52.4	49.7	57.9
Southern	61.8	56.4	62.4	44.4	49.5	55.5
East	62.3	57.2	66.0	52.0	49.6	58.9
West	62.0	56.3	63.6	46.5	49.7	56.3
Central	50.0	40.9	37.0	21.6	32.3	36.4
Islands	62.2	56.5	63.3	45.2	49.7	55.8

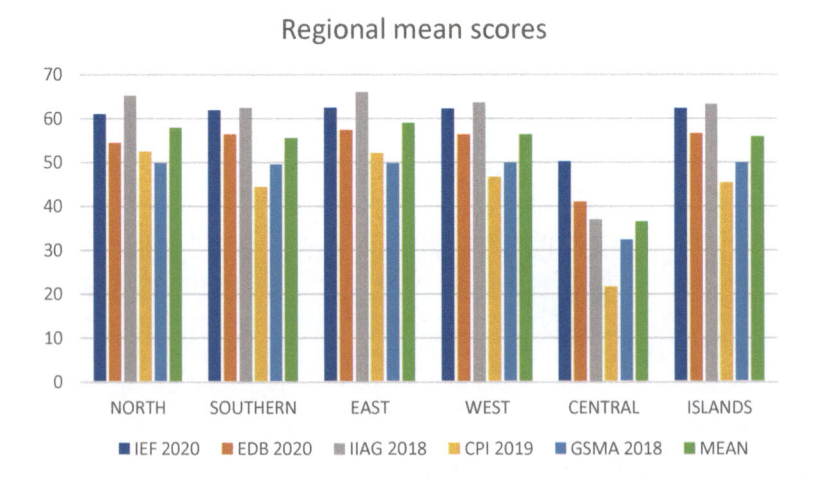

Fig. 12.4 Regional mean scores

the IEF score is the highest, at 50%, with all others being significantly lower, in the case of CPI just 21.6%. Two of these countries, Cameroon and Gabon, have mean scores of 43.4% and 44.8% respectively and lead the regional grouping. Other countries, including DRC and Congo, have been handicapped by the worst colonial legacy in Africa, postcolonial conflicts, and as in the cases of other countries in the region, by being landlocked and economically marginal, even if they constitute territorially and demographically large states.

So why do countries score highly or poorly, and what does this mean? At the risk of being over-simplistic, a high mean rating depends on relatively higher scores in the five contributing indices, whilst the poorest performers tend to have lower scores across the board, or are excluded from one or more indices. The IEF especially, and EDB, often exceeded other scores, raising the mean and indicating that market openness does not necessarily coincide with strengths in governance and anti-corruption. In terms of the largest and most developed economies, whilst South Africa and Kenya scored relatively highly, Nigeria's position, as the largest economy in Africa, at 23 is well down the ranking and held back by a very low CPI score. IIAG and GSMA scores are also quite low. Nigeria's position is bracketed by Burkina Faso and Djibouti, both tiny economies by comparison. Whatever the limitations of using these general indices, it does suggest that they can represent national-level deficiencies and areas for improvement with some accuracy.

For those countries with the lowest mean scores, of below 40, their histories of institutional fragility, conflict and disadvantage are compounded by a lack of entrepreneurial openness, making it much more difficult for enterprise alone to provide a dynamic for improving their outlook without improvements in their institutional, technological and human capital, as considered in the next section. However, even with these limitations, there is some evidence that progress can be made. In Somalia for example, there is collective action by business, open data and government people to improve the conditions for entrepreneurship in Mogadishu (https://www.sipaminstitute.org/).

Conceptualising Open Entrepreneurship with Institutional, Technology and Human Factors

The next stage of analysis is thematic, as shown in Table 12.4, by grouping the indicators into the three general themes of institutional, technological and human factors.

These themes are used to propose the conceptual model in Fig. 12.5.

This shows the scope of each index in contributing to the model of Open Entrepreneurship. Openness embraces both formal businesses and those in the informal, unregistered sector which constitute a majority of enterprises (Ratten & Jones, 2018). The themes are colour-coded to group them in relation to the seven Institutional, four Human Capital, and four Technological factors. These 15 factors indicate, in some cases on a proxy basis, the levels of national openness in entrepreneurship.

This is a propositional model, emergent rather than static or definitive, and likely to evolve as the factors and their inter-relationships change and develop.

The World Bank Doing Business (DB), IEF and IIAG were used as proxies for the governance and institutional aspects of open entrepreneurship, in the absence of any more specific measures. They provide preliminary indicators which should be taken with caveats, especially regarding the noted right-wing orientation of the IEF measure, which may be balanced by the African-centred IIAG. The technology aspect uses the GSMA as a proxy, again with limitations as previously stated.

However, this leaves a gap in the area of human development. The United Nations Human Development Index data from 2018 (UN HDI, 2019) was sourced from the UN portal for the 54 African countries available, except for Somalia, for comparison. The HDI is a composite index which comprises

Table 12.4 Mapping of indicators into thematic categories

Thematic categories	Indicators
Institutional factors	Policy; Rule of Law; Regulatory Efficiency; Property Rights; Business Registration; Contract Enforcement; Market Openness
Human (Capital) factors	Access to Formal Education: Access to Informal Learning; Participation in the formal economy and Human Rights
Technology factors	Telecoms Infrastructure; Mobile Internet Adoption; Technology affordability; Electricity

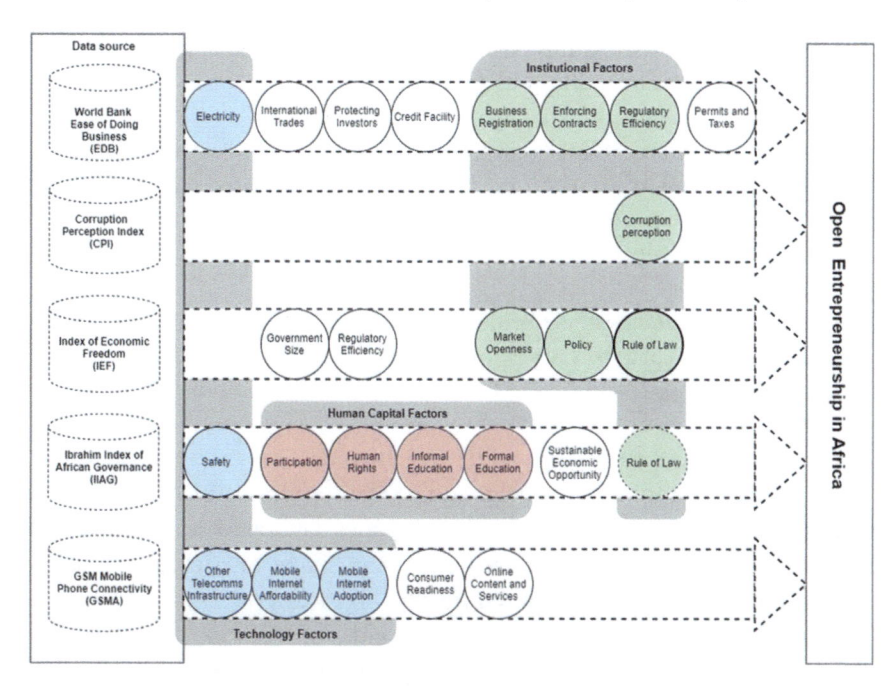

Fig. 12.5 Connecting data sources and themes

three contributing indices of health; education; and standard of living by gross national income per capita in US dollars.

We build on the foregoing iteration to propose a conceptual model that explains and integrates the relationships between institutional, human and technology factors on open entrepreneurship. In this model, we propose an aggregation of four indices—index of economic freedom, Ibrahim index of African governance, corruption perception index and World Bank Ease of Doing Business—as proximate measures of institutional factors. Human capital is captured as an aggregate of formal and informal knowledge, skills, experience, as well as health and well-being, for each of the countries. We therefore propose the following relationships for subsequent empirical interrogations:

Proposition 1: Institutional factors significantly influence open entrepreneurship in African countries through increased economic freedom, reduced level of corruption, efficient regulatory processes and stable and effective governance.

Proposition 2: Human capital, in the form of formal education and informal learning facilities and opportunities, positively influences open entrepreneurship in African countries.

Proposition 3: Increased diffusion of, and access to technology, significantly influence open entrepreneurship in African countries.

Proposition 4: Human capital moderates the impact of institutional factors on open entrepreneurship in Africa. In other words, increased level of human capital helps to mitigate or overcome negative institutional factors towards open entrepreneurship.

Proposition 5: Technology factors mediates the impact of human capital factors on open entrepreneurship. That is, the higher the level of access to formal and informal learning opportunities and facilities, the better the prospects of open entrepreneurship in African countries.

Whilst a detailed empirical investigation of these propositions is outside the scope of this chapter, we aim to draw on a panel data of African countries to examine these relationships, and how they can shape our understanding of open entrepreneurship in African countries (Fig. 12.6).

The final stage of analysis, in the present contribution, is a comparison with the results of the Legatum Prosperity Framework, which includes comparable concepts within its three domains of inclusive societies, open economies and empowered people.

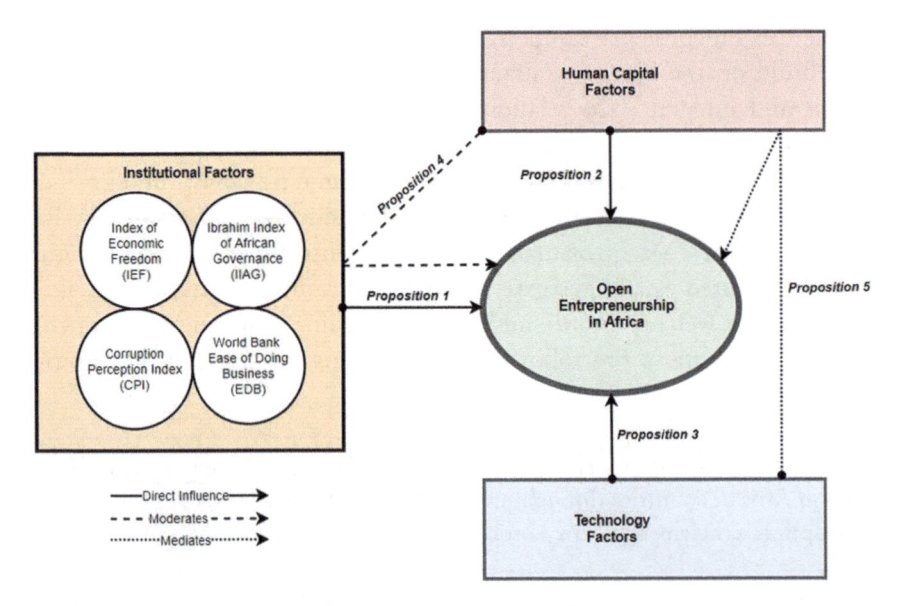

Fig. 12.6 Institutional, human capital and technology factors influencing open entrepreneurship

Comparison with the Legatum Prosperity Framework

The Legatum Prosperity Framework (LPF) explains that Open Economies 'encourage innovation and investment, promote business and trade, and facilitate inclusive growth' (Legatum, 2020a).

The index dates from 2007, enabling change to be tracked over a 14-year period to 2020. 167 countries are included in the 2020 ranking, including 54 African states. In addition to the global report, an Africa Prosperity Report was published (Legatum, 2020b), based on the 2019 data and including analysis of six regions. The report compares prosperity improvement, based on GDP per capita, over ten years in 47 countries and decline in seven, Central Africa having the weakest performance. In most other cases, conflict was a contributory cause. Preconditions for increased prosperity include strong personal freedom, absence of war and conflict, improvements in their institutions, governance and the inclusivity of their societies. Improvements in social well-being, health, education and living conditions have not contributed to improved prosperity, as they have also improved in states where prosperity has deteriorated. However, countries with weak institutions and governance saw prosperity decline. The report points to lessons which can be learned from the best performing and suggests that 'many answers to African prosperity can be found within the continent itself'.

The countries highest in the African rankings are, again, the small island states of Mauritius (1st), Seychelles (2nd), Cabo Verde (4th). They have more in common with each other than the African regions with which they are grouped. The next ranked are a core group of Southern African countries: Botswana (3rd), South Africa (5th) and Namibia (6th). Southern Africa is judged the most prosperous region in Africa, with the strongest governance, low levels of war and civil conflict, well-educated adult population and greatest openness to international investment.

The regional analysis places Southern Africa first followed by North, East, West, The Horn and Central Africa as the lowest performing region. This includes the weakest five countries which have all been subject to civil conflict. Violence and conflicts in South Sudan, the Democratic Republic of the Congo and Central African Republic have spread across borders, with refugee numbers increasing over the past decade. It assesses that the conflicts in these countries have prevented them from embedding strong institutions and growing their economies. Across many African states, Safety and Security has deteriorated with increased political violence and terror.

This is seen in the declining or low scores for countries including Libya, Somalia, DRC and South Sudan. The position of Nigeria, as Africa's largest economy, at a ranking of 39 in the index, one place below Libya and with a constant score over a long period, is striking. It is marked by poor scores for safety and security, economic quality and health; and suffers from oil dependency, rather than using this as a basis for investment in areas which can enhance non-oil prosperity. Overall, there are multiple points of agreement between the LPF and the Open Entrepreneurship Framework in relation to Africa.

Conclusions

This exploratory chapter aims to offer a way of assessing universal openness to entrepreneurship from extant data and frameworks. It is, inevitably, partial, indicative, emergent and incomplete. However, it proposes for the first time an initial Pan-African framework for Open Entrepreneurship, using existing datasets of known provenance, and enables comparison within and between these. It is compared and found congruent with the established Legatum LPF index.

One limitation of both frameworks is that they are only at national level. Many African countries with large land areas or dispersed populations have major regional variations, especially between city and rural areas which are not reflected in a single set of national indicators. Regional, provincial or city-level data is needed to show the more granular and specific local pictures, but the datasets are either not available or differ in format between states, making this analysis elusive. Alternatively, some of the data may exist as proprietary datasets, but not publicly available as open data.

Potentially, in future work, national, subnational, regional and local data resources may be identified and added to supplement this framework. Being able to identify how connections are made between national-level indicators and data, with resources available 'on the ground' for local entrepreneurs and organisations to use is essential (African Economic Outlook, 2017). These could be mapped to identify 'what works'; what could potentially be developed; and to establish gaps and priority areas for improvement and innovation.

An example is the crucial issue of internet access via mobile phone. The GSMA index is well-evidenced and a report published in 2019 (GSMA, 2019:1) highlights the gaps for African countries in connectivity, coverage, usage and gender access. However, at national level this is of limited value.

Raw data from mobile phone use must exist at local district and network provider level, and if aggregated could form proxy indicators for levels of business activity on mobile platforms in specific zones, such as markets and business districts, but is not publicly available. Progress on disclosure needs to be made on such issues.

It is important, and to be hoped that progress on wider access to useful official government, business and other datasets, not only at national but at regional and local levels will be made through initiatives such as the LDRI Africa Open Data Network, backed by the Open Data for Development (OD4D) global network. Business users need to be able to access useful and useable data at the level of their market and supplier network. The costs of data access also need to fall; the GSMA (2019:1) report shows that Africans have both the least affordable and slowest data access globally, thus imposing a double additional handicap on their competitiveness.

To make a difference, a framework for Open Entrepreneurship needs to embrace and engage the entrepreneur's perspective on their engagement with institutions, organisations, services and markets. This is captured very imperfectly through the business interviews in the DB index. Both the framework proposed in this chapter, and the LPI as a comparator, show that too many African countries lag well behind those on the African continent which offer the most open conditions for entrepreneurs, and their economies underperform and citizens suffer as a result. A facility which enables business owner-managers to provide feedback on their perceptions of openness, within the contexts where they do business, must be achievable in the era of advanced social media and user-generated customer rating applications such as Tripadvisor. The voices of entrepreneurs need to be heard to inform and energise progress towards a more open business world in Africa.

Finally, implications of the study for entrepreneurship policy and practice are proposed.

Implications for Policy

The framework is presented at an intermediate stage of development. In the context of recovering from the impact of Coronavirus, the ability of African countries to develop their economies and to generate the education, housing, health and other infrastructures which their growing young populations require is extremely challenging. The requirement to create employment and economic opportunities for a population growing at more than 30 million annually is even more so. The framework provides a means of smoothing and interpreting data gathered from different sources and making comparisons across Africa which can inform progress towards this.

Implications for Practice

One of the major issues at an African national level is the variation in developmental indicators between those states which perform highly or well in such areas as governance, human development, market access, digital communications, etc.; in relation to a number of fragile states with much poorer performance and endemic problems.

This is relevant for minority groups, including ethnic, linguistic and cultural minorities; women and disabled people; and migrants. There is a severe risk of their being omitted from national and international metrics, of becoming 'invisible' and hence further disadvantaged. This factor needs to be addressed by asking the question: which groups are not recognised by these indices?

Future implications for practice may potentially include the inclusion of subnational and regional data; case-based information from national and local studies; and connections with support organisations. Further work is required on sources and uses of openly available entrepreneurship learning, development and support materials for Open entrepreneurship.

Annex

Data table showing country scores on chosen indices and mean scores.

ISO	Country	IEF 2020	EDB 2020	IIAG 2018	CPI 2019	GSMA 2018	Mean
DZA	Algeria	46.9	48.6	50.2	35	51.6	46.5
AGO	Angola	52.2	41.3	38.3	26	43.8	40.3
BEN	Benin	55.2	52.4	58.7	41	39.4	49.3
BWA	Botswana	69.6	66.2	68.5	61	49.4	62.9
BFA	Burkina Faso	56.7	51.4	57.1	40	31.3	47.3
BDI	Burundi	49	46.8	39.8	19	26.0	36.1
CPV	Cabo Verde	63.6	55	71.1	58	50.8	59.7
MR	Cameroon	53.6	46.1	46.2	25	46.1	43.4
CAF	Cent African Rep	50.7	35.6	29.5	25	18.9	31.9
TCD	Chad	50.2	36.9	35.4	20	18.4	32.2
COM	Comoros	53.7	47.9	47.5	25	N/A	43.5
COG	Congo	41.8	39.5	39.8	19	41.3	36.3

(continued)

(continued)

ISO	Country	IEF 2020	EDB 2020	IIAG 2018	CPI 2019	GSMA 2018	Mean
CIV	Cote d'Ivoire	59.7	60.7	54.5	35	46.2	51.2
COD	DR Congo	49.5	36.2	32.1	18	26.1	32.4
DJI	Djibouti	52.9	60.5	45.1	30	N/A	47.1
EGY	Egypt	54	60.1	49.9	35	54.2	50.6
GNQ	Eq. Guinea	48.3	41.1	30.9	16	N/A	34.1
ERI	Eritrea	38.5	21.6	29.3	23	N/A	28.1
SWZ	Eswatini	55.3	59.5	48.7	34	35.9	46.7
ETH	Ethiopia	53.6	48	46.5	37	36.1	44.2
GAB	Gabon	56.7	45	42.4	31	49.0	44.8
GMB	Gambia	56.3	50.3	54.9	37	32.7	46.2
GHA	Ghana	59.4	60	68.1	41	51.2	55.9
GIN	Guinea	56.5	49.4	45.9	29	29.5	42.1
GNB	Guinea Bissau	53.3	43.2	40.2	18	25.1	36.0
KEN	Kenya	55.3	73.2	59.8	28	50.8	53.4
LSO	Lesotho	54.5	59.4	57.1	40	40.2	50.2
LBR	Liberia	49	43.2	51.6	28	38.7	42.1
LBY	Libya	N/A	32.7	28.3	18	53.6	33.2
MDG	Madagascar	60.5	47.7	49	24	32.9	42.8
MWI	Malawi	52.8	60.9	55.8	31	25.4	45.2
MLI	Mali	55.9	52.9	50.1	29	30.8	43.7
MRT	Mauritania	55.3	51.1	43.4	28	33.6	42.3
MUS	Mauritius	74.9	81.5	79.5	52	65.5	70.7
MAR	Morocco	63.3	73.4	58.4	41	57.7	58.8
MOZ	Mozambique	50.5	55	51	26	34.3	43.4
NAM	Namibia	60.9	61.4	68.6	52	45.2	57.6
NER	Niger	54.7	56.8	51.2	32	19.3	42.8
NGA	Nigeria	57.2	56.9	47.9	26	47.7	47.1
RWA	Rwanda	70.9	76.5	64.3	53	43.0	61.5
STP	Sao Tome & Principe	56.2	45	59.2	46	N/A	51.6
SEN	Senegal	58	59.3	63.3	45	41.7	53.5
SYC	Seychelles	64.3	61.7	73.2	66	N/A	66.3
SLE	Sierra Leone	48	47.5	50.9	33	37.9	43.5
SOM	Somalia	N/A	20	13.6	9	N/A	14.2
ZAF	South Africa	58.8	67	68	44	59.5	59.5
SSD	South Sudan	N/A	34.6	19.3	12	N/A	22.0
SDN	Sudan	45	44.8	30.8	16	38.9	35.1
TZA	Tanzania	61.7	54.5	58.5	37	41.0	50.5
TGO	Togo	54.1	62.3	49.1	29	34.7	45.8
TUN	Tunisia	55.8	68.7	63.5	43	60.3	58.3
UGA	Uganda	59.5	60	55	28	40	48.5
ZMB	Zambia	53.5	66.9	56.2	34	33.8	48.9
ZWE	Zimbabwe	43.1	54.5	44.7	24	39.2	41.1

References

Aerni, P. (2015). *Entrepreneurial rights as human rights: Why economic rights must include the human right to science and the freedom to grow through innovation.* Banson.

Alberto, A., & Weder, B. (2002). Do corrupt governments receive less foreign aid? *American Economic Review, 92*(4), 1126–1137.

Atiase, V., Kolade, O., & Liedong, T. (2020, December). The emergence and strategy of tech hubs in Africa: Implications for knowledge production and value creation. *Technological Forecasting & Social Change, 161*, 120307.

Atiase, V. Y., Mahmood, S., Wang, Y., & Botchie, D. (2018). Developing entrepreneurship in Africa: Investigating critical resource challenges. *Journal of Small Business and Enterprise Development, 25*(4), 644–666.

Budsaratragoona, P., & Jitmaneeroj, B. (2020). *A critique on the Corruption Perceptions Index: An interdisciplinary approach author links open socio-economic planning sciences* (Vol. 70), 100768.

Chigunta, F. (2017). Entrepreneurship as a possible solution to youth unemployment in Africa. *Laboring and Learning, 10*, 433–451.

de Maria, B. (2008). Neo-colonialism through measurement: A critique of the corruption perception index. *Critical Perspectives on International Business, 4*(2/3), 184–202.

DeJaeghere, J., & Baxter, A. (2014). Entrepreneurship education for youth in sub-Saharan Africa: A capabilities approach as an alternative framework to neoliberalism's individualizing risks. *Progress in Development Studies, 14*(1), 61–76.

Dollar, D., & Svensson, J. (2000). What explains the success or failure of structural adjustment programmes? *The Economic Journal, 110*(466), 894–917.

Dvouletý, O., & Blažková, I. (2018). *Entrepreneurship and corruption: Do corruption perceptions influence regional entrepreneurial activity?* The 12th International days of statistics and economics (pp. 433–440).

Dvouletý, O., & Orel, M. (2019). Entrepreneurial activity and its determinants: Findings from African developing countries. In V. Ratten, P. Jones, V. Braga, & C. Marques (Eds.), *Sustainable entrepreneurship. Contributions to management science*. Springer.

Edoho, F. M. (2015). Entrepreneurialism: Africa in transition. *African Journal of Economic and Management Studies, 6*(2), 127–147.

Heidhues, F., & Obare, G. (2011). Lessons from structural adjustment programmes and their effects in Africa. *Quarterly Journal of International Agriculture, 50*(1), 55–64.

Jones, J. (2010). 'Nothing is straight in Zimbabwe': The rise of the *Kukiya-kiya* economy 2000–2008. *Journal of Southern African Studies, 36*(2), 285–299.

Jones, P., Maas, G., Dobson, S., Newbery, R., Agyapong, D., & Matlay, H. (2018a). Entrepreneurship in Africa, part 1: Entrepreneurial dynamics in Africa. *Journal of Small Business and Enterprise Development, 25*(3), 346–348.

Jones, P., Maas, G., Dobson, S., Newbery, R., Agyapong, D., & Matlay, H. (2018b). Entrepreneurship in Africa, part 2: Entrepreneurial education and eco-systems. *Journal of Small Business and Enterprise Development, 25*(4), 550–553.

Jones, P., Maas, G., Dobson, S., Newbery, R., Agyapong, D., & Matlay, H. (2018c). Entrepreneurship in Africa, part 3: Conclusions on African entrepreneurship. *Journal of Small Business and Enterprise Development, 25*(5), 706–709.

Kuada, J. (2015). Entrepreneurship in Africa—A classificatory framework and a research agenda. *African Journal of Economic and Management Studies, 6*(2), 148–163.

Lansana, A., Migisha, C., Minjire, D., Juma, L., Adan, S., & Alemul, W. (2020). *Drivers of data for development: Exploring the factors that enable availability and utility of open data for development in Africa*. International Development Research Centre, Ottawa, Canada. http://www.idrc.ca.

Lashitew, A. A., & van Tulder, R. (2017). Inclusive business in Africa: Priorities, strategies and challenges. *Entrepreneurship in Africa, 15*, 71.

Legatum Institute. (2020a). *The Africa prosperity report overview 2019/20*. Legatum Institute.

Mårtensson, P., Forsb, U., Wallinc, S. B., & Nilssone, H. (2016). Evaluating research: A multidisciplinary approach to assessing research practice and quality. *Research Policy, 45*, 593–603.

Nkomo, S. M. (2011). A post-colonial and anti-colonial reading of 'Africa' leadership and management in organisation studies: Tensions, contradictions and possibilities. *Organisation, 18*, 365–386.

Ochonu, M. (2018). *Entrepreneurship in Africa: A historical approach*. Indiana University Press.

Open Knowledge Foundation. (2005). https://opendefinition.org/od/2.1/en/.

Osiakwan, E. (2017). The KINGS of Africa's digital economy. In B. Ndemo & T. Weiss (Eds.), *Digital Kenya*. Palgrave Studies of Entrepreneurship in Africa. Palgrave Macmillan.

Pollock, R. (2018). *The Open Revolution: Rewriting the rules of the information age*. https://openrevolution.net/. Accessed 23 June 2018.

Rae, D. (2019). Entrepreneurship in the open space: A new dynamic for creating value? In D. Higgins & P. Jones (Eds.), *Creating entrepreneurial space: Talking through Multi voices, reflections on emerging debates* (pp. 153–172). McGowan, P. Emerald.

Ramjoué, C. (2015). Towards open science: The vision of the European Commission, *Information Services & Use, 35*, 167–170.

Ratten, V., & Jones, P. (2018). Bringing Africa into entrepreneurship research. (pp. 9–27). In L.-P. Dana & V. Ratten (Eds.), *African entrepreneurship*. Palgrave Macmillan.

Riddell, J. B. (1992). Things fall apart again: Structural adjustment programmes in Sub-Saharan Africa. *The Journal of Modern African Studies, 30*(1), 53–68.

Sambajee, P., & Weston, A. (2015, January). A postcolonial analysis of entrepreneurship in Africa, AMC, 2015. *Academy of Management, 1*, online 2017.

Sheriff, M., & Muffatto, M. (2014). Reviewing existing policies for unleashing and fostering entrepreneurship. In selected African countries. *Journal of Developmental Entrepreneurship, 19*, 1450016/1–1450016/36.

Søreide, T. (2006). *CPI: Is it wrong to rank? A critical assessment of corruption indices* (CMI Working Papers), Chr. Michelsen Institute, Bergen, Norway

Takyi-Asiedu, S. (1993). Some socio-cultural factors retarding entrepreneurial activity in sub-Saharan Africa. *Journal of Business Venturing, 8*, 91–98.

UN Sustainable Development Goals. (2015). United Nations, New York.

World Bank. (2014). *Open data for economic growth.* Washington, DC. https://openknowledge.worldbank.org/handle/10986/19997.

Data sources

AEO. (2017). https://doi.org/10.1787/aeo-2017-en.

African Development Bank. (2020). *African Economic Outlook 2020.*

African Development Bank Data Portal. https://projectsportal.afdb.org/dataportal/.

Global Entrepreneurship Index. (2019). https://thegedi.org/global-entrepreneurship-and-development-index/.

Global Entrepreneurship Monitor. (2017). Middle East & Northern Africa Report.

GSMA. (2019). *The state of mobile internet connectivity 2019.* https://www.gsma.com/mobilefordevelopment/wp-content/uploads/2019/07/GSMA-State-of-Mobile-Internet-Connectivity-Report-2019.pdf.

Heritage Foundation. (2020). *Index of economic freedom.* https://www.heritage.org/index/.

Ibrahim Index of African Governance (IIAG). (2017). https://mo.ibrahim.foundation/.

Ibrahim Index of African Governance (IIAG). (2018). https://mo.ibrahim.foundation/sites/default/files/2020-05/2018-index-report.pdf.

Ibrahim Index of African Governance (IIAG). (2020). https://mo.ibrahim.foundation/iiag.

IEF. (2020). https://www.heritage.org/index/.

Legatum Institute. (2020b). *Legatum prosperity framework.* https://www.prosperity.com/download_file/view/4193/2025.

Open Data Barometer Impact Map. https://opendataimpactmap.org/afr.

Open Data for Africa. http://dataportal.opendataforafrica.org/.

Open Knowledge Foundation. (2005). *Open definition 2.1.* https://blog.okfn.org/2015/11/10/announcement-open-definition-2-1/.

Transparency International. (2019). *Corruption perceptions index.* https://www.transparency.org/en/cpi/2019.

United Nations. (2019). *Human development indicators.* http://hdr.undp.org/sites/default/files/hdr2019.pdf.

United Nations Strategic Development Goals. https://www.sdgmapping.ch/.

World Bank. (2020). *Doing business.* http://documents1.worldbank.org/curated/en/688761571934946384/pdf/Doing-Business-2020-Comparing-Business-Regulation-in-190-Economies.pdf.
Worldometer. (2020). https://www.worldometers.info/population/africa/.

13

African Youth Rising: The Emergence and Growth of Youth-Led Digital Enterprises in Africa

Wheeler R. Winstead and Jean T. Wells

Preface

Black Africa, often referred to as Sub-Saharan Africa, is projected to have the largest population of the eight Sustainable Development Goal regions by 2062 (United Nations, 2019). The region will account for most of the world's population growth in the coming decades which is seldom portrayed as an economic plus (United Nations, 2019). Its people are often viewed as the liability of Africa, not its assets. This negative portrayal is best illustrated in articles like "Africa to Lead World in Population Growth: Africa's population growth jeopardizes efforts to fight poverty, while immigration is expected to fuel U.S. population growth" which appeared in U.S. News & World Report (Chapman, 2019). The concern is that this rapid population growth will put undue pressure on poverty-stricken African countries.

This negative portrayal is especially true when it comes to the perspective of African youth. UN statistics revealed that in 2017, 60% of Africa's population was under the age of 25, compared to 42% in Asia, 32% in North America, and 27% in Europe (United Nations, Department of Economics

---

W. R. Winstead (✉)
Centre for African Studies, Howard University, Washington, DC, USA
e-mail: wheeler.r.winstead@Howard.edu

J. T. Wells
School of Business, Howard University, Washington, DC, USA

and Social Affairs, Population Division, 2017). Ahmad Alhendawi, former UN Secretary-General's Envoy on Youth, described this growth not as a dividend but as a youth population bulge (United Nations, Department of Public Information, 2017). Unfortunately, African youth are often the usual suspects to blame for the continent's problems. For example, in 1999, Africa's large population of unemployed youth was reported as a contributor to political instability and their exploitation as soldiers in ethnic, regional, and national conflicts (Human Rights Watch, 1999). A large youth population eclipsed all other factors in trying to explain political instability and conflict. Although the first 10 years of the new millennium gave birth to the narrative of "Africa rising," by 2015, Africa experienced an economic slowdown with a growth rate of only 3.4%—the lowest in 15 years (Bundervoet, 2016).

Can these woes simply be attributed to a growth in the number of African youth? Is this the proper, most helpful lens through which to view African youth? Mamadou Diouf argues that the "the condition of young people in Africa, as well as their future, is heavily influenced by the interaction between local and global pressures" (Diouf, 2003). He asserts that African societies, like all societies, are looking to their young people as instruments of change. Furthermore, he claims that the "bankruptcy of the nationalist project of development" coupled with economic and ideological adjustments accelerated youth migration toward the cities, the West and Europe and replaced the construct of youth as "the hope of the world" with youth as dangerous, criminal, decadent, and a threat to the whole of society (Diouf, 2003).

From the lens of the framework of a counter-narrative, this chapter provides some evidence and models of the blossoming of a new economic phenomenon occurring on continental Africa: youth entrepreneurship. The chapter examines African youth entrepreneurship and provides examples in the areas of mobile telephony, digital enterprises, renewable energy and more recently efforts to combat COVID-19. It provides an explanation for the occurrences, highlights potential opportunities, barriers and challenges while offering suggestions for expanding and leveraging this impact throughout the continent.

The Counter-Narrative

Counter-narratives refer to "narratives that arise from the vantage point of those who have been historically marginalized" (Mora, 2014). A counter-narrative also empowers and gives agency to the marginalized. According to Harper and Davis, the counter-narrative challenges the dominant narrative because of how it examines, critiques, and counters the master narrative. "Master narratives are dominant accounts that are often generally accepted as universal truths about particular groups" (Harper & Davis III, 2012). These master narratives are often crafted by those in positions of power thus having the effect of disempowering the subject of the narrative. Counter-narratives challenge the wisdom of the power brokers by providing a context to re-examine and transform established belief systems (Solorzano & Yosso, 2001). The counter-narrative framework has been embraced as a research methodology in the fields of Critical Race Theory, LatCrit, and Postcolonial Science (Mora, 2014). It is also closely related to the Oppositional Culture Theory of Ogbu which he used to explain the relationships between African Americans and social institutions in the US (Harper & Davis III, 2012).

The master narrative of African youth as portrayed by powerful institutions like the United Nations and western media becomes normative. Their stories and portrayals of African youth serve as a blueprint for the storylines, not only for non-Africans, but for Africans themselves. This master narrative is reproduced wittingly or unwittingly on an international scale (Andrews, 2004).

Their master narrative primarily presents African youth as a deficit. This chapter challenges that master narrative by presenting African youth as a dividend. The dividend counter-narrative of the twenty-first- century African youth has emerged as evidenced by their entrepreneurial endeavors. The dividend counter-narrative refers to a space of resistance or agency by African youth against the traditional dominant narrative often best seen in the direst of situations. The chapter provides support for the dividend counter-narrative in the form of case studies in the fields of technology, business and more recently in the medical response to the COVID-19 virus.

African Youth: A Dividend Counter-Narrative

In 2019, the Ichikowitz Family Foundation conducted a survey of African youth (African Youth Survey, 2020) to substantiate and quantify its belief of African youth as a dividend. The purpose of this study was to dispel erroneous assumptions with verifiable data in order to empower and change the stereotypes about Africa. The foundation's intent was to provide governments, the private sector and civil society with the insights into the aspirations, motivations and viewpoints of Africa's youth. According to the Foundation, "the findings should be understood as evidence-based insights into Africa's young adults, providing decision-makers with the data and analysis needed to undertake policy development" (Ichikowitz Family Foundation, 2020). Survey participants included 4,200 African youth between the ages of 18–24 who were interviewed face-to-face. The interviews were conducted on three hundred nationals from each of the following countries: Congo Brazzaville, Ethiopia, Gabon, Ghana, Kenya, Malawi, Mali, Nigeria, Rwanda, Senegal, South Africa, Togo, Zambia and Zimbabwe. Participants represented both rural and urban areas and were split evenly between males and females.

The study revealed that young Africans are optimistic about the future and their commitment and ambition to entrepreneurship to solve the problems of Africa's future. Researchers coined the term "Afro-Optimism": African youths' belief that despite life's challenges and an increasingly complex world, they are optimistic about the future. The report showed that 82% of all respondents believe that their standard of living will improve in the next two years and 67% of those whose standard of living is poor believe their positions will improve in the future. Eighty one percent of the respondents saw technology as being a positive force in improving their fortunes. According to Dr. Nick Westcott, these statistics show that young Africans were optimistic about their future and confident of their own potential (Ichikowitz Family Foundation, 2020, p. 106).

This potential even though infused with optimism and confidence is latent. Today, much of African youth innovation and entrepreneurship is motivated by the desire to survive or solve a pressing problem in the household or community. This is survival entrepreneurship. Many modern African cities are inundated with swarms of people, mainly youth, hawking wares in car-jammed streets and on corners selling everything from snacks to toilet seats. These informal markets are the primary source of employment for many African families. A hustle or starve existence is mandated by the lack of an economic safety net. Few of these efforts grow large enough to ever expand beyond the local homegrown market because they are fueled by cheaply manufactured products often imported from as far away as Malaysia and China.

African leaders are taking some steps to address the youth growth dilemma. On 31 January 2014, the African Union addressed the issue of youth dividend vs youth bulge in the Common African Position (CAP) on the Post-2015 Development Agenda. The CAP committed to "ensure that Africa's youth bulge is translated into demographic dividend" by developing "strategies that: strengthen entrepreneurial skills and capacity; increase youth's access to financial services; promote decent and commensurate jobs; increase access to business advisory services and credit facilities…" (African Union, 2014).

"Sub-Saharan Africa alone accounted for about 30% of the regulatory reforms making it easier to do business in 2014/15, followed closely by Europe and Central Asia" (World Bank, 2016). These changes in the business environment are yielding a new crop of youth entrepreneurs.

African Youth Entrepreneurship

Why examine youth entrepreneurship? By 2035, it's projected that Africans will comprise the majority of the working-age people in the world. Entrepreneurs will be needed to create jobs and grow businesses (Ichikowitz Family Foundation, 2020). Just as small businesses play a major role in the US economy by creating jobs and building economic independence, African entrepreneurs and especially African youth entrepreneurs could play the same role. Classic US examples are Steve Jobs and Mark Zuckerberg. Jobs was just 21 years old when he started Apple Computer in his family garage (Biography.com Editors, 2020). Zuckerberg was 19 years old when he started Facebook (Biography.com Editors, 2019). In the US, Apple is responsible for creating more than two million jobs including 80,000 employees, 450,000 jobs through suppliers, and 1,530,000 jobs attributable to the App Store ecosystem. In 2019, Apple paid more than USD$50 billion to more than 9,000 suppliers and manufacturers. US developers have earned over USD$16 billion in App Store sales worldwide since 2008 (Apple.com, 2020). Deloitte reported in *Facebook's Economic Global Impact* that the company enabled USD$227 billion of economic impact and 4.5 million jobs globally in 2014 (Deloitte LLP, 2015). Jobs and Zuckerberg were game changing, extraordinary entrepreneurs and are examples of how just two individuals can change and fuel the economy of the entire world.

This chapter juxtaposes a counter-narrative for African youth against the traditional dominant narrative inside the framework of entrepreneurship. The chapter embarks by addressing more concretely the framework of the counter-narrative as it pertains to an introduction to African youth and the basic business environment in which they operate. This section is followed by a review of some of the educational and enabling institutions which are emerging on the continent. The next section provides examples and specific cases that are particularly promising in the area of entrepreneurship. This is followed by a discussion of current issues facing African youths' response to the COVID-19 pandemic. The chapter concludes with recommendations and offers suggestions for further research particularly with regard to intellectual property (IP) protection of the inventions created by these youth entrepreneurs.

Educational and Enabling Institutions

Education is essential to unlocking the future entrepreneurial potentials of African youth. Africans will comprise the majority of working-age people in the world by 2035 (Ichikowitz Family Foundation, 2020, p. 59). Therefore, businesses must grow and entrepreneurship must increase. Education is critical for both to happen effectively and African educational institutions must be at the forefront.

According to Patrick Awuah, innovation in education is not an option. Awuah started Ashesi University in Ghana, in 2002 with a daring mission: "to educate a new generation of ethical, entrepreneurial leaders for Africa" (Ichikowitz Family Foundation, 2020, p. 58). Ashesi's 1,000 graduates are making a difference and demonstrating the potential of this educational model. In 2012, Ghanaians used a secure biometric voter registration system developed by Ashesi graduates that reduced voter fraud and boosted confidence in the election process. Other Ashesi graduates created secure cash transfer technologies that have facilitated millions of cash transfers across West Africa.

New innovative educational opportunities are appearing in other African countries. An example is the Makerere University in Uganda and the Rhodes University of South Africa co-sponsoring an app development challenge, which was to translate the Mozilla's Firefox Internet browser into Luganda, Uganda's most widely spoken language. To accomplish this, the universities organized a two-day translation marathon workshop that brought together software gurus from Uganda and South Africa, as well as top Luganda linguists. The purpose was to make the internet more accessible to non-English speaking Ugandans (Network World, 2008).

US universities are launching entrepreneurial programs in Africa. Stanford University, the Massachusetts Institute of Technology, Harvard University, the University of California, and the University of Wisconsin all have internship programs for young African entrepreneurs (Musau, 2017). Carnegie Mellon University (CMU), a world leader in engineering education and research, has been in the forefront of US higher education engagement in the promotion of Africa's entrepreneurial potential. In 2011, CMU, in partnership with the Rwandan government, opened CMU-Africa in Kigali with full-time resident CMU faculty and staff. The university offers a Master of Science in Information Technology and a Master of Science in Electrical and Computer Engineering. The CMU-Africa campus is in Kigali Innovation City, a Center of Excellence that hosts multinational and local companies (Carnegie Mellon Africa, 2018). CMU-Africa created the Industry Innovation Lab which seeks entrepreneurs with innovative ideas to create new products, services, joint ventures, and startups (Carnegie Mellon University, 2020).

The positive impact of CMU-Africa is evident in its number of graduates and their professional accomplishments. As of June 2019, CMU-Africa had graduated 196 students of which 83% were working in Africa; 30% were working in management positions; 10% were pursuing PhDs at world renowned universities like CMU and Oxford; and 8% were startup founders (Carnegie Mellon University, 2020).

Notable alumni include Andrew Kinai, software engineer at IBM Research, Africa who is the lead project manager for a blockchain-enabled microfinancing lending platform for Kenyan food kiosk owners. In 2017, the program was test piloted for 8 weeks on 220 small food kiosks; the average loan was about USD$30 repayable in four to eight days at interest rates of 1–2%. Borrowers experienced a 30% increase in their orders and an average 6% increase in profits. As a result of this successful pilot, plans are underway to expand the lending program across Africa and to other small businesses (Kinai, 2018).

Enabling institutions provide support (funding, mentoring, training) at an early developmental stage for the entrepreneurs. The Tony Elumelu Foundation (TFE) in Nigeria has been a leader in taking up the challenge of supporting Africa's youth entrepreneurs. The foundation offers training, funding, and mentoring to selected African youth and has committed USD$100 million to support entrepreneurs across Africa over a 10-year period. The foundation plans to support 1,000 startup companies per year during that period. The Tony Elumelu Entrepreneur is awarded a non-returnable investment of USD$5,000 to further develop a business idea. The recipient qualifies for a second-stage seed capital investment of USD$5,000 that is provided as returnable capital. The foundation's goal is to create one million new jobs and generate USD$10 billion in annual revenue growth across Africa by 2025 (The Tony Elumelu Foundation, 2016). As of June 2020, the TEF had trained, mentored, and funded 9,360 African start-ups from all 54 African countries (The Tony Elumelu Foundation, 2020).

In 2019, the inaugural Tony Elumelu Foundation (TEF)-United Nations Development Program (UNDP) Entrepreneurship Program was announced. The partnership is designed to empower 100,000 young African entrepreneurs in Burkina Faso, Cameroon, Chad, Mali, Mauritania, Niger and Nigeria, over a 10-year period. Each participant will receive seed funding between USD$1,500 and USD$5,000 (Cision PR Newswire, 2019).

Similarly, blueMoon, an Ethiopian agribusiness incubator, provides training, coaching, mentoring, and financial support to teams of young entrepreneurs in a competitive four-month incubator program in Addis Ababa (Blue Moon Ethiopia, 2018). The incubator program has graduated 33 startups since its inception in 2017. Eleni Gabre-Madhin, blueMoon incubator Founder and CEO, believes that Ethiopian youth agribusiness startups can change the world (Awosanya, 2019).

Africa's political environment is also contributing to this changing counter-narrative. The most dramatic change is the increase in the number of stable, democratically elected governments as witnessed in recent elections. This stability has led to African governments sponsoring youth entrepreneurship programs: for example, Uganda's Youth Venture Capital Fund (YVCF) provides concessional loans to individuals or groups between 18 and 30 years old. From its inception in August 2017 to May 2018, YVCF disbursed approximately USD$4,616,168 to fund 4,450 youth projects (Okoth, 2018).

In 2010, the government of Kenya mandated that the Kenya Private Sector Alliance partner with the World Bank to create the pilot Kenya Youth Empowerment Project (KYEP) (Kimando, 2012). This five-year pilot program was designed to provide training and business/life support services to vulnerable youth between the ages of 15 and 29, who were not in school or working and with at least eight years of schooling. The youth also received work placement internships in the formal and informal sectors. KYEP was offered in Nairobi, Mombasa and Kisumu. In KYEP's 2016 final report, 20,384 youth received training, a 36% increase above the target of 15,000 and 13,289 youth were successfully placed in internships, a 33% increase above the target of 10,000.

The success of KYEP led the Kenyan government to implement a new initiative in 2016, the Kenya Youth Employment and Opportunities Project (KYEOP) in partnership with the World Bank (Kenyan Private Sector Alliance, 2016). Like KYEP, KYEOP's objective is to increase employment and earning opportunities among targeted young people. Entrepreneurial training is augmented with support services in life skills, core business skills, internships and apprenticeships. Between 2016 and 2021, the plan is to reach over 280,000 youth between 18 and 29 years of age who are jobless, have experienced extended spells of unemployment or are currently working in vulnerable jobs (Kenya Youth Employment & Opportunities Project, 2020).

The Case for Digital Technology

Africa is now a leader in usage of mobile money service with more than half of the world's usage in Sub-Saharan Africa. According to the Pew Research Center, cell phones are now just as common in South Africa and Nigeria as they are in the US (Oates, 2015). Africa has the "second largest region behind Asia–Pacific in terms of unique subscribers (12% of the global subscriber base) but is also the least penetrated" according to The Mobile Economy: Africa 2016 report (GSM Association, 2016). The mobile phone market in Africa is now bigger than either the US or European Union (Kelly & Dalphond, 2013).

The 2020 African Youth Survey also documents the importance and potential of technology in African youth entrepreneurship in the future. The survey showed that 86% of respondents report owning a smartphone. The majority of these respondents report using their smartphones for a minimum of three or more hours every day (Ichikowitz Family Foundation, 2020, p. 61).

The accessibility of information and communication technology, particularly of mobile phones, is pushing African entrepreneurship and transforming urban and rural Africa. African youth are embracing and capitalizing on the economy of the mobile phone technology. Mobile technology emerged as the "platform of choice for creating, distributing and consuming innovative digital solutions and services in Africa" and skyrocketing phone usage is spurring rapid innovation in the field (GSM Association, 2016). The expansion of advanced mobile networks and the growing adoption of smart devices have resulted in the creation and growth of technology hubs and accelerators/incubators among African young entrepreneurs. Below are some examples of youth innovators who are propelling African communities vis-à-vis digital and mobile phone technologies into the future in ways unimaginable to skeptical scholars. Most of these individuals were named as one of Africa's Most Promising Young Entrepreneurs: Forbes Africa's 30 Under 30 for 2015.

Mubarak Muyika, Founder, Zagace Limited, Kenya

Mubarak Muyika was tragically orphaned at a young age. Fortunately, he was adopted by his aunt and uncle who operated a small business. Noting the deficiencies in website services provided to this business, Muyika took the initiative to learn how to build a website and to code. In 2011, he started his first venture, HypeCentury Technologies and Investments, which provided web hosting services to small businesses at an affordable price. His business flourished to the point where he secured a scholarship to attend prestigious Harvard University in the US. Surprisingly, he rejected this opportunity because he was laser focused on managing and growing his business. Muyika expanded the scope of services to include domain name registration, a key intellectual property component of protecting a business. In 2012, when Muyika was 18 years old, he was selected as an Anzisha Fellow. The Anzisha Fellowship program is a collaborative initiative between African Leadership Academy and Mastercard Foundation. The program's goal is to increase the number of jobs created by African entrepreneurs (The Anzisha Prize, 2019). This created additional opportunities and led Muyika to sell HypeCentury in a six-figure deal. By the following year, Muyika founded Zagace Limited, a cloud-based bundled enterprise software that helps companies manage accounting, payroll, stock management, and marketing in a bundled package.

Catherine Mahugu, Co-founder, Soko; Founder, Chiswara; Co-founder, Wazidata, Kenya

Mahugu founded Chiswara, an agricultural-technology and online platform that offers equitable experiences for local coffee farmers and global consumers. Mahugu also founded Wazidata, a design-led innovation company that "aims to help in international development by bridging the digital divide and providing equitable access to technologies by applying design thinking concepts and methodologies" (WaziData, n.d.).

Mahugu co-founded Soko, an online platform where global shoppers can buy handcrafted accessories directly from artisans in Kenya and Ethiopia. Soko is designed to empower the local artisan entrepreneur. Soko has sold over 250,000 products worldwide to over 450 international retailers. Soko's jewelry has been worn by Michelle Obama, Oprah Winfrey, Lupita Nyongo, and Nicole Kidman. Mahugu has been a World Bank Fellow, an Ashoka-American Express Emerging Innovator Fellow, a BBC 100 Women and Top 5 Upcoming Tech Women in Kenya to Watch.

Bheki Kunene, Founder, Mind Trix Media, South Africa

As a teenager, Kunene was expelled from school. Fortunately, he eventually completed high school and received a scholarship to attend the Ruth Prowse School of Art to study graphic design. While at Ruth, Kunene started Mind Trix Media with R600 (USD 57) along with two other classmates, a computer and no business knowledge. Mind Trix offers web development and design services, development of mobile applications, printing, and marketing. After his two classmates quit the business, Kunene persevered and continued to build his business singlehandedly. Within days of securing his largest client, Kunene was falsely accused of murder, arrested, and jailed. He was released almost a week later after the real murderer was captured. A few years later, he was hit by two cars and spent three months in the hospital recovering from his injuries. Despite these life-altering events, Kunene continued to grow his business. In 2014, Kunene was named as one of the top 10 national finalists of the South African Breweries Kick Start Business Competition. In 2016, Kunene was the first business leader to receive the Acacia Global Leadership Award. Acacia Global is a nonprofit that partners with NGOs and South African community leaders to develop the next generation of leaders, address social justice issues, and meet basic human needs (Acacia Global, 2021). Kunene has expanded his business beyond South Africa to reach clients in other African countries including Zimbabwe and Angola, and outside the continent to Vietnam and Italy, and as far away as the US (Hesketh, 2019).

Emeke Anako, Co-founder, Founder2Be, Nigeria

Emeke Anako is no stranger to starting businesses. Anako co-founded three businesses: Jara Mobile Limited, Founder2Be, and Entarado. Jara Mobile has revolutionized the way Africans pay bills with the Jara app which enables customers to pay bills and be instantly rewarded with discount coupons to various retailers—similar to a loyalty rewards program. Jara Mobile was selected to be featured in the 2018 Lagos Social Media Week inaugural "Launched in Africa Series" where an improved version of the Jara app was to be unveiled. Jara Mobile plans to expand operations to Ghana, Kenya, South Africa, and Rwanda. Founder2Be is a match-making service for business owners in Africa. Entarado provides web development services to small businesses (Akano, 2018).

Abiola Olaniran, Founder, Gamsole, Nigeria

Olaniran developed his first game code at age 15 and recognizing the need for specialized education, he studied computer science and mathematics at the Obafemi Awolowo University in Nigeria. In 2010, Olaniran won both the Microsoft Africa Imagine Cup software competition and the Samsung Nigeria Developer Challenge in the games and entertainment category. In 2012, Olaniran founded Gamsole, a game production company, which garnered over 3 million downloads within six months of debuting in the

Windows phone store. The company has developed over 35 game applications and has had over 10 million downloads. In 2015, Gamsole won Best Innovation at the Appsafrica Innovation Award. Olaniran is Nigeria's highest paid game developer (Rise Networks, 2015).

Takunda Chingonzo, Co-founder, Neolab Technology & Saisai Wireless, Zimbabwe

At 19 years old, Chingonzo co-founded Neolab Technology, a startup factory which has helped build numerous startups. Neolab has worked with the National University of Science and Technology in Zimbabwe where students are trained in groups to convert concepts into sustainable startups. In 2014, Chingonzo was named a Young African Leaders Initiative Mandela Washington Fellow. In 2014, Chingonzo co-founded Saisai Wireless, which provides free access to WiFi hotspots in public areas. Chingonzo is also a Yale University Young African Scholar, Yunus and Youth Fellow, and Kairos Fellow. Chingonzo's vision is to help build 100 startups in Africa by 2020 (Yale University, 2021).

Clarisse Iribagiza, Founder/CEO, DMM.HeHe (Formerly HeHe Labs), Rwanda

In 2010, while a junior studying computer engineering at the University of Rwanda, Iribagiza participated in a six-week program offered by the Massachusetts Institute of Technology Global Startup Labs program on the fundamentals of technological entrepreneurship. These were the impetus that led Iribagiza to launch HeHe Labs (now DMM.HeHe), a mobile technology company. In 2011, Iribagiza co-founded iHills, an association that mentors Rwandan youth in the technology sectors. In 2012, HeHe won a $50,000 grant from Inspire Africa for Global Impacts Initiative. In 2013, the Imbuto Foundation, a project supported by the Rwandan First Lady conferred on Iribagiza its Celebrating Young Rwandan Achievers Award for her accomplishments. Also in 2013, Iribagiza and her team won $7,500 for the innovative idea that they presented at the Transform Africa Summit in Rwanda. In 2014, Iribagiza was named among 100 global thinkers by Lo Spazio della Politica, an Italian think tank. Iribagiza serves on the Presidential Youth Advisory Group at the African Development Bank. DMM.HeHe serves over 2 million users across the African continent (Diallo, 2015).

Raindolf Owusu, Founder, Oasis Websoft, Ghana

Owusu is a software engineer who attended Methodist University. In 2011, he founded Oasis Websoft as an initiative to solve the daily problems of Africans. Owusu also developed Anansipedia, Africa's first web browser and an educational platform that provides resources to the less privileged and Bisa, a telemedicine platform that gives users information about how to access doctors. Owusu developed Dr. Diabetes, a web-based application that educates users about diabetes. In 2015, Owusu was named a Young African Leaders Initiative Mandela Washington Fellow and one of the 100 Most Influential Africans in the New African Magazine. In 2016, Owusu received the International Telecommunications Union Young Innovator Award (TechCamp, n.d.).

Julie Alexander Fourie, Founder, iFix, (Now Called WeFix), South Africa

In 2006, Fourie's iPod fell and broke, he was unable to find a company to repair it and ultimately fixed it himself by using do it yourself (DIY) steps he found online. Sensing the need for this type of service, Fourie founded iFix in his dorm room at Stellenbosch University. The company repairs and services Apple and Samsung electronics. By 2008, iFix had expanded with locations in Johannesburg and Pretoria. In 2011, Fourie founded RiCharge, a solar-based mobile charge station to recharge electronics in rural Africa where electricity is scant. Fourie also started UFIX, a DIY Apple repair kit so that users could learn how to repair their devices similar to how he learned in 2006 when he repaired his iPod. By 2015, iFix had expanded further with locations in Cape Town and Durban, employing over 40 workers and servicing over 4,000 clients monthly (Okunlola, 2019).

Kodjo Afate Gnikou, Inventor, Togo

Kodjo Afate Gnikou, a young Togo inventor, created a 3D digital printer from discarded scanner parts that can be built for less than USD$100. Gnikou participated in the NASA International Space Apps Challenge in Paris (Winstead, 2018).

Rupert Bryant, Co-founder, ISP Web, South Africa

Rupert Bryant of South Africa co-founded and developed ISP Web, an USD$11 million business. ISP Web is considered the biggest service provider in South Africa.

Verona Mankou, Founder/CEO, VMK, Republic of Congo

Verona Mankou, of the Republic of Congo, the Founder & CEO of the company VMK, created Elikia, the first African-made mobile phone and Way-C tablet, Africa's version of the iPad (Dolan, 2015).

Renewable Energy

Africa's economy is growing at unprecedented speed. One of the core challenges as African countries continue to grow and develop is energy: meeting rising demand for power, transport, and other uses in a way that is economically sustainable and safeguards livelihoods. By 2030, the demand for energy is expected to double due to economic growth, changing lifestyles, and the need for reliable modern energy access (International Renewable Energy Agency, IRENA, 2015).

The International Renewable Energy Agency (IRENA) believes that Africa could meet "nearly a quarter of its energy needs through the use of indigenous, clean, renewable energy by 2030" (IRENA, 2015). This statement was reiterated in 2019 (IRENA, 2019).

"Africa's reserves of renewable energy resources are the highest in the world" according to a 2013 report by the African Development Bank (Mukasa, et al. 2013). See Fig. 13.1 . The report bolsters this statement with the fact that 18 of the top 35 developing countries ranked highest in renewable energy reserves are in Africa (Mukasa et al., 2013).

Nyasha Bamhare, CEO of the Zimbabwe-based renewable energy company Samansco, asserts that small-scale power grids provide Africa with the sustainability and flexibility not possible with traditional energy grids (Kilian, 2017). According to Bamhare, the decentralized distribution of "off the grid" energy generation will be a key driver in Africa's energy future.

Developing Regions with the Higest Potential for Renewable Energy

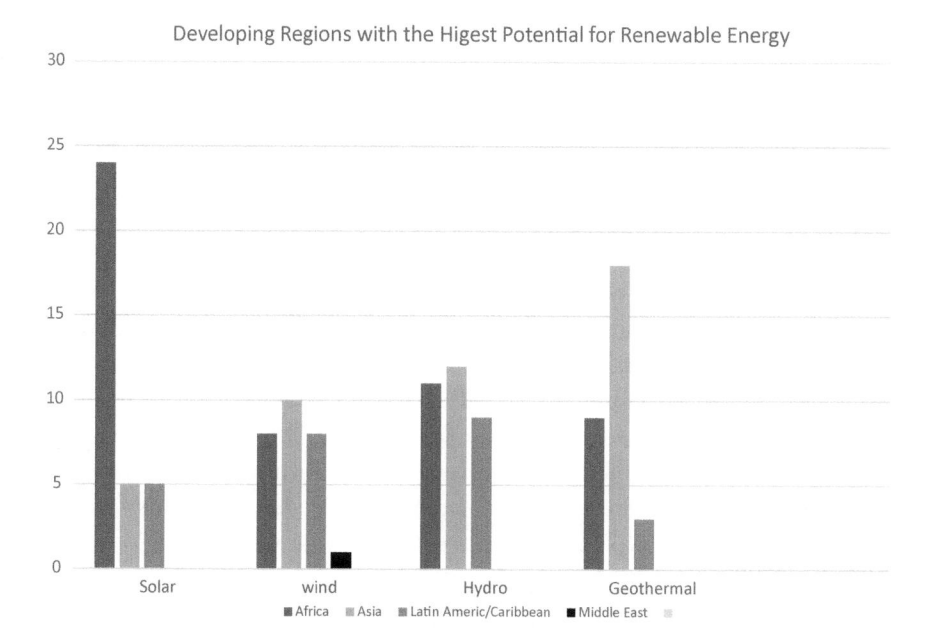

Fig. 13.1 Developing regions with the highest potential for solar, wind, hydro, and geothermal energy (*Source* Adapted from "Development of Wind Energy in Africa" by Alli D. Mukasa, Emelly Mutambatsere, Yannis Arvanitis, and Thouraya Triki, March 2013, in Working Paper Series N° 170 African Development Bank)

Solar

Africa leads the world in the sunshine index. Seven of the 10 sunniest countries are in Africa: Chad, Egypt, Kenya, Madagascar, Niger, South Africa, and Sudan (Kuwonu, 2016). Africa could eventually lead the world in the production of solar energy because it gets 117% more sunshine than Germany which currently has the highest installed solar power capacity. The combination of abundant sunshine, a huge energy need, a burst in solar innovation which provide better transmission, storage, payment systems and dropping costs could mean that solar-based solutions will play a leading role in addressing Africa's energy needs (Winstead, 2018).

Adnan Amin, the IRENA director general, predicts an African solar revolution the scale of which could be comparable in speed and importance to the rapid surge in mobile phone usage two decades ago. Solar companies like BBOXX in Rwanda believe that Africa may leapfrog over Europe and North America straight into solar, bypassing the electricity grid, just as it did in skipping landlines in favor of mobile phones. BBOXX, for example, has leapfrogged over the cash payment system and only accepts payment by mobile phone money transfers (Nuwer, 2017).

Historically, Africans created renewable and recyclable inventions out of necessity, not choice. The ideas of "green entrepreneurship" and sustainable development were labels which modernized or sanitized these desperate efforts. However, a growing youth population combined with the need for jobs and sustainable, renewable energy choices have triggered new development opportunities that have not gone unnoticed by African youth entrepreneurs. In addition, IRENA, the Energy and Environmental Partnership trust fund, (EEP, Africa), the UN and various African governments are encouraging youth entrepreneurship efforts in the renewable energy sector. In 2020, IRENA launched its youth forum in Abu Dhabi with participants from several African countries. The purpose of the forum was to "strengthen the existing network of young energy leaders with the latest insights from the renewable sector, as well as to connect young people with IRENA experts" (IRENA, 2020).

Henri Nyakarundi, Founder, African Renewable Energy Distributors

African Renewable Energy Distributors (ARED) founded by Henri Nyakarundi is a solar energy distribution company which produces a smart kiosk that runs on solar energy. ARED kiosks serve as a one-stop digital power center for mobile phone users in semi-urban and rural areas. Nyakarundi, a son of Rwandan refugees, grew up in Burundi until the civil war forced his family to move. Henri later relocated to the US and enrolled at Georgia State University to study computer science. He was driven by the desire to solve problems which also had social impact by creating micro businesses for the people of Rwanda. Henri moved back to Rwanda in 2012 once the kiosk prototype was ready (Eastaugh, 2017). ARED can charge up to 80 cell phones simultaneously. Nyakarundi leases his kiosks for a USD$100 down payment followed by USD$200 in installments under a micro-franchising system. Franchisees can make between USD$38 to $107 monthly, which in Rwanda, is enough to pay rent and feed a family. Henri offers free franchisees to women and the disabled (Winstead, 2018).

Mixon Faluweki, Inventor, Malawi

Mixon Faluweki, a Malawian physics student, lived in a community where only 11% of rural households had electricity but 47% own a bicycle. Mixon invented the Padoko bicycle phone charger to support the expanded use of mobile phones which need to be charged regularly (BBC, 2014).

Wind

Wind-based electricity, one of the world's fastest-growing energy resources, grew at an average annual rate of about 30% between 1996 and 2008. Nonetheless, it is still underdeveloped compared to the growth of other renewable fuels such as hydro and solar. In its 2013 report, the African Development Bank pointed out that at "least 8 African countries are among the developing world's most endowed in terms of wind energy potential" (Mukasa, et al., 2013). See Fig. 13.2. Countries along Africa's large coastline have the best potential for wind power production (Tiyou, 2016). In March 2019, Kenya opened the Lake Turkana Wind Power project, the largest wind farm in Africa. This facility consisted of 365 turbines each with a capacity of 850 kilowatts (Frangoul, 2019).

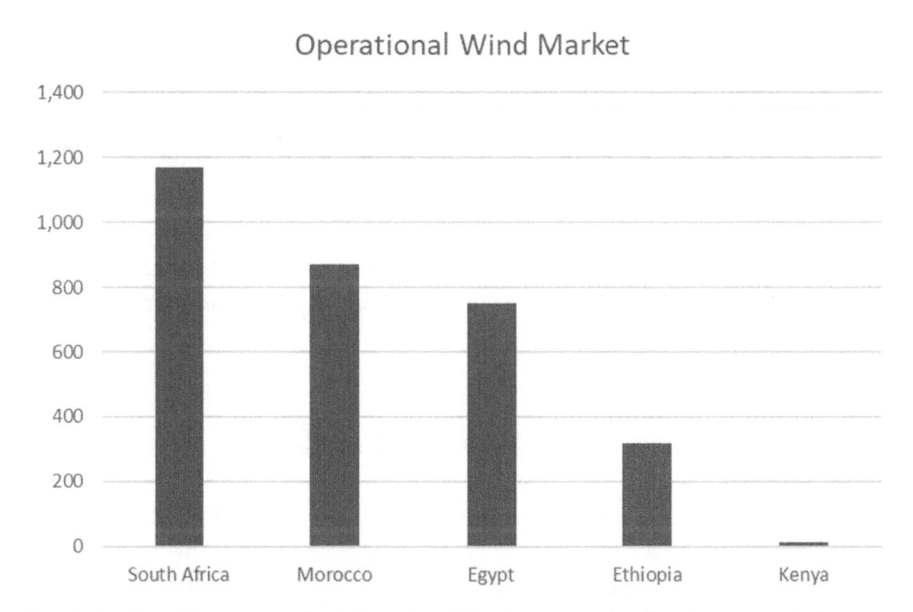

Fig. 13.2 Five Biggest Wind Markets in Africa (*Source* "The five biggest wind energy markets in Africa" by Tony Tiyou (2016), October 19, in Renewable Energy Focus.com, International Solar Energy Society)

The Boy Who Harnessed the Wind - William Kamkwamba

The wind market in Africa is dominated by the world's largest multinational companies like Siemens, General Electric, Mainstream Renewables, EDF, Iberdrola Renewables, Engie, and Acciona (Winstead, 2018). However, the story of William Kamkwamba's windmill project has captured the hearts and imagination of the world and exemplifies the best in African youth agency. Poverty forced William to drop out of school in the rural community of Masitala, Malawi. At the age of 14, despite his limited command of the English language, William built an electricity-producing windmill mainly from pictures he found in a library book titled "Using Energy." He constructed the windmill from wood, a tractor fan, shock absorbers, PVC pipes, a bicycle frame, and scrap. The windmill project was primarily to replace the flickering smoky light provided by the kerosene lantern. However, his windmill was able to power four lights, neighbors' cell phones, and pump grey water for irrigation. Kamkwamba's subsequent community projects included malaria prevention, lighting for the six homes in his family compound, deep-water well powered by a solar pump, and a drip irrigation system (Moving Windmill Project, 2013).

The story of William's windmill project went viral. In 2007 and 2009, William gave two TED Talks on his accomplishments. Subsequently, he was featured in two books: an illustrated children's book and his memoir both entitled "The Boy Who Harnessed the Wind." "William and the Windmill" was awarded the 2013 South by Southwest (SXSW) festival's Grand Jury Award for Documentary Feature (May, 2013). Also, in 2013, Kamkwamba was named one of the "30 People Under 30 Changing the World" by Time magazine (Rhodan, 2013). In 2014, Kamkwamba graduated from Dartmouth College with a degree in engineering. In 2019, Kamkwamba's story was featured in the Netflix drama, The Boy Who Harnessed the Wind (Netflix, 2019). William's story is just one example of an African youth counter-narrative.

Response to the COVID-19 Pandemic

Africa's entrepreneurs and innovators today are often forced into existence because of the tremendous needs they face. The threat and peril of the coronavirus is today's impetus for the emergence of several youth entrepreneurs/innovators. This current COVID-19 pandemic is forcing African entrepreneurs to rethink and explore alternative ways to meet the needs of their communities. Access to testing, healthcare, and accurate and timely information are major challenges in more developed countries and are exacerbated in less developed African countries. However, the following are examples of nimble African youth ingenuity in response to the coronavirus global healthcare pandemic.

Makerere University's School of Public Health has partnered with the Ministry of Science, Technology and Innovation (MOSTI) and Kiira Motors Corporation to create the Resilient Africa Network (RAN). RAN is exploring the science, technology, engineering, and innovation solution space in an effort to combat the pandemic in Uganda. This group is working to develop an Open Design Low-Cost Ventilator using the open access designs from the Massachusetts Institute of Technology, University of Florida, and other public license ventilator technology developers. The plan is to address the needs in Africa emphasizing supply chain localization to bring the product to scale. The intent is that the capacity created will be valuable to Africa even beyond the COVID-19 pandemic (Makerere University, 2020).

Nelson Kwaje, a 28-year-old South Sudanese, is tackling the problem of misinformation on COVID-19. Nelson, a Program Director for #DefyHateNow, a community organization based in South Sudan, with branches in Cameroon, Kenya, Sudan, and Ethiopia, helped to initiate the #211CHECK collective. #211CHECK is a digital community of youth working in various fields to raise awareness on coronavirus prevention and fight misinformation using the #COVID19SS (Wickramanayake, 2020).

Chidi Ohammah, the Nigerian-based CEO of Sevenz Healthcare, has devised an innovative way for people to get tested from the comfort of their homes. Hamadou Daouda, a Niger-based entrepreneur, developed a digital solution to connect local communities with relevant timely information. In March 2020, NOVATECH, Hamadou's company, launched a free call service, in 5 national languages, which allows the entire population to call and get advice on how to prevent COVID-19. This innovative platform, validated by the Ministry of Health, has received over 4,000 calls. Nadiatu Ali, a Ghanaian entrepreneur, created an enterprise that produces sanitizer gels and is donating face masks to people in his community (The Tony Elumelu Foundation, 2020).

Erico Pinheiro Fortes, a Cabo Verdean entrepreneur, founded PrimeBotics, to develop versatile drones which deliver customized technological solutions to farmers, governmental, and non-governmental institutions in the business of agriculture in Africa and the world. When the global COVID-19 crisis hit, Erico refocused PrimeBotics to provide new solutions aimed at mitigating the spread of the virus. The plan is to use drones to disinfect streets and deliver medical and non-medical supplies. PrimeBotics would also manufacture 3D-printed face shields for hospitals (The Tony Elumelu Foundation, 2020).

Mohammed Akamara, a Sierra Leonian entrepreneur, is addressing the need for hand sanitation to prevent COVID-19 spread. Mohammed founded Light Salone Innovation which manufactures the Lili Tap, a safe and unique handwashing system for small communities using locally available and recyclable materials. His non-touch design works with a foot lever which opens and closes the tap. The government of Sierra Leone has endorsed his system which is currently being implemented in communities, homes, offices, business places, markets and schools throughout the country (The Tony Elumelu Foundation, 2020).

Twenty-six-year-old Christian Achaleke of Cameroon began producing a homemade hand sanitizer using the World Health Organisation's (WHO) recipe after realizing that the state had not set up contingencies for containment and management. He launched a street campaign to encourage "young people to act responsibly and spread correct information, and to help people follow the preventive measures, which had become prohibitively expensive" (Wickramanayake, 2020).

The Ndlovu Youth Choir of South Africa, "known for reaching the finale of America's Got Talent [in 2019], composed, performed and filmed a musical rendition of the World Health Organisation's (WHO) coronavirus safety advice" (Wickramanayake, 2020). Certain features of the song were translated into various South African languages to ensure that the diverse communities were well informed about safety measures during the spread of this outbreak.

Recommendations and Conclusion

This chapter examines the issue of African youth entrepreneurship from the perspective of a counter-narrative: African youth as a dividend. The chapter also showcases the importance and positive impact of educational institutions and other enabling structures and programs that support African youth entrepreneurs. African youth agency is highlighted in the areas of digital technology and renewable energy. African youth ingenuity and flexibility are illustrated in response to the COVID-19 crisis.

Much more is still needed, however, to sustain and expand these advances. The authors of this chapter posit that the counter-narrative must also be accompanied by a change in the mindset of the present leadership. Tiyou in the ESI Africa, laments that while the "potential for wind in Africa is enormous, the resources are clearly underutilized." His solution is strong-willed African leadership with "bold and holistic vision" that would integrate initiatives to increase regional capacity (Tiyou, 2018). In a similar fashion, the potential for African youth entrepreneurship is abundant and should continue to be supported by government and other entities.

Educational institutions should consider collaborating their efforts with enabling entities to maximize and leverage their resources in order to sustain programs for African youth. More public–private partnerships are needed in every country which benchmark the best with demonstrated outcomes. Longitudinal studies of youth entrepreneurial efforts are needed to better understand and evaluate the relationships between variables as related to the success or failure of the project. Basic follow-up studies are important for replication and modeling. Governments and private enabling institutions will want to know and understand the details of initiatives and outcomes.

The youth entrepreneurial growth also raises several regulatory and policy implications particularly in the area of intellectual property (IP) protection: How do African youth entrepreneurs protect their intellectual/innovative resources so that they are not stolen similar to how African physical and human resources have been exploited for centuries? Conversely, are young African innovators violating IP laws? To what extent do the easing of business regulations make African youth entrepreneurs more vulnerable to unfair encroachment by powerful foreign corporations? How do the continent's widespread mobile technology users protect themselves from hackers?

In the Christian Bible, God asked Moses "What is that in your hand?" (Exodus 4:2, New International Version). Moses replied a staff. God's question was not one of a physical nature due to God's lack of sight or knowledge. Instead, God was questioning whether Moses fully understood the real power of God resident now with him in the form of a staff. In a similar vein, African youth represents an underutilized and often unseen resource with tremendous growth and potential.

Today's African youth entrepreneurs are forging ahead despite the many barriers and lack of opportunities they face. Dire need remains the primary impetus for the agency in African youth innovation. However, African youth agency, combined with opportunity, is creating a counter-narrative. This chapter supports the narrative that African youth are a dividend and their entrepreneurial efforts represent a major source of economic energy which could lead to increased individual wealth, collective economic revival in many African countries and the improvement of Africa's international status.

References

Acacia Global. (2021). *Global leadership award recipients.* Retrieved January 12, 2021, from https://www.acaciaglobal.org/award-recipients.

Adeya-Weya, C. (2015). *Report on the young African innovators, creators and entrepreneurs workshop: intellectual property (ip), innovation, creativity for entrepreneurship and job creation.* WIPO.

African Union. (2014). *Common African position (cap) on the post-2015 development agenda.* Addis Abba.

Akano, E. (2018). *Africa business communicaties.* Retrieved January 12, 2021, from https://africabusinesscommunities.com/features/startup-interview-emeka-akano-ceo-jara-mobile-ltd-nigeria/.

Andrews, M. (2004). Opening to the original contributions: Counter-narratives and the power to oppose. In M. B. Andrews (Ed.), *Considering counter-narratives: Narrating, resisting, making sense* (p. 1,2). John Benjamins.

Apple.com. (2020, August 15). Retrieved August 15, 2020, from Apple Job Creation: https://www.apple.com/job-creation/.

Awosanya, Y. (2019, September 5). *Techpoint.Africa.* Retrieved April 23, 2020, from *BlueMoon is a startup powering the Ethiopian startup space.* https://techpoint.africa/2019/09/05/bluemoon-ethiopia/.

BBC. (2014, November 14). *Using a bicycle to charge your phone.* Retrieved April 16, 2018, from BBC World Service: http://www.bbc.co.uk/programmes/p02c5gv5.

Biography.com Editors. (2019, October 24). (A. T. Networks, Producer) Retrieved August 15, 2020, from The Biograpy.com Website: https://www.biography.com/business-figure/mark-zuckerberg.

Biography.com Editors. (2020, June 10). *Steve Jobs Biography.* (A. T. Networks, Producer) Retrieved August 15, 2020, from The Biography.com website: https://www.biography.com/business-figure/steve-jobs.

Blue Moon Ethiopia. (2018, April 13). *Blue Moon Ethiopia.* Retrieved from Blue Moon Ethiopia: http://www.bluemoonethiopia.com/.

Bundervoet, T. (2016, January 19). Is Africa still rising? Taking stock halfway through the decade. *Future development.* Retrieved from https://www.brookings.edu/blog/future-development/2016/01/19/is-africa-still-rising-taking-stock-halfway-through-the-decade/.

Carnegie Mellon Africa. (2018). Retrieved April 13, 2018, from https://www.africa.engineering.cmu.edu/.

Carnegie Mellon University. (2020). *Carnegie Mellon University Africa.* Retrieved April 24, 2020, from Alumni Impact: https://www.africa.engineering.cmu.edu/alumni-impact/index.html.

Chapman, W. (2019). Africa to lead world in population growth. *U.S. News & World Report.*

Cision PR Newswire. (2019, December 30). *Tony Elumelu foundation announces final 2,100 African entrepreneurs for the inaugural TEF-UNDP entrepreneurship programme*. Retrieved April 24, 2020, from https://www.prnewswire.com/news-releases/tony-elumelu-foundation-announces-final-2-100-african-entrepreneurs-for-the-inaugural-tef-undp-entrepreneurship-programme-300979878.html.

Deloitte LLP. (2015). *Facebook's economic global impact.* Deloitte LLP.

Diallo, B. (2015). *A timeline of Clarisse Iribagiza's tech exploits.* Retrieved January 12, 2021, from https://www.afrikatech.com/health/a-timeline-of-clarisse-iribagizas-tech-exploits/.

Diouf, M. (2003, September). Engaging postcolonial cultures: African youth and public spaces. *African Studies Review, 46*(2), 1–12. Retrieved from https://www.jstor.org/stable/1514823.

Dolan, K. A. (2015, June 12). Africa's most promising young entrepreneurs: Forbes Africa's 30 under 30 for 2015. (T. Tshabalala, Ed.) *The little black book of billionaire secrets.*

Eastaugh, S. (2017, October 24). *The solar-powered cart that can charge 80 cell phones at once.* Retrieved April 16, 2018, from https://www.cnn.com/2016/08/09/africa/ared-solar-charging-kiosk-henri-nyakarundi/index.html.

Frangoul, A. (2019, July 22). *Sustainable energy.* (CNBC, Producer) Retrieved April 26, 2020, from *The biggest wind farm in Africa officially up and running.* https://www.cnbc.com/2019/07/22/the-biggest-wind-farm-in-africa-is-officially-up-and-running.html.

GSM Association. (2016). *The mobil economy: Africa 2016.* GSM Association.

Harper, S. R., & Davis III, C. H. (2012). They (don't) care about education: A counternarrative on black male students' response to inequitable schooling. *Education Foundations* (Winter-Spring 2012), 107.

Hesketh, B. (2019, March 29). *The leadership project, growth hack your life.* Retrieved January 12, 2021, from https://www.thelegacyproject.co.za/2019/03/29/bheki-kunene-founder-mindtrix/.

Human Rights Watch. (1999, April 18). *More than 120,000 child soldiers fighting in Africa.* Retrieved from Human Rights Watch. https://www.hrw.org/news/1999/04/18/more-120000-child-soldiers-fighting-africa.

Ichikowitz Family Foundation. (2020). *African youth survey 2020-the rise of Afro-Optimism.* Ichikowitz Family Foundation.

IRENA. (2015). *Africa 2030: Roadmap for a renewable energy future.* The International Renewable Energy Agency. Retrieved from www.irena.org/remap.

IRENA. (2019). *Scaling up renewable deployment in Africa.* International Renewable Energy Agency.

IRENA. (2020). *Renewables beyond 2030: The key role of youth in the global energy transformation.* International Renewable Energy Agency.

Kelly, T., & Dalphond, Z. V. (2013, January 16). *Africa: Using icts for transformational development.* (World Bank) Retrieved from Information and Communication for Development.

Kenya Youth Employment and Opportunities Project. (2020). *About KYEOP.* Retrieved April 23, 2020, from http://mis.kyeop.go.ke/about-nc/.

Kenyan Private Sector Alliance. (2016). *Kenya youth empowerment project*. Retrieved April 23, 2020, from https://kepsa.or.ke/kyep/

Kilian, A. (2017, July 19). Africa's energy future lies in solar energy says CEO. *Engineering News*. Retrieved April 5, 2018, from http://www.engineeringnews.co.za/article/africas-energy-future-lies-in-solar-energy-says-ceo-2017-07-19.

Kimando, L. N. (2012, June). Factors affecting the success of youth enterprise development funded projects in Kenya: A survey of Kigumo district Muranga County. *Internatinal Journal of Business and Commerce, 1*(10), 61–81.

Kinai, A. (2018, April 18). *IBM research blog*. (IBM, Producer) Retrieved April 24, 2020, from *IBM and Twiga Foods introduce blockchain-based microfinancing for food kiosk owners in Kenya*. https://www.ibm.com/blogs/research/2018/04/ibm-twiga-foods/.

Kuwonu, F. (2016, April). Harvesting the Sun. *Africa renewal on line*. Retrieved April 16, 2018, from https://www.un.org/africarenewal/magazine/april-2016/harvesting-sun.

Makerere University. (2020, April 23). *Coronavirus resource center*. Retrieved April 23, 2020, from *A collaborative effort spearheading the development of an open design low cost ventilator*. https://coronavirus.mak.ac.ug/articles/20200315/collaborative-effort-spearheading-development-open-design-low-cost-ventilator.

May, K. T. (2013, March 13). *Ted Blog*. Retrieved April 24, 2020, from *William and the Windmill" wins Grand Jury Award at SXSW*. https://blog.ted.com/william-and-the-windmill-wins-grand-jury-award-at-sxsw/.

Mora, R. A. (2014). *Counter-narrative* (Center for Intercultural Dialogue, No., 36), 2014.

Moving Windmill Project. (2013). *William Kamkwamba*. Retrieved April 24, 2020, from http://www.williamkamkwamba.com/about.html.

Mukasa, A. D., Mutambatsere, E., & Triki, Y. A. (2013). *Development of wind energy in Africa*. African Development Bank.

Musau, Z. (2017). Entrepreneurial universities: Marry Scholar Research with Business Acumen. *AfricaRenewal Special Edition, 2017*, 10.

Netflix. (2019, January 25). *The boy who harnessed the wind*. Retrieved April 24, 2020, from https://www.netflix.com/title/80200047.

Network World. (2008, August 5). *Networkworld*. Retrieved April 23, 2020, from *Universities to translate Firefox into African language*. https://www.networkworld.com/article/2274515/universities-to-translate-firefox-into-african-language.html.

Nuwer, R. (2017, October 9). *Rural Rwanda is home to a new solar power idea*. Retrieved April 15, 2018, from http://www.bbc.com/future/story/20171009-rural-rwanda-is-home-to-a-pioneering-new-solar-power-idea.

Oates, J. P. (2015). *Cell phones in Africa: Communication lifeline*. Pew Research Center.

Okoth, C. (2018, May 22). *New vision*. Retrieved April 23, 2020, from *Govt disburses sh17.5b to youth through Venture Capital Fund*. https://www.newvision.co.ug/new_vision/news/1478274/govt-disburses-sh175b-youth-venture-capital-fund.

Okunlola, B. (2019). *How Julie Alexander Fourie founded one of Africa's largest mobile servicing companies*. Retrieved January 12, 2021, from https://foundersafrica.com/how-julie-alexander-fourie-founded-one-of-africas-largest-mobile-servicing-companies/.

Rhodan, M. (2013, December 4). *Time Magazine*. Retrieved April 24, 2020, from 30 People Under 30 Changing the World. https://ideas.time.com/2013/12/06/these-are-the-30-people-under-30-changing-the-world/slide/william-kamkwamba/.

Rise Networks. (2015). *Abiola Olaniran, Founder of Gamesole is RISE youth of the week*. Retrieved January 12, 2021, from https://risenetworks.org/yotw/abiola-olaniran-founder-of-gamsole-is-rise-youth-of-the-week/.

Solorzano, D. G., & Yosso, T. J. (2001). Critical race and latcrit theory and method: Counter-storytelling. *International Journal of Qualitative Studies in Education, 14*(4), 471–495.

TechCamp. (n.d.). *Raindolf Owusu*. Retrieved January 12, 2021, from https://techcamp.america.gov/bios/1676/.

Ted Talks. (2007). *William Kamkwamba, Inventor*. Retrieved February 16, 2018, from Ted Talks. https://www.ted.com/speakers/william_kamkwamba.

The Anzisha Prize. (2019). *About*. Retrieved January 12, 2021, from https://anzishaprize.org/about/.

The Tony Elumelu Foundation. (2016). *Catalysing Entrepreneurship: 2010–2015 Impact Report*.

The Tony Elumelu Foundation. (2020). Retrieved April 25, 2020, from https://www.tonyelumelufoundation.org/.

The Tony Elumelu Foundation. (2020a, April 9). *Making and impact during Covid-19 pandemic*. Retrieved April 22, 2020, from here's how to get tested for Covid-19 from the Comfort of your Home. https://www.tonyelumelufoundation.org/making-impact-during-covid-19-pandemic/heres-how-to-get-tested-for-covid-19-from-the-comfort-of-your-home.

The Tony Elumelu Foundation. (2020b, April 9). *Making impact during Covid 19 pandemic*. Retrieved April 22, 2020, from *How I am helping my community survive the COVID 19 pandemic*. https://www.tonyelumelufoundation.org/making-impact-during-covid-19-pandemic/how-i-am-helping-my-community-survive-the-covid-19-pandemic.

The Tony Elumelu Foundation. (2020c, April 9). *Making impact during covid-19 pandemic*. Retrieved April 22, 2020, from *Erico is refocusing primebotics with new solutions to mitigate the spread of covid-19 in cabo verde*. https://www.tonyelumelufoundation.org/making-impact-during-covid-19-pandemic/erico-is-refocusing-primebotics-with-new-solutions-to-mitigate-the-spread-of-covid19-in-cabo-verde.

The Tony Elumelu Foundation. (2020, April 13). *Making impact during Covid-19 pandemic*. Retrieved April 22, 2020, from *Mohammed-akamaras lili tap provides Africans in sierra leone a safer and unique handwashing*. https://www.tonyelume

lufoundation.org/making-impact-during-covid-19-pandemic/mohammed-aka maras-lili-tap-provides-africans-in-sierra-leone-a-safer-and-unique-handwashing.

The Tony Elumelu Foundation. (2020, April 14). *Making impact during covid-19 pandemic*. Retrieved April 22, 2020, from If You are in Niger Dial 701 for Advice on how to prevent covid-19: https://www.tonyelumelufoundation.org/making-impact-during-covid-19-pandemic/if-youre-in-niger-dial-701-for-advice-on-how-to-prevent-covid19/.

Tiyou, T. (2016, October 19). *The five biggest wind energy markets in Africa*. (I. S. Society, Producer) Retrieved April 22, 2018, from Renewable Energy Focus.com: http://www.renewableenergyfocus.com/view/44926/the-five-biggest-wind-energy-markets-in-africa/.

Tiyou, T. (2018). The state of wind energy in Africa. *ESI Africa*(1), 4 and 5. Retrieved April 26, 2020

United Nations. (2019). *World population prospect 2019*. United Nations, Department of Economic and Social Affairs, Population Division.

United Nations, Department of Economics and Social Affairs, Population Division. (2017). *World population prospects: The 2017 revision, DVD edition*. United Nations.

United Nations, Department of Public Information. (2017). Youth dividend or ticking time bomb. *Africarenewal special edition 2017*. Strategic Communication Division.

WaziData. (n.d.). *WaziData*. Retrieved January 12, 2021, from http://www.wazidata.com/.

Wickramanayake, J. (2020, April 3). *Africa renewal*. Retrieved April 24, 2020, from *Coronavirus: Meet 10 young people leading the covid-19 response in their communities*. https://www.un.org/africarenewal/web-features/coronavirus/meet-10-young-people-leading-covid-19-response-their-communities.

Winstead, W. R. (2018). African youth entrepreneurship models. In A. L. Narendra K Rustagi (Ed.), *Entrepreneurship growth strategies for Africa* (pp. 49–68). Neeraj Publishing House.

World Bank. (2016). *Doing business 2016: Measuring regulatory quality and efficiency*. World Bank.

Yale University. (2021). *Yale young African scholars*. Retrieved January 12, 2021, from https://africanscholars.yale.edu/people/takunda-chingonzo.

14

Technology Entrepreneurs: Surviving the Valley of Death in the Nigerian Innovation Ecosystem

Oluwaseun David Adepoju

Introduction

Technology has transformed our lives in ways unimaginable. Many countries have built innovative and creative economies due to the technology boom in the last two digital decades. However, as some countries boast of a working creative economy today, the same is not the case for others who are still struggling in technology and innovation investment. This aforementioned is manifested through the lack of support and encouragement for technology entrepreneurs who are the propagators of innovation. Another factor that is evident in countries with shaky creative economies is a poor research environment to propel innovative ideas. Technology entrepreneurs in such countries have been having difficulties surviving the valley of death. The country of consideration in this study is Nigeria, a country whose economy is mostly dependent on crude oil. The study examined the challenges of technology entrepreneurs in Nigeria and also made policy recommendations in promoting the creative economy, particularly at a time when world economies are diversifying into a more innovative and creative one.

Entrepreneurship has been a significant factor in the economic development and the promotion of the innovation ecosystem of any country and

O. D. Adepoju (✉)
African Leadership University, Kigali, Rwanda
e-mail: oadepoju@alueducation.com

should be treated with utmost importance. To corroborate this, Alvarez and Barney (2020) noted that "entrepreneurship has been a concept centered around creating opportunities in any ecosystems(Alvarez & Barney, 2020) further engaged entrepreneurship ideas as the major foundation for creating a fruitful economy through opportunity creation for the citizens. It is pertinent to also note entrepreneurship does not only create opportunities but also solve pressing societal challenges through social innovation. Commenting on the role of entrepreneurship in solving the world's grand challenges (Markman et al., 2019, p. 1) defined entrepreneurship as the " development of sustained applications and solutions that collectively address grand challenges to make the world better". Alluding to the aforementioned, entrepreneurship is one of the most potent instruments to solving some of the most pressing global challenges that the world faces today and it must be explored appropriately in the execution of the Sustainable Development Goals. Entrepreneurship spans across various innovative products and services from individuals to create a robust collaborative and creative economy for a country. To support this assertion, Maciel and Fischer (2020) stated that collective actions in an entrepreneurial space create a robust and easily scalable venture ecosystems.One could use the aforementioned to support the "collaboration is the new competition" mantra, especially in the entrepreneurial space. Many countries have explored the collaboration and support models for entrepreneurial strategies, Nigeria included.

Nigeria, the largest economy in Africa is not excluded in entrepreneurial support for various young entrepreneurs and small-scale businesses in the quest to reduce youth unemployment. Tajudeen and Aare (2019) noted that "Nigeria in the last three decades, has had to grapple with the perennial problem of unemployment". The unemployment statistics in Nigeria has shown a consistent increase over time. According to the National Bureau of Statistics of Nigeria (2020), Unemployment Rate in Nigeria averaged 12.84% from 2006 until 2020, reaching an all time high of 27.10% in the second quarter of 2020. Tajudeen and Aare (2019), Nwambam and Eze (2017), Saidi Atanda and Enilolobo (2018) and Ayoade et al. (2020) have all stated that unemployment in Nigeria is a menace and the best way to solve it is through deliberate entrepreneurial support for Nigerian young people. One question that has consistently begged for an answer has been, " where is the outcome of the support that has been provided by the Nigerian government over the years?". The aforementioned is in line with Ayoade et al. (2020), who stated that it is worrisome, that despite the accessibility of technology and government contributions towards entrepreneurial development in Nigeria, entrepreneurship has not performed creditably well due to varying challenges.

Several studies have been done to study the challenges of entrepreneurs and startups generally in Nigeria. For example, studies by Mohammed et al. (2017), Ovwiroro (2017), Onimole and Olaiya (2018) and Oladunjoye and Adewumi (2018) have all observed that challenges such as lack of financial support, poor entrepreneurial curriculum, hostile environment and weak innovation ecosystem are the significant challenges facing entrepreneurs in Nigeria. However, little or no research has been done to understand why technology entrepreneurs/startups do not succeed. In lieu of the aforementioned, this study seeks to understand why most tech startups have not been surviving the valley of death in the Nigerian innovation ecosystem.

Literature Review

Entrepreneurial Development in Nigeria

One of the precursors of economic prosperity in any country is the investment in entrepreneurship (Chauke & Obadire, 2020; Khyareh, 2020; Loukil, 2020; Wanass & Shahaza, 2020). To corroborate the aforementioned, Buanyomi and Barnard (2020) stated that entrepreneurship creates competitiveness in an economy that eventually leads to national wealth and a healthy Gross Domestic Product. Entrepreneurship promotion and development do not only make the citizens of a nation independent, financially secure and innovative; it also contributes to the national wealth and economic development. The success of an economy depends on a number of factors including entrepreneurial development. According to Jayeola et al. (2018) there is a strong correlation between economic environment and entrepreneurial development. The economic environment of a country determines the entrepreneurial development of such a country and vice versa. The literature above all points to the fact that entrepreneurship is a very important foundation for economic development in any economy.

Some entrepreneurial scholars have pointed to the role of entrepreneurship in wealth creation and poverty reduction in Nigeria. Hu et al. (2017; Balogun (2019) and Agu and Nwachukwu (2020) stated that "entrepreneurship is pertinent to the analysis of how new ideas for reconfiguring objects in the material and social world can be harnessed to enhance a nation's wealth". In the same line of thought Kim et al. (2018) stated that the small-scale businesses that are focused on people have the potential to create innovative entrepreneurs that will contribute to national wealth and create more jobs. Summarily, entrepreneurship remains a critical factor in the creation and implementation of growth and development of a country. We could conclude from the reviewed literature that entrepreneurship is pivotal to economic prosperity.

As entrepreneurial innovation became very popular in the last two decades, Nigeria has also not been left out in this area. According to entrepreneurship has been a major driver in bridging the unemployment and innovation gap in Nigeria. The Nigerian government started making entrepreneurial investments in the early 80s to reduce poverty and to create more jobs. The first contribution of the federal government of Nigeria was seen in investment in entrepreneurial education. According to Onimole and Olaiya (2018), "Entrepreneurship education in Nigeria became necessary due to the challenges of globalisation and trade liberation experienced in the 1980s, which led to the creation of the Structural Adjustment Programme (SAP) that brought about a considerable reduction in public sector job placements". It is also noteworthy that the federal government integrated a lot of entrepreneurship education programmes into undergraduate programmes across universities and polytechnics in the country which took effect from the 2007/2008 academic session.

Subsequently, both the Nigerian Universities Commission (NUC) and National Board for Technical Education (NBTE), regulatory bodies for both Universities and Polytechnics/Monotechnics, respectively, enforced the implementation of government's directive with regard to the inclusion of entrepreneurship studies in higher institutions' curriculum as compulsory courses. Presently, entrepreneurship studies have been successfully introduced to almost all departments of the Nigerian higher institutions. Interestingly, the creation of entrepreneurship centres in higher institutions of learning in Nigeria has further enhanced the achievement of entrepreneurship education goals in the country since these centres are saddled with the responsibilities of coordinating the entire process and designing programmes that could help in promoting entrepreneurship education in Nigeria. The entrepreneurship courses avail students the opportunity of gaining both theoretical/conceptual knowledge of the course as well as the practical aspect of it which students are required to spend a few weeks learning practical knowledge in entrepreneurship businesses around their school environments.

In conclusion, Ojo and Oluwatayo (2016), stated that entrepreneurship is a veritable tool for the achievement of inclusive growth and consequently sustainable development. They further stated that there are many opportunities entrepreneurs can harness in Nigeria given the demographic dividends.

In fact, the youths constitute about 60% of the Nigerian population. Opportunities include but are not limited to agriculture, creation of place utility for manufactured products (toiletries, beverages, among others), repairs and servicing of mobile phones, computers, generators, cars, etc.

Technology Entrepreneurs: Prospects and Challenges

Entrepreneurship seems to be a spider with many tentacles; however, in the last two decades; technology entrepreneurship has been on the leading side all around the world. According to Wright and Clarrysse (2020), technology entrepreneurship is defined as those ventures that make use of or invest in emerging technologies before these technologies are implemented in products sold in mainstream markets. The authors further stated that the success of technology entrepreneurship in any ecosystem is dependent on the founder's resilience, government support and an enabling market system. Pathak and Muralidharan (2020) on the other hand considered technology entrepreneurship in terms of access to technological resources. They posited that technology entrepreneurship is a two-stage process that involves access to and use of new technologies and technological resources by entrepreneurs. The two-stage approach to technology entrepreneurship Pathak and Muralidharan (2020) reiterates the fact that access to technologies does not mean automatic use of such technologies by entrepreneurs and vice versa.

Nigeria, like other developing countries that are heavily reliant on the export of natural resources, decided to join the league of nations that are benefiting from the dividends of technological investment and incubation by commissioning the first technology incubation centre in Agege, Lagos state in 1993. However, according to the Federal Ministry of Science and Technology Report of 2005, the formal programme of technology incubation in the country was only launched with the promulgation of Decree No. 5 of 1995 which also entrusted the supervision and coordination of the programme to the Federal Ministry of Science and Technology with effect from July 1995. The report states further that there are currently 21 Technology Business Incubation Centres in 21 states out of the 36 states of the federation. This shows the efforts of the federal government of Nigeria in promoting technology entrepreneurship and innovation by investing in technology incubation centres. In spite of these, the pertinent question to ask is if these incubation centres are functioning to their full capacities or just there for decoration and record sake. As Obaji et al. (2016) posited, "Technology business incubation initiatives have been implemented in developing countries including Nigeria since the 1990s with uneven levels of success".

The challenges facing technology entrepreneurs in Nigeria has been scantily studied. However, inferences can be made from other works of literature that established the challenges of technology incubation and other issues relating to technology startups. In stating the problems of technological incubation and technology entrepreneurship in Nigeria, Obaji et al. (2016) noted that inadequate funding for tech startups, inconsistent government policies on science and technology and lack of technological innovation policy. Another major challenge facing technological entrepreneurship in Nigeria as stated by Obaji et al. (2016) is creating links between knowledge generation and business development. This link is called the valley of death. He further stated that it has been challenging to commercialise knowledge and ideas from researchers in the country's universities and other research institutes to value-added innovative products, processes and services.

The Innovation Ecosystem and the Valley of Death

According to Jucevicius et al. (2016), bridging the gap between the research economy and commercial economy otherwise known as the "valley of death" remains one of the key concerns of any mature and institutionalised innovation ecosystems. In addition, Cardozo (2019) defined the valley of death as the road between a discovery generated from basic research to a commercial product or process is long and, according to some, rife with significant roadblocks. The aforementioned points to the fact that ideas and discoveries are not enough, there is yet a long journey to take if the ideas and discoveries must come to fruition. The journey however, is full of uncertainties and risks. The concept of the valley of death is a heterogeneous one as many scholars have adapted it to various conditions but no matter the situation it is being used to describe, it represents and defines a familiar premise of plunging and break in a journey to corroborate the aforementioned, the valley of death describes the metaphorical depths to which promising science and technology too often plunge, never to emerge and reach their full potential. Aragón et al. (2019) noted that "there exists the concept of a valley of death that prevents the progress of science from the laboratory bench to the point where it provides the basis of a commercially successful business or product".

In another study, Hai and Li (2019) stated that "the gap in resources for technology demonstration and development (TD&D) is colloquially known as the valley of death". The actors engaged in moving innovations from discovery through commercialisation are academia, small businesses, the investor community and commercial industry. For these actors, it is within this valley that much potential innovation dies for lack of the resources to develop them to a stage where the industry or the investor community can recognise their commercial potential and assess the risk associated with bringing them to market.

A lot of innovation ecosystem scholars have written extensively on the solutions to bridging the valley of death in various innovation ecosystems. One prominent scholar is Klitsie et al. (2019), who propounded a design innovation perspective to bridging the valley of death. Supporting the design innovation perspective of Klitsie et al. (2019), Kolarz et al. (2015) noted that Innovation by design has the potential of mitigating the Valley of Death by structuring the process of innovation from creative ideas to valuable propositions. In recent times, other scholars who have contributed to the innovation ecosystem and valley of death, proffering different design solutions are Micheli et al. (2018), Liedtka (2018), Price and Wrigley (2016) and Rae (2016). These theoretical reviews will form the background for the explanations in the subsequent section of this study.

Methodology

This research asked pertinent questions such as the examination of the challenges faced by technology entrepreneurs in Nigeria and how Nigeria is fairing in the global innovation index. The objectives of this research are to examine the challenges faced by technology entrepreneurs in Nigeria and how Nigeria is fairing in the global innovation index.

This study used the complementary research method which seeks to understand why most technology entrepreneurs in Nigeria do not survive the gap between their ideal conceptions and transforming their ideas into a profitable product. The approach combined qualitative in-depth interviews for selected technology entrepreneurs and quantitative secondary data on Nigeria's position in the Global Innovation Index from the Global Innovation Ranking Document. The paper also has a practitioner tone because it seeks to speak directly not only to the technology entrepreneurship researchers but to the technology entrepreneurs working in the field. The complementary approach has been used to confirm the responses from the interview as a true representation of Nigeria's image in the Global Innovation Index. The Global Innovation Ranking data is used in supporting, affirming corroborating the interview data. Purposive sampling was used in selecting 10 startups in the technology industry for the in-depth interview. Purposive sampling is also often referred to as "judgemental sampling" or "expert sampling". As a practitioner in the field of research, the researcher selected the respondent for the interview based on their understanding of those who are able to respond to the question. A critical and empirical review of academic literature was made to make concept connections and inform policy recommendations made to solve the problems stated in this study. The Global Innovation Index was also consulted to understand the innovation trend in Nigeria between 2007 and the present. There was also a comparative analysis of Nigeria's innovation ranking with selected countries in Africa such as Kenya, Rwanda, Egypt and South Africa. Policy recommendations were given to the major actors (academia, business, government and startups) in the Nigerian innovation ecosystem based on the outcome of the study.

Qualitative data was analysed using thematic analysis while descriptive statistics and frequency count was used in analysing the secondary data (Innovation Index). The complementary method has helped the researcher in confirming that the interview data are a true representation of Nigeria's positioning in the Global Innovation Ranking since the success or failure of grassroots innovation contributes directly to the ranking globally.

Results and Discussion

See Tables 14.1 and 14.2.

Discussion of Findings

The discussion will be grouped in the flow of the themes identified in the table of representative quotes above. This will help in tying together similar experiences from the respondents and by implication create a better picture of the challenges faced by the technology entrepreneurs.

Theme 1: EdTech, E-learning and Learning Management Systems

A software developer ***TE/INT1*** narrated his journey into technology entrepreneurship. When he was asked what his experiences have been so far as a software developer in the education space, he had this to say,

> I started developing learning management software for secondary schools in 2010. The features of my software would greatly help schools in managing student data, ensure an effective grading system and an easy assessment system for staff and students. I took a loan to develop the prototype in 2011, and I started looking for clients in secondary schools in Lagos state Nigeria. I visited 20 schools and had several meetings in the space of one year with no subscription to my product even though all of them confirmed my solution to be

Table 14.1 Profile of respondents

Code	Industry	Business lifecycle	Location	Product	Challenge
TE/1	EdTech	Growth Stage	Lagos Nigeria	Learning Management System	Trust in foreign products by client
TE/2	FinTech	Growth Stage	Lagos Nigeria	Micro-Loans for SMEs	Police Harassment
TE/3	EdTech	Growth Stage	Ibadan Nigeria	Examination Preparation Platforms for University Admission Seekers	Failure of government acquisition promise
TE/4	HealthTech	Growth Stage	Ibadan Nigeria	Virtual medical records management system	Commitment issues from the government hospitals
TE/5	Delivery and Logistics	Growth Stage	Port Harcourt, Nigeria	Motorbike Delivery system and Digital Errand Services	Cultural Discrimination
TE/6	Business Solutions(UI/UX)	Growth Stage	Lagos, Nigeria	Business Branding and Customer Experience Design	Poor pricing of services
TE/7	FinTech	Growth Stage	Lagos, Nigeria	Digital Savings	Massive withdrawal of funds due to competition propaganda
TE/8	EdTech	Growth Stage	Ibadan, Nigeria	Digital Homeschooling System	Excuses on expensive Internet data subscription
TE/9	FinTech	Growth Stage	Abuja, Nigeria	Digital Debt Relief System	Defaulting in agreements from customers and regulatory issues from the Security Exchange Commision

(continued)

Table 14.1 (continued)

Code	Industry	Business lifecycle	Location	Product	Challenge
TE/10	FinTech	Growth Stage	Lagos, Nigeria	Blockchain Encrypted Cryptocurrency Exchange Platform	Perception issues on cryptocurrencies as scam

disruptive. In 2012, I eventually got a school that was ready to subscribe to my solution. On the day the deal was to be signed, I got to the Principal's office as early as possible. At around 11 am, the principal came in to inform me that the management of the school had changed their minds in going on with subscribing to my solution. I was emotionally broken, but I summoned the courage to move on. Two months later, I heard from an insider that the school eventually subscribed to the software by a Pakistani software developer at a higher price than my offering to them. It is sad to know that they did not use the software for a single day for the one-year subscription they made because they could not navigate the solution that did not infuse local uniqueness in its features.

This is a typical situation in the Nigerian innovation ecosystem where we don't appreciate the solutions being provided by indigenous technology entrepreneurs. There seems to be a culture of validating everything that comes from abroad which most times gives us less value compared to what we can access at home from our homegrown solutions. It is not impossible that this same situation described above is responsible for the massive brain drain and innovation emigration in Nigeria.

In the same vein, one of the most popular homegrown technology solutions in Nigeria in the education space did not survive the valley of death and died in 2013 after a long time of fighting for survival. The founder ***TE/INT3*** had this to say;

I built this platform in 2010 to help students preparing for university entrance exams to have access to a compendium of past questions that they can solve and get their grades in real-time. I believe this to be the solution to the massive failures in the entrance examinations. In my prototyping stage, a coaching centre used this platform to prepare 50 students for the JAMB exam, and none of the candidates scored less than 260 in the exam. I pushed this solution to the federal ministry of education in 2012 to enable a wide acceptance in schools. I was invited to a pitch competition with three other Edtech startups, and my idea was selected as the best. I was promised some money to keep the platform

Table 14.2 Representative quotes supporting the interview themes

Author(s)	Respondent Alignment	Theme(s)	Quote	Analysis
Mittal (2019)	TE/2, TE/9 and TE/10	Digital payment	"Digital payments, mobile lending and personal finance are currently the most popular areas where FinTechs are operating in"	Fintech entrepreneurs are disrupting the mobile and digital payments system in Nigeria
Franklin (2019)	TE/2, TE/9 and TE/10	Fintech regulations	"A formal regulatory framework, if done right, could encourage innovation and growth in the burgeoning fintech sector" "In March 2018, The CBN along with Nigeria Interbank Settlement System introduced a regulatory sandbox with the aim to facilitate digital innovation by the FinTech companies"	The regulatory system in the Nigerian Fintech space is still largely unstable as the financial sectors' stakeholders are still trying to understand the evolving fintech space
Pius (2019)	TE/1, TE/3 and TE/8	Learning Management System	"Even though Nigeria is a latecomer in the incorporation of learning management systems in its classrooms, it is gradually catching up with the rest of the world in terms of deploying much needed learning management systems in its classrooms to aid effective teaching and help improve the teaching–learning experience"	The Nigeria Educational landscape is evolving gradually in embracing and fully understanding the role of LMS's in the effective delivery of their curriculum. This struggle to understand the innovation is probably responsible for the poor acceptance of respondent TE/3 and TE/8 innovation

(continued)

Table 14.2 (continued)

Author(s)	Respondent Alignment	Theme(s)	Quote	Analysis
Yaya et al. (2016)	TE/4	Health Records Challenges	Findings show that the major challenges faced in handling health records in the surveyed hospitals include: poor funding, inadequate computer and other ICT devices, poor skill in computing, harsh environmental conditions, lack of preservation and conservation policy	The challenges in health records management in Nigeria seems humongous and this is evidently manifested with the experience of respondent TE/4 who received cold shoulders from the stakeholder of the Nigerian health sector
Techpoint (2020)	TE/5	E-commerce and logistics	Some companies decided to move on from the e-commerce and logistics business and others continued the struggle for profitability, thus causing a rethink in business models. Despite the odds, the resilience might be paying off as eCommerce companies are getting more attention	Nigeria has experienced a lot of e-commerce and logistics business death due to issues such as scepticism. Trust issues and cultural biases such as the one experienced by the respondent TE/5. The future however looks bright with innovative business models
Omeh (2017)	TE/5	Digital Errand Services	Errand service business in Nigeria is capable of generating millions of Naira on a monthly basis. People are very busy these days and the reality of the modern day is not helping matters in any way. Not even in the near future does any solution seem to be in sight. Instead, more people would be getting busier than ever. Thereby making the business of errand services to be more viable and among the best jobs in Nigeria	Delivery, logistic and errand services have been predicted to be among the most profitable businesses in Nigeria but despite the potentials, there have been challenges faced by the startup in this business which they battle every day to overcome through consistent model tweaking

running since I was still an undergraduate student then. I was also promised that the solution would be introduced to all the secondary schools in Nigeria. This is seven years after the promise; it is still a promise till today. I stopped running the platform in 2013 when I could not sustain the management. I have moved on to other things, and I hope to return to Edtech when I have enough resources and support from the government and external investors.

One would have thought that the government should be the best supporter of disruptive innovation, but this was not the case with the technology mentioned above. It is good to encourage young people to be innovative but is even better to give them support and an enabling environment to thrive and gain traction. The aforementioned Edtech platform did not also survive the valley of death in the Nigeria innovation ecosystem due to false promises from the government.

Theme 2: Fintech and Digital Payment Solutions
TE/INT2, a fintech technology entrepreneur who developed a platform that makes SMEs access micro-loans from investors narrated how he was always being harassed by the Nigeria Police force to give them money because they think he is the one giving loans to people on his platform. He had this to say about his journey as a technology entrepreneur so far,

> I created a platform that brings together loan givers and Small and Medium Scales businessmen and women. The platform was running smoothly for roughly six months before I started facing police harassment. I was accused of online fraud twice. I was arrested several times without any real reason. None of my clients accused me of an anomaly, and when the harassment got to a peak for me, I relocated to Kenya where I launched my platform in Kenya Shillings, and I have enjoyed the support and an enabling environment so far since I moved out of Nigeria. I was willing to help Nigerian SMEs with my platform, but the environment was hostile to me.

This aforementioned is another sad story of hostility to an innovative solution that ensures financial inclusion for SMEs. This is another case of innovation emigrating out of Nigeria to Kenya. One could say in this case that "the problem is not the scarcity of innovators but the discouraging innovation ecosystem that is not favourable to let innovation survive".

Theme 3: E-commerce, logistics and E-errand services
TE/INT 5, an e-commerce and logistics startup stated thus:

> I have invested a lot of time, research and resources into my platform until I realized that we left out one issue, and that is the issue of trust. People still have

issues trusting platforms where they have to pay online before they get their products and services. Despite our hard work to serve the customers better, our research shows that we have low patronage because of trust issues. We know that the platform economy is evolving in Africa but we expect people to have overcome the trust barrier.

The situation above may be the reason why some e-commerce companies that could not pivot into pay on delivery model closed shop. Many platforms, such as the one described above, continue to struggle because of trust issues from the people. One cannot categorically say if it is a Nigerian issue only but it seems platform e-commerce and platform economies seem to be booming in other countries than Nigeria.

Nigeria in the Global Innovation Ranking

It is very pertinent to examine in retrospect, Nigeria's position on the Global Innovation Index and where it is at the moment to ascertain the progress Nigeria has made so far in her innovation ecosystem. The ranking from 2007 to 2020 has been examined. Table 14.3 shows the position of Nigeria in the global Innovation index. It shows the general ranking and for 14 years between 2007 and 2020 (Table 14.4).

Table 14.3 Nigeria's Global Innovation Ranking (2007–2020)

Year	Rank
2007	72
2008	70
2009	70
2010	96
2011	96
2012	123
2013	120
2014	110
2015	128
2016	114
2017	119
2018	116
2019	114
2020	121

Source INSEAD WIPO Global Innovation Ranking

Table 14.4 Comparative Global Innovation Ranking of Nigeria, Kenya, South Africa, Egypt and Rwanda

Year	Nigeria	Kenya	South Africa	Egypt	Rwanda
2007	72	78	38	74	–
2008	70	–	43	76	–
2009	70	78	43	76	–
2010	96	83	51	74	–
2011	96	89	59	87	109
2012	123	96	73	103	102
2013	120	99	58	108	112
2014	110	85	53	99	102
2015	128	92	60	91	94
2016	114	80	54	107	83
2017	119	80	57	105	99
2018	116	78	58	95	99
2019	114	77	63	92	94
2020	121	86	60	96	91

Source INSEAD WIPO Global Innovation Ranking

Data Analysis

Scatter plot showing the pattern of Nigeria's rank in the Global Innovation Index (2007–2020).

A comparative analysis of the Global Innovation Ranking of Nigeria, Kenya, South Africa, Egypt and Rwanda (2007–2020).

Discussion of Secondary Quantitative Data

The scatter plot showed Nigeria's inconsistent rise and fall in the Global Innovation Ranking except for three years stability maintained between 2009 and 2011. The decline after a major increase seems like a year or two intervals. It can be concluded that there is no innovation policy sustainability in Nigeria as many innovative programmes do not last before it's truncated. This situation can be used in explaining and justifying the challenges faced by the respondents in this study as the entrepreneurial ecosystem of a country will always be a reflection of how innovative the country is. To corroborate this, Abiola Adebowale (2017) in his research on innovation policies for industrialisation in Nigeria discovered that the outcomes of the innovation policies in Nigeria are different because the efforts and commitments to the policies were different over time. INSEAD Global Innovation Report has reported almost every report that lack of coordinated vision, lack of project continuity policies during political power change and partisan attitude towards policies implementation as factors responsible for the inconsistency in Nigeria's innovation ranking. Innovation may not thrive well in Nigeria if deliberate actions are not taken to ensure its cross-tenure sustainability. The implementation of cross-tenure implementation policy will aid Nigeria in ensuring full implementation of its innovation policies and innovation ecosystem support systems, which by implication will help more entrepreneurs, especially technology entrepreneurs to survive the valley of death.

Worthy of note is the notable improvement that was noticed between 2012 and 2015 compared to the previous years. This could be as a result of the creation of the Ministry of communication technology which was created in 2011 as an independent ministry from the Ministry of Science and Technology under the President Jonathan administration. To corroborate this assertion, Techpoint (2020) chronicled the achievement of the Ministry of Information Technology between 2011 and 2015 under the leadership of Dr Mobolaji Johnson. Some of the notable achievements are;

- Digitisation Projects for in-house and external government services
- Investment in ICT skills acquisition programs
- National ICT Policy 2012
- National Broadband Plan 2013—21,018
- Guidelines for Nigerian Content in ICT 2013
- Migration of all governments Ministries, Departments and Agencies (MDAs) to the ".gov.ng" domain.

These achievements and many others positioned Nigeria to rank to improve in ranking from 96 in 2011 to 123 in 2012. This is a sign that with capable leadership, the Nigerian innovation ecosystem can blossom much more than what it is at the moment. Another pointer to the success of Nigeria in innovation ranking within these years is the springing forth of several technology startups all around the country. Examples include gomyway.com, the first Nigerian carpooling startup which launched in 2015. Even though gomyway died just before its second birthday, the startup encouraged other startups to launch. Other tech startups that launched between 2001 and 2015 are Ynaija, DealDey, IrokoTV, Hotels.ng, Jumia.ng and many more. All these startups are a result of an enabling innovation environment and hopefully Nigeria returns to the playbook that enabled many young technology entrepreneurs to thrive between 2011 and 2015. It is a thing of pride to note that a larger percentage of the technology companies that launched around this time are still standing and waxing stronger in 2020 and have survived the valley of death. The analysis also showed a good jump from 114 in 2019 to 121 in 2020. This is possibly a sign that the addition of the Digital Economy aspect to the roles of the Communication Ministry, under the leadership of the new Minister of Communication and Digital Economy, Aliyu Pantami is bearing some good fruits.

On a continental level, the comparative analysis showed that Nigeria has been a leader in comparison with the other three countries with which it was compared. Egypt and Nigeria seem to show the same pattern except for the big difference that occurred in 2014 and 2015 where both countries had a pouted difference at almost the same proportion of rising and falling. Egypt had another significant fall in 2018 compared to Nigeria's trend. South Africa seems far from Nigeria, Egypt, Rwanda and Kenya at all fronts and this serves as a great insight into the factors that determine high innovation ranking. Comparing Rwanda and South Africa, we can see that even with the late coming of Rwanda into the Global Innovation Ranks, it started top high compared to South Africa and despite its steady fall over the years, it has still done fairly better than South Africa in the last ten years. Lastly, Kenya has the most inconsistent pattern in its innovation ranking.

These patterns show that Africa still has a long way to go in Innovation Investment, Innovation Policies and Entrepreneurial Support Systems. If Africa will match up with the big innovative ten such as South Korea, New Zealand and Estonia, there is a need for re-engineering our different innovation ecosystems through deliberate decision-making and Innovation Investments.

The triangulation of interview data, the Global Innovation Index data and literature review are connected by creating a balance between the interview story and the logic of the quantitative data in the Global Innovation Index.

Policy Recommendations

Policy Recommendation for Government

With the above established, the following policy recommendations are being proposed for consideration to solve this issue.

1. An agency for technology entrepreneurial development should be inaugurated and work directly with the Ministry of Science and Technology and the various universities in the country. The agency should be charged

with the responsibilities of seeking financial support of technological ideas, managing technological incubation centres and promoting/marketing of technological ideas to the world market.
2. As part of the yearly education budget, special provision should be made for technological innovation development for technology entrepreneurs and fresh inventors.
3. The federal government of Nigeria should consider launching a national programme of the creative economy which would bring a national consciousness and technology readiness for the country.
4. The support system for technological innovation would improve if the digital divide between the old generations and the new generations who are technologically savvy.
5. The Federal Ministry of Science and Technology should ensure a well-organised tech-valley to encourage venture capitalists to come and invest in innovative ideas of technology entrepreneurs.
6. Nigeria as a country has not been using the instrument of crowdfunding for innovation promotion, and as such, it is one of the best ways to gather financial resources to help technology entrepreneurs survive the valley of death.

Policy Recommendations for Academia

Academia is responsible for the knowledge economy in an innovation ecosystem. They are the backbone for the product that would eventually be seen in the market. Their role is of greater import, and the following are the recommendations for them;

1. University education curriculum should include technological touch to encourage innovative thinking by students.
2. University students should be encouraged to do more of applied research than basic research, thus improving their inquiry skills which could lead to innovative ideas.
3. The academia should aim to solve problems in the society rather than being problem discussants by equipping laboratories and workbench rooms with cutting edge technologies.
4. University Professors should live by example to students by showing interest in practical research and not just writing theoretical papers.
5. Researchers should do more of a tailored study based on the problems and needs observed in society.

Policy Recommendations for Businesses

The entrepreneurial terrain of Nigeria is growing by the day, but most businesses are not doing well because of a poor business plan. A good company may not get funding if it is poorly planned while a poor business can get funded if it is well presented. The following are the policy recommendation for businesses in Nigeria;

1. A proper concept of what the innovative idea is all about
2. A convincing proof should always be presented to venture capitalists for funding
3. A consistent gathering of fellow technology entrepreneurs to discuss and sharpen ideas
4. Taking individual innovations to knowledge hubs and incubators where further development could be made on the concept
5. Imbibing an enduring entrepreneurial spirit in the face of business failures

References

Adebowale, B. (2017). Innovation policies and sector development in Nigeria's oil palm industry: Lessons from Malaysia. *International Journal of Learning & Intellectual Capital, 14*(2), 135–153.

Agu, A., & Nwachukwu, A. (2020). Exploring the relevance of Igbo Traditional Business School in the development of entrepreneurial potential and intention in Nigeria. *Small Enterprise Research, 27*(2), 223–239.

Alvarez, S., & Barney, B. (2020). Has the concept of opportunities been fruitful in the field of entrepreneurship? *Academy of Management Perspectives, 34*(3), 300–310.

Aragón, A., Iturrioz, C., Narvaiza, L., & Parrilli, M. D. (2019). The role of social capital in regional innovation systems: Creative social capital and its institutionalization process. *Papers in Regional Science, 98*(1), 35–51.

Ayoade, A., Odetunde, O., & Falodun, B. (2020). Modeling and analysis of the impact of vocational education on the unemployment rate in Nigeria. *Applications & Applied Mathematics, 15*(1), 550–564.

Balogun, A. (2019). Impact of ghe millenium development goals - Microfinance schem on entrepreneurial development of youths in the Federal capital Territory, NigeriaI. *ICAN Journal of Accounting & Finance, 8*(2), 158–181.

Buanyomi, A., & Barnard, B. (2020). The future scenario of entrepreneurship responsible for significant GDP growth. *IUP Journal of Entrepreneurship Development, 17*(1), 41–91. *Business Management, 56*, 10–29.

Cardozo, N. (2019). Economic aspects of the deployment of fusion energy: The valley of death and the innovation cycle. *Philosophical Transactions of the Royal Society A: Mathematical, Physical & Engineering Sciences, 377*(2141), 1–9.

Chauke, & Obadire. (2020). Using gender differential motivations in youth entrepreneurship as economic survival strategy in South Africa. *Gender & Behaviour: Lfe Centre for Psychological Studies/Services, Ile-Ife, Nigeria, 8*(1), 4–5.

Franklin, J. (2019). Nigeria is cautiously optimistic about new fintech regulation. *International Financial Law Review* (n.pag).

Hai, B., & Li, H. (2019). (2019) More innovation, more money? Innovation performance, financial constraints, and financial performance. *Academy of Management Annual Meeting Proceedings, 1,* 1.

Hu, Y., Ogedengbe, A. R., & Adamolekun, W. (2017). 'Communicating development' – A cultural shift: Emerging discourses on entrepreneurial development and poverty reduction by Nigeria's banking and microfinance sectors. *Critical Arts: A South-North Journal of Cultural & Media Studies, 30*(5), 709–727.

Jalilov, A., & Onder, G. (2016). *Pyrex Journal of Business and Finance Management Research, 2*(3), 10–013.

Jayeola, O., Olawale, O. T., & Adewumi, A. A. (2018). Economic environment and entrepreneurial development in Lagos and Ogun States, Nigeria. *Scholedge International Journal of Multidisciplinary & Allied Studies, 5*(3), 27–36.

Jucevicius, G., Juceviciene, R., Gaidelys, V., & Kalman, A. (2016). The emerging innovation ecosystems and "Valley of Death": Towards the combination of entrepreneurial and institutional approaches. *Engineering Economics, 27*(4), 430–438.

Khyareh, M. (2020). Entrepreneurship and economic growth: The mediation role of access to finance. *Janus. Net: E-Journal of International Relations, 11*(1), 98–111.

Kim, K., El Tarabishy, A., & Bae, Z. (2018). Humane entrepreneurship: How focusing on people can drive a new era of wealth and quality job creation in a sustainable world. *Journal of Small Businesses., 12*(1), 13–14.

Klitsie, J. et. al. (2019). Overcoming the valley of death: A design innovation perspective. *Design Management Journal,* 14, 28–41. https://doi.org/10.1111/dmj.12052.

Kolarz, P. et.al. (2015). *Innovation by design: How design enables science and technology research to achieve greater impact.* London: Design Council.

Loukil, K. (2020). Intellectual property rights, human capital and types of entrepreneurship in emerging and developing countries. *Theoretical & Applied Economics, 27*(1), 21–40.

Maciel, A., & Fischer, E. (2020). Collaborative market driving: How peer firms can develop markets through collective action. *Journal of Marketing, 84*(5), 41–59.

Markman, G., Waldron, T. L., Gianiodis, P. T., & Espina, M. I.. (2019). E Pluribus Unum: Impact entrepreneurship as a solution to grand challenges. *Academy of Management Perspectives, 33*(4), 371–382.

Mittal, V. (2019). *Nigerian FINTECH Landscape.* Blockchain Innovation. Published. https://doi.org/10.13140/RG.2.2.34864.00001.

Mohammed, K., Ibrahim, H., & Mohammada, A. (2017). Empirical evidence of entrepreneurial competencies and firm performance: A study of women entrepreneurs of Nigeria. *International Journal of Entrepreneurial Knowledge, 5*(1), 49–61.

National Bureau of Statistics of Nigeria Unemployment Report. (2020). https://www.nigerianstat.gov.ng.

Nwambam, A., & Eze, P. (2017). Education and school leavers' unemployment saga: Implication for educational planning in Nigeria. *Educational Research and Reviews, 12*(9), 549–553.

Obaji, N., Olugu, M. U., & Balogun, K. O. (2016). Sustainable innovative policy in technology business incubation: Key factors for successful entrepreneurship development in Nigeria. *International Journal of Scientific and Research Publications, 4*(11), ISSN 2250-3153.

Ojo, A., & Oluwatayo, B. (2016). Entrepreneurship as drivers of growth, wealth creation and sustainable development in Nigeria. *Socioeconomica, 4*(8), 325–331.

Oladunjoye, & Adewumi. (2018). Economic environment and entrepreneurial development in Lagos and Ogun States, Nigeria. *Scholedge International Journal of Multidisciplinary and Allied Studies, 5*(3), 7–8.

Omeh, S. (2017, December 23). *Running Errand services in Nigeria* (p. 1). www.wealthresult.com.

Onimole, S., & Olaiya, S. (2018). Harnessing full employment strategy for nigeria. Entrepreneurship imperatives, prospects and challenges. *Business Management Dynamics, 7*(10), 1–15.

Ovwiroro, A. (2017). Contemporary issues in diversification of Nigerian economy through entrepreneurship. *International Journal of Vocational Education & Training, 24*(2), 36–45.

Pathak, S., & Muralidharan, E. (2020). A two-staged approach to technology entrepreneurship: Differential effects of intellectual property rights. *Technology Innovation Management Review, 10*(6), 5–13. https://doi.org/10.22215/timreview/1364

Pius, K. (2019, May 10). *Learning management system in Nigeria* (p. 1). Gopius.

Saidi, M., & Enilolobo, O S. (2018). Welfare effects of gambling on Nigerian youths: A case study of Lagos State. *Journal of Gambling Business & Economics, 12*(1), 65–79.

Tajudeen, B., & Aare, K. (2019). Deploying orature to meet the challenges of unemployment in Nigeria. *International Journal of Education and Literacy Studies, 7*(2), 144–149.

Techpoint. (2020, July 12). *Challenges of e-commerce and logistics in Nigeria* (p. 2).

Wanass, K., & Shahaza, N. (2020). The role of applying targeted cost technology and the dimensions of entrepreneurship in achieving sustainable development. *Talent Development & Excellence, 12*(2), 23–30.

Wright, M., & Clarysse, B. (2020). Technology entrepreneurship and shaping industries. *Academy of Management Discoveries, 6*(3), 355–358. https://doi.org/10.5465/amd.2019.0120

Yaya, A. et. al. (2016). Job satisfaction as correlates of librarians productivity in public university libraries in Nigeria. *Library Philosophy and Practice (e-Journal)*, 5–6.

15

ICT Usage Behaviours by SMEs in Varying Operational Environments: A Nigerian Case Study

Ibrahim Rufai

Introduction

Informed by Social Shaping Theory (modified), this chapter presents research that examines the impact of communication technologies (mobile telephony, personal computer and internet facilities) on the performance of small and medium businesses in Lagos State, Nigeria. The overarching aim of this piece is to stimulate economic development through context-driven ICT policy and support initiatives for SMEs, especially those operating in African economies (i.e. Nigeria, Ghana, Eritrea, Mali) that still experience significant digital divide between urban and rural communities. Results indicate that SMEs operating in different socio-economic settings present varying performance results from the use of communication technology tools. The study was undertaken through a firm survey and also a number of semi-structured interviews with purposively selected 100 SMEs operating in both the affluent and disadvantaged districts of the city.

The chapter elucidates on the following questions of the study under focus:

1. What impact(s) do ICTs have in enhancing the business performance of SMEs?

I. Rufai (✉)
De Montfort University, Leicester, UK
e-mail: ibrahim.rufai@dmu.ac.uk

2. In what ways does socio-economic context influence the choice of ICTs by SMEs; and what is the impact on business performance?
3. What are the different SME outcomes that can be identified in varying local socio-economic contexts where there is similar ICT access; and how can these be explained?

Using basic descriptive statistics and thematic analytical techniques for the survey and interview data, respectively, the major findings suggest that:

1. as communication technologies positively impact the performance of SMEs, existing socio-economic factors within the districts where the firms operate also influence the choice of communications technology and significantly shape its impact on business performance;
2. class differences with respect to income and education disparity, as well as communication habits in the affluent and disadvantaged communities account for different outcomes in the business performance of firms;
3. the impact of communication technologies on the local economy seems to be more prominent and significant in regard to the performance of firms operating in the affluent districts compared to the performance of firms operating in disadvantaged districts.

Globally, entrepreneurs and other stakeholders now seem to have fully come to terms with the transformational impact potentials of ICT for rapid improvement in economic and social welfare of the digitally connected and digitally disadvantaged communities. ICT is now credited with facilitating access to numerous health services, learning materials, education and works to beneficiaries wherever they may be (Broadband Commission, 2013; Kessington et al., 2019). The Broadband Commission report also indicated that mobile subscriptions in Africa and the Middle East exceeded one billion in 2013. It predicted there could be over 2.1 billion mobile broadband subscriptions in 2014, about one-third of the global stock of mobile technologies—up from one-fifth in 2011 (ITU website, 2014). The subscription levels initially projected to reach 7 billion by 2018, has now exceeded this milestone.

According to Budde Communications (2013): cited in Broadband Commission Report (2013), "Africa is the region with the largest remaining growth potential in the world and it is estimated that the market in telecom services will grow by 1.5 billion people, almost half the remaining market worldwide, by 2050" (ITU website, 2014). The report also indicated that much of the growth in fixed broadband subscriptions globally are located in developing economies. However, it is stated that the overall fixed broadband penetration rates still remain low at 6.1% in developing countries, compared with 27.2% in industrialised nations in 2013 (ITU website, 2014).

Mobile telephony penetration in Africa sub-continent is now reported the fastest in the globe, accounting for over 620 million subscribers, second only to Asia (Atkearney & GSMA, 2011; GSMA, 2019). Also, over 3.5 billion people are now connected to mobile internet globally (GSMA, 2019). Its contribution to socio-economic well-being and business development has been widely noted. According to Jeffrey (2010): cited in Etzo and Collender (2010), "mobile phones are the single most transformative technology for development" (p. 661). It is reported as having capacity to support democratic values in the form of voters' enlightenment (Aker et al., 2011), curtail corruption tendencies and facilitate socio-economic growth and development (Okpaku, 2006).

According to Aker and Mbiti (2010), "As telecommunication markets mature, mobile phones in Africa are evolving from simple communication tools into service delivery platforms. This has shifted the development paradigm surrounding communication costs to one that could transform lives through innovative applications and services" (p. 208).

In the context of the above, SMEs operating within the African markets have huge possibilities to lower their costs, increase productivity and revenue generation drive by leveraging on the business transformational potentials of communication technologies. According to McKenzie (2012): cited in Broadband Commission Report (2013), "SMEs which invest more than 30% of their budget on web technologies can grow their revenue nine times as fast as SMEs spending less than 10%" (ITU website, 2014).

However, ICTs in general, and mobile telephony in particular, are also accused of promoting poverty and reinforcing socio-economic disconnection. Puri et al. (2010) noted instances in some African Millennium villages where dwellers prefer to forgo payment of their children's school fees in preference for purchasing mobile phones credit. In Ethiopia, the economically disadvantaged 75% of the country's total population with mobile telephony subscription and usage expend about one-third (27%) of their wages on it, showing "the continued high cost of services on the continent" (Gillwald & Stork, 2008, p. 14). This probably depicts that some individuals believe so much in the socio-economic utility of mobile telephony and are willing to expend a high proportion of their disposable income for its services. However, accusing ICT of engendering poverty by itself seems unfairly exaggerated. Varying socio-economic circumstances of users and other unknown intervening variables might provide plausible explanations concerning how ICT's benefits are distributed and perceived by different consumers.

Fuchs and Horak (2008) state thus "unequal pattern of material access, usage capabilities, benefits and participation concerning ICTs are also due to the asymmetric distribution of economic (money, property), political (power, social relationships), and cultural capital (skills)" (p. 101). Therefore, the impact of ICTs in general and mobile telephony in particular should be analysed and examined in the context of prevailing socio-economic factors and forces which are either strengthened or weakened by them (ICTs). ICTs or mobile telephony would either serve as tools/catalysts of socio-economic empowerment or instruments of socio-economic domination and exploitation, depending on the context of usage. They embed in the prevailing context of social support, resource extraction and conflict, and also contribute to reconfigure and reconstitute them (Carmody, 2010).

The overarching theme of this chapter suggests that while communication technologies could boost the performance of SMEs in developing economy, prevailing socio-economic factors and circumstances within the districts where firms operate significantly to shape such influence, and might account for varying outcomes in the business performance of different firms. Hence, developmental efforts should go beyond ensuring universal, equal access to ICTs, but also marshalling the machinery of government through policy initiatives to facilitate, enhance and support local capacity for effective usage of ICT tools to achieve socio-economic objectives.

Literature Overview

The potential of ICT as agent of international trade and socio-economic development in today's increasingly deregulated world's economy has been widely noted (Xing, 2018). Van Dijk (2006) highlighted the effectiveness of ICT as a potent driver of economic development in South Korea as well as other Southeast Asian nations. Also, Burke (2010) explained that ICT deployment (i.e. ownership of websites) serves as a major boost to increased sales volume and new customers' acquisition drive by firms.

Further, Kamal and Qureshi (2009) indicated a positive relationship between ICT usage and SMEs growth, development and sustainability. ICT is also perceived to be a life-saving intervention for ailing small and medium businesses. It is thought ICT possesses inherent capabilities that could bolster the survival chances of small firms (Good & Qureshi, 2009; Kamal & Qureshi, 2009).

According to the United Nations (2007), ICTs' adoption can be very beneficial to SMEs performance. Such potential performance-enhancing benefits include: increased productivity in the production processes; improved efficiency of internal business operations; better and accelerated access to domestic and global business contacts; improved inventory management systems; efficiency in production processes; improved intra-departmental communication; improved accounting and budgeting practices; significant communication cost reduction; increased client base through e-marketing; facilitating links to domestic and global outsourcing contacts; facilitating the acquisition of best practices in business dealings; facilitating capacity-building of entrepreneurs and workforce through e-learning platforms as well as enabling business registration and administration of tax remittances. Also, the European Commission (2008) echoes similar sentiment that ICT is capable of enhancing growth potentials of SMEs and accelerating their innovativeness.

The positive influence of ICT usage on business performance of SMEs has also been widely reported in a significant number of empirical studies. ICT is viewed as a catalyst to organisational change (Hazbo et al., 2008) and an enabler to improve business performance of SMEs. Evans and Wurster (1997) argue that it facilitates reach and engenders richness in e-business communication and collaboration with stakeholders, as well as enhances the capacity of local SMEs to engage gainfully in the digital economy (Golding et al., 2008). Pavic et al. (2007) reported that SMEs could leverage on ICT advances to gain competitive advantage in terms of innovation, marketing, business efficiency, product quality and customers' responsiveness. Also, empirical findings from a study by Frank and Wallace (2012) on 'The Livelihood Outcomes of ICT Use in Microenterprises: The Case of South Africa' suggest a positive impact of ICT on the livelihoods of small and medium firms. "Overall, the effects of using ICT were easy communication and time saving when interacting with customers and suppliers" (Frank & Wallace, 2012, p. 10).

Rim's (2009) analysis of secondary survey data set (covering different manufacturing sectors between 1998 and 2002) obtained from Tunisian National Institute of Statistics (TNIS) relating to its National Annual Survey Report of Firms (NASRF) indicated a strong impact on firms' efficiency as a consequence of ICT use. Firms/organisations with more relative deployment/usage of ICT were reported to enjoy an average of 5% productive efficiency than their contemporaries. Besides, it was found that ICT deployment/usage complemented with commensurate human capital improvement through training and development would improve firms' efficiency far more beyond the direct influences of these two factors (ICT and Human Capital) if isolated.

A causal relationship between mobile telephony in particular and productive efficiency was demonstrated by Thompson and Garbacz (2007). Their finding established a positive effect of telecommunication—mobile telephony on productive efficiency in developing countries. Samuel et al. (2007), in their study which appeared in a Vodafone report study tagged Africa: The Impact of Mobile Phones (2005) also reported that people use mobile technology as a substitute for travel, for business transactions—to start and open business, and to strengthen social bond with friends and family.

A more recent study of impact of ICT on small and medium enterprises in Kumasi, Ghana, suggests that most of the SMEs studied experienced a positive business performance as well as other benefits, as a result of using ICT. The study, a mixed-method investigation of 40 SMEs specifically reported a significant increase in sales volume as a result of using the internet/website; cost reduction and improvement in business operations and increase in firms' output/productivity. A related study (Isaac, 2012) on a random sample of 350 small-scale business owners in Southwest Nigeria concerning Information and Communication Technologies as Drivers of Growth: Experience from Selected Small-Scale Businesses in Rural Southwest Nigeria, reported cost reduction, ease of marketing and enhanced incomes by small-scale entrepreneurs as consequences of ICT adoption and usage.

Adewoye and Akanbi (2012) also reported a significant and positive effect of ICT's investment on the profitability of SMEs in Nigeria. Their investigation examined the effects of Information and Communication Technology investment on the profitability of 60 randomly selected sachet water businesses in Oyo state, Nigeria. Findings suggest a significant causal relationship between ICT investment and profitability of the firms. Results also indicate an increase in manpower requirement, salary and business capital invested after ICT adoption. However, there was also a corresponding increase in production volume and profitability (Adewoye & Akanbi, 2012).

In another study, Barrantes et al. (2012) conducted an explorative, qualitative case study of the impact of mobile telephony usage on small and medium businesses in the carpentry and cabinet-making sector in a disadvantaged district of South Lima, Villa El Salvador, Peru. Informed by the cluster theoretical perspective, the research suggests that the impact of mobile telephony usage manifests more in business areas of marketing and customer relationship management. Specifically, findings demonstrate that: "the mobile telephone facilitates the rapid flow of information in the vertical negotiation processes. The mobile also improves emergency responses or furniture production impasses with bespoke design" (Barrantes et al., 2012, p. 88).

Just like much of the empirical research and other theoretical arguments previously discussed in this chapter, these studies have made significant contributions towards our understanding of the relationship between communication technologies and society. However, their analyses focus so much on technological imperatives as determinants of socio-economic change, thereby providing an incomplete account of the largely mutually influencing relationships between technology and social factors. A balanced explanation would need to give due considerations to both technological and social imperatives in the analysis in order to deepen and strengthen our understanding of a more symbiotic interaction between technology and society.

Therefore, this chapter departs from the prevailing perspective of technological determinism which underpins many previous studies. Informed by the modified social shaping theoretical framework, this chapter discusses an empirical study that investigates the impact of communication technologies (mobile telephony, internet and/or computer) on the performance of small and medium businesses operating in both the affluent and disadvantaged districts of Lagos State, Nigeria. It aims at furthering the scope of investigation in this field by providing much deeper insights and understanding into a more symbiotic and mutually influencing relationship between technology and society.

Theoretical Framework

The theoretical and academic debate on the nature of relationship between technology and society has always been intense. Many of the earliest investigations (i.e. Adewoye & Akanbi, 2012; Barrantes et al., 2012; Hazbo et al., 2008; Isaac, 2012; Rim, 2009) tended to privilege technological determinism—technology viewed as an autonomous, separate entity that is independent of society and exacting effects on society. This thinking has been widely criticised as having the potential to stifle creative engagement with technology, leading to uncritical embracing of technological change and defensive adaptation to it.

By stressing technological influences on society, a deterministic assumption overlooks the Social Shaping of technology or how the social relations and networks forged by individuals in society affect, moderate and shape technological impact, design and usage. Constructionism, as a general theoretical viewpoint against technological autonomy or supremacy, opposes determinism.

Williams and Edge (1996) noted that social shaping of technology thinking denies that technology emanates from "a single social determinant, or through the unfolding of a predetermined technical logic" (p. 54). Sproul and Keisler (1991) established that the significant impacts of technological usage could hardly be anticipated, according to their investigation of technology usage in organisations.

However, this study modifies the Social Shaping Theory, reinforces it with a new concept of 'Symbiotic Interactionism', and adapts it for the investigation. Essentially, 'Symbiotic Interactionism' suggests a much clearer hybrid of the main ideas of technological determinism and social shaping theoretical perspectives in a mutually influencing relationship. The modified social shaping perspective, when described with the new concept argues for 'mutually-influencing inter-activity' in explaining the relationship between technology and society—the interaction/relationship between technology and social relations/context is mutually influencing. As technology impacts society and institutions within it (technological determinism), prevailing factors in the social contexts/relations also influence technological choice and shape its impact in change process (social shaping).

Social Shaping Theoretical Perspective

Some writers and researchers (for example Bijker, 1995; Winner, 1993) interpret and think of social shaping as operating only in the design, development and production of technologies—in the design and production of technologies according to certain social values and preferences, but not the selection, adoption and adaptation of the existing technologies to different community needs.

However, social shaping also applies to adaptation and selection of the existing technologies (i.e. communication technologies) by different communities according to their specific prevailing socio-economic and infrastructural circumstances. Social shaping extends beyond the design and production of technologies, to exploring how social outcomes are achieved in the selection and adoption of technology. Therefore, social shaping research encompasses a myriad of different social situations, circumstances and processes of technology adoption and selection, from design and development through production and usage, as well as the mediating influence of socio-economic forces (Williams & Edge, 1996). Thus, focusing on the immediate operating environments in the affluent and disadvantaged business districts of South-western Nigeria, a social shaping theoretical approach will help me to examine "ways in which social, institutional, economic and cultural factors shape: the form of technology – the content of technological artefacts and practices; the rate of innovation; and the outcomes of technological change" (Bjker, 1995). A key hypothesis of this chapter is that SMEs operating in different socio-economic communities in South-western Nigeria (i.e. Lagos State) would benefit more from ICT policy initiatives that are informed by socio-economic circumstances in their immediate operating environments. The region is reputable for large concentration of formal and informal SMEs with significant digital inequality between the rural and urban business districts (Research ICT Africa, 2018).

Methodology

Why a Nigerian Case Study Within Developing Economies and Sub-Saharan Africa?

According to the latest figures by the World Bank (2019), Nigeria currently accounts for half of the West Africa's population at approximately 202 million people, and arguably the biggest among the five major economies (Nigeria, South Africa, Algeria, Egypt and Morocco) in the entire African continent (African Economic Outlook, 2020). It is one of the world's major oil producers of crude oil and the biggest in Africa (Ploch, 2011). Much of the West Africa's economic transactions are warehoused in the country. It occupies a central and influential position as the economic and military superpower of the continent, always playing prominent roles in socio-economic and political stability of African countries (i.e. its mediating and stabilising roles in civil/political unrest in Liberia, Sierra Leone, Zaire (DRC), Tanzania, Angola, Chad etc.). Nigeria is also a "leading player in the African Union, the New Partnership for Africa's Development (NEPAD), and the Economic Community of West Africa States (ECOWAS)" (World Bank, 2013).

The country is arguably credited with the fastest growing telecommunication market in the continent, owing to the government liberalisation programme in the telecommunication sector. Its mobile telephony subscription base is currently over 183 million. Nigerians actively using mobile telephony have grown astronomically in number, but landline subscription and usage in the country has dropped (Charles et al., 2007). The growth in the telecommunication sub-sector has positively inspired and impacted entrepreneurship, leading to increasing opportunities for small and medium businesses in the form of franchises, retailer ships, dealerships and other associated value-added services (Tella et al., 2007).

Therefore, in addition to other factors mentioned in this narrative, the choice of Nigeria as a case study and representation of developing economies and Sub-Saharan Africa is informed by its strategic position as a regional and continental economic superpower within Africa. It is suggested that the choice of Nigeria as a case study can give an indication of the trend, as well as inform ICT policy design in other African/developing countries with similar political, cultural and socio-economic situations/circumstances, with respect to the potential impact of communication technologies on the performance of small and medium businesses operating in different context—the affluent and disadvantaged districts.

Study Area: Profile of Lagos State, Nigeria

People: In landmass, Lagos State is one of the smallest states in Nigeria—accounting for 356, 861 hectares, out of which 75,755 are wetlands. It is the most populous state in Nigeria. Every ethnic nationality in the country is represented in Lagos State (Roberts & Oladeji, 2001). The Yorubas constitute about 60%, while Hausa, Igbo and other ethnic minorities account for about 40% of its population.

Despite being one of the most expensive cities in the globe, most Lagosians live in abject poverty by local and international standards. Majority of its disadvantaged populace reside in low-cost, highly populated areas of the city such as: Bariga, Agege, Ajegunle, Isolo, Oshodi, Shomolu, Shogunle, Mushin and so on. Large sections of these areas are sometimes in appalling sanitary conditions, but are relatively convenient to industrial employment or amenable to self-employment (Peil, 1991).

There is however a considerable number of rich residents who choose to live among their kinsmen in low income, crowded areas "from Lagos Island and Ajegunle to Agege and other northern suburbs. This is partly a question of where successful men have found land to build and partly the need to stay close to business interests or the desire to remain with kinsmen" (Peil, 1991, p. 26).

The number of blights/slums inhabited by the low-income residents of Lagos has been on the increase since 1980s. The state government acknowledged 42 of such blighted neighbourhood in 1983. Results of a survey conducted by Nubi and Omirin (2006) established that over 70% of metropolitan Lagos is blighted.

Ikoyi, Victoria Island and Lekki Peninsula which are all within the boundaries of Eti-Osa Local Government area are dwelling and business settlements of the affluent, upper income class of Lagos State. They (Ikoyi, Victoria Island and Lekki Peninsula) represent the cream of the most exclusive and expensive residential and business locations in the state. Victoria Island in particular is the main financial hub and business enclave of the trio with major 5-star hotels, expensive commercial real estates, exquisite private schools and a host of others. It inhabits most of the major indigenous and international corporations' headquarters. Although Ikoyi and Lekki Peninsula share similar characteristics with Victoria Island as exclusive commercial and business enclaves, they are mainly residential settlements for the high-income elite and expatriates alike.

These two different districts (affluent and disadvantaged) are deliberately chosen for the study because of their obvious opposing socio-economic characteristics and contexts as mentioned above. In particular, the objective is to empirically measure how their varying socio-economic backgrounds might account for different outcomes in the performance of SMEs.

Field Work Design

For the purpose of this paper, SMEs were included in the sample according to the following criteria:

- Significant use of ICT: The cases (firms) significantly support their business operations with ICT architecture (mobile phone, internet and/or personal computer), to the extent that if the ICT systems in their operations were to experience failure or malfunctioning, their business operations, productivity and overall performance would be negatively impacted.
- Pre-existing ICT exposure: The firms (especially those selected for the interview—second phase of the research) have been in operations long before adopting/implementing ICT systems in their business dealings. This made it feasible empirically to track change/impact in business performance/productive efficiency occasioned by ICT adoption/usage.
- Similarity in ALL Respects: All drawn cases (firms) were similar in every known respect (business type, staff strength, knowledge/educational qualification of managers/employees, and so on), with the exception of differences in social contexts where they are embedded.

Table 15.1 Sample table

Research phase	Affluent area	Disadvantaged area	Sample total	Research methods
Phase 1	50 Firms	50 Firms	100 Firms	Survey—structured questionnaire
Phase 2	7 Firms	7 Firms	14 Firms	In-depth study—semi-structured interview

- The firms (cases) of interest (in equal number and size) originate from two different social contexts (upper, affluent community and poor, disadvantaged community). This ensures fair comparison on all grounds except the varying social contexts.
- Performing/Productive Business: Since the research interest was to explore ICT impact on business performance, the SMEs that were investigated were among the top, high-performing/productive entities in their industry.

As shown in Table 15.1, the study (conducted in 2014) was undertaken in two phases: the first phase involved a survey of select small and medium enterprises operating in the affluent and disadvantaged areas of Lagos State, Nigeria. SMEs were selected by snowball sampling. Initial subjects (firms) that were suggested through referrals were also requested to nominate other businesses in their group (subject to meeting strict predefined eligibility criteria as stated in the previous page). Questionnaires were administered to 100 firms—50 each from the affluent and disadvantaged areas, out of which 14 respondents, 7 each from the affluent and the disadvantaged areas were drawn for the second phase of the study. Therefore, the second phase of the research involved seven firms each (14 in total), drawn and interviewed from both the affluent and disadvantaged areas.

Research Design

The study examined ICT impact on SMEs business performance/productivity. A variant of longitudinal approach called 'Retrospective Panel Design' (De Vaus, 2001) was employed. It used some recollection techniques and devices to enable respondents to recollect and reconstruct the order and sequence of past experiences/activities. "We can work back from the present to the past or focus on 'anchor events' and then question around these" (De Vaus, 2001, p. 128). Very good and reliable data could be obtained by asking questions that explore significant milestones and memorable events in the respondents' life or business.

The non-probabilistic, purposive sampling technique that was adopted to recruit respondents for the study ensured only relevant respondents who were most likely to provide rich, quality and fruitful data in the context of examining causal relationship between the independent and dependent variables—(ICT impact and business performance) were recruited.

Also, this procedure was strategically adopted with a view to ensuring there is a match between research questions and sample of respondents. In other words, the relevance of respondents towards addressing research objectives and research questions guided sample recruitment (Bryman, 2008).

The sample was recruited in the same proportion from two communities in Lagos State, Nigeria, both with ICT access, but differentiated by socio-economic contexts or backgrounds—the upper, privileged class and the socio-economically disadvantaged class.

Sample composition includes the following: SMEs who have been in business before ICT (internet-based, mobile and personal computer) diffusion in Nigeria, and whose businesses still subsist till date as well as firms who started their businesses afterwards.

Research Strategy

The study adopted elements of both quantitative and qualitative paradigm: a mixed-method strategy. This was for the purpose of: triangulation (to enable the possibility for findings corroboration); offset (to allow potential weaknesses of methods associated with each strategy to be offset by each other); completeness (to allow an in-depth, broad and comprehensive investigation as well as better understanding of phenomenon); credibility (to enhance the likelihood of results/findings integrity) and to be able to elicit diversity of views/responses from the sample (Bryman, 2008).

Limitations of the Study and What These Mean for Future Research Direction

Limitations in the Context of Research Coverage: This research was limited to examining the ICT impact in the context of small and medium enterprises in Lagos State, Nigeria. Although small and medium businesses constitute a major sector in any economy and are central to national development, other major stakeholders in socio-economic development such as:

Large businesses/corporations, Multinationals, Non-governmental organisations, government institutions as well as other private sectors operating in different socio-economic contexts would need to be included in future investigations for a much deeper understanding of ICT impact in socio-economic process. Time and resource constraints did not allow for this extended scope.

Therefore, future research needs to accommodate these groups and note any emerging patterns and variations that could provide further insights into the relationship between technology and society. The following questions are suggested to guide future research direction:

1. What impact do ICTs have on business efficiency and performance; and to what extent does this improve organisational bottom-line?
2. In what specific business processes is ICT most effective; and how were these processes conducted before ICT?
3. What form of ICT is the most effective for facilitating business activities and why?

Limitations in Research Methods: This study used limited survey and comprehensive semi-structured interview methods to conduct investigation on a purposively select small sample of small and medium businesses operating in both the affluent and disadvantaged districts of Lagos State, Nigeria concerning the impact of ICT (mobile telephony, computer/internet facilities) on their performance. The survey was only intended to generate a bird's eye view of respondents' opinions on the research questions, complemented with a more comprehensive semi-structured interview. Time and resource constraints were the main reasons for such a restricted sample size.

However, on reflection, it was thought that future research endeavour in this field should consider a larger sample size that will be more representative, because a greater number of small and medium businesses now leverage the use of ICT to boost their business performance.

Also, future research could consider additional research methods such as non-participant observation to further strengthen and corroborate survey and interview findings. Views of other departmental heads/representatives concerning their ICT usage experience could also be measured to provide further insights about the business impact of ICTs on organisational performance.

Thus, this research could serve as a pilot for future larger scale investigation. Future studies should also reflect a representation of different states in Nigeria to observe and document general patterns in the findings for policy considerations.

In view of the above limitations, the findings from this research cannot be generalised. However, the study contributes to deepening theoretical understanding of the relationship between technology and society in general and ICT impact on socio-economic process in particular. Besides, its contribution through analytical generalisations will also be valuable to policy design efforts.

Results

The research was conducted from the theoretical perspective that the relationship between communication technology and society is symbiotic: technology impacts society and factors within society also shape/influence technology choice and impact. The quantitative (survey) data obtained from the research went through a very basic manual descriptive analysis—frequency and percentages. Participants' responses to each question were compared between the affluent and disadvantaged areas and patterns were noted.

Survey Findings

The major survey findings suggest that the largest proportion of all the sampled firms (44.1%) used the internet as the major communication technology medium. However, its usage is more evident (25.4%) among firms operating in the affluent areas than those operating in the disadvantaged areas (18.6%).

On the other hand, while mobile telephony closely follows the internet as the most used communication technology medium (37.3%) among all the sample firms, it is much more common among companies operating in the disadvantaged areas (28.8%) as against those in the affluent areas (8.5%). All respondents in both affluent and disadvantaged areas (100%) believe use of communication technology media improve business performance. This is also corroborated by works from (Esselaar et al., 2007; Locke, 2004; Rim, 2009).

Survey findings also indicate that most of the respondents (67.8%) in both the affluent and disadvantaged areas are of the opinion that the use of communication technology media has improved the performance of their business to a very great extent. Survey data also suggest that all 24 firms (8 from the affluent and 16 from the disadvantaged areas) whose business operations predated the advent of communication technology media, and are still in business till date believe use of communication technology media is making their firms to perform better now compared to the period when they were not making use of any form of ICT to support their business activities.

Also, evidence suggests that local factors such as: 'level of education of customers' who live within the immediate operating environment of firms and are served by such firms is a major factor that companies often consider in deciding which communication technology medium will be most cost-effective, relevant and appropriate to use in the course of their business activities. Other factors that are also considered by firms in this regard according to the survey findings are: Customers' purchasing power, customers' attitude to technology and the state of infrastructural support systems.

In conclusion, findings from the survey also suggest that the largest proportion of all sampled firms (45.8%) believe local factors influence their business performance to a great extent.

Data from Table 15.2 shows that the largest proportion of all the sampled firms (44.1%) used the internet as the major communication technology medium. This figure is even more significant when added to the 8.5% of firms from both areas that use Email services, an internet-based facility as their major communication technology medium. However, the table depicts that internet usage as a major communication technology medium is more evident (25.4%) among firms operating in the affluent areas than those in the disadvantaged areas (18.6%).

By contrast, while mobile telephony closely follows the internet as the most used communication technology medium (37.3%) among all the sampled companies, it is much more common among firms operating in the disadvantaged areas (28.8%) as against those in the affluent areas (8.5%).

Table 15.2 Most used communication technology medium by the sampled companies

Communication medium	Affluent area	Disadvantaged area	Total
Mobile telephone	5	17	22
	8.5%	28.8%	37.3%
Personal computer	2	3	5
	3.4%	5.1%	8.5%
Internet	15	11	26
	25.4%	18.6%	44.1%
Intranet	1	0	1
	1.7%		1.7%
Video conferencing	0	0	0
Email	3	2	5
	5.1%	3.4%	8.5%
Sub-Total	26	33	59
	44.1%	55.9%	100%

As shown in Table 15.3, all respondents in both the affluent and disadvantaged areas (100%) are of the view that use of communication technology media improves their business performance. This perception is supported by empirical evidence from extant research (Aker & Mbiti, 2010; Aker et al., 2011; Esselaar et al., 2007; Gomez, 2012; Locke, 2004; Rim, 2009). Findings from their studies corroborate positive causal relationships between ICT and SMEs in terms of boosting productive efficiency, profitability and growth.

Data from Table 15.4 only relate to 24 firms (8 from the affluent and 16 from the disadvantaged areas) who had been in operation as business entities in the sampled population before the advent of communication technology media (internet, mobile telephone and personal computer), and are still operating as business concerns till date. All of them (100%) believe use of communication technology media is making their firms perform better now compared to the period when they were not making use of any form of communication technology media to support their business activities. This buttresses wide-ranging extant empirical and theoretical research (Aker & Mbiti, 2010; Aker et al., 2011; Donner, 2004; Gomez, 2012; Horst & Miller, 2006; Jensen, 2007; Samuel et al., 2007; Thompson & Garbacz, 2007; Waverman et al., 2007).

Evidence from these studies shows that Information Communication Technologies (ICTs) are potent tools in boosting productivity and enhancing workplace efficiency in the developing nations. In the same vein,

Table 15.3 Respondents' views on communication technology media as catalysts for business performance improvement

Respondents' views	Affluent area	Disadvantaged area	Total
Yes	26	33	59
	44.1%	55.9%	100%
No	0	0	0
Sub-Total	26	33	59
	44.1%	55.9%	100%

Table 15.4 Current state of performance of communication technology-driven companies compared to their pre-ICT experience

Company now performing better	Affluent area	Disadvantaged area	Total
Yes	8	16	24
	33.3%	66.7%	100%
No	0	0	0
Sub-Total	8	16	24
	33.3%	66.7%	100%

(Papaioannou & Dimelis, 2007) reported in their study that there is an evidence of causality between ICT and organisational performance. In particular, they argued that there is a positive causal relationship between mobile technology and productive efficiency in the developing world. It is believed that people use mobile technology to facilitate business transactions, create business opportunities and also use it as a substitute for travel.

Data from Table 15.5 shows that 'Level of Education of Customers' who live within the immediate operating environment of firms, and are served by such firms is a major factor that companies often consider in deciding which communication technology medium will be most cost-effective, relevant and appropriate to use in the course of their business activities. The largest proportion (22%) of all sampled firms said the 'Level of Education of Customers' is a major factor that influences their choice of communication technology medium. This is followed by 18.6% of all respondents who are of the opinion that 'Customers' Attitude to Technology' within their areas of operation is a factor they consider most, as well as 13.6% of all sampled firms

Table 15.5 Major influencing factor in local context

Most considered local factor	Affluent area	Disadvantaged area	Total
Customers' level of education	6 10.2%	7 11.9%	13 22%
Customers' social status	1 1.7%	0 0	1 1.7%
Customers' purchasing power	6 10.2%	2 3.4%	8 13.6%
Customers' attitude to technology	7 11.9%	4 6.8%	11 18.6%
Traffic situation	0 0	3 5.1%	3 5.1%
Infrastructural support systems	3 5.1%	5 8.5%	8 13.6%
ICT competencies/technical knowledge of customers	1 1.7%	6 10.2%	7 11.9%
ICT technical knowledge of staff	0	0	0
ICT competencies of staff	0 0	4 6.8%	4 6.8%
Type of ICT used by similar companies	1 1.7%	2 3.4%	3 5.1%
Security situation	1 1.7%	0 0	1 1.7%
None	0	0	0
Sub-Total	26 44.1%	33 55.9%	59 100%

who expressed that they consider 'Customers' Purchasing Power' as a major factor in choosing which communication technology medium to use in their business activities. Some of the sampled firms (13.6%) also view the state of 'Infrastructural Support Systems' within their local operation areas as a major influencing factor in choice of useful and appropriate communication technology medium.

Interview Findings

This section presents a synthesis of major findings from both the semi-structured interview and the limited survey in the previous chapter. Highlights of the findings are captured below:

Findings from both the semi-structured interview and survey suggest that the adoption of ICT (mobile telephony, computer/and or internet facilities) signalled an improvement in business performance of studied firms in terms of operational cost reduction, sale/customer increase, business expansion, increase profitability, improve service quality/delivery, fraud reduction and general operational and administrative efficiency. It is also revealed that firms from different socio-economic backgrounds exhibit tendencies for using more of a particular form of ICT than others in their business engagements. Many of the businesses operating in the disadvantaged areas and having much of their customer base and other stakeholders within that vicinity tend to use more of mobile telephony than computer/internet facilities, while firms with more clientele in the affluent areas and operating from such locations use more computer/internet tools than mobile telephony for their business operations.

It is reported that the nature of socio-economic peculiarities (level of education, income level, communication habits and level of sophistication) of clients in each operating area largely determine the most effective and appropriate communication technology medium for business interaction. In addition, findings suggest that the nature of socio-economic peculiarities described above also shape and mediate the impact of ICT on business performance. In the affluent areas where most residents/clients are highly sophisticated, educated and financially buoyant, the impact of ICT on business performance appears to be more prominent and significant. The socio-economic peculiarities of the area seem to be catalysts to ICT-driven business performance. On the other hand, the prevailing low-income level, high level of illiteracy and weak infrastructural support in the disadvantaged areas are shown to limit the extent of improvement in communication technology could contribute to business performance of firms operating in the area.

Thematic Data Analysis

ICT Impact on Performance—Interview data shows that the firms (from both affluent and disadvantaged areas) interviewed experienced operational and administrative inefficiencies, sloppy communication, customers' dissatisfaction and restricted business expansion in their operations before deployment of Information Communication Technologies. They also endured numerous cases of fraud, resource wastages and inadequacy of requisite information for business operations. According to Interviewee 6:

> "Initially we run our operations manually, with lot of paperwork and time wastage. Marketing involved moving from place to place to woo potential customers. Customer as well as staff records were all manually documented and filed away in our filing room......tracking and retrieving staff or customer data was very tedious and time-consuming". (Interview 6 Transcript, p. 2)

However, adoption of Information Communication Technologies in their businesses heralded an improvement and positive turn around in terms of operational cost reduction, sale/customer increase, business expansion, increase profitability, improved service quality/delivery, fraud reduction and general operational and administrative efficiency. Some of the interviewees from both affluent and disadvantaged areas narrated their experience after adopting and deploying Information Communication Technologies thus:

> Interviewee 1: "I could interact with my staff, hold meeting through Skype and run the company's business from overseas. Right now am forwarding some templates I did about six years ago to some of my partners in Dubai and India. In the past, it would be impossible. So they have really enhanced our capacity. It has helped go more paperless. It has assisted in the areas of information and knowledge management system (Interview 1 Transcript, p. 1). I don't think we can live without ICT now. Its like saying without aeroplane, you should go to Birmingham by foot, it is just not possible. It is unimaginable. We couldn't have functioned at our level now without ICT. The impact has been huge". (Interview 1 Transcript, p. 2)

This is corroborated by the survey data in Table 15.4 which only relates to 24 firms (8 from the affluent and 16 from the disadvantaged areas) who had been in operation as business entities in the sampled population before the advent of communication technology media (internet, mobile telephone and personal computer), and are still operating as business concerns to date. The survey finding revealed that all respondents (100%) believe use of communication technology media is making their firms perform better now compared to the period when they were not making use of any form of communication technology media to support their business activities. The belief in the positive impact of Information Communication Technologies on performance of small and medium enterprises is also supported by empirical evidences from Rim (2009), Esselar et al. (2007), and Stuart Locke, (2004). Findings from their studies corroborate positive causal relationships between Information Communication Technology (ICT) and small/medium businesses in terms of boosting productive efficiency, profitability and growth.

Empirical and theoretical research by Gomez (2012), Aker et al. (2011); Aker and Mbiti (2010), Pyramid Research, UK (2010), Thompson and Garbacz (2007), Samuel et al. (2007), Waverman et al. (2007), Jensen (2007), Donner (2004), and Horst and Miller (2006) also buttress this argument. Evidence from these studies shows that Information Communication Technologies (ICTs) are potent tools in boosting productivity and enhancing workplace efficiency in the developing nations.

<u>Mediation of Socio-Economic Contexts on ICT's Choice</u>—Data also shows that firms from different socio-economic settings exhibit tendencies for using more of a particular form of Information Communication Technology than others in their business engagements. Interviewee 13: "We rely most on mobile telephone, especially for communication at operational level with staff as well as for strategic communication with our stakeholders such as our bankers with respect to getting update concerning our financial position for planning purposes. We also use mobile communication for regular contact with our customers – parents of our students…." (Interview 13 Transcript, p. 1).

In comparison, all the interviewed firms dealing with more clientele from the affluent areas and operating from such locations use more computer/internet tools than mobile telephone for their business operations. The following interview extracts explicitly state:

> Interviewee 2: "ICT, particularly internet is a tool of communication and research to us. It is the major medium we use to engage in business interaction with our clients in this area. We can't really do without it now". (Interview 2 Transcript, p. 2)

The evidence above for both the affluent and disadvantaged areas are supported by the survey finding in Table 15.2 which depicts that internet usage as a major communication technology medium is more evident (25.4%) among firms operating in the affluent areas than those in the disadvantaged areas (18.6%) while mobile telephony is much more common among firms operating in the disadvantaged areas (28.8%) as against those in the affluent areas (8.5%) as the most used communication technology medium.

One plausible explanation for this is that the nature of socio-economic peculiarities (level of education, income level, communication habit and level of sophistication) of clients in each operating area largely determine the most effective and appropriate communication technology medium for business interactions. This is also corroborated by the survey finding in Table 15.5 which shows that 'Level of Education of Customers' who live within the immediate operating environment of firms, and are served by such firms is a major factor that companies often consider in deciding which communication technology medium will be most cost-effective, relevant and appropriate to use in the course of their business activities. The largest proportion (22%) of all sampled firms said the 'Level of Education of Customers' is a major factor that influences their choice of communication technology medium, followed by 18.6% of all respondents who are of the opinion that 'Customers' Attitude to Technology' within their areas of operation is a factor they consider most, as well as 13.6% of all sampled firms who expressed that they consider 'Customers' Purchasing Power' as a major factor in choosing which communication technology medium to use in their business activities.

Regarding firms operating in the affluent areas:

> Interviewee 1: "Most of our clients are professionals in their respective line of businesses, with comparable high level of sophistication and appreciation of ICT-driven tasks/work process. So we are guided by this understanding and always relate with them at that level with respect to business communication and relationship management. I have had business meeting with a client in Dubai through SKYPE and the outcome was very productive and mutually-rewarding". (Interview 1 Transcript, p. 3)

Concerning firms operating in the disadvantaged areas:

> Interviewee 13: "It is more about literacy level. Being in that type of environment, not many people are very educated or well read. Second, the level of poverty – the income level is very low, so ability to explore communication

facility or technology is limited. The other thing is weak infrastructural support such as electricity as well as the lifestyle of people around here. It is more of a noisy, loud lifestyle, so it is possible for you to have music being to the highest volume possible around you. These affect the adoption of ICT because you always feel how can I use ICT effectively in this type of environment? ……. because if my customers don't have the literacy level to use internet, I can't use internet in communicating with them, because they won't understand it. Also if my customers don't have disposable income to procure desktop and connect to the internet, and I adopt internet, it is not going to be very useful for us. Also if there is no electricity to support the use of these things, it is not going to work. What is easiest for majority of our people/customer now is mobile communication and other facility you have on it such as 'text messaging'. That's what defines our choice/usage, that's what is supported by the environment where we operate. And that is why mobile telephony is what we deploy in great deal in our operations". (Interview 13 Transcript, p. 4)

In the affluent area where most residents/clients are computer-literate, technologically driven, highly educated and sophisticated with strong purchasing power, firms tend to adopt more computer/internet facilities in their business activities and dealings than mobile telephony. However, in the disadvantaged areas that are often characterised by illiteracy, low income and weak infrastructural support, mobile telephony is the major medium often adopted by firms in business interactions with most clients in the areas.

Mediation of Socio-economic contexts on ICT's impact—Interview data extracts also reveal that nature of socio-economic peculiarities of clients served by firms shape and mediate the impact of Information Communication Technology on business performance. It is suggested that the extent to which communication technology media could boost their business performance is influenced greatly by factors within the local operating environment of firms.

In the affluent areas where most residents/clients/customers are highly sophisticated, educated and financially buoyant, the impact of communication technology on business performance appears to be more prominent and significant. In other words, the socio-economic peculiarities of the area seem to be catalysts to ICT-driven business performance.

According to one of the interviewees:

Interviewee 5: "the level of sophistication of customers we serve informs our ICT deployment, which on the other hand helps us to meet their standard and taste, and then survive as a business entity. For example if don't have an internet or website that is constantly functioning and accessible, our performance will be affected because we deal with customers who always have access to the internet and might want to check a particular product anytime or make an online order to be delivered to them at a particular time". (Interview 5 Transcript, p. 3)

By contrast, the prevailing low-income level and high level of illiteracy in the disadvantaged areas are shown to limit the extent of improvement in communication technology could contribute to business performance of firms operating in the areas. This is expressed by some interviewees data extracts:

> Interviewee 10: "Yes. Because we could only go as far as what the parents could afford in terms of ICT deployment in the school. And apart from affecting students' learning outcomes in some respect, it even makes us less competitive as a school among our peers. You even desire parents to have computer at home that the children could use for their homework and so on. But the parents cannot afford it". (Interview 10 Transcript, p. 3)

Discussion and Conclusions

First, with respect to the impact of communication technology on business performance, the findings indicate that the use of mobile telephony, computer and internet-based communication channels makes a significant contribution to the performance of the small and medium enterprises that were studied. Results also suggest that small and medium enterprises from different socio-economic communities exhibit tendencies for using more of a particular form of communication technology medium than others in their business engagements. In addition, the interview and survey findings show that the nature of socio-economic peculiarities (income level, level of education, level of sophistication and communication habit) of clients/customers served by firms also shape and moderate the impact of communication technology on business performance to a great extent.

The above empirical evidence from the study strongly supports the idea of a mutually influencing relationship between communication technology and society—communication technology positively impacts on the performance of small and medium firms, and existing socio-economic context/factors within the districts where the firms operate also influence the choice of communication technology and subsequently shape its impact on business performance.

Contribution to the Literature

This research contributes to a small (i.e. Adewoye & Akanbi, 2012; Isaac, 2012) but growing body of empirical investigations that examine the roles of ICT in the performance of small and medium businesses in Nigeria. Its general findings that ICT usage by SMEs positively impacts business performance in terms of cost reduction, enhanced productivity as well as improved revenue and profitability are also corroborated by evidence from Adewoye and Akanbi (2012) and Isaac (2012).

Further, it makes a direct contribution to a refinement and modification of Social Shaping Theory in its application to African SMEs business context. Modified Social Shaping Theory suggests and predicts mutually influencing, symbiotic relationships between technology and social factors. The original SST disproportionately focuses on social factors' influence on technology, while dis-emphasising valid arguments of technological determinism concerning the impacts/influence of technology on social context and relations. In addition, the study also contributes to advancement in the frontier of knowledge by deepening an understanding of the relationship between technology and society.

Also, this research presents a new perspective (Modified Social Shaping Theory: implying mutually-influencing, symbiotic relationships between technology and social factors) that would guide future research concerning the impact of ICTs in socio-economic change. Some of the previous works fail to examine the peculiarities of social contexts in which technology is embedded, and how its impact might be shaped and moderated by such factors. In other words, hardly any previous studies have employed a modified Social Shaping framework for understanding ICTs impact on socio-economic change, particularly in regard to SMEs business performance. Instead, existing perspectives (such as technological determinism) that inform most ICTs impact studies are premised on the old paradigm assumption concerning socio-economic change—that development would be triggered across board, if technological architecture is copied and implemented wholesale.

Key findings in this research suggest a new, balanced perspective (using modified Social Shaping Theory) and enriched theoretical discourse by acknowledging both social and technological factors in the debate. It suggests that the views expressed by some authors that technological provision would generally impact or contribute to socio-economic advancement in developing society need to reflect varying contexts of infrastructure and socio-economic peculiarities of different communities, and how those might account for variation in socio-economic change (Ashby et al., 1980; Djamen et al., 1995; Lerner, 1958; Lomas, 1995; Pye, 1963).

Specifically, the modified Social Shaping Theory as a new model for understanding the relationship between technology and society is invaluable to researchers and policymakers in the following ways:

1. As an explanatory model to aid understanding and articulate the relationship between technology and society in socio-economic change process.
2. As an analytical tool to inform empirical investigations into the impact of ICTs in socio-economic development.

The findings lend support to the idea of a more symbiotic relationship between technology and society. It is argued that as communication technologies positively impact the performance of small and medium firms studied, existing socio-economic contexts/factors within the districts where the firms operate also influence the choice of communications technology, and significantly shape its impact on business performance.

Contribution to Policy

Findings suggest there are different outcomes in business performance of small and medium firms operating in different districts. High levels of education, sophistication and strong purchasing power of most clients/customers in the affluent areas are shown to be catalysts to ICT-driven business performance of firms operating in such communities. By contrast, the prevailing weak purchasing power and high rate of illiteracy that characterise disadvantaged districts served by studied firms are shown to limit the extent of improvement in communication technology could contribute to business performance of firms in such areas.

It therefore appears that socio-economic factors such as illiteracy and poverty should be issues of great concern to government interested in using ICT to address socio-economic inequalities and engender even development. Another issue of concern to ICT policy designers should be the relevance and appropriateness of ICTs services and content to varying and specific targets. The underlying cliché of the old development paradigm assumption that technology would leapfrog developing countries' socio-economic capabilities into the elite club of advanced knowledge-driven economies needs to give way to a more pragmatic, context and need-driven approach. In view of this, effective ICT for development policy should give serious consideration to the following:

First, ICT policymakers need to move beyond rhetoric and intensify real and concrete efforts at initiatives that would support eradication of mass illiteracy among the disadvantaged/poor communities. Findings suggest that the high level of illiteracy among the disadvantaged districts served by the studied firms constitutes hindrance to improvement communication technology which could contribute negatively to business performance. The policy initiatives should encompass basic computer/internet training, information processing management and creation of more awareness about the potentials of ICT in improving the quality of life. These messages should be conveyed in local languages best understood by the target audience for ease of assimilation. The emphasis should be on imparting requisite knowledge that would make it easier for the disadvantaged/poor communities to be able to exploit the benefits of ICT to improve their quality of life.

Second, policy also needs to address the issues of un-affordability of computer/internet facility by the disadvantaged/poor communities. Findings indicate that prevailing weak purchasing power among the disadvantaged districts is one of the factors that restrain them from gaining access to computer/internet facilities, thereby limiting the extent firms could attempt in using communication technology to boost business performance. Policymakers would need to be more creative in addressing the digital divide occasioned by these factors.

References

Adewoye, J. O., & Akanbi, T. A. (2012). Role of Information and Communication Technology investment on the profitability of small and medium scale industries - A case study of sachet water companies in Oyo State, Nigeria. *Journal of Emerging Trends in Economics and Management Sciences (JETEMS), 3*(1), 64–71.

African Economic Outlook. (2020). *Developing Africa's workforce for the future*. Available from: https://www.afdb.org/en/knowledge/publications/african-economic-outlook. Accessed September 4, 2020.

Aker, J. C., Collier, P., & Vincente, P. (2011). *Is information power? Using cell phones during an election in Mozambique (Mimeo)*.

Aker, J. C., & Mbiti, I. (2010). Mobile phones and economic development in Africa. *Journal of Economic Perspectives, 24*(3), 207–232.

Ashby, J., Klees, S., Pachico, D., & Wells, S. (1980). Alternative strategies in the economic analysis of information/education projects. In Emile G. McAnany

(Ed.), *Communications in the rural third world: The role of information in development*. Praeger Publishers.

Barrantes, C., Aileen, A., Cesar, H., & Martin, C. (2012). The Impacts of the use of mobile telephone technology on the productivity of micro and small enterprises: An explorative study into the carpentry and cabinet-making sector in Villa El Salvador. *Information Technology and International Development, 8*(4), 77–94.

Bijker, W. (1995) Socio-historical technology studies. In S. Jasanoff, G. E. Markle, J. C. Peterson & T. Pinch (Eds.), *Handbook of science and technology studies* (pp. 229–256). Sage.

Bryman, A. (2008). *Social research methods*. Oxford University Press.

Broadband Commission For Digital Development Report. (2013) (Online). Available from http://www.itu.int/en/pages/default.aspx. Accessed August 21, 2014.

Burke, K. (2010). The impact of internet and ICT use among SME agribusiness growers and producers. *Journal of Small Business and Entrepreneurship, 23*(2), 173–194.

Carmody, P. (2010). *Globalization in Africa: Recolonization or renaissance?* Lynne Rhenner Publishers Inc.

Charles, A. K., Ekong, U. O., Tolulope, F. I., & Ayodele, A. A. (2007). M-commerce implementation in Nigeria: Trends and issues. *Journal of Internet Banking*, 12(2).

De Vaus, D. A. (2001). *Research design in social research*. Sage.

Donner, J. (2004). Micro entrepreneurs and mobiles: An exploration of the uses of mobile phones by small business owners in Rwanda. *Information Technologies and International Development, 2*(1), 1–21.

Djamen, J., Ramazani, D., & Somé, S. (1995). Electronic networking in Africa: Emergence towards the internet. *FID News Bulletin., 45*(7/8), 228–233.

Esselaar, S., Stork, C., Ndiwala, A., & Dea-swarray, M. (2007). ICT Usage and its impact on profitability of SMEs in 13 African countries. *Information Technologies and International Development, 4*(1), 87–100.

Etzo, S., & Collender, C. (2010). The mobile phone 'revolution' in Africa: Rhetoric or reality? *African Affairs., 109*(437), 659–668.

European Commission. (2008). *Making SMEs more competitive* (Online) Available from http://ec.europa.eu/enterprise/sme/competitive_en.htm. Accessed October 30, 2008.

Evans, P. B., & Wurster, T. S. (1997, September–October). Strategy and the economics of information. *Harvard Business Review*, pp. 71–83.

Ezigbo, O. (2009). *Nigeria: MDGs – Poverty rate rises to 75 percent – UN. Thisday Newspaper* (Online). Available from http://www.allafrica.com/stories/200902270 161.html. Accessed December 15, 2010.

Frank, M., & Wallace, C. (2012). The livelihood outcomes of ICT use in micro-enterprises: The case of South Africa. *Electronic Journal on Information Systems in Developing Countries, 53*(1), 1–16.

Fuchs, C., & Horak, E. (2008). Africa and the digital divide. *Telematics and Informatics., 25*, 99–116.

Gillwald, A., & Stork, C. (2008). *Towards evidence-based ICT policy and regulation: ICT access and usage in Africa* (Online). Available from: www.researchICTafrica.net

Global Systems Mobile Association (GMSA) and ATKEARNEY. (2011). *Africa mobile observatory 2011: Driving economic and social development through mobile services* (Online). Available from http://www.gmsworld.com

Global Systems Mobile Association (GMSA). (2019). The state of mobile internet connectivity report*: Mobile For Development.* (Online). Available from https://www.gsma.com/mobilefordevelopment/resources/the-state-of-mobile-internet-connectivity-report-2019/

Golding, P., Donaldson, O., Tennant, V., & Black, K. (2008). *An analysis of factors affecting the adoption of ICT by SMEs in rural and urban Jamaica* (Online). Available from http://is2.lse.ac.uk/asp/aspecis/20080109.pdf. Accessed May 15, 2009.

Gomez, R. (2012). Users perception of the impact of public access computing in Colombia: Libraries, telecenters and cybercafes. *Information Technologies and International Development., 8*(3), 19–33.

Good, T., & Qureshi, S. (2009). *Investigating the effects of microenterprise access and use of ICT through a capability lens: Implications for global development*. Proceedings of the Second Annual SIG GlobalDev Workshop, Phoenix, USA

Hazbo, S., Arnela, C., & Chun-yan, H. (2008). ICT adoption model of chinese SMEs. *International Journal of Business Research, 44*, 161–165.

Horst, H., & Miller, D. (2006). *The unpredictable mobile phone* (Online). Available from http://www.ucl.ac.uk/anthropology/people/academic_staff/d_miller/. Accessed July 22, 2013.

International Telecommunication Union Report. (2014). *Measuring the information society report* (Online). Available from https://www.itu.int/search?

Isaac, B. O. (2012). *Information and communication technologies as drivers of growth: Experience from selected small-scale businesses in rural Southwest Nigeria.* Department of Agricultural Economics, University of Ibadan, Nigeria (Online). Accessed June, 2013.

Jensen, R. (2007). The digital provide: Information (technology), market performance and welfare in the South India Fishery Sector. *Quarterly Journal of Economics, 122*(3), 879–924.

Kamal, M., & Qureshi, S. (2009). *An approach to IT adoption in micro-enterprises: Insights into development*. Proceedings of the Fourth Midwest United States Association for Information Systems Conference, Madison, USA.

Kessington, O., Susan, K. F., & Rocky, J. W. (2019). Impact of information technologies in Nigerian small-to medium-sized enterprises. *Journal of Economics, Finance and Administrative Science, 24*(47), 29–46.

Lerner, D. (1958). *The passing of traditional society: Modernizing the Middle East.* The Free Press.

Locke, S. (2004). ICT Adoption and SME growth in New Zealand. *Journal of American Academy of Business, Cambridge* (4), 93–102.

Lomas, P. (1995). *Calling the Pacific: Pacific communications and computing forum.* Islands Business Pacific Ltd.

Nubi, T. O., & Omirin, M. M. (2006, July 25–28). *Urban violence, land rights and the environment*. Paper presented at the International Conference on Environmental Economics and Conflict Resolution., University of Lagos, Nigeria.

Okpaku, J. O. (2006). Leapfrogging into the information economy: Harnessing information and communication technologies in Botswana, Mauritania and Tanzania. In L. Fox, & R. Liebenthal (Eds.), *Attacking Africa's poverty: Experience from the ground*. World Bank.

Papaioannou, S. K., & Dimelis, S. P. (2007). Information technology as a factor of economic development: Evidence from developed and developing countries. *Economics of Innovation and new Technology* (pp. 179–194).

Pavic, S., Koh, S. C. L., Sampson, M., & Padmore, J. (2007). Could e-business Create a Competitive Advantage in UK SMEs? *Benchmarking: An International Journal*, 14(3), 320–351.

Peil, M. (1991). *The city is the people*. Belhaven Press.

Ploch, L. (2011). *Elections and issues for congress. Congressional research service* (Online). Available from http://fpc.state.gov.documents/organisation. Accessed June 15, 2011.

Puri, J., Mechael, P., Cocmaciuc, R., Sloninsky, D., Modi, V., & Berg, M. (2010, December 15). *A study of the connectivity in millennium villages in Africa*. Paper Presented at 4th International ICTD Conference. Royal Holloway, University of London.

Pye, L. W. (1963). Introduction. In L. W. Pye (Ed.), *Communications and political development*. Princeton University Press.

Research ICT Africa. (2018). *The state of ICT in Nigeria*. Available from https://researchictafrica.net/?s=state+of+ict+in+nigeria. Accessed July, 2019.

Roberts, F. O. N., & Oladeji, A. (2001). *Resurgent identity crisis and security management in Lagos, Nigeria: Lessons for West African Cities*. Proceedings of International Conference on Security, Segregation and Social Networks in West African Cities, 19th-20th Centuries', Ibadan, Nigeria.

Rim, B. A. M. (2009). Impact of the adoption of ICT on firms' efficiency in the Tunisian manufacturing sector. *Economic Modelling, 26*(5), 961–967.

Samuel, J., Shah, N., & Hadingham,W. (2007). *Mobile communications in South Africa, Tanzania, and Egypt: Results from community and business surveys*. Moving the debate forward: The Vodafone Policy Paper Series #3 2005 (Online). Available from http://www.vodafone.com/. Accessed August 17, 2007.

Sproul, L., & Kiesler, S. (1991). *Connections: New ways of working in the networked organisation*. MIT Press.

Tella, S. A., Amaghionyeodiwe, A. L., & Adesoye, B. A. (2007). Telecommunication infrastructure and economic growth: Evidence from Nigeria. *Being a Paper Submitted for the UN-IDEP and AFEA Joint Conference on "Sector-led Growth in Africa and Implications for Development"* to be held in Dakar, Senegal from November 8–11, 2007 (Online). Available from http://www.unidep.org/Release3/Conferences/Afea_2007/IDEP_07_17. Accessed March 5, 2011.

Thompson, H. G., & Garbacz, C. (2007). Mobile, fixed line and internet service effects on global productive efficiency. *Information Economics and Policy, 19*, 189–214.

The World Bank Report. (2019). The World Bank in Nigeria. https://www.worldbank.org/en/country/nigeria/overview. Accessed June 4, 2020.

United Nations Development Programme. (2007). *The role of government in promoting ICT access and use by SMEs: Considerations for public policy*. APDIP en-note 12/2007 (Online). Available from http://www.apdp.net/apdipenote/12.pdf. Accessed June 5, 2009.

Van Dijk, J. (2006). *The network society* (2nd ed.). Sage.

Waverman, L., Meschi, M., & Fuss, M. (2007). *The impact of telecoms on economic growth in developing nations. Moving the debate forward*. The Vodafone Policy Paper Series #3 (Online). Available from http://www.vodafone.com/etc/medialib/attachments/crdownloads. Accessed 2005.

Williams, R., & Edge, D. (1996). The social shaping of technology. *Research Policy, 25*, 865–899.

Winner, L. (1993). Upon open the black box and find it empty: Social constructivism and the philosophy of technology. *Science, Technology, and Human Values, 18*, 362–378.

World Bank. (2013). Nigeria: Basic economic report, Report No 3341- UNI.

World Bank Discussion Paper Series 246. Washington, DC: World Bank. www.lagosstate.gov.ng. January, 2012.

Xing, Z. (2018). The impacts of Information and Communications Technology (ICT) and E-commerce on bilateral trade flows. *International Economics and Economic Policy, 15*, 565–586. https://doi.org/10.1007/s10368-017-0375-5

Part IV

Entrepreneurship in Conflict Zones

16

Picking up the Pieces: Social Capital and Entrepreneurship for Livelihood Recovery Among Displaced Populations in Northeast Nigeria

Oluwaseun Kolade, Robert Smith, and Saliba James

Introduction

In the past few decades, there has been a significant increase in the global rate of forced displacement, often precipitated by persecution, civil wars, terrorism, transborder conflicts, as well as natural disasters. The United Nations High Commission for Refugees (UNHCR) reports that there are 68.5 million forcibly displaced people worldwide (25.4 million refugees and 43.1 million internally displaced people), and each year only a small fraction are able to return to their former homes (UNHCR, 2019). The Boko Haram insurgency in Nigeria has precipitated a humanitarian tragedy on a scale comparable to the Nigerian civil war (1967–1970) and arguably the worst of any man-made or natural disaster in Nigeria's history. The Internal Displacement Monitoring Centre estimates that up to 3.3 million people have been internally displaced due to terrorist violence perpetrated by Boko

---

O. Kolade (✉)
Department of Management and Entrepreneurship, De Montfort University, Leicester, UK
e-mail: seun.kolade@dmu.ac.uk

R. Smith
Aberdeen, Scotland, UK

S. James
Department of History, University of Maiduguri, Maiduguri, Nigeria

Haram (Internal Displacement Monitoring Centre, 2015). The number of people displaced by the conflict is the largest in Africa and the third largest in the world. Using qualitative data obtained from interviews conducted with respondents in Northeast Nigeria, this study examines the extent to which the displaced populations are drawing on social capital and human capital to withstand, cope with and recover from the adverse experiences and consequences of the insurgency and counterinsurgency.

Given that most forced displacements occur in developing countries like Nigeria, government resources are increasingly stretched to deal with such crises, and there are calls for a fundamental rethink of the traditional approach to interventions in disaster situations. In particular, scholars and practitioners are highlighting the need to shift from the current emphasis on material solutions and financial input, to an approach that combines both material and social solutions, bringing people and communities to the forefront of interventions (Aldrich & Meyer, 2015; Johnson et al., 2013; Wind & Komproe, 2012). Forced migration entails social processes in which human agency and social networks play a major part. These networks can be instrumental in the construction and (re)-construction of livelihood systems and communities shattered by insurgencies and protracted conflicts.

The large-scale displacement in Northeast Nigeria has precipitated the disruption and potential transformation of social capital as individuals and households are forced to leave the comfort zones of familiar neighbourhoods and physically separate from the strong ties of families, friends and neighbours with whom they have bonded for decades. They are instead compelled to meet new individuals and households, typically in camps and new communities, with whom they have to forge new relationships in order to survive and rebuild their lives (Aldrich et al., 2020). These new networks of relationships can play a key role in creating new entrepreneurial opportunities that can help displaced peoples recover and rebuild their lives. This chapter makes two important contributions: firstly, it sets out a conceptual framework that captures the transformation of social capital due to forced displacement, and the instrumentality of the resulting new networks for entrepreneurial activities. Secondly, the chapter also explores the unique empirical context of Boko Haram insurgency in Northeast Nigeria, and how displaced peoples are drawing on social capital to cope and rebuild their lives through entrepreneurship.

Theoretical Framework

Towards a New Approach to Humanitarian Action: The Humanitarian-Development-Peace Nexus

One of the larger-scale current trends in humanitarian action comprises efforts to engineer a more effective 'nexus' among humanitarian, development and peace-building action, to better achieve the objectives of each, on the argument that their respective objectives can be interdependent (Development ICVA, 2018; Initiatives, 2019; Wolf & Wilkinson, 2019). This trend, though it has antecedents going back decades, arises from a relatively recent realisation (e.g. United Nations Secretariat, 2016) that most large-scale humanitarian crises become protracted (and in some cases seemingly intractable); that developmental deficiencies can instigate and almost always exacerbate crises; that perennialising short-term humanitarian aid is unsustainable within the context of limited resources; and that a country where a major part of the population is in crisis cannot attain the Sustainable Development Goals ('SDGs'). These realisations are reflected in the New Way of Working promoted by the United Nations (UNOCHA, 2017). While the call for a nexus approach to humanitarian action has gained significant traction in recent years, scholars and practitioners are still grappling with the need for better conceptual clarity and simplicity that can inform better operationalisation of complementary interventions and bring achievement of the SDGs onto the horizon despite a prevailing crisis. In a recent contribution, Howe (2019) proposed a framework to capture the mutually reinforcing interactions among the three distinct but linked domains of humanitarian, development and peace actions (see Fig. 16.1). In this framework, nexus actions are seen as those actions that, by intentional design and by mobilising comparative advantage of multiple actors, contribute to achieving outcomes in at least one of the other nexus areas.

In practice, the triple nexus approach has generated some sustained experiments in joint humanitarian-development assessment and analysis; formulation of 'collective outcomes' (shared objectives) that resonate with both the SDGs and humanitarian imperatives and that address pressing problems that require both developmental and humanitarian actions to overcome; and aligned programming so as to combine the necessary ingredients to achieve the collective outcomes (though this stage is to date the least advanced). The United Nations is focusing on a selected set of countries with protracted crises for these experiments (Burkina Faso, Cameroon, Chad, Ethiopia, Niger, Nigeria, Somalia), though aid teams and governments in

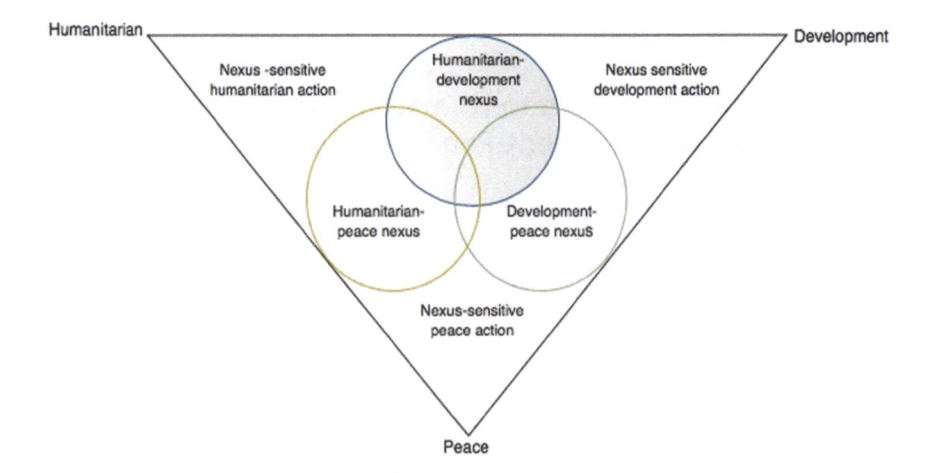

Fig. 16.1 The triple nexus framework (*Source* Howe, 2019)

other countries are also practising some or most elements (United Nations Secretariat, 2019). However, even though these initiatives tend to have more explicit objectives on resilience and empowering crisis-affected people than the humanitarian and developmental country strategies, respectively, from which the 'nexus' is drawn, they do not extend to systematic assessment and purposive strengthening of productive social ties (International Rescue Committee, 2019; Medinilla et al., 2019).

On the donor side, the Organisation for Economic Cooperation and Development has adopted a strong 'Recommendation on the Humanitarian-Development-Peace Nexus' for its members, which comprise the major official donors (OECD, 2019). The largest part of development aid is bilateral (government to government); flows from international financial institutions is the second-largest part; and multilateral aid through United Nations and non-governmental organisations is smaller (though it tends to enjoy a larger proportion in countries with protracted crises, where problems of governance and/or security constrain development action). So, whether nexus approaches reach critical mass in a given country mainly depends on the affected-country government and its bilateral donors; the United Nations cannot do much alone.

The idea of better appreciating, and possibly leveraging, social capital among crisis-affected people thus arises in this context of new emphasis upon coordinating different aid streams and maximising their synergies so as to bring into view a durable end to a given crisis. It is not so much a consequence of nexus thinking; rather, both arise from the search for new approaches to crises that seem insoluble with current methods. Nonetheless, the nexus is generally propitious for research and practice on social capital in crises. Social capital's interactions with individual and community outcomes are fairly well charted and credited in development contexts (Fafchamps, 2006; Fukuyama, 2001; Portes & Landolt, 2000; Woolcock & Narayan, 2000), although interventions based thereon are less practised and studied (Pronyk et al., 2008). In contexts of protracted humanitarian crises in less-developed countries, such charting is in its infancy. The emphasis on and spread of nexus approaches will not automatically rectify this, but it may help to mobilise social capital expertise in the developmental sector to study and start to apply social capital approaches more intensively in crisis settings.

Social Capital, Conflict and Disaster Response

As used in this study, social capital refers to systems that result from social and economic organisation, trust, solidarity, shared values and norms of reciprocal cooperation, informational and economic exchange and informal and formal groups and associations (Grootaert, 1998; Putnam, 1994, 1995, 2001; Uphoff & Wijayaratna, 2000). It has been defined as 'the sum of the resources, actual or virtual, that accrue to an individual or a group by virtue of possessing a durable network of more or less institutionalized relationships of mutual acquaintance and recognition' (Bourdieu & Wacquant, 1992). Social capital is recognised as a key livelihood asset in the sustainable livelihood framework, by means of which individuals and communities can overcome vulnerabilities by transforming structures and processes to achieve livelihood outcomes (Krantz, 2001). Scholars have offered various categorisations of social capital. For example, some have described social capital in its structural, relational and cognitive dimensions (Camps & Marques, 2014). Structural social capital refers to the structures and overall pattern of connections among actors in a network, while cognitive social capital refers to those resources providing shared representation, interpretations and systems of meanings among parties. This includes intangible forms such as trust and norms of reciprocity (Baum & Ziersch, 2001; Nahapiet & Ghoshal, 1998). Relational social capital refers to the type of personal relationships actors have, and how it influences their behaviours within the system (Nahapiet & Ghoshal, 1998). Social capital has also been classified into bonding social capital among people with similar socio-economic characteristics and family and religious identities; bridging social capital among people belonging to different ethnic, social and religious groupings; and linking social capital between ordinary citizens and those in authority (Claridge, 2013).

Although there has been a surge of interest in the phenomenon of social capital and how it may influence and improve the development process (Lautze & Raven-Roberts, 2006), the literature on social capital and how it interacts with violent conflicts, especially in the context of intra-state wars, remains limited, despite the attention to the major and persistent humanitarian crises that these wars generate. Unlike in interstate conflicts in which the need to confront an external national enemy tends to foster national unity and strengthen social cohesion, intra-state conflicts can be generally expected to weaken the social fabric of the communities concerned. Such violent conflicts often divide populations by eroding interpersonal and communal trust and weaken or even destroy the social norms and values that underpin cooperation and promote collective action in pursuit of common interest. Erosion of social capital lies at the heart of communal strife. Not only does the destruction of social capital increase the likelihood of violent conflict, but this can also hamper the process of reconciliation and recovery after the cessation of hostilities. Without the restoration of social capital, provision of other forms of capital is unlikely to promote economic and social development in post-conflict societies (Grootaert, 1998; Hoffmann & Muttarak, 2017; Uphoff & Wijayaratna, 2000).

Social Capital and Disaster Response

Recent studies in disaster management and response have highlighted the importance of social capital as a key resource in humanitarian response. When disasters strike, especially sudden natural disasters and man-made conflicts, the first responders are family members, friends and neighbours in proximity to the incident. Their interventions are often underpinned by norms of expectations and obligations they feel towards affected neighbours, especially those within their personal networks (Dynes, 2006). Conversely, in disaster situations, governments and external actors typically have to grapple with capacity and resource constraints in trying to respond fast. This is especially so in emergencies where urgent actions may be required to save lives, and local knowledge is critical to the effective coordination of humanitarian interventions (Bhandari, 2014). In addition, in response to disaster, affected people tend to evacuate in social groups such as family units, and external support needs to take these social organisations into account in order to be effective. As such, some researchers argue, and some practitioners have acknowledged, the need to link material and technological solutions with social solutions, and embed social networks into the fabric of humanitarian interventions (Aldrich & Meyer, 2015).

Other scholars have highlighted the informational potential of social networks in disaster situations. Networks are potential channels of critical information that can help individuals and communities prepare well for, and respond effectively to, disasters. However, strong social capital can also have negative impacts, for example through exclusion of members of the outgroup and information hoarding within the in-group (Bhandari, 2014). There, the recent interest on social capital in humanitarian situations should not uncritically assume that social capital—in its various forms—is inherently a positive thing. Humanitarian interventions should therefore be aimed not just at harnessing but also, where necessary, at transforming social capital. This critical engagement is important in all disaster situations, but may be especially important in conflict situations and other man-made disasters: conflict situations are typically associated with negative social capital and low levels of human capital, and these are often inter-linked with in-group bias, outgroup prejudice and other factors that precipitate and aggravate intergroup conflicts.

Furthermore, while there has been increasing attention to the role of social capital in emergency response, there is a need for more empirical data on the role of social capital in longer-term livelihood recovery and resettlement strategies. Humanitarian interventions tend to be, by default, oriented to short-term objectives such as evacuations, provisions of first aid and supply of urgent relief materials. However, crises increasingly tend to become protracted due to persistent root causes combined with lack of capacity of affected people to achieve long-term livelihood recovery and resettlement on their own. There is therefore a need for research that focuses on long-term outcomes. This paper examines the impact of social capital on entrepreneurial activities of affected households, and how this is contributing to their survival and livelihood recovery strategies.

Human Capital, Social Capital and Entrepreneurship

Scholars have also highlighted the need to put human capital at the heart of development interventions. One of the leading figures of modern human capital theory, Theodore Schultz, observed that there was an apparent contradiction between the assumption of donor countries that poor countries are poor mainly because they lacked capital, and the views of some practitioners that poor countries do not have sufficient ability to absorb additional capital. According to Schultz, this apparent contradiction can be resolved by clarifying and distinguishing between different forms of capital. Most development aid are provided in the form of financial—grants, loans, etc.—or physical—structures, equipment, inventories—capital. There is less investment in human capital. As a result, 'human capabilities do not stay abreast of physical capital, and they do become limiting factors…' (Schultz, 1961).

Human capital is defined as 'the aggregation of the innate abilities and the knowledge and skills that individuals acquire and develop throughout their lifetime' (Laroche & Ruggeri, 1999, p. 89). It is acquired and developed mainly through formal education, on-the-job training and other informal means (Acemoglu & Autor, 2011; Becker, 1964; Schultz, 1961). Human capital interacts closely with social capital (Coleman, 1988), and this in turn can influence disaster outcomes: scholars have observed that the impact of education on disaster preparedness is sometimes mediated by social capital. For example, individuals who are better connected and actively engaged within the community tend to have better access to information and expertise, and this enables them to be better prepared in the event of disasters (Hoffmann & Muttarak, 2017). Social networks are channels of information-sharing and knowledge transfer, and they can also function as a hub for skill development and training (Inkpen & Tsang, 2005).

This paper examines how affected peoples deploy their human capital in entrepreneurial activities, and how they develop and complement their ideas, skills and knowledge using opportunities and resources accruing from their social networks. It thus aims to elucidate the interaction of human and social capital in a crisis context.

The aggregate stock of human capital—in educational qualification, vocational skills, talents and entrepreneurial competencies—are effective drivers of new venture creation and entrepreneurial performance, especially in turbulent environments. This can complement the role of social capital, in terms of opening access to new markets and facilitating new linkages with suppliers and other key actors in the entrepreneurial ecosystem. Entrepreneurs have been described as socially embedded agents who leverage resources from their social environment. These resources include information, industry knowledge, financial assistance and social support, among others (Neumeyer et al., 2019; Theodoraki et al., 2018). Furthermore, entrepreneurship has been found to have transformative impacts in conflict situations by facilitating increased transactions and lowering outgroup prejudice in multi-ethnic and multi-ethnic communities and other similar contexts (Tobias et al., 2013).

In this chapter, we propose a conceptual model that explains how forced displacement disrupts and transforms social capital, and how transformed social capital can be instrumental for new opportunity creation through the development of new networks which are in turn harnessed for entrepreneurial

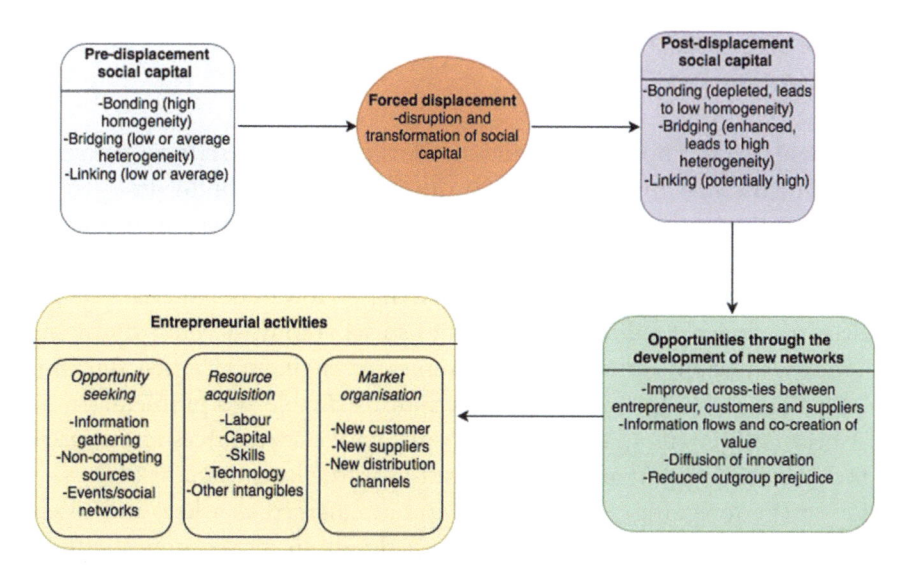

Fig. 16.2 Social capital and entrepreneurship in situations of forced displacement (authors)

activities (Fig. 16.2). Among other things, we suggest that, prior to displacement, there is a higher level of bonding in social capital associated with high homogeneity and strong ties within families and friendship networks. As people are forcibly displaced from their settled locations, families and friends separate, and individuals and households come into contact with new households from other backgrounds, typically in displaced persons camps, but also in less institutionalised, informal settlements outside of their familiar communities. In other words, as bonding social capital depletes, bridging social capital tends to expand. The resulting formation of new networks has productive economic function and creation of entrepreneurial opportunities, in terms of new customers and suppliers. Firstly, as the displaced persons forge new linkages with other households as well as new communities outside the camp, they are able to gather valuable information about demands and opportunities that enable them to expand their customer base, as well as their products/services range. Secondly, they can harness new bridging networks to access new options for suppliers in both existing and new supply chains. Thus, the new networks can enable entrepreneurial activities—opportunity seeking, resource acquisition and the development of new markets. These can play a significant outcome in livelihood outcomes of displaced households.

Entrepreneurship and Livelihood Recovery in Humanitarian Crises

Households caught up in humanitarian crisis typically face critical battles for survival in the first instance, and then the struggle to rebuild their lives in the aftermath. In the survival stage of post-disaster response, humanitarian agencies often have an indispensable role in providing urgent medical aid, shelter, food items and other relief materials. However, material aid that neglects to foster conditions (economic, social, infrastructural, incentives) for entrepreneurship misses an opportunity to engineer a better and more durable outcome or potentialities. This is unsustainable and problematic, not least because humanitarian agencies do not have the resources and capacity to meet all the needs of affected populations in the long term.

Given the foregoing, entrepreneurship has emerged as a key, and recent, area of interest in humanitarian practice. A significant proportion of affected people in post-disaster and post-conflict contexts are usually driven by the necessity to engage in various forms of subsistence entrepreneurship. They use these ventures to generate additional income to complement the support they get from humanitarian agencies, and they use this extra income to meet critical household needs such as food and shelter. While this practice has been reported by a number of NGOs and practitioners, it has not attracted commensurate attention among scholars. This chapter seeks to contribute towards this gap in knowledge.

Given the foregoing, this chapter examines the extent to which social networks are helping to shape and expand market opportunities for displaced persons engaged in entrepreneurship. In particular, we explore how displaced peoples are harnessing bonding networks to access information and build entrepreneurial capacity; and how they are using bridging and linking networks to create and expand new markets for their products and services. Finally, we discuss the link between these entrepreneurial opportunities and livelihood outcomes for the displaced.

Methodology

This paper draws on in-depth interviews to explore how social networks and individual skills are contributing to coping and recovery strategies of displaced households in Northeast Nigeria. In order to gain a broad perspective of IDPs' experience across the region, fifteen respondents were interviewed across three camps for internally displaced people (IDPs), in

Borno State and Yobe State—two key areas affected by the insurgency. The respondents include male and female representatives of displaced households, NGO workers and government officials. This approach enables us to complement information from the affected households with insights from NGOs, government officials and other stakeholders working with them. The female representation also enables us to grapple with gendered perspectives, often under-reported in these contexts. The interviews were carried out in Hausa, the lingua franca in the region. The respondents were asked to respond to open-ended questions such as: (1) Have your extended family members been of any help to you after you were displaced from your home? If so, how?. (2) Do you have friends from other towns and other parts of the country? How, if ever, have they been of help after you left your home? (3) Are you running any business at the moment? If so how has it helped you to recover from the insurgency? (4) Has your past and new networks helped with your business? If so, how? The transcripts of the interviews were then subjected to thematic analysis using NVivo11, to explore key issues relating to the role of social capital in promoting IDP entrepreneurship and livelihood recovery. The qualitative data collection whose results are presented in this paper is the first phase of a project that will next entail quantitative data.

Study Context

Northeast Nigeria is one of the six geopolitical zones in the West African nation, and it comprises six states: Adamawa, Bauchi, Borno, Gombe, Taraba and Yobe. It is the poorest geopolitical zone in the country, and the region with the highest levels of illiteracy and unemployment. Borno State, the epicentre of the Boko Haram insurgency, has an estimated population of 5.2 million and a landmass of 61,435 km^2, the largest state by landmass in Nigeria (University of Maiduguri, 2009). It is bordered by Niger Republic to the north, Chad to the northeast and Cameroon to the east. Within Nigeria, it shares borders with other Northeastern states of Adamawa, Yobe and Gombe states. Maiduguri is the capital city of Borno and the largest city in Northeastern Nigeria, covering an area of 543 km^2, and with an estimated population of 1 million (Mayomi & Mohammed, 2014).

In 2002, Boko Haram was formed in Maiduguri, Borno State, by the radical cleric Mohammed Yusuf. Its official name is *Jamaatu Ahlus-Sunnah Lidda Awati Wal Jihad*, the Arabic for 'People Committed to The Prophet's Teachings for Propagation and Jihad'. Its popular name, Boko Haram, derives from its core teaching that Western education is forbidden (Adesoji, 2010).

Although the group was founded in 2002 essentially as a protest movement, by 2009 it had evolved into a violent insurgency. This is against the background of historical and socio-economic conditions prevalent in the Northeast region in general and Borno State in particular. Between 2003 and 2009 Mohammed Yusuf articulated his ideology which included *tawhid* (Oneness of God), opposition to and refusal of service to secular government (*taghut*) and rejection of Western education, which gave rise to the term Boko Haram or Western education is forbidden (Adamu, 2009). Although the Ulama (Muslim scholars) and the majority of Muslims in Borno remained moderate and opposed to the new Salafist ideology, it resonated with the youths, most of whom were illiterate, unemployed and vulnerable to religious indoctrination. The ideology forms the basis for a strident and potentially violent demand for a Shariah state based on the Quran rather than a government guided by a secular constitution. In this respect religion became the powerful driver of the insurgency.

However, an even more significant driver was the underdeveloped economic condition in the Northeast region. In 2015 the National Bureau of Statistics indicated that 76.8% of people in Northern Nigeria lived below the poverty line compared to 19.3% in the Southwest. The Bureau in 2017 cited a poverty index of 74.2% in the North. The grim statistics derived from the reversal of agricultural growth by deindustrialisation, as major agro-allied industries, including textile, food and beverages and other small and medium-scale enterprises across the North including Maiduguri, collapsed. The level of poverty and unemployment propelled the impoverished youths into the waiting arms of Boko Haram and its leader whose oratory and social support programmes seemed more real than futile government promises.

The insurgency broke out in July 2009 with violent attacks on government institutions including police headquarters and stations in Maiduguri. Eventually schools and churches were targeted and destroyed. By 2014 the insurgents were in control of 13 Local Government Areas in Northern Borno, parts of Northern Adamawa and Yobe. Their activities extended to other states outside the Northeast including Kano, Jos and Abuja where the United Nations headquarters and police headquarters came under attack (Kolade et al., 2019).

The government response to the Boko Haram insurgency was more violence. The initial response indeed included violent crackdowns, harassment and arrest of youths in communities suspected to be harbouring Boko Haram. Many alienated youths joined the Boko Haram, but the majority joined the Civilian Joint Task Force (CJTF) or Yangora, reinforcing the counter-insurgency. While the military strategy provided modest short-term results, the crisis became intractable. By 2015 the insurgency had taken its toll on the region. More than 2.2 million people had been displaced from their homes and over 35,000 killed (Ibrahim et al., 2017). A humanitarian disaster had ensued as schools were shut down and villages were deserted. Agriculture was grounded in emptied rural communities. The tragedy was reflected in the emergence of IDP camps in Borno Adamawa, Yobe, Gombe and as far as Abuja. The scope and intractable nature of this disaster exposed the relative ineffectiveness of a purely military approach and limitations of the top-down interventions.

Findings and Discussion

Respondents' Profile

The summary of the respondents' profiles is provided in Table 16.1. Altogether, nine IDPs were interviewed. In addition, three NGO workers, two government officials and one member of the host community were interviewed across three locations. The majority of the respondents reported here are male heads of households, but this is an ongoing study and care has been taken to ensure adequate female representation in the rest of the field exercise. Most of the respondents are young, under 40 years of age, and most hold primary or no formal education.

The following key themes emerged from the interview transcripts. They highlight the role of social capital on access to funding and resources, and skill development and access to market opportunities. The interviews also illuminate how entrepreneurship activities are contributing to the livelihood outcomes of displaced persons.

Social Capital and Access to Funding and Resources

The respondents highlighted how their networks have helped them in different ways to access funding and various material resources that helped them to cope in the aftermath of displacement. This can be especially critical at the point of arrival in a new location, often in areas with no NGOs, or where NGOs and other organisations are unable to access easily. In such cases it becomes more critical for displaced persons to tap into existing support mechanisms within their host communities, as one respondent observed:

Table 16.1 Profile of respondents

ID	Category	Location	Gender	Age	Level of education
1	IDP	Gwoza, Borno State	Female	32	Primary
2	Government official	Gwoza, Borno State	Male	51	Post-secondary
3	NGO	Gwoza, Borno State	Female	31	Degree
4	Host community	Gwoza, Borno State	Male	48	Primary
5	IDP	Gwoza, Borno State	Male	28	Secondary
6	NGO	Gwoza, Borno State	Male	33	Post-secondary
7	IDP	Kasaisa, Yobe State	Male	52	No formal education
8	IDP	Kasaisa, Yobe State	Male	32	No formal education
9	IDP	Kasaisa, Yobe State	Male	41	Primary
10	IDP	Kasaisa, Yobe State	Male	51	No formal education
11	IDP	Kasaisa, Yobe State	Male	23	No formal education
12	IDP	Kasaisa, Yobe State	Female	26	Primary
13	Government official	Bakassi, Borno State	Male	25	Degree
14	NGO	Bakassi, Borno State	Male	32	Degree
15	IDP	Bakassi, Borno State	Female	36	Secondary

When the first attack was launched by Boko Haram in our community, we left without taking anything with us, and we arrived this community (Kasaisa). After two days, the ward head (Bulama) gave us an accommodation for a while and allocated a piece of land to all of us and we erected a makeshift structure and stayed in it. Two days later, the Chairman of our Local Government Area (Gujba) gave us two bags of maize each to all displaced persons. (Respondent 7, Kasaisa Camp, Yobe State Nigeria, June 2019)

This respondent, along with others, was introduced to the community in question by family and friends. In addition, these displaced persons with active external networks are able to access support from their friends based in other parts of the country. These include old friendships and professional relationships forged when the respondents visited, lived or worked in other parts of the country's six geopolitical zones or had people from other parts of the country coming to live or visit temporarily in their community prior to the insurgency. This support helps affected households to meet urgent primary needs such as shelter and food needs, which is an important threshold before they can begin the process of rebuilding their lives:

> …some few friends and business partners have been very helpful when we were first displaced due to Boko-Haram insurgency and relocated to this place. In-kind and cash assistance were brought to me, and that has greatly helped in addressing some of our immediate need like clothing, kitchen utensils and food stuff. (Respondent 8, Kasaisa Camp, Yobe State, June 2019)

The material and financial resources that some of the IDPs accessed from their network have also been used to support income-generating entrepreneurial activities. This is in recognition of the need to have an extra stream of income to meet ongoing households needs. Therefore, some of the cash they received from their networks are used as start-up funds or to revive businesses that were shut down after the respondents were forced to flee from their homes:

> My new friends helped me introduce me to their market; they also helped me with cash to start my business in my new place (Respondent 1, Gwoza Camp, Borno State, June 2019).
>
> Some of our families residing in Damaturu town have come to our assistance when we were displaced and settled in this place. Monetary and in-kind supports were brought to us and these have really made us to recover from the loss we encountered. One of my nieces among our family gave me N120,000 to start something and with that I started a business to sustain us. (Respondent 9, Kasaisa Camp, Yobe State, June 2019)

Social Networks, Market Opportunities and Skill Development

The subject of access to new market opportunities, mentioned by respondent 1 above, is another key theme that ran through the interviews with the displaced persons and other stakeholders. It is obvious that forced displacement has a disorienting impact on affected households. However, it also precipitated new market opportunities that can reinforce pathways to long-term recovery. Displaced households bring to their host communities different, and sometimes new, products, services, skills and tastes. Each of these, individually and as an aggregate, can have varying benefits to expansion and organisation of markets. As they settle in their host communities, it is possible, over time, for displaced people to assume full roles as consumers, suppliers, producers and service providers. However, this is not a guaranteed outcome, as a lot of other factors need to align in order for this to happen. These include appropriate policy instruments and interventions to support the development and expansion of new markets, and targeted capacity building and funding to support entrepreneurial activities.

Bridging social capital can help them to access market opportunities and achieve integration into the wider entrepreneurial ecosystem—that is, the system of micro-enterprise owners, customers, suppliers and other actors that support the creation and growth of new ventures. For example, IDPs who are micro-enterprise owners can draw on their new networks of friends in the host community to gather information that can support the creation of new products and services. They can also draw on these new networks to develop new skills and create new markets for their products and services. As one respondent observed, they also profit from the acquisition of relevant skills within their new networks:

> They helped me by accommodating me and being kind to me, and also teach me so many skills that I didn't have before and it really helps me. They also connect me to other customers. What I learn from these people is what is really helping me. (Respondent 5, Gwoza Camp, Borno State, June 2019)

Some of the NGOs have incorporated skills training into their intervention programmes, in recognition of the need to help IDPs help themselves, and not rely entirely on handouts:

> We empowered them with materials to start the business and monitoring them on how to do it. We also teach them so many skills that can help them do their business on their own. We also teach them how to serve - We also teach them marketing strategies. (Respondent 3, NGO Worker, Gwoza Camp, Borno State Nigeria, June 2019)

However, from the respondents' comments such as the one quoted above, there is a sense that much of the NGOs' interventions, including skills-training programmes, is underpinned by a top-down approach. There is therefore a need to actively engage affected households in a co-creation process that includes assessment of existing skills, analysis of areas where skill augmentations are more appropriate and a provision of opportunities for the IDPs to present their own business ideas. In effect, the existing skills and business ideas of displaced people can be used as a baseline for NGOs' intervention programming.

Entrepreneurship and Livelihood Outcomes

The respondents highlighted various ways in which their entrepreneurial skills and activities have contributed to livelihood outcomes. These include meeting basic existential needs primarily food, clothing and shelter. They also include the indirect impact on other important, if intangible, outcomes such as education and human capital development. For example, this respondent describes how his entrepreneurial activities have not only helped him to meet basic needs like food and clothing, but also how it has afforded him the income to support his education and those of his siblings:

> This really helps me, because these skills that I learned is of great help to me in this insurgency. Anywhere I go I can do work that will help me to provide food, clothing for myself and my brothers and so many things to help us in life. (Respondent 5, Gwoza Camp, Borno State, June 2019)
>
> In this insurgency, I was able to run a business that helped me to complete my secondary school and also support my brothers too for their primary school education. Because of the limited cash I have and many responsibilities awaiting me, I couldn't go further with my education, but I believe one day I will still go further. (Respondent 5, Gwoza Camp, Borno State, June 2019)

In addition, engaging in entrepreneurial activities appear to have boosted respondents' self-belief, dignity and sense of independence. This can be hugely significant in terms of mental and psychological recovery from the trauma and distress precipitated by forced displacement. As the following comment reveals, the quest for dignity and independence is a key priority for displaced persons:

> These [skills and business activities] have helped me in my day-to-day living as a displaced person. I can engage myself in my little business... And it helps me move on with my life, with a hope that I can be an independent person in life. (Respondent 1, Gwoza camp, Borno State, June 2019)

Conclusion and Recommendations

Traditional, mainly material approaches to interventions in disaster situations have come under increased scrutiny in recent years because they have failed to deliver desired long-term outcomes and, being expensive and logistically difficult, have encountered resource and capacity constraints in the face of continually expanding humanitarian crises. The study found that displaced households typically rely on their networks of family and friends as the first source of support in the immediate aftermath of the insurgency, before they are in a position to access any other possible external support. Furthermore, even after affected households have come in contact with humanitarian agencies, they continue to rely extensively on their social networks, including newly forged ones, in order to access new resources and opportunities to rebuild their lives. In this regard, we present a new theoretical framework that maps the changes in the social capital stock of affected peoples before and after displacement. The framework explains the instrumentality of new forms of social capital in shaping new relationships and interactions among entrepreneurs, suppliers and customers; fostering new channels of information flow and diffusion of innovation; and lowering outgroup prejudice. In turn, these are conducive to opportunity seeking, resource acquisition and market organisation for entrepreneurial outcomes. In line with this, the study found that entrepreneurial activities and market opportunities among displaced people provides a viable pathway to generate income and thereby improve household welfare and other livelihood outcomes. Governments and stakeholders can draw on this in the design and implementation of policies and humanitarian actions that foster long-term livelihood outcomes through entrepreneurial development among the displaced.

However, while social capital is a source of critical support, it need not be a replacement for humanitarian agencies. Rather, the findings in this paper can point to opportunities and methods for humanitarian actors to stimulate social and human capital among crisis-affected people purposively as part of their interventions, with the aim of better outcomes and value for aid money. The links and interactions of displaced peoples can be viewed as a form of linking social capital. In terms of specific policy recommendations, governments in the affected region can use public procurement to incentivise entrepreneurship. Procurement can be used in a strategic and targeted way to drive demand and reward entrepreneurial activities. For example, the government can contract IDP farmers to supply raw produce for government-sponsored free school meals, produce school uniforms for free government-sponsored provision thereof and deploy the services of IDPs in public construction works.

References

Acemoglu, D., & Autor, D. (2011). The basic theory of human capital. In *Lectures in Labor Economics* (pp. 1–34). London, UK.

Adamu, F. I. (2009). Ideology of Boko Haram. *Journal of Islamic Education, 2*(2), 31–44

Adesoji, A. (2010). The Boko Haram uprising and Islamic revivalism in Nigeria. *Africa Spectr., 45,* 95–108. https://doi.org/10.2307/25798918.

Aldrich, D. P., & Meyer, M. A. (2015). Social capital and community resilience. *American Behavioral Scientist, 59,* 254–269. https://doi.org/10.1177/0002764214550299.

Aldrich, D. P., Kolade, O., McMahon, K., & Smith, R. (2020). Social capital's role in humanitarian crises. *Journal of Refugee Studies.* https://doi.org/10.1093/jrs/feaa001.

Baum, F. E., & Ziersch, A. M. (2001). Social capital: Glossary. *Cambridge University Press.* https://doi.org/10.1017/CBO9780511815447.

Becker, G. S. (1964). *Human capital: A theoretical and empirical analysis with special reference to education.* New York: The National Bureau of Economic Research.

Bhandari, R. B. (2014). Social capital in disaster risk management; A case study of social capital mobilization following the 1934 Kathmandu Valley earthquake in Nepal. *Disaster Prevention and Management, 23,* 314–328. https://doi.org/10.1108/DPM-06-2013-0105.

Bourdieu, P., & Wacquant, L. (1992). Interest, habitus, rationality. In *An invitation to reflective sociology* (pp. 115–140). University of Chicago Press.

Camps, S., & Marques, P. (2014). Exploring how social capital facilitates innovation: The role of innovation enablers. *Technological Forecasting and Social Change, 88,* 325–348. https://doi.org/10.1016/j.techfore.2013.10.008.

Coleman, J. S. (1988). Social capital in the creation of human capital. *American Journal of Sociology, 94,* S95. https://doi.org/10.1086/228943.

Development Initiatives. (2019). *Donors at the triple nexus: Lessons from the United Kingdom.* Bristol, UK.

de Wolf, F., & Wilkinson, O. (2019). *The triple nexus, localization, and local faith actors: The intersections between faith, humanitarian response, development, and peace.* Copenhagen.

Dynes, R. (2006). Social capital: Dealing with community emergencies. *Homel. Secur. Aff., 2,* 1–26.

Fafchamps, M. (2006). Development and social capital. *Journal of Development Studies.* https://doi.org/10.1080/00220380600884126.

Fukuyama, F. (2001). Social capital, civil society and development. *Third World Quarterly, 22*, 7–20. https://doi.org/10.1080/01436590020022547.

Grootaert, C. (1998). *Social capital: The missing link?* (No. 3). World Bank Social Capital Initiative.

Hoffmann, R., & Muttarak, R. (2017). Learn from the past, prepare for the future: Impacts of education and experience on disaster preparedness in the Philippines and Thailand. *World Development, 96*, 32–51. https://doi.org/10.1016/j.worlddev.2017.02.016.

Howe, P. (2019). The triple nexus: A potential approach to supporting the achievement of the Sustainable Development Goals? *World Development, 124*, 104629. https://doi.org/10.1016/j.worlddev.2019.104629.

Ibrahim, J., Bagu, C., & Yau, Y. Z. (Eds.). (2017). *Understanding community resilience in the context of the boko haram insurgency in Nigeria*. Centre for Information Technology and Development (CITAD).

ICVA. (2018). *Navigating the nexus topic 1: The nexus explained*.

Inkpen, A. C., & Tsang, E. W. K. (2005). Social capital networks, and knowledge transfer. *Academy of Management Review, 30*, 146–165. https://doi.org/10.5465/AMR.2005.15281445.

Internal Displacement Monitoring Centre. (2015). *Boko Haram's terror ripples through the region*.

International Rescue Committee. (2019). *Operationalizing SDG16 and the triple nexus: Exploring lessons from current peacebuilding practice in conflict–affected contexts*.

Johnson, N., Elliott, D., & Drake, P. (2013). Exploring the role of social capital in facilitating supply chain resilience. *Supply Chain Management, 18*, 324–336. https://doi.org/10.1108/SCM-06-2012-0203.

Kolade, O., Kibreab, G., James, S., & Smith, R. (2019). Picking up the pieces: Social capital and entrepreneurship for livelihood recovery among displaced populations in Northeast Nigeria. *Institute for Small Business & Entrepreneurship Annual Conference, 11*.

Krantz, B. L., 2001. *The sustainable livelihood approach to poverty reduction: An introduction*.

Laroche, M., & Ruggeri, G. C. (1999). On the concept and dimensions of human capital in a knowledge-based economy context. *Canadian Public Policy, 15*(1), 87–100. Marcel Mérette, University of Ottawa.

Lautze, S., & Raven-Roberts, A. (2006). Violence and complex humanitarian emergencies: Implications for livelihoods models. *Disasters, 30*, 383–401. https://doi.org/10.1111/j.0361-3666.2006.00328.x.

Mayomi, I., & Mohammed, J. A. (2014). A Decade assessments of Maiduguri urban expansion (2002–2012): Geospatial Approach. *Global Journal of Human-Social Science: (B) Geography, Geo-Sciences Environmental Science & Disaster Management, 14*, 1–9.

Medinilla, A., Shiferaw, T., & Veron, P. (2019). *Think local. Governance, humanitarian aid, development and peacebuilding in Somalia*.

Nahapiet, J., & Ghoshal, S. (1998). Social capital, intellectual capital, and the organisational advantage. *Academy of Management Review, 23*, 242–266. https://doi.org/10.2307/259373.

Neumeyer, X., Santos, S. C., Caetano, A., & Kalbfleisch, P. (2019). Entrepreneurship ecosystems and women entrepreneurs: A social capital and network approach. *Small Business Economics, 53*, 475–489. https://doi.org/10.1007/s11187-018-9996-5.

OECD. (2019). *DAC recommendation on the humanitarian-development-peace nexus*. OECD/Legal/5019.

Portes, A., & Landolt, P. (2000). Social capital: Promise and pitfalls of its role in development. *Journal of Latin American Studies*. https://doi.org/10.1017/S0022216X00005836.

Pronyk, P. M., Harpham, T., Busza, J., Phetla, G., Morison, L. A., Hargreaves, J. R., Kim, J. C., Watts, C. H., & Porter, J. D. (2008). Can social capital be intentionally generated? A randomized trial from rural South Africa. *Social Science and Medicine, 67*, 1559–1570. https://doi.org/10.1016/j.socscimed.2008.07.022.

Putnam, R. D. (2001). *Bowling alone: the collapse and revival of American Community* (New ed.). Simon & Schuster.

Putnam, R. D. (1995). Bowling alone: America's declining social capital. *Journal of Democracy, 6*, 65–78. https://doi.org/10.1016/S0362-3319(02)00190-8.

Putnam, R. D. (1994). *Making democracy work: Civic traditions in modern Italy*. Princeton University Press.

Schultz, T. W. (1961). Invetsment in human capital. *The American Economic Review, 51*(1), 1–17. https://www.sciencemag.org/lookup/doi/10.1126/science.151.3712.867-a.

Theodoraki, C., Messeghem, K., & Rice, M. P. (2018). A social capital approach to the development of sustainable entrepreneurial ecosystems: An explorative study. *Small Business Economics, 51*, 153–170. https://doi.org/10.1007/s11187-017-9924-0.

Tobias, J., Mair, J., & Barbosa-Leiker, C. (2013). Toward a theory of transformative entrepreneuring: Poverty reduction and conflict resolution in Rwanda's entrepreneurial coffee sector. *Journal of Business Venturing, 28*, 728–742. https://doi.org/10.1016/j.jbusvent.2013.03.003.

Tristan Claridge. (2013). Types of social capital [WWW Document]. Social Capital Research Training. http://www.socialcapitalresearch.com/explanation-types-social-capital/. Accessed 1/4/2019.

UNHCR. (2019). *Trends at a Glance: Forced displacement in 2018*.

United Nations Secretariat. (2019). *Strengthening of the coordination of emergency humanitarian assistance of the United Nations*.

United Nations Secretariat. (2016). *Outcome of the Wolrd Humanitarian Summit—Report of the Secretary General*.

University of Maiduguri. (2009). *Faculty of Engineering Handbook*. University of Maiduguri. https://doi.org/10.1017/CBO9781107415324.004.

UNOCHA. (2017). *New way of working*.

Uphoff, N., & Wijayaratna, C. M. (2000). Demonstrated benefits from social capital: The productivity of farmer organisations in Gal Oya, Sri Lanka. *World Development, 28*, 1875–1890. https://doi.org/10.1016/S0305-750X(00)00063-2.

Wind, T. R., & Komproe, I. H. (2012). The mechanisms that associate community social capital with post-disaster mental health: A multilevel model. *Social Science and Medicine, 75*, 1715–1720.

Woolcock, M., & Narayan, D. (2000). Social capital: Implications for development theory, and policy. *World Bank Res. Obs., 15*, 225–249. https://doi.org/10.1093/wbro/15.2.225.

17

Barriers and Opportunities for Refugee Entrepreneurship in Africa: A Social Capital Perspective

Tracy Luseno and Oluwaseun Kolade

Introduction

Africa currently faces the old age phenomena of displacement and is yet to find a plausible solution neither create a dichotomy that distinguishes refugees from economic migrants. According to UNHCR (1951; Article 1(A)(2)) a refugee is *someone who is unable or unwilling to return to their country of origin owing to a well-founded fear of being persecuted for reasons of race, religion, nationality, membership of a particular social group, or political opinion.* The current global refugee population is 25.9 million of whom more than 26% are hosted on the African continent (UNHCR, 2020). Despite efforts to establish peace in parts of the continent, armed conflicts prevail resulting in 5 of the top 10 refugee hosting countries being in Africa with Uganda, Ethiopia and Kenya hosting majority of asylum seekers (UNHCR, 2020). The chapter builds upon literature analysis on social capital and entrepreneurship as well as contextual sources. Specifically, we

---

T. Luseno (✉)
De Montfort University, Leicester, UK
e-mail: tracy.luseno@dmu.ac.uk

O. Kolade
Department of Management and Entrepreneurship, De Montfort University, Leicester, UK
e-mail: seun.kolade@dmu.ac.uk

© The Author(s), under exclusive license to Springer Nature
Switzerland AG 2022
O. Kolade et al. (eds.), *The Palgrave Handbook of African Entrepreneurship*,
https://doi.org/10.1007/978-3-030-75894-3_17

look at how refugees in Kenya overcome barriers towards entrepreneurship given the unique long adopted 'encampment' policy by the government that restricts their right to work and freedom of movement (Carrier, 2016). Ultimately, we propose a conceptual framework on social capital and refugee entrepreneurship.

Studies on refugee entrepreneurship have suggested that institutional environment, relevant experience, language barriers or social embeddedness impact entrepreneurial and integration initiatives by refugees (Constant et al., 2008; Millar-Schijf & Choi, 2008). As such there exist a 'refugee gap' making it difficult for refugees to successfully enter the economic sector in the host country in comparison to other groups of migrants (Bakker et al., 2017). This gap may be associated with traumatic flight experiences, loss of educational qualifications or lack of recognition in host country and context of reception on administrative processes because of refugee influx or asylum procedures. Similarly, literature on refugee entrepreneurship in Africa offers the challenging nature of integration and labour seen as early as upon their arrival in the host country. These challenges include employment opportunities offered in camps, rural and urban settings, the attitudes of employers, lack of information on legal entitlements of refugees, institutional and language barriers (Carciotto & Cristian., 2017; Zetter & Ruaudel, 2016). Despite these challenges, entrepreneurship amongst refugees has also been found to be complex, highlighting characteristics that are distinct cognitively, affectively and socially (Bizri, 2017) thus becoming an effective tool in integration and management of the refugee crisis. One that may be the solution to the burgeoning population of those forcibly displaced where the individual endowments such as characteristics, skills, competencies and education (human capital) as well as social relations and networks (social capital) can be drawn from to generate access to resources, new market opportunities and business ideas for forced migrants (Bagwell, 2015; Williams & Williams, 2012).

Social capital and refugee entrepreneurship literature has an increasing body of work, however, Barrett and Vershinina (2016) argue that it is often ungeneralisable, highly fragmented and contextual, with many case studies that focus on a specific group. Yet, despite the emergence of social capital and its relevance in forced migration (Wauters & Lambrecht, 2006, 2008) there remains paucity on forced migration research and the role social capital plays on entrepreneurship for refugees especially within an African context. Our contribution is denoted through showcasing how refugees harness social capital and entrepreneurial competencies to their advantage to overcome institutional environment and achieve entrepreneurial and livelihood outcomes. We then develop a conceptual framework that can be crucial to understanding refugee entrepreneurship.

The remainder of the chapter is structured as follows. Firstly, social capital is conceptualised and discussed. Subsequently, we highlight key theoretical underpinnings. We then highlight forced migration in Africa followed by a discussion within the Kenyan context. We then propose a conceptual framework and conclusion.

Conceptualisation of Social Capital

Social capital is defined by Bourdieu (1985, p. 248) as *'the aggregate of the actual and potential resources linked to possessions of a durable network of more or less institutionalised relationships of mutual acquaintances.'* It has been used to describe and address an array of social phenomena within different academic traditions and research including socio-economic performance, democracy, competitive advantages and organisational dynamics (Adler & Kwon, 2000; Ostrom & Ahn, 2003).

There are three forms of social capital: bonding, bridging and linking. The internal focus of social capital primarily focuses on the relationship individuals possess and maintain with other individuals, additionally, there are resources that are available to them within the established networks. Coleman (1990) illustrated this view, emphasizing that collectivity within a network with a focus on density facilitates collective goals; Adler and Kwon (2000) termed this as a bonding form of social capital.

The external focus of these networks illuminates those resources which individuals would not be able to reach without a 'bridge' that of which is provided by another individual who has access to them, Burt (1997), Bourdieu (1985) and Lin et al (1981) look to outward access of resources through social network. Often the two foci are not mutually exclusive and as Adler and Kwon (2000) state, are highly dependent on the perspective and on the level of analysis.

Linking social capital is derived from the term Linkage in Szreter and Woolcock (2004); these proponents presented in this form of social capital often define the powers and resource distinctions within society amongst all actors. Unlike bridging social capital where individuals horizontally access resources from those who belong to same group in terms of status and power, linking social capital has been found to connect individuals 'vertically' across power gradients to explicitly connect individuals with formal institutions and as such is essential to the wellbeing and long-term development of marginalised groups (Lipsky, 1980; Szreter & Woolcock, 2004).

Levels of Analysis

There exists a debate as to whether social capital should be analysed and understood as an individual or collective resource (Poortinga, 2006). In its broadest form, social capital has been defined as resources held and produced by the social relations of an individual and as a collective as theories on social capital often are situated in the micro, meso and macro levels of analysis relative to the levels within society. The micro level analyses the linkages between the individual and their connectedness with members within a similar hierarchical level. The meso level aspects are concerned with formal and informal networks within members of community institutions, services and groups across adjacent hierarchical levels paving way to access resources. The macro level structure identifies the support provided by formal institutions such as government institutions and laws that enables community responsiveness to facilitate support. Figure 17.1 shows the conceptual model of the levels derived from the literature on social capital.

Forced Migration, Vulnerabilities and Livelihood Strategies of Refugees in Africa

All African countries are signatories of the 1951 United Nations Convention on the status of refugees and the 1969 Organisation of African Unity Convention where refugees are accorded the right to healthcare, non-discrimination, shelter, education and social protection (UN, 1948). However, different nations have interpreted these inconsistently resulting in poor adherence to humanitarian laws that have left nearly 2 million refugees in 10 countries dependent on unilateral agencies and food aid (Kimetrica, 2016). Refugees are rendered to humanitarian actors and development partners such as the United Nations High Commission for Refugees (UNHCR), United Nations Development Programme (UNDP) and International Organisation of Migration (IOM) that struggle to remain vigilant in preventing the spread of ongoing and recurring epidemics, temporary housing provisions and healthcare facilities.

Figure 17.2 displays the fluctuating populations of refugees in the continent from 1990 to 2018. At a peak of 6.4 million in 1994 the population

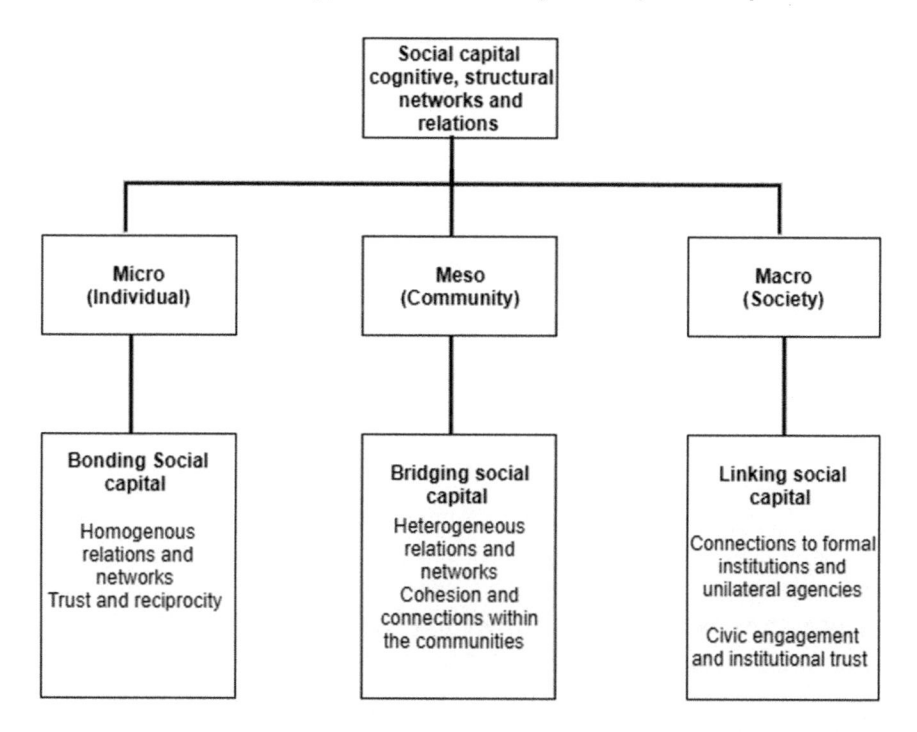

Fig. 17.1 Social determinants of refugee entrepreneurships and levels of analysis (*Source* Author(s))

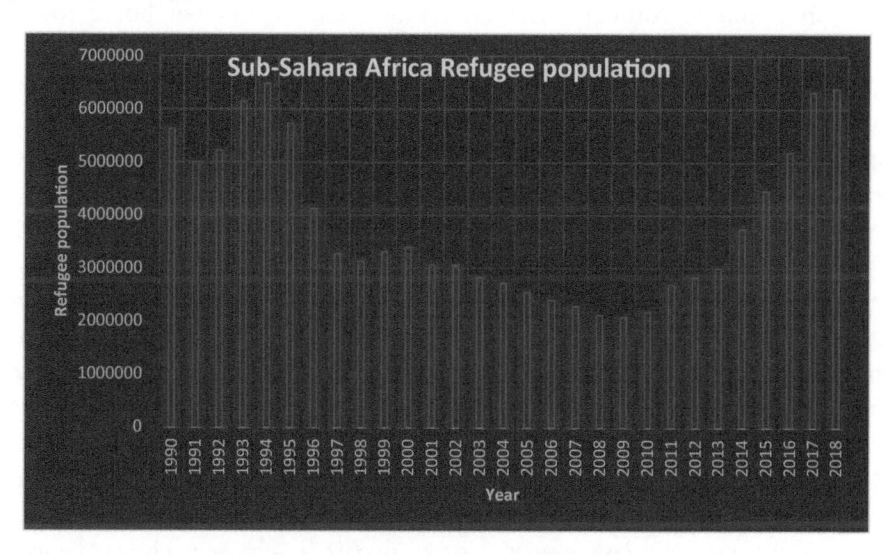

Fig. 17.2 Sub-Sahara Africa refugee population 1990–2018

declined by nearly 60% to 2.08 m in 2009. A number that has since tripled evidently showing a refugee crisis on the continent. The rise in number of refugees creates several problems and challenges for both the host community and refugee populations. Subsequently, refugees face violations of their basic human rights and fundamental social protection as host countries struggle to provide what little resources they have towards welfare for forced migrants (Cediey & Foroni, 2008). A failure that has been termed as a 'protection gap' (Türk & Dowd, 2014) due to the lack of legal entitlements and is often met '*by closed borders, hostility, discrimination and abuse*' (Oxfam, 2016).

Refugees find themselves in a dilemma composed of restrictive and impractical options to their avail. Majority of them are often unable to return to their home countries, despite efforts by the host governments, their governments and humanitarian agencies, as a result, the sustained uncertainty over their protection, safety and dignity in environments that continue to be volatile and fragile post-conflicts. Opportunities for resettlement in third countries are also on the decline, particularly in Western societies, due to the decline in quotas on refugee resettlement. Often refugees are challenged in accessing basic economic and social activities irrespective of the vast human capital that is present amongst refugee populations. Consequently, many refugees are still entirely dependent on declining humanitarian aid with minimal viable paths to self-reliance.

In situations of conflict, the links refugees have with their home countries are inadvertently destroyed thus leading to loss of family network, social contacts, community and human capital skills (Kolade, 2018; Maniraguha, 2011). However, in some cases the migration networks, socio-economic opportunities and liberal policies help inform forced migrants on how to travel, assimilate and create self-sustenance within host countries (Massey, 1988).

Refugees are likely to have less extensive social networks in their host country because of fleeing their homes. Furthermore, they no longer can acquire funds, capital or labour force as they fear persecution or harm from their country of origin. They may also be less likely to engage in self-reliance or self-employment due to potential traumatic experience from their home country during the flee thus they may likely have psychological problems (Lyon et al., 2008; Wauters & Lambrecht, 2008). Moreover, their decision to migrate was involuntary therefore, they remain uncertain as to where they may end up thus have less opportunity to prepare in advance. The challenges faced in starting a business (such as financial access and local market opportunity knowledge) often seem paradoxical to their success yet the research indicates that refugees are disproportionately entrepreneurial (IRC, 2018; Kamau & Fox, 2013; Vearey et al., 2011). Refugees and asylum seekers turn to entrepreneurship as a means of survival in attaining economic and social mobility thus able to overcome the negative conditions such as labour market obstacles (lack of educational credentials, discrimination and language barriers), unemployment and lack of job prospects (Moore & Mueller, 2002).

Though limited in access role, social capital and social networks play in rebuilding economic prospects amongst those forcibly displaced (Zetter et al., 2006) and largely link to the different tiers of vulnerability that exist amongst the displaced. For example, Somali refugees often possess better social connections in comparison to Burundi refugees in Uganda or South Sudanese refugees in Kenya (Betts, 2018). The reliance of refugees on their kin as a measure of exposure to customs and institutions creates networks that stand as structural links within new societies, hence, forging new prospects of friendship, marriage, employment and education opportunities, accommodation and financial aid (Marlowe, 2011). The explicit link that exists between family ties and social capital is crucial in establishing and improving their economic security and capital base. Several studies have found that financial resources from interconnected residential units are often pooled to cope with economic instabilities (Kleit et al., 2011). Furthermore, resources such as employment information, resettlement and welfare are exchanged in addition to aid received in household labour such as childcare and food preparation (Harris & Young, 2010).

Ties that exist outside of immediate family also offer forms of support such as ethnic group often foster economic adaptation through acting as kin networks, access to labour opportunities, community benefits and accommodation. Whereas networks obtained from humanitarian agencies and governments often offer support in early stages, such as acquisition of means to escape their countries, essential services and financial assistance. Additionally, these agents are crucial for integrating refugees into mainstream public spaces such as workplaces or schools as they provide access to households, material goods, employment opportunities and access to language training (Marlowe, 2011). This facilitates the capacity of refugees to re-establish disrupted networks whilst actively mobilising new forms of social capital that aid in rebuilding their lives.

Refugee History in Kenya

Kenya has a long-standing relationship with hosting refugees. It is the third largest refugee hosting country after Ethiopia (UNHCR, 2020). Currently hosting approximately 500,000 refugees. Kenya's relative stability, economic resilience and porous borders has had refugees since early 1970s (Ali et al., 2017). The geographic location of Kenya (see Fig. 17.3) sets it at a turbulent region, one that has Kenya on the receiving end of refugees and asylum seekers. These refugees enjoyed full status rights, including the right to reside in urban areas and free movement across the country, right to work, access to educational opportunities and application to legal rights to stay (IFC, 2018). However, the refugee regime in Kenya transformed from generous and hospitable with an emphasis on integration to that of hostility with growing levels of xenophobia, denial of basic human rights and few opportunities to integration in 1992 (Horst, 2003). This was as a result of an overwhelming

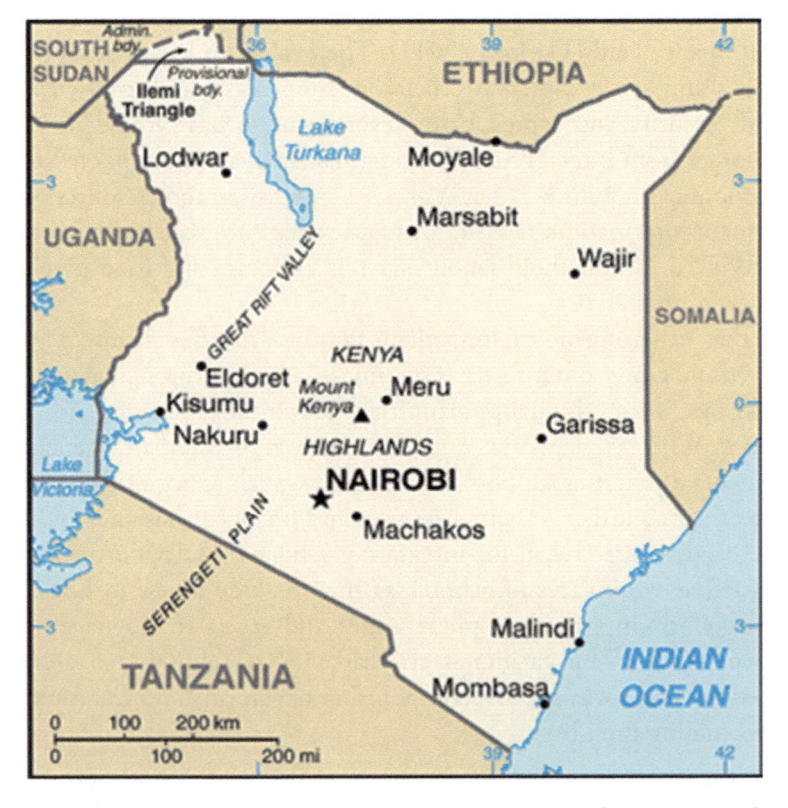

Fig. 17.3 Map of Kenya showing its neighbouring countries (*Source* cia.gov)

influx of refugees from Sudan and Somalia prompting withdrawal of the Kenyan authorities from refugee protection.

Though a member of the 1963 OAU and 1951 refugee convention, Kenya lacks its own national refugee legislation and instead heavily relies on the encampment policy that emerged in 1991. Kenya looks to the encampment policy as a solution to tackling its refugee crisis. One that has been criticised as a mechanism of the government to alleviate itself of refugee welfare and sees refugees designated to camps highlighted in Fig. 17.4 far from urban centres in predominantly arid and semi-arid areas that have often been subjected to socio-political marginalisation. A vast majority of refugees are not permitted to reside outside these camps and no longer granted working rights nor provided with opportunities to integrate.

The encampment policy stems from long-standing discrimination against the Somali over security and socio-economic credentials (Campbell et al., 2011). The policy was predicated on the condition of providing temporary protection and responsibility of refugees and asylum seekers are delegated

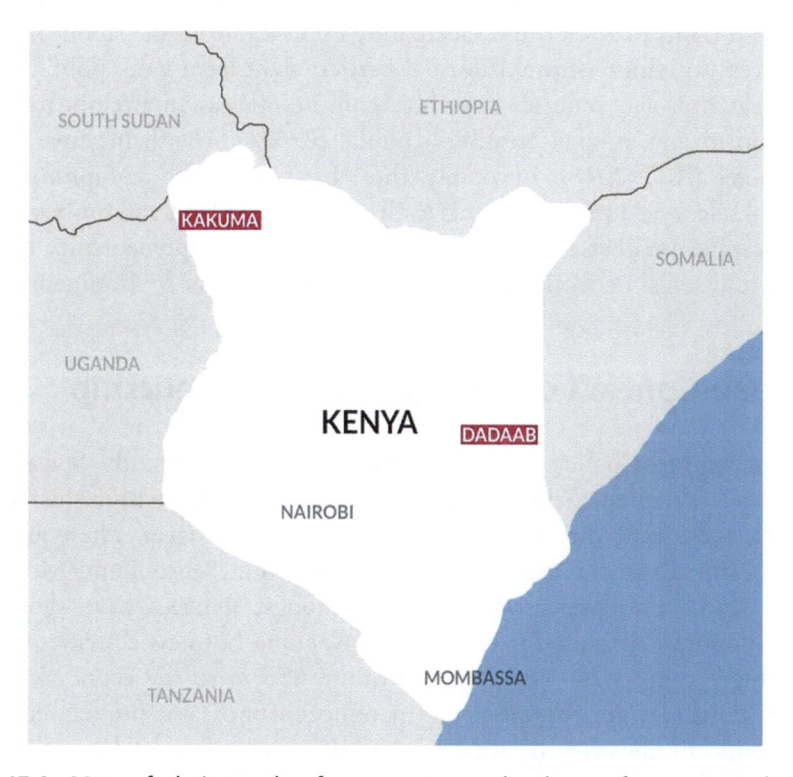

Fig. 17.4 Map of designated refugee camps and urban refugee areas (*Source* UNHCR.org)

to unilateral agencies including UNHCR, International Organisation for Migration (IOM) and Danish Refugee Council (DRC). This option is viewed as most appropriate by the agencies and Kenyan government as it allowed provision of assistance to the arriving refugees and guarded the Kenya's national interests. Refugees who had settled along the coast and in Mombasa (mostly Somali's) were transferred to Dadaab camp and those who primarily came from Ethiopia, Sudan, DRC were hosted in Kakuma camp. Permission to reside in urban areas was only granted to those seeking higher education and medical care unavailable within camps or formal employment though work permits are rare. Even so, residing outside the camp for refugees meant an implicit forfeiture of protection and assistance in exchange for freedom and pursuit of opportunities (UNHCR, 2020).

Kenya's development framework makes no mention of refugees leaving them no choice but to create networks within and outside the camp that open frontiers for both refugee and host communities despite the formal and informal barriers faced. Formal barriers stem from the Security Laws Amendment Act that withholds constitutional rights, including freedom of movement and rights to work thus exacerbating exclusion from the labour markets and access to infrastructure. Informal barriers stem from weak political will, that seeks to isolate refugees from host communities as an attempt to counterterrorism and as such creating a public perception with negative effects that linger (IRC, 2018). Inevitably, these barriers severely compromise the material safety (adequate standards for living, housing land and property) and social capital (market opportunities and access to entrepreneurship, human capital and social networks and institutional and societal environment).

Kenyan Context of Refugee Entrepreneurship

The encampment policy situates Kenya as a unique case study. Specifically, on refugee entrepreneurship. Despite challenges presented within the African context, there exist thriving business initiatives by refugees. There are over 5000 businesses in the camps and hundreds within Nairobi and Mombasa (IFC, 2018). Entrepreneurship activity amongst refugees have shown to boost economic activity, for example, in Kakuma business activities within the refugee camp were found to contribute $56 m to the economy (IFC, 2018). Furthermore, entrepreneurs in refugee camps also provide employment opportunities for the local communities, who largely depend on the existence of camps as they are marginalised and neglected by the government with little development initiatives (IRC, 2018).

Most recently, policies towards allowing partnerships and integration of refugees have been adopted. The Comprehensive Refugee Response (CRRF) Framework in 2017 (UNHCR, 2020) and the Global Compact on Refugees (GCR) in 2018, could change the encampment policy that severely incumbers and limits refugees creating promise of investment and integration for refugees and the host community. Additionally, in 2016 the government embarked on the first of its kind 'self-reliance' refugee settlement in Kaloboyei, Kenya that seeks to create self-reliance and interaction with the host community (Betts et al., 2020). These two institutional factors (UNHCRs' CRRF and Kaloboyei initiative) places Kenya in a strong position to create possible solutions towards the conundrum that surrounds its refugee crisis. If successful, refugees would access avenues for job creation, entrepreneurship and integration (Tippens, 2017 and improve the market-based livelihoods and increase private sector involvement (Sanghi et al., 2016; Staps, 2018).

Despite these efforts, there is very minimal improvement in refugee entrepreneur conditions who still face institutional environment from both policy and market contexts. Though it makes economic sense to improve labour market outcomes for refugees, the provision of labour market access is politically charged (Mckinsey Global Institute, 2016). Furthermore, the host communities surrounding refugee camps often perceive refugees as receiving better treatment whereas for those in urban areas the corrupt city council and officials often harass those engaging in business through bribery and extortion leaving little room for profit (Campbell, 2006). Though more recently, entrepreneurship amongst refugees in Kaloboyei camp is changing local perception of refugees from that of passive towards active participation (Betts et al., 2020).

The challenges faced by refugees in Kenya imply that entrepreneurship can lead to self-reliance from both humanitarian assistance and the state. There is an extensive depth of research on immigrant entrepreneurship in comparison to that of refugees (Romero & Valdez, 2016) and though refugees require even greater support for integration, similar experiences exist between the two groups. Romero and Valdez (2016) state that immigrant entrepreneurial success is perceived as overcoming structural inequality that comes from entering an economy and society as an immigrant with unequal rights and access coupled with an interaction between individual agency, social capital and strong community links. Similarly, Wauters and Lambrecht (2008) termed refugee entrepreneurship as 'killing two birds with one stone' where the domestic economy can be boosted and promote integration into host community. Kenya's rate of entrepreneurship and entrepreneurship education training has been on the rise given the rise in unemployment.

Entrepreneurship is also viewed to contribute to integration that goes beyond economics and improve other aspects of self-reliance (Betts et al., 2020) such as the case of Kakuma where both groups acquire skills and qualifications through language and vocational training (UNHCR, 2020). Integration and acceptance from both the refugee and host community perspectives have been cited as a primary reason for refugees seeking to be entrepreneurs (Betts et al., 2020; Heilbrunn, 2019). Integration and acceptance facilitate opportunities to accessing better networks and engaging communities beyond that of the entrepreneur within the camps whilst allowing those in urban areas to purchase assets such as housing.

Social Capital

This section looks at the three forms of social capital to identify the network structures and society relations using empirical evidence that result in entrepreneurial and livelihood outcomes. Table 17.1 provides a summary on how the three forms of social capital are mobilised amongst refugee populations in Kenya.

Bonding Social Capital

Bonding social capital is fundamental during resettlement amongst those forcibly displaced as it is often developed amongst those with similar backgrounds. The determinants of success for refugees in Kenya are because of their own agency, identity and capacity with most bonds formed amongst similar ethnic groups. Somali and Ethiopian refugees are perceived to be the most engaging in business activities in comparison to Congolese and South Sudanese communities a factor that is attributed to their access to remittance and networks (Betts, 2018). In the case of Somali entrepreneurs, they use global networks that are forged through their ethnic ties to further develop their business and market (Kamau & Fox, 2013). The formation of ethnic community organisations is often used to strengthen sense of identity and safety (Spencer, 2006), an example of this is the *hawala* banking system within Kakuma camp that allows borrowing of capital to finance small business initiatives amongst the Somali community.

Table 17.1 Social capital amongst refugees in Kenya

Social capital	Kakuma camp (aid model)	Kaloboyei settlement (self-reliance model)	Nairobi (urban area)
Bonding Social Capital	• Ethnic ties forged promote capital lending systems such as *hawala*	• Travel between the Kakuma camp and the Kalobeyei settlement allows for ethnic ties to form	• Ethnic ties are formed to facilitate lack of support from government and unilateral agencies • Entrepreneurs possess stronger ties with host community from neighbourhood cohesion
Bridging Social Capital	• Community spaces built in religious, employment and educational opportunities • Ties extend to urban and international areas due to long existence of the camp (28 years)	• Kaloboyei settlement integrates both refugee and host community members that forge networks through schools and businesses • Community spaces built in religious, employment and educational opportunities	• Access to market facilitates opportunities to extend to international markets and access to remittance • Well established businesses extend opportunities to facilitate goods and services to those in camp settings
Linking Social Capital	• Relationships forged by community leaders. Government and unilateral agencies provide instrumental access to information and market	• Challenges from lack of established relationships with Government and unilateral agencies provide instrumental access to information and market	• Challenges from strained relationships between refugees and law enforcement often result in bribery and harassment • Bribery and corruption provide opportunities to distribute goods and services to camp settings and countries such as Somalia

Source Ali et al. (2017), Betts et al. (2020), IFC (2018), and Kamau and Fox (2013)

Bridging Social Capital

The formation of looser connections within the groups allows for participation within the wider community that results in creation of values and governance processes. Refugees who have been living in camps for long periods have built community spaces that provide religious activities, employment and education opportunities (Betts, 2018; Kimetrica, 2016). These spaces facilitate integration amongst the refugee population as well as with the local host communities as entrepreneurs employ individuals from other ethnic communities to expand their customer base (Kamau & Fox, 2013). The longevity of refugees in camps has also fostered external networks such as those of Ethiopian and Somali groups that provide access to external markets in urban areas such as Nairobi and Mombasa (Kamau & Fox, 2013). These relationships have been found to be deeper and more intense in comparison to those that are formed at the neighbourhood level (Betts et al., 2020).

Linking Social Capital

Refugees in Kenya find themselves having weak connections with state structures and institutions. Often viewed as service recipients, refugee communities seldom have influence on policies and debates that involve their welfare (Betts, 2018). Refugees are often met with hostility and discrimination by government and law enforcement agencies that has led to undermining and erosion of the linking social capital between the two groups. Therefore, greater effort is often required from the refugee communities. Some ethnic groups possess stronger links with state and institutional structures as their extended links to urban areas often result in bribery of officials to allow access to goods and services such as Somali traders between Daadab camp who distribute goods to Somalia from Mombasa (IFC, 2018). Community leaders have also been found to provide a crucial link between the community and public service providers in the camps. For example, Kakuma camp has seen great development due to formation of personal relationships between community leaders, government and unilateral service providers that have been instrumental to development of the camp.

Institutional Barriers

Policy Barriers

Policies are in place to foster self-reliance and promote private investment, but considerable constraints remain. As stated in the Refugees Act of 2006, the right to employment, movement and ownership are granted. However, the ability of refugees to exercise them is limited by practical constraints and the encampment policy. Majority of entrepreneurs operate within the informal economy for various reasons (Betts et al., 2020; IFC, 2018; Kamau & Fox, 2013; Omeje & Mwangi, 2014). Majority of refugees within the urban settings lack legal status whereas, those in camps are denied labour rights and freedom of movement. For both groups, the challenge stems from the slow bureaucratic processes that are time consuming, unfriendly to the uneducated and riddled with extortionists making it challenging to integrate to the formal economy and occupy legal status for their businesses.

A second factor is motivated by the corrupt means through which refugees must navigate their businesses through bribery. In Kakuma, businesses are obliged to pay an informal tax, one that is influenced by the ethnic groups. The study by IFC (2018) found that Burundians, Rwandans and Kenyans (host community members who run businesses in the camp) pay the highest form rate. In turn they possess stronger political influence or sense of security whilst influencing employment, ownership and property rights. In Nairobi, the corrupt Kenyan legal system sees refugees navigate law enforcement agencies through bribery as a measure to avoid unsettling contact. Furthermore, the engagement of refugees in informal businesses in urban areas is propelled by their 'invisibility advantage' that is, their shared physical and ethnographic similarity to the Kenyan Somali does not make it easy to distinguish them. Therefore, acquiring fake documentation on rightful status is accessible and for those that are affluent bribery of government officials results in obtaining genuine documentation (Omeje & Mwangi, 2014).

Market Barriers

Traditionally, goods and services have been delivered directly by the aid agencies to camps through in-kind distribution or service provision. However, more recently the focus has shifted to the supply side of the labour market such as improving employability, skill and know-how of refugees that may result in their initiative to start a micro enterprise as an income generating activity that eventually leads to self-reliance. Whilst these approaches do lead to promoting short-term income earnings opportunities, they often result in significant long-term problems such as multiple individuals engaging in the same 'traditional' income generating activities such as selling vegetables. This may result in negative spill over effects with the host community (Nutz, 2017) that may already be operating such businesses, such as the case in Dadaab where Somali refugees engage in cattle farming that competes with the host community and Nairobi where Congolese refugees run hair dressing salons in competition to the local communities (Tippens, 2017).

Majority of refugees face administrative barriers that hinder access to resources, specifically, geographical barriers that see financial constraints and access points due to challenges of camp locations that limit goods and services obtained by those who venture into entrepreneurship. Similarly, outside camps, refugees find themselves unable to access credit and bank accounts because of their illegal status. More so, loan providers hold prejudice on refugees as high risk with low profitability ventures with little knowledge of the business sectors they engage (Nutz, 2017). However, more recently accessing finance from institutions and banks that aim to invest in development of refugee camps, one such example, is the recent public–private coalition in 2018 between Mastercard and the U.S Agency for International Development (USAID) in both Kakuma and Daadab camps. This seeks to transform refugee settlements into digitally connected communities through technology, solutions and experience from multiple sectors (Bhagat, 2019) that may transform barren spaces into untapped profit.

These administrative barriers often lead to refugees reluctance to engage with banking institutions that place further distance between the refugee community and formal financial institutions instead often influenced by their cultural beliefs and norms on taking on debt, paying interest or use of co-signers to secure loans, refugees rely on informal lending from family, friends, co-ethnic communities such as M-pesa and *hawala system* and the broader diaspora to set up their businesses (UNCTAD, 2018; Betts et al., 2020). The adoption of informal financial institutions for business support sees a rise in the number of business ventures amongst refugees. Predominantly within the Muslim community, given that the religion bars charging of interest to loans, the adoption of the *hawala* money is relied on to settle personal and business obligations (Kamau & Fox, 2013; Omeje & Mwangi, 2014).

Entrepreneurial Strategies

Refugees in Kenya support the notion that is displayed in both bricolage and effectuation such that the entrepreneurship is simply not a phenomenon waiting to be discovered but one that may also be created, enacted and constructed (Alvarez & Barney, 2006). Refugees in Kenya engage in a wide range of economic activity albeit, those in camps have similar business initiatives in comparison to those who are in Nairobi and Mombasa, a factor that may be attributed to the limited resources, access to market and infrastructure (Betts et al., 2020; Kamau & Fox, 2013; Omeje & Mwangi, 2014).

Three major indicators have been highlighted to determine the choice and level of business entrepreneurs engage in, namely, availability and access to market (i.e. goods and services), access to finance and social networks. For example, in Kakuma, entrepreneurs engage in the local business trade of firewood (bricolage) thus enacting and shaping their environment (Baker & Nelson, 2005) through creating a need with resources they have at hand. The type of bricolage in Kakuma implies success from opportunity identification to opportunity exploitation entrepreneurship through effectuation has also been identified within refugee camps through the use of their social ties to co-ethnic groups across the country (O'Callaghan & Sturge, 2018). Specifically, ties that lie outside the camp, Somali refugees expand their trade and markets to the diaspora through social networks of family and friends that are repatriated to countries in the West (Omeje & Mwangi, 2014). Through this form of financial system those in the diaspora remit business capital to their kin. Amongst other ethnic groups, use of table banking where the members of the community make monetary contributions to a kitty from which members can borrow (Isaacs, 2018).

Entrepreneurial Outcomes

Necessity entrepreneurship plays a significant role in the engagement and type of business refugees venture into which in turn informs the business performance, ownership and entrepreneurial satisfaction. Whilst little research is yet to fully identify the level of satisfaction (human capital, motivation, individual and venture characteristics) for refugees in Kenya their overall business performance and ownership has been researched. Findings suggest that those in urban settings fair better in achieving higher sales and retaining profits from their ventures (Omeje & Mwangi, 2014; Pavanello et al., 2010; Tippens, 2017). This is due to the diversified businesses they engage in such as Somalis who run retail shops, Ethiopians who engage in restaurant businesses and Congolese who partake in the music and hair industries. Their profits are furthered by their access to remittance from kin in the diaspora as they easily reinvest into their businesses (Omeje & Mwangi, 2014; Pavanello et al., 2010). This allows for prioritisation of the economic performance to diversify businesses and support members of their community which extends to those within the camps particularly within the Somali community.

Camp settings have also signalled increase in profit from self-reliance initiatives. Research in Kakuma, Kaloboyei and Dadaab suggest that profits are achieved but significantly vary depending on the type of business. Further influential factors are linked to the location, ethnic group and financial access (Betts et al., 2020). The camps have sub-divisions and depending on location, one can access certain goods and services. In the case of Kakuma, entrepreneurs located in Kakuma 1 (1 of 4 sub-divisions) possess better networks within the supply chain given that they have been there longer (IFC, 2018). The ethnic group determines the customer base and financial assistance one can receive, such as the case of Somali groups being majority of refugees and asylum seekers in Daadab and having networks in urban areas influence their profits.

Business ownership is challenged by the poor policy and regulation structures on refugee reception in the country. In Nairobi affluent refugee entrepreneurs wield the weak political and institutional state in Kenya and their significant influence in the private and public capacities that emancipate from their national and transnational networks and contact to their advantage in purchasing property and housing (Scheibel, 2009). However, majority of those in urban settings and camps are unable to do so are left vulnerable with a myriad of challenges on issues such as insecurity and repatriation. One unique case presents Getahun from Ethiopia who runs a multi-million Kenya shillings business in Kakuma camp who declined repatriation to the US as he could not access insurance and guarantee from the government over the safety of his business (*The Guardian*, 2017).

Livelihood Outcomes

In the case of both urban and encamped refugees, entrepreneurship fits as a solution to the oppression and restrictions on labour market integration. For those in camps the length of stay greatly affects livelihood improvements, Betts et al. (2020) noted an increase in self-reliance in both Kakuma and Kaloboyei camps given the increased dietary diversity from those who engaged in entrepreneurial activities. Furthermore, in Dadaab camp research has shown that individuals who have been in the camp for ten years or more are engaged in small to medium size business have greater income generating activities as opposed to the newly arrived dependent on humanitarian assistance (Kamau & Fox, 2013).

The protracted refugee crisis in the region generates scarcity for labour opportunities and access to common resources such as water, forestry and grazeland for support that generates income which is a key component to their livelihood and economic productivity. Access to land provides these natural resources that generate little income as clashes with host communities are common as they also engage in this trade (Betts et al., 2020). Similarly, in urban areas, refugees are presented with higher income opportunities from their diversified businesses (Omeje & Mwangi, 2014). Both settings indicate that as a result entrepreneurs reinvest back into their communities to assist the families and kinsmen (Betts, 2018; Kamau & Fox, 2013; Omeje & Mwangi, 2014).

Though research shows that more income and increased wellbeing are somewhat achieved, refugees are rendered vulnerable to insecurities both within and outside the camps. Fraught with challenges and tension, refugees undergo harassment from law enforcement, hostility from host community and xenophobic perception from the public. The perceived burden of refugees by the Kenyan government renders them vulnerable to encampment for those in urban areas and forced repatriation to their home countries as previously intended in 2013 (Cannon & Fujibayashi, 2018). Furthermore, unilateral agencies are turning to self-reliance model to cope with pressures of aid assistance and food dependency from refugees, though proving to be successful in that refugees voluntarily migrate to Kaloboyei and those in urban areas to camps, the semi-arid location proves difficult to engage in agriculture and as a result the Kaloboyei initiative is taking longer to transition to self-reliance than expected. The efforts by the government and unilateral agencies are further creating tension between refugees and host communities as they perceive refugees to receive better treatment (Betts et al., 2020).

Social Capital Framework for Refugee Entrepreneurship

Social capital has the potential for creating opportunities and supporting refugees through connections, information exchange and acquisition of resources. The development of social capital concept within refugee entrepreneurship often focuses on individual cases and refugee migration in developed countries. There exists a pressing priority to provide a sustainable approach of supporting refugee entrepreneurs in developing countries with a focus on how refugees mobilise social capital and navigate the institutional environment to improve their entrepreneurial and livelihood

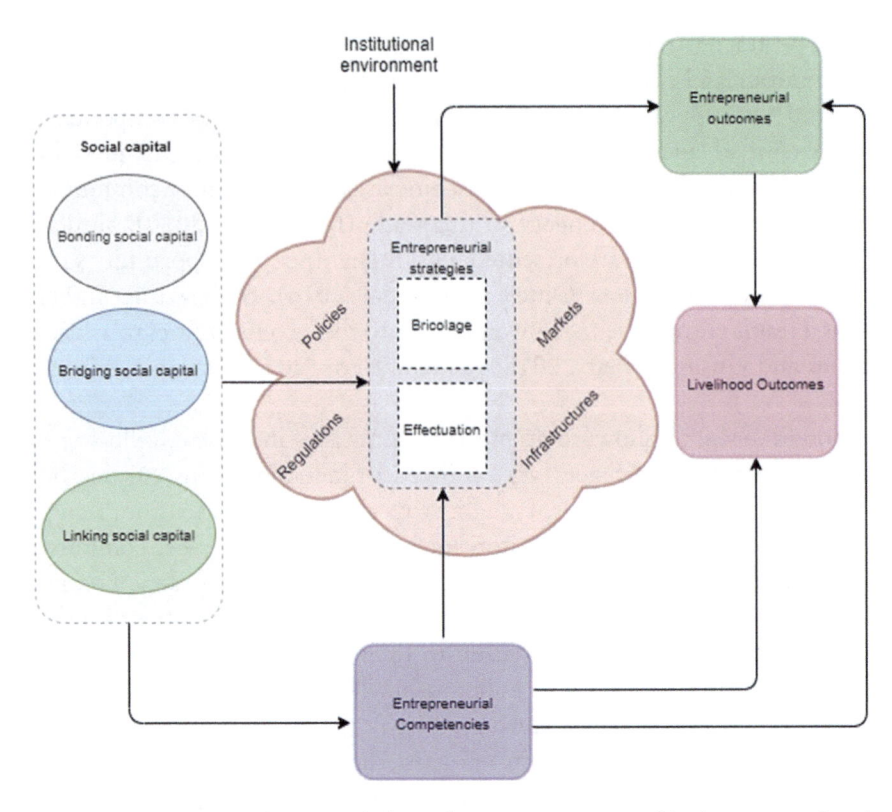

Fig. 17.5 Social capital framework for refugee entrepreneurship (*Source* Authors)

outcomes. To better understand this, we draw from the Kenya context of refugee entrepreneurship in both urban and camp settings. We then propose the model conceptual framework in Fig. 17.5.

Social Capital

Literature on entrepreneurship often reflects that migrants and refugees utilise social capital as a resource that provides access to co-ethnic networks that provide finances (Vershinina et al., 2011). The conceptual framework accounts for the three forms of social capital; bonding, bridging and linking social capital as adapted from Szreter and Woolcock (2004). The various views on these three forms of social capital are their values; they are perceived to be inherent from the networks and relationships that are drawn from socialising as a form of social support defined by the nature of the relationships, interactions and ties underlying particular networks (Williams & Williams, 2011). Thus, acting as a mechanism that provides information and resources that individuals can mobilise to enhance their personal returns within their environment (Jack & Anderson, 2002). Social capital is found to be fundamental to entrepreneurship in areas that face adverse economic and social conditions where bonding forms of social capital are developed from community support (Welter et al., 2008), bridging forms support interests of local business communities (Williams & Williams, 2011) and linking forms across power differentials (Szreter & Woolcock, 2004).

Entrepreneurial Competencies

The conceptual framework accounts for entrepreneurial competencies that influence an individual's motivation. The entrepreneurial competencies represent a constellation of characteristics that relate to successful business development (Aurik & Astri, 2018). Entrepreneurial competencies can highly impact entrepreneurial performance through venture opportunities, strategies and growth. The framework looks at four classifications of entrepreneurial competencies: attitudinal, behavioural, managerial and technical. Attitudinal competencies look to an entrepreneur's self-efficacy, motivation and risk attitudes in business. Behavioural competencies identify the underlying characteristics an entrepreneur has in having casual relationships with effective or superior performances in the process of carrying out business activities. The managerial competencies look to identify the ability entrepreneurs possess in identifying expected outcomes and clearly outlining, directing and executing tasks. Lastly, technical competencies highlight ones' ability to address rapid changes within their business environment (Tittel & Terzidis, 2020).

Entrepreneurial competencies are key as they provide entrepreneurs with the ability to identify and exploit opportunities, access social capital, customer management skills, decision-making abilities, leadership skills, delegation and motivational skills and commitment (Mitchelmore & Rowley, 2010).

Institutional Environment

The conceptual framework distinguishes between four institutional environments that impact refugee entrepreneurship; policy, regulations, infrastructural and market barriers as they have a constraining or facilitative impact through influencing strategies, interactions, possible activities and the consequences of such strategies in different contexts (Licht & Siegel, 2006). The institutional theory recognises that both formal and informal environments shape the level of individual entrepreneurial success (Aldrich, 1992) from opportunity recognition to venture creation.

Entrepreneurial Strategies

Shane and Venkataraman (2000, p. 218) define entrepreneurship as 'the field of entrepreneurship is the scholarly examination of how, by whom and with what effects opportunities to create future goods and services are discovered, evaluated and exploited.' In line with this, we define entrepreneurship as an outcome of human agency in a context-specific setting amongst the forcibly displaced through exploitation and creation of new opportunities.

Entrepreneurial strategy was defined by Murray (1986, p. 1) as *a means through which an organisation establishes its fundamental set of relations with its environment…simultaneous change of decisions taken…which will allow it to survive and prosper in its chosen environment.* Dependent on the entrepreneurs understanding of the environment the conceptual framework proposes two concepts effectuation, and bricolage. Through explanation of the process by which entrepreneurs go about in making do with limited financial and human capital, effectuation attributes a cognitive problem-solving approach by actors who are successful in business ventures despite being in a context of high uncertainty (Sarasvathy, 2008). One that is achieved through focusing on use of available resources (that is entrepreneurs self (competencies), their knowledge and networks) as opposed to conceptions on how to succeed. Bricolage on the other hand, provides actors with opportunity to combine resources that are available cheaply or free in novel ways that are applied to problems and opportunities for which they were not originally intended, as such new services can be derived from these existing resources (Baker & Nelson, 2005).

Entrepreneurial Outcomes

The conceptual framework captures entrepreneurial outcomes through four variables: business ownership, business performance and entrepreneur satisfaction as indicators of entrepreneurial outcome. The outcomes may range from the income generated from the enterprise to ownership of business or property. In turn, the entrepreneurial outcomes are influenced by the firm performance a factor that is wholly important to refugee entrepreneurship.

Livelihood Outcomes

The conceptual framework looks at livelihood outcomes through the level of 'sustainable livelihood' achieved drawing. Defined by Chambers and Conway (1992, p. 6) as 'capabilities, assets (including both material and social resources) and activities required for a means of living. A livelihood is sustainable when it can cope with and recover from stresses and shocks, maintain or enhance its capabilities and assets, while not undermining the natural resource base.' We draw from Carney et al.'s (1999) interpretation of an Sustainable Livelihood Framework (SLF) approach with a focus on four livelihood outcomes that alleviate the widespread constraints within refugee settings that can be captured through: more income, increased well-being, reduced vulnerability and improved food security. As such they provide an understanding on how refugees act on their asset limitations which are influenced by the aforementioned factors to build pathways that enable self-reliance.

Conclusion

The social and economic impact of refugee movement is felt in the towns and cities of host countries. Their presence is often assessed less as a benefit than a burden, however, this narrative is changing and the positive 'economic lives of refugees' (Alfaro-Velcamp et al., 2017) is a growing subject of interest. Often met with bureaucratic red tapes, corruption, hostility, minimal access to markets and finances, limitations on rights and welfare, aid dependency and vulnerability these factors prolong the refugee cycle. However, promoting entrepreneurship can result in elevation in integration for refugees and development.

We propose that the conceptual framework offers to provide insight on identifying the ways in which refugee entrepreneurship can be encouraged across Africa. The framework highlights how certain contextual influences shape and create both the opportunities and barriers for entrepreneurs. It highlights how the institutional environment influences the mobilisation of available social capital, self-competencies and culture the refugees possess. Finally, it indicates that these factors interact and impact the entrepreneurial and livelihood outcomes. In doing so, there exists an opportunity to stimulate discussions amongst policymakers towards both social and economic inclusion of refugees that eventuates in positive economic and social development for both the home and host countries.

References

Adler, P. S., & Kwon, S. (2000). Social capital: The good, the bad, and the ugly. In E. L. Lesser (Ed.), *Knowledge and social capital: Foundations and applications* (pp. 89–115). Butterworth-Heinemann.

Aldrich, H. E. (1992). Methods in our madness? trends in entrepreneurship research. In D. L. Sexton & J. D. Kasarda (Eds.), *The state of the art of entrepreneurship* (pp. 191–213). Boston: PWSKent.

Alfaro-Velcamp, T., Mclaughlin, R., Brogneri, G., Skade, M., & Shaw, M. (2017). 'Getting angry with honest people': The illicit market for immigrant 'papers' in Cape Town, South Africa. *Migration Studies, 5*(2), 216–236.

Ali, J. A., Imana, D. K., & Ocha, W. (2017). The refugee crisis in Kenya: Exploring refugee-host community causes of tensions and conflicts in Kakuma refugee camp. *Journal of International Relations, and Foreign Policy, 5*(2), 39–51.

Alvarez, S., & Barney, J. (2006). Discovery and creation: Alternative theories of entrepreneurial action. *Revista Organizações Em Contexto, 3.* https://doi.org/10.2139/Ssrn.900200.

Aurik, G., & Astri, G. (2018). An analysis of differences in students' entrepreneurial competencies between the management and entrepreneurship study programmes at the school of business and management (Sbm) Institut Teknologi Bandung (Itb). *Journal of Entrepreneurship Education, 21*(4), 1–11. https://search-proquest-com.proxy.library.dmu.ac.uk/docview/2178087403?accountid=10472.

Bagwell, S. (2015). Transnational entrepreneurship amongst Vietnamese businesses in London. *Journal of Ethnic and Migration Studies, 41*(2), 329–349.

Baker, T., & Nelson, R. E. (2005). Creating something from nothing: Resource construction through entrepreneurial bricolage. *Administrative Science Quarterly, 50*(3), 329–366. https://doi.org/10.2189/asqu.2005.50.3.329.

Bakker, L. Dagevos, J., & Engbersen, G. (2017). Explaining the refugee gap: A longitudinal study on labour market participation of refugees in the Netherlands. *Journal of Ethnic and Migration Studies, 43*(11), 1775–1791.

Barrett, R., & Vershinina, N. (2016). Intersectionality of ethnic and entrepreneurial identities: A study of post-war Polish entrepreneurs in an English city. *Journal of Small Business Management.* Online First. https://doi.org/10.1111/Sjbm.12246.

Betts, A., Omata, N., & Sterck, O. (2020). The Kalobeyei settlement: A self-reliance model for refugees? *Journal of Refugee Studies, 33*(1), 189–223.

Betts, A. (2018). The global compact on refugees: Towards a theory of change? *International Journal of Refugee Law, 30*(4), 623–626.

Bhagat, A. (2019). Governing refugee disposability: Neoliberalism and survival in Nairobi. *New Political Economy.* https://doi.org/10.1080/13563467.2019.1598963.

Bizri, M. (2017). Refugee-entrepreneurship: A social capital perspective. *Entrepreneurship & Regional Development, 29*(9–10), 847–868. https://doi.org/10.1080/08985626.2017.1364787.

Bourdieu, P. (1985). The forms of capital. In J. Richardson (Ed.), *Handbook of theory and research for sociology of education* (pp. 241–258). Greenwood Press.

Burt, R. (1997). The contingent value of social capital. *Administrative Science Quarterly, 42*(2), 330–365.

Campbell, E. (2006). Urban refugees in Nairobi: Problems of protection, mechanisms of survival, and possibilities for integration. *Journal of Refugee Studies, 19*(3), 396–413.

Campbell, E., Crisp, J., & Kiragu, E. (2011). *Navigating Nairobi: A review of the implementation of UNHCR's urban refugee policy in Kenya's capital city*. UNHCR.

Cannon, B., & Fujibayashi, H. (2018). Security, Structural Factors And Sovereignty: Analysing reactions to Kenya's decision to close the Dadaab refugee camp complex. *African Security Review*, 1–22. https://doi.org/10.1080/10246029.2017.1408475.

Carciotto, S., & Cristian, D. (2017). *Access to socio-economic rights for refugees: A comparison across six African countries*. Scalabrini Institute for Human Mobility in Africa. http://sihma.org.za/wp-content/uploads/2017/03/Final_report.pdf.

Carney, D., Drinkwater, M., Rusinow, T., Wanmali, S., Singh, N., & Neefjes, K. (1999). *Livelihood approaches compared. A brief comparison of the livelihoods approaches of the UK Department for International Development (DFID)*. CARE, Oxfam and the United Nations Development Programme (UNDP).

Carrier, N. (2016). *Little Mogadishu: Eastleigh, Nairobi's global Somali hub*. Hurst & Co.

Cediey, E., & Foroni, F. (2008). *Discrimination in access to employment on grounds of foreign origin in France*. International Labour Office, Geneva.

Chambers, R., & Conway, G. (1992). *Sustainable rural livelihoods: Practical concepts for the 21st century* (IDS Discussion Paper, 296). Brighton: IDS.

Coleman, J. S. (1990). *Foundations of social theory*. Belknap Press.

Constant, A., Kahanec, M., & Zimmermann, K. (2008). Attitudes towards immigrants, other integration barriers, and their veracity. *SSRN Electronic Journal*. https://doi.org/10.2139/Ssrn.1424986.

Harris, M., & Young, P. (2010). Building bridges: The third sector responding locally to diversity. *Voluntary Sector Review, 1*, 17.

Heilbrunn, S. (2019). Against all odds: Refugees bricoleuring in the void. *International Journal of Entrepreneurial Behavior & Research, 25*(5), 1045–1064.

Horst, C. (2003). *Transnational nomads: How Somalis Cope with refugee life in the Dadaab camps of Kenya* (PhD Dissertation). Research Institute for Global and Development Studies, University Of Amsterdam, Amsterdam, The Netherlands.

IFC. (2018). *Kakuma as a marketplace: A consumer and market study of a refugee camp and town in northwest Kenya* (English). Washington, DC: World Bank Group. http://documents.worldbank.org/curated/en/482761525339883916/Kakuma-as-a-marketplace-a-consumer-and-market-study-of-a-refugee-camp-and-town-in-northwest-Kenya

IRC. (2018). *Dreams deterred: Opportunities to promote self-reliance for Somali refugee youth in Kenya*. International Rescue Committee.

Isaacs, L. (2018). *Impact of the Regulatory Environment on Refugees' and Asylum Seekers' Ability to Use Formal Remittance Channels*.

Jack, S., & Anderson, A. (2002). The effects of embeddedness on the entrepreneurial process. *Journal of Business Venturing, 17*, 467–487. https://doi.org/10.1016/S0883-9026(01)00076-3.

Kamau, C., & Fox, J. (2013). *The Dadaab dilemma: A study on livelihood activities and opportunities for Dadaab refugees*. Intermediaries in Development Nairobi.

Kimetrica. (2016). *Refugee vulnerability study: Kakuma, refugee camp*. Commissioned by UNHCR and WFP. https://www.wfp.org/sites/default/files/refugee%20hh%20vulnerability%20study_kakuma%20refugee%20camp_%202016%2005%2006.pdf.

Kleit, R. G., & Carnegie, N. B. (2011). Integrated or isolated? The impact of public housing redevelopment on social network homophily. *Social Networks, 33*(2), 152–165.

Kolade, O. (2018). Venturing under fire: Entrepreneurship education, venture creation and poverty reduction in conflict-ridden Maiduguri, Nigeria. *Education + Training*. https://doi.org/10.1108/ET-08-2017-0124.

Licht, A. N., & Siegel, J. I. (2006). The social dimensions of entrepreneurship. In M. Casson & B. Yeung (Eds.), *Oxford handbook of entrepreneurship*. Oxford University Press. Available at SSRN: https://ssrn.com/abstract=824844.

Lin, N., Ensel, W. M., & Vaughn, J. C. (1981). Social resources and occupational status attainment. *Social Forces, 59*, 1163–1181.

Lipsky, M. (1980). *Street-level bureaucracy: Dilemmas of the individual in public services* (p. 131). Russell Sage.

Lyon, F., Sepulveda, L., & Syrett, S. (2008). Enterprising refuges: Contributions and challenges in deprived urban areas. *Local Economy, 22*(4), 363–375.

Maniraguha, J. P. (2011). *Challenges of reintegrating returning refugees: A case study of returnee access to land and to basic services in Burundi* (Master's Thesis). Universitetet I Tromsø.

Map of Kenya. (2019). CIA. https://www.cia.gov/the-world-factbook/countries/kenya/. Accessed on: 14 April 2019.

Map of Kakuma and Dadaab Refugee Camps. (2019). UNHCR. https://data2.unhcr.org/en/country/ken. Accessed on: 14 April 2019.

Marlowe, J. (2011). Sudanese settlement: Employing strategies of intercultural contact and cultural maintenance. *The Australian Review of African Studies, 32*, 101–117.

Massey, D. S. (1988). Economic development and international migration in comparative perspective. *Population and Development Review, 14*(3), 383–413.

Mckinsey Global Institute. (2016). *Jobs lost, jobs gained: Workforce transitions in a time of automation* [Online]. https://www.mckinsey.com/~/media/mckinsey/featured%20insights/future%20of%20organisations/what%20the%20future%20of%20work%20will%20mean%20for%20jobs%20skills%20and%20wages/mgi-jobs-lost-jobs-gained-report-december-6-2017.ashx.

Millar-Schijf, C. C. J. M., & Choi, C. J. (2008). Worker identity, the liability of foreignness, the exclusion of local managers and unionism: A conceptual analysis. *Journal of Organisational Change Management, 21*(4), 460–470. https://doi.org/10.1108/09534810810884858.

Mitchelmore, S., & Rowley, J. (2010). Entrepreneurial competencies: A literature review and development agenda. *International Journal of Entrepreneurial Behaviour & Research, 16*, 92–111. https://doi.org/10.1108/13552551011026995.

Moore, C. S., & Mueller, R. E. (2002). The transition from paid to self-employment in Canada: The importance of push factors. *Applied Economics, 34*(6), 791–801.

Murray, J. A. (1986). A concept of entrepreneurial strategy: Summary. *Strategic Management Journal (pre-1986), 5*(1), 1–13.

Nutz, N. (2017). *A guide to market-based livelihood interventions for refugees*. ILO.

O'Callaghan, S., & Sturge, G. (2018). *Against the odds: Refugee integration in Kenya* (HPG Working Paper).

Omeje, K., & Mwangi, J. (2014). Business travails in the diaspora: The challenges and resilience of Somali refugee business community in Nairobi, Kenya. *Journal of Third World Studies, 31*, 185–217.

Ostrom, E., and Ahn, T. K. (2003). Introduction. In E. Ostrom & T. K. Ahn (Eds.), *Foundations of social capital* (pp. xi–xxxix). Edward Elgar.

Oxfam International. (2016). *How the world should respond to humanitarian crises | Oxfam International* [Online]. https://www.oxfam.org/en/how-world-should-respond-humanitarian-crises.

Pavanello, S., et al. (2010). *Hidden and exposed: Urban refugees in Nairobi, Kenya* (HPG Working Paper). Overseas Development Institute (ODI).

Poortinga, W. (2006). Social capital: An individual or collective resource for health? *Social Science & Medicine, 62*(2), 292–302.

Romero, M., and Valdez, Z. (2016). Introduction to the special issue: Intersectionality and entrepreneurship. *Ethnic and Racial Studies, 39*(9): 1553–1565.

Sanghi, A., Harun, O., & Varalakshmi, V. (2016). *"Yes" in my backyard? The economics of refugees and their social dynamics in Kakuma, Kenya*. Washington, DC: World Bank Group.

Sarasvathy, S. (2008). *Effectuation: Elements of entrepreneurial expertise* (p. 243). https://doi.org/10.4337/9781848440197.

Scheibel, .A. (2009). *Diaspora-driven development in stateless Somalia: All relationships are local relationships* (Masters of Arts' Thesis). The American University, Cairo.

Shane, S., & Venkataraman, S. (2000). The promise of entrepreneurship as a field of research. *Academy of Management Review, 25*(1), 217–226.

Spencer, S. (2006). *Refugees and other new migrants: A review of the evidence on successful approaches to integration*. Centre on Migration, Policy And Society, Oxford University.

Staps, M. (2018). *Market-based livelihood interventions in a long-term refugee camp*.

Szreter, S., & Woolcock, M. (2004). WP2002–13 health by association? Social capital, social theory and the political economy of public health 1. *International Journal of Epidemiology, 33*, 650–667. https://doi.org/10.1093/Ije/Dyh013.

Tippens, J. A. (2017). Urban Congolese refugees in Kenya: The contingencies of coping and resilience in a context marked by structural vulnerability. *Qualitative Health Research, 27*(7), 1090–1103. https://doi.org/10.1177/1049732316665348.

Tittel, A., & Terzidis, O. (2020). Entrepreneurial competences revised: Developing a consolidated and categorized list of entrepreneurial competences. *Entrepreneurship Education, 3*, 1–35. https://doi.org/10.1007/s41959-019-00021-4.

The Guardian. (2017). 'They call him the millionaire': The refugee who turned his camp into a business empire.

Türk, V., & Dowd, R. (2014). Protection gaps. In *The Oxford handbook on refugee and forced migration studies*. Oxford University Press.

UN General Assembly. (1948). Universal declaration of human rights, 10 December, 217A (III). https://www.refworld.org/docid/3ae6b3712c.html.

UN General Assembly. (1951). *Convention relating to the status of refugees*. United Nations, Treaty Series (Vol. 189, p. 137). https://www.refworld.org/docid/3be01b964.html.

UNCTAD. (2018). *Policy guide on entrepreneurship for migrants and refugees*.

UNHCR. (2020). Figures at a glance [Online]. https://www.unhcr.org/uk/figures-at-a-glance.html.

Vearey, J., Richter, M., Nu'N'ez, L., & Moyo, K. (2011). South African HIV/AIDS programming overlooks migration, urban livelihoods, and informal workplaces. *African Journal of AIDS Research, 10*(Supplement): 381–391.

Vershinina, N., Barrett, R., & Meyer, M. (2011). Forms of capital, intra-ethnic variation and Polish entrepreneurs in Leicester. *Work, Employment & Society, 25*, 101–117. https://doi.org/10.1177/0950017010389241.

Wauters, B., & Lambrecht, J. (2006). Refugee entrepreneurship in Belgium: Potential and practice. *The International Entrepreneurship and Management Journal, 2*(4), 509–525.

Wauters, B., & Lambrecht, J. (2008). Barriers to refugee entrepreneurship in Belgium: Towards an explanatory model. *Journal of Ethnic and Migration Studies, 34*(6), 895–915.

Welter, F., Trettin, L., & Neumann, U. (2008). Fostering entrepreneurship in distressed urban neighbourhoods. *International Entrepreneurship and Management Journal, 4*, 109–128.

Williams, N., & Williams, C. C. (2012). Evaluating the socio-spatial contingency of entrepreneurial motivations: A case study of English deprived urban neighbourhoods. *Entrepreneurship and Regional Development, 24*(7/8), 661–684.

Williams, N., & Williams, C. (2011). Tackling barriers to entrepreneurship in a deprived urban neighbourhood. *Local Economy, 261*, 30–42.

Zetter, R., & Ruaudel, H. (2016). *Refugees' right to work and access to labor markets: An assessment* (KNOMAD Working Paper). World Bank Global Program on

Forced Displacement (GPFD) and the Global Knowledge Partnership on Migration and Development (KNOMAD) Thematic Working Group on Forced Migration. Washington, DC: World Bank Group.

Zetter, R., Griffiths, D., & Sigona, N. (2006). The policy discourse on refugee integration in Europe: The contradictory dynamics of convergence or divergence. Paper accepted by *Journal of European Social Policy*.

18

Entrepreneurial and SME Activity in Libya: Reviewing Contextual Obstacles and Challenges Leading to Its Fractured Enterprise Culture

Abdulmonem Ahmed Esaudi, Robert Smith, and Veronica Scuotto

Introduction

Entrepreneurship is a prime driving force in economic development particularly in Africa (Naudé & Havenga, 2012) and is strongly associated with Small and Medium Enterprises (SMEs) as a vehicle for entrepreneurship (Burns, 2011). This review of extant literature on entrepreneurship, and SME activity in a Libyan context explores entrepreneurial behaviour and practices. This is vital given the lack of studies on the topic (OECD, 2016). It makes a contribution by focusing on a unique context and adds substantially to discussions about entrepreneurship in a turbulent environment as well as illuminating a contemporary frontier of African entrepreneurship. Specifically, it addresses barriers to the rapid modernisation and evolution of Libyan entrepreneurship and business practices. Seem also Omar et al. (2020) for a discussion on frameworks for supporting enterprise in a Libyan context (2020). Not all African entrepreneurial ecosystems are flourishing and those in conflict zones are held in a perpetual state of instability. It is

---

A. A. Esaudi
University of the West of Scotland, Paisley, UK

R. Smith (✉)
Aberdeen, Scotland, UK

V. Scuotto
University of Turin, Turin, Italy

survival and transformation, not growth that matters. In Libya, there is a stark contrast between entrepreneurship in urban centres and surrounding rural districts. This review provides contextual insights from the literature, highlighting lessons to be learned which may inform policy and practice in other African states.

Libya is an Arab country, occupying a strategic location, between Southern Europe and the Arab Maghreb countries. It is part of the MENA [Middle East and North Africa] region with a 1770 km coastline on the Mediterranean Sea and a vast landmass of 1700 million square kilometres. Its desert covers 90% of its landmass. It is Africa's 4th largest country, sharing borders with Tunisia, Algeria, Egypt, Chad, Niger and Sudan. Its population [2020 census] was estimated at 6,871,292 and the majority live on its coast. Its largest city and economic centre is Tripoli (CIA, 2020). Demographically, a third of its population sare aged below 20 years. Its SMEs represent 96% of total enterprises (OECD, 2016; Omar et al., 2020; Wurfali, 2006). These are characterised by limited value-adding, low level of competitiveness, productivity and skills and are constrained by inadequate equipment and knowledge, exacerbated by a lack of government support (Elmansori & Arthur, 2014; OECD, 2016; Omar et al., 2020). Consequentially, Libyan enterprises are less likely to survive or grow (Ali & Omar, 2015; Wurfali, 2006). Yet, paradoxically, Libya is one of the richest oil and gas producers, being the third largest exporter of oil to Europe. It is an OPEC member contributing to around 5.3% of their total oil production (Squalli, 2007). It possesses roughly a third of Africa's oil reserves (Anyanwu, 2014; OECD, 2016) and is an upper, middle-income country (World Bank, 2014). Nevertheless, successive Libyan governments have not exploited its immense wealth effectively for the citizenry. Crucially, it is one of the least diversified economies among oil and gas producing countries and there is a concern for its underdeveloped entrepreneurial resources and SMEs (OECD, 2016). The Libyan economy remains heavily dependent on oil and gas and a fragile SME infrastructure. As a result, the performance of home-grown enterprises is weak, constraining future entrepreneurial growth.

This chapter addresses a unique and important empirical context. Within the past decade a number of theoretical propositions have emerged to explore entrepreneurship in the bottom of the pyramid and conflict contexts. Of relevance, are the theories of 'transformative entrepreneuring' (Tobias et al., 2013) and 'emancipatory entrepreneuring' (Al-Dajani et al., 2015). These underpin this review by identifying and interrogating contextual factors important to Libyan entrepreneurs and SME owners. Success factors and challenges faced by entrepreneurs are subjects of scholarly and practitioner interest across countries. However, there are differences between how entrepreneurs operate their enterprises across these countries due to their differing economic, political and cultural factors (Benzing et al., 2009). We also consider underlying proto-entrepreneurial factors, focusing on the historical, demographic and cultural variables to entrepreneurial activity using two separate units of analysis—entrepreneurship; and SMEs because entrepreneurs are central to economic development and SMEs are the medium through which future entrepreneurial growth and economic development is achieved. It is through them that legitimate entrepreneurial activity is channelled. We concentrate on identifying barriers from an owners perspective. This entails evaluating the role of socio-historical, socio-cultural, socio-political and socio-economic factors influencing business survival and success. We consider limiting environmental factors which impact the support provided to owners, addressing a research gap to better understand contemporary Libyan entrepreneurship and SME activity in terms of definition and development.

Historical, Socio-Political and Socio-Economic Contexts

From a historical perspective, Libya has long been subjected to foreign rule and instability making it a perpetual conflict zone (Elkrghli, 2016). Its coastal zone was part of the Ottoman Empire from 1551. However, at various times it was a partially autonomous State. In 1835, the Ottoman Turks reoccupied the region finding a war-torn country with its commerce and agriculture ruined by tribal strife and political instability, government neglect and feuding (Anderson, 1984: 325). The Ottoman's initiated reforms (the *Tanzimat*) whereby agriculture and land reform replaced the failing revenues of the old caravan route and nomadic tribalism. Ottoman rule lasted until the Italian occupation and colonisation of Libya from 1911 to 1943. For Abdussalam (1983) three significant events (international and national in origin) altered and transformed the Libyan economy—Italian colonialism; foreign administration and aid (1942–1960); and multinational corporations (1955 to date). This led to socio-economic and spatial polarisation.

To better understand the evolution of Libyan entrepreneurship, one must consider entrepreneurial activity during the colonial period (Higgins, 1955/1959). Historically, such activity during Italian and British rule (1911–1951) was limited and dominated by Italian entrepreneurs. Additionally,

Libya lacked entrepreneurial capital and an indigenous enterprise culture. This rule-bund foreign political and economic domination hampered the emergence of entrepreneurial markets to Libyans who were dependent on agricultural and animal husbandry and small traditional industries requiring low capital startup. This had a profound impact, resulting in a dearth of indigenous entrepreneurs as most people became salaried workers prone to dependency culture. Large businesses were controlled and monopolised by colonialists resulting in a dysfunctional anti-entrepreneurial culture.

Nevertheless, Libya became an independent kingdom in 1951 under King Idris who rebuilt it after the discovery of oil in 1956. Economic development emerged with independence and international aid. His government initiated an enterprise development plan (circa 1952–1957) giving special attention to creating and establishing SMEs. A lack of capital, natural resources other than oil and gas, technical/management and entrepreneurial skills prevented the creation of larger enterprises. A few small agrarian projects were established with technical assistance from the United Nations (Higgins, 1959). In reviewing entrepreneurial activity Higgins (1955/1959) discussed the problems faced by Libya after independence in building a *desert economy* (Lockwood, 1957). As a new, independent nation Libya was not ready to assume the economic and political burdens of self-government (Higgins, 1955). This was hindered because it had not been *tutored in the ways of being a nation* (ibid., 1955: 313). A lack of indigenous entrepreneurship combined with its dearth of private enterprise in conjunction with a privileged monopoly became a major obstacle—blocking future economic growth (Higgins, 1959). This was exacerbated by the inability to initiate large-scale projects due to poor indigenous management and research skills, combined with a lack of government support and severe lack of capital. Nevertheless, Higgins identified untapped major resources including the latent skills of its people who found it hard to break into an economy dominated by established ethnic entrepreneurs and powerful international corporations despite the transformative changes of the Idris era.

Prior to 1969, the Libyan economic system was capitalist with public ownership only in sectors requiring large-scale investment. The Libyan government regulated internal economic processes such as, exporting and importing laws (Senina & Shamiya, 2010). The majority of firms were established and concentrated in Tripoli prior to 1969 but employed few Libyans. The contribution of SME's to the GDP was miniscule due to production limitations and because most industries were focused on processing local agricultural products (Buferna, 2005). Nevertheless, there was limited economic expansion and an increase in ancillary firms. In the sixties, new industrial projects emerged but with very limited production capacity due to poor funding (Saleh, 2010). In any case, the discovery of oil in 1958 side-lined the importance of these potentially emancipatory developments and prior to then it was one of the poorest countries in the world (Bini, 2012). Mallakh (1969) documented a phenomenal turn around and growth in the economy post-oil and cites staggering indicators of growth such as growth per capita GNP rising rapidly. This increased government revenue but caused severe socio-economic strains. Post oil, the economy changed dramatically, undergoing a structural shift. This raised Libya's wealth and rippled through its sectors, until the turmoil of the Gadaffi era.

The Kingdom of Libya ended on 1st September 1969 in a Military coup led by Muammar Gadaffi which saw the establishment of his Cultural Revolution and the—*Libyan Arab Republic*. He ruled for over forty years during which the constitution and parliament were suspended to introduce his controversial political system based on social politics and political and economic changes. In 1972, in an attempt to control policy decisions, all political parties and institutions were disbanded. By 1977, he introduced a new political philosophy renaming Libya *the Socialist People's Libyan Arab Jamahiriya*. This drastically altered the political system, establishing *the Authority of the People* notionally allowing them to directly govern the country. This was Gadaffi's source of authority, legislated through the system of the General People's Congresses (Oakes, 2011). The economic system changed overnight from capitalist to socialist, leading to an expansion of the public sector at the expense of the private as the regime deliberately cut it back. Prior to then it played a significant role in the economy. However, in 1978, Gadaffi introduced further profound economic changes based on his personal criticisms of capitalist and communist systems. His unique system of *Socialism* abolished all forms of ownership such as private companies and shareholding, wholesale trading and retailing. These became state-owned fiefdoms. This ideology changed the country's economic foundations and repression led to an exodus of Libyans migrating overseas for work—especially educated people with entrepreneurial skills, creating an educated diaspora in Europe, the UK and the US (Aldoukalee, 2013). This triggered a shortage of skilled workers and managers and further reliance on oil and gas (Suleiman, 2009; Vandewalle, 2008).

Despite the change of direction by late 1978, the State was forced to change by liberalising its economy, reducing the socialist model gradually whilst adopting new regulations to revive privatisation. Libyans were again encouraged to own and operate private and co-operative productive enterprises, stimulating small industries and investment in the agricultural sector. The world recession and oil price decline of the 1980s affected the economy causing a financial crisis. The State moved towards a more open economy and private businesses were run by workers' committees. From 1990, the State nationalised most businesses (local and foreign) such as manufacturing, banking and insurances services. This led to State control of business (Buferna, 2005; Vandewalle, 1998). This mechanism initiated dramatic change although some private businesses emerged to help the regime enhance and support the private sector. Most new firms were created in the early 1990s and during one year around 140 SMEs were established without government assistance (AfDB, 2011).

In 1992, in an attempt to improve economic development, a privatisation law was approved and public enterprises privatised (Masoud, 2009). This had little influence on the economy because the private sector and SMEs were in a poor state. Their GDP contributions were very low due to difficulties and obstacles discussed herein. State intervention still prevailed. Barriers to trade, such as customs tariffs, remained substantially high and coupled to an absence of customs protection impacted negatively on the private sector. This led to the emergence of parallel markets of consumer goods imported from Tunisia, Algeria and Egypt. Banks provided more support and loans to State institutions but the private sector had restricted access to finance because ownership rights and an individual's rights to acquire, possess, enjoy, use, were not guaranteed. This accelerated uncertainty as the economy suffered from a lack of economic diversification under Gadaffi. Simultaneously, Libya suffered UN economic sanctions, including banning oil imports and the export of goods/technology. This was lifted in September 2003. During isolation, the economy faced various challenges as the sanctions and trade embargoes brought about rising import costs. This led to domestic inflation and a deteriorating standard of living. After the lifting of sanctions, in an attempt to develop the economy, the regime embarked upon a further wave of economic reforms between 2003 and 2011. This accelerated the privatisation programme by transferring ownership of SMEs to create more private businesses which were exempted from income and export taxes for a 5 year period to assist in the importation of necessary equipment and raw material for production (Alfaitori, 2012). Nevertheless, all firms remained State controlled and influenced by political policy thus the changes failed to unleash their transformative and emancipatory potential.

The period 1994–2000 saw a development plan focusing on establishing industrial SMEs, based on raw materials and local input. Existing industries were encouraged to achieve self-sufficiency and exports. This 'see-sawing' of policies decimated the private sector and despite reform the economy remained reliant on oil and gas (Ibrahim et al., 2013). Simultaneously, the regime prioritised the establishment of large and industrial strategic projects outwith the reach of ordinary citizens due to high investment costs. They were not allowed to own more than one house (Ghanem, 1985), severely limiting their economic emancipation and ability to accumulate capital. As a result, capitalist ownership almost ceased to exist except in agriculture as the regime neglected SMEs needs and failed to initiate effective strategic plans (Maghboub, 2009). This widened the gulf between urban and rural enterprises.

This period saw shifts and changes in economic regulations which effectively retarded the development of Libya's SMEs. Legislations and laws were issued for the restructuring of economic sector activities by shifting towards collective and individual property (Abdulsaed, 2010). This was intended to expand the economic base to diversify income sources by encouraging productive activities to address unemployment which by 2003 had grown to 17.3% (Abdulsaed, 2010). Nevertheless, between 2006 and 2010, the regime belatedly attempted to kick-start economic reform by paying more attention to SMEs (Saleh, 2010). This resulted from a realisation of their importance in economic growth. Resolution No. 109/2006 created a fund for supporting and encouraging production. The funds provide entrepreneurs with facilities and advantages including exemption from customs duties and taxes on all machinery and equipment imported. The reforms were continually disrupted by instability and political unrest, internally and externally including the 'Arab Spring' movement and the Libyan Civil War (February–May 2012). Brahimi (2011) cited factors influencing the downfall—namely (1) the intense personalisation of politics which ensured that Gadaffi was blamed for the hardships and humiliations of his rule; (2) An iron-fisted approach linked to tribal dynamics; (3) a resistance to centralised authority. This resulted in competing divisions, tribal alliances, militias and families. Figure 18.1 summarises the phases and illustrates the key milestones in Libya's politico-economic history.

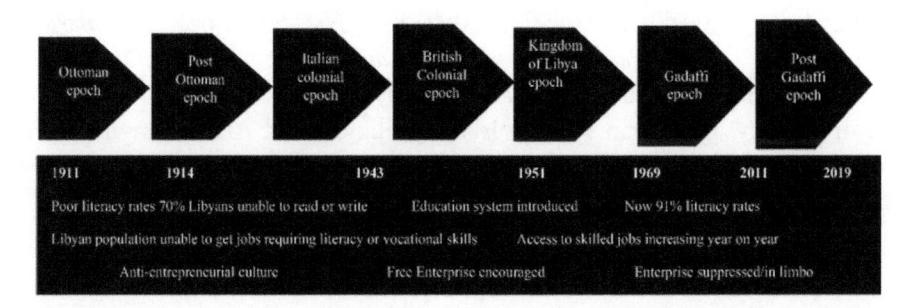

Fig. 18.1 Phases of Libyan enterprise development (author generated)

The collective effect of this perpetual epochal 'see-sawing' was that Libya failed to generate a transformative model of entrepreneurship as articulated by Al-Danya et al., let-alone an indigenous 'Enterprise Culture' and despite the 'stuttering' transformation of the enterprise legislation introduced, it has not had an emancipatory effect as articulated by Tobias et al. (2013). This is worthy of a deeper critical interrogation of factors and events that shaped the evolution of Libyan entrepreneurship, including the changing roles of state actors and institutions and the role played by institutional voids, institutional incongruence and environmental turbulence. There are other cultural and religious reasons which help further explain such incongruence.

The Influence of Culture and Religion

Culture is a community's shared way of life, values and symbols such as perceptions, preferences and people's behaviour. It results from human actions which influence their behaviour as a consumer within society and is linked with languages, religion, policies, economy, social institutions, education, class-value, ethics, customs and attitudes (Kanungo, 2006) and a contributory problem is the lack off unifying Libyan culture with its urban–rural, political-institutional and tribal divides. This may also apply in other African countries.

Arguably, unlike Western societies, Libyan traditional social institutions such as family, clan and tribe play an important role within communities and at a personal level. Culture affects the economics and politics of Arab business practices and social life and does not vary greatly among its cities albeit social structure is significantly influenced by tribal and social background. Tribes are composed of branches, families and groups. Family forms the base of Libyan society as individual lives, communities and social relations are familial-tribal. Within tribes, individuals show their respect and loyalty towards a particular social group (Obeidi, 2001) and good/bad familial or tribal reputation crucially influences the lives of individuals socially, politically and economically. For Obeidi (2001: 87) '*The clan or tribe can interfere even at an individual level, such as in decisions about marriage*'. There are around 140 different tribes, clans and militias in Libya.

Importantly, in Libyan society, Islamic religion and Arabic language are vital cultural factors influencing shared values and symbols. These factors have a formal role in playing the foundation of Libyan social homogeneity

(Attir & Al-Azzabi, 2004). Islamic religion, language and family coalesce exert significant influence on social structure, attitudes and behaviours, forming the base of Libyan masculinities. One must take into account behaviours, principles and religious influence as influential factors along with political and societal considerations (Twati & Gammack, 2006). This is vital in encouraging transformative and emancipatory forms of entrepreneurship in conflict zones because it ties in with recent conversations on how spiritual capital influences entrepreneurship activities in contexts of institutional voids (Kolade et al., 2019; Mika, 2015). Spiritual capital is a set of personal, intangible and transcendent resources that emanate from an individual's spiritual or religious beliefs and experiences and is particularly relevant to sub-Saharan Africa with its considerable institutional voids where religion and spirituality play a dominant role in society (Kolade et al., 2019). For Mika (2015), spirituality and entrepreneurship are inseparable elements of indigenous entrepreneurship which sits contrary to the omnipotent view of the heroic entrepreneur which pervades Western-centric notions and cultural logics. In this respect, there is scope for Libyan values and beliefs as forms of spiritual capital to activate entrepreneurship. Increasingly, twenty-first-century businesses are grappling with the challenges of operating in turbulent environments characterised by market volatility, political instability and warfare. These are relevant to countries, where institutional weaknesses exacerbate environmental turbulence (Kolade et al., 2019).

Societal relationships within Libyan culture are very important and recognised as a unique attribute. Abubaker (2011) examined the relationship between culture and the economic environment, critically reviewing prior studies regarding the impact of culture on employee communication behaviour. Abubaker concluded that masculinity, high-power distance and uncertainty avoidance influence the Libyan economic environment. Nevertheless, Twati and Gammack (2006) pointed out that in the Libyan business environment, managers and supervisors are not expected to consider their subordinates' opinion or feedback as accepting such advice denotes weakness. Twati and Gammack suggest most Libyan organisations are characterised by a classic hierarchical model with excessive bureaucracy, inflexibility, tall structure and high standardisation being commonplace. This results in a widening gap between top and lower management, centralisation of decision-making and communication difficulties.

The position of the family in the business environment has a significant role to play within socio-economic growth as many family businesses developed and became an extended family institution (Elasrag, 2011; Welsh & Raven, 2006). For Elasrag, family is an important organising unit providing workers and managers with a medium for passing on skills and knowledge (Fahed-Sreih et al., 2010). Families are a primary source of job creation and entrepreneurs are heavily dependent on them because family members are the primary funding resource and such businesses drive socio-economic development (Eltaweel, 2012).

The relationship between religion, economic activity and entrepreneurship is tenuous and complex (Salmah et al., 2013). Religion has an important effect on believers' entrepreneurship, the decision to become an entrepreneur and entrepreneurial networks. Islamic religion encourages Muslims to be entrepreneurs and provides guidance on all aspects of life including business (Abeng, 1997; Vargas-Hernández et al., 2010). According to Islamic work ethic characteristics, social relations in the workplace depend on trust, respect, integrity, honesty communication, diligence and respect for colleagues. Muslims must communicate effectively with colleagues and respect their managers (Yousef, 2001). Moreover, Islam proscribes appropriate ethical considerations for entrepreneurs engaging in business activity. There are several elements that an individual must foster at work such as being honest, having a high need for achievement, being a hard worker, being frugal and more productive, punctual and time-saving, committed and loyal to their occupation and organisation, avoiding greed and forbidden sources such as interest, avoiding malicious behaviour, being patient and taking risks (Vargas-Hernández et al., 2010).

Graafland et al. (2006) examined the relationship between Islam and responsible business conduct. Muslim entrepreneurs hold positive views of business conduct, respect legal obligations and public-sector relationships. Islamic entrepreneurship has its own culture and guiding principles based on Islamic law. Muslim entrepreneurs must abide by Islamic law and avoid prohibited activities harmful to society, such as refraining from alcohol, gambling, monopolies, speculation on commodities and practising usury (Hassan & Hippler III, 2014). Access to external finance is a major obstacle faced by owners (Ahmad & Atniesha, 2018; Smit & Watkins, 2012). A key difference between Islamic and other economic systems is that Islam favours an interest-free approach. The prohibition of interest is derived from three fundamental principles—(1) Paying interest based on money-for-money conflicts with Islamic jurisprudence; (2) According to Islamic jurisprudence on economic transactions, charging interest favours the already wealthy leading to inequality and an economic gap between rich and poor; and (3) Demanding fixed interest charges in exchange for capital affects poor people and high interest rates slow business growth.

Eltaweel (2012) and Abdulsaleh (2017) explored the funding of Libyan SMEs in terms of sources, uses, attitudes and constraints—highlighting that most owners are unable to borrow from banks because interest is too high and prohibited in Islam. Religious factors contribute to the reluctance of owners to obtain loans. Islamic financial practice has not taken root in the country (Wahab & Abdesamed, 2012), skewing the funding gap. Al Balushi et al. (2019) and Gait and Worthington (2009) reviewed the attitudes, perceptions and motivations of business owners towards Islamic finance suggesting that most supported the practice (Alzardak, 2018). Islamic banking is based around partnership and making profit via various modes (Table 18.1).

Religious factors play a major role in stimulating/depressing entrepreneurial activity which hinders owners from obtaining formal

Table 18.1 Methods of Islamic banking

Modes of finance	Narrative description
Musharakah—co-operation partnership	The business enters into a joint temporary enterprise between the bank and the client, where both contribute to the equity capital of the enterprise. The client puts up 20% of capital, and the banks 80%. Profit and losses are shared according to their equity shareholding in an agreed ratio over a limited duration between the investor and entrepreneur. Equity capital remains constant over the period, and the bank waives its share gradually until the client becomes sole owner
Murabaha—profit	The lender works as a commissioner. The bank buys property then re-sells it to its client at an agreed percentage of profit with no interest over a fixed term
Mudarabah—agencies	The bank contributes all project funding, whilst its client provides the managerial effort and labour at an agreed percentage of profit
Ijarah—lease or hire	The bank buys assets required by its client and leases them for an agreed period. At the contract end the bank transfers ownership to the client at an agreed price

Adapted from Aburime (2008), Farid (2007)

financing. Culture and family influence the extent to which individuals can successfully pursue entrepreneurship, impacting on Libya's ability to initiate 'transformative' and 'emancipatory' forms of entrepreneurship (Al-Danya et al., 2017; Tobias et al., 2013).

An Overview of Contemporary Libyan SMEs

Historical, socio-economic and socio-political contexts have effected political and economic instability in the sector but despite the perpetual flux caused by political instability and the collapse of the Gadaffi regime, Libya maintained a stable and growing SME sector and economy with unique characteristics. We use the Libyan definition posited by Salem (2006) based on employee numbers and value of capital—less than 25 employees, with value capital of 2.5 million Libyan Dinar (LYD). Medium-sized enterprises employ up to 50 employees, with a capital base not exceeding 5 million LYD.

The Libyan SME Sector: The number of SMEs in Libya is unknown but the Ministry of Trade and Economy estimates, suggest around 180,000, not counting informal and unregistered entrepreneurs who deliberately avoid taxes, rules and regulations (Ali & Omar, 2015; Porter & Yegin, 2006; Samawi et al., 2016). The sector accounts for 96% of enterprises, characterised by low levels of competitiveness, productivity, skills and add limited value (Saleh, 2010). Small enterprises are constrained by inadequate equipment and knowledge and by poor government support (Elmansori & Arthur, 2014). They comprise of three types (Wurfali, 2006), see Table 18.2, but until the Civil War began in 2011 tourism was beginning to feature (Alammari et al., 2016; Elkrghli, 2016).

Most SMEs are concentrated in the North West (Tripoli) accounting for 46%, with 36% in the North East; 16% are small corporations; 80% are individually run; and 3% family owned (El Nakhat, 2006; Saleh, 2010). These enterprises are characterised by flexibility and the ability to respond

Table 18.2 Types of Libyan SMEs

Type	Description
Craft-based enterprises	Traditional craft and Agrarian—located throughout Libya
Industrial enterprises	Oil based—Located in urban and northern Libya
Service enterprises	Industry and service based—Located in urban and northern Libya

Adapted from Wurfali (2006)

rapidly to changing market demands (Maghboub, 2009). Their contribution to the economy is small because most are concentrated on low productivity services, retail business and small construction. According to Saleh, levels of investment in non-oil sector between 1995 and 2003 were about 16.7% of GDP, highlighting low government investment. This is magnified because SME wage rates are lower than at larger companies causing recruitment problems. This leads to a dual economy in which high incomes based on oil and gas coexist with lowered private-sector incomes and productivity.

<u>Libya and its economic characteristics:</u> Oil and gas provide Libya's main income [70% of GDP]. The share of non-hydrocarbon GDP is low with the economy based on exporting natural resources rather than creating and supporting other products/services/investment/innovations. The World Bank (2006) reported a general decline in other sectors with the contribution of industrial and constructions enterprises being low. The contribution of agriculture/fisheries is less than 4%. These statistics are low for Middle Eastern and North African countries. Compared with other OPEC members the contribution of the non-oil sector into GDP is significantly lower, reflecting low investment into non-oil activities over the past four decades. Nevertheless, Libya still has a high level of GDP growth rate per capita. According to Porter and Yegin (2006) high oil revenues bolster its economy. Yet, most Libyans have low incomes unlike other oil producing countries and high unemployment [30%], especially among the young (Saleh, 2010; The World Bank, 2010). Libyan accountancy bodies are homegrown and accounting legislation does not mirror international SME best practices. There is no distinction between financial accounting and taxation which impacts negatively on institutional behaviours, obstructs investments and operating decisions. There are no requirements for external audits of financial statements causing a lack of precision in preparing financial reports, necessitating the need for a simplified accounting regime and support (Saleh, 2010). The tax authorities have adopted a discretionary basis for tax collection (Eltaweel, 2012). Unsurprisingly, owners are dissatisfied with such regulations/procedures which foster corruption and abuse of resource distribution and requires urgent reform from policymakers (Wahab & Abdesamed, 2012). There is a need for improvement and the governments must reduce constraining barriers on business, including paralysing obstacles and challenges (Abdulsaed, 2010; Wurfali, 2006). See Fig. 18.2.

Saleh (2010), Ali and Omar (2015) and Omar et al. (2020) classified finance sources into self-financing; informal; and formal. Informal sources are unregulated and most SMEs are informally financed (Ali & Omar, 2015). Borrowing informally involves high interest rates compared to formal sources,

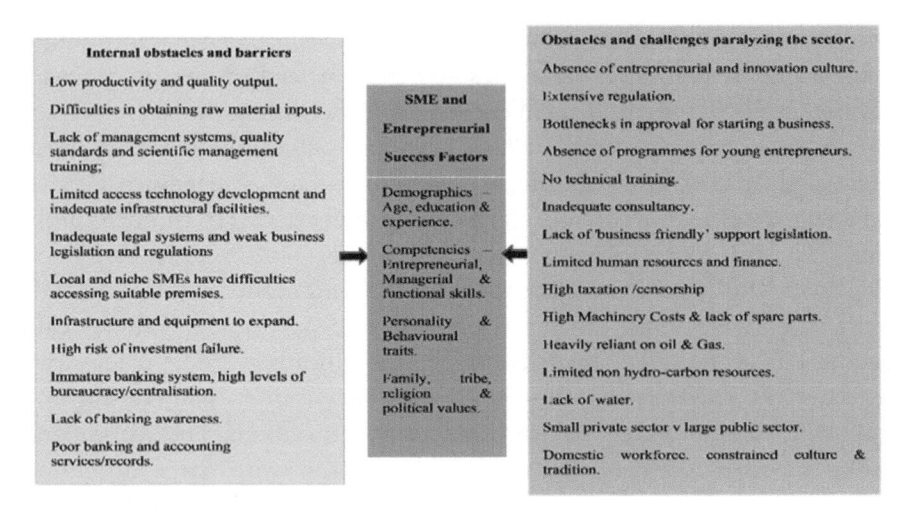

Fig. 18.2 Factors affecting Libyan SME success (author generated)

Internal obstacles and barriers	SME and Entrepreneurial Success Factors	Obstacles and challenges paralyzing the sector
Low productivity and quality output.	Demographics Age, education & experience.	Absence of entrepreneurial and innovation culture.
Difficulties in obtaining raw material inputs.		Extensive regulation.
Lack of management systems, quality standards and scientific management training;		Bottlenecks in approval for starting a business.
		Absence of programmes for young entrepreneurs.
Limited access technology development and inadequate infrastructural facilities.		No technical training.
	Competencies – Entrepreneurial, Managerial & functional skills.	Inadequate consultancy.
Inadequate legal systems and weak business legislation and regulations		Lack of 'business friendly' support legislation.
Local and niche SMEs have difficulties accessing suitable premises.		Limited human resources and finance.
		High taxation /censorship
Infrastructure and equipment to expand.	Personality & Behavioural traits.	High Machinery Costs & lack of spare parts.
High risk of investment failure.		Heavily reliant on oil & Gas.
Immature banking system, high levels of bureaucracy/centralisation.	Family, tribe, religion & political values.	Limited non hydro-carbon resources.
		Lack of water.
Lack of banking awareness.		Small private sector v large public sector.
Poor banking and accounting services/records.		Domestic workforce, constrained culture & tradition.

reliance upon short-term loans and prohibitive financial and material guarantees. This is caused by the aforementioned obstacles in the formal financial sector (Eltaweel, 2012). This makes developing a well-functioning financial system to provide accessible financial service paramount because commercial banks are reluctant to lend to SMEs (Abdesamed & Wahab, 2012). According to the Libyan Central Bank, commercial banks should obtain additional guarantees (up to 125%) in the form of land and property. State-owned banks provide financial legitimacy via a statement account, short-term loans and commercial credentials to allow the importation of raw materials and goods. These banks have weak processes and provide loans depending on the personal characteristics of borrowers who must open tied accounts. This sets up a pecking order (Ahmad & Atniesha, 2018). Most borrowers cannot provide the required business plans or financial data. Recently adopted banking laws and regulations are ineffective because banks do not apply them effectively and efficiently (Omar et al., 2020; Saleh, 2010). Lending to SMEs is risky and banks adopt risk-reduction procedures and tightened risk-assessment to reflect differential lending rates. There is a need for better legislation and setting proper terms and there are no rules to prevent multiple loans from different banks, encouraging fraud. Bankers do not receive training in facilitating evaluation and risk management of loans. Abdesamed and Wahab (2012) and Abdulsaleh and Worthington (2016) highlight the lack of a comprehensive registration system, covering movable and immovable assets which obstructs systems designed to facilitate and support them.

Surviving the Aftermath

Although the political system changed dramatically post-revolution, Libya still faces substantial socio-economic challenges as a result of the difficulty of socio-political transition. Successive power-brokers, including The National Transitional Council (NTC), General National Congress (GNC) and Libyan Council of Representatives (COR), respectively, and successive governments have failed to reach agreement. These institutions were powerless and unable to stabilise the situation. The NTC was formed in 2011 holding power briefly. In May 2012, the first government was formed to guide the country towards elections scheduled for July 2012. Despite a lack of democratic experience, political instability and security crises the election of the GNC in July 2012 went smoothly (Puddington, 2013). On 22nd May 2014, the GNC created a transitional political road map, announcing parliamentary elections on the 25th June 2014. There were countrywide protests demanding the GNC step down for failing to lead the country through the transitional period. As a result, the Libyan COR was elected on 25th June 2014, replacing the GNC. A few months later, the Constitutional Chamber of the Supreme Court in Tripoli ruled that the Parliament was seated unconstitutionally—leading to the National Congress reconvening in Tripoli to resume power. Since then there have been two rival governments; one formed by the COR, located in Tobruk; and the second formed by the GNC, located in Tripoli. This rivalry impacted negatively on the economy, particularly in fiscal management and expenditure patterns. Consequentially Libya faces challenging socio-economic conditions which hinder transformative entrepreneurship (Puddington, 2013).

Since the 2011 conflict, oil production has declined dramatically resulting in economic collapse [a 62% decline in GDP]. However, in November 2013, production declined dramatically due to the deteriorating security situation and the closure of oil ports in the East of Libya by separatist militias bent on achieving their political and economic demands. These included demanding the sale of oil independently, as well as independence for eastern Libya. This caused a further decline in GDP and in oil production during 2014. The country faced a significant fiscal deficit resulting in a decline in revenues leading Libya's internationally recognised NTC government to borrow from the commercial banks to discharge its obligations causing significant gaps in government expenditure. Foreign reserves were affected by the need to finance two governments (CBL, 2014). Consequentially, the private sector remained limited, facing difficulties and uncertainties due to its volatile politics. Instability was not the only reason for a decrease in the performance and private-sector atrophy as successive transition governments did not implement the required economic reforms. Following the uprising, the public sector initially saw dramatic growth in employees because of the need to integrate fighters into the economy. This led to the continuing neglect of the private sector and lowered entrepreneurial intentions (Puddington, 2013). In an effort to develop and promote private firms, the rival governments supported a change to balance the private and public sectors, reduce poverty and unemployment and increase diversity (Elmansori & Arthur, 2014; Zarook et al., 2013b). They supported and encouraged the private sector and overturn State domination. Zarook et al. (2013b) explain that to make its economy more diverse, the governments increased the support of the private sector to help launch small businesses. This resulted in the Libyan Enterprise Centres programme in 2012 to promote entrepreneurial culture and provide business support for start-ups. The Centres transformative mission is to develop entrepreneurship and innovation culture across Libya to create a supportive and an emancipatory environment for small businesses. See Fig. 18.3.

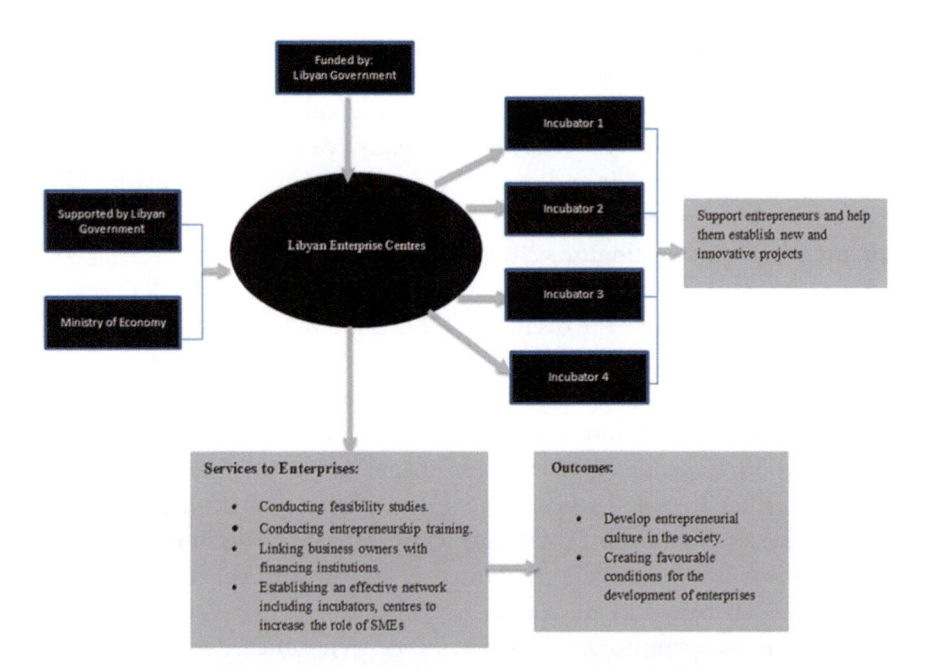

Fig. 18.3 The Libya Enterprise Centre and entrepreneurial ecosystem (Author generated)

It comprises of 13 centres and business incubators tasked with the provision of business support, training and mentoring services to existing SMEs and new entrepreneurs. Whilst the initiative was welcome, Omar et al. (2020) argue that it is not operating at full potential. This is because the economy had not reached the expected sustainable point due to continued political and economic instability (IMF, 2013b). This makes focusing on SMEs essential due to their crucial role in motivating economic activity, poverty alleviation and job creation. Salem (2006), Ali and Omar (2015) argued for the need for highly productive enterprises to service local markets. There is also a need to encourage the university educated diaspora to return and play a part in transforming the enterprise culture to emancipate its people (Aldoukalee, 2013). As a result of the political instability and conflict entrepreneurs are often reluctant to start firms in spite of the political efforts and because of contextual and cultural factors revolving around poverty, organised-crime, corruption, popular revolution, war influencing start-up decisions. Other cultural factors that influence entrepreneurial decision-making include the bureaucratic system, autocracy and the existence of entrepreneurial milieus such as social class, region and geographical regions (Touzani et al., 2015). According to Darendeli and Hill (2016) although all SME's had to cultivate strong ties to the Gadaffi regime to succeed, those that also invested in social-benefit projects and in social ties with families with few ties to the ruling family earned a broader legitimacy that helped them survive the political turmoil. By 2018, the situation in Libya was worsening according to a Forbes Magazine Survey was ranked the 2nd worst country in the world for doing business, behind Afghanistan (Omar et al., 2020). By 1999/2020, unemployment in Libya had risen to 48.7% (CIA, 2020).

Indeed, many of the above-mentioned strengths of the Libyan economy have been negated by the onset of the Civil War of 2019/2020 and renewed political instability which returned Libya to a 'fratricidal' war zone (Eriksson, 2015). The political situation is even more problematic. By 2019, the opposing governments had failed to reach agreement and the Libyan National Army controlled by the House of Representatives in Tobruk besieged Tripoli. HOR forces now control 90% of Libya (Weise, 2020). Sporadic fighting continues on the outskirts of Tripoli in a proxy war involving coalitions of foreign powers on each side. This has damaged the SME sector in Tripoli and Libya as a whole and once again the sector remains in limbo. Carboni and Moody (2018) describe Libya as an 'ungoverned space' where the collapse of State institutions reignited tribal, political, religious and ideological tensions (Carboni & Moody, 2018). Lacher (2011) blames the internecine politics of families, tribes and cities as playing a role in Libyan Revolution. Indeed, it is a similar situation to the politics of the Ottoman era as discussed above. Indeed, Varvelli (2013) emphasises the role of tribal dynamics in Libya's future, blaming it on an incompatible 'Trilemma' characterised by three competing elements: Islam, democracy and the rentier state. Moreover, the COVID-19 pandemic has also caused problems in the country which has a poor health system and infrastructure. Although the death rate is not particularly high (WHO figures list 91,357 cases and 1340 deaths), Libya is considered to be vulnerable. The low rates may result from under reporting. Along with the existing social issues, Covid will inevitably exacerbate the instability (Elmonsori, 2020) and has already led to a dramatic slowdown of SME activity in Libya. There is a pressing need to tackle the endemic lack of entrepreneurial culture within Libyan (Maghboub, 2009); and to improve the education, experience, management skills and training of entrepreneurs, their staff and to take cognisance of psychological traits, family and social networks (Eltaweel, 2012; Nisser & Ibrahim, 2018; Saleh, 2010; Zarook et al., 2013a).

Conclusion

It is evident that the development of an indigenous entrepreneurial spirit and culture in Libya has been hindered by long-term socio-historical, political and economic instability. Political instability has significant implications and constitutes a severe obstacle to economic growth by slowing down economic development post-crisis (Aisen & Veiga, 2013; Gyimah-Brempong & Traynor, 1999; IMF, 2013a). Indeed, political instability has negative effects and impacts on policymaking and productivity affecting capital growth, leading to economic decline. This is hampered by short-term economic policies. An unstable political environment reduces business confidence and frequent changes of regulations and economic policies lead to market fluctuations and poor economic performance. Ahamed and Alzardak (2018) stress the need for developing positive relationships between financial services and government regulators to assist SMEs. The market is extremely sensitive to disturbances to economic growth. For example, political instability negatively affected the level of consumer spending and the growth rate of GDP. Libya is a textbook teaching case on instability. This review by critically interrogating the factors and events shaping the evolution of Libyan entrepreneurship, including the changing roles of state actors from the Ottomans, the Italians, the British and its monarchy, the socialist state and a new generation of warlords and proxy States have created ever-changing political and institutional voids with consequential institutional incongruence, and inevitable environmental turbulence.

This review highlights the fractured enterprise culture within Libya (Maghboub, 2009). Enhancing indigenous entrepreneurial culture is vital to support and develop SMEs. This requires supportive input from all State agencies, educational institutions, legislative bodies, banks, industry and corporations to make it easier for entrepreneurs setting up, or running enterprises (Nisser & Ibrahim, 2018). Suleiman (2009) stresses a need for facilitating, motivating and supporting all entrepreneurs. The contexts discussed above are not exceptional but Libyan entrepreneurs suffer from ingrained obstacles and challenges that prevent them from realising their full entrepreneurial potential. They thus perform below expectation and exhibit low entrepreneurial growth (Saleh, 2010). Not every analysis of Libya post Gaddafi is bleak—indeed, Vandewalle (2012) articulated early successes in what he referred to as the 'New Libya'. Pack (2019) argues that progress in Libya will stall until it deals with the real issues of failing to address the root causes of the country's malaise, its flawed economic institutions and the lack of a social contract. Pack suggests that the economic structures established during the Qadhafi period have become more entrenched in the political vacuum and calls for an urgent mapping of Libya's economic structures.

A weakness of this review is its reliance on historical content and limiting its exploration of enterprise to urban areas restricts other lines of inquiry. There are other enterprising peoples and tribes including the nomadic 'Taureg' with an entrepreneurial heritage in Libya and North Africa (Scholze, 2015). Nevertheless, it has highlighted the changing nature of Libyan enterprise and the power of 'transformative' (Tobias et al., 2013) and 'emancipatory entrepreneuring' (Al-Dajani et al., 2015) to transform and change the Libyan SME sector. The theoretical position adopted in this review allows scholars and practitioners to build upon the historical and socio-cultural issues discussed herein and to make ontological and epistemological sense of the changing SME and entrepreneurial landscape. The theoretical positioning and the developing transformatory/emancipatory framework is useful because it will accommodate future studies. This is important because an understanding of a countries historical, cultural, religious and social heritage is of vital significance in determining and understanding their enterprise cultures, but also because such factors are continuously changing and capable of being changed. Libyans have survived the turmoil of the Ottoman era, the Italian colonisation and the Gaddafi era. The challenging contemporary socio-political turmoil from the Idris era through to the chaotic Gaddafi years and the Libyan Centre's for entrepreneurship initiative is proof of this. Accommodating Islamic religious and banking practices and developing a Libyan entrepreneurial ecosystem will help create a vibrant, inclusive enterprise culture which will transform and emancipate Libya and its peoples. It has also provided a proto-typological framework for exploring challenges and opportunities for entrepreneurship in similar North Africa and the Middle Eastern contexts.

There is an opportunity to reduce sectoral imbalances through the diversification of its economy and by expanding non-oil activities and by devising an effective, viable strategy to develop SMEs and achieve higher levels of investment and better productivity to reduce the volatility caused by fluctuating oil prices. Simultaneously, there is a need to tackle unemployment and diversify the economy through improving and supporting the sector. The Libyan governments must do more to support small businesses to stimulate sustainable economic development and encourage rapid economic growth of non-oil sector to create new job opportunities. They must pragmatically manage strategies for maximising the proceeds of oil investment to facilitate the transition into a market economy. Although the growth of non-oil activities has improved incrementally, it remains low in comparison with other MENA countries, reflecting inadequate investment and low levels of productivity. There is a need for new effective SME policies to encourage and support more setups/growth; a better support infrastructure; and for more integration and regional and rural enterprise support structures to achieve equity and stimulate balanced economic growth. The economy must be rebalanced and rural entrepreneurship must be encouraged but ultimately, an end to conflict is required before the latent Libyan entrepreneurial spirit can be unleashed.

References

AfDB. (2011). *African Economic Outlook. Libya: Post-war challenges.* http://www.afdb.org/fileadmin/uploads/afdb/Documents/Publications/Brocure%20Anglais%20Lybie_North%20Africa%20Quaterly%20Analytical.pdf.

Abdesamed, K. H., & Wahab, K. A. (2012). *Do experience, Education and Business plan influence SMEs start-up Bank loan?* The Case of Libya. @inproceedings Abdesamed2012DoEE.

Abdulsaleh, A. M. (2017). The introduction of Islamic finance in Libya: Capturing the opportunities for SMEs development. *Journal of Emerging Economies and Islamic Research, 5*(1), 39–48.

Abdulsaleh, A. M., & Worthington, A. (2016). Bankers' perceptions of successful SMEs loan applications: A case study from Libya. *The MENA Journal of Business Case Studies, 4*(7), 106–115.

Abdussalam, A. S. (1983). *External forces, economic development and regional inequality in Libya.* Dissertation. Oklahoma University.

Abdulsaed, M. A. (2010). *The importance of organising administrative and its impact on the performance of small and medium enterprises in Libya.* Tripoli University.

Abeng, T. (1997). Business ethics in Islamic context: Perspectives of a Muslim business leader. *Business Ethics Quarterly, 7*(3), 47–54.

Abubaker, A. (2011). *Influence of core cultural values on the communication behaviour of staff in Libyan Organisation.* Unpublished document.

Aburime, T. U. (2008). Islamic banking theories, practices and insights for Nigeria. *International Review of Business Research Papers., 5*(1), 321–339.

Alzardak, O. (2018). Influence of financial services on SMEs performance in Libya: The mediating role of government regulastions. *Journal of Islamic and Human Advanced Research, 8*(1), 01–17.

Al Balushi, Y., Locke, S., & Boulanouar, Z. (2019). Omani SME perceptions towards Islamic financing systems. *Qualitative Research in Financial Markets, 11*(4), 369–386.

Ahamed, S., & Alzardak, O. (2018). Influence of financial services on SMEs performance in Libya: The mediating role of government regulations. *Journal of Islamic and Human Advanced Research, 8*(1), 1–17.

Aldoukalee, S. A. (2013). *An Investigation into the challenges faced by Libyan PhD Students in Britain: [A study of the Three Universities in Manchester and Salford].* Unpublished PhD thesis, University of Salford, Salford, UK.

Alfaitori, A. (2012) *The state role in privatization process Libya enterprise: Entrepreneurship and innovation annual conference.* Libya Enterprise Centre.

Al-Dajani, H., Carter, S., Shaw, E., & Marlow, S. (2015). Entrepreneurship among the displaced and dispossessed: Exploring the limits of emancipatory entrepreneuring. *British Journal of Management, 26*(4), 713–730.

Ali, F., & Omar, A. (2015). *2013 GEM Libya-National Report. Technical report based on survey results.* Research and Consulting Centre-The University of Benghazi; Global Entrepreneurship Research Association-London Business School.

Anderson, L. (1984). Nineteenth-century reform in Ottoman Libya. *International Journal of Middle East Studies., 16*(3), 325–348.

Anyanwu, J. C. (2014). Oil wealth, ethno-religious: Linguistic fractionalization and civil wars in Africa: Cross country evidence. *African Development Review, 26*(2), 209–236.

Ahmad, N. S. M., & Atniesha, R. A. A. (2018). *The pecking order theory (POT) and start-up financing of small and medium enterprises (SMEs): Insights into available literature in the Libyan context* (pp. 191–200). Economic and Social Development: Book of Proceedings.

Aisen, A., & Veiga, F. J. (2013). How does political instability affect economic growth? *European Journal of Political Economy., 29*, 151–167.

Alammari, A., Khalif, A. A., & Othman, G. (2016). The importance of SMEs in Libyan tourism sector. In A. Alammari, K. A. Abdussalam, & G. Othman (Eds.), *The role of management functions in successful enterprise performance* (pp. 45–60). Agroinform.

Attir, M., & Al-Azzabi, K. (2004). The Libyan Jamahiriya: Cuntry, people, social and political development. *Doing Business with Libya* (pp. 8–17).

Benzing, C., Chu, H. M., & Kara, O. (2009). Entrepreneurs in Turkey: A factor analysis of motivations, success factors, and problems. *Journal of Small Business Management, 47*(1), 58–91.

Brahimi, A. (2011). Libya's revolution. *The Journal of North African Studies, 16*(4), 605–624.

Bini, E. (2012). *Oil workers, trade unions and the emergence of oil nationalism in Libya, 1956–1969*. European University Institute.

Buferna, F. M. (2005). *Determinants of capital structure: Evidence from Libya*. PhD thesis. The University of Liverpool.

Burns, P. (2011). *Entrepreneurship and small business: Start-up, growth and maturity* (3rd ed.). Palgrave Macmillan.

Carboni, A., & Moody, J. (2018). Between the cracks: Actor fragmentation and local conflict systems in the Libyan civil war. *Small Wars & Insurgencies, 289*(3), 456–490.

CBL. (2014). Central Bank of Libya: Economic Bulletin Report. Department, (ed.). Tripoli.

CIA. (2020). *Central Intelligence Agency. The world fact book; Libya.*https://www.cia.gov/library/publications/the-world-factbook/geos/ly.html.

Darendeli, I. S., & Hill, T. J. (2016). Uncovering the complex relationships between political risk and MNE firm legitimacy: Insights from Libya. *Journal of International Business Studies, 47*, 68–92.

El Nakhat, K. A. (2006). *Accounting information in micro manufacturing enterprises in Libya*. Unpublished PhD Thesis. Sheffield Hallam University, UK. Sheffield.

Elasrag, H. (2011). Enhancing the competitiveness of the Arab SMEs. *Open Journal of Economic Research, 1*(2), 7–21.

Elkrghli, S. (2016). The relationship between political conflict (2013/2016) and marketing performances of Libyan tourism SMEs. In *Conference: Refereed proceedings of the 13th annual world congress of the academy for global business advancement (AGBA) and 2016 AGBA—Indonesia chapter's inaugural conference* (p. 13, No. 1). http://www.agba.us/pdf. At: Indonesia, Surakarta.

Elmansori, E., & Arthur, L. (2014). Obstacles to innovation faced by small and medium enterprises (SMEs) in Libya. *International Journal of Knowledge Management in Middle East & North Africa, 3*(2), 181–194.

Elmansori, E. (2020). The impact of the Coronavirus pandemic (COVID-19) on the small & medium sized enterprise (SMEs) in Libya. In *Coronavirus: The management of pandemic and the impact on agendas 2020*. World Sustainable Development Outlook, 2020. WASAD.

Eltaweel, M. E. (2012). How are small businesses in Libya financed? *International Conference on Business, Finance and Geograph (ICBFG 2012)*. Phuket. Thailand, pp. 171–172.

Eriksson, M. (2015) A fatricidal Libya and its second civil war. In *Harvesting decades of Qaddafi's 'divide and rule'*. (PDF) A Fratricidal Libya and its Second Civil War 2016 | Hi and Welcome to my Website Mikael Eriksson - Academia.edu.

Fahed-Sreih, J., Pistrui, D., Huang, W. V., & Welsch, H. P. (2010). Family and cultural factors impacting entrepreneurship in war time Lebanon. *International Journal of Entrepreneurship and Innovation Management, 12*(1), 35–51.

Farid, M. (2007). Entrepreneurship in Egypt and the US compared: Directions for further research suggested. *Journal of Management Development., 26*(5), 428–440.

Gait, A., & Worthington, A. C. (2009). *Libyan business firm attitudes towards Islamic methods of finance*. Griffith Business School, Griffith University.

Ghanem, S. M. (1985). *Planning and development in modern Libya*. London, England; Wisbech, Cambridgeshire, England; Boulder, Colo., USA: Society for Lybian Studies; Middle East & North African Studies Press; Lynne Rienner Publishers.

Graafland, J., Mazereeuw, C., & Yahia, A. (2006). Islam and socially responsible business conduct: An empirical study of Dutch entrepreneurs. *Business Ethics: A European Review., 15*(4), 390–406.

Gyimah-Brempong, K., & Traynor, T. L. (1999). Political instability, investment and economic growth in Sub-Saharan Africa. *Journal of African Economies., 8*(1), 52–86.

Hassan, M. K., & Hippler, W. J., III. (2014). Entrepreneurship and Islam: An overview. *Econ Journal Watch., 11*(2), 170–178.

Higgins, B. (1955). *Entrepreneurship in Libya*. MIT.

Higgins, B. (1959). Economic review: Entrepreneurship in Libya. *Middle East Journal, 11*(3), 319–323.

IMF. (2013a). *The dynamic effect of social and political instability on output: The role of reforms*. Working paper.

IMF. (2013b). Libya: 2013 article Iv consultation. IMF Country Report. http://www.imf.org/external/pubs/ft/scr/2013/cr13150.pdf.

Ibrahim, M., Mutalib, M. A., & Abdulaziz, A. M. (2013). The over dependency of Libya on oil revenue: Economic vulnerability. *Australian Journal of Basic & Applied Sciences, 7*(11), 537–540.

Kanungo, R. P. (2006). Cross culture and business practice: Are they coterminous or cross-verging? *Cross Cultural Management: An International Journal, 13*(1), 23–31.

Kolade, O., Egbetokun, A., Rae, D., & Hussain, J. (2019). Entrepreneurial resilience in turbulent environments: The role of spiritual capital. In *Research handbook on entrepreneurship in emerging economies: A contextualised approach*. Edward Elgar Publishing.

Lacher, W. (2011). Families, tribes and cities in the Libyan revolution. *Middle east policy,* Vol. XVIII, No. 4, Winter 2011.

Lockwood, A. N. (1957). Libya: Building a desert economy. *International Conciliation,* No. 512.

Maghboub, M. (2009). Small firms in Libya, reality and requirements of change. In *Creating an appropriate environment for the success of small and medium-sized enterprises conference.* Sabha, Libya.

El Mallakh, R. (1969). The economics of rapid growth: Libya. *Middle East Journal, 23*(3), 308–320.

Masoud, N. M. (2009). *Libya's economic reform programme and the case for a stock market.* Ph.D thesis University of Huddersfield.

Mika, J. P. (2015). *The role of publicaly funded enterprise assistance in Maori entrepreneurship in Aotearoa New Zealand.* Unpublished PhD thesis, Massey University, New Zealand.

Naudé, W. A., & Havenga, J. J. D. (2012). An overview of African entrepreneurship and small business research. *Journal of Small Business and Entrepreneurship, 18*(1), 101–120.

Nisser, H. I., & Ibrahim, N. (2018). The effect of education level and experience on SME performance in Libya. *International Journal for Studies on Children, Women, Elderly and Disabled, 4,* 260–264.

OECD. (2016). *The development dimension SMEs in Libya's reconstruction preparing for a post conflict economy.* An OECD Report.

Oakes, J. (2011). *Libya: The history of Gaddafi's pariah state.* The History Press.

Obeidi, A. (2001). *Political culture in Libya.* Curzon.

Pack, J. (2019). *It's the economy stupid: How Libya's civil war is rooted in its economic structures.* IAI Papers, Paper 19.

Omar, A., Ali, F., & Imhamed, S. (2020). Exploring entrepreneurial framework conditions In Libya: A national perspective. *Journal of Entrepreneurship, Business and Economics, 8*(1), 15–53.

Porter, M., & Yegin, D. (2006). *National economic strategy: An assessment of the competitiveness of Libya.* The general planning council of Libya. Cera, UK.

Puddington, A. (2013). *Freedom in the world 2013: Democratic breakthroughs in the balance.* Freedom House.

Saleh, I. M. (2010). *Small and medium enterprises and its role in the development process.* Unpublished MSc thesis. Arab Open Academy in Denmark.

Salem, A. A. (2006). The role of small and medium business in reducing unemployment. In *Development of small and medium business conference, 7–8/06/2006.* University of Garyounis.

Salmah, S., Wahab, K. A., & Haris, A. (2013). Islamic entrepreneurial motivation: An analytical review. In *5th Islamic economics system conference—Sustainable development through the Islamic economics system 4–5th September.* Universiti Sains Islam Malaysia.

Samawi, A., Mdanat, M., Yosef, F., & Abutayeh, B. (2016). Formal versus informal financing of SMEs in the Libyan context: The case of Ghrian city. In *Proceedings* of 33rd international business research conference 4–5 January 2016, Flora Grand Hotel, Dubai, UAE, (Vol. 8).

Senina, M., & Shamiya, A. (2010). *The general framework of the policies of restructuring the Libyan economy*. The Research Centre of Economic Sciences.

Scholze, M. (2015). Sand, Sun, and Toyotas: Tuareg entrepreneurship in desert tourism in Niger. In U. Röschenthaler, & D. Schulz (Eds.), *Cultural entrepreneurship in Africa*. Routledge.

Smit, Y., & Watkins, J. (2012). A literature review of small and medium enterprises (SME) risk management practices in South Africa. *African Journal of Business Management., 6*(21), 6324–6330.

Squalli, J. (2007). Electricity consumption and economic growth: Bounds and causality analyses of OPEC members. *Energy Economics., 29*(6), 1192–1205.

Suleiman, R.A. (2009) Mechanisms and the development of SMEs in the North African countries and Gulf Cooperation Council (GCC) An empirical study on small firms in Sabha. In *Creating appropriate environment for the success of SMEs Conference*. Sabha-Libya.

Tobias, J., Mair, J., & Barbosa-Leiker, C. (2013). Toward a theory of transformative entrepreneuring: Poverty reduction and conflict resolution in Rwanda's entrepreneurial coffee sector. *Journal of Business Venturing, 28*(6), 728–742.

Touzani, M., Jlassi, F., Maalaoui, A.., & Rabi Hassine, B. H. (2015). Contextual and cultural determinants of entrepreneurship in pre-and post-revolutionary Tunisia: Analysing the discourse of young potential and actual entrepreneurs. *Journal of Small Business and Enterprise Development, 22*(1), 160–179.

Twati, J. M., & Gammack, J. G. (2006). The impact of organisational culture innovation on the adoption of IS/IT: The case of Libya. *Journal of Enterprise Information Management., 19*(2), 175–191.

Vandewalle, D. (1998). *Libya since independence: Oil and state-building*. Cornell University.

Vandewalle, D. J. (2008). *Libya since 1969: Qadhafi's revolution revisited*. Palgrave Macmillan.

Vandewalle, D. (2012). After Qaddafi: The surprising success of the new Libya. *Foreign Affairs, 91*(6), 8–15.

Vargas-Hernández, J. G., Noruzi, M. R., & Sariolghalam, N. (2010). An exploration of the affects of islamic culture on entrepreneurial behaviors in muslim countries. *Asian Social Science., 16*(5), 120.

Varvelli, A. (2013). *The role of Tribal dynamics in the Libyan future*. ISPI Papers.

Wahab, K. A., & Abdesamed, K. H. (2012). Small and medium enterprises (SMEs) financing practice and accessing bank loan issues-The Case of Libya. In *Proceedings of World Academy of Science, Engineering and Technology*. World Academy of Science, Engineering and Technology (WASET), 1535.

Welsh, D. H. B., & Raven, P. (2006). Family business in the middle east: An exploratory study of retail management in Kuwait and Lebanon. *Family Business Review, 19*(1), 29–48.

World Bank. (2006). *Libya—Country economic report*.http://documents.worldbank.org/curated/en/2006/06/7011992/libya-country-economic-report.

World Bank. (2010). *World development indicators. Country profile: Libya*. http://epri.org.za/wp-content/uploads/2011/03/27-Libya.pdf.

World Bank. (2014). *World development indicators*. http://data.worldbank.org/country/libya.

Weise, Z. (2020: 17/1). *Talks to de-escalate the hostilities are set to be held in Berlin on Sunday*. https://www.politico.eu/article/the-libyan-conflict-explained/.

Wurfali, T. A. (2006). Small and medium enterprise in Libya between reality & ambition. *Qualification requirement of SME in Arabic countries,* Algeria 17, 18 April 2006, pp. 86–98.

Yousef, D. A. (2001). Islamic work ethic-A moderator between organisational commitment and job satisfaction in a cross-cultural context. *Personnel Review, 30*(2), 152–169.

Zarook, T., Rahman, M. M., & Khanam, R. (2013). The impact of demographic factors on accessing to finance in Libya's SMEs. *International Journal of Business and Management, 8*(14), 55.

Zarook, T., Rahman, M. M., & Khanam, R. (2013). Management skills and accessing to finance: Evidence from Libya's SMEs. *International Journal of Business and Social Science, 4*(7), 106–115.

19

Application of the People, Context, Deal and Opportunity (PCDO) Model for Entrepreneurship Advancement in Africa

Ovo Imoedemhe

Introduction

The chapter postulates that the legal and institutional framework of the African Union (AU) is inadequate to tackle the current crisis and conflict-ridden situations in most African countries to provide an enabling environment for entrepreneurship advancement in Africa. The chapter proposes the application of the people, context, deal and opportunity (PCDO) model by African countries in order to ensure the safety and security of people and create the right context and to leverage entrepreneurial opportunities in Africa. The proposal is founded on Aspirations 4 and 6 of Agenda 2063 by which the AU aspires to become an integrated, peaceful, progressive, safe and secure Africa by the year 2063 with development programmes that are led by African people.

While Africa is on the road map to entrepreneurial advancement like the rest of the world, there are certain challenges that the continent continues to grapple with, such as conflicts, crisis, corruption, insecurity and instability. In view of these challenges, this chapter examines whether the African Union (AU) can adequately tackle the problems and ensure peace, security and stability in Africa. Arguably, institutional environmental conditions and

---

O. Imoedemhe (✉)
School of Law University of Bradford, Bradford, UK
e-mail: o.c.imoedemhe@bradford.ac.uk

entrepreneurship are inseparable because entrepreneurship advancement is fostered by the right institutional environment. Security is identified as a foremost context or environment in which entrepreneurship can thrive. It is argued that there are widespread patterns of insecurity in most African countries, and that entrepreneurship advancement in Africa is dependent upon stable, peaceful and secure environment where the rule of law is upheld, and rights are guaranteed. It is proposed that stable, safe and secure environment will in turn shape the local attitudes and cultural context favourable for entrepreneurship advancement in Africa.

The influence of institutional environment on the level and types of entrepreneurship and the entrepreneurial activities is well established. Writing within the context of entrepreneurship education and training (EET) in Ghana, Kenya and Mozambique, Robb et al. (2014) postulated that among the barriers to entrepreneurship advancement in Africa were local attitudes and cultural disincentives. The local attitudes include the pervasive fear of venturing into self-employment when there are family financial obligations, which make it difficult, for example, to deny goods or services to extended family members because of fear that they are unlikely and genuinely unable to pay for them (Robb et al., 2014, 34). Indeed, in most African countries, such as Ghana, Kenya, Mozambique, Nigeria, the Central African Republic and the Democratic Republic of the Congo, there are negative cultural perceptions of entrepreneurship (Robb et al., 2014, 39). Cultural disincentives refer to factors associated with local perceptions. Accordingly, Robb et al. observed that the cultural belief stems from the lack of wide acceptance of entrepreneurship as a respected career path (Robb et al., 2014, 39). Other barriers include corruption, conflicts and crisis, poverty and dysfunctional leadership.

The chapter proceeds in four sections. The introductory section is followed by an examination of the prevailing pattern of insecurity, crisis and conflicts in a few African countries and its consequence for decent life and entrepreneurship advancement. Incidences of crisis, conflicts and wanton killing of African people in Central African Republic (CAR), Nigeria and Sudan are highlighted to suggest that if these patterns are not dealt with, entrepreneurship advancement would remain underdeveloped in these and other African countries that face similar security and instability problems. The second section analyses entrepreneurship in general and the nature of the social and commercial entrepreneurship, in particular. It also analyses bricolage concept as it applies to the African continent. The third section examines the legal and institutional framework for entrepreneurship advancement within the African Union (AU) including the Peace and Security Council

(PSC) which is responsible for conflict prevention, resolution and management. Analysis of Aspirations 4 and 6 of Agenda 2063 and the 'Kagame Report' shows that the continent continues to aspire to achieve an inclusive Africa and an Africa whose development is driven by its people.

The application of the people, context, deal and opportunity (PCDO) model to Africa is the focus of the fourth section. The section highlights the need for a shift in the AU's institutional reform framework that is currently focused on policies, rules, regulations and the proliferation of organs to one that includes cognitive elements. It argues for the reforms that are people and context centred to ensure the creation of safe and secure environment. The chapter concludes with the proposal of a decentralised AU to allow individual African countries to implement entrepreneurship advancement that is built around people informed by the PCDO model.

Circumstances of Africa's Conflict-Ridden Countries

Africa consists of 55 countries and it is the second largest continent in the world, both in area and population, behind Asia. The countries in Africa are diverse in geography, politically, socio-culturally and economically. Most African countries were previously under the subjugation of colonial powers. The 1960s and 1970s marked African countries' emancipation, as individual African countries gained independence from their colonial masters. The impact of the years of colonisation, the negotiations leading up to independence, the people and contexts differ from one African country to another. Such historical and contextual differences could be seen in their levels of development. Therefore, it is erroneous and misleading to discuss Africa as a country, hence a contextual analysis of the continent through the prism of the Africa Union (AU) is undertaken. This means that discussions about Africa should encompass or at least contemplate all 55 countries and their varying stages of socio-cultural, political and economic developments in view of promoting entrepreneurship in Africa.

Although only three countries are used as case study due to space constraints, discussions in this section reveals a pattern of conflict and crisis in most African countries. It is argued that for effective entrepreneurship advancement in Africa, the conditions of Africa's conflict-ridden countries must be confronted and transformed to peaceful, secure and stable Africa. With the adoption of the theme 'silencing the guns' in Africa by 2020, the African Union (AU) aimed to achieve a peaceful, safe and secure Africa.

Formulating such a theme highlights the fact that conflicts and crisis have been a major part of most African countries' trajectories post-independence by experience. The countries under focus, namely, the Central African Republic, Nigeria and Sudan are identified as a few of Africa's remaining conflict hotspots, for which reason the AU devised the theme with the hope that the guns will truly be silenced. Regrettably, the theme was not achieved. Instead, there have been more instances of violence both in these countries and others such as Somalia, Mali and Libya. Coffey (November 2019) listed CAR, Mali, Somalia and South Sudan as some of the most dangerous countries in the world.

The Central African Republic

The population of Central African Republic (CAR) continues to be depleted due to civil wars since its independence in 1960. It is reported that the insurgency led by the *Seleka* (alliance in Sango) a coalition of armed Muslim groups resulted in the severe depletion of the country's security infrastructure and heightened ethnic tensions. In 2012, the *Seleka* forces launched an offensive against the CAR government (BBC News 18 December 2012). In response, the *anti-balaka* group (invincible in Sango) coalitions of Christian fighters carried out reprisal against the *Seleka* forces (Violence in Central Africa Republic, 14 January 2021). Since September 2013, both forces have continued widespread attacks against each other that plunged the CAR into atrocities resulting in hundreds of thousand deaths, thousands of refugees, while hundreds are displaced and dispersed in neighbouring countries such as Cameroon and Democratic Republic of Congo (United Nations Human Rights, CAR: Mapping Human Rights Violations 2003–2015; CAR Refugees and Internally Displaced Persons, 31 December 2020).

Reports from human rights groups and United Nations agencies suggest that crimes committed by both the *Seleka* and *anti-balaka* groups constitute war crimes and crimes against humanity. Consequently, in April 2014, the United Nations Security Council (UNSC) established a peacekeeping force in Bangui. However, due to the inability of the CAR government to stop the crisis, there has been escalation and several deaths were recorded as the two recognised groups in 2014 increased to about fourteen armed factions with hundreds of allied groups outside the country (Dukhan, 2017). Therefore, Baddorf (2017) noted that despite the peace agreement signed in June 2017, and the United Nations establishment of the Multidimensional Integrated Stabilization Mission in the Central African Republic (MINUSCA) in Bangui in April 2018, the end to the atrocities in CAR is still not in sight.

The priority task of the MINUSCA was to ensure the protection of civilians and disarm militia groups (United Nations Peacekeeping: MUNISCA). Regrettably, with over fifteen thousand peacekeepers operating in CAR, MINUSCA appears unable to fulfil its mandate as they continue to face significant challenges (Global Conflict Trackers, 14 January 2021). Also, the United Nations documents several attacks against UN peacekeepers and humanitarian workers, noting that fifteen peacekeepers were killed in CAR in 2017, while six others were killed by various armed groups in 2018 (United Nations Peacekeeping, 31 October 2018).

Significantly, the crisis in CAR has been referred to the ICC twice. Both were self-referrals. Self-referrals are situations referred to the ICC by the government of the country in which the crimes occur or where the alleged perpetrators are nationals of the country. In 2004 and 2014, the government of CAR referred situations in its country to the ICC, resulting in Situations and Cases CAR I and II, respectively, at the ICC. Details of the crisis in CAR and the rationale for self-referrals cannot be undertaken here. The CAR ratified the Rome Statute on 3 October 2001 and in line with the complementarity regime of the ICC, the government of CAR should be able to investigate and prosecute international crimes that occur in its territory (Imoedemhe, 2017, 23). However, being supposedly overwhelmed with renewed violence in 2012, the government again referred the situation to the ICC in May 2014, exactly a decade after the first referral (Human Rights Watch, CAR: ICC Sets Trial 28 July, 2020). Self-referral depicts not only the inability or unwillingness of a government to act, but it also demonstrates weak institutions and arguably misdirected priorities. According to Keppler (2021) the people of CAR 'suffered unspeakable atrocities and horrors during the civil conflict that began in 2012'.

Nigeria

There are repeated patterns in most African countries where incidences of grave injustices and violations of human rights are propagated either directly or indirectly by some African governments. Admittedly in Nigeria, the insurgence of the group called Boko Haram (Western education is sinful) has been on for decades, therefore, both rebel groups and government forces are responsible for the violence and violations of human rights. News is replete with accounts of killings and kidnappings of people, including men, women, children and young adults, so much so that Nigeria was named the 'global capital of kidnapping' (Al Okoli, 2019). This notorious distinction that placed Nigeria as the 'kidnap-for-ransom capital' meant that Nigeria accounted for a quarter of globally reported kidnap cases (Imoedemhe, 2017, 183).

The Nigerian government is partly responsible for the state of affairs, due to its apathy and failure to act. Jatto (2018, 85) documents several atrocities and unlawful killings in Nigeria, which have risen to heightened proportion and have attracted the international community as allegedly constituting crimes against humanity, war crimes and the crime of genocide. Yet the Nigerian government has done little to nothing to stop the atrocities. Abraham Jatto (2018) documented statistically how Muslim Fulani Herdsmen mostly from the Northern part of Nigeria have consistently and systematically killed innocent Nigerians who are predominantly in the Southern and other parts of Nigeria, destroying farmlands and thereby making the entire country insecure and unsafe.

Human security is lacking in Nigeria. Human security means the 'protection of fundamental freedoms which define human lives, in the process protecting people from critical (severe) and pervasive (widespread) threats and situations through the usage of processes that build on people's strength and aspirations' (Human Security Centre, 2010, 205). This implies that the protection, preservation of lives and ensuring individual freedom are components of human security. Human Rights Watch document several killings in the Northern and Southern parts of Nigeria noting that Boko Haram, Fulani Herdsmen and the Nigerian Military have committed unimaginable atrocities against men, women and children, yet nobody is being held to account (Roth, Human Rights Watch [HRW] World Report, 2020).

Like a few other African governments, the Nigerian government appears complicit in the atrocities. According to Imoedemhe (2017, 184–185) Nigeria is susceptible to being a failed state due to the inability of the government to ensure security and safety of people and property. Since 2010, Nigeria has been under preliminary examination by the International Criminal Court (ICC). In the 11 December 2020 report, the Chief Prosecutor of the ICC Fatou Bensouda noted among others that both Boko Haram and the Nigerian Security Forces (NSF) have committed acts constituting crimes against humanity and war crimes. Consequently, Bensouda requested authorisation by the Judges of the Pre-Trial Chamber of the ICC to open investigations in Nigeria (Statement of the Prosecutor, 11 December 2020). The ten-year long preliminary examination is certainly not the fault of the Office of the Prosecutor (OTP), whose lean resources have been and continues to be overstretched due to the increasing demands placed on it. Rather, it is the failure of the Nigerian government who, being a party to the Rome Statute of the ICC since 2000, failed to take responsibility for its complementarity role (Imoedemhe, 2017, 19–20).

Sudan

For decades, Sudan remained the largest country in Africa in terms of land mass. However, with the secession of South Sudan in July 2011, it has become the third largest country behind Algeria and the Democratic Republic Congo (DRC) who rank first and second, respectively. Conflicts in Darfur, Southern Kordofan and Blue Nile have been recorded by Human Rights Watch (HRW, World Report 2020). Succinctly, the conflicts have been between the government forces and rebel groups. The conflicts between the Sudan Liberation Movement/Army (SLM) and the *Janjaweed* (militia men on horseback) in Darfur from 2003 to 2005 resulted in several deaths and displacements of several Sudanese (Gardner, 2020). This also culminated in the first warrant of arrest issued by the ICC against a sitting president—Former President of Sudan, Omar Al-Bashir in 2009 and 2010 (Imoedemhe, 2015, 89). The situation in Darfur Sudan had been referred to the ICC by Resolution 1593 of the United Nations Security Council (UNSC) in March 2005, being the first referral by the UNSC to the ICC.

Omar al-Bashir is charged with genocide, accused of ethnic cleansing, by which he allegedly attempted to wipe out three non-Arab ethnic groups (Fur, Masalit and Zaghawa) in the Darfur region where more than 200,000 people have died since 2003. Despite being the only sitting president faced with genocide charges, Omar al-Bashir travelled freely and was re-elected in April 2015. Nevertheless, conflicts in Sudan continued unabated resulting in several deaths, internal displacements and gross human rights violations. In April 2019, President Omar al-Bashir was ousted after being president for over 30 years. Roth (HRW, 2020) reports that several conflicts between the groups, as well as the Rapid Support Forces (RSF) a paramilitary force, continued in Khartoum, Darfur and other regions. By an agreement between the African Union and the United Nations Security Council, the African Union/United Nations Mission in Darfur (UNAMID) was established to stop human rights abuses and ensure the protection of civilians in Sudan. UNAMID's mandate has been extended for another one-year period.

In summary, the pattern of insecurity, wanton killings, displacement of people and destruction of properties highlighted in CAR, Nigeria and Sudan is replete in most African countries. Jalloh (2009, 475) labelled the continent the most conflict-ridden in the world. As argued by Imoedemhe (2015, 85), this assertion appeared justified because 10 out of the 24 most war-ridden countries recorded between 1980 and 1994 were in Africa. The question is how African countries can ensure entrepreneurship advancement in an atmosphere or environment that is devoid of peace, safety and security. The chapter argues for African governments to safeguard the rule of law, uphold the sanctity of life and ensure safety and security of its citizens. The African context—partly crisis-ridden, less secure, politically, and economically volatile as well as with less developed institutions, requires context-tested approaches, of which the PCDO model may be considered appropriate for adoption by African countries.

Entrepreneurship: Social and Commercial

The aim of entrepreneurship is wealth creation through innovation and creativity. The word entrepreneur is taken from the French word *enterprendre*, which means 'to undertake' (Singh & Belwal, 2008). Accordingly, an entrepreneur is an individual who is driven by ideas and who takes steps to bring together the finances, people, equipment and facilities to establish and manage a business enterprise in order to achieve his goals and ambitions (Singh & Belwal, 2008). Entrepreneurial activity necessarily involves people, resources and the appropriate environment.

Broadly, two types of entrepreneurship could be identified: social and commercial. Social entrepreneurship refers to innovative, value creating activity that occur within or across the non-profit, business or government sectors (Austin et al., 2006). The underlying objective of social entrepreneurship is to create social values, rather than personal wealth. Thus, social entrepreneurship is entrepreneurial activity with social purpose embedded in it, as it addresses social needs that are not met by commercial enterprises (McMullen, 2011). Also, Desa (2012, 734) observed that, unlike traditional commercial entrepreneurships that have the goal of financial return, social entrepreneurs have goals of providing mission-related social outcomes, as well as market-based outcomes.

Conversely, the focus of commercial entrepreneurship is the creation of profitable business operations that results in private gain and brings financial returns to investors or shareholders (Austin et al., 2006). These authors also suggest that commercial entrepreneurship tends to focus on breakthroughs and meeting needs, whereas social entrepreneurship focuses on serving basic needs more effectively through innovative approaches. This implies that for commercial enterprise to flourish, there are gaps in the social sphere that must be bridged. Therefore, the challenge or failure of commercial entrepreneur presents as an opportunity for the social entrepreneur to facilitate social change through innovative approaches that satisfy unmet needs (Nicholls, 2008).

In terms of bottom lines, Sahasranamam and Nandakumar (2020, 104) made a useful distinction saying that social enterprises reinvest their profits towards the achievement of their social mission while commercial enterprises divide the profits among investors or stakeholders. The inability of social entrepreneurship to redistribute profits further results in social enterprises being placed in potentially precarious competitive disadvantaged position when compared to commercial enterprise (Austin et al.). There seems to be a fine line because social entrepreneurial activities reflect economic realities and economic activities do generate social value. Thus, the parameters for measuring organisational performance are different. Commercial enterprises use conventional performance measures, such as market share, return on assets or stock market returns, whereas social enterprises use qualitative indicators, which are at times, difficult to measure as well as quantitative measures on outreach and social service delivery.

Furthermore, Desa (2012), Sahasranamam and Ball (2016, 2018), Sahasranamam and Raman (2018) assert that due to the limited financial gains, social enterprises often depend on bricolage approaches, volunteers and social alliances for mobilisation. These two types of entrepreneurship are discussed because, in relation to the application of the PCDO model, it is believed that African countries would benefit from both types. Moreover, the social sphere or environment within which all commercial entrepreneurships develop and flourish needs to be safeguarded. Therefore, rather than draw the strain distinctions, it is proposed that both commercial and social entrepreneurship are mutually inclusive, interdependent and mutually beneficial to each other and to society at large. Significantly, the African context seems to accommodate and facilitate the use of bricolage approaches.

Bricolage

Bricolage approaches can be constructively applied in the African context to enhance entrepreneurship advancement because Africa being the second largest continent in the world is blessed with huge potentials in labour, materials, skills and unharnessed natural resources. African countries are also rated as developing third world states with weak institutions and emerging economies. Desa (2012, 742) found that in the face of weak, uncertain or evolving regulatory and technological institutions, the results indicate that social entrepreneurs move towards bricolage activity. Bricolage describes the process of using whatever tools and processes that are immediately available to achieve a construction work or arts. It is about making do with pre-existing resources and creating new products from the tools and materials at hand (Desa, 736).

Shane (2003) identified three distinct dimensions of bricolage, namely, materials, labour and skills. Further analysis by Desa (2012, 736) demonstrates that material bricolage refers to forgotten, discarded, worn-out, or presumed 'single-application' materials with new use. Labour bricolage involves customers and suppliers that provide free on-site work on projects and that bricoleurs usually permit and encourage the use of self-taught skills on the job. Regardless of their suitability, 'making do with whatever is at hand' is a commonality among all dimensions of bricolage. To some degree, most entrepreneurial activities, such as necessity entrepreneurship or entrepreneurs operating in resource-constraint environments employ the use of bricolage. Similarly, both commercial and social entrepreneurship often rely on bricolage approaches.

In addition to the bricolage approaches, there are factors at multiple levels both internal and external that can influence and ensure the protection of new business creation processes. They include individual-level, national-level, regional-level and international-level contextual factors (Bhagavatula et al., 2010; Bowen & De Clercq, 2018; Davidson & Honig, 2003). The interaction between the individual-level and the country-level contexts makes it impossible to examine entrepreneurship through the individual level alone without the broader context in view. Within the African continent, the significance of the broader contextual environment for entrepreneurial advancement is brought to the fore by Aspiration 6 of Agenda 2063, which leans towards achieving development that is led by African citizens. Therefore, similar ideals of individual and country-level interactions highlighted in Agenda 2063 support elements and structures for entrepreneurship advancement in Africa. An evaluation of Aspirations 4 and 6 of Agenda 2063 and how the PCDO model can be deployed for their attainment is critical but first, a highlight of the PCDO model is in order.

Introducing the People, Context, Deal and Opportunity (PCDO) Model

This section introduces the elements of people, context, deal and opportunity model. The Sahlman's (1996) people, context, deal and opportunity (PCDO) framework further developed by Austin et al. (2006, 3–4) have elements that are interdependent and context-dependent. These elements are discussed below.

'People' refers to those who actively participate in or who bring resources to the venture. They include those within and outside the organisation who contribute to the success of the project. Implicitly, the skills, attitudes, knowledge, contacts, goals and values acquired by the people provide the resource-blend, which contributes to the overall success of the business.

'Context' refers to the environment and the cultural context in which the business operates; it includes the external elements that are outside the control of the entrepreneur that influence success or failure. Contextual factors include the macroeconomy, tax and regulatory structure and socio-political environment. Economic environment, tax policies, employment levels, technological advances and social movements, such as those involving labour, religion and politics are examples of specific contextual factors that can frame the opportunities and risks that new ventures grapple with (Austin et al., 2006, 5). It is imperative to define those contextual elements that must be consciously dealt with, and those that can simply play out as they will and at their time. Thus, according to Austin et al., attention to everything means attention to nothing. Conversely, leaving out a single critical contextual element can be the precursor to failure. A critical contextual element in Africa is security i.e. ensuring a safe, peaceful and stable environment for entrepreneurship to thrive and hence the proposal for the application of the PCDO model to African countries for entrepreneurship advancement within the continent. Not only are African governments expected to ensure the development of the people, but the contextual environment must also be free of conflicts, crises and insecurity for the safety of people generally to enhance entrepreneurship advancement.

'Deal' is the substance of the bargain that defines who gives what, who gets what, and when deliveries, supplies and receipts occur in a venture (Austin et al.). Each transaction delivers a bundle of values, such as economic benefits, social recognition, autonomy and decision rights, satisfaction of deep personal needs, social interactions, fulfilment of generative and legacy desires and delivery on altruistic goals (Austin et al.).

'Opportunity' is defined by Sahlman (1996, 140) as 'any activity requiring the investment of scarce resource in hopes of a future return'. Thus, opportunity is the desired future state that is different from the present that motivates commercial and social entrepreneurs to invest scarce resources, with the hope and belief that the achievement of a better future state and returns on investment are possible (Austin et al., 7). Therefore, change is motivated by the vision of the future that is better for the decision-maker, and by the credibility of the path presented to that desired future state. One of the difficulties surrounding entrepreneurial study is that the definition of opportunity is not necessarily shared by the multiple constituencies who must work together to create change. Often, change affects power relations, economic interests, personal networks and even self-image. A critical factor that creates motivation for joint action arises when people create a common definition of opportunity that can be shared (Austin et al., 5). The successful application of the PCDO elements requires the understanding of the wider context of legal and institutional environment in view of advancing entrepreneurship in Africa. The next section analyses the legal and institutional framework for entrepreneurship advancement in Africa.

Legal and Institutional Framework for Entrepreneurship in Africa

The question may be asked whether the African Union (AU) is regionally situated with legal and institutional framework that promotes entrepreneurship advancement in the continent. Birthed in July 2002, the African Union (AU) replaced the defunct Organisation of African Unity (OAU). The OAU focused on the struggles and fight against apartheid, colonialism and worked towards the attainment of political independence for countries in the continent. Arguably, the focus of the OAU on the political independence of individual states and holding assiduously to the principles of non-interference with the political and territorial integrity of states accounted for some of the reasons for the AU's replacement of the OAU (Amao, 2020, 20; Imoedemhe, 2015, 86).

The AU was established by means of a multilateral treaty—the Constitutive Act of the African Union (2002), which was opened to ratification and accession by other emerging countries within the continent. Olivier (2015) observed that guided by a common vision for an integrated Africa, the AU's agenda was driven by efforts towards economic cooperation, as well as a new political emphasis on democratisation, human rights, good governance and the rule of law. The Constitutive Act also created nine (9) bodies or organs through which the AU functions (Olivier, 2015; 518). They include the Assembly of States of the AU, the Executive Council, The Pan African Parliament, the Court of Justice, the Commission, the Permanent Representatives' Committee, the Specialised Technical Committees, the Economic, Social and Cultural Council and the Financial Institutions (Constitutive Act, 2002; art

5). Udombana (2020, 4–5) notes that the AU emerged from a 'refurbished regional organisation… to Africa's inter-governmental institution for political security and economic governance'.

Legal framework refers to instruments such as laws, rules and regulations and specifically in the regional context, it also includes treaties, policies and decisions adopted for the purpose of promoting peace, prosperity and entrepreneurship advancement in Africa. Significantly, institutions are conceptualised to include not just organs, structures, formal and informal laws, but also cultural frames and behavioural patterns that are prevalent among a people. According to North (1990, 2001, 321), institutions are the rules of the game that structure human interactions in a society. Therefore, institutional framework should transcend the proliferation of organs and bodies, to include normative and cognitive institutions, which are the less formal and the 'taken-for-granted' but ingrained belief system, customs and norms that shape behaviours in society. National cultures could positively or negatively influence the proliferation of entrepreneurship in given countries (Dheer, 2017; Vershinina et al., 2018). Although it could be erroneous to discuss Africa as a country, a contextual analysis of the continent was done through the prism of the AU and taking the conflict-ridden three countries as representative cases. The AU's construct of legal and institutional framework almost always referred to laws, policies and decisions of the AU, including its founding treaty—the Constitutive Act. The chapter argues that the people, local attitudes and cultural context among others are important components of institutional framework that can shape and promote entrepreneurship advancement. These conditions are taken care of by the PCDO model as discussed later on.

Agenda 2063 Aspirations

The AU's primary objective is the emergence of an 'integrated peaceful and prosperous Africa, driven by its own citizens and representing a dynamic force in the global arena' (Agenda, 2063). The AU's more specific vision for conflict management reflects an awareness that the precondition for achieving this overarching goal is security and stability on the continent. The peace and security architecture establishes a long list of tasks related to the prevention, management and resolution of conflict across Africa. The strategic elements of this vision have been endorsed by the supreme organ of the AU the Assembly of Heads of State and Government composed of the 55 AU member states. The Assembly convenes only twice a year, making it unsuitable to oversee the day-to-day conflict management. Therefore, the Peace and

Security Council (PSC) a fifteen-member organ manages strategic and operational decisions about where, when and how to manage conflicts (Williams, 2011).

In May 2013, the AU launched Agenda 2063, by which Africa began to rigorously pursue seven (7) aspirations with the aim of attaining the common goal of an integrated, peaceful and prosperous continent in the 'Africa we want' by 2063. The idea is that 50 years from 2013, the continent would have achieved peaceful, prosperous, secure, stable and an integrated Africa with development agenda and programmes championed by African people. Critically, Aspirations 4 and 6 of Agenda 2063 read thus:

Aspiration 4: A peaceful and secure Africa: A stable and peaceful Africa with Institutional Structure for AU Instruments on Peace and Security

Aspiration 6: An African whose development is people driven, relying on the potential offered by African people, especially its women and youth and caring for children. Full Gender Equality in all spheres of life, removing all forms of discrimination against women and girls and ensuring women, youth and girls' empowerment

Arguably, among the seven aspirations of the AU's Agenda 2063, attaining a peaceful and secure Africa appears the most significant for several reasons. First, a people-driven development agenda must first ensure the safety and security of the people who are primarily dependent on for the development. Second, as it relates to entrepreneurship advancement, the necessity for a peaceful and secure environment, including political and economic stability cannot be overemphasised. Therefore, having begun the pursuit of a peaceful and secure Africa since 2013, it is important to examine how the AU ensures that these aspirations are not only achieved, but sustained in the long run.

Critically, seven years after the launch of Agenda 2063, the AU formulated the theme for 2020 as the year of 'silencing the guns' in the continent. Arguably, this was in pursuit of the attainment of Aspiration 4 of Agenda 2063, which declares 'A Peaceful and Secure Africa' with the goal to attain a stable and peaceful Africa. Priority areas for the achievement of the aspiration were institutional structure for AU instruments on peace and security, maintenance and preservation of peace and security and ensuring defence, security and peace. Aspiration 4 Goal 1 further requires that peace, security and stability should be preserved throughout the continent. Although the need to strengthened governance, accountability and transparency as foundational mechanisms for strengthened security and peace have been listed under Aspiration 4 Goals 2&3, there seems to be no concrete mechanism or strategies to ensure that these aspirations become Africa's reality, as policy rhetoric and reality do not match. It is therefore not surprising that 2020 passed without the actualisation of 'silencing the guns' in Africa.

Given the highly fragmented institutions of the AU with many focussed areas, The AU felt that a strengthened mechanism for the attainment of Agenda 2063 was through institutional reforms. With repeated patterns of crisis and conflicts, collective Africa acknowledged 'the need for radical transformation at all levels and in all spheres' in order to accelerate development and meet the aspirations of citizens (Agenda, 2063, para 66b). In Agenda 2063, the AU pledged to use the lessons from past and present development efforts and challenges to forge an African-centred approach to transformation (Agenda, 2063, para 3). However, Udombana (2020, 33) postulates that chronic remorse is also an undesirable thing. There are mistakes, which humanity has made and repented of so often that there is no excuse for repeating them. Consequently, in July 2016, the Assembly of Heads of States mandated President Paul Kagame of Rwanda to lead a process of institutional reforms with a pan-African advisory team of nine members (Assembly/AU/Dec.606 (XXVII)).

The Paul Kagame Report (2017; 4) reiterated 'the urgent need to act' for the integrated peace and prosperity of Africa. However, analysing the 'Kagame Report', Turianskyi and Gruzd (2019, 24) noted that 'some of the Kagame's reforms have already met with resistance, while others have been changed substantially and they risk getting mired in the AU's notorious politicised bureaucracy'. This implies that so far, the AU's only mechanism for accomplishing Agenda 2063 Aspirations, which is the Kagame Report may end up being different from the original proposal due to the myriad of the national interests of 55 countries at play.

Furthermore, Aspiration 6 of Agenda 2063, envisions an 'Africa whose development is people driven, relying on the potential offered by African people, especially its women, youth, and caring for children'. The goals include to achieve full gender equality in all spheres of life, to engage and empower youth and children, priority areas include women, youth and girls' empowerment, as well as bringing violence and discrimination against women and girls to an end. This implies that Africa's development must be driven by African people. Therefore, reliance is placed on the potentials of African people, especially women, youth and children. Within this aspiration, Africa is meant to promote a culture of inclusivity where nobody is discriminated against on grounds of age, sex, gender, locality, religion, ethnic or political affiliations. In order to guarantee gender equality, Aspiration 6 Goals 1&2 propose the elimination of all forms of discrimination and the actualisation of an Africa in which all citizens are empowered to engage and actively participate in decision-making at all levels.

It is proposed that while African governments must continue to take responsibility to protect African people in line with the aspirations, the application of the people, context, deal and opportunity (PCDO) model may be of great value to Africa's entrepreneurship advancement. The next session will analyse the PCDO model in detail and how African leaders may adopt or adapt it to actualise Agenda 2063 aspirations.

The Application of the PCDO Model in Achieving Agenda 2063

As noted earlier, Agenda 2063 has seven aspirations. Analysis in this chapter focuses on two, Aspirations 4 and 6 together with their goals and priority areas, which include, achieving a peaceful, safe and secure Africa and an Africa whose development is driven by African people. Similar to other continents of the world, Africa engages in efforts to advance and promote entrepreneurship. The AU's legal and institutional framework are reflected in its laws, policies and decisions, including its Constitutive Act and its organs. However, institutions transcend laws and organs to include cognitive and cultural frames that shape people's interactions in society and determine development. Thus, although the AU's legal and institutional framework may have encouraged a few pouches of entrepreneurial activities in certain African countries, there needs to be a change in focus areas to achieve Aspirations 4 ad 6 for cohesive advancement.

Significantly, in December 2017, a few African policy-makers came together under the aegis of the United Nations Conference on Trade and Development (UNCTAD), the Rwanda Development Board (RDB), the Rwanda Convention Bureau (RCB) and the Global Entrepreneurship Network (GEN) in Kigali Rwanda (Africa Entrepreneurship Policy Forum, 2017). Formulating what may be termed 'best practices' for entrepreneurship advancement, the gathering developed strategies on how to implement national entrepreneurship policies based on the entrepreneurship policy framework (EPF), methodology and good practices of the UNCTAD in Africa. It is commendable that integrating entrepreneurship in the broader sustainable development agenda was devised, as well as incorporating entrepreneurship education into schools' curricula, such as in Botswana, Rwanda and Tanzania. The Empretec model and the Tony Elumelu Entrepreneurship Programme (TEEP) in Nigeria are programmes geared towards the transformation, reorientation of mindsets and development of entrepreneurship skills (Africa EPF, 2017).

Nevertheless, the analysis of conflicts and crisis in Central African Republic (CAR), Nigeria and Sudan, reveals that Africa's main challenges are reflected in the lack of security, safety and stability. These challenges in turn constitute a bane to development generally and specifically to entrepreneurship advancement. It is argued that suitable environment in terms of political and economic stability, safety and security of individuals, property, are precursors to entrepreneurship advancement. Where these are lacking, there is so much that the AU or any of its organs could do for all 55 African countries to realise the objectives of Agenda 2063, even when these have been rhetorically legislated in policy documents as ideals and aspirations.

The values and ideals of Aspiration 4 include that a stable and peaceful Africa with institutional structure for AU instruments on peace and security would supposedly be achieved by the Peace and Security Council (PSC). The PSC is AU's decision-making organ that is saddled with the prevention, management and resolution of conflicts in the continent. It is a collective security and early warning arrangement intended to facilitate timely and efficient responses to conflict and crisis situations in Africa. However, the PSC together with its key pillar, the African Peace and Security Architecture (APSA)—a framework to promote peace, security and stability, has not been able to curtail crisis in the continent, as the organ seems overwhelmed with the series of continuing conflicts and crisis, some of which have resulted in several deaths, displacements and referrals to the International Criminal Court (ICC).

People

Applying the 'People' concept in the PCDO model to Africa, people are the greatest resource of any country. Therefore, to ensure entrepreneurship advancement in the continent, safety and security of the people and property, as well as people development must be prioritised by the respective African governments. Arguably, due to weak institutions, uncertainties and insecurity, Africa's entrepreneurship development is currently based on the bricolage concept of 'making do with' whatever is available. A decentralised AU by which individual African government takes the responsibility to protect the people, ensure safety and security and engage in deliberate programmes for the development of its people, including the youths, women and children is recommended. The protection of and investment in people should be country-specific with individual government's recognition and respect for the sanctity of life and the protection of human rights and dignity.

The requirement that both human and capital inputs are essential to entrepreneurship advancement underscores the importance of the need for a decentralised application of the PCDO model. This is because entrepreneurs are people who must consider people, such as managers, employees, funders and other organisations and talents that are critical to their success. In other words, the success or failure of an entrepreneur is determined and dependent on the people. Sahlman (1996), Hart, AQ articulated two critical determinants of a successful entrepreneur. They are (1) an entrepreneur must have an awareness and in-depth knowledge of the industry and (2) the entrepreneur must be known by others for the people, abilities, skills that they possess and are willing to deploy to customers and the industry at large. The people and potentials of individual African countries should be discovered, developed and deployed towards entrepreneurship advancement and the starting point is to ensure the protection and safety of the people.

The challenges of crisis, conflicts, insecurity and instability prevalent in most African countries implies that the legal and institutional framework currently available to the AU may seem plausible, but inadequate. A paradigm shift from a framework that is based on laws, policies, structures and organs, to an inclusive framework that is founded on cognitive pillars, which include the change of mindsets of the people and the imbibing of right values, customs and belief systems is recommended. These values have been highlighted in the different aspirations of Agenda 2063, nevertheless, no concrete mechanisms or strategies are in place to attain them. It is proposed that by adopting the People pillar in the PCDO model, African development would be people-focused and the respective African governments would be able to ensure safety and security within their territories and communities to achieve Aspirations 4 and 6 of Agenda 2063, which will in turn ensure entrepreneurship advancement. The different entrepreneurship efforts and advancements in a few African countries reveal that focus is on the development of youth and women. For example, the symposium organised by the Department of Trade and Industry of the African Union Commission provided an avenue for the exchange of ideas and experiences related to Youth Entrepreneurship. It provided a platform for how public and private partners should collaborate to address some challenges, such as the challenges of youth and women unemployment (African Union and Digital Entrepreneurship, 2018).

Context

Arguably Aspiration 6 Agenda 2063 mirrors the context pillar of the PCDO model, as it strives for Africa's development in a context that promotes women, youth and children empowerment, eliminates all forms of discrimination and ensures equality at all levels. Context is everything insofar as entrepreneurship advancement is concerned. No business thrives amidst chaotic, insecure or unstable environment. Context relates to the environment and culture that are the determining factors for the success or failure of all entrepreneurial activities. Although context relates broadly to laws, regulatory structures, technological advancements and socio-political environment, the focus here is on security. This is because the objective of laws, policies and regulatory structures is to promote peaceful, safe and secure environment, which will in turn ensure a context of technological advancement that facilitates exchanges, innovativeness and competitiveness. As noted by Austin et al. (2006), social movements such as labour, religious and political associations are examples of specific contextual factors in society. Thus, focus on the social environment and specifically on security is because every government must guarantee the safety and security of lives and property, as a basic need for life itself, from which all other human endeavours including entrepreneurship can flow and flourish.

Although there are pouches of developments in some African countries, the institutional environmental context necessary for nurturing and developing entrepreneurship seems inadequate in Africa. Admittedly, a few African Union (AU) developments through various policies and institutional frameworks, such as the various AU infrastructure, organs and institutions and the availability of rich resources in different African countries suggest that the AU could ensure the right context for development. For example, the 'one million by 2021' initiative articulated by the African Union Entrepreneurship (2020), aimed to ensure transformation of institutional environmental conditions necessary for entrepreneurial growth and development in the continent. The initiative was designed to promote interconnectivity and inclusivity among young African entrepreneurs across the continent and in the diaspora, as well as build affiliations with business leaders and international entrepreneurship networks. This implies that youth entrepreneurship and start-up developments are central to national development strategies. Therefore, policies that provide sustainable infrastructures, build human capital and improve the business environment must be prioritised at all levels.

Nevertheless, as noted earlier, institutional environment transcends policies and organs to include belief systems, attitudes and mindsets that shape interactions and behaviours in society. Austin et al. posited that attention to everything means attention to nothing. Conversely, leaving out a single critical contextual element can be the precursor to failure. In Tanzania for example, it was reported that despite positive development such as the launch of the National Entrepreneurship Strategy, the business environment is considered unfriendly especially because it fails to promote youth employment (AU and Digital Entrepreneurship, 2018, 3). Thus, Tanzania has consistently ranked above 100 among 195 economies in the 'Annual World Bank Doing Business Reports'. Furthermore, the African Digital Entrepreneurship Cairo Report (2018; 3) noted that about 90% of businesses in Tanzania are informal and the private sector complains about complexity, multiplicity, unpredictability and high cost of the regulatory requirements. Similarly, the World Bank's ease of doing business ranking of 190 countries for 2018, benchmarked to June 2017, has no African country among the first top twenty. (World Bank Ease of Doing Business, October 2020). Virtually all the countries at the bottom are from Africa. South Africa and Nigeria, two of Africa's leading economies were ranked at 82 and 145, respectively, Mauritius ranked 25 and Rwanda 41 (Udombana, 2020; 30).

African countries need to improve the business environment along peace and security in order to foster entrepreneurship and social and economic development. It is argued that the context pillar in the PCDO model could be applied to ensure safety and security of individuals, cultural mindsets and attitudinal changes on a country-by-country basis. It is anticipated that such changes would translate to the creation of the needed stable and predictable environment for entrepreneurship advancement in Africa.

Deal

Deal relates to the market, competitive, technological, regulative contexts. The functioning market allows exchanges, contracts enforcement, and formalisation of businesses. Non-functioning market does have an opposing effect; contract enforcement and property rights also have legal connotations and pre-suppose functional legal system. Attainment of a peaceful and secure Africa whose development is driven by African people would require advancements in technological, regulative and functional legal systems. This means that the deal pillar would have to be adapted to individual African countries' legal systems.

How entrepreneurs engage the deal quadrant differ by context, crisis-ridden or peaceful? For social and profit-oriented entrepreneurship, context is important because a peaceful and friendly environment will always attract the right people, investments and deals. Deals are the implicit and explicit contractual relationships between the venture and all resource providers (Chaulagain, 2020). Deals also relate to the contractual relations among the parties, it involves the allocation of resources, cash and risk and therefore it affects the venture's value. Examples of deals include investment contracts, terms of employment for managers, deals with customers and vendors. Two critical questions to ask are whether the deals are legal, comprehensive and coherent, and to what degree do the deals make sense given the people involved, the nature of the opportunity and the context? (Harvard Business School, 2017). Value transactions differ in entrepreneurships in terms of kind, consumers, timing, flexibility and measurability.

Thus, deals involve the exchange of value. As regards the kind of value involved in exchanges, social entrepreneurs rely on creative strategies to offset limited financial rewards and incentives with nonfinancial incentives to recruit, retrain and motivate staff, volunteers and funders. Also, social entrepreneurs provide value to more diverse stakeholders than commercial entrepreneurs. Similarly, social entrepreneurs' relationships with consumers have little economic capability with few alternatives. Thus, consumers of social entrepreneurs' goods and services have little economic power to exercise in transactional relationships. Nevertheless, beneficiaries of social entrepreneurship may not have a bargaining power, but they could be considered as clients or consumers of their services. Lack of transaction does not necessarily imply they are no customers. Funders are key stakeholders, but the general public could also consume the services and products of the social enterprises as the revenue generated helps to fund social and charitable activities.

With respect to timing and flexibility, deal differs significantly, as commercial entrepreneurs have wide discretion to deploy capital towards activities that they think would add the most value to the business. Social entrepreneurs do not have this luxury of discretion. Therefore, they spend most of their time on ongoing operational activities, which come with restrictions and varied expectations of accountability. The ongoing evaluation leads to the challenge of complexity associated with measurability. While it is easy for commercial entrepreneurs to focus on gains, return on investment and equity distribution of the deal, there are uncertainties in the deal framework with investors in social entrepreneurship due to the lack of factors, such as profit or return on investment that align the interests and actions of the various parties involved. This makes the precise measurement of social impact complicated because of the nature of social phenomenon, multicausality of underlying factors, and lengthy temporal manifestations (Austin et al.).

Due to the diversity in the levels of development, cultural and political contexts, it would be challenging measuring the deal element across the 55 African countries. Therefore, a generic application of the deal model, could at best, result in lopsided analysis. In formulating the deal necessary to launch and sustain a venture, social entrepreneurs have the responsibility to balance the costs to attain various resources with the potential benefits that accrue to the organisation and its clients on a case-by-case basis. Similarly, deal must be country-, as well as situation-specific. It is proposed that rather than hide under the aegis of the AU's legal and institutional framework, the 55 constituent member states of the AU must identify the deal in the PCDO model in their specific localities in order to create the environment necessary for entrepreneurship advancement.

Opportunity

The resource context, market context, entrepreneurship development policies ongoing in Africa combined are factors that provide opportunities to create integrated peaceful, safe and secure environment in the continent. Opportunity at individual level could be identified or created. Opportunities are identified from the environment, where entrepreneurs intend to venture into new businesses, such as seeing unmet demands, observing changes in technology, government incentives, availability of markets for the products, etc. (Woldesenbet et al., 2012). From the effectuation and bricolage perspectives, opportunities could be created. The African environment, especially due to crisis and conflict, tend towards effectuation or bricolage to foster entrepreneurship development.

Austin et al.'s articulation of the opportunity framework refers to a future that is better than the present. This implies that opportunity presents a future that is usually fundamentally different given the underlying generative effect of market failure. Certainly, contextual forces impinge on other variables and are applicable to all forms of entrepreneurship, albeit to varying degrees. Thus, what might be deemed unfavourable contextually to commercial entrepreneurship could be an opportunity for social entrepreneurship and vice versa. Application of the opportunity framework implies that the AU's desired future for an Africa that is greater and better than the present; a peaceful, prosperous, stable, safe and secure Africa was the motivation for the launch of Agenda 2063 in May 2013. Similar to opportunities in the commercial and social sectors that make entrepreneurs to invest scarce resources with the hope of future returns, African leaders certainly see a great future in the 'Africa we want' in which Africa would be the cynosure of the world. Therefore, change is motivated by the vision of the future that is better for the decision-maker, and by the credibility of the path presented to that desired future state.

Again, akin to the lack of general acceptance of what constitute opportunity in entrepreneurial study, the AU continues to grapple with diversities of interests because its legal and institutional framework and reforms are not necessarily shared by the multiple constituencies in African countries who must work together to create change. This presents African countries as both negative and positive opportunity; negative because, entrepreneurship advancement would be slow or non-existent without cohesion or consensus of interests. However, this also presents as a positive opportunity because African leaders could potentially turn the current situation around by adopting the PCDO model to effect a change for the great future that they want. Change affects power relations, economic interests, national cultures, and communities' cultural contexts play vital roles in promoting entrepreneurship initiatives in different countries. Critically, motivation for joint action arises when people share common vision and goals. Regrettably, the sharing of common vision and goal between the AU and all 55 member states seems far-fetched. Therefore, a decentralised application of the PCDO model is advocated. While the AU is poised to effect institutional reforms and pursue the aspirations of Agenda 2063, a few of its member states seems divided, some are contending with crisis and conflicts, while others continue to grapple with poverty, corruption and insecurity. Arguably the lack of consensus acts as constraints to entrepreneurship advancements in Africa.

Instances of the lack of consensus among AU member states are replete and documented in the operations of the AU. Specifically, The African Continental Free Trade Area (AfCFTA) Agreement of 2018 established the Continental Free Trade Area (CFTA) to provide the institutional framework for a code of conduct that reduces tariffs and other barriers to trade and eliminates discrimination in trade relations among AU member states (AfCFTA, 2018; art 3). The AfCFTA Agreement entered into force on 30 May 2019 for the 24 countries that had deposited their instrument of ratification with the African Union Commission (AUC) Chairperson (AfCFTA; art 23&24). The AfCFTA advances the Pan African Vision of an integrated, prosperous and peaceful Africa enshrined in Agenda 2063 (Udombana, 2020; 33–34). However, only 28 states have ratified the AfCFTA Agreement, representing 51% of the 55 AU member states. Twenty-seven states are yet to ratify the AfCFTA Agreement (AfCFTA, Ratification Status). The AU Rules prescribe two-thirds, which is 37 states of the total AU membership for the Assembly sessions to form a quorum. This means that the Assembly will need at least nine additional member states to form a quorum for any proposed deliberation and decision on the CFTA (AU Assembly Rules of Procedure, R.6) as it has potential to increase entrepreneurial and trade opportunities.

Arguably, the lack of consensus applies to Agenda 2063, because not all 55 African countries are at one with the aspirations as some countries have other priorities areas, such as the fight against poverty, corruption, which are far removed from Agenda 2063 aspirations. Therefore, having formulated and begun the 50-year journey towards the transformed 'Africa we want', and despite the resistance to the implementation of the 'Kagame Report, it may be beneficial for ongoing AU reforms to transcend mere reforms on paper to include the adoption of the PCDO model. Although AU continues to hold its place as a rallying point, a decentralised approach is advocated whereby individual African governments adapt and implement the PCDO at the country levels, first by ensuring safety and security of people and property. The positive application of the opportunity quadrant in the PCDO model to Africa, means that CAR, Nigeria and Sudan and indeed other African governments can take advantage of current negative crisis and conflicts situations as an opportunity to create a better and bigger future for the African people to actualise aspirations of Agenda 2063. Therefore, what might seem unstable, unfavourable, insecure and unpredictable Africa today might well be translated to the peaceful, secure, integrated, inclusive and economically developed Africa of the future.

Conclusion

As Aspiration 6 highlights, the future of Africa is in the hands of African people, Africa's development must be driven by its own citizens. The question is how? The chapter has analysed that with respect to general development and specifically, entrepreneurship advancement, the AU structures, legal and institutional framework are inadequate. Therefore, a decentralised method by which the AU continues to be the umbrella and central regional organisation, while individual countries take ownership of Agenda 2063 for national implementation will be a blessing. This is imperative because the diverse challenges a few African countries continue to grapple with mean that a one-size-fit all policy may not be the answer. Custom policies are needed. Undoubtedly, the attainment of an inclusive and integrated Africa includes development in all spheres of endeavours including in the field of entrepreneurship advancement. For the people of Africa to take ownership of their development, their safety must first be guaranteed. In the varying stages and levels of development in African countries, there is scope for innovation, creativity, expansion and advancements. Therefore, in addition to the AU legal and institutional framework and reforms, it is proposed that the PCDO model should be adopted by the AU and individual member states for implementation and actualisation of Agenda 2063. The application of the PCDO model should be country and situation-specific rather than a generic application.

The PCDO framework is a combination of interconnected factors. They are factors that cannot be applied in isolation. Certainly, Africa is bestowed with abundant resources and opportunities. Therefore, the question that individual African government should ask is whether the countries have the right 'context' that guarantee the rule of law, security and safety of lives. People do matter, and entrepreneurship is people-centric. People's experience of enterprising can be positive or negative depending on mindsets, the training they have been exposed to, and the environment in which they live and interact. The capabilities, experiences and expertise of individuals are context-dependent. The importance of the total wellbeing of African people is highlighted in all Aspirations of Agenda 2063. However, the reality is a far cry due to crisis and conflicts that have culminated in several deaths and displacements. This negative pattern must be addressed at country levels supported by right institutions at national and continental levels.

The proposal that the PCDO model should be applied to Africa does not imply that other reform initiatives are less important. Rather, it is recommended that the PCDO model should be specifically adopted as focused reforms parameters for individual African countries alongside other ongoing AU legal and institutional reforms towards the attainment of Agenda 2063. The limited scope of the analysis in this chapter provides opportunity for further research, to evaluate how the PCDO model could be implemented in practical terms and on a country-by-country basis first for the actualisation of Agenda 2063 and then to enhance entrepreneurship advancement in Africa.

References

Africa Entrepreneurship Policy Forum. (2017, December 13–14). *Entrepreneurship policies for regional inclusive and sustainable development*. Kigali Rwanda. 2017 https://unctad.org/meetings/en/SessionalDocuments/diaeepf2017d01_report_en.pdf. Accessed April 20, 2020.

African Union and Digital Entrepreneurship. (2018). *Report on 1st African Union start up fest 6–10 December 2017 Cairo Egypt*. 1–24 (hereinafter 'Cairo Report

2017'). https://au.int/en/documents/20180215/african-union-and-digital-entrepreneurship. Accessed April 24, 2020.

African Union. (2020). *Entrepreneurship.* https://1millionby2021.au.int/entrepreneurship. Accessed April 30, 2020.

African Union. *Agenda 2063: The Africa we want.* https://au.int/en/agenda2063/overview. Accessed April 20, 2020.

African Union. *Our aspirations for the Africa we want.* Agenda 2063. https://au.int/en/agenda2063/aspirations. Accessed April 30, 2020.

Al Okoli, C. (2019). Kidnapping for ransom has become Nigeria's latest security problem. *QUARTZAFRICA.*

Amao, O. (2020). *African Union law: The emergence of a sui generis legal order.* Routledge.

Austin, J., Stevenson, H., & Wei-Skillern, J. (2006). Social and commercial entrepreneurship: Same, different or both? *Entrepreneurship Theory and Practice, 30*(1), 1–22.

Baddorf, Z. (2017). Pessimism about CAR peace deal widespread. *Voice of Africa.*

Bhagavatula, S., Elfring, E., Tilburg, A., & Bunt, G. (2010). How social and human capital influence opportunity recognition and resource mobilisation in India's handloom industry. *Journal of Business Venturing, 23*(5), 245–260.

Bowen, H. P., & De Clercq, D. (2018). Institutional context and the allocation of entrepreneurial effort. *Journal of International Business Studies, 39*(4), 747–768.

Chaulagain, M. (2020). POCD—A Proven Framework to Build Your New Venture.

Davidson, P., & Honig, B. (2003). The role of human capital among nascent entrepreneurs. *Journal of Business Venturing, 18*(3), 301–331.

Desa, G. (2012). Resource mobilisation in international social entrepreneurship: Bricolage as a mechanism of institutional transformation. *Entrepreneurship Theory and Practice, 36*(4), 727–751.

Dheer, R. J. S. (2017). Cross-national differences in entrepreneurial activity: Role of culture and institutional factors. *Small Business Economics, 48*(4), 813–842.

Dukhan, N. (2017). Dangerous divisions: The Central African Republic faces the threat of secession. *Enough: The project to end genocide and crimes against humanity.*

Gardner, T. (2020). Sudan's revolution runs aground in Darfur: We cannot build a democracy if we have militias everywhere. *The new humanitarian.*

Global Conflict Tracker. (2021). *Sub-Saharan Africa: Violence in the Central African Republic.*

Human Security Centre. (2010). *Human security report 2009/2010: The causes of peace and the shrinking costs of war.*

ICC. (2020, December 11). *Statement of the prosecutor of the international criminal court.*

Imoedemhe, O. (2017). *The complementarity regime of the international criminal court: National implementation in Africa.* Springer. Doi: https://doi.org/10.1007/978-3-319-46780-1.

Imoedemhe, O. (2015). Unpacking the tension between the African Union and the international criminal court: The way forward. *African Journal of International & Comparative Law, 23*(1), 75–105.

Jalloh, C. C. (2009). Recognising international criminal law? *International Criminal Law Review, 9,* 445–499.

Jatto, A. A. (2018). *Sustainable construction and human security in Sub-Saharan Africa.* Lambert Publishing.

Keppler, E. (2021). Central African Republic: First *Seleka* suspect in ICC custody. *Human Rights Watch.*

McMullen, J. S. (2011). Delineating the domain of development entrepreneurship: A market-based approach to facilitating inclusive economic growth. *Entrepreneurship Theory and Practice, 35*(1), 185–193.

Nicholls, A. (2008). *Social entrepreneurship: New model of sustainable social change.* OUP.

North, C. (2001). Why some countries are rich and some are poor. *Chicago-Kent Law Review, 77,* 319–332.

North, D. C. (1990). *Institutions, institutional change and economic performance.* CUP.

Olivier, M. (2015). The role of African Union law in integrating Africa. *South African Journal of International Affairs, 22*(4), 513–533.

Robb, A., Alexandria V., & Parton, B. (2014). *Entrepreneurship education and training: Insights from Ghana, Kenya and Mozambique* (p. 34). World Bank Publications.

Roth, K., Human Rights World Report 2020. *Human Rights Watch.* https://www.hrw.org/world-report/2020/countrychapters/nigeria.

Sahasranamam, S., & Ball, C. (2016). Sustainable procurement in social enterprises: Comparative case studies from India and Scotland. In L. Bals & W. Tate (Eds.), *Implementing triple bottom line sustainability into global supply chain* (pp. 219–231). Greenleaf Publishing.

Sahasranamam, S., & Ball, C. (2018). National context matters: Influence of national business system on social enterprises. In Scotland and India in L. J. Spence, J. G. Frynas, J. N. Muthuri, & J. Navare (Eds.), *Research handbook on small business social responsibility: Global perspectives.* Edward Elgar Publishing Limited.

Sahasranamam, S., & Nandakumar, M. K. (2020). Individual capital and social entrepreneurship: Role of formal institutions. *Journal of Business Research, 107,* 104–117.

Sahasranmam, S., & Raman, V. (2018). Individual resources, property rights and entrepreneruship in China. *International Journal of Emerging Markets.*

Sahlman, W. A. (1996). Some thoughts on business plans. In W. A. Sahlman, H. Stevens, M. J. Roberts & A. V. Bhide (Eds.), *The entrepreneurial venture* (pp. 138–176). Boston: Harvard Business School Press.

Singh, G., & Belwal, R. (2008). Entrepreneurship and SMEs in Ethiopia: Evaluating the role, prospects and problems faced by women in this emergent sector. *Gender in Management: An International Journal, 23*(2), 120–136.

The Constitutive Act of the African Union. (2002). https://au.int/sites/default/files/pages/34873-file-constitutiveact_en.pdf. Accessed April 25, 2020.

Turianskyi, Y., & Gruzd, S. (2019). *The 'Kagame Reforms' of the AU: Will they stick?*

Udombana, N. J. (2020). A step closer: Economic integration and the African continental free trade area. *Duke Journal of Comparative & International Law, 31*(1), 1–90.

Vershinina, N., Woldesenbet K. B., & Murithi, W. (2018). How does national culture enable or constrain entrepreneurship. *Journal of Small Business and Enterprise Development, 25*(4).

Williams, P. D. (2011). The African Union's conflict management capabilities. *International Institutions and Global Governance Programe* 1–32.

Woldesenbet, K., Ram, M., & Jones, T. (2012). Supplying large firms: The role of entrepreneurial and dynamic capabilities in small businesses. *International Small Business Journal, 30*(5), 493–512. https://doi.org/10.1177/0266242611396390.

World Bank Ease of Doing Business, October 2020.

Part V

Gender and Diversity Issues in African Entrepreneurship

20

'Longing to Grow My Business': The Work–Life Interface of Women Entrepreneurs in Ethiopia

Konjit Hailu Gudeta, Marloes van Engen, Pascale Peters, Kassa Woldesenbet Beta, Brigitte Kroon, and Atsede Tesfaye Hailemariam

Introduction

Women entrepreneurship is often encouraged for various reasons. Some authors (e.g., Shabana et al., 2017; Singh & Belwal, 2008) stress that entrepreneurship empowers women and enhances their status in their communities. Others argue that entrepreneurship improves the household's welfare and fosters a nation's wider social and economic development. Yet, literature also shows that women face many challenges, such as gender inequality (e.g., educational background), the gendered role of women (e.g., normative and social expectations), and limited access to resources (e.g., time- and labour-saving technologies, household appliances and child care facilities), to name a few (Carter et al., 2015; Gudeta et al., 2019; Jennings

---

K. H. Gudeta (✉) · A. T. Hailemariam
School of Commerce, Addis Ababa University, Addis Ababa, Ethiopia

M. van Engen · P. Peters
Nyenrode Business Universiteit, Breukelen, The Netherlands

M. van Engen · B. Kroon
Department of Human Resource Studies, Tilburg University, Tilburg, The Netherlands

K. Woldesenbet Beta
De Montfort University, Leicester, England, UK
e-mail: kwoldesenbet@dmu.ac.uk

& Brush, 2013; Kelley et al., 2017; Zewdie & Associates, 2002). These challenges are particularly severe in developing economies, such as those in Sub-Saharan Africa. Ethiopia, a Sub-Saharan African country and the context of this study, is no exception.

Generally, the enhanced autonomy to decide when and where to work, associated with self-employment, is identified as one of the important motivating factors for women to enter entrepreneurship, as this allows women to better manage the work–life interface (Álvarez & Sinde-Cantorna, 2014; Tremblay & Genin, 2008). This is even more true for married women with dependent children (Annink & Den Dulk, 2012). Although some research findings support the idea that self-employment can help women achieving the control and flexibility they aspire (Annink & Den Dulk, 2012; Loscocco, 1997), evidence still indicates that this may not bring the intended ease in managing women entrepreneurs' work–life balance (Annink & Den Dulk, 2012; Lee Siew Kim & Seow Ling, 2001; Marlow, 1997; Parasuraman & Simmers, 2001; Shelton, 2006). Inability to attain work–life balance through self-employment is oftentimes attributed to the varied and many responsibilities that women take on in both domains. Self-employment implies that one needs to be 'always on' for both family and clients, which creates time pressures (Hillbrecht & Lero, 2014) and that it comes with long, irregular, and a-typical working hours and interwoven work and nonwork commitments (Gold & Mustafa, 2013; Hyytinen & Ruuskanen, 2007). Thus, the mere flexibility afforded by self-employment may not simply solve women's work–life issues (Annink & den Dulk, 2012).

The interwoven work/nonwork commitments and the associated work–nonwork boundary interruptions (cf. Ashforth et al., 2000; Kossek et al., 2012) may apply to women in Ethiopia where traditional gender roles are widely accepted (Bayeh, 2016; Burgess, 2013; Kassa, 2015). The traditional view of the feminine gender role prescribes women to shoulder the lion share of the domestic and care responsibilities in a household regardless of them having a job or running their own business. Men's involvement in domestic work in this traditional view is an exception (Gudeta & Van Engen, 2017, 2018). Women are not only expected to play primary roles in terms of being a spouse, a caretaker, and a parent, they are also expected to undertake and/or supervise household chores, care for close family members, and to provide community services (Gudeta & Van Engen, 2017, 2018). Managing the family–work interface is exacerbated as women entrepreneurs lack access to time and labour-saving technologies and household appliances (Zewdie & Associates, 2002) and also lack or have limited access to child and elder care facilities (Gudeta et al., 2019). All these factors combined can be expected to negatively influence women entrepreneurs' business operation and growth ambitions.

In view of the account above, by using grounded theory to analyse in-depth interviews with women entrepreneurs in the capital of Ethiopia, Addis Abeba, the present study seeks to explore how the enactment of the work–life roles of women entrepreneurs in Ethiopia play a role in women's business operations and growth aspirations. In doing so, we aim to contribute to the literature on work–life interface and women business success by examining how women entrepreneurs in Sub-Saharan Africa explain the way they operate their business, how they perceive their roles in their family and community help or hinder their business operation, and what motivates them in pursuing business (and family and community) success. In this chapter, women business growth intention is conceptualized as women entrepreneurs' attitudes about engaging in actions or behaviours with the belief that these result in positive changes in business performance. Women's business growth intention is thus considered to be the link between their beliefs and behaviour (cf. Bird, 1988). Following Bird (1988), we can expect that women are pre-disposed to growth intentions based upon a combination of personal (e.g., perceived abilities) and contextual factors and may utilize work–nonwork boundary management strategies to help improve their performance (Shelton, 2006).

Literature Review

Until now, work–nonwork boundary management and work–family balance have been primarily studied in the context of organisational employment. Consequently, the larger part of the existing work–family interface research focuses on the experiences and challenges of those employed in organisations. However, with the growth of men and particularly women entrepreneurs and self-employed workers across the globe (Elam et al., 2019; Millán et al., 2014), the work–family interface has become an emerging theme in the area of entrepreneurship, and there is a growing research interest in investigating work–life interface experiences of women entrepreneurs (Jennings & McDougald, 2007; Shastri et al., 2019; Shelton, 2006). One possible explanation for the heightened interest in work–life interface in the entrepreneurship field emanates from the fact that entrepreneurs are their own bosses with a latitude of discretion and control and flexibility in terms of what business and tasks they want to do, where they do this, and with whom they do business and collaborate (Peters et al., 2020).

However, all these agentic choices come with a multitude of challenges for women entrepreneurs, especially since they may hold multiple roles, values, and identities (Peters et al., 2020; Shastri et al., 2019). For many women, their ability as professional entrepreneurs is not recognised and acknowledged by society. The literature on women entrepreneurship suggests the importance of including family when investigating women entrepreneurs' work–life balance as these are often intertwined and, consequently, considerably affecting one another (Aldrich & Cliff, 2003; Jennings & McDougald, 2007). To better understand the work–life experiences of individuals, various theories and perspectives have emerged (Bianchi & Milkie, 2010; Harrington, 2007; Shockley et al., 2017). For example, Jennings and McDougald (2007) argue that female entrepreneurs are likely to experience more work–life conflict as compared to male entrepreneurs, which demands them, intentionally or unintentionally, to employ coping strategies that limit the growth of their businesses. Therefore, the reported performance differences between male-headed and female-headed businesses may be explained by examining how women and men entrepreneurs experience work–life conflict as well as the coping strategies they choose (Jennings et al., 2010). Jennings and colleagues, therefore, suggest that women entrepreneurs may 'choose' to integrate their work–life responsibilities, which may result in reduced commitment to and involvement in one of the life domains—usually the work domain (Bögenhold & Klinglmair, 2015), while men may separate their work–life roles more to focus on managing and growing their businesses.

Work–family literature reviews reveal that experiencing conflict between work and family roles has negative consequences for individuals, such as reduced physical and mental wellbeing, enhanced stress, lower job satisfaction, and engagement with family (Eby et al., 2005; Ford et al., 2007; Shockley et al., 2017). Also Peters et al. (2020) report that overload with parental responsibilities can lead to conflict between work and family roles for women self-employed entrepreneurs, affecting the relationship between work-related values, their sense of work control, and, in turn, their subjective career satisfaction. In general, studies on (women) entrepreneurs have reported that the challenges involved in managing domestic and care responsibilities, while taking care of a business, can be sources of tension and stress for women entrepreneurs (McGowan et al., 2012), resulting in lower economic performance of their businesses (Elam et al., 2019; Longstreth et al., 1987; Rogers, 2005; Shelton, 2006).

Drew and Humbert (2012) provided great insight into the family–work interface management by men and women entrepreneurs in Ireland. They showed that mothers rather than fathers worked flexible hours and took on the lion's share of unpaid work and care, and consequently, reported higher work–nonwork role conflict (Drew & Humbert, 2012). Their work is important as it extends the gender and employment issue from mainstream organisational studies to entrepreneurship. It provided empirical evidence on the predictable continuity of fathers' career trajectory, while mothers had 'more fragmented working patterns, reflecting absences for caring and adjustments such as part-time or working from home (p. 49)'.

The many contributions that women could make through their entrepreneurial activities are widely acknowledged. However, to facilitate women better to make these, the structural mechanisms which shape women entrepreneurial activities need to be taken into account (De Bruin et al., 2007; Thebaud, 2010). For instance, the study by Bade et al. (2014), conducted in India, showed that women entrepreneurs face a challenge in finding a balance between their work and personal life as a result of conflicting needs/demands from their familial, social, personal, and entrepreneurial roles. This study drew on secondary sources, such as literature review and Internet sources, and showed that although Indian women are satisfied with their work–life balance, they are also struggling with the overtime associated with their business. It suggested more awareness of the personal goals in the family, societal, and personal domain may help better management of work–life balance. Some of the work–life interface strategies identified by Jennings and McDougald (2007) include women reducing the hours spent on their business to fulfil family and/or domestic roles and postponing women's decision to expand their businesses until children get older (prioritising fulfilling family/care demands). This resembles work by Bleijenberg et al. (2016) who study part-time work in relationship to gender and ambition. Also in this case, reducing working hours is revealed as a strategy for women to combine work and nonwork demanding them to postpone the realization of their ambitions in the work domain.

The use of boundary theory (Ashforth et al., 2000; Kossek et al., 1999, 2012; Nippert-Eng, 1996) would help us to understand how women entrepreneurs would be able to manage the work–life interface by using different work–life role management strategies and the effect of such strategies on the performance of women entrepreneurs' businesses. Boundary theory states that people create, maintain, and frequently transit across boundaries of the work and nonwork domains to manage their work–life roles. For the purpose of this study, two dimensions are distinguished: work–family role flexibility and work–family role permeability. Flexibility refers to roles being enacted in variable physical and temporal locations (Sundaramurthy & Kreiner, 2008). Permeability refers to the degree to which roles are enacted during the execution of another role. Importantly, roles can be psychologically and/or behaviourally located in other roles, referring to the extent to which a role can spill over into another role (Sundaramurthy & Kreiner, 2008). To manage their physical, temporal, or psychological work–nonwork boundaries, mainstream boundary theory assumes that people enact a boundary management strategy. The options can lie on a continuum ranging from high on segmentation (i.e., where work–life roles are separately undertaken) to high on integration (i.e., where people deal with their work–life roles simultaneously) (Kossek et al., 2012; Nippert-Eng, 1996). Moreover, individuals may have different preferences for either segmenting or integrating their work–life roles. In practice, however, individuals' preferred boundary management strategies are not necessarily reflected in their enacted boundary management strategies (Peters & Blomme, 2019).

Methods

The study followed a grounded theory approach to explore the work–life boundary management experiences of women entrepreneurs in Ethiopia. In-depth interviews were conducted with 31 women entrepreneurs who are operating micro, small, and medium enterprises in Addis Ababa. To tap into heterogeneity in experiencing and managing work–life interface, we included women participants operating in different sectors, for a varied number of years, having diverse demographic characteristics, such as age, marital status, availability of children, and level of education. For sampling the women interviewees, snowball-sampling technique, referrals through friends, and contacts with established women-related business associations were used. Employing a variety of criteria in selecting our samples and using different mechanisms of sampling enabled us to capture different experiences of participants as well as increase the credibility of our findings (Rubin & Rubin, 2005).

Semi-structured interview questions were used to explore the work–life boundary management experiences, challenges, and boundary management strategies of the selected women entrepreneurs. Interviews lasted 50 min on average and were audio-recorded after informed oral consent was obtained from the participants. Data were analysed using constant comparison (Corbin & Strauss, 1990), where incidents in the data are constantly compared with other incidents for similarities and differences. Line-by-line coding was initially conducted by the researchers, followed by the construction of the core categories which matched the collected data set. The core themes that emerged from the qualitative data analysis included: permeability of multiple roles, 'I'm here and there' and longing for success.

Findings and Analysis

This section presents the main findings of the study. These are organized by core themes, supported by representative quotes and descriptions.

Permeability of Multiple Roles

One of the study's main findings concerns the women entrepreneurs' struggle with managing the permeability of the various work and nonwork roles that they were expected to play. More specifically, the women experienced that there were too many roles spanning the boundaries of their roles in business (work), family and domestic care, social obligations, and community services. Some of these are highly culturally sensitive, such as paying respect to the dead, making financial or material contributions during weddings, cultural celebrations, and mourning for the dead. For some of our interviewees, domestic and childcare responsibilities (i.e., caring for children, husband, dependents, and other extended family members) took their primary attention. One of the respondents said:

> It's a must [to take care of home/family responsibilities], you must give a priority to your home/family, you have to fulfill [your family roles]. If I have to leave my business and go buy groceries for home, I do that; if your child is taken ill, you must give priority for that (Women's clothing store owner, aged 31, two children aged 3 and 1).

Interestingly, in most accounts, the interviewees indicated that they needed to fulfil the societal expectation to be the (primary) care provider and take (sole) responsibility for overseeing domestic chores. Another respondent mentioned:

> [F]or instance, today, I left home to go to work very late. Because I had to tell the housemaid what she had to prepare for my children and had to arrange things in the house. If something happens at home, [...] if something happens to the children, it concerns me. I am responsible. So, such things at home affect [my] business (Advertising and Printing business owner, aged 30, two children, aged 3 and 1.5).

The women's family–home responsibility was followed closely by the responsibility of giving attention to managing their business. In practice, this implied that they had to take the roles of manager, purchaser, operations, customer service, and supervision of employees, if present. Some interviewees, however, indicated that business was given priority over social or community services. These women chose to find a way to deal with community roles outside of work hours. One reflected on her experience as follows:

> I do it [deal with community roles outside of work hours, authors] in a way that doesn't affect my work [business]. And if I have to help, for instance, if you tell me to go right now and chop some onions for a wedding, I wouldn't do it. It's my work that is going to hold me responsible and not anybody else. The responsibilities [at work] are a priority. (School owner, aged 46, three children, aged 28, 22, and 18).

For most interviewees, however, fulfilling social and community expectations did constitute an important and demanding role. The commonly described roles included attending important life events of community members, such as childbirth, weddings, and funerals, which also involves paying respects for the dead, visiting the ill, involving in a community or kinship-based voluntary associations. Some aspects of this role, at times, also required making monetary and material contributions. The social and community service is considered to be important as it helps to develop the interviewees' social capital, since a large part of the community members come together at times of difficulties and loss. One of the interviewees shared her experience of managing boundary-spanning roles at home, business, and community (religion, in this case), and how she experienced difficulties navigating these roles simultaneously. She proclaims:

> It is very difficult to be a mother and a businesswoman at the same time [...] For example, we wake up every day at 5:45 AM and wake the children so they can have breakfast. [I] then have to drive them to school. Though my husband is home, I am the one who must get to work in the mornings, so I drive the children to school and arrive at the shop around 8 AM. I work [at the shop] all day and close the shop around 6 pm. When I get home, more work awaits me as I must bath the children, help them study, and teach them the bible. Moreover, there are days when I also have to go to church for a bible study session, so on those days, I must go there at the end of the business day. [...] I am also responsible for making sure we have enough to eat and drink at the house and check whether the house is being kept properly. [...] Whenever I hear someone is sick, I make time to go and visit them. I also do my best not to miss funerals. I make time after I get home or I close my shop early to go [attend]. (Stationary Store owner, aged 36, three children, aged 16, 9, and 7).

Most of the interviewees expressed similar experiences and challenges of managing competing expectations simultaneously. Hence, the role permeability can be regarded to be real and poses a significant challenge of managing work and nonwork boundaries. How do women entrepreneurs attend simultaneously to competing and at times, conflicting expectations? The findings reported above imply the potential trade-offs: attending to a certain role effectively comes at a cost of not being able to attend some of the other roles. For instance, the interviewee referred to above experienced that she had to close her shop on a regular basis in a bid to attend to her social obligations which have to come at a cost in the form of reduced sales. Other interviewees had to skip the time they were supposed or want to spend with their family in order to fill urgent customer orders which put pressure on their domestic roles and family relationships.

'I'm Here and There'

One of the consequences of work–nonwork role permeability is the intersection of spatiality, temporality, and behaviours of women entrepreneurs in their day-to-day routines. Most of the interviewed women, especially those with care roles at home, reported how their responsibilities at home interfered with their business roles, and required space- and time-bound coping strategies. In particular, this appears true for women who have small children at home. A women entrepreneur with two young children, who were three and one-year old at the time of the interview, and who worked from home designing and producing leather products, explained how challenging it was for her to juggle her business and her family responsibilities. Initially, her decision to move the business to her home was motivated by the ever-increasing rent she had to pay for her small shop as well as by the availability of open space at her in-laws' compound. She admitted that she benefitted from bringing the business to her home. At the same time, however, she felt the pressure working from home put on her business. She says:

> [My work-family life] is full of pressure. Now, I am not working as fully as I should be. My children are close-by and need on-off supervision… there are times when I am here and there. A full-time commitment to work is impossible due to children-home responsibilities. So, there are things like that, and I think to some extent it has affected my work (Leather Products company owner, aged 31, two children, aged 1 and 3).

Table 20.1 Summary of results

No	Main findings	Summary
1	Permeability of multiple roles	Most participants were identified as having multiple roles in their work, family, and community domains. Most women, with care responsibilities with the family, were found struggling to manage the permeability of the domains and the various roles that span the work–life boundaries of the work–nonwork domains. Doing so require the women to make some trade-offs, to manage demands from one domain (e.g., attending funeral) while impacting their other roles (i.e., closing business to go attend)
2	'I am here and there'	The women's multiple roles in the three domains and the high permeability allow the women to considerably integrate their roles, demanding them to be 'here and there'. Women with pre-school children and who do not have familial or reliable house help support heavily use integrating coping strategies
3	Longing for success: Effect of permeability of work–life interface management	For some women, competing demands from their work, family and community domains impact their business growth intentions and/or decisions. On the other hand, some women with considerable experience in the business and with less family responsibility or with reliable support were indeed able to grow their businesses showing the significance of the favourable family context

The same interviewee moved on and said that she could have 'focused more on [her] work' if she had decided to move her business out of her house (Table 20.1). But she decided not to do so, she wanted to have her young children 'at a close distance' to provide them with better care at home.

> A woman, however great she is as a businessperson, she also has a lot of other responsibilities. In the house, from the family and culturally expected role of women, there are lots of pressure on women, what we call family... things like managing housemaids and household activities. So, when I see it from that aspect, it is quite a challenge for the woman [all women]! And a business led by a woman encounters similar challenges as well. When I say I didn't hit the target that I had in the beginning, I also know that I need to be satisfied and be grateful for what [I have] now. But sometimes, I think what if I kept going on the momentum I had when I began. But for me not to go at that speed I wanted to, could be explained by something that happened here – children and home and these are also significant aspects of life".

The above narrative of this mother-entrepreneur reveals the tensions, conflicts, and ambiguities of straddling across different roles. At times, she feels joy about having children and caring for them as a mother; and, at other times, the narrative shows how such a role also holds her back not making progress on running a profitable business. She brought business home, perhaps believing that it would be easier to do in that way. However, this proved more difficult temporally and spatially because she must monitor and care for children and manage home-related activities along with running a business. This finding questions one of the premises of the boundary theory as this suggests women to be able to enact their roles flexibly in variable physical and temporal locations (Sundaramurthy & Kreiner, 2008). However, it also confirms insights from boundary theory that individuals' enacted work–nonwork boundary management strategies do not always resemble their preferred boundary management strategies (Peters & Blomme, 2019).

Another interesting and relevant issue raised by a few interviewees related to their social capital need, in particular networking, for running a business. They considered the importance of networking for business resource access, but also indicated that they could not do it because of a lack of time due to their caring responsibilities.

> The difference between working men and women, [...] is that men network much. They support each other well. Plus, they make time [for each other]. They may say "let's have some beer", but they spend a great deal of time discussing about their work, sitting with just one bottle of beer. [...] So, when they are out and about, they build support [networks]. But when you look at a woman, she immediately goes to home when she leaves work. There are children, she must make sure that food is prepared, there is marriage [to tend to] and all that. And I used to see that clearly sometimes. When I go and present my case [at work], I am all alone. Because I couldn't mobilize support using

that time, through networking [as men do]. (Social entrepreneur, aged 68, four children aged 40, 35, 35, and 32).

Another businesswoman experienced that she had to be reflective regarding to dealing with work–home demands. She said:

> I often get fed up as I must buy and sell everything at the shop and I also have to make sure the house is full. Sometimes, it becomes too much to handle, but you have to do it anyways [...] It was difficult at first, but I have now managed to handle it. (Stationary business owner, aged 36, three children, aged 16, 9, and 7).

Longing for Success: Effect of Permeability of Work–Life Interface Management

Managing the work–life interface by women entrepreneurs requires them to deploy essentially two strategies: integration and/or separation or segmentation. Role permeability essentially refers to how women can manage work–life challenges simultaneously, though this could be at a different level of prioritising. The analysis suggests that women were not only interpreting their experience of dealing with competing roles, but were also reflecting on whether it was a right decision to start a business in the first place and on how they could manage it to have a potential for growth. Such narrative strongly featured from women who were relatively young with pre-school children and/or less fortunate in having familial support or trustworthy housemaids. One respondent shared her experience of the ups and downs of managing her business, while at the same time trying to raise her two young boys. She said that running her own business as a self-employed was radically different from being employed in someone else's organisation. She opined that young aspiring women with pre-school children or with a plan to have a child in the near future should not go into business. She mentioned that a caring burden impacts women's business operation (performance). She puts it as follows:

> I wouldn't advise for a person who's newly married or has recently given birth to go into business. Because my children are what worries me most. It's recently that my youngest who's three-years old started going to school. So, I was worried about him very much... what if he fells... what if... I believe all other mothers think like that. So at least if they are done with and already sent their children to school, that would be fine. That way you could have at least fulfilled one of your responsibilities... when [the children] start spending the day at school that will take some burden off you. Because this is not like

office work [employment] that you go straight home leaving work at five and reach home at six. If that's the case, you could have helped your children with their studies and homework while cooking their food. (Children's clothing store owner, aged 38, two children aged 3 and 8)

The above expressed opinion is shared by another respondent who also believed that a woman aiming to open a new business should reconsider doing so. She described that running a profitable business requires a woman to dedicate her time which would be challenging if she has familial and/or care responsibilities. She described this as follows:

If a woman has children, if she has responsibilities at home, to tell the truth, it's very difficult [to open and run a business]. I sometimes say that I should just quit [the business] and sit down and raise my children at home. [...] So, for a woman with family responsibilities, if she starts a business, she better makes time to be there. Otherwise, I would advise not to start it at all. The business needs her. So, she should first be done raising her children and then come back to start a business when things are settled. I don't think women abandon their children to focus on their business. (Women's clothing store owner, aged 31, two children aged 3 and 1).

However, not all participants equally experienced the freedom to control their work, family, and community responsibilities from impacting one another. Most importantly, for the women interviewees with small children, family and care responsibilities frequently interfered with their business time, causing a few of the women to question their decision to stay in business. This was also reported by the women who had grown (adult) children at the time of the interview when sharing their struggle in running and growing their businesses when they were in the phase of raising small children.

An interviewee who worked as a business consultant and who owned a food retailing shop and had three children (aged 17, 11, and 4) said that 'being a woman' comes with many responsibilities, and this poses a significant challenge to run a successful business. She considered herself a lucky person because she had a trustworthy domestic worker who was able to take care of domestic and care responsibilities 'off [her] shoulders, so that [she has] no worries if [she] wants to work or stay out late'. However, she admitted that for most women this challenge will remain and that businesswomen do need 'extra support', because of the additional burden they have in the family domain while running their businesses.

Handling domestic and care responsibilities and responding to emergencies at the community were both found to be interfering with the women's businesses. The following two interviewees expressed supporting evidence:

> The children, when they come home from school, they need somebody who opens the door for them, who prepares supper for them and that is difficult for us. Here it is not the husband who faces the problems, it is us. They just go to work, stay there until 5 PM and come home and something like that. But you can't do that. You leave your work and go there. Most of the time this is the reason why women's work [business] faces obstacles. Also, when there is a funeral, you just get up pick your cloth and leave (Restaurant and Construction equipment rental owner, aged 38, three children aged 17, 16, and 8).

> [Women's] challenges are so many. By just being a woman, you have many challenges. Your responsibilities are many… [men's] responsibilities… [their] major role is in [their] work… when you take the women's responsibility [she has] to fill that a hole [at the family], the gap that nobody else fills in for [her]. [A woman] needs four ears instead of two, four more hands instead of two, especially when there're children, four children may talk to you at the same time (Import, Export and Health Services, co owner, aged 31, four children aged 11, 7, 4, and 2.5).

Some women entrepreneurs provided stark narratives on tensions between an ability to grow a business and to take up caring responsibilities at home. In one case, a leather products designer and manufacturer was not able to exploit the opportunity structure accessible to her. When she was offered a production site by the government, as she was operating in the leather industry which the government considers as one of the strategic sectors, she decided not to take the incentive in place in a bid to take care of her children working from home. She explained:

> "…. and it is because of such benefits [combining care and business], that I was inclined to [keep working from home] even when the government offered us production site. I am saying that I don't need a production site but rather a place where I can sell my products. Why? Because if I take this work out of my home, here I have very young children and we wouldn't see each other in the day time and I would like it if they won't be affected like that…" (Leather Products, co-owner, aged 31, two children, aged 1 and 3)

Some other women cited their familial responsibilities as a reason limiting their business growth (intention). A respondent with two small children reported:

I know how much I should work to be profitable in the business. But time is a constraint. I know how many hours I should be working here but I am not doing that… But I plan to do that in the future… I spent less time of the required because of my responsibilities at home. Further, the success and growth of my business is determined by the number of clients I have, and how much it's increasing… but my business growth slowed down, it has been impacted because I had to close before the end of the business day and go home to care [for the family]. If I had enough time, I could have grown it; I could have opened it in another location where there's a better market. I also have other business ideas that I want to venture into… I could have expanded it into that as well if I had more time. But I couldn't (children store owner, aged 32, two children aged 5 and 1.5).

Here, we can see that the interviewee's care responsibility is limiting her from expanding her business into new territories and also from growing her market/customer base by taking her time away from the business. Her analysis of space and time for growth indicated the intertwined negative association between care and home responsibilities and business growth and expansion. She described:

I feel that my business operations are sometimes limited because of my responsibilities with my children. There were times that I thought about travelling to Thailand to import goods for my store, instead of buying them from wholesalers in town. That would have made my business more profitable and grow, but then I say what about my children? It's not that I am not happy that I have them. I am. But because I have them, that limits me… from travelling and importing on my own. This type of business is more profitable if you could open your store from 8:00 am to 8:00 pm. It could have been more successful, but my responsibilities at home and with the children are limiting me from doing that.

In many respects, the accounts presented above can be viewed as the typical narratives of women entrepreneurs who face the challenges of managing the work–life interface. In fact, our analysis shows that role permeability and the use of integration strategies are more often used than flexibility and separation of work and nonwork role activities. The majority of respondents was struggling to manage the work–family interface. Their decisions for starting, running, and growing their business were not as rational as often suggested, but appear determined and profoundly influenced by the intersection of family, business, culture, normative societal expectations, and more. It is also clear that there is no simple panacea for the complex issue of managing boundaries between business (work) and nonwork (life roles, such as family and community roles). Overall, the above empirical evidence points out that aspiration for women entrepreneurs' business growth demands a holistic perspective.

Although there were a considerable number of the women's accounts that show the challenges they face and how they feel being limited from growing their businesses, our data also shows the cases of women entrepreneurs who were able to grow their businesses. A closer look at our data shows that those women who have considerable experience in the business often raise factors such as finance, access to working space, and others as reasons limiting their growth aspirations compared to the women with a few years of business experience and care responsibilities. An entrepreneur who has been in business for seven years and who appreciates the child care support she gets from her aunt and hired help(s) shares her experience as:

> We are in transition of getting it scaled up to the online business ... we have markets also... people who own stores [of traditional clothes] they want to buy from us. So it has good feasibility... thanks to God it's growing... it's really growing. So supplying them and going with the international fashion calendar... you need to invest more on the system and production capacity so we're there now (Designer, aged 34, three children, aged 7, 5, and 1.5)

Apart from the challenges from role permeability, determination in achieving success in all domains came forth as a shared personal strength in the interviewees, as is expressed by an experienced entrepreneur:

> Nothing else pushed me forward. I wanted to achieve financial freedom and now I am where I wanted to be (Management consultant and foodstuffs shop owner, aged 36, three children, aged 17, 11, and 14)

In general, we observed that there remain strong motivations but also formidable challenges. The overall findings support the view of a strong 'superwoman' who attempt to integrate all the demands of work–life challenges.

Discussion and Conclusion

Drawing on work–life interface literature and boundary theory, this study examined the work–life challenges of Ethiopian women entrepreneurs and the consequences of such challenges on the management and growth of their businesses. First, our analysis showed that Ethiopian women entrepreneurs experienced multiple role identities, as a mother, care-taker, business woman, household chore operator/manager, a member of community/social/religious group, et cetera. This may not be surprising, as many women in various countries face similar multiple identities with corresponding normative expectations. What is interesting, however, in our view, is how these women experienced and managed the expectations of multiple work and nonwork roles and how their work–life interface management clearly impacted their business operation and growth. Our qualitative analysis especially showed the pervasiveness of work–nonwork roles permeability which led the women entrepreneurs to deploy more of an integrating strategy to manage work–life interface. Experience of flexibility for managing the work–nonwork boundary interfaces was less commonly practiced, since this still demands segmentation which requires someone else to keep an eye on the children or to enact other roles in the nonwork domain. Further, the ways in which our interviewees interpreted and experienced their work and nonwork roles showed that most of them were likely to prioritise their children and other family issues followed by their business. In some cases, community obligations also competed with running the business. Importantly, however, there were also cases where women entrepreneurs were able to separate their business roles from family/domestic care management, both in terms of behaviour, cognition, or regarding time. We also noted that the ability to separate the enactment of business management from other domains could be facilitated because these women had dependable support from family members (spouse, mother) or from trustworthy housemaids. Integrating family into work was also observed in a few cases, for example, by working from home. Also, this strategy was not ideal about running and growing a business.

Second, this study also showed that it is difficult for the women entrepreneurs, if not impossible, integrating various roles in a day-to-day routine and achieving business success and, let alone, growth. There were many cases where the women entrepreneurs' decisions to expand their businesses were postponed, and this was for many reasons, such as lack of time, resources, and multiple roles vying for women's commitment. In short, many women were longing for business success, yet, without being enabled and supported by their environment, be they firm-specific, family, community, or social.

A third main finding of this study is that women's enterprises are more likely to be survival or life-style type and less growth-oriented because of their competing role requirements (Morris & Kuratko, 2020). This may explain why a majority of women enterprise start small and remain small. Hence, women's motivation to venture into business may likely to be driven by family/lifestyle preferences than with an intention to grow it. This raises the question whether 'business growth' associated with economic measures could be an apt way to examine women's venturing into business and its outcomes. We think it might be appropriate instead to explore what women consider as 'success' when enterprising, which includes qualitative indicators, not only business profitability/turnover and growth (De Bruin et al., 2007; Hailemariam & Kroon, 2018; Walker & Brown, 2004). Our chapter extends the view that suggests the relevance of using other measures of success given the interdependence between performance, success, and goals when studying about growth intention of women entrepreneurs (De Bruin & Hirsch, 2000).

Contributions

Our study's findings and insights contribute to the work–life and women entrepreneurship literatures in three important ways. First, it questions the view of imaginary 'gender neutral' entrepreneurship. In addition to considering the market, money, and management aspects of women entrepreneurship, it is important to consider family responsibilities (theirs and others) and reproductive work environment as these are found to be key determinants of women business success (Brush et al., 2009; Minniti, 2010). Therefore, it is of great importance to apply a gender-sensitive and multi-level analysis of women entrepreneurship.

Second, our study identified the main coping strategies women entrepreneurs' use in the study context and how such use is not only temporally and spatially bound, but they are also put limits on effective management and growth intentions of women businesses. It seems that integrating multiple role expectations emanates from the gendered ascription of women to family, childcare, and community responsibilities. This creates tensions and negative feelings such as guilt that put pressure on women entrepreneurs to conform with prevailing (un-codified) value standards (Jamali, 2009). This implies the need for radical changes in the culturally accepted norm and/or institutionalised practices that disadvantage women business.

Third, despite the fact that women entrepreneurs often create significant contributions beyond economic growth (Sheikh et.al., 2018), the prevailing view that sees entrepreneurship as an engine of economic growth may need to be questioned. This view is problematic, since it diverts attention from examining *how* women businesses operate at the intersection of gender, sex, family, culture, religion, and institutions. Moreover, their businesses also contribute to emancipating women in male-dominated cultures by providing role models and opportunities for personal development (Hailemariam &

Kroon, 2018). Future research using a more intersectional lens by paying women entrepreuneurs' multiple identities could not only further our understanding of the interplay of their motivation, identity, family, and community responsibilities with prescriptive expectations that individuals and institutions may have, to prescriptive approaches with emphasis on how women enterprises could be supported so that they contribute to family–community wellbeing and economic development.

One of the ways to extend the current strand of research might be using expectancy theory as this theory would help to identify factors related to how and why women pursue business growth opportunities. Previous studies have suggested that individuals' perceptions of their abilities and skills link with their expectancy perceptions and that they deploy their resources and efforts into tasks that they believe they can do (Bandura, 1986) with successful outcomes (Gatewood et al., 2002; Hailemariam & Kroon, 2018). Studying the association between the women's perceived abilities and their performance expectations of enterprise by size (Cliff, 1998) and industry, thus, might provide important insights into women business growth intentions, attitudes, and ways of achieving them. By showing the myriad ways in which Ethiopian women entrepreneurs manage the boundaries between their different work and nonwork life domains, this chapter highlights how 'longing to grow their business' is a strong motivator in juggling the varied demands from their family and community and their persistence in running their business.

References

Aldrich, H. E., & Cliff, J. E. (2003). The pervasive effects of family on entrepreneurship: Toward a family embeddedness perspective. *Journal of Business Venturing, 18*, 573–596.

Álvarez, G., & Sinde-Cantorna, A. I. (2014). Self-employment and job satisfaction: An empirical analysis. *International Journal of Manpower, 35*(5), 688–702.

Annink, A., & Den Dulk, L. (2012). Autonomy: The panacea for self-employed women's work-life balance? *Community, Work and Family, 15*(4), 383–402.

Ashforth, B. E., Kreiner, G. E., & Fugate, M. (2000). All in a day's work: Boundaries and micro role transitions. *Academy of Management Review, 25*(3), 472–491.

Bade, M. U. R., Reddy, J. V., & Rao, M. P. D. (2014). Work-life balance of women entrepreneurs in India. In R. Aluvala (Ed.), *Managing human resources in global era-prospects & challenges* (pp. 158–170). Zenon Academic Publishing.

Bandura, A. (1986). *Social foundations of thought and action: A social cognitive theory*. Prentice-Hall, Englewood Cliffs.

Bayeh, E. (2016). The role of empowering women and achieving gender equality to the sustainable development of Ethiopia. *Pacific Science Review b: Humanities and Social Sciences, 2*(1), 37–42.

Bianchi, S. M., & Milkie, M. A. (2010). Work and family research in the first decade of the 21st century. *Journal of Marriage and Family, 72*(3), 705–725.

Bird, B. (1988). Implementing entrepreneurial ideas: The case for intention. *Academy of Management Review, 13*(3), 442–453.

Bleijenbergh, I. L., Gremmen, C. C. M., & Peters, P. (2016). Timing ambition: How organisational actors engage with the institutionalised norms that affect the career development of part-time workers. *Scandinavian Journal of Management, 32*(4), 179–188. https://doi.org/10.1016/j.scaman.2016.08.004.

Bögenhold, D., & Klinglmair, A. (2015). Women's self-employment and freelancers: Observations on female entrepreneurship. In A. Burke (Ed.), *The handbook of researchers on freelancing and self-employment: Chapter 5* (pp. 51–62). Senate Hall Academic Publishing.

Brush, C., & Hisrich, R. (2000). *Women-owned businesses: An exploratory study comparing factors affecting performance* (Working Paper Series 00–02). RISE Business.

Brush, C. G., De Bruin, A., & Welter, F. (2009). A gender-aware framework for women's entrepreneurship. *International Journal of Gender and Entrepreneurship, 1*(1), 8–24.

Burgess, G. (2013). A hidden history: Women's activism in Ethiopia. *Journal of International Women's Studies, 14*(3), 96–107. http://vc.bridgew.edu/jiws/vol14/iss3/7.

Carter, S., Mwaura, S., Ram, M., Trehan, K., & Jones, T. (2015). Barriers to ethnic minority and women's enterprise: Existing evidence, policy tensions and unsettled questions. *International Small Business Journal, 33*(1), 49–69.

Cliff, J. E. (1998). Does one size fit all? Exploring the relationship between attitudes towards growth, gender and size. *Journal of Business Venturing, 13*(6), 523–542.

Corbin, J., & Strauss, A. L. (1990). Grounded theory research: Procedures, canons, and evaluative criteria. *Journal of Qualitative Sociology, 13*(1), 3–21.

De Bruin, A., Brush, C. G., & Welter, F. (2007). Advancing a framework for coherent research on women's entrepreneurship. *Entrepreneurship Theory and Practice, 31*(3), 323–339.

Drew, E., & Humbert, A. L. (2012). Men have careers, women have babies. *Community, Work, & Family, 15*(1), 49–67.

Eby, L. T., Casper, W. J., Lockwood, A., Bordeaux, C., & Brinley, A. (2005). Work and family research in IO/OB: Content analysis and review of the literature (1980–2002). *Journal of Vocational Behavior, 66*(1), 124–197.

Elam, A. B., Brush, C. G., Green, P. G., Baumer, B., Dean, M., & Heavlow, R. (2019). *Global entrepreneur monitor: 2018/2019 women's entrepreneurship report.* Global Entrepreneurship Research Association, London Business School, Regents Park.

Ford, M. T., Heinen, B. A., & Langkamer, K. L. (2007). Work and family satisfaction and conflict: A meta-analysis of cross-domain relations. *Journal of Applied Psychology, 92*(1), 57–80.

Gatewood, E. J., Shaver, K. G., Powers, J. B., & Gartner, W. B. (2002). Entrepreneurial expectancy, task effort, and performance. *Entrepreneurship, Theory and Practice, 27*(2), 187–206.

Gold, M., & Mustafa, M. (2013). Work always wins: Client colonization, time management and the anxieties of connected freelancers. *New Technology, Work and Employment, 28*, 197–211.

Gudeta, K. H., & Van Engen, M. L., (2017). The omnipresent community in the work-life experiences of women entrepreneurs in Ethiopia. In M. Las Heras, N. Chinchilla, & M. Grau (Eds.), The *work-family balance, technology, and globalization* (pp. 181–201). Cambridge Scholars Publishing.

Gudeta, K. H., & Van Engen, M. L. (2018). Work–life boundary management styles of women entrepreneurs in Ethiopia—"choice" or imposition? *Journal of Small Business and Enterprise Development, 25*(3), 368–386.

Gudeta, K. H., van Engen, M., Peters, P., van Veldhoven, M., & Moors, G. (2019). Hired domestic help: Critical factor in women entrepreneurs' life and business satisfaction in sub-Saharan countries. In M.-T. Lepeley, K. Kuschel, N. Beutell, N. Pouw, & E. Eijdenberg (Eds.), *The wellbeing of women in entrepreneurship: A global perspective* (pp. 391–402). Routledge.

Hailemariam, A. T., & Kroon, B. (2018). Redefining success beyond economic growth and wealth generation: The case of Ethiopia. In S. Yousafzai, A. Fayolle, A. Lindgreen, C. Henry, S. Saeed, & S. Sheikh (Eds.), *Women's entrepreneurship and the myth of 'underperformance': A new look at women's entrepreneurship research*. Edward Elgar Publishing.

Harrington, B. (2007). *The work–life evolution study*. Boston College Center for Work and Family.

Hilbrecht, M., & Lero, D. S. (2014). Self-employment and family life: Constructing work-life balance when you're 'always on. *Community, Work, & Family, 17*, 20–42.

Hyytinen, A., & Ruuskanen, O. (2007). Time use of the self-employed. *Kyklos, 60*, 105–112.

Jamali, D. (2009). Constraints and opportunities facing women entrepreneurs in developing countries: A relational perspective. *Gender in Management: An International Journal, 24*(4), 232–251.

Jennings, J. E., & Brush, C. G. (2013). Research on women entrepreneurs: Challenges to (and from) the broader entrepreneurship literature? *The Academy of Management Annals, 7*(1), 663–715.

Jennings, J. E., Hughes, K. D., & Jennings, P. D. (2010). The work–family interface strategies of male and female entrepreneurs: Are there any differences? In C. G. Brush, A., De Bruin, E. J. Gatewood, & C. Henry (Eds.), *Women entrepreneurs and the global environment for growth: A research perspective* (pp. 163–186). Edward Elgar.

Jennings, J. E., & McDougald, M. S. (2007). Work-family interface experiences and coping strategies: Implications for entrepreneurship research and practice. *Academy of Management Review, 32*(3), 747–760.

Kassa, S. (2015). Challenges and opportunities of women political participation in Ethiopia. *Journal of Global Economics, 3*(4), 1–7.

Kelley, D., Benjamin, B., Candida, B., Patrica, G., Mahdavi, M., Majbouri, M., Cole, M., Dean, M., & Heavlow, R. (2017). *Global entrepreneurship monitor 2016/2017: Report on women's entrepreneurship.* Babson College.

Kossek, E. E., Noe, R. A., & DeMarr, B. J. (1999). Work–family role synthesis: Individual and organisational determinants. *International Journal of Conflict Management, 10*, 102–129.

Kossek, E. E., Ruderman, M. N., Braddy, P. W., & Hannum, K. M. (2012). Work–nonwork boundary management profiles: A person-centered approach. *Journal of Vocational Behavior, 81*(1), 112–128.

Lee Siew Kim, J., & Seow Ling, C. (2001). Work–family conflict of women entrepreneurs in Singapore. *Women in Management Review, 16*(5), 204–221.

Longstreth, M., Stafford, K., & Mauldin, T. (1987). Self-employed women and their families: Time use and socioeconomic characteristics. *Journal of Small Business Management, 25*(3), 30–37.

Loscocco, K. A. (1997). Work–family linkages among self-employed women and men. *Journal of Vocational Behavior, 50*(2), 204–226.

Marlow, S. (1997). Self-employed women: New opportunities, old challenges? *Entrepreneurship & Regional Development, 9*(3), 199–210.

McGowan, P., Redeker, C. L., Cooper, S. Y., & Greenan, K. (2012). Female entrepreneurship and the management of business and domestic roles: Motivations, expectations and realities. *Entrepreneurship & Regional Development, 24*(1–2), 53–72.

Millán, J. M., Congregado, E., & Roman, C. (2014). Persistence in entrepreneurship and its implications for the European entrepreneurial promotion policy. *Journal of Policy Modeling, 36*, 83–106.

Minniti, M. (2010). Female entrepreneurship and economic activity. *European Journal of Development Research, 22*(3), 294–312.

Morris, M. H., & Kuratko, D. (2020). The entrepreneurial journey: Intention versus emergency. In M. H. Morris & D. Kurato (Eds.), *What do entrepreneurs create? Understanding four types of ventures.* Monograph book, Published online, 10 January, Edward Elgar Publishing, www.elgaronline.com.

Nippert-Eng, C. E. (1996). *Home and work: Negotiating boundaries through everyday life.* The University of Chicago Press.

Parasuraman, S., & Simmers, C. A. (2001). Type of employment, work–family conflict and well-being: A comparative study. *Journal of Organisational Behavior, 22*(5), 551–568.

Peters, P., & Blomme, R. J. (2019). Forget about the "Ideal Worker": A theoretical contribution to the debate on flexible workplace-designs, work–life conflict and opportunities for gender equality. *Business Horizons, 62*(5), 603–613. https://doi.org/10.1016/j.bushor.2019.04.0030007-6813/#2019.

Peters, P., Blomme, R., De Jager, W., & Van der Heijden, B. (2020). The impact of work-related values and work control on the career satisfaction of female freelancers. *Small Businiss Economics, 55*, 493–506. https://doi.org/10.1007/s11187-019-00247-5.

Rogers, N. (2005). The impact of family support on the success of women business owners. In S. L. Fielden & M. J. Davidson (Eds.), *International handbook of women and small business entrepreneurship* (pp. 91–102). UK: Edward Elgar.

Rubin, H. J., & Rubin, I. S. (2005). *Qualitative interviewing: The art of hearing data* (2nd ed.). Sage.

Shabana Asma, K., Neha, V., & Siddique, R.A. (2017). Women empowerment through entrepreneurship for their holistic development. *Asian Journal of Research in Business Economics & Management, 7*(2), 1–17.

Shastri, S., Shastri, S., & Pareek, A. (2019). Motivations and challenges of women entrepreneurs. *International Journal of Sociology and Social Policy, 39*(5/6), 338–355.

Sheikh, S., Yousafzai, S., Sist, F., AR, A. A., & Saeed, S. (2018). Value creation through women's entrepreneurship. In *Women entrepreneurs and the myth of 'underperformance'*. Edward Elgar Publishing.

Shelton, L. M. (2006). Female entrepreneurs, work-family conflict, and venture performance: New insights into the work-family interface. *Journal of Small Business Management, 44*(2), 285–297.

Shockley, K. M., Shen, W., DeNunzio, M. M., Arvan, M. L., & Knudsen, E. A. (2017). Disentangling the relationship between gender and work–family conflict: An integration of theoretical perspectives using meta-analytic methods. *Journal of Applied Psychology, 102*(12), 1601–1635.

Singh, G., & Belwal, R. (2008). Entrepreneurship and SMEs in Ethiopia: Evaluating the role, prospects and problems faced by women in this emergent sector. *Gender in Management: An International Journal, 23*(2), 120–136.

Sundaramurthy, C., & Kreiner, G. E. (2008). Governing by managing identity boundaries: The case of family businesses. *Entrepreneurship Theory and Practice, 32*, 415–436.

Thébaud, S. (2010). Gender and entrepreneurship as a career choice: Do self-assessments of ability matter? *Social Psychology Quarterly, 73*(3), 288–304.

Tremblay, D.-G., & Genin, É. (2008). Permeability between work and non-work: The case of self-employed IT workers. *Canadian Journal of Communication, 33*(4), 701–720.

Walker, E., & Brown, A. (2004). What success factors are important to small business owners? *International Small Business Journal, 22*(6), 577–594.

Zewdie and Associates. (2002). *Jobs, gender and small enterprises in Africa: Preliminary report on women entrepreneurs in Ethiopia*. ILO.

21

Deconstructing the Myth: African Women Entrepreneurs' Access to Resources

Kassa Woldesenbet Beta, Natasha Katuta Mwila, and Olapeju Ogunmokun

Introduction

High-level interest in women entrepreneurship (WE) by academics, policymakers and development practitioners indicates its significant role in economic development, gender equality, women empowerment and household well-being, to name the salient ones. These perspectives on the role of WE, however, obligate various stakeholders to engage in affirmative actions, but less in understanding how individual, meso-, and macro-environments shape, in complex ways, women's entrepreneurship (Brush et al., 2009). For instance, the focus on women's economic empowerment seeks to address women's equal participation in markets and access to basic productive resources, wages and opportunities of economic development (Byrne et al., 2019). As is the case with other businesses, it is argued that women entrepreneurs need a variety of resources to start, run and grow businesses. But such requisite financial, human, social capital and market resources are neither readily available nor used effectively for business purposes by women.

K. Woldesenbet Beta (✉) · O. Ogunmokun
De Montfort University, Leicester, UK
e-mail: kwoldesenbet@dmu.ac.uk

N. K. Mwila
Centre for Enterprise and Innovation, De Montfort University, Leicester, UK
e-mail: natasha.mwila@dmu.ac.uk

In addition, the societal, cultural and institutional environmental factors enable or constrain women entrepreneurs' access to such resources. Resource access and use by women thus become recurrent issues in entrepreneurship and development circles. The availability of entrepreneurial resources is not uniform across countries and severely limited in developing countries such as found in Africa. This chapter deals with this important issue and addresses the key research question: What evidence exists that shows the relationship between the availability of various resources and their accessibility and use by women entrepreneurs for enterprising in Africa?

The scale of, and attitudes towards, entrepreneurship by women in Africa has been increasing (Ratten, 2020). It is the sole continent in the world where more women than men prefer to become entrepreneurs. GEM Women's Entrepreneurship Report 2018/2019 shows that the highest rates of total early-stage entrepreneurial activities (TEA, 21.8%) and established business ownership (11.3%) are by women in sub-Saharan Africa. The same report showed 42% of women entrepreneurs cited necessity motives and 55.6% cited opportunity motives to venture into business; these proportions, however, vary across the countries in Africa. For example, countries such as Angola and Madagascar stand out with both high rates of women's necessity-driven entrepreneurship and large gender gaps. We believe that whilst such development in female enterprise in Africa is promising, it does not show the multitude, multi-layered, challenges women in Africa face in the process of enterprising. Of the many challenges, this chapter focuses on resource potential, resource access and use challenges women face as resources such as financial, human and market are considered as the building blocks of viable business (Bates et al., 2007; Carter et al., 2015). Resource potential is defined as 'the set of knowledge, relations and financial resources gathered together by the entrepreneur' (Uzunidis et al., 2014, 1).

Methodology

We adopted a systematic literature review protocol to gather, analyse and review studies on gender and entrepreneurship in Africa. The literature review followed methodological recommendations of Tranfield et al. (2003) and Podsakoff et al. (2005) to ensure a systematic, transparent and replicable process. Prominent databases such as ScienceDirect, Web of Science, Google Scholar and ProQuest were selected to retrieve relevant publications on gender and entrepreneurship in Africa. We used a period from 1990 to 2020, applied inclusion and exclusion search criteria and publications written in English language to retrieve the maximum possible search results or journal articles.

The following keywords were used to look for relevant studies by checking for their presence in the title or abstract of the articles: wom*n entrepreneurship AND Africa; female entrepreneurship AND Africa; Gender AND Entrepreneurship AND Africa; Wom*n AND Business AND Africa; women business AND family; Gender enterprising AND Africa and other similar terms. The search of these databases resulted in retrieving relevant 105 articles published in 62 journals across 28 African countries in the period between 1990 and 2020 (30 years). Of the 105 retrieved articles, approximately 40 (38%) of the articles dealt with the issues relating to women enterprising resources. This final sample of 40 articles were fully read to identify and code the key issues addressed. Such coding and thematic analysis led to emergence of four core themes: Resource Potential, Access to Resources, Resource Utilisation and Performance.

Geographical Coverage and Time Horizons of Publications

Whilst Africa is the second-largest and most populous continent after Asia, it receives less scholarly attention by many academic disciplines. The same is true about research and publications on entrepreneurship in Africa. Our database searches on women enterprising resources and performance over the period of past 30 years (1990–2020) found that only 14 countries out of 54 countries in Africa were covered in the studies reviewed. This is a stark indication that research on women entrepreneurship is concentrated in some parts of the continent whilst other African countries were scarcely researched and were out of scholarly conversations. The review found that many of the studies have been conducted in South Africa (10, 25%), Ethiopia (6, 15%), Uganda (6, 15%) and Ghana (5, 13%) with research scantily conducted in the other parts of Africa (Table 21.1).

Further highlighting the scarcity of research on women's enterprising resources is the fact that its growth has been a recent but uneven phenomenon although our search for relevant publications spans the last thirty years. We focused on the last thirty years because WE entrepreneurship is a new phenomenon, and prior to late 1980s, studies had mainly addressed entrepreneurship by male as a dominant form of enterprising. As a result, our premise that the longer the time span for search may result in retrieving the larger amount of studies, however, was not materialised. A few studies on African women enterprising resources emerged from 2010 onwards, but

Table 21.1 Geographical coverage of publications

Countries	Count
South Africa	10
Ethiopia	6
Uganda	6
Ghana	5
Sub-Saharan Africa (SSA)	3
Tanzania	3
Africa	2
Kenya	2
African regions (West Africa, Southern Africa, and Middle East and North Africa)	3
Other 8 African countries each covered by a single study (Burkina Faso; Mali; Niger; Rwanda; Senegal; Eswatini; Lesotho; Zimbabwe)	8

most of the research outputs were produced in 2017 and 2018 suggesting a continuous and growing advance in the field of WE. The publications on this area, however, saw a downward trend from 2019 onwards. In summary, the search results showed studies with focus on women's enterprising resources are scarce, do not cover the full continent and are a very recent phenomenon. Thus, we urge scholars to engage in this emerging area of research in Africa to further scholarship and inform policy and practice (Fig. 21.1).

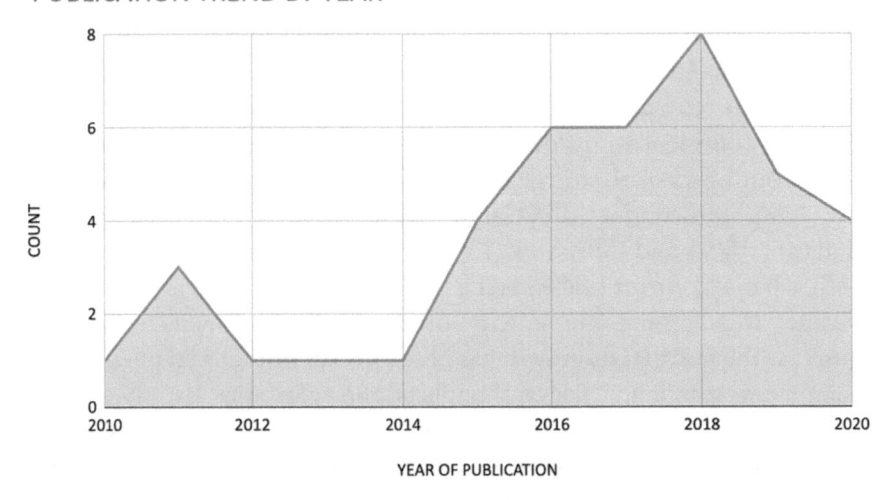

Fig. 21.1 Yearly trend of publications (*Source* Authors)

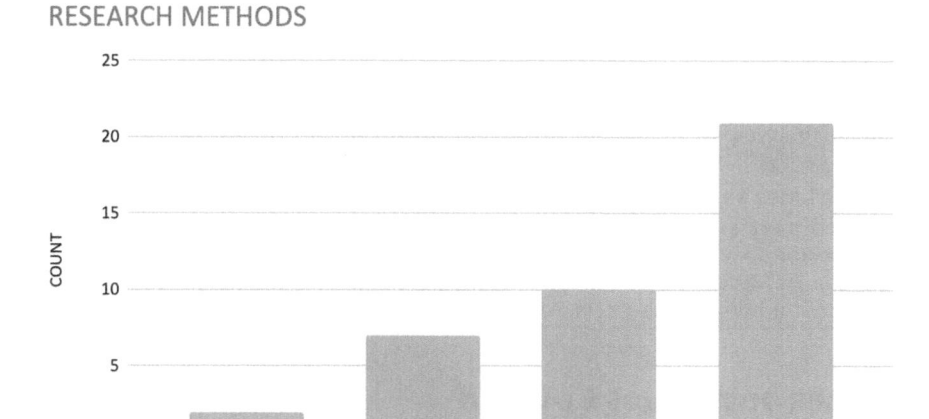

RESEARCH METHODS

[Bar chart showing counts by methodology: Conceptual/Review ≈ 2, Mixed methods ≈ 7, Qualitative = 10, Quantitative ≈ 21. Y-axis: COUNT (0–25). X-axis: METHODOLOGY.]

Fig. 21.2 Research methods across articles (*Source* Authors)

We also probe into the research methods used in the studies of women enterprising resources in Africa. Of the 40 articles, 21 articles were quantitative, 10 qualitative, 7 used mixed methods and the remaining three conceptual/review articles (Fig. 21.2).

Mapping Theoretical Grounding of the Articles

Following Sutton and Staw (1995) and Whetten (1989), we examined the theoretical perspectives employed in the 40 articles reviewed. This was achieved by identifying the building blocks that underpin and provide answers to the questions 'what, why, who, where, when'; and by scrutinising the purpose, research questions, methods, findings and contributions and/or implications of the reviewed articles. Half of the articles were devoid of underpinning theories and were driven by prescriptive approaches to describe the potentials and constraints for accessing resources by women. Ten articles each were informed by one theory/concept: four papers by feminist theories, four papers by human capital theory; and two papers by resource-based view. The review thus found the diversity but fragmented nature of the use of theoretical perspectives and the lack of cumulative knowledge development on women's enterprising resources in Africa (Table 21.2).

Table 21.2 Theoretical perspectives

Theories	Count
None or not stated	20
Feminist theories	4
Human capital	4
Resource-based view	2
Other ten theories/perspectives (Utility Maximisation Theory; Double-Hurdle Model; Gestalts Theory; Property Right Theory; Financial Literacy; Fit/Misfit' Approach; Social Capital; Stakeholder Theory; Resource Paradox; Value-Chain Positioning)	10

Themes and Issues Covered

The next stage in our systematic review involved identifying the main issues studied by the reviewed forty articles. The in-depth review of articles and subsequent coding led to identify several issues and core themes covered by these reviewed articles. The core themes that emerged from coding analyses were *resource potential, access to resources, resource utilisation, and performance* (see Table 21.3).

Resource Potential

Resources are the premise on which enterprising occurs. Uzunidis et al. (2014) define resource potential as 'the set of knowledge, relations and financial resources gathered together by the entrepreneur' (Uzunidis et al., 2014). Based on the systematic review of the literature, we define resource *potential as 'the set of financial, human, relational, locational and physical resources accessible for enterprising activities by the entrepreneur'*. This section critically discusses the resource potential for women entrepreneurs in Africa based on this definition and main issues/factors identified above (see Table 21.3).

Finance

By far, finance is the most prominent issue recognised as a valuable resource not only for enterprising activities but also for maintaining livelihood in the reviewed articles. Finance is further disaggregated into the following distinct areas: start-up capital, operating capital, savings, formal credit, informal revolving credit, short-term credit, long-term credit, microfinance and cash transfers. These distinctions in the types of financial resources are crucial in

Table 21.3 Main issues covered in thematic areas

Core themes and main issues	Authors and dates
Core Theme 1: Resource Potential	
Money (start-up capital, working capital, bank loans, savings, microfinance, credit, informal credit)	Abubakar (2015), Acheampong (2018), Aterido et al. (2013), Brixiová et al. (2020a, 2020b), Dedehouanou and Araar (2020), Hodges et al. (2015), Pueyo et al. (2020), Solano and Rooks (2018), Saviano et al. (2017), Sequeira et al. (2016), Teixeira and Sharifu (2017), Washington and Chapman (2014), Witbooi and Ukpere (2011) and Wu et al. (2019)
Management Skills/Human Capital, Education, Entrepreneurial Cognition	Mezgebo et al. (2017), Dedehouanou and Araar (2020), Brixiová et al. (2020b), Aterido and Hallward-Driemeier (2011), Adom and Asare-Yeboa (2016), Nyakudya et al. (2018), Wu et al. (2019), Adom and Asare-Yeboa (2016) and Meier zu Selhausen (2016)
Information/Mobile Technology	Abubakar (2015), Mezgebo et al. (2017), Dedehouanou and Araar (2020), Okeke-Uzodike et al. (2018) and Ajumobi and Kyobe (2017)
Land (rights) and Premises	Mezgebo et al. (2017), Gebrehiwot et al. (2018), Bambio and Bouayad Agha (2018) and Meier zu Selhausen (2016)
Social Networks	Mezgebo et al. (2017), Solano and Rooks (2018), Hodges et al. (2015), Dedehouanou and Araar (2020), Gottlieb (2016) and Agyire-Tettey et al. (2018)
Energy	Pueyo et al. (2020), de Groot et al. (2017), Gray et al. (2019) and Brixiová et al. (2020a)
Time	de Groot et al. (2017), Hodges et al. (2015) and Gottlieb (2016)
Knowing Other Entrepreneurs	Sequeira et al. (2016) and Hodges et al. (2015)
Location, Urban/Rural/Infrastructure	Rijkers et al. (2010), Agyire-Tettey et al. (2018) and Mezgebo et al. (2017)
Value Chain Participation, Market	Sesan et al. (2019) and Abubakar (2015)

(continued)

Table 21.3 (continued)

Core themes and main issues	Authors and dates
Core Theme 2: Access to Resources	
Gender Difference or Inequality	Pueyo et al. (2020), Mohlakoana et al. (2019), Teixeira and Sharifu (2017), Solano and Rooks (2018), Witbooi and Ukpere (2011), Saviano et al. (2017), Okeke-Uzodike et al. (2018), Brixiová et al. (2020), Aterido and Hallward-Driemeier (2011) and Bardasi et al. (2011)
Gender Neutral Policies, Women Empowerment Policies, and Representation in Politics and Development	de Groot et al. (2017), Abubakar (2015), Mezgebo et al. (2017), Sequeira et al. (2016); Gebrehiwot et al. (2018), Hodges et al. (2015), Dedehouanou and Araar (2020), Okeke-Uzodike et al. (2018), Acheampong (2018), Gottlieb (2016), Adom and Asare-Yeboa (2016), Meier zu Selhausen (2016) and Olowu et al. (2017)
Gender Stereotype/Blind	de Groot et al. (2017), Gray et al. (2019), Witbooi and Ukpere (2011), Agyire-Tettey et al. (2018)
Culture, Norms, Customary Practices, Patriarchal Norms	Mohlakoana et al. (2019), Mezgebo et al. (2017), Witbooi and Ukpere (2011), Wu et al. (2019), Sequeira et al. (2016), Gebrehiwot et al. (2018) and Gottlieb (2016)
Firm Size	Sesan et al. (2019), Brixiová et al. (2020a), Rijkers and Costa (2012) and Bardasi et al. (2011)
Land Ownership Right	Bambio and Bouayad Agha (2018) and Brixiová et al. (2020)
Collateral Requirement, High-Interest Rate, Complicated Loan Application	Teixeira and Sharifu (2017), Mezgebo et al. (2017), Sesan et al. (2019) and Witbooi and Ukpere (2011)
Household Context, Marital Status	Teixeira and Sharifu (2017), Aterido et al. (2013) and Wu et al. (2019)
Skills, Education Level	Aterido et al. (2013), Brixiová et al. (2020) and Teixeira and Sharifu (2017)
Business Strategy, Creativity	Ajumobi and Kyobe (2017) and Hodges et al. (2015)
Value chain, Location and Investment Climate	Mohlakoana et al. (2019), Sesan et al. (2019) and Rijkers et al. (2010)

(continued)

Table 21.3 (continued)

Core themes and main issues	Authors and dates
Core Theme 3: Resource Utilisation	
Gender Gap, Discrimination	de Groot et al. (2017), Washington and Chapman (2014), Gottlieb (2016), Ahmed and Kar (2019) and Nyakudya et al. (2018)
Training, Skills, Non-Cognitive Skills, Tertiary Education and Low Literacy	Brixiová et al. (2020), Aterido and Hallward-Driemeier (2011), Mohlakoana et al. (2019), Teixeira and Sharifu (2017)
Decision-Making; Use and Control over Resources; Women's Rights	Abubakar (2015), Teixeira and Sharifu (2017), Mezgebo et al. (2017) and Gebrehiwot et al. (2018)
Financial Literacy, Financial Management	Mezgebo et al. (2017), Saviano et al. (2017) and Ajumobi and Kyobe (2017)
Business Experience, Supportive Social Contacts, Financial Confidence	Mezgebo et al. (2017), Solano and Rooks (2018) and Witbooi and Ukpere (2011)
Family Context, Gendered Social Norms, Home-Based Enterprise, Lack of Value Chain	Acheampong (2018), Teixeira and Sharifu (2017), Fiala (2018), Adom (2015), Mohlakoana et al. (2019), Mezgebo et al. (2017) and Abubakar (2015)
Risk Aversion	Saviano et al. (2017), Fiala (2018) and Simo Kengne (2016)
Sectoral Disadvantage	Bardasi et al. (2011)
Inefficient/Dysfunctional Regulative Institutions	Ahmed and Kar (2019)
Core Theme 4: Business Performance	
Gender Differentiated Outcome in Value Chains/Returns	Sesan et al. (2019), Agyire-Tettey et al. (2018), Bardasi et al. (2011), Rijkers et al. (2010), Rijkers and Costa (2012) and Olowu et al. (2017)
Women Empowerment/Decision and Control Over Resources	Bambio and Bouayad Agha (2018), Mezgebo et al. (2017), Okeke-Uzodike et al. (2018) and Sesan et al. (2019)
Complementary Skills and On-the-Work Experience	Adom and Asare-Yeboa (2016), Brixiová et al. (2020) and Olowu et al. (2017)
Marketing Strategies	Hodges et al. (2015) and Brixiová et al. (2020)
Livelihood	Dedehouanou and Araar (2020)
Economic Development	Adom (2015)
Enterprise Productivity	Rijkers et al. (2010) and Bardasi et al. (2011)

understanding what forms of finances have an impact on women's enterprising and under which circumstances in an African context. Notably absent in the reviewed articles were studies that focussed on bank loans, angel finance, venture capital and crowdfunding with clear indication of underdevelopment of entrepreneurial finance alternatives in Africa.

One interesting insight from the reviewed literature is that not all forms of finance lead to thriving enterprises and that the findings are inconclusive. Such inconclusive findings on the effects of forms of finance may suggest two underlying reasons. First, the context in which women use the given form of finance is important for it to have either positive or negative outcomes on their enterprise. Second, it is observed that studies that use different research methods on the same form of finance may report contrasting results. Fiala (2018), for instance, found that financial interventions may have a negative impact on women's investment in their enterprises. Although only a short-run study, the findings revealed that capital boosts are neither effective on improving the likelihood of women enterprising nor in scaling up their enterprises (Fiala, 2018). Washington and Chapman (2014) also confirmed negative impacts of finance on women's enterprising but only regarding later stage enterprises. Unlike Fiala (2018) and Washington and Chapman (2014) did find positive short-run effects of finance on women's enterprising in early-stage enterprises. Brixiová et al. (2020) also found contradictory evidence to Fiala's (2018) that short-term loans led to sales growth, innovation and much needed operational capital. Personal savings present a crucial resource for women as they have been found to have limited access to other alternative sources (Teixeira & Sharifu, 2017). Other literature pointed to the need to have customised financial products and the usefulness of financial inclusion for women entrepreneurs (Saviano et al., 2017). This may resolve the conundrum on conflicting evidence on the efficacy of finance. The literature review findings on the financial resources, whilst they were less robust and patchy, provided some important issues to consider issues such as:

- Nature of finance (grant intervention versus repayable credit).
- Use of finance (start-up versus operation versus scaling up).
- Amount of finance (small periodic interventions versus lump sum).
- Source of finance (formal versus informal).

Further research is thus required to provide a conclusive perspective on the potential financial resources.

Relational Resources

Social networks are an important resource for women entrepreneurs in Africa to have access to other resources (Agyire-Tettey et al., 2018; Ajumobi & Kyobe, 2017; Dedehouanou & Araar, 2020; Mezgebo et al., 2017; Okeke-Uzodike et al., 2018). Social networks provide support for enterprising (Ahmed & Kar, 2019) and in societal life beyond women's enterprises (Solano & Rooks, 2018). Sequeira et al. (2016) and Hodges et al. (2015) found that personal knowledge of another entrepreneur greatly increases women's enterprising potential.

Closer to home, family labour is important in making women's enterprising feasible (Aterido & Hallward-Driemeier, 2011; Gebrehiwot et al., 2018; Hodges et al., 2015), both from the perspective of having voluntary assistance in the running of the enterprise and in assisting women meet their other social–cultural obligations. Where voluntary labour is unavailable, women's enterprises need to have the capacity to hire labour to make enterprising possible (Hodges et al., 2015). If they cannot afford to hire labour, women entrepreneurs tend to multi-skill (Hodges et al., 2015). Because of the high costs associated with labour, women's enterprises structured around temporary labour perform better (Brixiova et al., 2020). Gottlieb (2016), however, cautions of the tendency for women's social networks to be confined to women's only groups, limiting their enterprising potential. Women entrepreneurs benefit more from social contacts who can provide mentorship (Okeke-Uzodike et al., 2018).

Human Capital

Like finance, human capital is ubiquitous in the literature as knowledge, skills and competence are key resources for enterprising. Human capital is discussed in the context of management skills (Brixiová et al., 2020; Mezgebo et al., 2017; Okeke-Uzodike et al., 2018), general education (Adom, 2015; Meier zu Selhausen, 2016; Sequeira et al., 2016), on-the-job experience (Adom & Asare-Yeboa, 2016; Meier zu Selhausen, 2016) and entrepreneurial cognition (Wu et al., 2019).

Again, like finance, the reviewed literature does not provide conclusive evidence on human capital's role on women's enterprising. Sequeira et al. (2016) found no impact of early and secondary education on women's venture success. Although early and secondary education are not found to have significant impacts on women's enterprising, tertiary education provides value as it enhances the impact of financial literacy training on the performance of women (Brixiová et al., 2020b). Mezgebo et al. (2017) as well as Saviano, Nenci and Caputo (2017) found that higher levels of education improve women's enterprise success but only when they enable acquisition of key skills like financial literacy. Lower education levels are problematic not only for women entrepreneurs with insufficient education, but are also problematic if their husbands, who are at most times in charge of key decisions, have low levels too (Aterido et al., 2013). Related to development of human capital is entrepreneurship training programmes. Entrepreneurship training programs have been met with some success (Abubakar, 2015). A crucial finding by Brixiová et al. (2020b) has been that training is only effective in improving women's entrepreneurial performance when they have complementary skills learned on the job. They further found that most training interventions benefit men but not women entrepreneurs because of this lack of complementary skills (Brixiová et al., 2020b). The longer women are in business, the better their performance which may be linked to the human capital acquired over time (Brixiová et al., 2020). The resounding conclusion is that overall lower levels of knowledge and skills amongst women explain a substantial part of the gender gap (Nyakudya et al., 2018). Such findings also show interplay of various factors that boost the efficacy of human capital.

Land and Premises

Land is a strategic resource in an African context. The importance of land as a resource potential is linked not only to the need to have fixed property as collateral to use in securing loans (Brixiová et al., 2020a; Mezgebo et al., 2017) but also increases social status and decision-making of women. Ownership of property and assets is also used as collateral and is so crucial for finance (Sesan et al., 2019). Land is also a prerequisite for agriculture-based enterprises which dominate women's enterprising in Africa. Women in some societies, however, are cut off from more profitable agrarian activity which is reserved for men's enterprising (Gebrehiwot et al., 2018). The socio-cultural norms in many African societies thus prohibit women from land ownership (Bambio & Agha, 2018), and therefore invariably cut them off from access to this stream of finance and limits enterprising in agribusiness. Even where women may be allowed land ownership, it is often as joint owners with their husbands (Meier zu Selhausen, 2016) which limits their ability to use land to secure finance.

Premises are an important consideration for women's enterprising, particularly those that run home-based entities (Mezgebo et al., 2017). Home-based enterprises are constrained in their areas and scale of operation (Okeke-Uzodike et al., 2018). The challenges of operating home-based enterprises by women can be explained by difficulties women face when managing work–family interface with quality of life. Running home-based enterprises thus poses challenges on time and involvement levels in both business and family activities as well as limiting satisfaction with work and family.

Media

Media has been identified as a valuable information source and contributes to women's enterprising knowledge (de Groot et al., 2017). Mezgebo et al. (2017) recognise that media in all forms, including mass media sources like radio and television, and social media platforms such as Facebook, fills the void where women's formal education is low.

Information and Mobile Technology

Technology in its broadest sense presents immense resource potential as it facilitates access to all elements of resource potential under discussion. Several scholars (Dedehouanou & Araar, 2020; Mezgebo et al., 2017; Okeke-Uzodike et al., 2018) found that technology is an important avenue for accessing some forms of credit, information, communication with social contacts and acquiring business skills. Sesan et al. (2019) reviewed how household technologies lighten the load of household labour for women, freeing them up more for enterprising. Ajumobi and Kyobe (2017) find that mobile technology in particular presents a great resource potential for women entrepreneurs.

Energy

Energy is not typically listed as a crucial enterprising resource in the broader entrepreneurship literature. As a matter of fact, it does not fit in with our adopted definition of resource potential. However, the literature on women enterprising in Africa reveals this to be a crucial resource particularly for women with extremely low levels of start-up capital (Pueyo et al., 2020) and informal enterprises (Mohlakoana et al., 2019). Further, the lack of energy sources are found to exacerbate the burden of women's household labour and in turn to limit their enterprising. This phenomenon has been labelled as 'energy poverty' (de Groot et al., 2017; Gray et al., 2019) and is specific to women's enterprising in developing contexts. Similarly, other scholars have listed other household utilities such as water as being a crucial enabling resource for the same reason as energy is (Mezgebo et al., 2017).

Time

Time has become increasingly appreciated as a critical resource in women's entrepreneurship as they are required to manage work–family balance. Hodges et al. (2015) point out that without accounting for and managing time constraints, women enterprising efforts are futile. This sentiment is echoed by Gottlieb (2016) and de Groot et al. (2017). Time is a dimension of a family–business balance where women are required to manage their time across family and business activities as the trade-off has significant implications whether the enterprise becomes successful or not.

Markets

Market access provides opportunity structures for women's enterprises. They are outlets for the enterprising effort without which the entrepreneurial reward loop would be incomplete. Markets are therefore included in our discussion of resource potential as evident in the resource analyses of Abubakar (2015) and Okeke-Uzodike et al. (2018). Meier zu Selhausen (2016) finds that markets in Uganda are crucial resource for women because women are cut off from the more profitable market streams such as commodity markets and are often left to engage only at the level of petty trade. This is also the case in Ethiopia where Gebrehiwot et al. (2018) found that women have limited opportunities for high value trade due to market exclusion. Related to markets is the question of where women entrepreneurs are positioned in the value chain (Sesan et al., 2019).

Locational Resources

There is an apparent distinction in the enterprising opportunities and experience of women who reside and enterprise in urban locations in comparison to those who do so in rural locations (Agyire-Tettey et al., 2018; Aterido et al., 2013). This has been linked to the access to roads and easier transportation (Mezgebo et al., 2017; Rijkers et al., 2010), and proximity to cities (Dedehouanou & Araar, 2020) where there is higher value enterprising activity. There is evidence that firms in remote rural areas are less productive and have slower growth (Rijkers et al., 2010). Rijkers et al. (2010) established that this is linked to the quality of infrastructure in rural areas and their poorer access to credit.

Sector Choices

The industry or the sector in which enterprises operate differentiate their performance and growth potentials. Studies found that women's enterprises in manufacturing (Brixiová et al., 2020) and those that are involved in exporting (Agyire-Tettey et al., 2018) perform better than in other sectors. Sector choice appears to influence the size of the enterprises and research finds that size matters; larger women enterprises outperform small- and medium-sized entities (Costa & Rijkers, 2012). Bardasi et al. (2011) supported this finding and found that women enterprises tend to struggle because of their concentration in sectors in which firms are smaller and less efficient.

Access to Resources

We recognise that resource potential means little if women entrepreneurs cannot access these resources. In our review, we, therefore, identified the enablers and barriers to resource access by women entrepreneurs in Africa. We further explored the strategies in place to access resources given these barriers and enablers following the logic of Rawhouser et al. (2017).

Barriers

The thematic analysis in this area found several factors that hold back women entrepreneurs' access to essential resources for enterprising and decent life maintenance. Of these identified constraints, cultural/social norms and customary practices, gendered-blind policies, gender stereotype, gendered discrimination, informality, collateral requirements and lack of land ownership rights were found to limit women's access to resources significantly. The identified barriers to resources access by women entrepreneurs are discussed below.

Cultural and social norms, and customary practices: The informal institutions have been the most cited barrier to women's access to resources. The impact of social norms can be seen in the unequal gendered division of labour (Adom, 2015; Gebrehiwot et al., 2018; Okeke-Uzodike et al., 2018; Pueyo et al., 2020; Sequeira et al., 2016) which limits their time in pursuing enterprise-related activities. These norms are linked to patriarchy which creates gender-related drudgery (Mezgebo et al., 2017; Mohlakoana et al., 2019). Traditional role distribution puts women in an inferior position for resource access (Aterido et al., 2013). Traditional role distributions create the 'motherhood burden' that has been brought into focus in women entrepreneurship literature (Wu et al., 2019). There are some customary practices that deny women from accessing resources (Gebrehiwot et al., 2018). Some social norms create limiting perceptions about women's capacity to comprehend business, 'laziness' and lacking ideas (Gottlieb, 2016) which in turn bars them from accessing resources. Social norms limit the nature of interactions possible for women, and therefore restrict the nature of their networks, further hindering their access to resources (Witbooi & Ukpere, 2011). Some of the detrimental social norms are embedded in religious practices (Sequeira et al., 2016). Gottlieb (2016) found that some Islamic practices in particular were detrimental to women's access to resources. In addition, some social norms have disarmed women of *decision-making power* in their enterprise, and this has the effect of limiting their access to resources (Teixeira & Sharifu, 2017). In many African countries, husbands are required to approve formal financial credit for married women (Aterido et al., 2013). Gottlieb (2016) finds that this is especially problematic if husbands are not supportive of the enterprise activities of their wives, have a bad credit history or/and are low in literacy.

Gender blind policies and interventions: de Groot et al. (2017) argue that the failure of women in accessing resources is linked to the gender-neutral approach of policies and interventions that they are supposed to benefit from. Witbooi and Ukpere (2011) concur with this surmising and argue that entrepreneurial policies do not consider the needs of women. Related to this is the *gendered discrimination*. Some of women's limitations in accessing resources is because of discrimination (Teixeira & Sharifu, 2017). Brixiová et al. (2020a) found that there is societal gender discrimination associated with some social norms. Aterido et al. (2013) explain that financial institutions tend to also discriminate women through taste and statistical discrimination.

Women's access to resources has been hindered by their *lack of awareness* of interventions intended to improve enterprising. Pueyo et al. (2020) and Okeke-Uzodike et al. (2018) found that most enterprise interventions reach men and not women because women do not know about these interventions in the first instance. Witbooi and Ukpere (2011) found that lack of awareness also extends to not knowing about the different financial institutions available. Lower levels of women's education may be a factor in the extent of unawareness (Aterido et al., 2013). Women's inability to access resources has also been linked to the *informal* nature of the majority of their enterprises (Okeke-Uzodike et al., 2018). Entrepreneurial policies tend to miss them as they tend to target formal enterprises (Aterido et al., 2013; Mohlakoana et al., 2019). This seems to be the fate for necessity-driven enterprises (Teixeira & Sharifu, 2017), which are the majority of women's enterprises. The *size* of the enterprise appears to be a factor in women's ability to access resources (Aterido et al., 2013). This is often because firm size is linked to profitability and used as a proxy to determine the ability of women to repay loans (Sesan et al., 2019).

Another constraint is the multiple costs incurred by women in accessing resources. These costs include the higher interest rates they are charged for credit (Mezgebo et al., 2017) and the lower income levels they have that make it difficult to access resources (Aterido et al., 2013; Witbooi & Ukpere, 2011). Not all the costs are financial in nature. Teixeira and Sharifu (2017) explore the complexity of meeting the requirements for credit which women often fail to meet. Sesan et al. (2019) in their study also found that women are confronted with unreasonable formal loan requirements. Ahmed and Kar (2019) concurred that women faced disproportionate administrative and bureaucratic burdens in accessing formal finance. Women enterprises tend to face *local disadvantages*. For instance, rural areas are underserviced, and this presents a barrier to accessing resources. Rurality limits women's ability to physically access resources (Witbooi & Ukpere, 2011) and market opportunities. Operating home-based enterprises also limits market and growth potential as well as access to basic resources.

Formal institutional imperfections also pose formidable challenges to accessing resources. There are a number of citations of barriers in the structure and operation of formal institutions. Sequeira et al. (2016) found that institutional imperfections like corruption and political unrest presented barriers to women accessing resources. Ahmed and Kar (2019) added that other imperfections like insufficient and discretionary tax subsidies disfavoured women. Institutional imperfections result in lack of trust, especially in sectors dominated by women (Okeke-Uzodike et al., 2018).

Enablers

Gender specific policies, legislation and interventions: The failure of several entrepreneurship-favouring policies, legislation and interventions points to the need for a gender-specific approach to these attempts to enable women's access to resources (Abubakar, 2015; Gray et al., 2019; Mezgebo et al., 2017). Gender needs to be mainstreamed (Olowu et al., 2017) taking into account specific gender-specific needs and contexts. A gender explicit approach to interventions acknowledges that some enterprising products and services are not appropriate for women and would consider their persistent hardships in accessing resources (Witbooi & Ukpere, 2011). The efficacy of government-led approaches may be enhanced through women's representation in development and political administrations (Gebrehiwot et al., 2018). Targeting of interventions would also call for the promotion of rural entrepreneurship (Dedehouanou & Araar, 2020), by encouraging the development of enterprises in rural areas and supporting the existing rural enterprises where most women entrepreneurs are active. Government support is important for addressing some of the formal institutional imperfections (Sequeira et al., 2016). Governments can influence the regulatory environment that prevails and can create an enabling environment for women's access to resources and enterprising overall (Bambio & Agha, 2018; Okeke-Uzodike et al., 2018). Governments should recognise that there is an access gap for small- and medium-sized enterprises in general and for female entrepreneurs in particular (Brixiova et al., 2020). Acheampong (2018) adds that female headed households need specialist attention in policies, legislation and interventions. Policies need to be attuned to their social constraints (Gottlieb, 2016) and support female dominant sectors as well as microfinance (Acheampong, 2018; Hodges et al., 2015). Financial policies should be open to the sector to be more inclusive of development of financial institutions and flexible financial policies (Brixiová et al., 2020). To increase the likelihood of success, there is need for a unifying of efforts and collaborative policies across sectors (Dedehouanou & Araar, 2020). Increasing the levels of women's education may enhance their ability to meet the requirements for credit through the acquisition of entrepreneurial skills especially (Teixeira & Sharifu, 2017). Policies that encourage education and training of women entrepreneurs could increase their levels of formal education (Adom & Asare-Yeboa, 2016).

Strategies—Relational Tactics: The reviewed articles do not provide evidence of strategies implemented by women to access resources and this may be an area worthy of further investigation. However, we were able to identify relational strategies in gaining access through husbands (Aterido et al., 2013; Teixeira & Sharifu, 2017), male neighbours or close male relatives (Gebrehiwot et al., 2018) and through the social groupings that women entrepreneurs belong to (Meier zu Selhausen, 2016; Solano & Rooks, 2018).

In summary, African women entrepreneurs face multifaceted and multi-layered challenges to access enterprising resources. These challenges, the systematic review found, are intertwined in complex ways, and suggest the need for a holistic understanding of women entrepreneurship and the ways in which this can be enabled.

Resource Utilisation

Informed by the work of Klyver and Schenkel (2013) and guided by thematic analysis, we explore how women utilise the resources they do have access to, so as to identify where their efficiencies are and where they could be improved. Overall, there appears to be a resource underutilisation because of the gendered division of labour (Pueyo et al., 2020; Wu et al., 2019). There has been a persistent theme of an inadequate entrepreneurial culture (Abubakar, 2015; de Groot et al., 2017; Dedehouanou & Araar, 2020; Okeke-Uzodike et al., 2018) due to the survivalist and informal nature of women enterprises which also leads to resource underutilisation. This is exacerbated by the family orientation of many African women entrepreneurs which prioritises resource commitment to household livelihood over enterprise (Adom, 2015; Fiala, 2018; Hodges et al., 2015; Teixeira & Sharifu, 2017). The weight of family commitment increases risk aversion and lack of confidence, further leading to underutilisation of resources (Kengne, 2016; Saviano & Caputo, 2017). Limited decision-making and control compromise resource utilisation even further (Aterido et al., 2013; Gebrehiwot et al., 2018; Meier zu Selhausen, 2016; Mezgebo et al., 2017). There is evidence that single women make better utilisation of resources (Aterido & Hallward-Driemeier, 2011), but more needs to be done to substantiate such a finding. Low literacy levels and business skills also hinder the full utilisation of resources (Mezgebo et al., 2017; Mohlakoana et al., 2019; Nyakudya et al., 2018; Teixeira & Sharifu, 2017). Gaining skills in budgeting and financial management has been shown to improve resource utilisation (Ajumobi & Kyobe, 2017). Supporting social contacts enhance resource utilisation (Solano & Rooks, 2018) but limited social networks hamper resource utilisation (Gottlieb, 2016).

Enterprise Performance

The final theme which emerged from the thematic analysis was enterprise performance. The review found that the link between access to, and utilisation of, various resources and women enterprise performance was tenuous and rarely examined adequately. Only a few studies attempted to look into the enterprise performance using indicators such as sales (Brixiová, et al., 2020b), productivity (Bardasi et al., 2011; Rijkers et al., 2010), livelihood (Dedehouanou & Araar, 2020) and contribution to development (Adom, 2015). A few other studies tended to explore the link between the resource access and its outcome by using qualitative strategic impact indicators such as women empowerment (Mezgebo et al, 2017; Okeke-Uzodike et al., 2018; Sesan et al., 2019), decision-making and control over resources (Mezgebo et al., 2017), and market competitiveness (Saviano et al., 2017). Other studies also indicated how strategy (business and marketing) could play a role in enhancing the performance of women enterprises (Hodges et al., 2015) but we argue that such an achievement is likely to be influenced by location, sector and entrepreneurial orientation of the women entrepreneurs. Thus, we can state that the findings from the above studies were inconclusive on the relationship between resources and women enterprise performance. For instance, despite the taken-for-granted assumption by some scholars and development practitioners that resource access or mainstreaming gender empowers women and enhances their decision-making power and control over resources, convincing empirical evidence is yet to emerge. Sesan et al., (2019), for instance, argue that women's market participation is not a sufficient condition for their economic empowerment; resource access and utilisation are impacted by the household and family context where husbands have a final say in decision-making. It was thus expected that several studies under our review to report gendered differentiated outcomes (Agyire-Tettey et al., 2018; Bardasi et al., 2011; Olowu et al., 2017; Rijkers et al., 2010; Rijkers & Costa, 2012; Sesan et al., 2019).

Conclusions and Issues for Further Research

This chapter sought to examine critically the literature and empirical findings on the African women entrepreneurs' access to resources by conducting the systematic literature review. The systematic literature review and the thematic analysis of the published 40 articles within a period of 30 years (1990–2020) provided vital evidence on focus, methods, theoretical underpinnings, findings and their implications. Four overarching conclusions are drawn from careful examination that, overall, suggest, studies on the women's access to resources have been a very recent phenomenon, slowly evolving, theoretically fragmented and lacking cumulative knowledge development. Methodically, quantitative approaches that sought cause–effect and gender difference explanations were prevalent with limited qualitative approaches that did not help the nuanced understanding of women entrepreneurs' access to resources. The four conclusions are summarised as follows:

First, African women entrepreneurs' access to resources has received an extremely limited attention by scholars and has been a recent phenomenon and focused on restricted corners of Africa. No studies were found prior to 2010, with sharp increases in the years 2017 and 2018; South Africa, Ethiopia, Uganda and Ghana accounted for 68% of the all studies undertaken, only the remaining 13 papers covered the rest of Africa regions and the other ten countries within this continent.

Second, half of the studies conducted were devoid of theoretical underpinning only being motivated by description and prescription. Of the remaining 20 papers, four papers were based on feminist theories, four papers used human capital theory and two papers used the resource-based view as their theoretical bases. Of the other nine studies reviewed each was based on a single theory/model, ranging from stakeholder theory to double-hurdle model. Because of such fragmentation and underdevelopment in the use of theoretical perspectives, the field of women enterprising resources lacked cumulative knowledge and is under-theorised.

Third, the dominance of quantitative studies and the focus on description of the phenomenon of women enterprising resources suggest that the reviewed studies were more interested in identifying factors that enable and/or constrain women's access to resources for enterprising opportunities and the motivations for mainstreaming women entrepreneurship (Jennings & Brush, 2013) for purpose of social and economic development and household well-being. Such interest and focus, in turn, led not only to narrow understanding and theoretical underdevelopment but also to 'focus on assumed, innate sex differences that inevitably reproduce the "othering" of women' (Henry et al., 2016, 235).

Fourth, the nuanced understanding of the issues related to women enterprising can be achieved by integrating the process and practices associated with *resource potential, resource access, resource utilisation and enterprise performance* within an interdependent chain of actions and interactions. The core argument here is the availability of resources (financial, human, relational, locational and physical) in each context is not a sufficient enabler of women entrepreneurship without their ability to access and use them with strategic foresight and for empowerment. This conclusion, in turn, implies WE is subject to multifaceted and multi-layered influences (Brush et al., 2009), and hence the focus on mainstreaming women entrepreneurship does not result in intended outcomes (cf, Datta & Gailey, 2012). A variety of perspectives and approaches (in theories and research methods) that help a holistic understanding of women entrepreneurs' access to resources should be considered in order to further scholarly knowledge and inform policy and practice.

The above four conclusions are also the main contributions of this chapter. Women entrepreneurship in Africa has rarely received well-thought-out rigorous research underpinned by theories and appropriate research methodologies, and hence can provide golden opportunities for scholars to question the taken-for-granted assumptions on this area.

Issues for Further Research

Developing and furthering a holistic understanding of women entrepreneurs' access to resources in Africa requires multifaceted perspectives and a variety of research methods to study under-explored issues. We conclude, thus, this chapter by posing the following research questions to guide future research on women enterprising resources.

1. What are the lived experiences of African women entrepreneurs' access and use of entrepreneurial resources?
2. Why do the effects of use of specific resources by women entrepreneurs vary across the context?
3. To what extent do the mainstreaming of women entrepreneurship initiatives in Africa enable women empowerment? What lessons could be learnt from such gender mainstreaming approaches?
4. What theoretical perspectives and research methodologies are more appropriate to studying the lived experience of women entrepreneurs in Africa and why?
5. How do we map the kinds of resources required to the stages of women enterprises (start-up, operation and growth)?
6. How and to what extent the advance in mobile and information technology affects the ways in which women entrepreneurs' access and use resources? Does mobile and information technology play a transformative role?

7. How can information asymmetry be addressed to facilitate African women's access to resources?

References

Abubakar, H. A. (2015). Entrepreneurship development and financial literacy in Africa. *World Journal of Entrepreneurship, Management and Sustainable Development, 11*(4), 281–294.

Acheampong, G. (2018). Microfinance, gender and entrepreneurial behaviour of families in Ghana. *Journal of Family Business Management, 8*(1), 38–57.

Adom, K. (2015). Recognizing the contribution of female entrepreneurs in economic development in sub-Saharan Africa: Some evidence from Ghana. *Journal of Developmental Entrepreneurship, 20*(01), 1550003.

Adom, K., & Asare-Yeboa, I. T. (2016). An evaluation of human capital theory and female entrepreneurship in sub-Sahara Africa. *International Journal of Gender and Entrepreneurship, 8*(4), 402–423.

Agyire-Tettey, F., Ackah, C. G., & Asuman, D. (2018). Gender and returns to entrepreneurship in Africa. *International Journal of Social Economics, 45*(12), 1609–1630.

Ahmed, Y. A., & Kar, B. (2019). Gender differences of entrepreneurial challenges in Ethiopia. *Academy of Entrepreneurship Journal, 25*(2), 1–6.

Ajumobi, D. O., & Kyobe, M. (2017). Alignment of human competencies with mobile phone technology and business strategies by women-LED SMEs in South Africa. *The Electronic Journal of Information Systems in Developing Countries, 80*(1), 1–25.

Aterido, R., Beck, T., & Iacovone, L. (2013). Access to finance in Sub-Saharan Africa: Is there a gender gap? *World Development, 47*, 102–120.

Aterido, R., & Hallward-Driemeier, M. (2011). Whose business is it anyway? *Small Business Economics, 37*(4), 443.

Bambio, Y., & Agha, S. B. (2018). Land tenure security and investment: Does strength of land right really matter in rural Burkina Faso? *World Development, 111*, 130–147.

Bardasi, E., Sabarwal, S. & Terrell, K. (2011). How do female entrepreneurs perform? Evidence from three developing regions. *Small Business Economics, 37*, 417.

Bates, T., Jackson, W. E., & Johnson, J. H. (2007). Introduction: Advancing research on minority entrepreneurship. *Annals of the American Academy of Political and Social Science, 613*, 10–17.

Brixiová, Z., Kangoye, T., & Tregenna, F. (2020a). Enterprising women in Southern Africa: When does land ownership matter? *Journal of Family and Economic Issues, 41*(1), 37–51.

Brixiová, Z., Kangoye, T., & Said, M. (2020b). Training, human capital, and gender gaps in entrepreneurial performance. *Economic Modelling, 85*, 367–380.

Brush, C. G., de Bruin, A., & Welter, F. (2009). A gender-aware framework for women's entrepreneurship. *International Journal of Gender and Entrepreneurship, 1*(1), 8–24.

Byrne, J., Fattoum, S., & Garcia, C. D. (2019). Role models and women entrepreneurs: Entrepreneurial superwoman has her say. *Journal of Small Business Management, 57*(1), 154–184.

Carter, S., Mwaura, S., Ram, M., Trehan, K., & Jones, T. (2015). Barriers to ethnic minority and women's enterprise: Existing evidence, policy tensions and unsettled questions. *International Small Business Journal, 33*(1), 49–69.

Costa, R., & Rijkers, B. (2012). Gender and rural non-farm entrepreneurship. *World Development, 14*(12), 2411–2426.

Datta, P. B., & Gailey, R. (2012). Empowering women through social entrepreneurship: Case study of a women's co-operative in India. *Entrepreneurship Theory and Practice, 36*(3), 569–587.

de Groot, J., Mohlakoana, N., Knox, A., & Bressers, H. (2017). Fuelling women's empowerment? An exploration of the linkages between gender, entrepreneurship, and access to energy in the informal food sector. *Energy Research & Social Science, 28*, 86–97.

Dedehouanou, S. F. A., & Araar, A. (2020). Gender, entrepreneurship and food security in Niger. *Review of Development Economics, 24*(3), 815–830.

Fiala, N. (2018). Returns to microcredit, cash grants and training for male and female microentrepreneurs in Uganda. *World Development, 105*, 189–200.

Gebrehiwot, M., Elbakidze, M., & Lidestav, G. (2018). Gender relations in changing agroforestry home gardens in rural Ethiopia. *Journal of Rural Studies, 61*, 197–205.

Gottlieb, J. (2016). Why might information exacerbate the gender gap in civic participation? Evidence from Mali. *World Development, 86*, 95–110.

Gray, L., Boyle, A., Francks, E., & Yu, V. (2019). The power of small-scale solar: Gender, energy poverty, and entrepreneurship in Tanzania. *Development in Practice, 29*(1), 26–39.

Henry, C., Foss, L., & Ahl, H. (2016). Gender and entrepreneurship research: A review of methodological approaches. *International Small Business Journal, 34*(3), 217–241.

Hodges, N., Watchravesringkan, K., Yurchisin, J., Karpova, E., Marcketti, S., Hegland, J., Yan, R.-N., & Childs, M. (2015). Women and apparel entrepreneurship. *International Journal of Gender and Entrepreneurship, 7*(2), 191–213.

Jennings, J. E., & Brush, C. G. (2013). Research on women entrepreneurs: Challenges to (and from) the broader entrepreneurship literature? *The Academy of Management Annals, 7*(1), 663–715.

Kengne, B. D. S. (2016). Mixed-gender ownership and financial performance of SMEs in South Africa. *International Journal of Gender and Entrepreneurship, 8*(2), 117–136.

Klyver, K., & Schenkel, M. T. (2013). From resource access to use: Exploring the impact of resource combinations on nascent entrepreneurship. *Journal of Small Business Management, 51*(4), 539–556.

Meier zu Selhausen, F. . (2016). What determines women's participation in collective action? Evidence from a western Ugandan coffee cooperative. *Feminist Economics, 22*(1), 130–157.

Mezgebo, G. K., Ymesel, T., & Tegegne, G. (2017). Do micro and small business enterprises economically empower women in developing countries? Evidence from Mekelle city, Tigray, Ethiopia. *Journal of Organisational Change Management, 30*(5), 767–778.

Mohlakoana, N., de Groot, J., Knox, A., & Bressers, H. (2019). Determinants of energy use in the informal food sector. *Development Southern Africa, 36*(4), 476–490.

Nyakudya, F. W., Simba, A., & Herrington, M. (2018). Entrepreneurship, gender gap and developing economies: The case of post-apartheid South Africa. *Journal of Small Business & Entrepreneurship, 30*(4), 293–324.

Okeke-Uzodike, O. E., Okeke-Uzodike, U., & Ndinda, C. (2018). Women entrepreneurship in Kwazulu-Natal: A critical review of government intervention policies and pograms. *Journal of International Women's Studies, 19*(5), 147–164.

Olowu, A., Ijeoma, E., & Vanroose, A. (2017). Entrepreneurship performance and gender differences in West Africa: Examining the nexus at country level. *Gender and Behaviour, 15*(3), 9786–9807.

Podsakoff, P. M., MacKenzie, S. B., Bachrach, D. G., & Podsakoff, N. P. (2005). The influence of management journals in the 1980s and 1990s. *Strategic Management Journal, 26*(5), 473–488.

Pueyo, A., Bawakyillenuo, S., & Carreras, M. (2020). Energy use and enterprise performance in Ghana: How does gender matter? *The European Journal of Development Research, 32*, 1249–1287.

Ratten, V. (2020). African entrepreneurship. *Small Enterprise Research, 27*(2), 103–109.

Rawhouser*, H., Villanueva, J., & Newbert, S. L. . (2017). Strategies and tools for entrepreneurial resource access: A cross-disciplinary review and typology. *International Journal of Management Reviews, 19*(4), 473–491.

Rijkers, B., Söderbom, M., & Loening, J. L. (2010). A rural–urban comparison of manufacturing enterprise performance in Ethiopia. *World Development, 38*(9), 1278–1296.

Saviano, M., Nenci, L., & Caputo, F. (2017). The financial gap for women in the MENA region: A systemic perspective. *Gender in Management: An International Journal, 32*(3), 203–217.

Sequeira, J. M., Gibbs, S. R., & Juma, N. A. (2016). Factors contributing to women's venture success in developing countries: An exploratory analysis. *Journal of Developmental Entrepreneurship, 21*(01), 1650001.

Sesan, T., Clifford, M., Jewitt, S., & Ray, C. (2019). "We learnt that being together would give us a voice": Gender perspectives on the East African improved-cookstove value chain. *Feminist Economics, 25*(4), 240–266.

Solano, G., & Rooks, G. (2018). Social capital of entrepreneurs in a developing country: The effect of gender on access to and requests for resources. *Social Networks, 54*, 279–290.

Sutton, R. I., & Staw, B. M. (1995). What theory is not. *Administrative Science Quarterly*, 371–384.

Teixeira, A. A., & Sharifu, H. A. (2017). Female entrepreneurship and access to bank loans in Tanzania: A double-hurdle model approach. *Journal of Developmental Entrepreneurship, 22*(03), 1750019.

Tranfield, D., Denyer, D., & Smart, P. (2003). Towards a methodology for developing evidence-informed management knowledge by means of systematic review. *British Journal of Management, 14*(3), 207–222.

Uzunidis, D., Boutillier, S., & Laperche, B. (2014). The entrepreneur's 'resource potential' and the organic square of entrepreneurship: Definition and application to the French case. *Journal of Innovation and Entrepreneurship, 3*(1), 1.

Washington, M. L., & Chapman, Z. (2014). Impact of microfinance on entrepreneurial activity in emerging economies: Panel data from Argentina, Brazil, Colombia & South Africa. *International Journal of Entrepreneurship, 18*(1), 59–67.

Whetten, D. A. (1989). What constitutes a theoretical contribution? *Academy of Management Review, 14*(4), 490–495.

Witbooi, M., & Ukpere, W. (2011). Indigenous female entrepreneurship: Analytical study on access to finance for women entrepreneurs in South Africa. *African Journal of Business Management, 5*(14), 5646–5657.

Wu, J., Li, Y., & Zhang, D. (2019). Identifying women's entrepreneurial barriers and empowering female entrepreneurship worldwide: A fuzzy-set QCA approach. *International Entrepreneurship and Management Journal, 15*(3), 905–928.

22

An Empirical Insight into the Factors Affecting the Oscillation of Women Between Self- and Paid Employment in South Africa

Bridget Irene, Promise Opute Abdullah, and William K. Murithi

Introduction

Before participating in entrepreneurial activities, entrepreneurs oftentimes work for other companies and those who become entrepreneurs sometimes return to paid employment. Therefore, research on how and why people transition between jobs and entrepreneurship throughout their careers is needed (Burton et al., 2016). By exploring career perspectives, researchers can situate entrepreneurship within a collection of alternatives to jobs that include employment and unemployment in organisations (Sørensen & Sharkey, 2014). Employees are more likely to enter entrepreneurship, for example, when opportunities to advance with their employer are limited or otherwise unattractive or when there is a conflict in terms of personal responsibilities.

Career mobility research shows that people assess entrepreneurial career choices based not only on their current jobs but also positions with other

---

B. Irene (✉)
Coventry University, Coventry, UK
e-mail: bridget.irene@coventry.ac.uk

P. O. Abdullah
GPROM Academic and Management Solutions, Paderborn, Germany

W. K. Murithi
Centre for Enterprise and Innovation, De Montfort University, Leicester, UK
e-mail: william.murithi@dmu.ac.uk

employers (Rider & Tan, 2015), and men and women have divergent motivations and intentions for new venture (Irene, 2018) creation. Nowadays, careers usually span several organisations, contrary to the internal labour market era (Cappelli, 2000). Thus, a career perspective on entrepreneurship identifies three career choices people face throughout their careers: (1) engage in entrepreneurship, (2) continue to work with current employer or (3) change employers. This study explores the mobility perspective to understand women's motivation for entrepreneurship and how the appeal of entrepreneurship evolves—relative to the three alternatives—as they accumulate work experience. In contrast to these alternatives, we apply this versatility viewpoint to understand how entrepreneurship's appeal grows as one accumulates work experience, thereby highlighting some methodological problems and promising directions for future study.

There is also a need to understand entrepreneurial motivation among men and women, not only through an economic lens but also about the psychological impact on entrepreneurs. While motivational theories help us to understand the factors that influence distinctive employment options between men and women, it is important to consider the psychological constructs of an individual's choices that improve their abilities to meet individual goals (Fosić et al., 2017). Earlier exploratory studies revealed significant differences by gender in venture creation (Schwartz, 2006). Accordingly, Carsrud and Brannback (2011) suggested that personality traits explain entrepreneurial behaviour to a certain degree but failed to explain the positive correlation in motivation between entrepreneurs and people in paid employment i.e. they are both "need" driven; these needs are varied and can be gender-disaggregated. Specific behaviours, such as deciding to engage in entrepreneurial activities, are primarily influenced by motivation. Motivation is a broad term for describing all internal factors combining intellectual and physical energy, initiating and organizing individual activities, directing and channelling individual behaviour (Bahtijarević-Šiber, 1999 cited in Fosić et al., 2017). Therefore, motivational factors are the driving force that propels women entrepreneurs to venture into entrepreneurship. Motivational factors are also a means by which women entrepreneurs reconcile conflicting needs or emphasize one need over the other so that needs are prioritised (Weihrich & Koontz, 1994 cited in Fosić et al., 2017).

Little has been done to understand why women begin their economic activities in the labour market and then opt-out to venture into entrepreneurship and subsequently opt back into the labour market. We posit that this hopping back and forth has huge implications for business performance as well as the emotional well-being of women. Based on the non-economic, socio-cultural and gendered factors, this study seeks to understand women's entrepreneurial motivation as well as the factors that influence their oscillation between paid employment and entrepreneurship in the context of South Africa. Most studies on women entrepreneurial motivations have adopted the "pull" versus "push" approach to understanding women's choices for entrepreneurial engagement. By exploring the career mobility perspectives juxtaposed with a motivational theory approach, this paper seeks to understand how women's career choices evolve. To this end, this research aims to answer the following question: What are the factors that influence women entrepreneurs' oscillation between self- and paid employment?

Theoretical Backdrop

There has been a major shift in the discourse on entrepreneurial motivation from a static, content-oriented theory[1] approach to a more dynamic, process-oriented theory[2] approach (Su et al., 2020). Various attempts have been made by scholars to classify triggers of entrepreneurial engagement from two broad perspectives: economic and non-economic motivations. To this end, Allan et al. (2016) advocates for the division of entrepreneurial motivation theory into two schools, one based on economics and the other rooted in psychology; however, these two schools have opposing views. The classical economic theory is premised on the view that the goal of entrepreneurial behaviour is to maximise wealth, and the pursuit of economic returns is at the core of entrepreneurial behaviour (Kuratko et al., 1997 and Baumol 1990). In particular, Douglas and Shepherd (2000) suggests that the potential of high economic returns will "pull" people to start a business, and the lack of adequate economic returns (such as income solidification) can also "force" people to start a business. Accordingly, Hessels et al. (2008) argue that the development of entrepreneurial motivation depends to a large extent on the entrepreneur's desire for wealth increase. Praag and Cramer (2001) also found that entrepreneurial motivation develops if the anticipated return on entrepreneurial activities exceeds the employment wage or salary. Still, entrepreneurship is a complex and dynamic practice, and this view does not

---

[1] Content theory focuses on the needs that motivate people and cause then to sustain stop certain behaviours. Content theories imply that individuals are unique and have unique sources of motivation. It is premised on the fact that the absence of motivational factors creates tension that can trigger negative behavioural performance.

[2] Explore how behaviour is caused, sustained or stopped by the motivational factors. There are four predominant process theories that include reinforcement, expectancy, equity and goal setting; and that individual choices are based on preferences, reward factors and sense of accomplishment.

explain some entrepreneurial process phenomena. For instance, why do individuals choose entrepreneurship as a career option despite the high risk and lack of guarantee of economic returns? Secondly, evidence from numerous researches shows that in the early phase of entrepreneurship some businesses make no profit or even sustain losses. Why then are there still individuals wanting to start a business? This contradicts the notion that wealth creation is the fundamental reason for the cultivation of entrepreneurial behaviours.

Women's Entrepreneurial Motivation

The study of Patrick and Stephens (2016) found that women's motivation for engaging in entrepreneurship differs significantly from their male counterparts. Relatively speaking, autonomy/flexibility and social factors rank high for women than men (Patrick & Stephen, 2016). However, the findings are more conflicting in terms of business growth ambitions. The study of Bosma et al. (2009) found that women were more likely to be necessity entrepreneurs in a range of countries including South Africa. Family needs were identified as the major driver for women's entrepreneurial activities. In particular, the flexibility to control working hours that is associated with business ownership was touted as a major motivation for women entrepreneurs. The study of Jayawarna et al. (2011), for instance, showed that among young mothers, flexibility and autonomy ranked high in their choice of entrepreneurship. Reynolds and Curtin (2008) also found from their study that women placed more emphasis on flexibility and autonomy than achievement and profit/wealth creation when deciding to engage in entrepreneurship. In the same vein, Hirschi and Fischer (2013) concluded from their study of German university students that women perceived entrepreneurship as a way of doing good rather than as a means of self-fulfilment.

Wealth creation alone is not the justification for women's entrepreneurial drive and actions of women (Jayawarna et al., 2011). As stated earlier, Rindova et al. (2009) suggest that the belief that entrepreneurial motivation emanates from self-esteem and personal achievement may be an influencing factor in the entrepreneur's action and decision-making. Several other factors also influence entrepreneurial motivation, such as individual circumstances and the socio-economic environment, i.e. unemployment, prior work experience, resource availability and government policies. Research indicates, however, that these variables have little influence on the entrepreneurial motivation of women. This is in line with the suggestions of Deci and Ryan (2010) that altruism and pro-social considerations motivate individuals (including women) towards opportunity identification to solve social problems and improve society. The need for autonomy and other intrinsic factors such as self-efficacy and values has been found to influence the entrepreneurial motivation of women (Irene, 2016).

Most researchers have interpreted entrepreneurial motivation with economic rationality, based on conventional entrepreneurial motivation studies (Su et al., 2020); however, this does not explain why women entrepreneurs engage in new venture creation given the high uncertainty and the fact that profits are neither specified nor guaranteed. On the other hand, non-economic factors provide a plausible explanation for women's entrepreneurial motivation to a certain extent and help to understand the choice of entrepreneurship over the safety that paid employment offers (Hoyte et al., 2019). However, the role of women's subjective entrepreneurial experience and the duration, as well as the intensity of their motivation (especially positive emotions) in the process of business ownership, remains unclear. This could be because as stated earlier, existing research on entrepreneurial motivation tends to be more static than dynamic.

The results from Hughes's (2006) study identified three large categories of business owners based on their motivation for engaging in entrepreneurial activities: (a) classic; (b) forced and (c) work–family. "Classic" women entrepreneurs are those who, for much of the same "classical" motives as men, are driven to become entrepreneurs. They also cite a lack of challenges (in present employment), self-realization, financial independence and need to be their bosses as entrepreneurial motivation. "Forced" women entrepreneurs are those who are pushed into entrepreneurship, primarily because of unemployment, retrenchment, "glass ceiling" and lack of job opportunities (Hughes, 2006; Murray & Syed, 2010). The enticement of the flexibility and prospects of achieving work–life balance and the value of the family-based business is their motivation for entrepreneurship (Loscocco & Bird, 2012).

Early exploratory studies such as Meyer (2009), Meyer and Landsberg (2015) and Irene (2018) have shown that often women embark on their entrepreneurial journeys in response to the demands of parenthood and due to spouse/partner responsibilities (Hilbrecht, 2016). Based on the evidence shown in the literature, this paper explores the relationship between women's entrepreneurial motivation in terms of their oscillation between self-employment and paid employment through the theoretical lens of Expectancy Theory and work–life balance theory.

Expectancy Theory

The Expectancy Theory, which is also known as Rational Intention Theory or Theory of Motivation, is utilised in this study because rational prioritisation is known to have an impact on individual intentions in terms of motivation-decision-action process (Barba-Sánchez & Atienza-Sahuquillo, 2017). The proponents of this theory infer that individuals' actions are based on anticipations rather than deprivations as indicated in the traditional theory that, naturally, individuals are inclined towards meeting their basic needs (Locke & Baum, 2014). According to Lawler and Suttle (1973) as cited in Barba-Sánchez and Atienza-Sahuquillo, 2017), people are driven or motivated to act in certain ways because they anticipate the outcomes or result of their actions. Essentially, the motive for choosing actions is dictated by the desirability of the outcome. At the heart of the theory, however, is the cognitive mechanism of how a person views the various motivating factors, and this occurs before the final decision is made. Outcomes, however, are not the only determining factor in the decision-making process (Hirschi & Fischer, 2013). Expectancy Theory is concerned with the cognitive processes involved in an individual's decision-making. Therefore, in each situation, people combine their needs with their values/beliefs, and expectations or perceptions of the probabilities of success.

Therefore, Vroom (1964) describes motivation as a function of a person's beliefs and expectations that certain actions would lead to certain expected behaviours, the instrumentality of the behaviours in achieving the results and the desirability of this outcome for the person, known as valence. Furthermore, the extension of the Expectancy Theory, suggested by Graen (1969), is based on the dissimilarity between first- and second-order outcomes. He defines first-order work as a set of behavioural expectations that are deemed appropriate for the person carrying out certain activities. The second order is known as work role outcome, and it is the product of the work on intrinsic and extrinsic rewards and punishments a person receives from playing a role. Although several studies have investigated the empirical application of Expectancy Theory in the entrepreneurship domain (e.g. Edelman et al., 2010; Gatewood et al., 2002), not all have demonstrated Vroom's (1964) proposed interrelationships. They mostly affirm the basic assumptions in different real-life circumstances in the industry field (Renko et al., 2012). Also, Locke and Baum (2014) argued that Expectancy Theory offers a brilliant framework for understanding why and how some people choose to engage in entrepreneurial activities rather than being employed in a regular paying job. According to Hsu et al. (2016), "expectancy theory would predict that an individual will be motivated to invest the effort necessary to start a business if he/she believes that high input of effort will make it feasible for him/her to attain desirable goals through business ownership (e.g. make more money, be independent, gain high social status, etc.)" (p. 123). Similarly, researchers like Gatewood et al. (2002) and Manolova et al. (2007) suggest that the process of new venture creation is largely based on the effort-performance-outcome model, essentially suggesting that entrepreneurial motivation is predicated on three elements: expectancy, instrumentality and valence. Holland (2011) concluded from his study of entrepreneurial motivation that entrepreneurs persevere with their businesses "when the outcome valences are high" (p. 347). Thus, it can be concluded that a person's motivation for remaining self-employed is dependent on the subjective probability of achieving these expectations and the attractiveness of self-employment. Accordingly, Millán et al. (2012) concluded from his examination of the transition from self-employment to paid employment that "a rational individual will quit self-employment to enter paid employment if the expected utility from self-employment is smaller than the expected utility from a wage employment offer received" (p. 85).

Drawing on the Expectation Theory, this study investigates South African women's entrepreneurial motivations in line with their expectations with a view of rationalising the decision to quit self-employment, re-enter the paid employment, then, quit paid employment and re-enter self-employment.

Work–Life Balance Theory

Several motivational theories, including content and process theories, have been advanced from past researches on the cross relationships between work and family life (Su, 2020). While there are overlaps between the theories, they are different enough to warrant individual attention. Some theories are, however, more widely accepted than others even though there is empirical evidence to support each of the theories (Rincy & Panchanatham, 2014). According to Pradhan (2016), "work" and "family" were treated as distinct segments before the 1970s, and the interdependence of both segments was only highlighted by Kanter (1977) by demonstrating how aspects of work affect family life and vice versa. About the same time, Pleck (1977) examined work–family roles as a collective that included male and female work roles as well as their family roles; the conclusion from the study was that for women, and there is a spill-over role from the family role into work role while for men, the spill-over is from work role into the family role. This spill-over theory was further strengthened by the 1980 study of Staines which concluded that the consequences of the spill-over from one segment of life to another can be both positive and negative. Thus, he advanced a new "compensation theory" suggesting that in compensating for the deficit in one aspect of life, a person may make the added investment into the other aspect. A new direction for the research on work–family relations was put forth by Greenhaus and Beutell (1985) in the work–life conflict theory. The work–life conflict theory suggests that an individual has different roles to perform with family and work placing a demand on the time, focus and commitment required to perform these roles. Roles' behaviours in family and work interfering with each other, thereby causing tension between family and work. Byrne (2005) also proposed a simplified way of understanding work–life balance by using the ancient balanced wheel linking each of the eight sections of the wheel to vital sections of life: work, family, finance, hobbies, spiritual, social and health. According to Byrne, for individuals, each of these sections are equally important, therefore, finding a balance between them is essential. However, it must be noted that for individuals, the weight of these sections may vary depending on the time and season of their lives. Therefore, regardless of this limitation, the balanced wheel of life offers a simplified way to understand work–life balance concept as it encompasses different segments of life.

As stated earlier, a person's life is multi-segmented, with some segments requiring only a minimal amount of time, energy and effort and other segments consuming the most time, energy and effort. For men and women, their professional roles are different and not necessarily gendered but rather based on qualification, experience and designation (Naithani, 2010). On the contrary, there are some traditionally and socially defined roles that are gendered in each of the eight segments of life. Thus, while men may participate in housework especially in homes where both couples are working, a significant portion of the household work (including childcare) remains in the domain of women's responsibility. While this gendered role distribution at the family level creates a new challenge of work–life balance for men and women, there remain some non-gendered roles in the other.

Although work and life are in binary domains (i.e. work domain and home/life domain), they are not properly segmented making integration a regular feature. For women, segmenting their professional and childcare duties fully is challenging given the social and traditional expectations for their participation in both domains. The same may be said of a single father who has no childcare facilities and is similarly involved in work as well as family responsibilities. In addition to work and family life being segmented at certain times, they are also used to compensate each other as the situation may demand. Thus, discontentment in one aspect can increase engagement in other segments where higher satisfaction can be derived. Consequently, a situation arises where work and family life become interdependent and a spill-over from one segment to another (positive or negative) becomes inevitable. For example, the physical and mental stress that a person undergoes due to pressurised work environments will affect the health segments of personal life regardless of gender. This is a classic case of negative spill-over. Conversely, the social and finance segments can be positively impacted by promotion or increment.

In the case of women, given their socially ascribed roles that make them primary caregivers, high segmentation between work and family life can ensure a better work–life balance. However, the competitive nature of today's world continuously demands more work time, making a high level of segmentation untenable, given the social and traditional expectations of women. In certain cases, women can keep family life segmented from work life (family does not impinge on work time, vigour and effort) or keep work life segmented from family life (work that does not impinge on family life, energy and effort). When the integration of work life and family life is high, the resultant imbalance creates high levels of work–life conflicts. Thus, while women are attempting to achieve a balance between the continuum of segmentation and integration of work and life, they inadvertently compensate for the loss in one segment with performance or results from another. In extreme cases, they could face losses in all segment as a consequence of their inability to manage both segments effectively. As the processes of segmentation, integration and compensation continue (to varying degrees), work and life will produce outcomes, which can be both positive and negative. These negative and positive outcomes have a spill-over effect on other segments thus leaving the work–life balance at a stage where the total of influential factors are either positive or negative.

The causal relationship between the theories of entrepreneurial motivation, expectancy/rational intention and work–life balance is depicted in Fig. 22.1. Work–life balance remains the overarching factor in the decision to engage in entrepreneurial activities for women (and some men alike) and informs the expectancy and rational intention of the women entrepreneurs. Entrepreneurial motivation is increased with the expectation of intrinsic and extrinsic rewards (such as work–life balance).

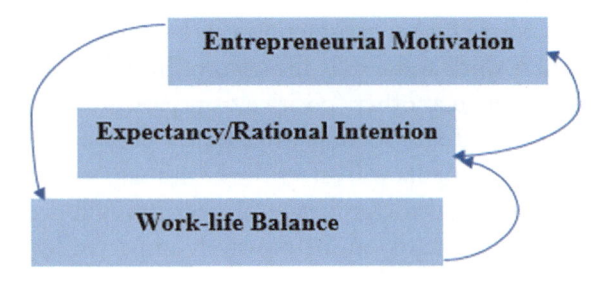

Fig. 22.1 Theoretical framework

Research Methodology

Qualitative phenomenology has been selected as the approach for this study as it enables the researchers to gain a deeper understanding of the lived experiences of the participants (Goulding, 2005). While several researchers have studied South African women entrepreneurs, the challenges, the barriers they face, their motivation and business complexities, little is known about the phenomenon of oscillation of women between entrepreneurship and paid employment. Therefore, to further explore this phenomenon, the study must employ appropriate methods of qualitative inquiry (Creswell et al., 2007). This methodological approach has also been utilised in various studies on work–life balance (Lewis & Humbert, 2010; Neubauer et al., 2019). Therefore, taking into consideration the fact that there is a strong positive correlation between work–life balance and oscillation, it makes theoretical sense to adopt the same methodology for this research.

Sampling Frame

The sample for this research was drawn from a population of South Africa businesswomen using stratified purposeful sampling. According to Patton (2001), this can be described as a sample within samples and purposive samples can be stratified or nested by selecting specific units or cases that vary according to key dimensions. This sampling approach can lend credibility to a research study (Patton, 1990), and it allows the researchers to get maximum variations in the data as well as identify cases of interest from the participants. The data was collected in two phases: (a) 50 women entrepreneurs were selected to participate in face to face interviews utilizing semi-structured questions; (b) 78 women entrepreneurs participated in 10 focus group discussions of between 6–8 participants per group. The criteria for inclusion included: (a) women who founded their own business; (b) businesses 2 years old or more; (c) women who had founded multiple businesses at different stages (serial entrepreneurs); (d) women who had engaged in paid employment between businesses and after engaging in entrepreneurship; (e) women with family responsibilities (all the respondents reported having children including single-parenthood) (Table 22.1).

Data Analysis

In choosing a data analysis method, the theoretical context of the study was taken into consideration. Given the objectives of the study, a narrative, interpretivist approach was chosen to analyse the qualitative data because according to Braun and Clarke (2006), this form of data analysis tends to provide a more detailed description of the overall data; it organises and describes data sets in rich detail. Also, coming from the interpretivist paradigm of this research framework, narrative analysis cannot be separated from "discourse analysis" or "thematic discourse analysis," which allows for broader assumptions, structures/meanings to be theorised behind what is expressed in the data (Braun & Clarke, 2006, p. 8). From an interpretivist perspective, an individual's experiences are socially produced and reproduced (Chowdhury, 2014). Therefore, data analysis within the interpretivist framework focuses on the individual's motivation or the individual's psychology rather than focusing solely on the socio-cultural and structural conditions that allow the individual accounts that are provided. The main focus of this qualitative data analysis was to extract behaviours and events that reflect entrepreneurial motivation among women entrepreneurs in South Africa. Thus, the day-to-day experience of management (i.e. integration, separation, compensation, necessity, opportunity, etc.) was extracted and explored. This was deemed necessary so that we can understand women's oscillation between entrepreneurship and paid employment. These behaviours may be the same as those already known or different (new).

The data was collected via face-to-face interviews and focus group discussions. The data was transcribed and open-coded using Maxqda software. Open coding is a process of word-by-word analysis of samples, the abstraction and recombination of data into concepts and categories, the purpose of which is to analyse phenomena and problems and to converge them. The coding system was developed based on the models of motivation and work–life balance and rational intention and used to classify the behaviours/events and was done with the research questions in mind (Braun & Clarke, 2006).

The data was analysed using the interpretative phenomenological analysis (IPA) approach proposed by Smith (2004). This approach involves a detailed

Table 22.1 Description of Sample

No. of respondents	Percentage (%)		Type of businesses	Percentage (N)
Age of respondents				
20–30	17	13.28	Renewable energy	2
31–40	37	28.90	Psychologist/counselling	2
41–50	56	42.75	Oil and Gas	2
Above 50	18	14.07	NGO	2
Marital status of respondents			Communication/PR	2
Single[a]	27	21.09	Transportation and logistics	5
Married	33	25.78	Medical services	2
Divorced	41	32.03	Legal services	5
Widowed	27	21.09	Insurance	5
Dependents			Business services/printing	8
Children	Yes		Travel and tourism	8
Elderly	Yes		Finance and investment	6
Extended family	Yes		Business consultancy services	6
			Art and entertainment	8
Years in Business (business experience)			Interior decoration	7
			Real estate	8
<2 years	18	14.06	Hotel and accommodation	5
2–5 years	43	33.59	Computer services/ITC	8
6–10 years	40	31.25	Construction and maintenance	5
>10 years	27	21.09	Manufacturing	5
Number of start-ups to date			Health and beauty	8
1	8	6.25	Wholesale and retail	5
2	41	32.03	Education and training	5
3	25	19.53	Restaurant and catering	9
4	35	27.34		
5	18	14.06		
The average age of each business				
<2 years	13	10.16		
2-5 years	48	37.5		
6–10 years	41	32.03		
>10 years	26	20.31		
Average years in paid employment experience (work experience)				
<2 years	31	24.22		
2-5 years	42	32.81		
5–10 years	30	23.44		
>10 years	18	14.06		

(continued)

Table 22.1 (continued)

No. of respondents	Percentage (%)	Type of businesses	Percentage (N)
The period between paid /self-employment (years)			
1 year	21	16.41	
2 years	42	31.81	
3 years	38	29.69	
4 years	16	12.5	
>5 years	1	0.78	

[a]Single moms with childcare responsibilities

examination of each participant's response and how their personal experience addresses the questions of oscillation between entrepreneurship and paid employment.

Findings and Discussions

As stated earlier, most studies on women entrepreneurial motivations have adopted the "pull" versus "push" approach to understanding women's choices for entrepreneurial engagement. This research, therefore, explores the career mobility perspectives juxtaposed with a motivational theory approach, to understand how women's career choices evolve. This research sought to answer the following question: ***What factors influence women entrepreneurs' oscillation between self- and paid employment?*** Given the purpose of the study, factors that influenced the oscillation of women between entrepreneurship and paid employment was the central focus, therefore, the average number of businesses per woman entrepreneur was highlighted in the interviews as well as the average number of years in paid employment at any given time was also discussed. The findings showed that the women who worked in paid jobs for the average 3–5 years were able to generate enough income to either start-up a new venture or stabilise the existing business. Also, given their work experience, they were able to return to paid employment while running their businesses side by side. The breakdown of the demographic profiles of the respondents is given in Table 22.1.

To better understand the variable, the responses from the interviews and focus group discussions were grouped into different themes relating to the research aims and objectives: (1) drivers of entrepreneurial motivation and (2) conceptualisation of oscillation. These themes are discussed in the following sections:

Drivers of Entrepreneurial Motivation of Women in SA

The participants in this research revealed several reasons behind their motivation to engage in entrepreneurial activities. The analysis of the factors reveals that the family-related needs such as work–life balance (53.9%) and flexibility (45.9%) ranked high on women's motivational factors (although interviewees identified multiple factors that motivated them to engage in entrepreneurial activities). Job stability and security also ranked high (44.3%). This is not surprising because, in South Africa, maternity leave is an unpaid leave with a maximum period of four months (one month before the baby is born and three months after the baby is born). Consequently, for women desiring extra time to spend with newborn babies or recovering from complicated childbirth, their jobs would be at risk. The need to achieve (38.5%); glass ceiling (33.1%); the desire to pursue own passion (31.3%); better working conditions (38.3%) and financial benefits (35.1%) were also high-ranking motivational factors for South African women entrepreneurs (see Fig. 22.2). The most highly rated factors, i.e. relating to work–life balance identified by almost all respondents are discussed below.

Our review of the literature on South African women entrepreneurs showed that most of them were driven by necessity (Meyer & Landsberg,

Drivers of Entrepreneurial Motivation

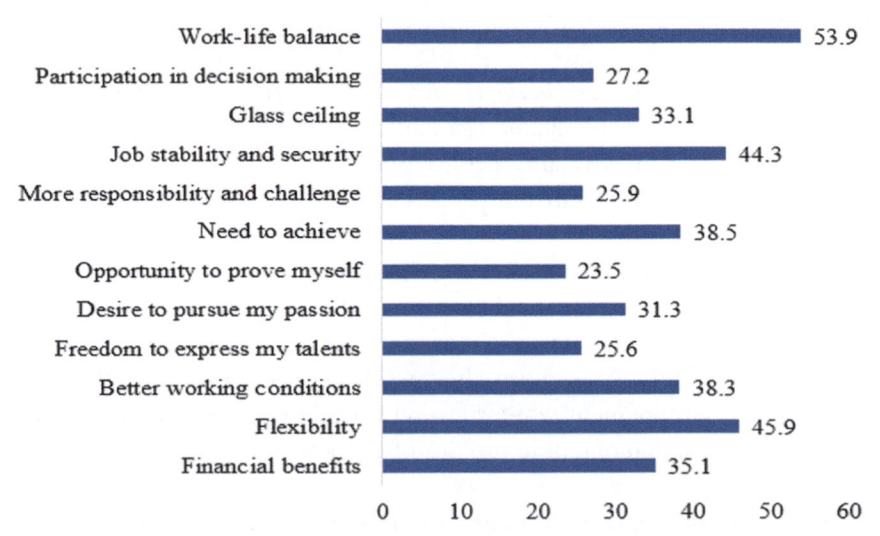

Factor	Value
Work-life balance	53.9
Participation in decision making	27.2
Glass ceiling	33.1
Job stability and security	44.3
More responsibility and challenge	25.9
Need to achieve	38.5
Opportunity to prove myself	23.5
Desire to pursue my passion	31.3
Freedom to express my talents	25.6
Better working conditions	38.3
Flexibility	45.9
Financial benefits	35.1

Fig. 22.2 Drivers of entrepreneurial motivation identified by the respondents (Figures represent the number of counts not participants) (*Notes* Each participant identified multiple factors that motivated them to engage in entrepreneurial activities)

2015). While these factors have economic undertones, the socio-cultural contexts cannot be overlooked. South Africa as with other African countries have patriarchal society and women's roles are predefined. Despite the efforts of the government to improve the life of previously disadvantaged individuals (especially women), women still lag in terms of education, job opportunities and entrepreneurship. Women of working age are thrown into fierce competition with men for the available employment opportunities and those unable to be gainfully employed resort to self-employment. Furthermore, this situation is exacerbated by the traditional view of women as primary homemakers putting the burden of maintaining stability and balance between work and family squarely on the women's shoulders. They are therefore pushed to the point where venturing into business out of necessity to meet their family needs becomes the only viable option (family needs and flexibility). Thus, it is their expectation or anticipation that the outcomes or result of their actions will be the flexibility to manage their time around family needs. As one of the participants explained:

> My reason for starting my own business was to have a work-life balance because I got pregnant. I had my second baby after 8 years and I was sure that this time around it will be more demanding handling 2 children under the age of 10. I needed the flexibility to be able to juggle this as well as earn an income to support the family. (Life coach)

The data thus shows that 76% of the participants who were with young families opted to give away the stability of employment to undertake the risk of venture creation because they desire the flexibility that self-employment offers to cope with family demands. While this does not indicate that business management is easier than paid employment in any way, being an entrepreneur allows them to manage their time and only take on tasks that do not interfere with family obligations. These are the following findings from previous researches. According to DeMartino and Barbato (2003) most women view entrepreneurship as a "flexible career choice" that enables them to manage work–life conflict. Most of the respondents (82%) also felt that being self-employed not only affords them the flexibility required to ensure work–life balance, it also enhances their sense of independence and boosts their confidence in dealing with a patriarchal society. This view is expressed by some participants:

> I had a "special needs" daughter so I felt that working outside the home would not give me the freedom and time required to care for her. I could not arrange

my hours in a job. So, with a shop, I had that freedom I could have somebody to look after the shop I could go out with my daughter for her doctor's appointments or spend time with family. This shop gives me a lot of time. It gives me confidence; this gives me freedom with money, freedom with time and interacting with people. Another thing is you learn a lot about life, about people, and about dealing with men. (Interior decorator)

Having my own business means I keep control of my own time. I can juggle my meetings and everything around me. I can set my appointments according to my availability. I can do things according to what my family demands from me and what my business needs are ... Sometimes, I need to go parent-teacher meeting at my son's school, and I have to go so I would take off for two or three hours. This is how I balance my life, and this is the privilege you have in your own business. (Contractor)

Family comes first. I don't close too late so that I will have a little time to cook and take care of the kids. If the work is too much for me, I get an extra hand. This is the main reason why I started my business- to be able to dedicate more time to my family. (Eatery owner)

I do my business when the kids are in school and spouse in office. A paid employment will not give me that flexibility. (Supermarket owner)

Economic factors also influenced women's entrepreneurial motivation (i.e. need for power). While the literature suggests that women were assigned domestic roles and men are considered as breadwinners, current shifts in the African socio-cultural contexts cannot be overlooked. Women are now working and earning a living like men which is seen as breaking away from their traditionally ascribed gender roles. In some South African homes, women are the actual breadwinners as could be seen from the demographic profile of the respondents in this research. While all the respondents had dependents (such as children and extended family dependents), most were either single parents, divorced or widowed. In the words of one respondent:

Of course, money was my biggest motivation because I had lots of needs and as you know without needs, nobody would do anything. I am a single parent with no support from my ex. When you are doing good and your business is growing then it's like an addiction. You would like to grow and feel proud of yourself and on top of all, you come out of financial difficulties. (Respondent)

Conceptualisation of Oscillation

The term oscillation is generally used to describe a periodic fluctuation between two things. Oscillation in its broadest sense can occur in anything from a person's decision-making process to tides and the pendulum of a clock. It is a simple back and forth motion over a central neutral point, created by changes in life circumstances (the context of this study). For this research, we have substituted the term "entrepreneurship" with "self-employment" and its relationship with gender. Evidence from existing literature suggests that greater autonomy is a major benefit for self-employed women, and they enjoy flexibility at work and have a higher level of participation in work and job satisfaction compared to employees in an organisation (Parasuraman & Simmers, 2001). According to Binder and Coad (2013), self-employed workers consistently report higher job satisfaction despite earning lower incomes.

Notwithstanding the above suppositions, it must be noted that self-employed workers experience higher levels of conflict concerning work–life balance and lower family satisfaction compared to employees in an organisation (Parasuraman & Simmers, 2001). According to Nguyen and Sawang (2016), conflict relating to work–life balance has a direct negative impact on mental health, work, family and life satisfaction. On the flip side, high business performance and job satisfaction can make entrepreneurs disregard other vital areas of life becoming engrossed in gratifying work to the exclusion of other important domains, thus resulting in a "spill-over" effect as stated earlier (Binder & Coad, 2013). As one participant explained:

> Us women, we need to know how to manage stress better and this is important because it's no use putting your family under unnecessary pressure because you are facing pressure in your business. The atmosphere in the home should not be affected and it will be if you start experiencing issues in the business. (Hairdresser)

The findings for this research are also in alignment with Douglas and Shepherd (2000) who suggested that people might "make the jump" for entrepreneurship or self-employment if they expect to achieve greater satisfaction. In the case of women entrepreneurs in South Africa, this satisfaction had to do with the family. As some of them put it:

> Being able to manage my husband and kids is the best achievement I could ever ask for, and becoming an entrepreneur is the only way I can accomplish that. (Wholesaler)

> My kind of business allows me to work mainly from home. It actually gives me time to be a homemaker it is not always easy, but because I have control over my time, I can always make sacrifices and adjustments. (Fashion designer)

> I do my business when the kids are in school and spouse in office. A paid employment will not give me that flexibility. (Supermarket owner)

The data from this qualitative study revealed that 89% of the participants were motivated to engage in entrepreneurial activities by the need to achieve work–life balance. For them, being in paid employment did not give them the flexibility they needed to achieve the quality of life they desired (work and family). The data also showed that "work–life balance" meant different things to different respondents depending on their demographic factors, i.e. family structure, nature of the business, marital status and the number of active years in business as well as dependents (children and other dependents from the extended family). Despite the differences between the respondents, the data also showed that self-employment is positively related to subjective well-being (psychological factors). For example, self-employed respondents who have employees report a higher level of life satisfaction compared to those without employees. One commonality, however, was the fact that all respondents believe that their primary responsibility was that of motherhood and the need to nurture their young babies superseded any other need. While most working mums (at the nursing stages) were given fewer working hours, women found it extremely hard returning to work 3 months after giving birth, as the most time the babies were not weaned at 3 months. The employee is entitled to 4 months of unpaid maternity leave, one month before the expected date of birth of the child and three months after the birth of the child. Employers are not obliged to remunerate employees for maternity leave. This is further complicated by the fact that maternity leave is unpaid, and most women are forced to return to work as early as one month after giving birth. This, therefore, makes the option of entrepreneurship the preferred option for most of the respondents.

The findings revealed that the major motivating factor for the oscillation between self-employment and being an employee in an organisation is the financial constraints experienced by women entrepreneurs (refer to Fig. 22.3 and Table 22.2). Most of them are unable to employ assistants due to the lack of cash flow for business operations and their inability to secure funding from financial institutions. Consequently, additional pressure is put on them to fulfil several roles in the business, thereby making it impossible to achieve the desired work–life balance. For others, the inability to raise capital also puts their businesses in survival mode increases the pressure on the women

Drivers of Oscillation from self to paid Employment

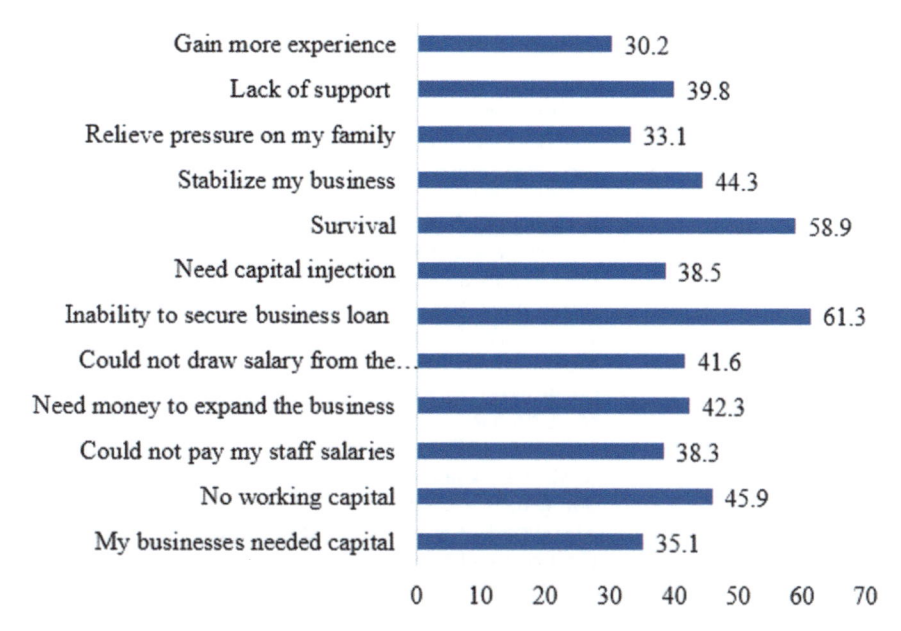

Factor	Value
Gain more experience	30.2
Lack of support	39.8
Relieve pressure on my family	33.1
Stabilize my business	44.3
Survival	58.9
Need capital injection	38.5
Inability to secure business loan	61.3
Could not draw salary from the…	41.6
Need money to expand the business	42.3
Could not pay my staff salaries	38.3
No working capital	45.9
My businesses needed capital	35.1

Fig. 22.3 Drivers of Oscillation identified by the respondents in this study (Figures represent the number of counts not participants) (*Notes* Each participant identified multiple factors that influenced their oscillation between paid and self employment)

and their families. Some women resort to regular paid employment to raise enough money for salaries for their employees or to keep the businesses afloat. They employ people to manage their businesses while they take high paying jobs to raise money that can be injected into the business. For some other respondents, they have had to close the businesses and take up regular paid employment for several years (usually between 2 and 5) to generate enough capital to restart their businesses (refer to Fig. 22.3).

> I think it was about six years ago, and I had I would say about 7 or 8 staff. And the bond rate (mortgage), the interest rate had just gone sky high, people were losing their jobs, they couldn't pay for their cars, couldn't pay their rent, and so a lot of parents were forced to withdraw their children. They weren't able to pay their fees, and for myself as the business owner, I needed to pay my staff because I did not want to retrench them, knowing it would be hard for them under the circumstances to find other jobs, but there wasn't enough money being generated. The banks weren't helpful as you know, so what I had to do was run the business in the morning and go and moonlight at night (doing night shifts in the hospital with my nursing degree) to supplement the business to pay my staff. It was a really hard time, but I owed it to my staff. (Pre-school owner)

Table 22.2 Challenges facing women entrepreneurs in SSA

Challenge categories	Reference points[a]	Typical quotes
Access to finance	93	"Women have less disposable time than men. The banks are not lending to us because we are considered high risk with no collateral. The best I can get is a personal loan and that is not enough for the business" (Consultant) "The biggest challenge that we as women face is the finance. We cannot get loans, we have no savings, and we have to depend on the men in our lives to fund us. If you have no man or he does not have enough, then you struggle with the business" (Boutique owner)
Lack of support	87	I love South Africa and I believe in it so much, but the government can't be everywhere, the government can't do everything. The government doesn't have the money to help every single entrepreneur with funding to start a business. The only way that this country is going to survive is if we all find a way to create a job. And whether that's you and me going into business together and then we employ somebody else or whether that's a woman who comes to my doorstep to say, "I have secretarial skills, can I type for you"? It's whatever it is (Contractor)
Family Responsibilities	90	"Balance, balance, because all of us have a partner and children, and that is difficult to juggle. And then you have to work hard, be actively involved in the business" (Fashion designer) "...you can have plans of schedules but again, with every woman, there're so many things that you have to focus on, so your family (and children) would have to be factored in when making plans and long term goals" (Retailer) "Raising children with little or no help at home leads to poor time management" (Retailer) "As a woman, and a mother sometimes you have to be home and cooking and all that, and this can have a negative effect on the business if not managed properly" (Contractor) "I think being a female adds lots of extra pressure because you need to do both sides: at home, you need to be a wife and mother and at work, you need to be a boss. And you are supposed to be able to balance that" (Interior decorator)

(continued)

Table 22.2 (continued)

Challenge categories	Reference points[a]	Typical quotes
Gender bias, stereotyping and discrimination	73	"Prejudices still remain between different cultures and male and female discrimination is still a huge problem" (Retailer) "Sometimes I feel that women are not taken seriously. Most companies are male-driven, quite reluctant to go into partnership with ladies as some think women cannot run businesses. So, the worst thing that can happen is for a woman to have a lack of confidence and motivation. She has to keep fighting, which is really unfair" (Retailer)

Notes [a]Indicates the number of related quotes found in the data. Participants indicated more than one motivation driver

I had to return to work several times because I think for a woman you definitely have to have empathy with staff and their families. They need the salaries you pay them to survive. So, when the business is not doing well because I cannot get loans from the bank to pour into the business, I have to go back to work to be able to generate more capital. I believed that over time, we will breakeven, but the time before we become profitable, I have to work to get money to keep the business float. (Retailer)

Finally, the data analysis revealed that most of the challenges that the respondents faced were concerning the inability to raise capital finance for their businesses. This is consistent with the literature that suggests that women are often prevented from acquiring capital finance due to lack of knowledge, inadequate education and also because of social and cultural factors (DTI, 2005). They are treated like second class citizens by the financial community (Hisrich & Brush, 1984) and most of the staff in financial institutions are not gender-aware and are ill-trained to handle the uniqueness of female entrepreneurship (Witbooi & Ukpere, 2011).

Therefore, to solve this problem, women entrepreneurs oscillate between taking active measures (active coping) or temporarily distance (i.e. avoiding confrontation). In this context, the active measures include taking up temporary employment as a bridging mechanism for a period and returning to active entrepreneurship when the need is fulfilled or avoiding confrontation and consequently creating a situation of acute imbalance with a negative impact on family and well-being. As stated in the introduction, to understand entrepreneurial motivation, it is vital to explore the consideration of entrepreneurship not just the economic but also the psychological impact on individuals. By taking active measures, psychological well-being is improved given that incorporating short breaks and temporary respite can be beneficial. In the long term, women entrepreneurs can use their ability to avoid "issues," along with active coping and learn to take advantage of both methods to deal with problems (Uy et al., 2013).

Conclusions and Recommendations

The main objective of this study was to highlight the main factors that motivate women entrepreneurs in South Africa to engage in entrepreneurial activities. We believe that understanding these factors will enhance our understanding of the factors that influenced oscillation between self-employment and paid employment. The study's findings confirm that most of the women participants were motivated to entrepreneurship by a desire for flexibility and the need to achieve work–life balance. Most women with family responsibilities would give up paid employment to engage in self-employment for the sake of meeting family needs. The question, therefore, arises "why would women give up the flexibility and achievement of work–life balance to take up paid employment that limits flexibility and puts a strain on family life?" The findings showed that while most women are "pushed" into entrepreneurship out of "necessity," they are also "pushed" back into paid employment out of "necessity." Thus, "Necessity" remains the main motivation for either self- or paid employment.

According to Meyer and Landsberg (2015), South African women entrepreneurs are plagued with many challenges and barriers such as (a) limited access to start-up capital, (b) government regulations, (c) illiteracy, (d) lack of business knowledge and (e) pressure in childcare responsibilities. This further justifies exploring the economic and the non-economic impact of entrepreneurship on women as it raises the question of their "psychological well-being". According to Hsu et al. (2016), the entrepreneur is less likely to give up the business, if engaging in entrepreneurship improves the quality of life and family well-being, Therefore, it can be seen that continuous oscillation from entrepreneurship to paid employment can increase work–life conflict that has a direct negative impact on well-being, work, family and life satisfaction (Nguyen & Sawang, 2016).

Our study reveals that barriers such as inequitable distribution of resources and the lack of ability to secure funding, faced by women entrepreneurs in South Africa, fuel oscillation between self- and paid employment. While these barriers and challenges have been the subject of various studies and known by the South African government, little has been done to mitigate or remove these barriers/challenges. The South African government in March 1995 passed the government White Paper on a "National Strategy for the Development and Promotion of Small Business in South Africa". By highlighting these barriers and challenges in their report, the government by implication recognised the importance of women entrepreneurs in the economic development of South Africa (O'Neill & Viljoen, 2001). Our recommendation, therefore, will be that government should implement policies that have already been formulated especially aspects relating to women entrepreneurs to mitigate the oscillatory behaviours that have been observed. These include problems concerning the legal status and access to finance (DTI, 2005: DTI - Department of Trade and Industry, 1995: 12).

Limitations and Directions for Future Studies

As this study only focused on investigating the factors that influence South African women's motivation to engage in entrepreneurial activities with a view to understanding oscillation, the inclusion criteria were women with family responsibilities (immediate or extended family). Therefore, we did not consider women entrepreneurs without family responsibilities. Thus, the findings cannot represent all women entrepreneurs in South Africa. The validity of this study is also limited to the interpretation of the responses and the ability to identify emerging themes. Additionally, this study focused on women. A study including samples drawn from men and utilising the same inclusion criteria could provide useful insights into factors that influence oscillation from self- to paid employment with male entrepreneurs.

References

Allan, B. A., Autin, K. L., & Duffy, R. D. (2016). Self-determination and meaningful work: Exploring socioeconomic constraints. *Frontiers in Psychology, 7*, 71.

Barba-Sánchez, V., & Atienza-Sahuquillo, C. (2017). Entrepreneurial motivation and self-employment: Evidence from expectancy theory. *International Entrepreneurship and Management Journal, 13*(4), 1097–1115.

Baumol, W. J. (1990). Entrepreneurship: Productive, unproductive, and destructive. *Journal of Political Economics, 98*, 893–921.

Binder, M., & Coad, A. (2013). Life satisfaction and self-employment: A matching approach. *Small Business Economics, 40*(4), 1009–1033.

Bosma, N., Acs, Z. J., Autio, E., Coduras, A., & Levie, J. (2009). *Global Entrepreneurship Monitor—2008 Executive Report*. Babson University and Universided de Desrrollo.

Braun, V., & Clarke, V. (2006). Using thematic analysis in psychology. *Qualitative Research in Psychology, 3*(2), 77–101.

Burton, M. D., Sørensen, J. B., & Dobrev, S. D. (2016). A careers perspective on entrepreneurship. *Entrepreneurship Theory and Practice, 40*(2), 237–247.

Byrne, D. (2005). *Social exclusion*: McGraw-Hill Education (UK).

Cappelli, P. (2000). The new deal at work. *Chi.-Kent L. Rev, 76*, 1169.

Carsrud, A., & Brännback, M. (2011). Entrepreneurial motivations: What do we still need to know? *Journal of Small Business Management, 49*(1), 9–26.

Chowdhury, M. F. (2014). Interpretivism in aiding our understanding of the contemporary social world. *Open Journal of Philosophy*.

Creswell, J. W., Hanson, W. E., Clark, V. L. P., & Morales, A. (2007). Qualitative research designs: Selection and implementation. *The Counselling Psychologist, 35*(2), 236–264.

Deci, E. L., & Ryan, R. M. (2010). Intrinsic motivation. *The corsini encyclopedia of psychology*, 1–2.

DeMartino, R., & Barbato, R. (2003). Differences between men and women MBA entrepreneurs: Exploring family, flexibility and wealth creation as a career motivator. *Journal of Business Venturing, 18*(6), 815–832.

Douglas, E. J., & Shepherd, D. A. (2000). Entrepreneurship as a utility-maximizing response. *Journal of Business Venturing, 15*(3), 231–251.

DTI. (2005). *South African Women Entrepreneurs: A Burgeoning Force in Our Economy* (SAWEN, Ed.). Department of Trade and Industry.

DTI - Department of Trade and Industry. (1995).*White paper on national strategy for the development and promotion of small business in South Africa*. Pretoria: Government Printer.

Edelman, L. F., Brush, C. G., Manolova, T. S., & Greene, P. G. (2010). Start-up motivations and growth intentions of minority nascent entrepreneurs. *Journal of Small Business Management, 48*(2), 174–196.

Fosić, I., Kristić, J., & Trusić, A. (2017). Motivational factors: Drivers behind women entrepreneurs' decision to start an entrepreneurial venture in Croatia. *Scientific Annals of Economics and Business, 64*(3), 339–357.

Gatewood, E. J., Shaver, K. G., Powers, J. B., & Gartner, W. B. (2002). Entrepreneurial expectancy, task effort, and performance*. *Entrepreneurship Theory and Practice, 27*(2), 187–206.

Goulding, C. (2005). Grounded theory, ethnography and phenomenology: A comparative analysis of three qualitative strategies for marketing research. *European Journal of Marketing, 39*(3–4), 294–308.

Graen, G. (1969). Instrumentality theory of work motivation: Some experimental results and suggested modifications. *Journal of Applied Psychology, 53*(2p2), 1.

Greenhaus, J. H., & Beutell, N. J. (1985). Sources of conflict between work and family roles. *Academy of Management Review, 10*(1), 76–88.

Hessels, J., van Gelderen, M., & Thurik, R. (2008). Entrepreneurial aspirations, motivations, and their drivers. *Small Business Economics, 31*, 323–339.

Hilbrecht, M. (2016). Self-employment and experiences of support in a work-family context. *Journal of Small Business & Entrepreneurship, 28*(1), 75–96.

Hirschi, A., & Fischer, S. (2013). Work values as predictors of entrepreneurial career intentions. *Career Development International*.

Hisrich, R. D., & Brush, C. (1984). The woman entrepreneur: Management skills and business problems. *Journal of Small Business Management, 22*(1), 30–37.

Holland, D. V. (2011). Utility maximization? An expectancy view of entrepreneurial persistence. *Management Research Review*.

Hoyte, C., Noke, H., Mosey, S., & Marlow, S. (2019). From venture idea to venture formation: The role of sensemaking, sensegiving and sense receiving. *International Small Business Journal, 37*(3), 268–288.

Hsu, H.-M., Hsu, J. S.-C., Wang, S.-Y., & Chang, I.-C. (2016). Exploring the effects of the unexpected outcome on satisfaction and continuance intention. *Journal of Electronic Commerce Research, 17*(3), 239.

Hughes, K. D. (2006). *Exploring motivation and success among Canadian women entrepreneurs* (p. 324). Canada, University of Alberta.

Irene, B. (2016). A cross-cultural review of the impact of entrepreneurial motivation on the success of female SMMs operators in South Africa. *International Journal of Current Advanced Research, 5*(7), 1122–1130.

Irene, B. (2018). Women entrepreneurs in South Africa: Maintaining a balance between culture, personal life, and business. In S. Yousafzai, A. Fayolle, A. Lindgreen, C. Henry, S. Saeed, & S. Sheikh (Eds.), *Women Entrepreneurs and the Myth of 'Underperformance': A New Look at Women's Entrepreneurship Research* (pp. 90–106, 17 p.). Edward Elgar Publishing Ltd.

Jayawarna, D., Jones, O., & Macpherson, A. (2011). New business creation and regional development: Enhancing resource acquisition in areas of social deprivation. *Entrepreneurship & Regional Development, 23*(9–10), 735–761.

Kanter, R. M. (1977). Some effects of proportions on group life. In *The gender gap in psychotherapy* (pp. 53–78). Springer.

Kuratko, D. F., Hornsby, J. S., & Naffziger, D. W. (1997). An examination of the owner's goals in sustaining entrepreneurship. *Journal of Small Business Management, 35*, 24.

Lawler III, E. E., & Suttle, J. L. (1973). Expectancy theory and job behavior. *Organizational behavior and human performance, 9*(3), 482–503.

Lewis, S., & Humbert, A. L. (2010). Discourse or reality: "Work-life balance" flexibility and gendered organisations. *Equality, Diversity and Inclusion, 29*(3), 239–254.

Locke, E. A., & Baum, J. R. (2014). Entrepreneurial Motivation. In J. R. Baum, M. Frese, & R. A. Baron (Eds.), *The psychology of entrepreneurship* (pp. 93–112). Psychology Press.

Loscocco, K., & Bird, S. R. (2012). Gendered paths: Why women lag behind men in small business success. *Work and Occupations, 39*(2), 183–219.

Manolova, T. S., Carter, N. M., Manev, I. M., & Gyoshev, B. S. (2007). The differential effect of men and women entrepreneurs' experience and networking on growth expectancies in Bulgaria. *Entrepreneurship: Theory and Practice, 31*(3), 407–426.

Meyer, N. (2009). *An investigation into the determinants of women entrepreneurship* (Doctoral dissertation, North-West University).

Meyer, N., & Landsberg, J. (2015). Motivational factors influencing women's entrepreneurship: A case study of female entrepreneurship in South Africa. *World Academy of Science, Engineering and Technology, International Journal of Social, Behavioral, Educational, Economic, Business and Industrial Engineering, 9*(11), 3857–3862.

Millán, J. M., Congregado, E., & Román, C. (2012). Determinants of self-employment survival in Europe. *Small Business Economics, 38*(2), 231–258.

Murray, P. A., & Syed, J. (2010). Gendered observations and experiences in executive women's work. *Human Resource Management Journal, 20*(3), 277–293.

Naithani, D. (2010). Recession and work-life balance initiatives. *Romanian Economic Journal, 37*, 55–68.

Neubauer, B. E., Witkop, C. T., & Varpio, L. (2019). How phenomenology can help us learn from the experiences of others. *Perspectives on Medical Education, 8*, 90–97. https://doi.org/10.1007/s40037-019-0509-2

Nguyen, H., & Sawang, S. (2016). Juggling or struggling? Work and family interface and its buffers among small business owners. *Entrepreneurship Research Journal, 6*(2), 207–246.

O'Neill, R. C., & Viljoen, L. (2001). Support for female entrepreneurs in South Africa: Improvement or decline? *Journal of Family Ecology and Consumer Sciences, 29*, 37–44.

Parasuraman, S., & Simmers, C. A. (2001). Type of employment, work-family conflict and well-being: A comparative study. *Journal of Organisational Behavior: THe International Journal of Industrial, Occupational and Organisational Psychology and Behavior, 22*(5), 551–568.

Patrick, C., Stephens, H., & Weinstein, A. (2016). Where are all the self-employed women? Push and pull factors influencing female labour market decisions. *Small Business Economics, 46*(3), 365–390.

Patton, M. (2001). Purposive sampling. *Ethnography: Sage benchmarks in research methods*.

Patton, M. Q. (1990). *Qualitative evaluation and research methods*. Sage.

Pleck, J. H. (1977). The work-family role system. *Social Problems, 24*(4), 417–427.

Pradhan, G. (2016). *Conceptualising work-life balance*. Institute for Social and Economic Change.

Renko, M., Kroeck, K. G., & Bullough, A. (2012). Expectancy theory and nascent entrepreneurship. *Small Business Economics, 39*(3), 667–684.

Reynolds, P. D., & Curtin, R. T. (2008). *Business creation in the United States: A panel study of entrepreneurial dynamics II initial assessment*. Now Publishers Inc.

Rider, C. I., & Tan, D. (2015). Labor market advantages of organizational status: A study of lateral partner hiring by large US law firms. *Organization Science, 26*(2), 356–372.

Rincy, V. M., & Panchanatham, N. (2014). Work life balance: A short review of the theoretical and contemporary concepts. *Continental Journal of Social Sciences, 7*(1), 1–24.

Rindova, V., Barry, D., & Ketchen, D. J., Jr. (2009). Entrepreneuring as emancipation. *Academy of Management Review, 34*(3), 477–491.

Schwartz, S. (2006). A theory of cultural value orientations: Explication and applications. *Comparative Sociology, 5*(2–3), 137–182.

Smith, J. A. (2004). Reflecting on the development of interpretative phenomenological analysis and its contribution to qualitative research in psychology. *Qualitative Research in Psychology, 1*(1), 39–54.

Sørensen, J. B., & Sharkey, A. J. (2014). Entrepreneurship as a mobility process. *American Sociological Review, 79*(2), 328–349.

Su, X., Liu, S., Zhang, S. & Liu, L. (2020). To be happy: A case study of entrepreneurial motivation and entrepreneurial process from the perspective of positive psychology. *Sustainability, 12*(2), 584.

Uy, M. A., Foo, M.-D., & Song, Z. (2013). Joint effects of prior start-up experience and coping strategies on entrepreneurs' psychological well-being. *Journal of Business Venturing, 28*(5), 583–597.

Van Praag, C. M., & Cramer, J. S. (2001). The roots of entrepreneurship and labour demand: Individual ability and low-risk aversion. *Economica, 68*(269), 45–62.

Vroom, V. H. (1964). *Work and motivation*. Wiley.

Witbooi, M., & Ukpere, W. (2011). Indigenous female entrepreneurs: Analytical study on access to finance for women entrepreneurs in South Africa. *African Journal of Business Management, 5*(14), 5646–5657.

Part VI

Researching African Entrepreneurship:
Methodological Considerations

23

Conducting Surveys in Africa: Reflections from National Surveys in Nigeria

Abiodun Egbetokun

Introduction

> Whether we like it or not surveys are part of our life. (Iarossi, 2006, p. 4)

Empirical research in entrepreneurship, innovation and development research often rely on survey data. These data come from two main sources: administrative and micro surveys. Administrative surveys are implemented by public or international organisations such as national statistical agencies and multilateral agencies like the World Bank. They are normally broad-based and tailored towards supporting the implementing authorities in their line of work. For instance, surveys conducted by national statistical offices form the basis for estimating indicators of human capital and the labour market. In contrast, micro surveys are implemented by individual researchers or research teams for the purpose of addressing specific research questions. Thus, they have narrower scope than administrative surveys. Table 23.1 provides an indicative comparison of administrative and micro surveys. Admittedly, there are cases where large-scale surveys are implemented by individuals or small research teams but these are exceptions rather than the norm, particularly in

---

A. Egbetokun (✉)
National Centre for Technology Management, Ile-Ife, Nigeria

© The Author(s), under exclusive license to Springer Nature Switzerland AG 2022
O. Kolade et al. (eds.), *The Palgrave Handbook of African Entrepreneurship*, https://doi.org/10.1007/978-3-030-75894-3_23

Table 23.1 A comparison of administrative and micro surveys

Attribute	Administrative surveys	Micro surveys
Geographical coverage	National or supra-national	Sub-national
Scope	Large number of variables, applicable to several issues or research questions	Small number of variables, applicable to few issues or research questions
Scale	Large scale, typically with thousands of observations	Small scale, with fewer observations
Implementing authority	Governments, donors, development partners	Individuals or research teams

Source Author's compilation

Africa. It is indeed more common for researchers to produce large or longitudinal datasets by combining data from several separate sources or from several rounds of the same survey.

Administrative surveys are especially interesting because of their coverage, scope and scale. High-quality national survey data enable researchers to answer a wide array of policy-relevant questions. However, in many African countries, the available administrative data often focus on macroeconomic issues such as GDP, national employment figures, nationwide education statistics, among others. Large-scale datasets that permit rigorous analyses in entrepreneurship, innovation and development research are seldom systematically gathered by public institutions. Moreover, gaining access to the available data is difficult, if not impossible in many places. To make up for the resulting gap in data access, researchers resort to collecting their own data through small and focused surveys. However, surveys are generally difficult to implement in Africa for several reasons, including weak demand for research evidence, poor infrastructure, limited local capacity and societal apathy.

Against this background, this chapter addresses three major issues. First, the chapter discusses the typical procedure for implementing surveys in Africa and the attendant challenges. This discussion is based on more than 10 years of personal experience with surveys in Nigeria, covering a wide range of topics including innovation, entrepreneurship, research on research, and impact evaluations. Second, the chapter recommends specific strategies to overcome the challenges that inhibit the implementation of surveys in African countries, drawing from the author's experience in Nigeria. These include conventional strategies, such as careful sample design and the use of responsive survey instruments. Others, such as the necessity of adopting a sequential procedure, and the need to provide nudges, are more contextualised. Finally, the chapter highlights some sources of rich administrative and/or large-scale survey data that researchers in entrepreneurship, innovation, development and policy will find interesting. The discussion in this regard is not meant to be exhaustive; rather, it serves the purpose of highlighting some classic examples of high-quality data sources. It is hoped that established and upcoming researchers with an interest in developing countries, particularly sub-Saharan Africa, will find this chapter relevant.

Procedures and Challenges of Surveys in a Typical African Country

Data analysis is at the heart of empirical research. Beyond the quality of research questions and the appropriateness of methods, the epistemological value of any empirical research project depends heavily on the data it is based upon. Indeed, even the most sophisticated analytical devices and writing prowess cannot salvage a piece of research that is based on poor data. For this reason, a discussion of how and where to obtain data of good quality, especially in developing countries, is relevant. As a starting point, it is instructive to understand how surveys—being an important source of data for innovation, entrepreneurship and development research—are undertaken in a typical developing country. There are many good texts on the subject of surveys—the texts by Iarossi (2006), UNSD (2005) and Bradburn et al. (2004) are exceptionally good. Thus, rather than dwell on theoretical and conceptual details, the following discussion offers a brief practitioner perspective on surveys in the African context based on the author's experience in Nigeria.

The Typical Survey Procedure

The standard survey procedure involves first getting a sampling frame that lists eligible units in a population of interest and then selecting a sample from this frame. For several reasons, these two steps are perhaps the most crucial in a survey. In particular, if a representative sample is not used, the entire research process could be compromised because eligible units whose attributes are influential may be excluded from the study sample. Moreover, it is impossible to draw population-level inferences from a non-representative sample, and a representative sample cannot be obtained without a comprehensive sampling frame.

With a sample in hand, the researcher or enumerator then proceeds to establish contact with each sampling unit and to collect the required data. This is done via telephone, questionnaires or interviews, among other means. Questionnaires, and interviews (if structured), may be self-administered or administered by a researcher or enumerator. Surveys are also sometimes deployed via the Internet using platforms like Google Forms, Surveymonkey and Zoho, among many others. In large-scale surveys, it is common to use survey firms (i.e. a company that specialises in the implementation of field surveys) and computer-assisted technologies (CAT) which often involve researchers or enumerators conducting interviews and directly recording responses on a computing device (usually a tablet). In a CAT survey, completed interviews may be stored locally on the device or automatically synchronised into an offsite server. A detailed comparative analysis of the above data collection alternatives is beyond the scope of this chapter but it is instructive to note that the choice of approach involves a careful consideration of the nature of data being collected, the survey targets, available resources, merits and demerits associated with each alternative approach as well as the prevailing ambience.

For instance, telephone surveys are becoming an attractive option given the increasing internet penetration in Africa. Indeed, extensive recent research highlights the benefits of telephone surveys, including scalability, sustainability, comparable accuracy to face-to-face fieldwork, low cost relative to face-to-face fieldwork, reduction in human error due to leaner and/or automated data capture, and easier non-response follow-up (Garlick et al., 2016; Gibson et al., 2017; Hoogeveen et al., 2014; Leo et al., 2015). However, the success of telephone surveys depends on a number of contextual factors including survey targets (individuals, firms or households), location (urban or rural), research topic, length of the survey, legitimacy of the authority implementing the survey, and prevalent social biases. For instance, a telephone survey of individuals in Nigeria on a subject that is finance-related is likely to suffer high rejection rates, and if longitudinal, could face serious attrition problems. This is because of the perceived prevalence of telephone scams, which has created a general sense of suspicion towards calls from unknown persons (Ojebode, 2012).

In general, telephone surveys are mostly effective within the literate or corporate population, and when the focus of the survey is neither sensitive nor controversial. In rural settings, structured interviews are appropriate. On their part, web surveys are easy to diffuse and particularly suitable where physical access or mobility is difficult—such as in cases of violent conflict or public health shocks. Indeed, the 2020 Covid-19 pandemic has created a strong demand for web surveys globally. However, web surveys are particularly sensitive to infrastructure (such as electricity and Internet connectivity[1]) and are prone to noise (the researcher sometimes not being able to ensure that every respondent is unique). Ostensibly mundane issues such as the balance between the number of items on a page and the scroll length of the page can also be challenging in web survey design (Peytchev et al., 2006). Specific ethical issues such as preservation of digital rights and cloud storage security need to be considered before deploying web surveys. Moreover, field experience in Nigeria shows that due to funding and infrastructural constraints as well as the small scale of most research projects, questionnaires are better hand-delivered by researchers or enumerators to respondents who self-administer (complete it by themselves without assistance). The researcher or enumerator then returns to retrieve by hand.

Hand delivery of questionnaires is important in the Nigerian context because the domestic logistics system is poor. Besides, it offers a way to quickly determine whether the respondent is able or willing to self-administer and for the researcher or enumerator to swiftly react accordingly. The poor domestic logistics network is also a major reason personal retrieval is important. In addition, personal follow-up and retrieval help the researcher or enumerator to quickly identify cases that require multiple visits and those whose responses need some clarifications. This sort of strategy is only efficient in settings with significant logistics and infrastructural challenges, and with relatively small-scale projects. Larger projects, even in the face of logistics and infrastructural deficiencies, definitely require creativity and resourcefulness on the part of the researchers.

Challenges of Surveys in a Typical African Country: A Nigerian Perspective

Depending on whom one asks, the process of conducting credible surveys in a developing country may be seen as easy, hard or next to impossible. Nonetheless, the emergence of a rapidly expanding body of empirical research from developing countries suggests that despite the challenges, getting the relevant data is, in fact, possible (Siyanbola et al., 2014). The rest of this section highlights four of the major challenges that complicate the conduct

---

[1] Specific tools tailored towards infrastructure-deficient contexts are now available. The KoBo Toolbox (https://www.kobotoolbox.org) is a good case in point. The toolbox includes a data collection app, KoBoCollect, which can be installed on an Android device and allows an enumerator to complete surveys offline for later upload when Internet connection becomes available. I thank Seun Kolade for highlighting this.

of surveys in a typical African country, based on my experience in Nigeria. Box 23.1 provides a case that highlights how some of the challenges crop up in practice and how they were dealt with.

Box 23.1 The Nigerian Innovation Survey: A practical case of survey challenges and solutions in Nigeria

[I]t is hard to plan a stratified sample in Nigeria due to non-availability of a consistent and reliable register of firms. Notwithstanding, the survey attempted a stratified sample based on the list of establishments with at least 10 employees obtained from the National Bureau of Statistics (NBS) and the Nigerian Stock Exchange. The Stock Exchange list includes only formal firms whereas the NBS list includes both formal and informal firms. These two sources were cross-referenced and any firm listed in both sources was automatically selected into the sample. The logic behind this is that if a firm was listed on the stock exchange then it must still be in the market. This criterion is important considering the fact that firm exit rate is particularly high in Nigeria, a factor that partly makes it difficult to compile a consistent register of all firms. To ensure a fair geographical and sectoral distribution in the final sample, the population of firms was stratified into geographical zones and sectors (in the first wave ISIC Rev. 3.1 was used and in the second wave ISIC Rev. 4). The final sample (about 1500 in each round of the survey) was then selected based on proportional probability, with a combined response rate of approximately 45%. The survey instruments were delivered by and to all the firms, and in many instances, some of the selected firms did no longer exist. In every possible case, the missing firm was substituted with another one in the same sector and geographical location. The two waves of the survey represent two repeated cross sections. Although it was ensured that every firm that responded in the first wave was contacted for the second wave, the response was particularly low, necessitating a re-sampling.

Source Egbetokun et al. (2019)

---

i. The most fundamental of the challenges that confront surveys in developing countries like Nigeria is a weak demand for research evidence among policymakers. The absence of systematic large-scale surveys similar to those routinely implemented in developed countries is rooted in this weak demand. It is also the reason for poor funding of research in general. The resulting lack of data has led to a proliferation of very small surveys for nearly every research topic, especially in the social sciences. Most of these micro surveys, typically conducted in the context of postgraduate studies, are either too small or too rudimentary to permit any meaningful inferences.

ii. Poor infrastructure constitutes a significant obstacle to surveys in many developing countries. As Iarossi (2006) notes, the survey infrastructure in developing countries is often hard to assess, which implies that several necessary elements are either missing or obscure. Two broad types of relevant infrastructure are usually deficient. Hard infrastructure includes transportation, fixed telephone lines, stable electricity and Internet access. Soft infrastructure is connected mainly to logistics, notably address lists, postal services and sampling frames. Lack of access to reliable sampling frames is an especially grievous problem (see Box 23.1 and Adeoti, 2012).

iii. Apart from monetary resources and infrastructure, conducting surveys requires a good knowledge of the right principles and theories. Relative to more developed countries, local capacity for well-designed and well-implemented surveys is rather weak in many African countries. This shows up mostly in poorly designed survey instruments and poor data management.

iv. Finally, the proliferation of many small surveys administered to the same or similar respondents has created a situation of survey overload that seems to have precipitated some form of societal apathy. Consequently, it is increasingly difficult to secure and sustain the interest of potential respondents in a survey.

Overcoming the Challenges

Dealing with the above challenges and others that may hinder the conduct of surveys is not necessarily straightforward. However, a number of steps may be taken to mitigate the problems, at least. What follows is a brief discussion of seven tips for overcoming common survey challenges.

i. Careful and rigorous sampling methods: A good survey requires a well-designed sample which must be carefully and rigorously selected. For entrepreneurship, innovation and development research, *epsem* (equal probability of selection method) sampling is the best, and is easily realisable. Non-probability sampling may be sometimes unavoidable but it has major limitations, not least of which is subjectivity (Kalton, 1983). Four of the most commonly used *epsem* sampling procedures include simple random sampling (SRS), stratified random sampling, systematic sampling and probability proportional to size (PPS) sampling (Iarossi, 2006). In most practical settings, stratification is possible based on some attribute of the population but the resulting clusters are of unequal size. PPS is especially suited for such settings as it ensures that every stratum is proportionately represented in the final sample.

ii. Resolving population frame problems: Sampling accuracy rests on the accuracy of the sampling frame, also known as the population frame.

This is a sort of register or database that contains the eligible units in a target population. Examples of population frames include business registers, population census records, and address lists, among others. A reliable frame will include all, or at least, most of the eligible units in a population. Obtaining a reliable frame requires as much diligence as the sampling procedure itself. The most fundamental problem with sampling frames in African countries is that of missingness, that is, reliable frames are sometimes non-existent or completely outdated. It is possible to overcome this problem with some creativity and extensive knowledge of the study context. For example, one may adopt a frame from previous surveys, redefine the target population or combine more than one frame. A practical application of the latter is briefly described in Box 23.1.

iii. Well-designed survey instruments: To improve survey response and quality, it is crucial to use a high-quality instrument. Typically, unless two different research projects address the same or similar questions, it is not advisable to 'copy and paste' survey instruments. Of course, there are well-tested scales to measure certain phenomena, such as the Big 5 Personality Traits (John & Srivastava, 1999), that may be adopted wholesale. Notwithstanding, question wording must be precise and contextually relevant. Indeed, previous research suggests that a single word may change the sense of survey questions and influence responses (Iarossi, 2006). Experts also agree on the necessity for survey instruments to be brief and focused (Bradburn, 2004; UNSD, 2005). It is redundant to ask questions about respondents' religion in firm-level surveys on innovation, for example.

iv. Solid technique: Where there is survey overload or the research topic is sensitive, it may be very difficult to secure responses. However, with appropriate survey methods and interview techniques, it is possible to get respondents to open up on the most sensitive matters, although this is most easily achievable via face-to-face interviews. For example, past research has documented data in which firm managers were willing to discuss corruption with a good measure of openness (Fisman & Svensson, 2007; Kaufmann, 1997). In practice, for instance, certain cultural settings would dictate that only female enumerators can approach female respondents. It is counterproductive to attempt otherwise.

v. Stakeholder engagement: Sometimes, gaining access to the target population and obtaining meaningful response rates depend on the extent of buy-in from the relevant stakeholders. This is particularly true in cases where the target population is part of a government programme. Failure to engage with the key stakeholders could cause a survey to fail, irrespective of the stage of implementation. It is advisable to identify relevant stakeholders and engage with them at the survey design stage. Not only does this ensure that the survey is relevant, but it also facilitates its smooth running and the uptake of the end results. In a recent survey, we were able to administer a questionnaire to over 10,000 individuals in 10 Nigerian states and retrieve the same over two days. No doubt this was a fairly expensive process, but all the investment could have been wasted without extensive support from the main domestic institutional stakeholder. Interest groups, workers' union and regulatory agencies are just a few of the stakeholders that could help facilitate surveys.

vi. Offer incentives: Incentives have a nudging effect and can improve response rates by up to 5% in face-to-face interviews (Iarossi, 2006). However, incentives must be creatively designed. As tempting as it is to give out money in return for survey responses, this comes with significant ethical and practical complications. It is therefore strongly advised to use non-monetary incentives such as writing materials or printed matter that inform respondents about how the data will be used, how similar data has been used in the past and what they stand to benefit. In a recent survey of fresh university graduates in Nigeria, we gave a free pen to each respondent alongside the paper questionnaire, and this worked well in ensuring that most completed the questionnaire on the spot. In another survey, we included with every questionnaire a wide-format infographic on the survey subject (large enough to hang on a wall). In web surveys, vouchers and free reports from past studies may be offered. Deciding on what is best depends on the researcher's knowledge of the context, the attributes of the target population, and available resources.

vii. Sequential procedure: In research projects that combine structured surveys with qualitative data collection like key informant interviews and focus group discussions, it is advisable to follow a sequential procedure where the survey comes first. The survey data should then be quickly explored to identify emergent themes, confusing findings and missing estimates. This two-step procedure has three main advantages. First, the interviews could pick up on some emergent themes from the survey data, for clarification and deeper exploration. Second, the follow-up interviews could help to fill in some gaps in the survey data, wherever possible. Finally, it becomes possible to refine the interview protocols (including sample and guide) in order to optimise the qualitative data collection process.

Selected Secondary Data Sources

This section contains some sources of rich large-scale survey data that are relevant for research in entrepreneurship, innovation and development in Africa. In general, compared to similar primary data, secondary datasets are much larger and typically inter-temporal, thereby enabling longitudinal and comparable multi-country studies. An important characteristic of the highlighted data sources is that they have all been widely applied—either alone or in combination with other sources—in rigorous research with strong relevance for policymaking in developing countries. In addition, they all have the common attribute of being dynamic: at the time of writing, almost all of the data sources were actively expanding, which raises the expectation that they are likely to cover in future any country that is presently missing. Along with a brief description of each data source, the coverage and access link up to 22 April 2020 are provided.[2] Admittedly, this list is not exhaustive, and it is not intended to be so. The purpose of this section is twofold: first, to highlight some examples of high-quality data sources; and two, to illustrate the type of rich data that African countries should seek to routinely gather and democratise as a way to spur high-quality research. Indeed, the body of research evidence that will emerge in a country is directly proportional to the quality of data that is available to researchers.

i. World Bank Enterprise Surveys (WBES)

The World Bank Enterprise Surveys (WBES) are a collection of firm-level surveys of a representative sample of manufacturing and services firms in several countries. Since its inception in 2002, the WBES has progressively increased its geographical coverage to include almost all low- and middle-income countries in the world and several high-income countries. Many of these countries have been covered several times such that panel datasets may be constructed (Fig. 23.1). At the time of writing, detailed Enterprisev Survey

---

[2] The coverage and access information (including weblinks) provided for each data source are correct at the time of writing. Specifically, I have taken care to confirm that the information is valid as of April 22, 2020. Given that data curation is a dynamic exercise, some of the information may change over time. Even if or when that happens, a simple search on Google should help the reader to locate the respective data source.

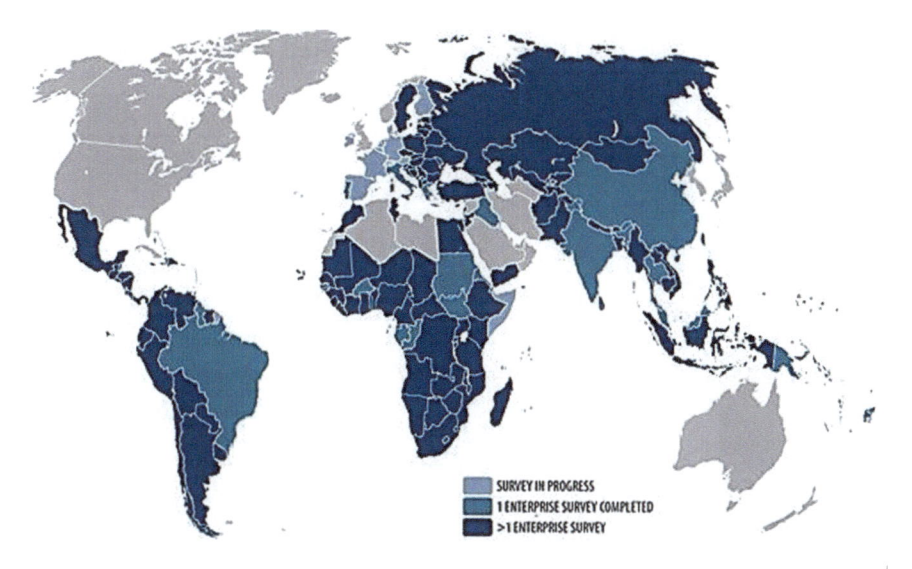

Fig. 23.1 Geographical coverage of the World Bank Enterprise Surveys (WBES) (*Source* https://www.enterprisesurveysorg/en/survey-datasets, accessed April 22, 2020)

datasets were available on around 160,000 firms in over 140 countries, giving an average of over a thousand firms per country. Over 35,000 firms in more than 40 African countries and territories are covered in Enterprise surveys carried out between 2006 and the end of 2019 (Table 23.2).[3]

The datasets include data on a wide range of variables from which the EAU generates and publishes at least 140 indicators across countries (World Bank, 2017). Notable among these are several aspects of firm characteristics, trade, workforce, performance, business environment (including taxes, regulations, corruption, obstacles and infrastructure, among others), gender, innovation and technology. Its expansive coverage makes the WBES the world's most comprehensive source of firm-level data from developing countries, as far as I know. The data is also one of the most widely applied in empirical research on entrepreneurship, innovation and development in Africa (see, e.g. Adegboye & Iweriebor, 2018; Hjort & Poulsen, 2019; Lemi & Wright, 2020). The full datasets can be accessed at https://www.enterprisesurveys.org/en/survey-datasets.

---

[3] See Section 2 in Bigsten and Söderbom (2006) for a review of enterprise surveys in Africa in the decade between 1990 and 2000.

Table 23.2 African countries in the World Bank Enterprise Surveys (WBES), 2006–2020

Country	Total	2006–2009	2010–2013	2014–2017	2018–2020
Angola	785	425	360	–	–
Benin	300	150	–	150	–
Botswana	610	342	268	–	–
Burkina Faso	533	533	–	–	–
Burundi	427	270	–	157	–
Cape Verde	254	254	–	–	–
Cameroon	896	535	–	361	–
Central African Republic	150	–	150	–	–
Chad	303	150	–	–	153
Congo, Dem. Rep	1228	340	888	–	–
Congo, Rep	151	151	–	–	–
Côte d'Ivoire	887	526	–	361	–
Eritrea	179	179	–	–	–
Eswatini	457	307	–	150	–
Ethiopia	1976	484	644	848	–
Gabon	179	179	–	–	–
Gambia, The	325	174	–	–	151
Ghana	1214	494	720	–	–
Guinea	373	223	–	150	–
Guinea-Bissau	159	159			
Kenya	2439	657	781		1001
Lesotho	301	151	150		
Liberia	301	150		151	
Madagascar	977	445	532		
Malawi	673	150		523	
Mali	1035	490	360	185	
Mauritania	387	237		150	
Mauritius	398	398			
Mozambique	1080	479	601		
Namibia	909	329		580	
Niger	301	150		151	
Nigeria	4567	1891		2676	
Rwanda	813	212	241		360
Senegal	1107	506		601	
Sierra Leone	302	150		152	
Somaliland	500		500		
South Africa	937	937			

(continued)

Table 23.2 (continued)

Country	Total	2006–2009	2010–2013	2014–2017	2018–2020
South Sudan	738			738	
Sudan	662			662	
Tanzania	1232	419	813		
Togo	305	155		150	
Uganda	1325	563	762		
Zambia	1204	484	720		
Zimbabwe	1199		599	600	
Total	35,078	14,828	9089	9496	1665

Source Author's compilation from https://www.enterprisesurveysorg/en/survey-dat asets, accessed April 22, 2020. The years in the table heading do not necessarily coincide with the survey years; rather, they indicate the period during which the surveys took place. For instance, a survey that took place in 2015 will be recorded under the column heading 2014–2017

ii. Africa Sector Database (ASD)

The Africa Sector Database (ASD) includes annual data on value added, deflators and employment across gender in the same 10 sectors across 11 countries in sub-Saharan Africa (Tables 23.3 and 23.4). At the time of writing, the data covered the period from 1960 to 2010. This sort of internationally comparable time series data enables unprecedented rigorous analyses of structural change and productivity in sub-Saharan Africa, as illustrated in Van Neuss (2019), Diao et al. (2019) and de Vries et al. (2015). Merging this data with other data sources such as the WBES enables richer analyses of

Table 23.3 Country and variable coverage in the African Sector Database (ASD)

Country	Value Added (current prices)	Value Added (constant prices)	Employment by sector
Botswana	1964–2010	1964–2010	1964–2010
Ethiopia	1961–2010	1961–2010	1961–2010
Ghana	1960–2010	1960–2010	1960–2010
Kenya	1960–2010	1964–2010	1969–2010
Malawi	1960–2010	1966–2010	1966–2010
Mauritius	1960–2010	1970–2010	1970–2010
Nigeria	1960–2010	1960–2010	1960–2010
Senegal	1960–2010	1970–2010	1970–2010
South Africa	1960–2010	1960–2010	1960–2010
Tanzania	1960–2010	1960–2010	1960–2010
Zambia	1960–2010	1965–2010	1965–2010

Source https://www.rugnl/ggdc/productivity/10-sector/other-releases/africa-sector-dat abase

Table 23.4 Sector coverage in the African Sector Database (ASD)

ISIC Rev. 3.1 code	ASD sector name	ISIC Rev. 3.1 description
A + B	Agriculture	Agriculture, Hunting and Forestry, Fishing
C	Mining	Mining and Quarrying
D	Manufacturing	Manufacturing
E	Utilities	Electricity, Gas and Water supply
F	Construction	Construction
G + H	Trade services	Wholesale and Retail trade; repair of motor vehicles, motorcycles and personal and household goods, Hotels and Restaurants
I	Transport services	Transport, Storage and Communications
J + K	Business services	Financial Intermediation, Real Estate, Renting and Business Activities
70	Dwellings	Owner-occupied Dwellings (is part of Business services)
L,M,N	Government services	Public Administration and Defense, Education, Health and Social work
O,P	Personal services	Other Community, Social and Personal service activities, Activities of Private Households
TOT	Total Economy	Total Economy

Note ISIC Rev. 3.1—International Standard Industrial Classification Revision 3.1
Source https://www.rugnl/ggdc/productivity/10-sector/other-releases/africa-sector-database

the role of firms in national productivity and structural change in Africa. The data is available at https://www.rug.nl/ggdc/productivity/10-sector/other-releases/africa-sector-database.

iii. Living Standards Measurement Study (LSMS)

The Living Standards Measurement Study (LSMS) programme started in 1980 and has since conducted multiple rounds of geo-referenced surveys in several countries. At the time of writing, over 100 LSMS surveys covering more than 40 low- and middle-income countries—12 of these being African (Table 23.5)[4]—are available directly from the LSMS data portal. The surveys include information on household characteristics and entrepreneurship activity, community-level information, and agricultural

---

[4] Statistical offices in some countries, such as Burundi, Cameroon, Chad, maintain LSMS-type survey data. This could bring the number of African countries with such rich household data up to 20.

Table 23.5 African countries in the Living Standards Measurement Study (LSMS)

Country	Year	Household Count
Burkina Faso	2014	10,411
Côte d'Ivoire	1985	1,588
	1986	1,600
	1987	1,600
	1988	1,600
Ethiopia	2011	3,969
	2013	3,969
Ghana	1987/1988	3,200
	1988/1989	3,200
	1991/1992	4,565
	1998/1999	5,998
	2009–2010	5,009
Malawi	2004–2005	11,280
Mali	2014	3,804
Morocco	1991	3,323
Niger	2011	3,968
	2014	3,617
Nigeria	2010–2011	5,000
	2012–2013	5,000
South Africa	1993	9,000
Tanzania–Kagera	1991–1994	800
Tanzania–National	1993	5,200
	2008–2009	3,280
	2010–2011	3,924
Uganda	2009/2010	3,123
	2010/2011	2,716
	2011/2012	2,715
	2013/2014	3,119

Source Author's compilation from http://surveys.worldbank.org/lsms/our-work/data, April 23, 2020

activities captured via three eponymous questionnaires. Just like the WBES is in terms of firm-level data, the LSMS is currently the world's most comprehensive source of household-level data, to the best of my knowledge. Several recent studies like Osabuohien et al. (2019) and Gaddis et al. (2019) illustrate the kind of analyses that are possible with LSMS data. The data is accessible at http://surveys.worldbank.org/lsms/our-work/data.[5]

---

[5] At the time of writing, the LSMS has launched high-frequency telephone surveys on the coronavirus pandemic in some African countries (see http://surveys.worldbank.org/covid-19). The surveys draw a stratified sub-sample of households from the latest LSMS sample in each country and interview these households monthly for a year. The resulting datasets are well-suited for longitudinal analyses of the impact of external shocks on households.

iv. Global Entrepreneurship Monitor (GEM)

The Global Entrepreneurship Monitor (GEM) is a global network of research teams founded in 1999. Each country team adopts the standardised GEM questionnaires and methodology to conduct two surveys annually: (a) the Adult Population Survey (APS) which collects data on the characteristics, motivations and ambitions of at least 2,000 existing and potential entrepreneurs as well as on social attitudes towards entrepreneurship in the country, and (b) the National Expert Survey (NES) that collects data from a selection of at least 36 experts in the country on the economic and social context for entrepreneurship. At the time of writing, GEM surveys have been conducted in over 100 countries over 20 years in total.[6] This includes a total of 20 African countries that have implemented at least one GEM survey, with South Africa having the longest time series by far (Table 23.6). This breadth of coverage makes the GEM database the world's most comprehensive source of individual-level data on entrepreneurship aspirations, activities and framework conditions, as far as I know. Globally, the GEM datasets are some of the most widely applied data in rigorous entrepreneurship research. Many recent studies such as Cinar et al. (2019), Dvouletý and Orel (2019) and Herrington and Coduras (2019) rely on GEM to analyse several aspects of entrepreneurship in Africa and to draw useful policy implications. The full data from both the APS and the NES are available at https://www.gemconsortium.org/data.

v. World Management Survey (WMS)

The World Management Survey (WMS), a multi-country, multi-sector survey on the quality of firm-level management practices, was initiated in 2002. At the time of writing, the WMS had been conducted across the same 4 sectors (manufacturing, retail, healthcare and education) in over 35 countries, with more than 20,000 observations in total. The indicators in the WMS—broadly related to modern techniques, performance management, goals setting/management, and human resources management—allow unprecedented analyses of the role of management practices in firm-level productivity and other aspects of performance. However, the surveys have limited coverage of Africa. For instance, in one of the latest versions of

---

[6] To give first-mover advantages to members of the consortium, the GEM data from each survey round is openly shared only after three years.

Table 23.6 African countries in the Global Entrepreneurship Monitor

Country	Years of GEM survey	Average TEA (%)*
Algeria	2009, 2011–2013	9.9
Angola	2008, 2010, 2012–2014, 2018	28.6
Botswana	2012–2015	28.6
Burkina Faso	2014–2016	28.3
Cameroon	2014–2016	30.1
Egypt	2008, 2010, 2012, 2015–2019	9.9
Ethiopia	2012	14.7
Ghana	2010, 2012, 2013	32.1
Libya	2013	11.2
Madagascar	2017–2019	20.7
Malawi	2012, 2013	31.8
Morocco	2009, 2015–2019	8.8
Namibia	2012, 2013	25.7
Nigeria	2011–2013	36.6
Senegal	2015	38.6
South Africa	2001–2006, 2008–2017, 2019	7.5
Sudan	2018	22.2
Tunisia	2009, 2010, 2012, 2015	7.6
Uganda	2003, 2004, 2009, 2010, 2012, 2013	31.7
Zambia	2010, 2012, 2013	4.7

Source Author's compilation with data from https://www.gemconsortium.org/data/key-aps, accessed April 24, 2020.
*TEA is Total early-stage Entrepreneurial Activity, that is, the percentage of 18–64 population who are either a nascent entrepreneur or owner-manager of a new business. This column reports the average across all surveys

the data, applied in Bloom et al. (2014), there are 11,300 firms from 34 countries. These include only 7 African countries—Ethiopia, Ghana, Kenya, Mozambique, Nigeria, Tanzania and Zambia with a combined sample of just over 800 observations—surveyed between 2013 and 2014, a reflection of the fact that the surveys are just expanding to the African continent. Partly because of this, empirical research using WMS data on Africa is missing at the time of writing this chapter, but it is hoped that this will change in the nearest future as more data becomes available from the continent. Indeed, an interesting feature of the WMS is that individuals or teams can adapt the standardised methodology to conduct their own independent surveys. Although these independent surveys may not necessarily be comparable to the core set of large-scale surveys, they offer an opportunity to deploy state-of-the-art methodologies despite limited research budgets. The full WMS data can be accessed at https://worldmanagementsurvey.org/survey-data/download-data/.

vi. In-country data

In addition to the sources of multi-country data mentioned above, a number of countries in sub-Saharan Africa maintain datasets of very good quality for innovation, entrepreneurship and development research. I highlight two of these: South Africa and Ethiopia.

(a) South Africa: South Africa is currently at the forefront of research on Science, Technology and Innovation (STI) Indicators in Africa. Annual surveys of research and development (R&D), and triennial surveys of business innovation have been implemented by the Centre for Science, Technology and Innovation Indicators (CeSTII) since 2002 (Manzini, 2015). Thus, as of 2010 when the first edition of the African Innovation Outlook (AIO) was compiled based on the first ever R&D and innovation surveys in many African countries, South Africa was already in its eighth round of R&D surveys and its third round of innovation surveys. The survey datasets are curated at http://datacuration.hsrc.ac.za/search/browse. In some instances, it is necessary to contact CeSTII or the Human Sciences and Social Research Council (HSRC) directly to gain access to the microdata. See Ghebrihiwet (2020) for an example of how the microdata has been applied in previous research.
(b) Ethiopia: The Central Statistical Agency (CSA) maintains one of the most consistent detailed industrial survey programmes in Africa. Among other data collection efforts, the Ethiopian Large and Medium Industrial Survey (LMMIS) has been conducted annually since 1996. The Small Scale Manufacturing Industry Survey (SSMIS) has been implemented periodically since 2002, with 7 rounds having been competed at the end of 2017. The survey reports are curated at http://www.csa.gov.et/component/phocadownload/category/14-all-survey-reports. Access to the microdata requires contacting the CSA directly. Grover (2019) and Hjort and Poulsen (2019) illustrate the application of the data.

Concluding Remarks

In this chapter the focus has been on how surveys are currently conducted in developing countries in Africa and what can be done to mitigate the attendant challenges, drawing upon the author's experience in Nigeria. Although this is not an exhaustive discussion of survey practice, the chapter has raised some issues that are practically relevant for surveys in developing countries.

These give rise to some key takeaways, the first of which should be the realisation that in driving high-quality research that could inform entrepreneurship, innovation and development policy in developing countries, good data is a sine qua non. In this regard, it is essential for government and other relevant authorities to invest in routine data collection through high frequency and periodic surveys. For instance, the triennial innovation surveys and the annual R&D surveys should not be under-resourced in Africa where we know very little about the state of the innovation systems.

The second key takeaway is the need to build capacity for surveys, both at the individual and systemic level. In addition to national statistical offices, specialised agencies such as CeSTII in South Africa and the National Centre for Technology Management (NACETEM) in Nigeria have an important role to play. Specifically, such agencies are best positioned to manage niche data collection efforts that national statistical offices can then leverage upon. The efforts of these kinds of organisations require considerable attention from policymakers and deserve as much publicity as can be afforded in their respective contexts. It is hoped that this chapter will stimulate the necessary debate around these issues.

The third takeaway is that there are several sources of good quality data that researchers in developing countries can explore, wherever possible. Clearly, these sources are superior in quality and scope to what any single researcher can produce, especially in the context of poor funding and intense infrastructural deficiencies. It is therefore reasonable to leverage on these data sources, not only for data but also for methodological spillovers including questionnaires, methodological notes and support for capacity building. It is unfortunate that too many researchers are either not sufficiently aware of these data sources or are not willing to invest the time required in adapting the data sources to their own research. For instance, I have personally seen cases where individuals design and conduct very small surveys to collect data that is readily available in existing sources. Without doubt, empirical analyses based on such rudimentary data will be weak. Hopefully, this chapter will point the inquisitive researcher in the right direction, that is, if it does not already contain what that researcher needs.

References

Adegboye, A. C., & Iweriebor, S. (2018). Does access to finance enhance SME innovation and productivity in Nigeria? Evidence from the World Bank Enterprise Survey. *African Development Review, 30*(4), 449–461.

Adeoti, J. O. (2012). Technology-related factors as determinants of export potential of Nigerian manufacturing firms. *Structural Change and Economic Dynamics, 23*(4), 487–503.

Bigsten, A., & Söderbom, M. (2006). What have we learned from a decade of manufacturing enterprise surveys in Africa? *World Bank Research Observer, 21*(2), 241–265.

Bloom, N., Lemos, R., Sadun, R., Scur, D., & Van Reenen, J. (2014). *The New Empirical Economics of Management* (NBER Working Paper 20102). National Bureau of Economic Research, Massachusetts. http://www.nber.org/papers/w20102. Accessed from February 14, 2014.

Bradburn, N. M., Sudman, S., & Wansink, B. (2004). *Asking questions: The definitive guide to questionnaire design—For market research, political polls, and social and health questionnaires*. Wiley.

Cinar, E. M., Hienkel, T., & Horwitz, W. (2019). Comparative entrepreneurship factors between North Mediterranean and North African Countries: A regression tree analysis. *The Quarterly Review of Economics and Finance, 73*, 88–94.

De Vries, G. J., Timmer, M. P., & de Vries, K. (2015). Structural Transformation in Africa: Static gains, dynamic losses. *The Journal of Development Studies, 51*(6), 674–688.

Diao, X., McMillan, M., & Rodrik, D. (2019). The recent growth boom in developing economies: A structural change perspective. In *The Palgrave handbook of development economics* (pp. 281–334). Palgrave Macmillan.

Dvouletý, O., & Orel, M. (2019). Entrepreneurial activity and its determinants: Findings from African developing countries. In *Sustainable Entrepreneurship* (pp. 9–24). Springer.

Egbetokun, A., Oluwatope, O., Adeyeye, D., & Sanni, M. (2019). The role of industry and economic context in open innovation: Evidence from Nigeria (chapter 5). In G. Rexhepi, R. Hisrich, & V. Ramadani (Eds.), *Open innovation and entrepreneurship: Impetus of growth and competitive advantages* (pp. 67—87). Springer.

Fisman, R., & Svensson, J. (2007). Are Corruption and taxation really harmful to growth? *Firm-Level Evidence, Journal of Development Economics, 83*, 63–75.

Gaddis, I., Siwatu, G. O., Palacios-Lopez, A., & Pieters, J. (2019). *Measuring farm labor: Survey experimental evidence from Ghana*. The World Bank.

Garlick, R., Orkin, K., & Quinn, S. (2016). *Call me maybe: Experimental evidence on using mobile phones to survey African microenterprises* (Economic Research Initiatives at Duke (ERID) Working Paper No. 224).

Ghebrihiwet, N. (2020). Foreign direct investment and industry-science R&D cooperation: The case of South Africa. *Innovation and Development, 10*(3), 373–394.

Gibson, D. G., Pereira, A., Farrenkopf, B. A., Labrique, A. B., Pariyo, G. W., & Hyder, A. A. (2017). Mobile phone surveys for collecting population-level estimates in low-and middle-income countries: A literature review. *Journal of Medical Internet Research, 19*(5), e139.

Grover, A. (2019). *Firms Far Up! Productivity, Agglomeration and High-Growth Firms in Ethiopia. Productivity, Agglomeration and High-Growth Firms in Ethiopia* (World Bank Policy Research Working Paper No. 9099). Retrieved on August 17, 2021 from https://openknowledge.worldbank.org/handle/10986/33119.

Herrington, M., & Coduras, A. (2019). The national entrepreneurship framework conditions in sub-Saharan Africa: A comparative study of GEM data/National Expert Surveys for South Africa, Angola, Mozambique and Madagascar. *Journal of Global Entrepreneurship Research, 9*(1), 60.

Hjort, J., & Poulsen, J. (2019). The arrival of fast internet and employment in Africa. *American Economic Review, 109*(3), 1032–1079.

Hoogeveen, J., Croke, K., Dabalen, A., Demombynes, G., & Giugale, M. (2014). Collecting high frequency panel data in Africa using mobile phone interviews. *Canadian Journal of Development Studies, 35*(1), 186–207.

Iarossi, G. (2006). *The power of survey design: A user's guide for managing surveys, interpreting results, and influencing respondents*. The World Bank. https://elibrary.worldbank.org/doi/abs/10.1596/978-0-8213-6392-8. Accessed from April 22, 2020.

John, O. P., & Srivastava, S. (1999). The Big Five trait taxonomy: History, measurement, and theoretical perspectives. *Handbook of Personality: Theory and Research, 2*, 102–138.

Kalton, G. (1983). *Introduction to survey sampling*. Sage.

Kaufmann, D. (1997). Corruption: Some myths and facts. *Foreign Policy* (Summer), 114–131.

Lemi, A., & Wright, I. (2020). Exports, foreign ownership and firm-level efficiency in Ethiopia and Kenya: An application of the stochastic frontier model. *Empirical Economics, 58*(2), 669–698.

Leo, B., Morello, R., Mellon, J., Peixoto, T., & Davenport, S. T. (2015). *Do mobile phone surveys work in poor countries?* (Center for Global Development Working Paper 398).

Manzini, S. T. (2015). Measurement of innovation in South Africa: An analysis of survey metrics and recommendations. *South African Journal of Science, 111*(11/12), Article #2014–0163. https://doi.org/10.17159/sajs.2015/20140163

Ojebode, A. (2012). Mobile phone deception in Nigeria: Deceivers' skills, truth bias or respondents' greed? *American Journal of Human Ecology, 1*(1), 1–9.

Osabuohien, E. S., Efobi, U. R., Herrmann, R. T., & Gitau, C. M. (2019). Female labor outcomes and large-scale agricultural land investments: Macro-micro evidence from Tanzania. *Land Use Policy, 82*, 716–728.

Peytchev, A., Couper, M. P., McCabe, S. E., & Crawford, S. D. (2006). Web survey design: Paging versus scrolling. *International Journal of Public Opinion Quarterly, 70*(4), 596–607.

Siyanbola, W. O., Adeyeye, A. D., Egbetokun, A. A., Sanni, M., & Oluwatope, O. B. (2014). From indicators to policy: Issues from the Nigerian research and experimental development survey. *International Journal of Technology, Policy and Management, 14*(1), 83–98.

UNSD (United Nations Statistics Division). (2005). *Household Sample Surveys in Developing and Transition Countries: Design, Implementation and Analysis.* United Nations. https://unstats.un.org/unsd/HHsurveys/. Accessed from April 22, 2020.

Van Neuss, L. (2019). The drivers of structural change. *Journal of Economic Surveys, 33*(1), 309–349.

World Bank. (2017, September 11). *Enterprise Surveys Indicators Descriptions.* https://www.enterprisesurveys.org/content/dam/enterprisesurveys/documents/Indicator-Descriptions.pdf. Accessed from April 23, 2020.

24

A New Look at Case Study Approach in African Entrepreneurship Research

Oluwasoye P. Mafimisebi and Frank Nyame-Asiamah

Introduction

Entrepreneurship is a complex, dynamic and broad field that is studied with a wide range of research design strategies and methodologies to understand its innovative ways of using resources to capture value (Audretsch et al., 2020; Maula & Stam, 2019; Suddaby et al., 2015; Thompson et al., 2020; Welter, 2011). Common among research design strategies that have been applied to understand African entrepreneurship is the case study approach (Amoako & Lyon, 2014; Khavul et al., 2009; Mafimisebi, 2017; Nyame-Asiamah et al., 2020). Case study research uses multiple sources of evidence to examine a contemporary phenomenon, within its real-life context, particularly when the boundaries between the phenomenon and context are not clearly obvious (Yin, 2014). It is an outward looking research strategy that requires rigorous scientific methodologies to explain how entrepreneurship research investigation has been conducted and reported. The rigour of scientific research and its independent judgement is traditionally interwoven in the study's philosophical assumptions, the fundamental beliefs of research that influence the choice of methodologies.

O. P. Mafimisebi (✉) · F. Nyame-Asiamah
Leicester Castle Business School, Faculty of Business and Law, De Montfort University, Leicester, UK
e-mail: oluwasoye.mafimisebi@dmu.ac.uk

Studies that explore cause–effect relationships or identify patterns in entrepreneurial phenomena tend to use positivist philosophy which seeks to formulate rules to generalize findings and predict entrepreneurial behaviour (Khavul et al., 2009; Wong & Ellis, 2002). Positivist research traditions largely use quantitative tools and rational economic models to measure entrepreneurial phenomena because they rely on the objective view that social researchers can be detached from what they observe (Saridakis et al., 2014; Thompson et al., 2020). Human experiences and perceptions that form part of entrepreneurs' behaviour are lost when analysing positivist research processes which are themselves not sensitive to human processes and changing entrepreneurial actions.

Entrepreneurship studies that favour the closeness between researchers and the social phenomena they study embrace interpretivist research philosophy. This research orientation decodes and analyses human behaviour, including entrepreneurs' daily experiences, their economic decisions, and non-verbal expressions to gain an in-depth understanding of entrepreneurship contexts (Munoz & Kimmitt, 2019; Thompson et al., 2020). Interpretivists mostly rely on qualitative research methodologies to understand entrepreneurs and their socio-economic contexts. Interpretivism suits African entrepreneurship contexts where cultural beliefs, norms, motives and practices influence enterprise activities. The arguable challenge is that interpretivism encourages a small number of cases that do not allow generalization to the whole study population and therefore can place limitations on scientific knowledge (Bennett & Elman, 2006; George, 1979; Yin, 2014).

There are many other methodological (philosophical) approaches to facilitate African entrepreneurship studies such as realism which assumes that *reality* exists around us and can be revealed with common sense, and constructivism which holds a subjective view that meaning is co-constructed with research participants (Creswell, 2014). The challenge however is that realism shares the same scientific reasoning with positivists for observing a phenomenon to prove every reality (Myers, 2019) while constructivism builds on prior knowledge and rejects the idea that actual truth exists (Fisher, 2007). As researchers debate on various philosophical approaches to find appropriate methodologies that can resolve the challenges around sample size, contextual, generalizability, *priori* and actuality, attention is turned on pragmatist research orientations which can address complex entrepreneurship research contexts.

Pragmatism combines research methods in 'whatever' form with the main aim to address research problem(s) and avoid philosophical conflicts (Johnson

& Onwuegbuzie, 2004). It is characterized as a 'problem centred', 'pluralistic' and 'practice-oriented' research methodology that tests ideas on an empirical scale through a rigorous design of the data capturing and analysis (Dencker et al., 2020; Kaushik & Walsh, 2019; Welter et al., 2019). Pragmatist research also captures the economic, social, political, historical and other contexts within which a phenomenon is studied (Creswell, 2014). In context, we believe that pragmatism is truly important to shed light on the economic, social, political, historical and cultural contexts in which African entrepreneurship is embedded. This brings pragmatism to the fore in African entrepreneurship studies where complex institutional arrangements and cultural practices offer opportunities to explore embedded cases of entrepreneurship that can compare or contrast the existing philosophical assumptions of entrepreneurship research in other non-African settings (cf. Argyres et al., 2020; Bluhm et al., 2011; Edmondson & Mcmanus, 2007; Mafimisebi & Nkwunonwo, 2015; Murphy et al., 2017).

African entrepreneurship is pluralistic in nature with multiple variations in entrepreneurial orientations, ecosystems, practices and cases across Africa. For example, entrepreneurial practices differ across most of the different African cultures, nations and economies. These multiple variations in African entrepreneurial practices blur the boundaries between entrepreneurial phenomenon and context. This suggests the need for case study approach in view that such approach is most appropriate in situations where distinction between phenomenon and context are not clearly evident (Yin, 2014). As such, African entrepreneurship is increasingly unique to allow for the use of case study approach to investigate unconventional entrepreneurial phenomena within the African context. In this regard, our work makes two unique contributions to African entrepreneurship and research methodology literature.

First, this chapter opens a new debate within entrepreneurship scholarship around the pragmatism of case study as a method to appropriately capture the unique dimension of African entrepreneurship phenomena in their real-life contexts. This challenges the narrow, stable and largely taken for granted context of most entrepreneurship (Welter et al., 2019) and extends the conversation to implications of methodological approach in uncovering the heterogeneity of entrepreneurship phenomena (Khavul et al., 2009; Maula & Stam, 2019; Welter et al., 2017; Williams et al., 2019). Second, we argue that case study is most fascinating when investigating entrepreneurship phenomena in non-Western or alternative contexts where boundaries between phenomenon and context are not clearly evident (Yin, 2014). This perspective positions African entrepreneurship as both specialized niche entrepreneurship and scalable mass-market manifestation of entrepreneurship (cf. Audretsch et al., 2020). From a practical perspective, our claim is that African entrepreneurship can be geared towards necessity and impact-driven process of opportunities, search and discovery in the Africa market. This theoretical claim emphasizes that African entrepreneurship requires that entrepreneurs search for opportunities perhaps in response to latent or prevailing dominant problems as well as focus on entrepreneurial opportunity discovery (Audretsch et al., 2020; Mafimisebi et al., 2020). We elaborate upon this claim by acknowledging that African entrepreneurship differs from the 'decontextualized standard model of entrepreneurship …, which considered entrepreneurship as high-growth, technology driven, and venture capital-backed', often 'referred to as the Silicon Valley Model' (Welter et al., 2019, p. 320).

This chapter examines the use of case studies in African entrepreneurship research and fosters new directions—theory building, falsification and extension that reflect on the challenges, methods and prospects of utilizing case studies in investigating entrepreneurship phenomena. We draw on our own field experiences to provide reflective accounts on how to implement case study research in African entrepreneurship context that can guide researchers to approach complex African entrepreneurship studies with pluralistic, problem-solving, and practice-oriented mindset while satisfying the scientific rigour requirements. The rest of the chapter is organized into five sections: In the next section, we discuss our conceptualization of African entrepreneurship and case study. Next, we examine case study approach by reviewing existing evidence on the contextual nature of case study. Thereafter, we present success factors when using case study approach in African entrepreneurship. This is followed by discussion of key contributions. Finally, we conclude the study and highlight new guidance for the use of case studies in African entrepreneurship.

African Entrepreneurship and Case Study

Historically, there have been explicit entrepreneurship practices and enactment in Africa for several decades. However, these entrepreneurship practices and enactment are distinct and unique to the African context. Entrepreneurship has become a global phenomenon and global practice contributing to social development and economic growth and helping to reduce unemployment and poverty (Maula & Stam, 2019; Suddaby et al., 2015). This recognition of the global dimension of entrepreneurship practice calls for rethinking our approach to investigating entrepreneurship phenomena given possible variations in emergence and discovery of entrepreneurial opportunities (Thompson et al., 2020; Welter, 2011). We suggest that using case study approach in uncovering entrepreneurial phenomena can help us theorize more broadly and make significant theoretical contributions to entrepreneurship literature. For example, much of early entrepreneurship studies conceptualize entrepreneurship as the enabler and discoverer of the market process, the means by which market equilibria are reached from states of disequilibria through the profit opportunities recognized by entrepreneurs. A number of previous studies (Audretsch et al., 2020; Thompson et al., 2020; Welter, 2011) argued that entrepreneurs discover opportunities to make extra profit by exploiting market disequilibria and as a result drive the economy towards equilibrium conditions in which such opportunities become limited or ceased to exist.

In many regards, entrepreneurship theorists emphasize that the exploitation of profit opportunities by entrepreneurs' alerts others to the opportunities and draws in imitators until eventually, competition reduces profit levels to normal level and equilibrium is restored (Thompson et al., 2020; Welter, 2011). This perspective does not truly capture the nature and dynamics of African entrepreneurship. Our conceptualization of African entrepreneurship positions it as a necessity, value creation and impact-driven process of opportunities search and discovery in the Africa market. Typically, African entrepreneurship is characterized by measured growth, high returns, volatile, uncertain and double institutional voids environment in which entrepreneurs must remain resilient to ensure their business survival or continuity. In this context, entrepreneurs search for opportunities perhaps in response to latent or prevailing dominant problem as well as focus on entrepreneurial opportunity discovery.

In this chapter, we note that African entrepreneurship is a specialized niche entrepreneurship and scalable mass-market manifestation of entrepreneurship which differs substantially from the Silicon Valley Model of entrepreneurship (Audretsch et al., 2020; Welter et al., 2019). We make the distinction that African entrepreneurship is not necessarily venture-capital backed and high-growth driven entrepreneurial endeavours compared with the Silicon Valley Model of entrepreneurship. This suggests that to understand African entrepreneurship, we must not reduce entrepreneurship to high-growth, technology driven, and venture capital-backed but seek to accommodate and embrace the indigenous and colourful pluralism of entrepreneurship and its underlying contextualization. African entrepreneurship is a distinct form of entrepreneurship in the sense that it is embedded in indigenous innovation, value creation, impact driven and mundane entrepreneurial activities involving diverse entrepreneurial actors serving consumers mostly at the base of the pyramid. These African entrepreneurial actors seek opportunities in resource constraints and resource munificent contexts. This suggests that African entrepreneurs operate under conditions of double resource dilemmas. On one hand, there is abundance of natural resources in Africa. This provides tremendous opportunities for entrepreneurs in Africa. On the other hand, African entrepreneurs are constrained by institutional voids, excessive taxation, incoherent government policy on entrepreneurship, lack of access to finance, and ineffective entrepreneurial ecosystems. Collectively, African entrepreneurship manifest itself under conditions of uncertainty and epitomize the colourful pluralism of entrepreneurship.

Audretsch et al. (2020) acknowledged that contextualization is necessary to understand the type or emergence of a particular manifestation of entrepreneurship, its intensity and frequency, and geographical location and its dynamics, in which entrepreneurship actually occurs. Therefore, we suggest that African entrepreneurship is distinct because of its contextual nature which is rooted in African culture and model of business operation. Recent research argues that in light of the colourful diversity of entrepreneurship and its underlying contextualization, it may be that entrepreneurship research has been asking the wrong (Audretsch et al., 2020, p. 2). This is why case study is essential to African entrepreneurship which is well suited to understand how to successfully eliminate poverty, unemployment and reduce inequality in African societies. Case studies are useful to understand and probe the right question relating to African entrepreneurship. Studies (Audretsch et al., 2020; Mafimisebi et al., 2020; Mafimisebi & Thorne 2015, 2017) discovered that albeit some national contexts are more conducive to generating world market leaders pursuing incremental innovation and niche strategies, other national contexts are more conducive to the Silicon Valley type of entrepreneurship with its emphasis on radical innovation and scale-up. This situation allows for the investigation of entrepreneurial phenomena using case study due to its inherently small sample sizes.

In view of this, case studies can help us better understand the unique contextualization of African entrepreneurship because of its methodological uniqueness (Brown, 2008; Farquhar, 2012). For example, case studies can help us uncover contextual issues, such as ease of doing business, entrepreneurial ecosystems, national innovation systems, tax regimes, business regulations, national culture, educational systems and supports for start-ups, affecting African entrepreneurship (Eisenhardt et al., 2016; McKeown

2004; Reinhardt et al., 2018; Baker et al., 2017; Bennett & Elman, 2007; Eisenhardt, 1989; Eisenhardt & Graebner, 2007; Bansal & Corley, 2012). Recent studies (Amoako & Lyon, 2014; Khavul et al., 2009; Mafimisebi, 2017; Nyame-Asiamah et al., 2020) have used cases to uncover the salient nature of entrepreneurial phenomena such as entrepreneurial orientations, thinking and actions, behaviours and resilience.

In addition, the use of case studies in African entrepreneurship is germane for several other reasons. Firstly, as a result of unique characteristics of African entrepreneurship, case study approach allows for the exploration and understanding of complex issues embedded in such African contexts. Secondly, rather than the outdated image of seeing case study research as mainly consisting of small 'N-number' in nature (George & Bennetty, 2005), case study research is well positioned to make significant theoretical contributions to understanding African entrepreneurship and in ways that unravel not just unconventional phenomena but emerging entrepreneurial phenomena in African context. Most African countries differ in their norms and institutions, legal rules and taxes, attitudes to entrepreneurship, governance structures, different economic and entrepreneurial outcomes. Specifically, African entrepreneurship is not homogeneous across national borders and institutional contexts in Africa, but various similar culture and orientations exist that enable entrepreneurship. However, we believe that four specific characteristics of African entrepreneurship fit especially well with case study research, namely the unique indigenous innovation, value creation, impact driven and mundane volatility. In the subsequent section, we then discuss more generally how case study approach can be linked to these unique aspects of African entrepreneurship.

Rethinking Case Study Approach in African Entrepreneurship

In light of the evidence that entrepreneurship is heterogeneous and often complex beyond the homogeneous Silicon Valley model of entrepreneurship, we believe that even African entrepreneurship is characterized by several path dependence, interaction effects, cultural interaction, weak vs robust entrepreneurial ecosystems, two-directional causality, equifinality (i.e. many different paths to the same outcome), multifinality (i.e. many different outcomes from the same value of an independent variable, depending on context), and variation in entrepreneurial practices. These variations and presence of complexities in entrepreneurial practice affect how knowledge about entrepreneurship can be constructed, nullified, and verified. Therefore, case study represents one of the unique methodological ways to draw causal inferences in African entrepreneurship.

Like Collier et al. (2004), we believe that causation cannot be simply established through small-n comparison (often referred to as intuitive regression) but through uncovering traces of a hypothesized causal mechanism within the context of a historical case or cases. This implies that researchers should concentrate on the causal mechanism aspect of African entrepreneurship cases. In this context, following Bennett and Elman (2006), we note that within-case research methods do not suffer from some of the pathologies associated with various quantitative research designs because they do not rely on establishing causation through comparison. This is consistent with empirical evidence that case studies are often wrongly criticized for having a 'degrees of freedom' problem, when in fact within-case methods may provide evidence that bears on multiple testable implications of a theory within a single case (George & Bennett, 2005; Johansson, 2003; Merriam, 2009; Stewart, 2014). Albeit there are challenges of undertaking case study research such as access to case organization(s), time consuming, and lack of researcher(s) control over the subject being studied. Nonetheless, the case study approach has been formalized in previous studies (Eisenhardt, 1989; Eisenhardt & Graebner, 2007; George & Bennett, 2005; Gioia et al., 2013) more completely and linked to underlying arguments in the philosophy of science that suits investigation of African entrepreneurship phenomena.

In the context of African entrepreneurship, the use of case studies has comparative advantages in developing internally valid and context-sensitive measures of entrepreneurship, heuristically identifying new variables through within-case analysis of deviant or other cases. This provides an avenue for possible check on spuriousness and endogeneity through within-case analysis, and testing and elaborating entrepreneurship theories. Although as we have also noted there are still challenges associated with case studies especially in context that case research methods are criticized for being misguided and outdated. However, the literature advocates that a number of criticisms levelled against case studies do not apply where case study researchers rethink selection of cases, include both positive and negative cases of a phenomenon, or contexts in which the outcome of interest was possible but did not occur (cf. Harley & Cornelissen, 2018; Mahoney & Goertz, 2004). This suggests that cases in African entrepreneurship should not just be selected because of their historical importance or simply due to convenience.

The inclusion criteria for case selection in African entrepreneurship research should consider extreme or deviant cases to allow for exploration of entrepreneurial phenomenon where an outcome is merely absent or impossible. There should be demarcation between rule of case inclusion and rule of exclusion. The rule of case inclusion should specify why a case is relevant, noting if at least one independent variable of the theory under investigation predicts its occurrence. Likewise, the rule of case exclusion should clearly state conditions under which cases are considered irrelevant and excluded from tests of a theory if one variable is at a level known from previous studies to make the outcome of interest impossible (Mahoney & Goertz, 2004). For example, as previously suggested some of the specific characteristics of African entrepreneurship are well suited to case study approach; unique indigenous innovation, value creation, impact driven and mundane volatility. In turns, we discuss each of these characteristics of African entrepreneurship as follows.

Unique Indigenous Innovation

African entrepreneurs contribute to indigenous innovation and make new or improved products/services available to indigenous people at the base of the pyramid who may not have access to them. There are unique indigenous innovation and solutions emerging from African entrepreneurs solving grand societal challenges in Africa and contributing to sustainable development goals in areas of poverty reduction, job and wealth creations. There is need to examine some of these indigenous innovations from Africa using case study research. We can uncover the uniqueness of indigenous innovation by investigating cases where an outcome is not known to have occurred or almost occurred (cf. George & Bennett, 2005). The base of the pyramid innovation is common in African contexts and most entrepreneurs targeted low income earners because of the prevalence of poverty and unemployment. Typically, African entrepreneurs differ from Western entrepreneurs because of heterogenous entrepreneurial orientations, behaviours and cultural outlook exhibit by them. Therefore, cases of these African entrepreneurs are needed to explore entrepreneurial behaviours and strategies as well as entrepreneurial finance, access to credit, technological innovation and impact, risk perception, business ecosystems and resilience, etc. These contextualized aspects of African entrepreneurship are useful to bring novel insights into the nature and dynamic of entrepreneurship. Data on case studies can be collected through historical research methods or combinations of interview and archival methods (Argyres et al., 2020).

Value Creation

African entrepreneurs are constantly creating values through unique products and services solving grand societal and sustainability challenges in Africa. How to capture and measure these values created by entrepreneurs in Africa remain vague. Cases of how African entrepreneurs capture and create values are needed to understand the unique contextualization of African entrepreneurship. This is really important to the understanding the nature and dynamics of African entrepreneurship. Dataset of entrepreneurial activities are normally scarce and researchers often find it difficult to gain access to credible database(s). Therefore, the use of deviant or extreme cases of African entrepreneurs are crucial to better understand entrepreneurship in Africa. It is well documented that case studies have practical versatility because case study research does not often subscribe to a fixed ontological, epistemological or methodological position (Mafimiseb, 2017). In this context, researchers can utilize case studies from a realist or positivist perspective where there is belief in the existence of single reality or perhaps from a relativist or interpretivist view which adopts notion that multiple realities and meanings exist (cf. Yin, 2014). The presence of philosophical plurality provides the avenue to decide the methodological orientation to be used when conducting case studies in African entrepreneurship. This implies that researchers can truly capture issues such as value creation, entrepreneurial ecosystems and tax regimes when using cases to understand their embedded nature in African entrepreneurship.

Impact-Driven

We found from reviewing extant studies that most African entrepreneurs are impact-driven in the sense that they create opportunities for people in the most meaningful and life-changing way (Amoako & Lyon, 2014; Khavul et al., 2009). These African entrepreneurs are not just helping to create jobs, reduce unemployment and poverty but also positively affecting local communities through co-creation of products and/services, and mentoring of youths. In this regard, we need a study that truly captures the impact-driven aspect of entrepreneurship in Africa; and cases are thus valuable here to give comprehensive view of the impact generated from African entrepreneurship. Albeit this may be challenging because of the need to demonstrate novelty and how this form of impact-driven entrepreneurship largely differs from entrepreneurship in the 'west'. Nonetheless, case studies provide avenue to design research that can be specifically tailored to the inherent complexity of entrepreneurship. As such, we expect that we can better understand the ontological status of African entrepreneurship via the use of case studies. We expect that researchers will use historical data, government documents, other studies, press releases, newspaper articles, and retrospective interviews, and focus group to capture the impact-driven aspect of African entrepreneurship.

Mundane Volatility

It is well documented that doing business in Africa is fraught with mundane volatility for entrepreneurs. We define mundane volatility as routine challenges, institutional voids, and resource constraints that exert forces on African entrepreneurs and complicate ease of doing business (cf. Amoako & Lyon, 2014; Mafimisebi & Nkwunonwo, 2015). This important aspect of African entrepreneurship is less understood and studied. Several significant aspects of African entrepreneurship are highly skewed; including for example resource constraints, crisis, resilience, social capital, human capital, entrepreneurial finance, business ecosystems, resources, munificence and the outcomes of entrepreneurial activities (cf. Crawford et al., 2015; Mafimisebi, 2017; Thompson et al., 2020; Welter, 2011). Case studies have potential to shed light on outliers and explain remarkable outcomes such as business resilience, small business performance in the face of volatility and business discontinuity. In this context, we suggest that the best way to understand how African entrepreneurs and organizations operate under condition of mundane volatility and turbulence is through in-depth single case studies or comparative case studies. Research can seek event-based process explanations rather than variance explanations in African entrepreneurship (cf. Van de Ven & Engleman, 2004).

Increasingly, we believe that entrepreneurship scholars can also use image—and video-based data as well as texts data to capture the facets of African entrepreneurship phenomena by writing out a 'thick' narrative description of the entrepreneurial processes involved either at the micro, meso and/or macro level of analysis (Gartner, 2007; Garud et al., 2014). Such narration is imperative because African entrepreneurs face fundamentally different circumstances as they navigate turbulence and diverse institutional, cultural and economic environments in Africa. In this situation, researchers can utilize 'more specific techniques of narrative bracketing and storying to depict in a more analytical sense a general sequence of events and to substitute a rich empirical description for a full-bodied narrative explanation' (Glaser & Strauss, 1967; Graebner et al., 2012). Likewise, next to such a narrative analysis, grounded theory procedures of coding and constant comparison can also guide the identification of distinguishing and common features in such unique cases (Strauss & Corbin, 1998; Glaser & Strauss, 1967; Graebner et al., 2012). In the next section, we discuss the success factors when using case studies in African entrepreneurship.

Success Factors When Using Case Studies in African Entrepreneurship

The quality of case study research, like all other scientific investigations, is judged by the fundamental principles of objectivity and rigour where robust methods of data collection and analysis have been followed to arrive at reliable conclusions that can be externally scrutinized to confirm their trustworthiness or validity (Eisenhardt, 1989; Eisenhardt & Graebner, 2007; Gioia et al., 2013). Without rigour and objectivity, the public confidence in scientific research is compromised. Observing these principles is essential in African entrepreneurship research settings where existing examples lay the emphasis on informal environments and largely apply a naturalistic or interpretivist methodology. Yin (2014) sets out six success criteria for judging the trustworthiness or validity of case study research: (i) The case should reveal something new and interesting that researchers did not know before; (ii) there should be sufficient evidence with compelling verbatim quotations to exemplify real-life situations; (iii) the story about the case should be complete with evidence discussed around the underpinning theoretical points of the study; (iv) there should be diverse and contrasting evidence of alternative views that reflect real-life situations; (v) the evidence should be written in a creative and engaging manner to convince the reader; and (vi) the study should stress the contribution to scientific knowledge and describe how it can be generalized to existing theory.

Other researchers have grounded the criteria for judging a successful case study in the researchers' self-consciousness and reflexive accounts of the people and organizations they study (Eisenhardt & Graebner, 2007; Gioia et al., 2013) and a critical reflection of the unique context (Khavul et al., 2009; Maula & Stam, 2019; Welter et al., 2017; Williams et al., 2019) to bring credibility to research findings. Although many different criteria exist to evaluate the success of case study research such as Yin's (2014) prescription for a positivist case study design that highlights unit(s) of analysis and logical connection between data and research propositions, the debate around rigour and objectivity has remained the focus for credible case study research. The principle of rigour has underlined many interesting African entrepreneurship case study research where elements of originality, sufficient evidence, multiple interpretations, engaging story, 'data-theory' linkages, reflexivity and contextual reflection have been demonstrated.

Firstly, Nyame-Asiamah et al. (2020) used 13 multiple cases from two enterprise sectors operated by African diaspora entrepreneurs from Cameroon, Gambia, Ghana, Kenya, Malawi, Nigeria, Sierra Leone and Zimbabwe to theorize how diaspora entrepreneurs take motivation from the push and pull institutional factors of their countries of origin and countries of residence to develop business enterprises in Africa. Using interviews, focus group discussion and documentary analysis, they provided rich insights into the African diaspora entrepreneurs' experiences, perceptions, and motivations for developing small- and medium-scale enterprises in Africa that supported their new theory contribution to African entrepreneurship. This unique and engaging study illuminates rigour and evaluative criteria in African entrepreneurship case studies that offers generalizability to theories and other contexts.

Secondly, Mafimisebi (2017) used case studies of two multinational oil companies to theorize moral disengagement as embedded in risk, crisis and disaster management strategy in Nigeria. Using semi-structured interviews, observation, archival documents and reports from commission of inquiry, the research showed how moral disengagement exacerbate organizational crisis. In context, the research used case studies to generate unique insights that extend crisis management theories to new domain. One significant lesson from the research was the use of multiple sources to triangulate data which increases the reliability of the findings (Mafimisebi, 2017). In essence, researchers should focus on providing depth in narratives from the multiple sources used and link evidence from the case to theoretical foundation of the research.

Thirdly, drawing on the analysis of 12 small and medium-scale enterprise cases exporting businesses from Ghana, Amoako and Lyon (2014) explored how entrepreneurs employ networks and trust-based relationships to cope in a context of institutional weakness. The findings from their multiple case study design reveal that African entrepreneurs and their organizations can avoid recourse to the courts and resort to using culturally specific relationships embedded in African settings to settle disputes when exporting. Through the trustworthiness of interviews and observations, Amoako and Lyon (2014) contributed to theoretical discussions that seek the hybridity of African traditional cultural institutions and the formal legal systems as an effective way to understand how entrepreneurship conflicts are resolved in weak legal and state-backed institutions. By taking owner-managers of small firms as the unit of analysis in institutional contexts, introducing new ways of repairing trust and contributing to theoretical discussions in trust building in international entrepreneurship this research demonstrates a successful case study in African entrepreneurship.

Fourthly, Khavul et al. (2009) conducted eight comparative case studies of informal microfinance enterprises in East Africa to develop a theoretical basis for understanding the establishment and evolution of family businesses in Africa. Applying a grounded theory methodology to analyse interview data, they showed that East African entrepreneurs used strong family and community ties to establish and develop businesses as well as using strong community ties to compensate the obligations that strong extended family ties create for entrepreneurs. Khavul et al. (2009) further demonstrated the understanding that embedded network ties and their complex dynamics in Africa shape enterprise growth. This study typifies contextual reflection, logical links between data and research propositions, diverse interpretations, and theoretical application to further studies to justify how African entrepreneurship case study satisfies rigour and objectivity. In sum, we integrate insights from different stream of research in case study methodology (Creswell, 2014; Eisenhardt & Graebner, 2007; Gioia et al., 2013; Yin, 2014), entrepreneurship (Amoako & Lyon, 2014; Khavul et al., 2009; Nyame-Asiamah et al., 2020; Welter et al., 2017) and crisis management (Mafimisebi, 2017; Mafimisebi & Nkwunonwo, 2015) in Africa to provide guidance on using case studies in African entrepreneurship (Table 24.1). The guidance cover stages in case study development, case evaluation criteria, explanation of measure and distinctiveness, and new directions and/or factors informing future case-based research.

Discussion

In this chapter, we argued that African entrepreneurship is unique because of its pluralistic nature and multiple variation in entrepreneurial orientations, ecosystems, practices and cases across Africa. Nonetheless, we find from our review of existing entrepreneurship studies that the implications of methodological approach in uncovering the heterogeneity of entrepreneurship phenomena has been taken for granted in most previous research. As such, we examined the use of case study in African entrepreneurship research and fosters new directions that reflect on the challenges, methods, and provide guidance on using case studies in investigating African entrepreneurship phenomena (Table 24.1). We found that across the literature several connotations of case study exist. For example, case study is considered as a method, a methodology, an approach, research design, research strategy

Table 24.1 Guidance on using case study in African entrepreneurship

Stages in case study development	Case evaluation criteria	Explanation of measure and distinctiveness	New directions
Pre-case	Before using case	Think about the types of questions to be answered The degree of focus on contemporary events	Have a case study protocol from the onset Decide whether the case study is for theory building and/or testing
	Deciding to use case	Formulate the research questions Research questions should translate into propositions	Provide rich, vivid and holistic case description Align case study to research questions
Research Design	Theoretical foundation	Formulate the study propositions Be clear about the unit of analysis for the case Provide explanation of why the case method is the most appropriate method to adopt	Unit of analysis as the basis for the case The case study should mainly ask questions about the unit of analysis
	Pilot study	The case may be an individual person, an event, an organization, team, or department within the organization Conduct a pilot study before the main study	Mini case study pilot can be used to test the appropriateness of case study method

(continued)

Table 24.1 (continued)

Stages in case study development	Case evaluation criteria	Explanation of measure and distinctiveness	New directions
	Theoretical sampling	Provide explanation of which case(s) were chosen and why	You can use extreme and/or deviant case(s) to obtain information on unusual events Use maximum variation case(s) and critical case(s) to obtain information on various circumstances for case process and outcome; and information that permits logical deductions
Data Collection	Triangulation	Use multiple sources of data in the research	Focus on providing depth in narratives from the sources used
	Review and evidence validation	Use replication logic in multiple case studies Review evidence and validate by external parties	Link evidence from the case(s) to theoretical foundation of the research
	Data collection transparency	Made how the data collection process was conducted clear	Develop case database Use case study protocol

Stages in case study development	Case evaluation criteria	Explanation of measure and distinctiveness	New directions
Data Analysis	Inter-coder agreement	If possible, use multiple coders (investigators, research assistants, etc.) to code the data	Provide clarity in data coding and procedures Use evidence from previous case research studies to inform coding criteria
	Case presentation	Present findings and empirical evidence in such a way that readers can see how the author(s) reach their conclusions	Thematic analysis is most popular in case research Qualitative Comparative Analysis (QCA) is also becoming increasingly popular in case research
	Case interpretation	Make sure case interpretation and/or analysis move beyond description and conceptual ordering	Use case studies as the basis the formulation of working hypotheses Case studies be used as the basis for the formulation of working hypotheses
Post-case	Reflecting on validity and reliability	Discuss the research quality and reflect on the insights generated from the research	Think more broadly about how to generate theory from the case Think about how to use case for theory extension, testing, falsification and building

and/or a form of inquiry (Anthony & Jack, 2009; Brown, 2008; Creswell, 2014; Gerring, 2004; Merriam, 2009; Simons, 2009; Stake, 1995, 2006; Stewart, 2014; Yin, 2014). In context, some studies see case study as a research method while emphasizing the procedures used (Yin, 2014); others discuss case study in the context of presenting cases. Likewise, some suggested that case studies are a qualitative design (Creswell, 2014), an approach (Simons, 2009), and/or strategy (Flyvbjerg, 2011; Stakes, 1995, 2006; Stewart, 2014), or even as inherently qualitative in nature (Merriam, 2009).

The alternative view, as we argued, is to perceive case studies as an instrument for building new theory, testing and/or refuting established theories in entrepreneurship. This implies that researchers need to be clear about the use and purpose of case study when investigating entrepreneurship phenomena. While there is lack of agreement on the definition of case studies, existing studies collectively advance our understanding of case study in research involving complex phenomena especially in situations where heterogeneity and methodological plurality exist. In particular, in line with recent studies (Amoako & Lyon, 2014; Audretsch et al., 2020; Khavul et al., 2009; Mafimisebi, 2017; Nyame-Asiamah et al., 2020; Welter et al., 2017), we suggest that case studies are a suitable methodological approach because African entrepreneurship is inherently heterogeneous across distinct entrepreneurial orientations, culture, ecosystems, practices and cases. In view of African entrepreneurship, focusing on the context suggests that the manifestation of entrepreneurial behaviour and thinking is inevitably embedded in the institutional and cultural environment of Africa (cf. Welter, 2011). As we have noted, African entrepreneurship cannot be homogenized because of the variations in national culture, tribes, regulation, institutional supports for micro and small businesses, and entrepreneurial ecosystems. Therefore, we propose that concepts such as entrepreneurial orientation and ecosystems are also heterogeneous in nature and can only be understood by undertaking case studies. African entrepreneurship is increasingly unique to allow for the use of case study approach to investigate unconventional entrepreneurial phenomena within the African context. In this regard, our work makes two unique contributions to African entrepreneurship and research methodology literature.

First, this chapter opens a new debate within entrepreneurship scholarship around the pragmatism of case study as a method to appropriately capture the unique dimension of African entrepreneurship phenomena in their real-life contexts. This challenges the narrow, stable, and largely taken for granted context of most entrepreneurship (Welter et al., 2019) and extends the conversation to implications of methodological approach in uncovering the heterogeneity of entrepreneurship phenomena (cf. Khavul et al., 2009; Maula & Stam, 2019; Welter et al., 2017; Williams et al., 2019). Second, we argue that case studies are most fascinating when investigating entrepreneurship phenomena in non-Western or alternative contexts where boundaries between phenomenon and context are not clearly evident. This perspective positions African entrepreneurship as both specialized niche entrepreneurship and scalable mass-market manifestation of entrepreneurship (Audretsch et al., 2020).

In practical perspective, our claim is that African entrepreneurship is necessity and impact driven process of opportunities search and discovery in the Africa market. This theoretical claim emphasizes that African entrepreneurship requires that entrepreneurs search for opportunities perhaps in response to latent or prevailing dominant problem as well as focus on entrepreneurial opportunity discovery (Audretsch et al., 2020; Mafimisebi et al., 2020). We elaborate upon this claim by acknowledging that African entrepreneurship differs from the 'decontextualized standard model of entrepreneurship …, which considered entrepreneurship as high-growth, technology driven, and venture capital-backed', often 'referred to as the Silicon Valley Model' (Welter et al., 2019, p. 320).

Conclusion

Approaching African entrepreneurship research with pragmatist orientations will enable researchers to achieve rigour and valid attributes of research outcomes that reflect the diverse and complex contexts in Africa. Such philosophical application delivered through a case study method rejects paradigm conflicts and gives opportunities for African specific entrepreneurship studies to focus more on values, reality and rigour that helps in addressing research questions. By developing business research understanding and conducting entrepreneurship research around the pragmatism of case studies in Africa, we support the idea of using mixed methods within the quantitative or qualitative approaches or adopting a case study strategy that combines some quantitative and qualitative methods in pragmatist traditions to explore unique contexts of African entrepreneurship. Through this, multiple sources of evidence can be used to investigate underexplored and contemporary phenomena which are not clearly apparent in African contexts and to allow researchers to generate new theories, extend our existing knowledge or contest the way African entrepreneurship research is perceived.

Studying African entrepreneurship through case studies also emphasizes the significance of informal networks in developing small- and medium-scale business enterprises, seeking market opportunities and building partnerships between local and African diaspora business ventures in the continent. It further paves the way to explore the merits of a single case study that uses repetitive processes to unveil patterns in complex African entrepreneurship settings to support theory development or to apply multiple cases to discuss differences, similarities and relationships between entrepreneurship phenomena in detail for generalization. Either way, multiple sources of evidence is necessary to maintain rigour and objectivity inherent in the case study approach, to unfold the complex factors embedded in African entrepreneurship and to achieve research outcomes that can be accepted as valid and trustworthy.

References

Amoako, I. O., & Lyon, F. (2014). 'We don't deal with courts': Cooperation and alternative institutions shaping exporting relationships of small and medium-sized enterprises in Ghana. *International Small Business Journal, 32*(2), 117–139.

Anthony, S., & Jack, S. (2009). Qualitative case study methodology in nursing research: An integrative review. *Journal of Advanced Nursing, 65*(6), 1171–1181. https://doi.org/10.1111/j.1365-2648.2009.04998.x

Argyres, N. S., De Massis, A., Foss, N. J., Frattini, F., Jones, G., & Silverman, B. S. (2020). History informed strategy research: The promise of history and historical research methods in advancing strategy scholarship. *Strategic Management Journal, 41*(3), 343–368. https://doi.org/10.1002/smj.3118

Audretsch, D. B., Lehmann, E. E., & Schenkenhofer, J. (2020). A context-choice model of niche entrepreneurship. *Entrepreneurship Theory and Practice, 00*, 1–28.

Bennett, A., & Elman, C. (2007). Case study methods in the international relations subfield. *Comparative Political Studies, 40*(2), 170–195. https://doi.org/10.1177/0010414006296346

Brown, L. (2008). A review of the literature on case study research. *Canadian Journal for New Scholars in Education, 1*(1), 1–13.

Bansal, P., & Corley, K. (2012). Publishing in *AMJ*—Part 7: What's different about qualitative research? *Academy of Management Journal, 55*(3), 509–513. https://doi.org/10.5465/amj.2012.4003

Baker, T., Powell, E. E., & Fultz, A. (2017). Whatddya know? Qualitative methods in entrepreneurship. In R. Mir & S. Jain (Eds.), *The Routledge handbook of qualitative research* (pp. 248–262). Routledge.

Bluhm, D. J., Harman, W., Lee, T. W., & Mitchell, T. R. (2011). Qualitative research in management: A decade of progress. *Journal of Management Studies, 48*(8), 1866–1891. https://doi.org/10.1111/j.1467-6486.2010.00972.x

Bennett, A., & Elman, C. (2006). Qualitative research: Recent developments in case study methods. *Annual Review of Political Science, 9*, 455–476.

Brady, H. E, & Collier, D. (Eds.). (2004). *Rethinking social inquiry: Diverse tools, shared standards*. Rowman Littlefield.

Collier, D., & Brady, H. E., & Seawright, J. (2004). Sources of leverage in causal inference: Toward an alternative view of methodology. See Brady and Collier (2004, pp. 229–266).

Crawford, G. C., Aguinis, H., Lichtenstein, B., Davidsson, P., & McKelvey, B. (2015). Power law distributions in entrepreneurship: Implications for theory and research. *Journal of Business Venturing, 30*(5), 696–713. https://doi.org/10.1016/j.jbusvent.2015.01.001

Creswell, J. W. (2014). *Research design: Qualitative, quantitative and mixed methods approaches* (4th ed.). Sage.

Dencker, J., Bacq, S. C., Gruber, M., & Haas, M. (2020). Reconceptualizing necessity entrepreneurship: A contextualized framework of entrepreneurial processes under the condition of basic needs. *Academy of Management Review*. https://doi.org/10.5465/amr.2017.0471

Edmondson, A. C., & Mcmanus, S. E. (2007). Methodological fit in management field research. *Academy of Management Review, 32*(4), 1246–1264. https://doi.org/10.5465/amr.2007.26586086

Eisenhardt, K. M. (1989). Building theories from case study research. *Academy of Management Review, 14*(4), 532–550. https://doi.org/10.5465/amr.1989.4308385

Eisenhardt, K. M., & Graebner, M. E. (2007). Theory building from cases: Opportunities and challenges. *Academy of Management Journal, 50*(1), 25–32. https://doi.org/10.5465/amj.2007.24160888

Eisenhardt, K. M., Graebner, M. E., & Sonenshein, S. (2016). Grand challenges and inductive methods: Rigor without rigor mortis. *Academy of Management Journal, 59*(4), 1113–1123. https://doi.org/10.5465/amj.2016.4004

Farquhar, J. D. (2012). What is case study research? In J. D. Farquhar (Ed.), *Case study research for business* (pp. 3–14). Sage. https://doi.org/10.4135/9781446287910.n2

Fisher, C. (2007). *Researching and writing a dissertation: A guidebook for business students*. Pearson Education.

Flyvbjerg, B. (2011). Case study. In N. K. Denzin & Y. S. Lincoln (Eds.), *The Sage handbook of qualitative research* (4th ed., pp. 301–316). Sage.

Gartner, W. B. (2007). Entrepreneurial narrative and a science of the imagination. *Journal of Business Venturing, 22*(5), 613–627. https://doi.org/10.1016/j.jbusvent.2006.10.003

Garud, R., Gehman, J., & Giuliani, A. P. (2014). Contextualizing entrepreneurial innovation: A narrative perspective. *Research Policy, 43*(7), 1177–1188. https://doi.org/10.1016/j.respol.2014.04.015

George, A. L. (1979). Case studies and theory development: The method of structured, focused comparison. In G. Lauren (Ed.), *Diplomacy: New approaches in history, theory and policy* (pp. 43–68). Free.

George, A. L., & Bennett, A. (2005). *Case studies and theory development in the social sciences* (4th ed.). MIT Press.

Gerring, J. (2004). What is a case study and what is it good for? *American Political Science Review, 98*(2), 341–354. https://doi.org/10.1017/S0003055404001182

Gioia, D. A., Corley, K. G., & Hamilton, A. L. (2013). Seeking qualitative rigor in inductive research notes on the Gioia ethodology. *Organisational Research Methods, 16*(1), 15–31.

Glaser, B. G., & Strauss, A. L. (1967). *Discovery of grounded theory: Strategies for qualitative research*. Aldine.

Graebner, M. E., Martin, J. A., & Roundy, P. T. (2012). Qualitative data: Cooking without a recipe. *Strategic Organisation, 10*(3), 276–284. https://doi.org/10.1177/1476127012452821

Greve, H. R. (2018). Show me the data! Improving evidence presentation for publication. *Management and Organisation Review, 14*(2), 423–432. https://doi.org/10.1017/mor.2018.18

Harley, B., & Cornelissen, J. P. (2018). Reframing rigor as reasoning: Challenging technocratic conceptions of rigor in management research. In T. B. Zilber, J. M. Amis, & J. Mair (Eds.), *The production of managerial knowledge and organisational theory: New approaches to writing, producing and consuming theory* (Vol. 59, pp. 59–76). Emerald Publishing.

Johansson, R. (2003, September 22–24). Key note speech at the international conference "*Methodologies in Housing Research*". Royal Institute of Technology in cooperation with the International Association of People–Environment Studies, Stockholm. http://www.psyking.net/htmlobj-3839/case_study_methodology-_rolf_johansson_ver_2.pdf. Accessed: December, 19, 2016.

Johnson, R. B., & Onwuegbuzie, A. J. (2004). Mixed methods research: A research paradigm whose time has come. *Educational Researcher, 33*(7), 14–26.

Kaushik, V., & Walsh, C. A. (2019). Pragmatism as a research paradigm and its implications for social work research. *Social Sciences, 8*(9), 1–17.

Khavul, S., Bruton, G. D., & Wood, E. (2009). Informal family business in Africa. *Entrepreneurship Theory and Practice, 33*(6), 1219–1238. https://doi.org/10.1111/j.1540-6520.2009.00342.x

Lieberson, S. (1992). Small N's and big conclusions: An examination of the reasoning in comparative studies based on a small number of cases. In C. C. Ragin & H. S. Becker (Eds.), *What Is a Case? Exploring the foundations of social inquiry* (pp. 105–118). Cambridge Univ. Press.

Maula, M., & Stam, W. (2019). Enhancing rigor in quantitative entrepreneurship research. *Entrepreneurship Theory and Practice, 57*(1). https://doi.org/10.1177/1042258719891388

Mahoney, J., & Goertz, G. (2004). The possibility principle: Choosing negative cases in comparative research. *American Political Science Review, 98*(4), 653–669.

Mafimisebi, O. P. (2017). Self-inflicted disasters: *Moral disengagement in unconventional risk, crisis and disaster management strategy.* University of Portsmouth: Unpublished PhD Dissertation.

Mafimisebi, O. P., & Nkwunonwo, U. C. (2015). Environmental risk: Exploring organisational resilience and robustness. *International Journal of Scientific & Engineering Research, 6*(1), 1103–1115.

Mafimisebi, O. P., & Thorne, S. (2015). Oil terrorism-militancy link: Mediating role of moral disengagement in emergency and crisis management. *Journal of Emergency Management, 13*(5), 447–458.

Mafimisebi, O. P., & Thorne, S. (2017). Vandalism-militancy relationship: the influence of risk perception and moral disengagement. *International Journal of Mass Emergencies and Disasters, 35*(3), 191–223.

Mafimisebi, O. P., Obembe, D., & Aluko, O. (2020). Organisation and product design pairings: A review of product innovation capabilities, conceptualization, and future directions. *Strategic Change, 29*, 13–24. https://doi.org/10.1002/jsc.2306

Merriam, S. B. (2009). *Qualitative research: A guide to design and implementation* (2nd ed.). Jossey-Bass.

McKeown, T. J. (2004). Case studies and the limits of the statistical worldview. See Brady and Collier (2004, pp. 139–167).

Muñoz, P., & Kimmitt, J. (2019). Social mission as competitive advantage: A configurational analysis of the strategic conditions of social entrepreneurship. *Journal of Business Research, 101*(C), 854–861.

Murphy, C., Klotz, A. C., & Kreiner, G. E. (2017). Blue skies and black boxes: The promise (and practice) of grounded theory in human resource management research. *Human Resource Management Review, 27*(2), 291–305. https://doi.org/10.1016/j.hrmr.2016.08.006

Myers, M. D. (2019). *Qualitative research in business and management.* Sage.

Nyame-Asiamah, F., Amoako, I. O., Amankwah-Amoah, J., & Debrah, Y. A. (2020). Diaspora entrepreneurs' push and pull institutional factors for investing in Africa: Insights from African returnees from the United Kingdom. *Technological Forecasting and Social Change, 152*, 119876.

Reinhardt, A., Kreiner, G., Gioia, D. A., & Corley, K. (2018). Conducting and publishing rigorous qualitative research. In A. Cassell, A. L. Cunliffe, & G. Grandy (Eds.), *The SAGE handbook of qualitative business and management research methods* (Vol. 1, pp. 515–532). Sage.

Sandelowski, M. (2011). Casing the research case study. *Research in Nursing & Health, 34*(2), 153–159. https://doi.org/10.1002/nur.20421

Saridakis, G., Marlow, S., & Storey, D. J. (2014). Do different factors explain male and female self-employment rates? *Journal of Business Venturing, 29*(3), 345–362.

Simons, H. (2009). *Case study research in practice.* Sage.

Stake, R. E. (1995). *The art of case study research.* Sage.

Stake, Robert E. (2006). *Multiple case study analysis.* Guilford.

Stewart, A. (2014). Case study. In J. Mills & M. Birks (Eds.), *Qualitative methodology: A practical guide* (pp. 145–159). Sage.

Suddaby, R., Bruton, G. D., & Si, S. X. (2015). Entrepreneurship through a qualitative lens: Insights on the construction and/or discovery of entrepreneurial opportunity. *Journal of Business Venturing, 30*(1), 1–10. https://doi.org/10.1016/j.jbusvent.2014.09.003

Strauss, A., & Corbin, J. (1998). *Basics of qualitative research: Techniques and procedures for developing grounded theory* (Vol. 2). Sage.

Thompson, N. A., Verduijn, K., & Gartner, W. B. (2020). Entrepreneurship-as-practice: Grounding contemporary theories of practice into entrepreneurship studies. *Entrepreneurship & Regional Development, 32*(3–4), 247–256. https://doi.org/10.1080/08985626.2019.1641978

Van de Ven, A. H., & Engleman, R. M. (2004). Event- and outcome-driven explanations of entrepreneurship. *Journal of Business Venturing, 19*(3), 343–358. https://doi.org/10.1016/S0883-9026(03)00035-1

Williams, D. W., Wood, M. S., Mitchell, J. R., & Urbig, D. (2019). Applying experimental methods to advance entrepreneurship research: On the need for and publication of experiments. *Journal of Business Venturing, 34*(2), 215–223. https://doi.org/10.1016/j.jbusvent.2018.12.003

Welter, F. (2011). Contextualizing entrepreneurship—Conceptual challenges and ways forward. *Entrepreneurship Theory & Practice, 35*(1), 165–184. https://doi.org/10.1111/j.1540-6520.2010.00427.x

Welter, F., Baker, T., Audretsch, D. B., & Gartner, W. B. (2017). Everyday entrepreneurship—A call for entrepreneurship research to embrace entrepreneurial diversity. *Entrepreneurship Theory and Practice, 41*(3), 311–321. https://doi.org/10.1111/etap.12258

Welter, F., Baker, T., & Wirsching, K. (2019). Three waves and counting: The rising tide of contextualization in entrepreneurship research. *Small Business Economics, 52*(2), 319–330. https://doi.org/10.1007/s11187-018-0094-5

Wong, P. L. K., & Ellis, P. (2002). Social ties and partner identification in Sino-Hong Kong international joint ventures. *Journal of International Business Studies, 33*(2), 267–289.

Yin, R. K. (2014). *Case study research: Design and methods.* Sage.

Index

A
Algeria 25, 29, 30, 35, 155, 359, 438, 442, 469
Angola 55, 101, 103, 155, 313, 518

B
Benin 97, 102, 273
B Faso 102, 155, 289, 387
Boko Haram 7, 385, 386, 395, 396, 398, 467, 468
Botswana 97, 102, 180, 241, 287, 293, 478
Bricolage 422, 423, 428, 464, 471, 472, 479, 484
Burundi 102, 318, 413, 586

C
Cameroon 289, 310, 321, 322, 387, 395, 466, 586, 607
Cape Verde 97
Capital 20, 24, 32, 48, 50–53, 58, 59, 69, 74, 78, 81–83, 99, 103, 118, 120, 126, 133, 134, 136, 150, 309, 354, 356, 386, 389–392, 395, 402, 409, 412, 413, 417–419, 426, 440, 443, 445, 446, 448, 454, 467, 480, 483, 495, 522, 526, 529, 560, 561, 563, 564
Central African Republic 101, 293, 464, 466, 479
Chad 101, 310, 317, 359, 387, 395, 438, 586
Co-creation 5, 246, 256, 257, 259, 400, 604
Comoros 102, 277
Conflict 3, 6–8, 104, 105, 192, 195, 272, 281, 284, 287, 289, 293, 304, 354, 385, 386, 390–392, 394, 407, 412, 437–439, 445, 446, 451, 453, 456, 463–467, 469, 473, 475, 477, 479, 480, 484–487, 496, 497, 503, 543, 550, 551, 557, 559, 564, 576, 596, 607, 613
Cong-Brazzaville 306
Congo-Democratic Republic 94, 101, 293, 464, 466, 469

Côte d'Ivoire 102, 287
Curriculum 5, 165, 173–178, 180–183, 223, 229, 233, 234, 241, 242, 247, 249, 251, 255, 257, 258, 331, 332, 346

D

Development 2–4, 6, 8–11, 19–22, 24, 25, 30–36, 46–48, 50–53, 55, 58–61, 68, 70, 73, 74, 78, 79, 83, 85, 94, 99, 103, 107, 116–118, 120–122, 129, 130, 132–136, 146–148, 150, 162, 164, 165, 175, 177, 181–184, 188, 190, 192–195, 205, 207, 216, 218, 221–223, 234, 241, 244, 245, 247–251, 253–260, 270, 271, 273, 276, 277, 279–281, 284, 290, 295, 296, 303, 304, 306, 308, 309, 312–314, 316, 318, 319, 330–332, 334, 345, 346, 353–355, 358, 359, 363, 375–377, 387–392, 397, 399–402, 410, 416, 420, 422, 427, 429, 439, 440, 442, 443, 454, 463, 465, 472, 473, 476–482, 484, 486, 510, 517, 518, 521, 528, 534, 536, 537, 545, 565, 573–575, 579, 582, 583, 590, 591, 598, 603, 608, 614
Diaspora/diaspora remittance 4, 117, 145, 147–151, 153–155, 160, 162–165, 422, 423, 441, 453, 481, 607, 614
Digital 5, 6, 9, 60, 216, 217, 221, 224–226, 228, 231–234, 253–255, 270, 272, 276, 282, 311, 312, 318, 321, 329, 341, 345, 346, 351, 355, 359, 377, 480, 482, 577

Diversity 3, 8, 77, 108, 134, 136, 273, 363, 424, 452, 484, 521, 600
Djibouti 102, 289
Dynamic capabilities 3, 21–24, 29, 36

E

E-commerce 340–342
Economic development 24, 45, 48, 51, 83, 148, 193, 223, 224, 230, 240, 244, 270, 273, 275, 329, 331, 351, 354, 363, 376, 437, 439, 440, 442, 456, 465, 482, 493, 511, 517, 537, 565
Ecosystem 4, 5, 46, 49, 51, 52, 54, 55, 58–60, 146–148, 150, 151, 164, 189, 192, 193, 195, 196, 202, 203, 204, 207, 218, 247, 259, 307, 330, 331, 333, 341–346, 392, 400, 437, 456, 600, 601, 603–605, 608, 612
Education 2, 4, 5, 11, 57, 58, 61, 155, 160, 162, 164, 165, 173–178, 180, 182–184, 189–201, 203–207, 215, 216, 222, 223, 226, 228, 229, 234, 240–242, 245–248, 250, 251, 253, 256, 258–260, 275, 291, 293, 308, 313, 332, 336, 346, 352, 369, 372, 376, 392, 395, 397, 401, 410, 420, 444, 464, 478, 498, 527, 529, 534, 557, 588
Egypt 25, 29, 155, 317, 336, 343, 345, 438, 442
Employment 5, 7–9, 45, 73, 74, 94, 103, 173, 174, 189, 190, 204, 216, 217, 222–225, 234, 245, 248, 250, 270, 274, 275, 295, 306, 310, 360, 408, 412, 413, 416, 420, 421, 473, 482, 483, 494, 495, 497, 505, 543–545,

547, 549, 552, 553, 555, 557, 560, 561, 563, 564, 574, 585
Enterprise 4, 10, 23, 48, 49, 57, 94, 95, 99–103, 105, 107, 115, 118, 121, 126, 130, 133, 146–148, 150, 165, 175, 178, 182, 191–193, 197, 201, 220, 228–230, 233, 234, 248, 250, 252, 269, 271, 272, 277, 289, 321, 428, 437, 440, 443, 444, 452, 453, 455, 456, 470, 509, 511, 526–528, 530, 532, 533, 535–537, 582, 583, 596, 607, 608
Entrepreneurial ecosystems 2, 47, 49, 58, 147, 148, 150, 189, 192–196, 202–204, 206, 207, 259, 437, 600, 601, 604, 612
Entrepreneurship/entrepreneurship education/entrepreneurship research v, vi, 2–11, 45–51, 53, 54, 57–60, 70, 75, 76, 79, 94, 96, 99, 100, 103, 104, 107, 108, 116–122, 125, 129–131, 134–137, 174, 335, 588, 595–598, 600, 602, 608, 613
Equatorial Guinea 101
Eritrea 97, 102, 287, 351
Ethiopia 8, 97, 102, 306, 312, 321, 353, 387, 407, 414, 416, 424, 494, 495, 498, 519, 530, 537, 589, 590

F

Family business 4, 67–70
Fintech 341
Formal institution 59, 68–70, 73, 80, 81, 84, 99, 100, 119, 120, 204, 410, 533, 534
Free market 2, 271

G

Gabon 101, 102, 289, 306
Gambia 97, 102, 607
Gender 3, 8, 9, 273, 294, 476, 477, 493, 494, 497, 510, 517–519, 528, 531–534, 536–538, 544, 551, 558, 559, 563, 585
Ghana v, vi, 102, 155, 276, 287, 308, 313, 351, 356, 464, 519, 537, 589, 607
Governance 4, 46, 47, 49–51, 54, 55, 59–61, 80, 189, 197, 202, 204, 207, 270, 272–274, 276, 279, 280, 284, 289–291, 293, 296, 388, 420, 474–476, 601
Gross domestic product (GDP) 74, 96, 97, 101, 102, 104, 124, 293, 440, 442, 449, 451, 454, 574
Growth 4, 6–8, 10, 19–24, 31, 32, 45–50, 53–55, 58–61, 74, 75, 78, 81, 83, 93–95, 99, 100, 103, 107, 108, 121, 146, 148, 149, 181, 193, 202, 218, 219, 224, 225, 231–233, 242, 243, 248, 250, 253, 258, 260, 269–271, 273, 274, 276, 278, 280, 293, 303, 304, 306, 309, 311, 316, 319, 323, 332, 352–356, 360, 367, 371, 396, 400, 427, 438–441, 443, 445, 446, 449, 452, 454–456, 481, 495, 496, 502, 504, 506–511, 519, 526, 531, 533, 538, 546, 598, 599, 608
Guinea 102
Guinea Bissau 297

H

Human capital 21, 30, 78, 118, 147, 149, 184, 222, 245, 289–292, 355, 386, 391, 392, 401, 402,

408, 412, 416, 423, 428, 481, 521, 527, 528, 537, 573, 605

I

Informal institution 46, 49, 54, 59, 69, 70, 73, 78, 82
Information and communication Technology (ICT) 6, 253, 344, 351–356, 359–364, 367–377
Innovation/innovation ecosystems/innovation surveys 3, 5, 6, 8–11, 34, 38, 49, 54, 55, 58, 60, 122, 147, 151, 153, 160, 164, 195, 216, 218, 225, 240–245, 250, 254, 257, 270, 272, 276, 277, 293, 294, 306, 309, 311, 312, 314, 317, 321–323, 329–336, 338, 341–346, 355, 402, 452, 470, 487, 526, 573–575, 579, 580, 582, 583, 590, 591, 600, 601, 603
Institutional environment 2–4, 10, 24, 46, 49–52, 54, 60, 67–69, 71, 76–80, 83, 85, 93, 95, 99, 103–108, 119, 127, 149, 240, 244, 408, 409, 417, 425, 427, 429, 464, 474, 481, 518
Institutional void 3, 4, 47, 49, 54, 59–61, 68, 78–81, 83–85, 132, 192, 196, 197, 204, 444, 445, 455, 599, 600, 605
Internationalisation 21
Investors/investment 2, 32, 35, 47, 50, 51, 53, 59, 81, 100, 102, 149, 163, 184, 215, 253, 259, 271, 273, 276, 279–281, 283, 284, 293, 309, 311, 331, 332, 341, 344, 345, 356, 392, 417, 421, 440, 441, 443, 449, 456, 471, 473, 479, 483, 526, 550, 581

K

Kenya vi, 7, 10, 73–75, 81, 83, 102, 103, 183, 241, 276, 281, 289, 310–313, 317, 319, 321, 341, 343, 345, 407, 413–418, 422–424, 426, 589, 607

L

Legal 8, 73, 82, 93, 100, 106, 127, 274, 284, 408, 412, 421, 446, 463, 474, 478, 480, 482, 484–487, 601, 607
Lesotho v, 102
Liberia 102, 359
Libya 8, 25, 29, 30, 155, 294, 438–442, 444, 448, 449, 451–456

M

Madagascar 55, 102, 277, 317, 518
Malawi 102, 306, 319, 320, 607
Mali vi, 29, 102, 306, 310, 351, 466
Market vi, 2, 3, 10, 20–26, 29–35, 37, 48, 49, 51, 55, 61, 67–70, 80, 85, 93, 108, 118, 146, 151, 184, 189, 218, 219, 221, 222, 225, 230, 232, 233, 240, 247, 253, 254, 256, 259, 272, 280–283, 289, 295, 296, 306, 311, 320, 333, 335, 346, 352, 359, 394, 399, 400, 402, 408, 413, 417, 418, 421, 423, 427, 454, 456, 471, 482, 484, 507, 517, 530, 533, 536, 544, 573, 598–600, 613, 614
Mauritania 310
Mauritius 46, 97, 102, 281, 293, 482
Micro enterprises 10, 95, 97, 98, 107, 421
Morocco 25, 29, 32–35, 359

Mozambique v, 55, 56, 102, 464, 589

N

Namibia v, 97, 102, 293
Nano Enterprises (NE) 4, 93, 95, 96, 107
New venture 5, 45, 47–52, 57–59, 61, 76, 99, 216–221, 225, 229, 232–234, 245, 247, 257, 274, 392, 400, 473, 544, 547, 549, 555
Niger 101, 102, 310, 317, 387, 395, 438
Nigeria vi, 4, 5, 7, 55, 73, 74, 94, 95, 97, 99, 102, 103, 115, 116, 120, 121, 124, 125, 130, 131, 135, 137, 155, 183, 187, 189–207, 215–218, 220, 222–225, 227–230, 232–234, 241, 242, 246–248, 250–254, 257, 258, 275, 276, 289, 294, 306, 309–311, 313, 314, 329–336, 338, 341–347, 356, 357, 359, 360, 363, 364, 385–387, 394–396, 400, 466–469, 479, 486, 574, 577, 578, 589–591, 607

O

Open Entrepreneurship (OE) 273, 290–292, 294–296

P

Policy/economic policy/entrepreneurial policy 2, 4, 6, 7, 10, 37, 38, 46, 47, 49–52, 54, 55, 57–61, 94, 107, 119–122, 125, 130, 132, 135, 146–148, 164, 165, 184, 190, 194, 198, 200, 202, 203, 223, 241, 242, 248, 250–252, 256, 258, 270, 279, 280, 283, 295, 306, 329, 334, 336, 344–346, 359, 360, 365, 376, 377, 400, 402, 415, 416, 421, 424, 441, 449, 478, 486, 520, 574, 588, 591, 600
Post-colonial 274
Poverty 1, 2, 6, 7, 47, 48, 57, 61, 94, 100, 103, 124, 129, 145, 146, 150, 189, 190, 192, 195, 198, 202, 204, 206, 207, 217, 223, 233, 248, 279, 303, 331, 353, 372, 396, 452, 453, 464, 486, 600, 603, 604
Private sector 10, 55, 94, 146, 147, 241, 305, 310, 364, 417, 482
Privatisation 2, 146, 441, 442

R

Refugee/refugee entrepreneurship 408, 411, 416, 417, 425–429
Regulation 32, 50, 51, 53, 55, 66, 69, 70, 73, 99, 100, 119, 126, 127, 135, 151, 216, 281, 323, 424, 427, 441, 443, 448–450, 454, 475, 564, 600, 612
Risk society 5, 187–189, 191, 192, 195–201, 206, 207
Rwanda 46, 75, 102, 281, 287, 306, 313, 314, 317, 318, 336, 343, 345, 478, 482

S

Sao Tome and Principe 101
Senegal 94, 102, 287, 306
Seychelles 97, 102, 277, 293
Sierra Leone vi, 102, 322, 359, 607
SMEs 19, 21–25, 36–38, 48, 51, 60, 94, 341, 351, 353–356, 359, 361, 362, 367, 375, 438, 439, 442, 443, 447–450, 453–455

Social capital 4, 52, 53, 61, 68, 221, 279, 386, 388–393, 397, 400, 402, 407–410, 413, 416, 418, 420, 425–427, 429, 500, 503, 517, 605
Somalia 102, 283, 287, 289, 290, 294, 387, 415, 420, 466
South Africa 5, 9, 55, 58, 73, 74, 94, 97, 102, 103, 173–175, 180–183, 276, 279, 289, 306, 308, 311–313, 315–317, 322, 336, 343, 345, 359, 482, 519, 537, 545, 546, 552, 553, 556, 557, 559, 564, 565, 588, 590, 591
South Sudan 97, 102, 283, 287, 293, 294, 321, 466, 469
Start-up 3, 5, 10, 11, 46–51, 53, 57–61, 100, 103, 146, 148, 174, 190, 191, 204, 205, 217, 247, 254, 255, 257, 309, 314, 331, 336, 399, 452, 481, 522, 526, 529, 538, 555, 564, 600
Sudan 56, 101, 317, 321, 415, 416, 438, 464, 466, 469, 479, 486
Survival 3, 4, 20–23, 25, 32, 33, 35–37, 58, 61, 71, 75, 100, 107, 108, 189, 193, 216, 247, 306, 338, 354, 391, 394, 413, 439, 509, 560, 599
Sustainable 5, 6, 46, 48, 57, 71, 174, 190, 200, 205, 241, 244, 254, 256, 270, 280, 303, 316, 318, 330, 332, 425, 429, 453, 456, 603
Swaziland 102

T

Tanzania 30, 75, 97, 102, 359, 478, 482, 589
Technology 2, 5, 6, 20, 24, 122, 148, 149, 153, 160, 164, 180, 181, 216, 217, 221, 223–226, 228, 231, 233, 253, 270, 290–292, 305, 308, 311, 312, 314, 321, 322, 329, 331, 333–336, 338, 341, 344–346, 351, 352, 356–358, 365–369, 371–376, 442, 529, 538, 591, 599, 613
Togo v, vi, 102, 306
Transformation 9, 10, 34, 37, 160, 183, 240, 242, 244, 260, 386, 438, 477, 479, 481
Tunisia 25, 29, 31, 32, 155, 438

U

Uganda 30, 75, 78, 102, 103, 155, 241, 308, 310, 321, 407, 413, 519, 530, 537
University/ies 5, 11, 184, 216, 217, 221, 223, 224, 226–229, 240–243, 313–315, 321, 346, 453, 581

V

Venture capital 48, 55, 310, 526, 598, 599, 613

W

Women 2, 8, 9, 312, 318, 341, 468, 476, 477, 480, 481, 493, 545–547, 550–553, 555–560, 563–565

Y

Youth 5, 6, 51, 174, 175, 184, 189, 190, 223, 248, 259, 275, 280, 304–311, 314, 318, 320–323, 396, 476, 477, 480, 481

Z

Zambia 21, 24, 25, 36, 102, 306, 589

Zimbabwe 30, 73, 74, 102, 272, 306, 313, 314, 316, 607

Printed by Printforce, the Netherlands